THE FRONTIERS OF
LIABILITY

Volume 2

- The Vienna Convention on the Sale of Goods
- The Condition of the Law of Tort
- Innovations in Contract
- The Remedial Constructive Trust

Edited by P. B. H. BIRKS

OXFORD UNIVERSITY PRESS

This book has been printed digitally and produced in a standard design
in order to ensure its continuing availability

OXFORD
UNIVERSITY PRESS

Great Clarendon Street, Oxford OX2 6DP
Oxford University Press is a department of the University of Oxford.
It furthers the University's objective of excellence in research, scholarship,
and education by publishing worldwide in

Oxford New York

Athens Auckland Bangkok Bogotá Buenos Aires Calcutta
Cape Town Chennai Dar es Salaam Delhi Florence Hong Kong Istanbul
Karachi Kuala Lumpur Madrid Melbourne Mexico City Mumbai
Nairobi Paris São Paulo Singapore Taipei Tokyo Toronto Warsaw

and associated companies in Berlin Ibadan

Oxford is a registered trade mark of Oxford University Press
in the UK and certain other countries

Published in the United States
by Oxford University Press Inc., New York

ISBN 0-19-825951-4

Printed and Bound by Antony Rowe Ltd

EDITOR'S PREFACE

PETER BIRKS

THE series of seminars for which these papers were written is intended to make progress in areas where the law has become confused. The frontiers of liability are often enough obscured by the dust of doctrinal conflict which is itself raised by shocks whose epicentre is far from the courts and of whose nature lawyers know little. Fin de siècle tort is a paradigm in point. Half a century after *Donoghue* v. *Stevenson* [1932] A.C. 562, yet another in a long series of leading Scottish cases gave the House of Lords the ideal opportunity to mark out more clearly the frontiers of the modern law of negligence. In this volume, in 'The Condition of the Law of Tort,' Lord Rodger, who was junior counsel resisting liability in *Junior Books Ltd.* v. *Veitchi Co. Ltd.* [1983] A.C. 520, recalls what turns out to have been, not merely a missed opportunity, but the beginning of a decade and more of turbulence, coinciding, as the Lord Advocate notes, with the retirement of Lord Wilberforce.

In the intervening decade our higher courts have been beating some notable retreats in the search for defensible lines. However, Dr Stapleton justly observes that they have not yet succeeded in articulating a strategy for a more stable future. The prevailing instability has left room for competing analyses and different policy choices: Sir Robin Cooke's paper is thus both a critique of London and a guide to alternative positions. It also opens up a theme which recurred in other seminars and has recently been challengingly explored by Sir Anthony Mason, A.C.J., in the *Law Quarterly Review* ((1994) 110 L.Q.R. 238), namely the impediments derived from the division of law and equity.

In these tort papers the world of the seventies does indeed seem very distant. The shape of the law of negligence has altered. Politico-economic assumptions have changed. More importantly and more profoundly, their intellectual substructure has shifted. Dr Hepple's important paper, for example, could not have been written in that age; it belongs to the nineties.

'Innovations in Contract' shows that some of that subject's problems are far from new and that they probably require no more than much firmer intellectual management, as, for example, the conditions for outflanking privity and the confusion caused by the collision of consideration and the unrequested detrimental reliance which perfects an estoppel, but the papers of Chief Justice Gleeson and Professor McBryde throw new and interesting comparative light on long-standing English preoccupations. Scots law ought to have learned earlier to blow its trumpet louder and without the tired note of complaint against English pollution. A neighbouring system without a doctrine of consideration and with a doctrine which confers rights on third parties ought by rights to be of absorbing interest south of the border.

As for Australia, the most striking feature of its recent law of contract is the willingness of courts and legislatures at both State and Federal level to strike a new balance between rigorous certainty on the one hand and individual mercy on the other, favouring the latter to a degree calculated to alarm many English judges and, perhaps no less, the Chief Justice and the Bar of New South Wales. Professor Beatson, who has held these problems in his Law Commission portfolio, looks out at these developments from England. Identifying a number of shifting frontiers in English contract, his paper shows that, whatever caution may be exercised as to the substance of their innovations, there is no reluctance to listen what is going on in other jurisdictions. With the special insight of an experienced Law Commissioner, he also highlights the need, more urgent in our European situation, to resolve the common law's love-hate, mostly hate, relationship with statutes.

The law of contract is becoming increasingly aware of the problems created by the diversity of its responsibilities. A world of difference lies between consumers hiring cars and buying washing machines on the one hand and on the other maritime import and export between the United Kingdom and the United States or Japan. Professor Reynolds, summing up the contract papers, rightly emphasizes the English preoccupation with international commercial litigation. That preoccupation lies at the centre of the debate which surrounds the United Kingdom's attitude to the Vienna Convention on international sales. Should we adopt it or should we not? We seem to be better at opting out than opting in, and this despite the United Kingdom's new geo-political reality. However, the account is complex. There are different judgments as to national self-interest, and there are different judgments as to the practical interests of those engaged in international commerce. The arguments are considered fully and fairly in the papers. The balance is struck in the Convention's favour.

'The Remedial Constructive Trust' is perhaps the most intractably difficult and obscure of these four contested areas. Here the external shocks which have shaken doctrine derive from the combination of secularization and moral pluralism which has changed the structure of family life and, perhaps less importantly, from the ups and downs of the housing market. The constructive trust, be it remedial or substantive, has been enlisted in the quest for acceptable solutions to the proprietary problems of unmarried divorce. It has been compelled to make large but arguably false claims both to be equity's response to unjust enrichment and to be able to mobilize that concept to solve the economic problems of partners who split up.

However, the real source of the turbulence through which the constructive trust is currently hurtling may be more more mundane: language is being used, if not with disregard of meaning, at least without being properly explained and understood, certainly not with the degree of clarity upon which Lord Wilberforce would insist. Why is this? Either there has been a mercifully unintended lapse in the usual standards of lawyerly analysis. Or, more worryingly, 'equity on the move' (to adapt Mr Davies' graphically threatening phrase) has stirred up the forces of the myopic rationality of intuitive fairness, decked out in the mumbo-jumbo of unfamiliar vocabulary, to inflict a deeper and premeditated defeat upon the rationality, and justice, of lucidity and precision. The defenders of the latter are now embattled but, at least in England and despite the fact that their strategies differ, they are not in danger of imminent defeat.

The vigorous seminar showed that even the rougher frontiers of equity can engage deep intellectual loyalties and sustain not inconsiderable campaigns. But the military metaphor must not conceal a feature in which this and all the seminars in the series can take pride in sharing with academic life at its best, that strong differences and vehement argument carried no trace of personal rancour.

Special thanks are due to the distinguished chairmen who gave up their time to lead these seminars, and also to those who came from distant places to defend the papers which they had written (for these

events take place under what have come to be called 'Finn Rules' after the precedent set by Professor Paul Finn in his famous series of seminars at the Australian National University: the participants come to the event having already studied the papers, and, since they therefore come for discussion, not monologue, the papers are not given on the day but merely introduced briefly by someone other than their author, the author having the briefest right of reply before the issues are thrown open). The chairmen were, on 1st May 1993 (The Vienna Convention on the Sale of Goods) Professor Barry Nicholas, F.B.A., formerly Principal of Brasenose College, Oxford, who himself played a large part in the making and drafting of the Convention; on 3 July 1993 (The Condition of the Law of Tort) The Rt. Hon. Sir Thomas Bingham, Master of the Rolls; on 16th October 1993 (Innovations in Contract) the participants had to put up with the editor, standing in at short notice for Lord Mustill who was prevented from attending by the death of his father; and on 18th December 1993 (The Remedial Constructive Trust) the Vice-Chancellor, The Rt. Hon. Sir Donald Nicholls. Substitutes aside, the debt to the chairmen is real and deep, since the experience of each seminar and the quality of the discussion was immeasurably enhanced by the learning and sympathetic leadership which they brought to it.

The authors who travelled furthest were Professor Dr Peter Schlechtriem, from Albert Ludwig's University in Freiburg in Breisgau; the Rt. Hon. Sir Robin Cooke, President of the New Zealand Court of Appeal; the Hon. Murray Gleeson, Chief Justice of New South Wales; and Professor Donovan Waters, Q.C., from Victoria University, British Columbia. We owe them thanks not only for their willingness to come so far but also, and even more so, for the learning and authority of their papers. This latter debt is also owed to all the other authors of the papers which now appear in this volume and those who accepted the office of reporter and thus bore the burdensome duty of delivering at the end of each day an extempore summary of the discussion.

In extending his own and the Society's thanks to all the authors and reporters, the editor is bound to add that, though some months have passed—and obviously more since the earlier seminars—the exigencies of publication have meant that no contributor has had the opportunity to make more than very minor textual changes since very shortly after the day of the seminar in question. The dates of near-finality are all given in the previous paragraph.

The reporter for 'The Condition of the Law of Tort' was Mr Weir. In years to come, unless perhaps the photocopier that's friend to sparkling pages anticipates the covetous razorblade, 'Errare Humanum Est' will disappear from sight, although by then, if it does, some scholar will no doubt be able to earn merit, even a doctorate, by a palingenesia patiently culled from old examination papers. Let him cast his net wide, since it may not be in the Law Tripos that he will find candidates invited to discuss 'Daily commuters to Damascus do not frequently have blinding visions.' After five minutes of Mr Weir's coruscating pessimism, some university lawyers, the better kind, properly brought up, will fall on their swords, and nearly all the rest will look for some convenient hole or stone to hide in or under.

Life will recommence. It has that tendency. And, if to those who emerge some sight returns, they may later muster a little timid zeal for one or two old causes. First, the intellectual unity of the common law world does not depend on Milner's imperial vision, much less on an imperial court of last recourse in London, does not and never did require a monolithic doctrinal uniformity, and will not be broken by this country's new relationship with Europe. There is indeed one threat in the offing. It will not come from Europe. It will come from foolish neglect of existing contacts at all levels, between postgraduates, academics, practitioners and judges. The presence in these seminars of Sir Robin Cooke, Chief Justice Gleeson and Professor Donovan Waters warrants the closeness of the continuing intellectual links. The top postgraduate courses must be protected, and funded; and much more must be done to send some of our best young law graduates to Commonwealth jurisdictions. Exchanges at the postgraduate level, more than anything else, hold the key to the continuing unity of the world-wide common law.

Secondly, the rationality of the law is worth fighting for, and the security of knowing where you stand is not attainable where that battle is abandoned. And, finally, as the law library bears witness, academic lawyers are not the lowest form of legal life. They may indeed have been brainwashed into thinking otherwise by the curious culture of the English Bar, whose practice in the matter of citing sources would make believe no barrister ever opened any textbook. Since continental jurists were never wished so out of sight, this is one piece of nonsense which the new relationship with Europe will help dispel. Wonderful, therefore, though it be to behold, the danger of damaged eyes is only one of a number of reasons for trying to avoid being hoist with Mr Weir's spectacular petard.

The Contributors

Professor Jack Beatson is Rouse Ball Professor of English Law in the University of Cambridge and is completing his period of office as a Law Commissioner; *Professor Peter Birks, F.B.A.,* Honorary Secretary of the S.P.T.L., is Regius Professor of Civil Law in the University of Oxford and a Fellow of All Souls College, Oxford; *The Rt. Hon. Sir Robin Cooke* is President of the New Zealand Court of Appeal; *Mr J. D. Davies* is a Fellow of St Catherine's College, Oxford; *Mr John Eekelaar* is Reader in Law in the University of Oxford, a Fellow of Pembroke College, Oxford, and editor of the Oxford Journal of Legal Studies; *Mr Simon Gardner* is a Fellow of Lincoln College, Oxford; *The Hon. Murray Gleeson* is Chief Justice of the Supreme Court of New South Wales; *Dr Bob Hepple* is Master of Clare College, Cambridge; *Professor W. W. McBryde* is Professor of Law in the University of Dundee and has been Vice-Principal of that University; *Professor F. M. B. Reynolds, Q.C., F.B.A.,* is Professor of English Law in the University of Oxford, Fellow of Worcester College and Editor of the Law Quarterly Review; *The Rt. Hon. the Lord Rodger of Earlsferry, Q.C., F.B.A.* is Lord Advocate; *Professor Dr Peter Schlechtriem* is Professor of Law and Director of the Institute for Foreign Law and Private International Law in the Albert-Ludwig's University in Freiburg in Breisgau; *Dr Jane Stapleton* is a Fellow of Balliol College, Oxford; *The Rt. Hon. Sir Johan Steyn* is Lord Justice of Appeal and Chairman of the Lord Chancellor's Advisory Committee on Legal Education and Conduct; *Professor Donovan Waters, Q.C., F.R.S.C.* is Professor Emeritus in Victoria University, British Columbia, and author of the leading Canadian work on Trusts; *Mr Tony Weir* is Reader in Law in the University of Cambridge and a Fellow of Trinity College, Cambridge.

TABLE OF CONTENTS

TABLE OF UNITED KINGDOM CASES

TABLE OF CASES FROM OTHER JURISDICTIONS

TABLE OF UNITED KINGDOM LEGISLATION

TABLE OF LEGISLATION FROM OTHER JURISDICTIONS

TABLE OF INTERNATIONAL INSTRUMENTS

PART I

THE VIENNA CONVENTION ON THE SALE OF GOODS

1. A Kind of Esperanto?

JOHAN STEYN

THERE is bound to be some hostility among English lawyers to the ratification of the U.N. Convention on Contracts for the International Sale of Goods, 1980. Such hostility is not simply the result of the conservatism of those who practise law: it is an aversion to what are conceived to be impractical and theoretical solutions offered in the name of misguided internationalism. Anthony Trollope explained this inclination of English lawyers in Orley Farm through the views of an experienced barrister of Lincoln's Inn. The passage reads as follows:[1]

'Mr Furnival, with many others—indeed, with most of those who were so far advanced in the world as to be making bread by their profession—was of opinion that all this palaver that was going on in the various tongues of Babel would end as it began—in words. 'Vox et praeterea nihil'. To practical Englishmen most of these international congresses seem to arrive at nothing else.'

The judgement of 'practical Englishmen' must be read in the context of Trollope's description of Lord Boanerges, a congenital law reformer and attender of international conferences. It has been suggested that Victorians would immediately have thought of Lord Brougham.[2] His full title was Baron Brougham and Vaux. A contemporary joke was apparently to say, unfairly, that he was *Vox et praeterea nihil*.

The Hague Rules received the force of law by the Carriage of Goods by Sea Act 1924. The Hague Rules were embodied in a convention adopted at an international conference. The Rules placed substantial limitations on the freedom of contract of shipowners. There was fierce opposition from English lawyers to the proposed ratification of the convention. The eleventh edition of Scrutton on Charterparties was edited by Lord Justice Scrutton and by the future Lord Justice MacKinnon. It was published in 1923, the year before the enactment of the Carriage of Goods by Sea Act. The editors of this influential textbook criticized the enactment of the Hague Rules in extreme language. They described the intended change in the law as 'a terrifying prospect'.[3] The objection of these eminent lawyers was to the very conception of the enactment of a multi-lateral international convention which interfered with the free-

dom of contract of citizens of this country. An acknowledged master of shipping law and its history, Lord Roskill, has explained that the United Kingdom's enactment of the Carriage of Goods by Sea Act 1924 was the result of the acceptance by the Government and shipowners in 1923 that Britannia no longer ruled the waves, and that her shipowners were no longer able to dictate terms to the traders of the world.[4] Today, nobody would seriously defend the position taken by Scrutton and MacKinnon. They were demonstrably wrong in what Lord Roskill described as hysterical opposition to the enactment of the Hague Rules. But it is important to remember that they spoke at the time for 'practical Englishmen', and for a legal profession confident that an international multi-lateral convention should not be allowed to detract from rights accorded by the common law.

It must not be thought that this hostility to international conventions was restricted to judges and practising lawyers. Based on a study of official papers released under the socalled thirty year rule, and with reference to the period to the middle fifties Dr Patrick Polden has commented as follows:[5]

'Most of the Lord Chancellors of this period, and their permanent secretaries, shared with the majority of judges and lawyers a profoundly insular outlook towards the law which made them instinctively hostile towards almost any proposition which might trench on the sovereignty of the English courts. Bilateral treaties to facilitate the enforcement of private rights might be tolerated, though seldom encouraged, but multilateral treaties and conventions were anathema.'

A good illustration is to be found in the field of international commercial arbitration. The Geneva Protocol of 1923 had two objectives. The first was to ensure that arbitration clauses would be enforceable internationally. The second was to ensure that arbitration awards made pursuant to such arbitration agreements would be enforced in the territory of the states in which they were made. Although the Geneva Protocol was limited in its application, it proved a highly successful convention. The Geneva Convention of 1927 broadened the field of application of the Geneva Convention of 1923. These two conventions provided the backbone of the New York

---

[1] Chapter XVII.
[2] Mullen, *Anthony Trollope, A Victorian in his World*, 1990, 484, footnote.
[3] Introduction, v.

[4] (1992) 105 L.Q.R. 501.
[5] *Guide to the Records of the Lord Chancellors Department*, Chapter 10. The Guide was published in 1988.

Arbitration Convention of 1958, which must rank as a great success story in the field of international conventions. But it is now clear from official papers released under the thirty year rule that the Lord Chancellor, Lord Cave, and the Permanent Secretary, Sir Claud Schuster, bitterly opposed the ratification of the Geneva Protocol of 1923. The flavour of the opposition appears from a letter written by Sir Claud Schuster in 1924. The Permanent Secretary referred to the birth of the Protocol. He then stated:[6]

'I was most unfortunately present at that birth. I protested in season and out of season against any such protocol being entered into. When it had been entered into, in spite of my opposition, there was not much object in attempting to obstruct the passage of the Bill.

The then Lord Chancellor (Lord Cave) was also opposed to the making of the protocol. Unfortunately the whole thing took place when he was ill, and his opposition, therefore, was greatly hampered . . . I do not see what more we can do. I think we had better await the catastrophe which will undoubtedly follow and only hope that the officious persons who hatched this senseless document will then have to bear the consequences of their misdeed.'

This hostility to international conventions did not cease in 1923. A period of seventeen years elapsed before this country ratified the New York Arbitration Convention of 1958. It would be naive to suppose that the antipathy of English lawyers multilateral conventions had disappeared. But the success of the 1958 convention, the accelerating rate of ratifications, and the fact that the United Kingdom was being left out in the cold in international commercial arbitration, compelled ratification. And belated ratification of this convention in 1975 has been of enormous benefit to the United Kingdom.

Recently, there has been another manifestation of such antipathy towards international conventions. It concerns the Vienna Sales Convention. It took the form of a detailed note in a prestigious law journal under the heading 'International Conventions and Commercial Law: The Pursuit of Uniformity'.[7] The author was Sir John Hobhouse, an immensely experienced and most distinguished High Court Judge who sits in the Commercial Court. Apart from the Vienna Sales Convention the author specifically considers the following conventions and draft texts: U.N. Convention on the limitation period on the International Sale of Goods, New York, 1974; EEC Convention on the Law Applicable to Contractual Obligations, Rome, 1980; UNIDROIT Convention on Agency in the International Sale of Goods, Geneva, 1983. For present purposes I am only concerned with the writer's views on the Vienna Sales Convention. The writer poses the question whether the Vienna Sales Convention serves a useful purpose in the field of commercial law or provides a satisfactory basis for municipal legislation. He argues that the sole objective of the Vienna Sales Convention is the 'achievement of a stark uniformity'. He contends that the very concept of the convention is subversive of certainty which is the first and paramount requirement of a sound commercial law. He says that the convention is 'an inadequate legal tool without compensating gain'. He objects to the fact that the convention is in mandatory form. He likens the 'utopian ideal', which led to the adoption of the convention, to the movement for the adoption of Esperanto as a universal language. In conclusions he says:

'What should no longer be tolerated is the unthinking acceptance of a goal of uniformity and its doctrinaire imposition on the commercial community. Only conventions which demonstrably satisfy the well proven needs of the commercial community should be ratified and legislation should only be agreed to if it is demonstrably fit to be enacted as part of the municipal law of this country.'[8]

As far as I am aware the arguments of Mr Justice Hobhouse have not been answered or critically examined. That is my only justification for venturing to express disagreement in print with the views of an esteemed colleague. But having abandoned any self-denying ordinance it is right that I should express my contrary views as clearly and forthrightly as Mr Justice Hobhouse expressed his views.

B. The Quality of the Text of the Convention

Given the controversy about the acceptability of the Vienna Sales Convention for incorporation into our municipal law, it is necessary to assess the quality of the text of the convention. This is the threshold question. It is important, however, to approach this qualitative enquiry realistically. The convention is not a rival text, domestically inspired and drafted, to the Sale of Goods Act. The convention was adopted on 11 April 1980 by 62 states. Thirty-four states have deposited instruments of ratification, accession, etc. It is therefore to be judged as an international text which has already received wide currency.

The subjectmatter of the convention is the international sale of goods. It is difficult to think of any good reason why the international sale of goods should intrinsically be less suitable as the subjectmatter of an international convention than, say, carriage of goods by sea. Domestically, the sale of goods was regarded as a suitable subjectmatter for

---

[6] Letter dated 25.10.1924 to Chitty. I am indebted to Mr V. V. Veeder, Q.C., for drawing my attention to this material.

[7] (1990) 106 L.Q.R. 530.
[8] op. cit., 535.

codification as long ago as 1893. And in international terms, although there is a substantial divergence in sales regimes of different nations, there is also sufficient common ground to make it a suitable subjectmatter for an international convention. I will not struggle with the point. The very fact that a convention was adopted by 62 nations, and ratified, acceded to, etc, by 34 nations to date, makes it impossible to argue that international sale of goods is intrinsically not a suitable subjectmatter for an international convention.

That brings me back to the quality of the particular text which was adopted. The drafting style of the convention is not that favoured by English Parliamentary draftsmen. I suspect that many English judges, who have to grapple with English statutes, would not regard this point as fatal to the intrinsic merits of the text of an international convention. I agree with the assessment of Mr Glower W. Jones that the Vienna Convention is expressed in the simple phraseology of commerce: it should be comprehensible to traders and lawyers alike.[9]

The delegates to the Vienna conference had to make compromises. The text is a blend of the techniques of the common law and the civil law. The nature of the compromises is usually clear. Occasionally, there is ambiguity. In international contract negotiations parties often leave a draft contract in ambiguous form in order to achieve agreement. The reasoning is: 'If we insist on our meaning being spelt out in the agreement the transaction will be lost. We will take the risk that a neutral judge or arbitrator will uphold our view if there is a dispute'. Similarly, in the drafting of an international convention studied ambiguity is a standard technique employed to achieve a consensus. Professor Nicholas gives a good illustration of this process at work in respect of the Vienna Sales Convention.[10] Article 16 (2) of the convention provides that an offer cannot be revoked

'(a) if it indicates, whether by stating a fixed time for acceptance or otherwise, that it is irrevocably; or

(b) if it was reasonable for the offeree to rely on the offer and being irrevocable and the offeree has acted in reliance on the offer.'

The provision in (a) is ambiguous. It has been pointed out that for the common lawyer, stating a fixed time for acceptance is *prima facie* no more than an indication that after that time the offer, unless revoked, will lapse. On the other hand, for the civil lawyer it indicates that the offer is irrevocable until that time. Professor Nicholas points out that at the Vienna conference a United Kingdom amendment designed to clarify the text in the common law sense was rejected, as was a West German amendment in the opposite sense. The ambiguity was recognized. Deliberate ambiguity is a fact of life in the negotiation of an international conventions. And in character it is not all that different from the occasion when Parliamentary draftsmen, acting on departmental instructions, simply say 'No. We will not clarify that point. We will leave it to the courts.' Making due allowance for this feature in the Vienna Sales Convention, it is important not to exaggerate its importance.

From an English point of view the intrinsic merits of the text have been examined and analyzed in depth by Mr J D Feltham[11] and Professor Nicholas,[12] who were delegates of the United Kingdom to the vienna conference. They have also explored the material differences between the convention rules and English law. Mr Feltham's ultimate verdict was as follows:

'given the difficulty of achieving agreement across a large number of nations, common law and civil law, capitalist and socialist, developed and developing, the code is probably as good as can be expected.'[13]

Writing several years later Professor Nicholas was prepared to delete 'probably'.[14]

It does not seem to me that it would be a useful exercise for me to attempt a comprehensive assessment of the merits of particular aspects of the text. But from the point of view of English law I will comment at this stage on three matters which are regarded as significant in the continuing debate on the convention. The first relates to Article 7. It reads as follows:

(1) 'In the interpretation of this Convention, regard is to be had to its international character and to the need to promote uniformity in its application and the observance of good faith in international trade.

(2) Questions concerning matters governed by this Convention which are not expressly settled in it are to be settled in conformity with the general principles on which it is based or, in the absence of such principles, in conformity with the law applicable by virtue of the rules of private international law.'

[9] Impact of the Vienna Convention in Drafting International Sales Contracts, International Business Lawyer, September 1992, 421.
[10] Nicholas, (1989) 105 L.Q.R. 203, at 215.
[11] [1981] J.B.L. 346; (1991) J.B.L. 413.
[12] (1989) 105 L.Q.R. 203.
[13] op. cit., 361.
[14] op. cit., 243.

The concept of duty of good faith plays a restricted role in the common law.[15] In civil law systems there is an overriding principle that in the making and carrying out of contracts parties should act in good faith. Article 7 (1) creates no such duty. It merely spells out a canon of construction of the convention.[16] That seems to me a limited provision which ought to cause no concern to a common lawyer. It is true, of course, that the national courts of some civil law countries may hold that in the convention system there is a duty of good faith in the making and performance of the contract. If such a difference emerges it seems to me perfectly tolerable and not one which need imperil the success of the convention. The resort under Article 7 (2) to 'the general principles' on which the convention is based may seem strange to a common lawyer. But it makes good sense in a convention. For example, Article 13 provides that for the purposes of the convention 'writing' includes 'telegram and telex'. Facsimile exchanges were not yet in use when the convention was drafted. The application of 'the general principles' on which the convention is based make it easy to conclude that writing includes facsimile exchanges.

The second point relates to documentary sales. The convention, like the Sale of Goods Act 1979, does not contain special provisions spelling out the incidents of documentary sales. If the absence of such provisions in the convention make the conclusion and performance of C.I.F. and F.O.B. contracts, and other documentary sales, more difficult that would be a most serious reproach to the draftsmen of the convention. But it is important to remember that documentary sales are not uniquely English institutions. Such sales have their origin in trade usages and are accommodated in legal systems world wide. Article 9 reads as follows:

(1) 'The parties are bound by *any usage* to which they have agreed and by any practices which they have established between themselves.

(2) The parties are considered, unless otherwise agreed, to have impliedly made applicable to their contract or its formation a usage of which the parties knew or ought to have known and which in international trade is widely known to, and regularly observed by, parties to contracts of the type involved in the particular trade concerned. (My emphasis)

This provision ensures that documentary sales can be accommodated in the convention system.

In the third place I would refer to Article 49 (1). It reads as follows:

(1) The buyer may declare the contract avoided:
   (a) if the failure by the seller to perform any of his obligations under the contract or this Convention amounts to a fundamental breach of contract; or
   (b) in case of non-delivery, if the seller does not deliver the goods within the additional period of time fixed by the buyer in accordance with paragraph (1) of Article 47 or declares that he will not deliver within the period so fixed.

It seems to me that paragraph (b) contains a notion that would be perfectly acceptable to English contract lawyers. It has been said that the notion of 'fundamental breach' in paragraph (a) is new. That is true. But it seems to me a more satisfactory provision that our triple classification of terms as conditions, warranties and innominate terms. It is true that the convention does not expressly provide for terms with which strict compliance is required, i.e. conditions in English legal terminology. It is also true that such conditions sometimes have a useful role to play. But parties are, of course, free under the convention to require by the terms of their agreement strict compliance with particular terms.

No international convention will ever satisfy all countries. But from an English point of view I regard the Vienna Sales Convention as providing an acceptable basis for the negotiation and performance of international sale of goods as well as for resolution of disputes arising from such transactions.

C. The Objections in Principle

Mr Justice Hobhouse considered that the sole objective of the Vienna Sales Convention was the achievement of a stark uniformity. That observation seems to me an inadequate description of the objective of this trade law convention. The uncontroversial premise must be that the promotion of international trade is a desirable goal. One of the impediments to transnational trade is the differences between the commercial laws of different countries. And perhaps more important than objective divergences in national laws is uncertainty as to what the laws of different countries are. Uncertainty as to the nature and scope of legal risks is bad for trade. No convention can eliminate such differences: national courts may apply the convention differently. No convention can

---

[15] I explored this theme elsewhere: The Role of Good Faith and Fair Dealing in Contract Law: A Hair-Shirt Philosophy?, 1991 Denning Law Journal 131.

[16] Article 31 (1) of the Vienna Convention on the Law of Treaties, 1969, provides that a treaty shall be interpreted in good faith.

eliminate uncertainties in its application. But a convention such as the Vienna Sales Convention will tend to reduce differences and to eliminate uncertainty. Such considerations are the rationale of the convention rather than a simplistic notion of uniformity for its own sake.

The argument is, however, that a convention like the Vienna Sales Convention will by its nature 'introduce uncertainty where no uncertainty existed before'. The argument is that certainty is a hallmark of our sales code, which is based on legislation nearly 100 years old. That is not a generalization which should readily be conceded. For example, the English distinction between conditions, warranties and innominate terms still leads to considerable uncertainty in commercial practice. Our sales law is in other ways far from perfect. For example, the right to reject goods on the ground of a minor breach of a statutorily implied term is hardly a satisfactory rule.[17] Not surprisingly, judges often struggle to avoid the rigidity of the rule by doing justice in accordance with the merits of the individual dispute.

It seems to me that the argument against the ratification of the Vienna Sales Convention based on the importance of certainty in commercial dealings rests on a false premise. It appears to assume that English traders will always be able to insist that English sales law shall govern the contract. That assumption is wrong. This country is still an important trading nation but it is no longer in a dominant position in the international marketplace for the sale of goods. For every international sale of goods in respect of which an English trader is able to insist that English law must govern the transaction, there will be one where the English trader has to concede the applicability of a foreign legal system, which will usually have a different sales regime and, unfortunately, in the case of some developing countries will involve sales regimes which are little more than embryonic.

But that still leaves for consideration the assertion that the very concept of a multi-lateral convention like the Vienna Sales Convention is likely to be productive of uncertainty. The argument falls into the category of 'the sky will fall down' type of advocacy. In the field of trade law conventions it is also nothing new. Similar arguments were put forward by Scrutton and MacKinnon about the proposed enactment of the Hague Rules when they gave evidence to

the joint committee of the two houses presided over by Lord Sterndale, the Master of the Rolls. Lord Justice Scrutton told the committee:

'If you are going to make one contract which everybody must adopt, for Heaven's sale make it an intelligible one.'[18]

Both Scrutton and MacKinnon questioned the intelligibility of the Hague Rules with detailed references to the Rules. Lord Roskill has given the verdict of history about those predictions. He said:

'They gave dire and in the event wholly unwarranted warnings of the problems which would arise as to their construction with uncertainty and endless litigation replacing what they saw as the clarity of the existing law based upon freedom of contract. In truth, as every commercial lawyer knows, it is remarkable how few cases there have been in this country upon the construction of the Rules.'[19]

There is in my view no reason to think that the interpretation of the Vienna Sales Convention will give rise to significantly greater problems than were thrown up by the Hague Rules.

There is another policy argument based on certainty which must be considered. Article 8 (3) of the convention provides as follows:

'In determining the intent of a party or the understanding a reasonable person would have had, due consideration is to be given to all relevant circumstances of the case including *the negotiations*, any practices which the parties have established between themselves, usages and *any subsequent conduct* of the parties.'   (My emphasis)

Mr Derek Wheatley, Q.C., who shares the views of Mr Justice Hobhouse on the Vienna Sales Convention, has argued that the certainty of our own law of contract would be undermined if the provisions of Article 8 (3) becomes part of such law.[20] He had in mind the rules of English law (a) that pre-contractual negotiations are not admissible in aid of the interpretation of a contract (the rule in *Prenn* v. *Simmonds*)[21] and (b) that the subsequent conduct of parties in the performance of a contract are also not admissible in aid of the interpretation of the contract (the rule in *Schuler* v. *Wickman*).[22] But English law is not quite so simple. Dealing first with the rule in *Prenn* v. *Simmonds* it is of some importance to note that in the *Karen Oltman*[23] the court rules that pre-contractual telex exchanges are admissible in aid of interpretation of an ambiguous word in a contract on the basis that the parties had contracted on an agreed basis. On this basis pre-contractual exchanges are

[17] Law Commission, No 160: Sale and Supply of Goods (1987).
[18] Parliamentary Papers, 1923, V, 836.
[19] (1992) 105 L.Q.R. 501.
[20] *The Times*, 27 March 1990. A riposte to Mr Wheatley's

article by Professor Roy Goods was published in *The Times* on 22 May 1990.
[21] [1971] 1 WLR 1381.
[22] [1974] A.C. 235.
[23] [1976] 2 Ll.L.R. 708.

regularly adduced in relation to disputes about the interpretation of contracts. The rule in *Wickman* v. *Schuler* is also subject to an important qualification. It is now established that if parties have acted on a common assumption as to the meaning of a provision in a contract, then subject to considerations of justice and equity, a party may be precluded from relying on the true interpretation.[24] This qualification permits evidence of 'practical construction', as it is called in the United States, to be introduced in English courts. Despite these qualifications it is probably true that extrinsic evidence in aid of the c construction of contracts is more readily admitted in civilian systems than in England. But the concession in Article 8 (3) to civilian jurisprudence hardly threatens the fabric of English contract law. In my view it will be a fairly rare case in which the admission of such material, which is not at present admissible under English law, will lead to different results.

A further objection in principle, which was canvassed by Mr Justice Hobhouse, is the fact that the Vienna Sales Convention, if ratified, will have mandatory effect. I readily accept that it is not a sufficient answer to this objection say that parties may by agreement exclude the application of the convention. It is also true that it would have been possible to draft a Model Law of the International Sale of Goods, akin to UNCITRAL's Model Law of Arbitration, leaving it to countries to decide whether to adopt it as part of their municipal systems. Such a course was necessary in the field of arbitration because of the drastic difference in national arbitration laws which made the adoption of a convention beyond the scope of the 1958 New York Convention impractical. But in the field of sales law a convention was a feasible preposition, as the extent of the ratification of the Vienna Sales Convention has already demonstrated. But, in any event, a model law, if enacted, also represents a mandatory regime. Similarly, to the extent that a trade law convention is adopted it simply replaces the existing mandatory sales regimes of ratifying countries. This objection in principle attacks the very conception of the utility of a trade law convention, and it does so on the false premise that it introduces for the first time mandatory sales regimes. There is a very good reason why the Vienna Sales Convention has mandatory effect. It has mandatory effect because it provides solutions in transnational transactions which parties have failed to solve in their contract. In my view this objection in principle is not warranted.

Mr Justice Hobhouse raised another objection to the ratification of the convention. He referred to the difficulty of amending and updating them. This point applies to all international conventions and cannot by itself be a good reason for abandoning such international initiatives. The law must not set its sights too high. If a trade law convention can play a productive role in facilitating trade over a few decades that is a great success.

D. The case for ratification

In evaluating the case for ratification by the United Kingdom of the Vienna Sales Convention it is essential to take into account the extent to which the convention has gained currency. The convention has already been ratified by 34 nations. Within the European Economic Community the convention has been ratified by Germany, France, Italy, Netherlands, Denmark, Spain and Greece. In the common law family of states the United States, Canada, Australia and Singapore have ratified the convention. There is also the undoubted prospect of further ratifications in the next few years.

Another relevant aspect of the contextual scene is the relative strength of the United Kingdom in international trade. If Britannia still ruled the waves in international trade—to quote again Lord Roskill's phrase—it would have been possible to argue that our traders should generally be able to insist on English law applying to transactions entered into by them and that there is no compelling need for the United Kingdom to ratify the convention. Sadly, however, the decline of our position in international trade has been considerable. Britain's share of the world trade in manufacture has apparently declined, from about 40 per cent in 1880, to less than 7 per cent a century later.[25] And the inexorable downward trend since 1945 is particularly noteworthy.[26] It is idle to pretend that our position in the international marketplace for the sale of goods is stronger than that of other medium sized trading nations. This factor is one of the principal reasons which led the Law Commission, in response to the Consultative Document issued in June 1989 by the Department of Trade and Industry, to recommend that the United Kingdom should ratify the convention.[27]

The consequences of the decline in the United

---

[24] *Norwegian American Cruises A/S* v. *Paul Mundy Ltd* (*The Vistafjord*) [1988] 2 Ll.L.R. 343, at 350–53.

[25] Smith, *The British Economic Crisis: Its Past and Future*, Penguin Books, 1989, 55.

[26] *The British Economy since 1945*, edited by Craft and Woodward, Clarendon Press, 1991, 148 (Fig. 5.4).

[27] Law Commission memorandum submitted to the Department of Trade and Industry under cover of a letter dated 30 October 1989; Law Commissions Twenty-Sixth Annual Report 1991, par. 2.6.

Kingdom's position in international trade are obvious. It means that for every contract, subject to English law, which an English trader is able to negotiate, there will be another contract governed by foreign law. Looking at the matter from the point of view of English traders the argument based on the asserted superiority of English law over the convention therefore breaks down. Frequently, our traders will be confronted with an irresistible demand by the other Party that his law or the law of a neutral country must apply. The content of that foreign law may not always be easy to ascertain: in the case of developing countries the law may be skeletal in the extreme. These considerations are an impediment to the successful conclusion of the transaction. On the other hand, the Vienna Sales Convention has the badge of neutrality and tends to facilitate the conclusion of transnational transactions. There is another aspect of the problems presently confronting our traders which is worth considering. A prudent trader faced with a demand to contract subject to a foreign law will often take advice on the legal risks involved. Taking advice on foreign legal systems is time consuming: the transaction may be lost before the advice is received. Moreover, the taking of advice on foreign law is a costly business. The convention therefore tends to reduce the costs of business transactions.[28]

It is also necessary to consider what happens if a dispute arises. If the contract is governed by a foreign law, it is often necessary to call expert witnesses to prove the relevant foreign law. A substantial part of the Commercial Court's time is taken up by the hearing of such disputes. The need to prove foreign law tends to delay the disposal of cases, and adds enormously to the cost of litigation. On the other hand if the convention is ratified and the convention rules apply, the court will not need expert evidence. And that will be so even if a party wishes to refer to decisions of foreign courts as persuasive authority on the interpretation of the convention.

E. Conclusion

The right questions seems to me to ask whether it is the best interests of the United Kingdom as a trading nation to ratify the Vienna Sales Convention. Like the Law Commission I take the view that the United Kingdom ought to ratify the convention.[29] At present our traders are at a disadvantage in the international market place. In my view it is important that ratification should not be delayed. But I am far from sanguine that anything will be done until the march of events, and acceleration of ratifications, absolutely compels it. Even in the face of overwhelming evidence that it is in the best interests of this country to ratify the convention, the antipathy of lawyers towards mandatory multi-lateral conventions may well delay what needs to be done for many years. Having started with a quotation from Trollope, I will end with another which dwells on the prejudice of English lawyers against learning from international experience. The reflection of an English lawyer was as follows:

'It would be useless at present, seeing that we cannot bring ourselves to believe it possible that a foreigner should in any respect be wiser than ourselves. If any such point out to us our follies, we at once claim those follies as the special evidences of our wisdom. We are so self-satisfied with out own customs, that we hold up our hands with surprise at the fatuity of men who presume to point out to us their defects.'[30]

Mr Wheatley's article in *The Times* was headed 'Why I oppose the wind of change'. Sadly, I doubt that there is yet much of a wind of change. Possibly there is still an educational task to be performed in demonstrating where the best interests of our country lie. But whatever we do the Vienna Sales Convention is a reality and its influence can only increase.

---

[28] Ndulo, (1989) 38 I.C.L.Q.R.1, 24–5.
[29] The Law Commission recommended that a declaration excluding Article 1 (1) (b) should be made under Article 95. I respectfully agree.

2. A Note of Caution

F. M. B. REYNOLDS Q.C.

Introduction

'Does the Lord Chancellor have no feeling for the superiority of law grown by experience and developed by judicial wisdom over statutory tests drawn up by a committee of theorists speaking different languages and trained in different legal systems?'

Dr F. A. Mann, December 1989.

THE above question from a letter to *The Times* actually concerns the Rome Convention on the Law Applicable to Contractual Obligations, which is now operative in this country by virtue of the Contracts (Applicable Law) Act 1990. It does not however seem inappropriate to cite it in the present context of the international sale of goods. For although the starting point for the solution of a problem in sale of goods in English law is not in fact judge-made law but the Sale of Goods Act 1979 (actually of course an Act of 1893), as regards international sales the provisions of the Act have almost all been overlaid by special law developed by means of judicial decision. It is therefore largely judge-made law with which we shall be, initially at any rate, dispensing (though we shall need more) if we adopt the Vienna Convention on Contracts for the International Sale of Goods.

Following the tone set by Dr Mann's words, I shall commence with some hard comments about the Vienna Convention: but in case any reader concludes that this is another typical English lawyer's last ditch counter-attack on the Convention, I should say at once that I shall conclude with the view that the United Kingdom ought to adopt it (though certainly not initially for the domestic law of sale of goods).

There is already an enormous amount written on the Convention, mostly by persons involved in its genesis, and I shall not seek to summarise or digest all of this,[1] nor to go over all the provisions of the Convention even in outline. I shall confine my observations to general ones about the desirability and value of such a convention and the ways in which such a convention may be useful and may do harm; about its general character and scheme; and about the extent to which it is appropriate to regulate its subject-matter, the international sale of goods. I conclude with some suggestions as to the role that the Convention might acceptably play in this country.

A. The Value of the Project

A great deal of time and effort has over a considerable period of years gone into the production of this convention. So it is really too late to ask whether such a project was ever desirable in the first place. Nevertheless it may assist one in assessing the merits of the Convention to consider what advantages might have been expected from a set of legal rules produced by an international committee largely slanted towards the approach of the theorist.

Such a product might, first, appear a step towards the international unification of commercial law. It is difficult to deny that that is a worthy object: but the serious differences in legal method, and even in views of the function of law in the community, make its attainment a very distant vision indeed. Within areas of some legal and cultural homogeneity, for instance on the continent of Europe, some forms of unification may be more attainable: but even in Europe there are very considerable differences in legal technique from one country to another, and all over the world the present fashion is towards emphasis on local individuality. For example, far from moving towards a common language, countries are taking steps to preserve and revive local languages. The same is to some extent true of law. It has been pointed out that conventions like that which we are discussing have a similarity to Esperanto. Just as an artificially devised language has not been found a suitable medium of international communication, so also an artificially devised law may not be.[2]

Secondly, in countries where the law of sale of goods is to be derived from different sources—in particular, partly from the general principles of a civil code and partly from a more detailed commercial code—a unified code for the contract of sale may be a general benefit, one which may even be translatable into domestic law. This may be an advantage for such countries, but it is not necessarily an advantage for all. The United States already has a fairly modern set of provisions on sales in the Uniform Commercial

---

[1] A good starting-point for an English lawyer is Professor Nicholas' summary of the Convention provisions in (1989) 105 L.Q.R. 201, which contains citations to material available at that date.

[2] See Sir John Hobhouse (1990) 106 L.Q.R. 530.

Code. The United Kingdom has the Sale of Goods Act. This is old, and far from being as perfect as was once thought. But it is not clear that it is yet totally unsatisfactory: wider projects of reform appear to have (so far) failed in Canada;[3] even small changes to the Act in the interests of consumers have only recently secured Parliamentary time in England;[4] and international sales are in any case provided for by an extensive overlay of case law in which flaws can be detected, but not such as to require a completely fresh start. A different code, emanating from meetings of theorists rather than (as in the case of the Sale of Goods Act) from decisions in actual disputes, and without (as in the Uniform Commercial Code) any input from persons involved in commerce, may be a doubtful advantage.[5]

It is also rightly said in this context that the Convention is drafted in terms that are (at least in English) simple and clear. But this can also be said of the Uniform Commercial Code and the Sale of Goods Act. In any case, much further knowledge is required for the understanding of how to apply these codes (especially the Sale of Goods Act); and it will be required also for the Vienna Convention also. For the superficial simplicity of its provisions hides very many difficulties.[6]

Thirdly, where the parties do not make clear their choice of the law to govern an international contract, so that the court has to determine with which country the contract is most closely connected, or apply some similar test, much trouble could be saved if the potentially relevant laws were the same, or at least strongly similar with local variations of interpretation. This point is also significant in countries where a choice of law by the parties need not be accepted, and some other law may be held to govern: though the adoption by many European countries of the Rome Convention referred to above will reduce the incidence of this phenomenon. The difficulties faced by courts in this context may perhaps be more serious where the judge may be able or obliged to take the point about the applicability of foreign law himself, and even to conduct his own independent researches into the foreign law. But in a jurisdiction, such as England, where if foreign law is not pleaded and proved the court applies its own law, this point has less validity. And in any case the problems of the conflict of laws remain for questions outside the scope of the Convention, such as the passing of property, agency and the capacity (which usually in

practice means corporate capacity) of the parties.

Fourthly, those from developing countries may feel themselves at a disadvantage by being exposed to the laws of a developed country which have been chosen by the overseas exporter or importer with whom they deal. Even the law of a 'neutral' country unconnected with the facts of the transaction may appear unsatisfactory. If both the developing country and the developed country have adopted the Convention, which was elaborately negotiated internationally at meetings attended by representatives of developing as well as of developed countries, this feeling of disadvantage may be alleviated. Alternatively, the developed country may offer the Convention as part of its law, pointing out that though part of that law it is in fact an international convention. Either way, the availability of the Convention will provide a friendly gesture to the developing country and also facilitate trade in general.

This is the strongest point so far mentioned in favour of conventions of this sort. There may well be advantages here: but they may not be so great as might be hoped. For the developing country is likely to deal as exporter in primary commodities, and these bring in many other international contracts—insurance, letters of credit, contracts of carriage and especially string sales. To alter the sales regime without taking into account the law relating to the connected transactions also may create more difficulties than it solves.

It must next be emphasised that the Vienna Convention is a product having its origin entirely in theory. It is in fact a development of work which started in Europe in the late 1920s, inspired to a considerable extent by Rabel, and led first to the Uniform Law on International Sales of 1954, which had little effect in Europe and none at all in the United Kingdom. If one seeks to understand a provision of the Convention better by investigating its provenance (as one can in the U.K. Sale of Goods Act, where the actual decisions, in real-life disputes, on which sections are based are, if rather old-fashioned, easily accessible), the documentation simply takes one back through previous provisions and drafts,[7] and to reports of discussions at which different views are expressed and questions decided by vote. So what one goes back to is simply earlier theory. It does not appear that the value of the exercise was often questioned; nor that investigation was commissioned as to commercial practices and preferences. The Ameri-

[3] The Ontario Law Commission's Report on Sale of Goods (1979).
[4] See the reforms proposed in 'Sale and Supply of Goods', Law Com. No. 160, Scot Law Com. No. 104 (1987).
[5] See Kahn, *La Vente Commerciale Internationale* (1961).
[6] Many examples are given in an important article by Hell-

ner, 'The UN Convention on International Sales of Goods—an Outsider's View': *Ius inter Nationes*, Festschrift für Stefan Riesenfeld (1983) 71.
[7] See, e.g. Honnold, *Uniform Law for International Sales under the 1980 United Nations Convention* (2nd ed.), Appendix B ('Concordance').

can Uniform Commercial Code does not purport to codify case law, but commercial views were taken during its drafting. Such a product would, equally, in this country surely only have been undertaken in consultation with representatives of traders, insurers, banks and the like, along the same lines as the genesis of the Hague Rules and the establishment and regular revision of the Uniform Customs and Practice on Documentary Credits. Even the Hamburg Rules on Carriage by Sea, which arguably have a political or even moral objective to rectify the balance of power in favour of shippers rather than carriers, and hence of developing countries, were formulated with the full participation of shipping interests. This had been true also the Hague and Hague-Visby Rules.

Finally, it must be borne in mind that conventions such as this are extremely difficult to change. Domestic legislation can be altered, even if with difficulty; case law can be developed. A convention such as this is almost carved in stone: will what was appropriate in 1993 be appropriate in 2013? States can modify their own versions: but then the uniformity is lost.

Mr J. D. Feltham, one of the British negotiators, said that 'given the difficulty of achieving agreement across a large number of nations, common law and civil law, capitalist and socialist, developed and developing, the code is probably as good as can be expected.'[8] Professor Nicholas subsequently ventured to delete the word 'probably'.[9] No doubt this is correct: but the value of an enterprise so conceived is not beyond doubt.

B. The Scheme of the Convention

Part II. Formation of the Contract

I turn now to the substantive provisions of the Convention itself. I propose to spend little time on Part II, which deals with formation of contract. I suggest that it is of little importance. The problems which it attacks, those of the offer and acceptance model, are well known to common lawyers, and probably to all lawyers, from their student days. The main differences from what is understood to be the current position in English law are that an offer can by its terms be irrevocable, i.e., without consideration to support

the promise to keep it open, or may become irrevocable because the offeree has acted in reliance on it;[10] and that acceptance of an offer becomes effective at the moment the indication of assent reaches the offeror rather than on dispatch.[11] So long as one has rules, it need not matter much what they are: even if one disagrees with them, I doubt whether accommodation to these solutions would be difficult.

Although the Law Commission not very long ago did not accept a view that 'firm offers' ought to be binding,[12] I find it difficult to see much actual objection to their being made so. In any case common lawyers, who attach much less significance to the doctrine of consideration than foreign observers, can often find consideration, and there is plenty of supportive material which could be deployed to render ineffective the revocation of an offer which has been relied on.[13] The 'postal acceptance rule has always seemed to me an anachronism deriving from the regular use, and perhaps greater reliability, of the mail in the late nineteenth century. Its general significance in the modern context has been much reduced:[14] I doubt if its passing will be mourned.

There are provisions concerning the well-known problem of the 'battle of the forms'. This problem is unsolved, and what is suggested is probably no worse than the solutions which might be applied at present.[15] The solutions which Part II offers seem to me neither better nor worse than others. They will not be difficult to accommodate should there be a wider reason for adopting them. They will, of course, raise problems of the conflict of laws.

A well-known inconsistency exists between Article 14 (1) and Article 55. It seems to reflect a pacific reconciliation between different doctrinal approaches to the significance of agreement on price. The second sentence of Article 14 (1) indicates that a proposal for a sale is only an offer if it 'implicitly fixes or makes provision for determining the ... price.' Article 55 however provides that where it does not, 'the parties are considered ... to have impliedly made reference to the price generally charged at the time of the conclusion of the contract for such goods ...' Common lawyers will have little difficulty in combining the two; but it has been suggested by the Scottish Law Commission that for clarity the second sentence of Article 14 (1)

---

[8] [1981] J.B.L. 346, 361 (but with reservations).

[9] Op. cit. supra, n. 1 at p. 243 (a misleading quotation).

[10] Article 16 (2).

[11] Article 18 (2). However, in general an offer can be revoked if the revocation reaches the offeree before he has *dispatched* an acceptance: Article 16 (1).

[12] 'Firm Offers', W.P. No. 60 (1975) (a Working Paper that never led to a Report).

[13] e.g. *Errington* v. *Errington* [1952] 1 K.B. 290.

[14] See, e.g. *Holwell Securities Ltd.* v. *Hughes* [1974] 1 W.L.R. 155; *Brinkibon Ltd.* v. *Stahag Stahl GmbH* [1983] 2 A.C. 34.

[15] See *Butler Machine Tool Ltd.* v. *Ex-Cell-O Corp.* (*England*) *Ltd.* [1979] 1 W.L.R. 401. For a different view, that they are worse, see Hellner, 'The Vienna Convention and Standard Form Contracts': *Dubrovnik Lectures* (1986), Ch. 10.

would be better omitted in any legislative acceptance of the proposals.[16]

The suggestion of the Scottish Law Commission just referred to comes from a useful Consultation paper,[17] discussing Part II and tentatively recommending that its solutions be adopted for the general law of Scotland. If Part II was adopted with the rest of the Convention, it would certainly seem odd to have different rules for the formation of international sales than for domestic sales and other contracts and there could be a case for generalising its results. But if agreement cannot be secured on any of these matters, it is possible to avoid the whole problem of formation by making a reservation[18] and excluding Part II.

It is too easy to be sidetracked by Part II. In one of the early seminars on the Convention conducted in London, Professor Honnold spent a considerable time drawing attention to the rules in it, considering in particular the merits of the rule that an offer expressed as irrevocable cannot be withdrawn. Immeasurably more significant, I suggest, are the provisions of Part III dealing with the contractual aspects of the sale of goods: and of those easily the most important, and hardly touched on at the seminar to which I have referred, are the provisions on remedies. To Part III I therefore now turn.

Part III. Sale of Goods

The general provisions of Part III as to the duties of seller and buyer are similar to what one would expect and do not require comment here. What all traders need to know, however, is what to do if things go wrong; and here the provisions of the Convention produce something very different from what we are accustomed to in this country.

Broadly, the position as to remedies under the United Kingdom Sale of Goods Act, as interpreted and developed for international sales, is as follows.

The *buyer* cannot normally obtain specific performance, i.e. an order of the court that the goods be delivered to him. This, partly because of its impact in bankruptcy situations, is normally only available in the case of unique goods, and at the discretion of the court.[19] He has however quite extensive rights to

treat the contract as discharged, i.e. terminate it. He can do this in two contrasting situations. First, if the seller's misperformance has involved breach of a term in the contract in respect of which the parties are interpreted as having intended exact compliance (a condition), the buyer can treat the contract as discharged however slight the breach of the term and whether he is prejudiced by the breach or not.[20] This is particularly effective where the term is sharply defined (as where goods are specified, or dates laid down for performance of various stages in the performance of a sale); it is less so where the term is of its nature imprecise (such as 'merchantable quality'[21]).

At the other extreme, the buyer can treat the contract as discharged if the breach is such as to deprive him of '*substantially the whole* benefit of the contract' (which I shall call the '*Hong Kong Fir* formula', after the case from which the words come[22]). In the middle comes a vague formula which simply asks whether the seller's conduct is repudiatory or renunciatory.[23] Apart from situations of straight refusal to perform, and of anticipatory breach, this has its main use in long-term (e.g., instalment) contracts. Beyond this there is an entitlement in all cases to damages.

The remedies of the seller are similar. However, he is rather more readily entitled to specific performance, in that the performance to which he is entitled is usually payment of the price, and common law developed an action (the action in debt) for this, without doing so for other forms of performance. The availability of the action is somewhat restricted; but it certainly can fairly readily be available.[24] As to discharge by breach, the seller is perhaps less likely than the buyer to be able to rely on a condition (there are none in his favour in the Sale of Goods Act) and hence perhaps more likely to have to rely on the *Hong Kong Fir* formula or the 'repudiatory conduct' technique. Again there is beyond this an entitlement to damages.

The right to treat the contract as discharged is however lost by affirmation or election, which requires a clear manifestation of intention to affirm. There are complexities here, as a party may be estopped from saying that he has not affirmed,[25] and by statute the buyer may lose the right to reject in

---

[16] Consultation Paper on 'Formation of Contract: Scottish Law and the United Nations Convention on Contracts for the International Sale of Goods' (1992), s. 3.3.

[17] *Supra.*

[18] Under Article 92.

[19] s. 52.

[20] A leading case is *Bunge Corp.* v. *Tradax Export S.A.* [1981] 1 W.L.R. 711.

[21] As in *Cehave NV* v. *Bremer Handelsgesellschaft mbH*

(*The Hansa Nord*) [1976] Q.B. 44.

[22] See *Hong Kong Fir Shipping Co. Ltd.* v. *Kawasaki Kisen Kaisha Ltd.* [1962] 2 Q.B. 26, 66 per Diplock L. J.

[23] e.g. *Decro-Wall International S.A.* v. *Practitioners in Marketing Ltd.* [1971] 1 W.L.R. 361; Sale of Goods Act 1979, s. 31.

[24] See Sale of Goods Act 1979, s. 49.

[25] e.g. *Panchaud Freres S.A.* v. *Etablissements General Grain Co.* [1970] 1 Lloyd's Rep. 53; *Peyman* v. *Lanjani* [1985] Ch. 457.

certain circumstances even without knowing that he has it.[26] Modifications of contract (i.e. in this context a complete waiver of rights) require in principle to be supported by consideration, though a recent decision on this point makes consideration not difficult to find,[27] and in any case the doctrine of promissory estoppel may apply.

Where there is no right to treat the contract as discharged there is still a right in damages; and here it is the only remedy.

The English law on affirmation or election and on waiver (a term which can be sued in several senses) or promissory estoppel is imprecise and still in process of evolution. It cannot be regarded as clear or entirely satisfactory.[28] (In this respect the provision of the Convention[29] which provides that 'A contract may be modified . . . by the mere agreement of the parties' would assist in the development of English law, which has long been moving in that direction anyway.) But beyond this the rights of the innocent party to a breach of contract are fairly clear. English judges are indeed much given to stressing the predictability in commercial transactions which results from the approach of English law. Some of this may be over-optimistically expressed: experienced international sales litigators will say that it is not at all easy to predict when an English court will hold a term a condition or say that one party has been deprived of substantially the whole benefit of the contract, and that the latter technique requires waiting to see what happens, while parties want to negotiate sooner. But the scheme is by and large fairly easy to grasp.

When we turn to the Convention, however, we find something which may indeed have more facilities for fine-tuning, but is going to be far more complicated for the average person in commerce to apply. The first remedy mentioned for both buyer and seller is to require performance.[30] Though this seems unfamiliar to common lawyers, there is a 'let-out' allowing a court not to enter a judgment for specific performance unless it would do so under its own law in similar circumstances.[31] We also are familiar with an action for the price, though its availability in English law is more circumscribed than in the Convention.[32] For the purposes of the Convention it seems fairly clear that such an action comes under the general ability to require performance, though it is unclear whether the procedural 'let-out' referred to above applies to actions for the price also. Some of the differences here may therefore prove to be of a technical nature.

However, the buyer's right to treat the contract as discharged ('declare the contract avoided') requires either a 'fundamental breach',[33] or, if the breach is one of non-performance, the service of a notice (the 'quasi-*nachfrist*') which is not complied with.[34] The idea of setting time, i.e. making time of the essence, is not unfamiliar in English conveyancing contracts,[35] and it is usually thought possible that similar procedures may be exercised in other contexts.[36] But the idea of 'fundamental breach', for all the familiar appearance of the words, is a new notion, apparently for civil lawyers and common lawyers alike. To us, it seems to be half-way between the English extremes of a breach of condition and a breach under the *Hong Kong Fir* formula. The breach must 'result in such detriment to the other party as substantially to deprive him of what he is entitled to expect under the contract'; and there follows an exception for situations where 'the party in breach did not foresee and a reasonable person of the same kind in the same circumstances would not have foreseen such a result.'[37] The first part of the provision has neither the predictability (and favour towards discharge) of the 'condition' technique, nor does its wording indicate anything like such a serious breach as that indicated by the *Hong Kong Fir* technique. It is half way between the two. The wording of it is also slanted towards breach by the seller: it is not at all clear what it means in connection with the breaches which the buyer can commit.[38] The second part merely adds criteria of an imprecise nature which are inconsistent with the strict duties that common lawyers regard as appropriate to commercial transactions. Such matters as contemplation and foreseeability may well be appropriate to the calculation of damages; but it may be thought that they are less so to the question of whether the innocent party must carry on with the contract.

This scheme does not allow for terms with which strict compliance is required (*anglice*, conditions), at least unless the notion of fundamental breach is given a very creative interpretation. (There are

---

[26] Sale of Goods Act 1979, s. 35.

[27] *Williams* v. *Roffey Bros. & Nicholls (Contractors) Ltd.* [1991] 1 Q.B. 1. But *cf. Re Selectmove*, C.A., 21 December 1993.

[28] See however the useful account given by Lord Goff of Chieveley in *The Kanchenjunga* [1990] 1 Lloyd's Rep. 391, 397–99.

[29] Article 29 (1).

[30] Articles 46 (1), 62.

[31] Article 28.

[32] Cf. Article 62 with Sale of Goods Act 1979, s. 49.

[33] Article 49 (1).

[34] Articles 47, 49.

[35] See, e.g. *Behzadi* v. *Shaftesbury Hotels Ltd.* [1992] Ch. 1; *Re Olympia & York Canary Wharf (No. 2)* [1993] BCC 159.

[36] See Beale, *Remedies for Breach of Contract* (1980), pp. 89–90, referring to *Charles Rickards Ltd.* v. *Oppenhaim* [1950] 1 K.B. 616 (actually a case on termination of a waiver).

[37] Article 25.

[38] See Hellner, op. cit. supra, n. 6, pp. 91–2.

commentators who suggest that it could be, though usually in connection with the buyer's duty to pay the price.) The notion of 'fundamental breach' seems likely to create situations of great uncertainty, and to make it difficult to draft a contract under which exact compliance can be required. It is sometimes said that the scheme favours the continuation rather than the termination of contracts. This is true in one sense—there may be no conditions; but not true in another—the requirements of fundamental breach are easier to satisfy than those operative at common law.

Beyond this, however, comes a battery of remedies which greatly further complicate the scene. The buyer may, if the breach is fundamental (but not otherwise) require the delivery of substitute goods;[39] or may in the case of any disconformity, require repair.[40] He may also reduce the price.[41] The seller may cure defects, sometimes even after the date for delivery.[42] It may be that the presence of all these remedies is largely a 'window dressing' operation and that damages will be the normal remedy. But they certainly complicate the appearance created by the régime.

The rights of the seller are rather simpler, and in general nearer to the present English law. They are to require performance, largely by way of action for the price, which has already been referred to; to avoid the contract;[43] and to sue for damages. The action for the price, as stated above, is more readily available than under the Sale of Goods Act, which requires that the property have passed or the price be payable on a 'day certain':[44] the Uniform Commercial Code has further restrictions still.[45] There is also a right to require other forms of performance, such as the taking of delivery.[46] Hence a seller may be able to insist on performance where to a common lawyer he ought to mitigate his damages by taking a practicable opportunity of making a cover purchase; and it appears that he can in some situations revest the property in himself though he has parted with possession,[47] a notion entirely unfamiliar to common lawyers. The seller can avoid the contract on fundamental breach or on the elapsing of a time which he

has set;[48] and he has an unexpected right in situations where the buyer is to specify the form, measurement or other features of the goods, of doing so himself.[49]

The Convention is full of references to the prompt exercise of rights and to action within a reasonable time;[50] and in the case of non-conformity of the goods there is an absolute two-year time bar placed on the buyer.[51] Such a fixed period is unfamiliar to common lawyers (except those who had the benefit of studying Roman law), and may provide traps, at any rate at first. Some of the early cases concern this point. But it cannot be said that the common law rules of affirmation, waiver and estoppel are much, if at all, better; and in any case a recent first instance decision on section 35 of the Sale of Goods Act interprets the policy of the Act as requiring prompt exercise of rights in a way not unlike what seems to be the assumptions of the Convention.[52] And the Convention, in Article 82, lays down clearly the position as to when rejection is barred by impossibility of restitution, a matter of notorious obscurity under the Sale of Goods Act.

Other features of the Convention represent the adoption of rules which have often been considered, and in some cases adopted, as reforms to the existing common law sales regime. Thus a right of partial rejection only exists under the Sale of Goods Act in very special circumstances:[53] the Law Commission long ago recommended a change in the law to allow it in more situations, though response was very slow.[54] The Convention accepts it. Article 71 gives a right to adequate assurance of performance not dissimilar from that of the Uniform Commercial Code.[55] The difficulties faced under the existing rules of common law by a party to a contract who is doubtful whether the other party can perform and thus would like to suspend his own performance are well known,[56] and this provision is one way of dealing with them, of which the arguments for and against have been well rehearsed. The main criticism of the Uniform Commercial Code provision is that the remedies may be too drastic for the situation, which may involve no more than temporary cash-flow prob-

---

[39] Article 46 (2) (if the breach is fundamental).
[40] Article 46 (3).
[41] Article 50.
[42] Article 48.
[43] Article 64.
[44] Section 49.
[45] s. 2–709.
[46] Article 62.
[47] See Hellner, op. cit. supra, n. 6 at p. 95. For a justification of the common law rule see Beale, op. cit. supra, n. 36 at pp. 116–18.
[48] Under the 'quasi-*nachfrist*': Articles 63, 64.
[49] Article 65.

[50] e.g. Articles 39 (1), 46, 48, 49, 64.
[51] Article 39 (2).
[52] *Bernstein* v. *Pamson Motors* (*Golders Green*) *Ltd.* [1987] 2 All E.R. 220 (consumer sale: too late to reject car after 26 days).
[53] Where goods are delivered mixed with goods of a different description: s. 30 (3).
[54] Op. cit. supra, n. 4.
[55] s. 2–609.
[56] He may put himself in repudiatory breach by doing so: see e.g. *The Nanfri* [1979] A.C. 757; *cf. Woodar Investment Development Ltd.* v. *Wimpey Construction U.K. Ltd.* [1980] 1 W.L.R. 277.

lems. The provision of the present Convention, how-ever, (surprisingly) gives no indication of what hap-pens when assurance is not given.[57] The following article, Article 72, actually adopts the common law notion of anticipatory breach, though the relation-ship between these two provisions is unfortunately obscured by the choice of very similar wording: 'it becomes apparent' and 'it is clear'. The first group of words seems an unsatisfactory translation of the French. There is a provision about 'Exemptions'—in effect *force majeure*;[58] even though the notion behind it is unknown to the Sale of Goods Act, it is fairly well understood by common lawyers working in the international sphere, and indeed its absence from English law may be counted a defect. The pro-visions for restitution on 'avoidance'[59] appear gener-ous and unfamiliar, as does the term itself in a legal system where reasoning proceeds on the basis that the contract is terminated *ex nunc*: but no doubt such problems can be overcome. Finally, the special provisions regarding preservation of the goods by the seller[60] are unfamiliar but not unacceptable.

There are indeed merits in all these ideas. The principal general objection so far is, I suggest, the complexity of the regime introduced. 'In my opinion, says Professor Hellner, 'the uncertainty of what the Convention means and the difficulties in under-standing how its rules are supposed to work are its chief weaknesses.'[61] It is said that the remedies involved are no more than formulations of what par-ties to contracts in fact do—seek replacement, repair, reduction of price, set further time limits, and the like. This may well be so in many types of contract. But in others the commercial remedy is to withdraw from the transaction and buy or sell elsewhere. And to give legal shape to all these procedures cannot but introduce complexity. For instance, in its last work on sale of goods the Law Commission at one point proposed to introduce a 'cure' regime. The members of the working party thought of more and more com-plications as time went on (e.g. at whose risk are the goods while they are being cured?) and the reform was eventually abandoned as in the long run detri-mental to the interests of buyers.

The question then arises as to how all this will work in those sales for which the Convention is

designed, international sales, and it is to that that I now turn.

C. International Sales[62]

The Convention is directed towards international sales. To a common lawyer this brings to mind, not disputes concerning consignments of shoes sent from Italy to England or Germany, nor sales of tractors by salesmen from developed countries to Nusquamian peasants[63] nor whether a contract involving supply of heavy plant for construction is or is not a contract of sale, but rather, documentary sales of commodities and other goods carried, often for long distances, by sea on c.i.f. or f.o.b. terms. Such contracts are regu-larly submitted to the law of a developed commercial jurisdiction.

The c.i.f. contract is a stylised type of international sale performed by the transfer of documents, usually through banks by virtue of a letter of credit, and linked also with contracts of carriage and insurance. At common law its rules have been worked out judi-cially.[64] There are no provisions directed towards it in the Sale of Goods Act, beyond a few rudimentary rules on documentary bills,[65] and indeed much of the Act (e.g. the association of risk and property[66]) is excluded in such sales by implication. The case law is twentieth century, i.e. subsequent to the Act. The f.o.b. contract is a simpler matrix, more like a domes-tic sale except for the addition of the f.o.b. delivery term, though it can be performed in ways that make it very similar to a c.i.f. contract.[67] Surely a conven-tion on the international sale of goods should be appropriate here. How suitable is the Convention for such transactions? The answer is that it is ill designed for them. For a start, there is little reference in it to documents, the most significant being Article 34, which refers to situations where the seller is bound to 'hand over' documents relating to the goods.[68] This omission does not of itself matter: the Sale of Goods Act contains as little or less reference to documents. Article 34 covers the initial situation of a documentary sale, and requires that the docu-ments be conforming: it also provides for a right of cure in respect of defective documents in appropri-ate situations. So far so good: indeed a leading case

[57] See Honnold, op. cit. supra, n. 7, p. 494, suggesting that Article 72 comes into operation.

[58] Article 79. See Hellner, op. cit. supra, n. 15 at pp. 353–5 for a discussion of the appropriateness of this clause to differ-ent types of contract.

[59] Article 81 (2).

[60] Articles 85–8.

[61] Op. cit. supra, n. 6 at p. 75, giving detailed examples in connection with the rights of the seller against the buyer.

[62] A valuable, though extremely terse, account of the appli-cation of the Convention to c.i.f. and f.o.b. contracts is given by Feltham [1991] J.B.L. 413.

[63] Feltham [1981] J.B.L. 346, 349.

[64] See *Benjamin's Sale of Goods* (4th ed.), Chs. 18, 19.

[65] s. 19.

[66] s. 20

[67] See Benjamin, op. cit. supra, Ch. 20.

[68] The heading to Section 1 of Chapter II makes a distinction between '*Delivery* of the goods and *handing over* of docu-ments.'

on such right of cure or retender as now exists now relates to substitution of documents,[69] though such a right could be most inappropriate in, for example, string contracts. But the fact that the goods cannot usually be seen till they are discharged from the ship, and even more the close connection of the letter of credit contract and the possibility of such long 'strings' of commodity sales, mean that special significance is attached in the English law of documentary sales to the exact compliance of the documents with the contract requirements. A bank will instantly reject non-conforming documents, and a buyer should be able to do so as well. Yet in such situations it appears under the Convention that the buyer can only avoid the contract if the breach is *fundamental*, whether in respect of what the documents say or the time of their tender (though in the latter case he may set a period for performance if the word 'non-delivery' in Article 49 (1) (b) refers to documents as well as goods, which it may not since the terminology used for the documents is 'hand over' rather than 'delivery'). The common law rules as to strict compliance arise from judicial interpretation and one does not expect them in the Convention any more than in the Sale of Goods Act: but here the provisions of Article 25 are actually a hindrance to the reaching of the appropriate result. Such a result may be achieved by saying that a slight non-conformity in the documents (for example, as to the date of shipment[70]) is in such contracts a fundamental breach; or by recourse to the notion of trade usage under Article 9, if the understandings of the c.i.f. (and possibly f.o.b.) terms rank as 'usages';[71] or by the use of express terms. But such an interpretation seems to me to be contrary to the assumptions of the Convention; and at the very best sympathetic and creative judicial development is likely to be required. It will take some time to generate appropriate understandings of the rules.[72]

Thinking in terms of a c.i.f. seller who ships, the next rule of the documentary sale is that the risk passes to the buyer on shipment. The reason for this is that it is then that the marine insurance policy normally comes into operation, though of course

other insurance, such as 'warehouse to warehouse', may be operative. Also, the liability of the carrier under the bill of lading, usually governed by the Hague or Hague–Visby Rules, commences at that point, or very close to it.[73] However, the rule of the Convention is that the risk passes when the goods are 'handed over to the carrier',[74] which in English law at least is not the same thing as shipment, or even as the time at which the contract of carriage comes into operation: for the goods may be received on to a wharf or into a dock warehouse controlled by the carrier. It is not at all clear that risk should be held to pass at this point. Even if the carrier is in such a case a bailee, the goods are probably not held under a contract of carriage, the maritime régime of Hague and Hague–Visby may not apply and the marine insurance policy may not be applicable.

Furthermore, where more than one carrier is involved, the Convention provides that the risk passes when the goods are handed over to the *first* carrier.[75] If the first carrier is a ship and later transhipment is envisaged, there are no difficulties beyond those given above. If multimodal transport is involved, and the first carrier is a land carrier, such a rule may often be convenient but has certainly not yet been established. Laid down here, this rule may be an appropriate solution for some cases,[76] but not necessarily for all.

In any case, not all sellers ship. They may contract to sell c.i.f. and buy from another supplier f.o.b.; and equally the buyer may resell the goods before they arrive. The situations envisaged in the commentaries are usually very simple ones.

Next, a c.i.f. seller may buy goods afloat and tender the documents on them. Here the risk should pass retrospectively from shipment, since the combined documentation tendered covers post-shipment risks. The common law position seems to be that documents relating to goods already deteriorated may be tendered, except perhaps by a seller who knows this, but documents relating to a shipment which had been lost at the time of the contract may not be.[77] Suspicion by some delegates of the idea of retroactive effect for the passing of risk led to the basic rule

---

[69] *Borrowman, Phillips & Co.* v. *Free & Hollis* (1878) 4 Q.B.D. 500.

[70] See *Bowes* v. *Shand* (1877) 2 App. Cas. 455. See Treitel in *Benjamin's Sale of Goods* (4th ed.), s. 18–116, nn. 31, 34, 37.

[71] For a criticism of the Convention in this respect see Hellner, op. cit. supra, n. 15.

[72] Other references to documents appear in Articles 30 (duty to hand over any documents relating to goods); 32 (1) and 67 (1) (identification of goods by shipping documents or otherwise); 58 (payment against documents); 67 (authorisation to retain documents does not affect passing of risk); 68 (passing of risk in the case of goods sold afloat by transfer of documents); 71 (2) (right of adequate assurance of performance where buyer

holds document). The common law principle that a rejection for an invalid reason may subsequently be justified by a valid reason existing at the time of rejection may sometimes be displaced by the requirement in Article 39 (1) that the defect be specified on rejection.

[73] See *Pyrene Co. Ltd.* v. *Scindia Navigation Co. Ltd.* [1954] 2 Q.B. 402.

[74] Articles 67, 68.

[75] Article 67 (1).

[76] See Treitel in *Benjamin's Sale of Goods* (4th ed.), s. 21–085, n. 30.

[77] See *Benjamin*, op. cit. supra, ss. 19–071 et seq., 19–096.

of the Convention being that the risk in respect of goods sold in transit passes at the time of conclusion of the contract,[78] a most impractical rule where the goods are at sea: its application requires knowledge of the exact times of the contract and of the event giving rise to (or perhaps the occurrence of?) the damage to the goods. There is however an exception[79] allowing retrospective operation of risk 'if the circumstances so indicate' which may perhaps be interpreted as applying to all cases where insurance documents are part of the tender: but this would need to be established, and arguably the rule then goes too far in covering cases where the goods did not exist at all when sold or a contractual appropriate was made of a lost cargo or of part of it. It is not clear that the buyer should in such cases be fixed with such an extreme risk.[80]

The Convention also does not appear to any considerable extent to envisage or deal with sales of part of a mass, which are of course common in the case of commodities shipped in bulk carriers.[81] Article 67 deals with sellers who ship the goods which they are selling. It provides, as already stated, that the risk passes when the goods are handed over to the first carrier. However, by clause (2) the risk does not pass to the buyer until the goods are 'clearly identified to the contract.' This would seem to mean that unless the provision is displaced by one of the possible methods (such as usage), the normal risk rules cannot apply where a seller ships in bulk and sells to several buyers whose goods cannot be identified till they are measured out from the ship at the port of discharge. In such a case risk would seem to pass on delivery from the ship, which would turn a c.i.f. into an ex ship contract. This result does not appear on its wording to apply where goods are sold afloat, though the point is not addressed.

There are also difficulties regarding the duty to or right of cure and other dilatory remedies if they are sought to be applied in string sales;[82] and in general after the initial reference to the tender of documents the Convention confines itself to laying down rules for the goods, leaving questions of breaches regarding the documents to be worked out. This is conspicu-

ously so of the right to reduce the price, which is again stated to apply in respect of defects in the *goods*; and of the rules as to damages, some of which again assume that the defect must be in goods not the documents.[83] Equally, Article 60 (b), referring to the buyer's obligation to 'take over' the goods, refers to a contractual obligation which a c.i.f. buyer does not usually have, since the goods are already his when he presents the bill of lading: this is part of his obligation to take delivery, but he does not really have that duty in respect of the *goods*. Of course such problems occur with the Sale of Goods Act also: but here we have since the first leading case on c.i.f. sales in 1912 eighty years of development. Under the Convention many years will again be required: and the reports of some of the arguments employed at the various meetings suggests that there may be some interpretation of a misconceived nature to contend with.

The position regarding f.o.b. sales is simpler, since these do prima facie involve delivery of goods in the way apparently envisaged by those who drafted the Convention; but in so far as use is made of documents as separate entities, problems similar to those arising under c.i.f. sales may arise. There are also difficulties regarding the passage of risk. It would appear that Article 67 is intended to apply to such contracts, though it is not clear that in the 'classic' type of f.o.b. contract where the buyer arranges transport it can be said that the words of the Article, 'the contract of sale involves carriage of the goods', apply. If it does, it must then be determined whether the requirement that the seller be 'bound to hand over the goods to the carrier at a particular place' covers situations where he does so by employing his own carrier to take the goods to the f.o.b. port, or, perhaps more likely, buys from another seller who contracts to deliver the goods direct to the ship.[84]

All these points show that the Convention of itself is not equipped with techniques for dealing with the problems of documentary sales, and it is difficult to believe that sufficient attention was paid to such sales in the consultations and drafting.[85] It will need much interpretation. The usual response is that all these problems will be met by the application of

---

[78] Article 68.

[79] Ibid.

[80] It only applies however when the goods are sold afloat: the requirement of identification to the contract in Article 67 (2) seems to prevent appropriation after loss in other cases: see Treitel in *Benjamin's Sale of Goods* (4th ed.), s. 19–075, n. 9, s. 19–096, n. 38.

[81] See *Benjamin*, op. cit. supra, ss. 18–131 et seq.

[82] They are usually hedged about with requirements of reasonableness in one form or another, e.g. Article 48 (1), right of cure after date for delivery 'if he can do so without unreasonable delay and without causing the buyer unreasonable inconvenience or uncertainty of reimbursement by the seller of

expenses advanced by the buyer'. These of course raise their own problems of uncertainty.

[83] As for damages for defective documents see, e.g. *James Finlay & Co. Ltd.* v. *N.V. Kwik Hoo Tong H.M.* [1929] 1 K.B. 400. Article 76 (2) refers to the price prevailing at the place where delivery should have been made: but is this the initial shipment, delivery of documents, or delivery of the goods at destination?

[84] See for an assessment of some (but not all) of the problems Nicholas in Bianca–Bonell, *Commentary on the International Sales Law* (1987), pp. 483 et seq.

[85] The point was taken by Kahn, op. cit. supra, n. 5.

Article 6, on total and partial exclusion of the Convention, and Article 9, on trade usages. Unless the Convention is excluded completely problems will arise as to the extent to which it is displaced. Questions arising out of the incorporation of inconsistent terms (e.g. INCOTERMS) may be fairly straightforward; but where the extent to which the *remedies* survive special contractual frameworks is in issue, problems may be more difficult.[86] There will be a period of great uncertainty even for skilled commercial lawyers, let alone for non-lawyers on the ground who actually decide what to do when things go wrong.

IV. Should the Convention be Adopted?

I suggest that the result of the above is that we may be neutral about Part II of the Convention, which is of comparatively slight importance, though there is no point in adopting it if Part III is not adopted also; but that we should have grave reservations about the suitability of Part III for the large-scale international sales which are subjected to English law and regularly arbitrated and litigated in this country. The objections to it are twofold. First, some of its rules, especially that on fundamental breach, are actually antipathetic and obstructive to the techniques which we would regard as conducive to certainty and resolute action and hence appropriate to commercial contracts governed by English law. Secondly, the rest of it almost totally ignores the documentary aspects of international sales, and fails to take into account the transactions which are likely to be related, such as connected sales in a string, letters of credit, carriage and insurance. This is true of the Sale of Goods Act too. But there we have 100 years of judicial development which has accommodated the rules to international sales. To adopt this Convention is therefore to start again: everything has to be relitigated to establish how the Convention applies to documentary sales with associated contracts. Yet unlike the Sale of Goods Act the Convention was actually *devised* to regulate international sales.

On the other hand the Convention is with us and operative in influential and significant commercial jurisdictions: whatever we think about the desirability of the original project, it is impossible to pretend that its results are not there, and narrow-minded to ignore it. English exporters and importers will undoubtedly come into contact with it when they are parties to contracts governed by the law of Convention countries which have not made a reservation

under Article 95. The Convention may obviously facilitate the handling of legal disputes within Europe, and with developing countries reluctant to accept the application of English law, or the law of some other developed country. It would also, I suggest, be unfortunate to let the Convention be developed entirely by judges and lawyers from other jurisdictions: English lawyers have a distinctive input to apply to it, and their experience in certain sorts of international dispute may enable them to give a lead in some of the many points that will require creative interpretation and development. To ignore the Convention is to bury one's head in the sand. And there may well be a whole category of lesser international sales—I mention again imports of unsatisfactory shoes from a nearby country—to which the scheme of the Convention is really quite appropriate and where its use will definitely facilitate dispute resolution. For such cases, it may find its main use in County Courts.

I suggest therefore that the United Kingdom should certainly ratify the Convention, and as soon as possible. But its introduction should obviously be carefully monitored. Those involved in international contracts of the type which I have discussed, to which I suggest that the Convention is not appropriate, should be warned (though many know already) to exclude the Convention altogether, to draft their contracts to achieve exactly the results which they think appropriate, or both. And while I am indifferent to whether or not the United Kingdom adopts Part II if it adopts the Convention in general, I suggest that a reservation should certainly be made, as is permitted by Article 95, in respect of transactions with non-Convention countries—as was done by the United States but not by Australia.[87] The Convention might thus facilitate the solution of disputes involving Convention countries while not affecting those involving other countries.

It seems to me, however, that it would be quite wrong at this stage to adopt the Convention, even in amended form, for purely domestic sales, as has been done, or nearly done, in some countries. It is certainly true that the result of not doing so would be one régime for domestic sales, one for Convention international sales, and (in effect) another for non-Convention international sales—for despite diligent references to the Sale of Goods Act by foreign commentators on the Convention it is difficult to regard the English rules for international sales as anything but a separate regime from the normal Sale of Goods

---

[86] See further Hellner, op. cit. supra, n. 15, who deals not only with INCOTERMS but also with the ECE 188 Contract on supply of plant and machinery, which contains remedial provisions.

[87] The excludable provision of the Convention, Article 1 (1) (b), in any case raises difficulties of the conflict of laws when applied by the courts of a non-Convention country.

A Note of Caution

Act régime. But this is not very different from the situation in international transport. Here the vast majority of litigation concerns sea transport and the Hague and Hague–Visby Rules, but some surface transport is governed by the CMR Convention on international carriage by road, which has a somewhat different régime, on which litigation sometimes appears, and on which foreign cases are sometimes cited.

Nevertheless, the 1893 Act cannot last for ever. Complaints against it have mostly been in respect of its application to consumer transactions—as regards the definition of 'merchantable quality' as it applies in consumer transactions, and as to the provisions regarding loss of the right to reject. The only proposal for reforming the law in respect of commercial transactions has concerned situations where the right to reject for breach of implied condition has been exercised totally unreasonably.[88] Whether or not these complaints are valid, time was only recently found for amending legislation on this matter,[89] on the research for and preparation of which a large amount of public money was spent in the early 1980s. More elaborate proposals in Canada also seem to have run into the sand. If the Convention proves a success, it could, probably with local amendments, be the eventual successor to the 1893 Act. But it must prove itself first.

[88] See Law Com. No. 160, Scot. Law Com. No. 104, referred to supra, n. 4.
[89] Still not adopted at the time of correction of proofs.

3. Some Observations on the United Nations Convention on Contracts for the International Sale of Goods[1]

PETER SCHLECHTRIEM

Preliminary Remarks

TO submit a paper addressed to such a distinguished auditorium as I have to expect in a seminar of the Society of Public Teachers of Law is a daring and difficult enterprise. The topic of 'Uniform Sales Law' is especially difficult, because I am confronted with the problem of what exactly is expected of such a paper. It could not be a report on the contents of the UN-Convention, because the participants of this seminar can read the text of the convention themselves. Usually, in seminars on CISG there is a comparison of the provisions of CISG with domestic law, but this could not be my task here: A comparison of CISG with English law by a German law teacher would be preposterous, and a comparison with German law would be boring for most members of the auditorium. Therefore, I would like to approach my obligation from two starting points:

(a) How was the Uniform Sales Law received by the legal community, and what kind of problems confronted the litigants and courts during the first years of application of the Uniform Sales Law?

(b) I am convinced that in the coming years, it will no longer be sufficient to teach our students our respective law of obligations. We will have to try to base our classes on contracts and torts on principles and solutions common to most European legal systems, in other words to teach principles of an European law of obligations. Therefore, I will try to deal with some basic principles of CISG and compare them with the Principles for International Commercial Contracts (PICC) elaborated by a working group of UNIDROIT, the European Institute for the Unification of Private Law on the one side, and the Principles of European Contract Law (PECL) laid down by a group of experts for the EC commission on the other side.

Part 1

Reception and Application

I. Historical remarks

My conviction that in the coming years we have to teach principles of the law of obligation common to all European legal systems was somewhat influenced by another conviction, namely that the Uniform Sales Law could be the centre piece of such a course because it is based on an extensive comparison of sales laws, and the intention of its authors was to find, if not common principles, then the solution best suited to the respective issue. That they did not fail completely is, so I think, demonstrated by the willingness of national legislators to use the Uniform Sales Law as a model of reforming their own sales law. A short reminder of the history of Uniform Sales Law, therefore, seems to be justified:

As is well known, the history of the unification of sales law began in 1928. The International Institute for the Unification of Private Law (UNIDROIT) in Rome had been founded on 3 September 1926 and was officially opened on 30 May 1928. Ernst Rabel, after discussions with the Secretary of State of the German Ministry of Justice, Schlegelberger, suggested to the President of the Institute, Vittorio Scialoja, that the first work program of the Institute should address the unification of the law of the international sale of goods.

The subsequent developments can be divided into two phases:

1. The first phase started with Rabel's already mentioned initiative. This led to the first provisional report on the possibility of unifying sales law, which Ernst Rabel presented to the Council of UNIDROIT at its second meeting on 21 February 1929. This was followed on the 17 December of the same year by the famous »Blue Report« and on 29 April 1930 by the founding of a committee comprising representatives of the English, French, Scandinavian and German legal systems. At a series of meetings between 1930

---

[1] Paper read in the SPTL-Seminars on The Frontiers of Liability on May 1, 1993. Parts of the informations used in the paper and published here have been the subject of other papers and publications by this author elsewhere.

and 1934 this committee worked out a first draft which was published in 1935. Already at this stage the rules concerning the formation of international sales contracts had been separated from those concerning the content of the contract. Although progress was to be interrupted by the second World War, a series of subsequent drafts, committee meetings and conferences finally led to the drafts from 1958 and 1963 and the Hague Conference in 1964, which led to the Hague Conventions.

28 states were present at the Hague Conference. These states also signed the Final Act. Four additional countries sent observers. In the end, however, only nine states ever ratified the Conventions, which came into force on 18th August 1972. In the German Federal Republic the Hague Conventions and the appended sales laws, ULIS and ULFIS, came into force on 16th April 1974.

2. The Hague Conventions, contrary to the assertion that they scarcely achieved any practical significance, were in fact frequently applied by courts. In the German Federal Republic alone, we have been able to identify more than 200 such court decisions. One can assume that the actual number of cases and out of court settlements in which ULIS and ULFIS were applied was considerably greater than that.

Nevertheless, even before the Hague Conventions were ratified in 1972 or came into force in Germany in 1974, they were already at a dead end. Already by the late 1960s it had emerged that the number of countries who were prepared to adopt the Hague Conventions would remain small. Some important States which had been heavily involved with the development of the Hague Conventions let it be known that they would not ratify, for example France, the Scandinavian countries and the USA. In 1968 the UN Commission for International Trade Law (UNCITRAL)—which had been established as a permanent UN committee at the request of Hungary by Resolution No. 2205 from 17 December 1966—decided to make the unification of sales law one of its responsibilities with a view to developing a new sales law.[2] This decision can be seen as the death knoll for the Hague Conventions.

The project at UNCITRAL began with an analysis of the Hague Conventions from which it became clear that no more countries were likely to adopt them. First, the Developing Countries and the Soviet Union criticised the Hague Conventions for being tailored to the needs of the western industrial nations.[3]

Secondly, several states which had been instrumental in the development of the Hague Conventions criticised the results of the Hague Conference.[4] Nevertheless the aim of UNCITRAL, and of the working groups which UNICITRAL set up, was not a completely new beginning, but a reworking of the Hague Conventions.

At the 11th meeting in New York in 1978 the so-called Vienna Draft, containing the rules for the formation of sales contracts, was combined with the draft, containing the rules for the content of the contract, so that—unlike the Hague Conventions—a single draft contained all the rules. This 'New York Draft' was sent to the governments of the UN member states for their comments. The draft and the comments which governments had submitted formed the basis of the Conference which was held in Vienna in early 1980 and was to work out the final text of the CISG.

62 nations participated at the conference which was held in March and April 1980 in the Vienna *Hofburg*. At the final ballot 42 states voted for the Convention.[5] Under Article 99, 10 ratifications were necessary for the Convention to come into force.

On 11 December 1986 three states—the USA, China and Italy—deposited their ratification documents with the UN General Secretary in a formal ceremony as the 9th, 10th and 11th state thereby fulfilling the requirements of Article 99. The CISG, therefore, came into force on 1 January 1988. There are now almost 40 member states.

II. Reception of the Uniform Sales Law

1. Legislation

If one looks through the every-growing list of Contracting States, it is clear that a large proportion of countries with extensive foreign trade are represented. Especially in Western Europe only a few exceptions remain, e.g. the United Kingdom and Belgium. In general it can be assumed that in Europe today, the Uniform Sales Law would govern most of the international trade of goods, if it were not excluded by the parties in many contracts.

Regarding the reception of the CISG by European legislators and practitioners, a very thorough report by the Swiss *Bundesrat* (i.e. the Swiss Government) is available. Before it started the procedure of ratifying the CISG, the Swiss Justice Department consulted law faculties, trade associations and the Swiss Comparative Law Institute for advice on the merits of the

---

[2] See YB 1968–1970 p. 76 ff.

[3] Contrary to the view of *Enderlein/Maskov/Stargardt*, Kaufrechtskonvention der UNO, Berlin 1985, p. 16 pont 1.2, the socialist countries, in particular Hungary and former Yugoslavia, were influential participants in the development of

the Hague Conventions.

[4] See UNCITRAL YB 1968–1970 p. 162 f. regarding the criticisms of Austria, Sweden and the USA.

[5] For further details see *Schlechtriem*, Einheitliches UN-Kaufrecht, Tübingen 1981, pp. 3 et seq.

Convention. While submitting the Convention to the Swiss Parliament for ratification, the Bundesrat reported on the answers received in the course of their consultations. The overwhelming majority of those approached to give their opinion had expressed positive views. There were only three negative answers: the Swiss Bar Association, the Association of Swiss Watch Makers and one unnamed enterprise.

2. Influence on domestic law

In addition to its direct reception through ratification of the CISG, the Uniform Sales Law has had a relatively strong influence on the development of domestic law. For example, the Scandinavian countries relied extensively on the Uniform Sales Law when they codified their sales laws in the 1980's.[6] Likewise, the law of obligations and property in the new Dutch *Burgerlijk Wetboek* is strongly influenced by the Uniform Sales Law.[7] The proposals of the German Commission for the Reform of the Law of Obligations, which were presented in autumn 1991, reveal a similarly strong influence of the Uniform Sales Law, for example, in the rules concerning the avoidance of contracts because of a breach of obligation.

This sort of influence confirms and reinforces the role of Uniform Sales Law as a kind of *lingua franca* among lawyers with different training and traditions. It could become, therefore, a model for the development and transformation of domestic contract laws and may bring about legal harmonization extending beyond the field of international goods traffic.

3. Influence of the Uniform Sales Law on scholars and the academic community

When the ULIS and the ULFIS were agreed upon in 1964 at the Hague and were subsequently put into force by a number of European States, the reaction of the academic community was rather weak. Only a handful of specialists were familiar with that Uniform Sales Law and compared its solutions with their domestic law. The reception of the CISG has been entirely different. Before it came into force, it had already been publicized throughout Europe and other countries in numerous academic lectures and publications and it had been presented at symposia and conferences.[8]

Numerous treatises and commentaries have analyzed the Uniform Sales Law. It is no longer possible to keep track of all the articles in legal journals and monographs, doctoral and masters theses which deal with issues arising from the Uniform Sales Law. They started to make lawyers familiar with the Convention, even before its ratification. It is especially important that textbooks on domestic sales law are already discussing the Uniform Sales Law.[9]

4. Courts

A similar picture is presented by the practical application of the Uniform Sales Law. It took several years before ULIS and ULFIS were really noticed. After the Hague Conventions had come into force in the Federal Republic of Germany, about five years passed before the German Federal Supreme Court first applied them in a decision. Amongst the replies to a survey conducted by my institute in 1987 were questions from some courts, asking what the Uniform Sales Law actually was. Although it was valid law, some had not even heard of it. No doubt many practitioners shied away from applying the Hague Conventions because it was unknown and unfamiliar to them.

This is entirely different in regard to the CISG. As a result of the already mentioned symposia, the publications in legal periodicals, the references in treatises and so on, it became well known to the German judges and the community of legal experts dealing with issues of the international trade of goods. So, it is not surprising that even prior to its entry into force in Germany, it was frequently applied on the basis of references by German conflict of laws rules to the

---

[6] *Hellner*, Contracts and Sales, in: *Strömholm* (ed.), An Introduction to Swedish Law, Stockholm 1988, pp. 257 et seq.; *Hellner*, The Structure of Law in a Legislative Perspective. The Structure of Law, in: *Frändberg, Van Hoecke* (eds), Skrifter fran Juridiska Fakulteten i Uppsala, Uppsala 1987, p. 113.

[7] *Hartkamp*, Einführung in das neue Niederländische Schuldrecht, Teil I, AcP 191 (1991), 396–410.

[8] Symposium in Baden bei Wien from 17–19 April 1983, documented in: *Doralt* (ed.), Das UNCITRAL-Kaufrecht im Vergleich zum österreichischen Recht, Wien 1985; Kolloquium des schweizerischen Instituts für Rechtsvergleichung in Lausanne on 19–20 November 1984, documented in: Schweizerisches Institut für Rechtsvergleichung (ed.), Wiener Übereinkommen von 1980 über den internationalen Warenkauf, Zürich 1985; Dubrovnik Lectures from 11–23 March 1985, documented in: *Sarcević/Volken* (eds), International Sale of Goods, New York 1986; 12th Congress of the International Academy for Comparative Law in Sydney/Mel-

bourne, Australia, 18–26 August 1986, discussed by *Honnold*, Uniform Words and Uniform Application, The 1980 Sales Convention and International Juridicial Practice, in: *Schlechtriem* (ed.), Einheitliches Kaufrecht und nationales Obligationenrecht, Baden-Baden 1987, pp. 115–46; Conference in Freiburg in Breisgau, Germany, 16–17 Feb. 1987, documented in: *Schlechtriem, id.*; Colloque des 1er et 2me décembre 1989 in Paris, documented in: *Derains/Ghestin* (eds), La Convention de Vienne sur la Vente Internationale et les Incoterms, Paris 1990; Conference at the University of Bern, Switzerland, 18–19 Oct. 1990, documented in: *Bucher* (ed.), Wiener Kaufrecht, Bern 1991.

[9] See, e.g., *Larenz*, Lehrbuch des Schuldrechts, Besonderer Teil, Band II/I, 13th edn., München 1986; *Fikentscher*, Schuldrecht, 8th edn., Berlin 1992; *Ghestin*, Traité des Contrats, La Vente, Paris 1990; *J. Murray*, Murray on Contracts, 3rd Charlottesville, Va. edn. 1990, Ch. 14.

Some Observations on the UN Convention on Contracts for the International Sale of Goods

law of a Contracting State. There is now already a whole series of German decisions. And at least one arbitration award handed down by the International Chamber of Commerce in Paris in 1989 applied the CISG as trade usages.[10] The tribunal stated: 'The tribunal finds that there is no better source to determine the prevailing trade usages than the terms of the United Nations Convention on International Sale of Goods . . .'. As a result of its reliance on the CISG, the tribunal found that the buyer had given notice of the non-conformity of a shipment within the 'reasonable period' of Article 39 (1), even though notice had been required immediately, according to the domestic law of the seller's country, and the buyer would therefore have notified too late. The tribunal also held that the seller should be regarded as having forfeited its right to invoke any non-compliance with the requirements of Articles 38 and 39 of the Vienna Convention, since he knew or could not have been unaware of the non-conformity of the shipment and therefore Article 40 applied. By applying the CISG as trade usages, regardless of whether it was applicable as law, the doors for the application of the CISG are wide open. It has to be assumed that this is not an exceptional case.[11]

A review of the decisions we collected concerning the ULFIS and ULIS reveals that predominantly smaller or middle-sized businesses were involved in actions under the Uniform Sales Law. Until now, the cases decided under the CISG in Germany have also mostly involved small businesses and relatively small sums.[12] One reason for this is that the large enterprises, such as those in the motor, chemical and construction industries, usually have subsidiaries in the countries to which they generate most exports. Thus, they do not sell across borders, but instead deliver to their subsidiaries which then sell according to domestic laws. Another reason is that large firms usually exclude the application of the Uniform Sales Law in favour of their domestic law on advise of their inhouse counsellors.

III. Requirements for the application and the sphere of application

The Uniform Sales Law only governs the international sale of goods. As a result, if often cuts a spe-

cific sector out from a complex transaction and subjects that part to the regime of the Uniform Sales Law. Consider the situation where a French S.A. (Société anonyme), represented by its P.D.G. (Président Directeur Général), sells a machine which was manufactured in England to a Swiss GmbH (limited partnership). If defects in this machine result in a fire at the Swiss buyer's business, then issues arise concerning sales and products liability law as well as the power of agency of the P.D.G., etc. Out of this complex sequence of events, the CISG only governs the sales contract between the Swiss party and the French company. It does not govern the power of agency of the parties involved, nor the legal nature of the companies, nor the tortious products liability of the English manufacturer. Substantive law that is only partially unified must not only determine the requirements for its applicability, but also delineate its sphere of application. Therefore, the prerequisites for its application and its sphere of application represent the front line, so to speak, of the problems with which business people and lawyers are confronted. It is no surprise to find that the initial decisions of the courts dealing with the Hague Uniform Sales Law concerned primarily these very issues, nor that the same issues have attracted a great deal of attention in the literature.

1. Article 1 (1) (a) CISG

The Vienna Uniform Sales Law applies only to the 'international sale' of goods. Thus, according to Article 1 CISG, the first, basic rule for its application is that the parties to the contract must have their places of business in different Contracting States. In contrast to the Hague Conventions, which required further 'international' characteristics, this is the only 'international' feature which is necessary under the Vienna Uniform Sales Law.[13]

The decisions handed down in Germany to date have not had any particular problems with this element. The parties have had their places of business in Germany on the one hand, and in Italy or France on the other.

2. Article 1 (1) (b) CISG

According to Article 1 (1) (b) CISG the Uniform Sales Law is also applicable when:

[10] J.D. 5.4.1991, pp. 1054, 1057 et seq.
[11] ICC Arbitration Case No. 5713 of 1989, *van den Berg* (ed.), Yearbook Comm. Arb'n XI, Deventer/Netherlands 1990, pp. 70 et seq.
[12] See, e.g., OLG Frankfurt a.M., NJW 1991, 3102 (56.000 FF); LG Aachen, RIW 1990, 491 (1.000.000 it. Lire); LG Baden-Baden, RIW 1992, 62 (16.900 DM); LG Hamburg, RIW 1990, 1015 (95.000 DM); LG München I, IPRax 1990, 316 (25.500 DM); AG Oldenburg i.H., IPRax 1991, 336 (4.600 DM); AG

Frankfurt a.M., IPRax 1991, 345 (10 107 DM); LG Frankfurt a.M., RIW 1991, 952 (4 710 000 ital. Lire).
[13] According to Article 1 ULIS additional objective criteria were required, namely that the goods sold were forwarded from the territory of one state to the territory of another state or that the offer and acceptance were 'transnational'. That meant that the delivery of the goods should be made in a state other than the one where the contract was made or that the offer and acceptance were made in different states.

32

(a) the parties have their places of business in different States,[14] and

(b) the rules of private international law (of a forum state) lead to the application of the law of a Contracting State.[15]

It is an issue of some controversy in the literature as to whether or not a contractual choice of law clause, selecting the law of a Contracting State, also brings in the Uniform Sales Law. Some argue that the parties' choice of law is insufficient, and that there must be an objective connecting factor—such as, for example, the seller's place of business in Swiss or German conflicts law—before the CISG and Article 1 (1) (b) can be applied. In my opinion, this view results from confusion over a different technical issue which often concerned German courts during the time after ULIS came into force:[16] It could be argued that a choice of law clause which refers solely to 'German' law, does not make clear whether German law in its entirety, or merely the domestic sales law of the civil code (BGB), is being referred to, and so leaves room for doubt whether the choice includes or excludes the Uniform Sales Law. Since, however, the Uniform Sales Law is part of the German domestic law referred to by such a wide clause, it must, in principle, also be applicable.[17] Therefore, in such a case, there should be no doubt that where reference is made to the law of a Contracting State which has implemented Article 1 (1) (b) CISG in its domestic law, this provision is to be observed and the CISG to be applied, even when the other party does not have its place of business in a Contracting State. Thus, if the choice of law clause in a contract between parties with their places of business in Australia and England refers to the law of Australia, the CISG is to be applied. The interpretation of a choice of law clause—provided the text were unambiguous—could however lead to the result that the parties did not mean the entire law of the State they chose, i.e. including the CISG and its Article 1 (1) (b), but only its domestic sales law.[18] Then—and only then—the choice of law is one of domestic sales law, excluding the CISG.

3. Application as a draft for contracts or as trade usages

Regardless of the requirements of Article 1 CISG, the Convention (or parts of it) can be applicable if the parties incorporate it (or parts of it) into their contract. This is not exactly a choice of law clause unless the parties chose the law of a Contracting State, having the state's implementation of the CISG in mind. Instead it is to be viewed as a drafting technique which uses the provisions of the CISG as a kind of model contract.

Another interesting way in which the CISG can find itself being applied was demonstrated by the arbitration tribunal of the Paris Chamber of Commerce. As mentioned above, it applied the CISG as trade usages in a case where non-conforming goods were delivered, and the issue was whether the buyer had notified the seller of the defects in a timely manner.

4. Sale of Goods

Article 1 CISG refers to 'contracts of sale of goods' as a further prerequisite to the application of the Uniform Sales Law. This element needs to be given substance, which the Uniform Sales Law itself only partially achieves. So far, however, this prerequisite has not presented a problem in the cases to which the CISG has been applied in Germany. These have involved shoes, textiles, wall-tiles and other items clearly within the meaning of 'goods'.[19]

(a) 'Goods'

(1) Basically, 'goods' means movable property. In contrast to Article 1 ULIS, this is not expressly stated in the Convention but is clear from the drafting history.[20] Contracts for the sale of real estate or rights (for example, intangible property rights or rights to know-how) do not come under the Convention.[21]

---

[14] This requirement must also be apparent as required by Article 1 (2) CISG, see *Karollus*, UN-Kaufrecht, Wien 1991, p. 29.

[15] Decisive here is the definite reference to a certain substantive law, *Karollus* (note 14), p. 33; *Czerwenka*, Rechtsanwendungsprobleme im internationalen Kaufrecht, Berlin 1988, pp. 161 et seq.

[16] BGH, 26.10.1980, in: *Schlechtriem/Magnus*, Internationale Rechtsprechung zu EKG und EAG, Baden-Baden 1987, Art. 3 EKG Nr. 3, pp. 131, 133 et seq.; BGH, 13.5.1981, id., Art. 3 EKG Nr. 4, pp. 134 et seq.; BGH, 26.10.1983, id., Art. 3 EKG Nr. 5, pp. 135 et seq.; BGH, 4.12.1985, id., Art. 1 EKG Nr. 6, pp. 103 et seq.

[17] See also *Audit*, La Vente Internationale de Marchandises, Paris 1991, p. 23.

[18] See also *Stoffel*, Le droit applicable aux contrats de vente internationale de marchandises, in: *Dessemontet* (ed.), Les con-

trats de vente internationale de marchandises, Lausanne 1991, p. 31, who in addition makes proposals for the interpretation of Swiss choice of law clauses, see p. 32.

[19] See AG Oldenburg i.H., IPRax 1991, 336 (textiles); LG Bielefeld, IPRax 1990, 315 (shoes); LG München I, IPRax 1990, 316 (textiles); LG Stuttgart, RIW 1989, 984 (shoes); LG Aachen, RIW 1990, 491 (shoes); LG Hamburg, RIW 1990, 1015 (textiles); LG Baden-Baden, RIW 1992, 62 (tiles); OLG Frankfurt a.M., RIW 1991, 591 (textiles).

[20] See *Herber*, in *v. Caemmerer/Schlechtriem* (eds), Kommentar zum Einheitlichen UN–Kaufrecht, München 1990, Art. 1 CISG RN. 20; *Czerwenka* (note 15), p. 147; *Hoyer*, Der Anwendungsbereich des UNCITRAL-Einheitskaufrechts, WiRechBl. 1988, pp. 70, 71.

[21] See *Honnold*, Uniform Law for International Sales under the 1980 United Nations Convention, 2nd edn., Deventer/Netherlands 1991, Art. 2 CISG no. 56.

Article 2 (d) CISG provides that even when stocks, shares, investment securities, negotiable instruments or money are treated as movable property by domestic law, they do not fall within the Convention.

(2) Those objects which the seller must first manufacture or produce also qualify as 'goods'. A case decided by the German court of appeal in Frankfurt, in which a German buyer had ordered shoes from an Italian manufacturer, to be manufactured according to the buyer's specifications, provides a clear illustration.[22]

Contracts concerning industrial plants can also fall within the scope of the Uniform Sales Law. In a contract for the sale of an industrial plant which is to be built on the buyer's land, neither the value of the land, nor the fact that the plant will become a part of the immovable property once it is built, is taken into consideration.

(b) 'Sale'

The question whether an obligation ultimately concerned with the procurement of rights to exploit, possess and own goods, is one arising from a 'sales contract', can also give rise to problems. Auctions—including private auctions[23]—are expressly exempted from the scope of the Uniform Sales Law, as are enforcements of judgements and other judicial measures which bring about a transfer of ownership. This is the case irrespective of whether domestic laws qualify events such as an auction as a sale (Article 2 (b) and (c) CISG). Difficulties can arise with contractual forms such as the lease with an option to purchase, where in effect the sales price is paid in instalments which are declared to be hire payments.

A 'sales contract' must in any event contain an obligation to deliver goods in exchange for money. Therefore, the Convention is not applicable to exchange[24] or barter contracts.[25] This view is con-

firmed by the fact that UNCITRAL has plans for a separate Convention for barter contracts in its work schedule. Distribution agreements and dealership contracts[26] also fall outside the scope of the Convention, although problems of classification can arise here, as the German judicial decisions concerning ULIS show.[27]

5. Exceptions to the Sphere of Application of the Uniform Sales Law

(a) According to Article 2 (a), the CISG does not apply to contracts for sales of goods purchased for personal, family or household use. This exception was inserted in order to avoid conflicts with domestic consumer protection laws.[28]

(b) Article 5 CISG contains another important exclusion from the sphere of application of the Uniform Sales Law. The liability of the seller for death or personal injury caused by the goods is determined by whichever domestic law is referred to by private international law. Products liability laws had been developed to a different extent by the states which participated in the Vienna Conference and, furthermore, they were the subject of other efforts to harmonize laws. So products liability was excluded from the CISG in order to avoid imposing the strict liability provisions of the Uniform Sales Law on states with less stringent products liability laws,[29] and in order to avoid problems arising from conflicts between the Uniform Sales Law and domestic tort laws[30] or domestic rules on concurrence of actions (such as the French principle of '*non-cumul*'[31]). Admittedly, this understandable intention has not been entirely realized because the Uniform Sales Law still applies when defective goods cause consequential property damage.

---

[22] OLG Frankfurt a.M., NJW 1992, 633 = EWiR 1991, 1081, § 25 CISG 1/91 (*Schlechtriem*).

[23] This is different from the ULIS which only exempted judicial sales/auctions of seized goods, see *Schlechtriem/Herber* (note 20), Art. 2 CISG Rn. 19 *et seq*. For the basis of this exemption, see *Schlechtriem* (note 5), p. 15. Auctions seldom have an international element since such sales are usually completed at the place the auction is held. In such instances, the application of the law of the state where the auction takes place is generally accepted. For additional details see *Audit* (note 17), p. 29.

[24] See *Karollus* (note 14), pp. 24 et seq.

[25] For a conflicting view see *Honnold* (note 21), Art. 2 CISG no. 56.1.

[26] See further *Honnold* (note 21), Art. 2 CISG no. 56.2.

[27] See BGHZ 74, 136 et seq. This was a case of a dealership agreement, under which individual sales contracts governed by the ULIS were entered into. For the distinction between an agreement on commission and a sale with right of return,

see Münster, in: *Schlechtriem/Magnus* (note 16), Art. 24 EKG Nr. 4.

[28] The ULIS provided only for an exemption in the case of instalment purchases, Article 5 (2) ULIS.

[29] It is interesting that authors from states which have strict products liability argue for the *exclusive* application of the CISG within its sphere of application, i.e. also for the consequential property damage caused by defective goods, see *Honnold* (note 21), Art. 5 CISG no. 73.

[30] *Lookofsky*, Loose Ends and Contorts in International Sales: Problems in the Harmonization of Private Law Rules, 39 (1991) Am. J. Comp. L. 403, 414 et seq. foresees that national tort law will considerably overlap with the Uniform Sales Law.

[31] For a consideration of the particular difficulties which the French are presented with by this principle in connection with Article 5 CISG, see *Niggemann*, Die Bedeutung des Inkrafttretens des UN–Kaufrechts für den deutsch-französischen Wirtschaftsverkehr, RIW 1991, 372, 377 et seq.

Since the topic of these seminars is frontiers of liability, I should at this point include some observations as to the borderland of tort and contract which we enter in cases of consequential damages to property caused by non-conforming goods. There is a growing discussion in German but also in American legal literature in regard to the concurrence of action under CISG and domestic tort law in case of injury to property and economic loss.

Liability based on breach of an international sales contract falling under CISG may 'collide' or 'concur' with liability based on domestic tort law rules. If, for instance, an American dry cleaner has purchased from a French manufacturer a machine which by a defect in its wiring sets his shop on fire, products liability under domestic tort law rules or the responsibility of the seller under Article 45 (1) (b) CISG could be invoked by the purchaser. One may ask, why not? But if the buyer had failed to examine the machine, therefore overlooked the defect which an examination would (perhaps) have revealed, and consequently did not give notice of the 'non-conformity', he looses his remedies under the Convention, Article 39 (1) CISG. Can he circumvent this cut-off provision by basing his claim on domestic tort law? How, if only the machine itself was destroyed or damaged? This effect of circumvention of one set of liability rules (and its restrictions on liability) by opting for the concurring liability system constitutes the core of the so-called problem of concurrence of actions, 'Anspruchskonkurrenz', of 'cumul ou non-cumul' or 'election of remedies'.[32]

The circumvention of one liability system by relying on concurring actions, which thereby gain factual priority over the other system, might be welcome and therefore not be regarded as a problem at all. This is true especially if the superseded rules of liability are outdated, inadequate and need correction. In Germany the growth of contract law liability, the generous postulation of contractual or pre-contractual bonds between two parties or on behalf of third party beneficiaries were partly stimulated by the need to overcome shortcomings of the traditional tort law. 'Concurrence' and the possibility of an 'election' of remedies was not a problem but a blessing. Where, however, the rules of one liability system are regarded as adequate, well-balanced and just, there is a need to protect them from being pushed aside by

concurring actions. This is especially the case if tort law uses broad general clauses, protecting even purely economic interests (in contrast to such tangible goods as life, health and property) and thereby (theoretically) allows tort actions for every interest violated by a breach of contract. Special liability rules for breach of contract, their prerequisites and restrictions become useless, when the party to a contract could always revert to tort law. This is the main reason for the rule of non-cumul under French law, excluding the application of tort law rules (almost) altogether if there is a contractual relation between the parties. The conflict, therefore, is decided by a courtmade rule of law giving the contractual liability system legal priority over a concurring tort liability system. In most countries, however, a concurrence of actions under tort and contract principles is allowed.

In regard to CISG, however, municipal courts are, in my opinion, not as free as in cases involving only domestic law, to grant remedies founded in tort if thereby regulations of CISG and prerequisites of or restrictions on its remedies are in effect pushed aside. For CISG is created by a Convention binding the states which have acceded to it by the proper acts, and leaves no room for national legislators or courts to deviate from the Convention, unless use was made of one of the few reservations.[33] The Convention has, so to speak, 'preempted' the field for all matters regulated by the Convention, if and as far as it is applicable. A legislator or a court would breach the obligation incurred by a state in acceding to the Convention, if it would create or allow remedies for a sales contract falling under the Convention, which are inconsistent with the rules on liability under CISG.

Leading scholars are of the opinion that property damages caused by non-conformity of goods are recoverable under Article 74.[34] But they disagree whether tort (products) liability is displaced in these cases by CISG.[35] And if we assume that the Convention displaces domestic tort law in these cases, then to what extent? If the property damages were not foreseen or foreseeable at the time of the conclusion of the contract and therefore not recoverable under the Convention—Article 74 sent. 2—can the injured buyer *now* revert to domestic tort law, which perhaps allows recovery of consequential—remote—damages more generously?

[32] See as to French law *Durry*, La Distinction de la responsabilité contractuelle et de la responsabilité délictuelle, 1986, p. 146 et passim; as to American Law *Prosser/Keeton*, The Law of Torts, 5th ed. St. Paul, Minn. 1984, Ch. 16, § 92, p. 664 et passim.

[33] See Articles 92–6 CISG.

[34] See *Honnold*, Uniform Law for International Sales, ?Deventer/Netherlands 1982, Art. 5 No. 73; *Bianca/Khoo*, Commentary on the International Sales Law, Milan 1987, Art. 5 sub. 3.2; *Stoll*, Inhalt und Grenzen der Schadensersatzflicht sowie Befreiung von der Haftung im UN–Kaufrecht im Vergleich zu EKG und BGB, in: *Schlechtriem* (note 8), pp. 257, 259; *von Caemmerer*, Probleme des Haager Einheitlichen Kaufrechts, AcP 178 (1978), 121, 147.

[35] See *Honnold id.*: CISG displaces domestic products liability rules; *Stoll id.*: Domestic tort law remains applicable.

The problem is even more difficult, if a domestic tort law protects (some) purely economic interest of one or the other party (especially consumers), e.g. the interest that goods brought on the market have an 'adequate' value.

It seems that one has to start with protected interests, the respective duties and the interrelations of interests and obligations. The obligation of the seller to deliver goods conforming to the contract in time corresponds to interests of the buyer—to use, to consume, to resell etc. the goods purchased, and therefore to receive them in time and conforming to the contract. These economic interests are basically contractual, for they are created by a contract. Their shape and extent depends on the parties' agreement—time of delivery, conformity of the goods and the corresponding interests of the parties are 'offspring' of the contract. There were in general[36] no extracontractual obligations of private parties to provide other parties with goods and their use. Extracontractual duties—duties of care or duties to manufacture and market goods free of defects—are, however, designated to protect interests existing independently of contractual obligations such as health and property, but also certain economic interest. There is a well known correlation between interests and duties, for the recognition of interests worth to be protected shapes the corresponding duties, and the formulation of the duties circumscribes the protected interests.

It is the essence of contractual interests as outlined above which is regulated by CISG and its rules and remedies for international sales, and which should not be altered or changed by a tort protection granted by domestic legislators or courts for economic interests. If a domestic law sets certain standards for goods—in regard to quality, safety, prices to be charged—a violation would not necessarily render goods sold under a CISG contract 'non-conforming'. They might be destined for re-export to countries with less stringent laws. And if they are non-conforming—as will normally be the case—damages for purely economic loss of the buyer could be claimed only in accordance with the articles of CISG.

The picture changes if other interests and respective duties are concerned. If the goods are unsafe—non-conforming to the contract or not—and cause bodily injury, we are outside the scope of CISG, Article 5. But even if only property damage was caused which as consequential damages were within the contemplation of the parties and therefore recoverable under Article 74 CISG, we are outside the prin-

cipal domain of interests created by contracts and protected by contractual remedies, and would have entered the field of genuinely extracontractual remedies.[37] Therefore, a tort action for property damages caused by defective and non-conforming goods should not be barred by an omission to give notice within reasonable time—Article 37 CISG—so that the remedies granted by Article 41 et seq. CISG are lost. Even if the goods themselves were destroyed by unsafe properties of the goods, thus giving rise for a tort action based on strict liability, the interest protected is basically an extracontractual one, for it should not be decisive whether the 'dangerous' defect destroyed the goods sold or another piece of property of the buyer or someone else.

Part 2

Principles and Basic Rules of the Convention

I. Formation of contracts

1. Offer and acceptance

In the provisions on formation of contracts the Convention is based on traditional foundations, i.e. the interplay of offer and acceptance. Other modes of reaching a binding agreement such as consecutive negotiations in which the agreement is achieved point by point or the common signing of a draft prepared before could not be regulated for lack of common convictions and experiences. Therefore, in situations of contract forming without identifiable offer and acceptance one has to try to work within the given framework of Articles 14 et seq.

2. Revocability of offers

Looking through the provisions on contract formation, we find several well known and time honoured battle grounds. The revocability of offers has for a long time been a favourite topic in comparative law classes and subject of engaged discussions in the conferences in the Hague and Vienna and in the preparations of the respective drafts. Both conventions reached a compromise between principles of English contract law and those legal systems in which the binding effect of an offer is a matter of course. It is my conviction that this is more or less a problem for scholars because I could not find a single transnational case to be decided under either the Hague Uniform Law nor under CISG on the formation of contracts, where an offer was retracted despite being qualified by the offeror as binding. There is only one point of uncertainty in Article 16 CISG dealing with this problem which is worth men-

---

[36] I.e. besides times of crises such as war or other disasters where special laws might be enacted.

[37] *Contra Honnold* (note 34), Art. 5, no. 73; *accord Stoll* (note 34), p. 257 et passim.

tioning here: Under Article 16 (2) a, the offeror can make his offer binding if the offer indicates *by stating a fixed time* for acceptance *or otherwise* that it is irrevocable.[38] It is unclear whether by stating a fixed time for acceptance the offer always becomes binding for the fixed time, or whether a fixed time is only an indication of the offeror's intention, but could also be interpreted differently as stating a time period after which the offer lapses, but not binding the offeror at all. In my opinion, the stating of a fixed time by the offeror can have different meanings and has to be interpreted according to the rule of interpretation of statements in Article 8.

3. Pretium certum

Another battlefield of sometimes heated discussions was the question of whether a proposal by one side is an offer only if it contains a fixed or determinable price, Article 14 (1) 2 CISG. Since this provision requires that an offer in order to be an offer has to indicate the price expressly or implicitly or has at least to make provision for determining the price, there seems to be an open contradiction to Article 55, under which an open price contract is recognized as valid. The relation of Articles 14 and 55 can only be explained by the history of the drafting: Countries defending the rule *'pretium certum'* were in the majority, when the rules on formation were discussed and voted upon in Vienna, because the Scandinavian countries did not participate. When, however, part III of the Convention was dealt with, the Scandinavian countries did participate and the majorities had changed, nations favouring the validity of open price contracts now having the majority and advocating a gap filling rule such as Article 55.[39] Again, I think the much discussed discrepancy of Articles 14 and 55 CISG is mainly a topic of scholarly concern and less of practical importance. In most cases, provided a liberal construction of contracts by the courts, there will be found some or the

other provision in the contract allowing the determination of the price, especially, if we regard Article 8 (2) and Article 8 (3) CISG, under which provision all relevant circumstances including the negotiations of the parties, even their subsequent conduct have to be taken into account. In the very few—and in my opinion, highly hypothetical—cases, where there is no price and no mechanism to be found in the contract to determine the price, and where it has to be assumed that for lack of an offer we do not have a contract there is still the possibility that by beginning performance or even performing the contract fully, the 'subsequent conduct' of the parties has to be interpreted as waiving the requirement of a fixed price and the provision of Article 14 (1) CISG, which is allowed under Article 6 CISG.

4. Standard forms and unfair clauses

While days and weeks were spent in the working groups and the conference to discuss such time honoured problems as revocability of offers and the necessity of a fixed price, other problems more important to merchants were not addressed. One of these is the treatment of standard forms or unfair clauses and their inclusion in the contract. Two situations can be distinguished:

(a) Standard forms used only by one party of the contract

What has to be done to make sure that a set of standard conditions becomes part of the contract and shape its contents? Is it enough to refer to one party's conditions somewhere and somehow accessible but not attached to the communication of offer or acceptance? The solution has to be found, in my opinion, again under Article 8 CISG, and it would be dangerous to apply domestic law and its different criteria for the validity of a reference to an inclusion of standard forms, although this could be defended under Article 4 (a). The UNIDROIT draft of Principles of

---

[38] The same solution is to be found in the UNIDROIT's working group draft, see Article 2.3 PICC:
'(1) Until a contract is concluded an offer may be revoked if the revocation reaches the offeree before he has dispatched an acceptance.
(2) However, an offer cannot be revoked:
   (a) if it indicates, whether by stating a fixed time for acceptance or otherwise, that it is irrevocable; or
   (b) if it was reasonable for the offeree to rely on the offer as being irrevocable and the offeree has acted in reliance on the offer.'
[39] The Principles of European Contract Law and the UNIDROIT draft contain comparable provisions:
Article 2.101 PECL:
  'Where the contract does not fix the price or the method of determining it, the parties are to be treated as having agreed on a reasonable price. The same rule applies to the mode of performance of the contract.'
Article 5.1.12 PICC:

'(1) If a contract does not fix or make provision for determining the price, the parties are considered, in the absenced of any indication to the contrary, to have made reference to the price generally charged at the time of the conclusion of the contract for such performance under comparable circumstances in the trade concerned, or if no such price is available, to a reasonable price.
(2) Where the price is to be determined by one party whose determination is manifestly unreasonable, then notwithstanding any provision to the contrary, a reasonable price shall be substituted.
(3) Where the price is to be fixed by a third person, and he cannot or will not do so, the price shall be a reasonable price.
(4) Where the price is to be fixed by reference to factors which do not exist or have ceased to exist or to be accessible, the nearest equivalent factor shall be treated as a substitute.'

International Commercial Contracts (PICC) at least recognizes the problem and declares 'surprising provisions' in standard terms as ineffective.[40] Problems of inclusion of standard terms into a contract had to be decided in the first American case under the Convention.[41] The court singled out from lengthy negotiations and letters exchanged a memo by the American purchaser of shoes from an Italian seller as being the offer. This offer referred to conditions in the contract between the American purchaser and his sub-purchaser (a Russian firm) providing for arbitration in Moscow. The seller, however, replied by also referring to this contract and its standard conditions but excluding in his reference parts of it and especially the arbitration clause. The court, however, did not see this as the decisive acceptance, having meant that there were a material deviation from the terms of the offer and therefore a counter offer under Article 19 (1), but stated that acceptance in fact did take place earlier under Article 18 (1) CISG by 'other conduct of the offeree indicating assent' to the offer and its reference to the standard form arbitration clause. This conduct indicating assent was seen in the beginning of performance by the offeror (!) who had provided a letter of credit and thereby commenced his performance: 'In this case, in light of the extensive course of prior dealing between these parties, Filanto (seller) was certainly under a duty to alert Chilewich (buyer) in timely fashion to its objections to the terms of the memorandum agreement, particularly since Chilewich had repeatedly referred to the Russian contract and Filanto had had a copy of the document for some time.' Therefore, there was an agreement about arbitration in Moscow.

Even more pressing is the problem of standard form or »unfair« clauses prohibited under domestic law. The EC-directive on unfair contract terms is an example of legislation voiding certain clauses in order to protect some parties (consumers). These provisions of domestic law (even if instigated by an EC-directive) have to be observed under Art. 4 sent. 2 (a)

CISG. If, however, they leave some discretion to the courts in evaluating »unfairness«, the rules of CISG could be used as a yardstick. If a contract clause in a contract falling under CISG requires of the buyer to give notice of defects within a reasonable period of time this can never be regarded as »unfair« in the sense of respective domestic provision and therefore voided.[42]

(b) Battle of the forms

The problem of the battle of the forms was raised in Vienna, and there were proposals by some delegations to resolve it, but to no avail. If the offeror and the offeree, both and respectively refer to their standard forms of contracts, and these collide, the only provision that can be applied and has to be applied is Article 19 CISG. This means that an acceptance accompanied by the offeree's standard forms has in most cases to be regarded as a counter offer to the offeror's communication and standard terms. There will be no contract if both parties go on exchanging references to their respective standard forms. Only if one party falls silent and begins or accepts performance could his behaviour be interpreted as acquiescence and agreement under Article 18 (1) 1 CISG to the other party's last communication. It is, therefore, the last shot that decides the battle. Neither last shot nor first shot solutions are satisfying. UNIDROIT's working group was more daring: It proposed to decide the battle of the forms in favour of formation of the contract without the colliding terms,[43] Article 2.18 PICC.

5. Letters of confirmation

Another gap in the formation of contract section is the lack of provisions on letters of confirmation. While under ULFIS national legal rules under which silence to a letter of confirmation is regarded as consent, could be applied as usages under Article 9 ULFIS, the narrower requirements for recognition of usages in Article 9 CISG will in most cases exclude such an effect of national usages on letters of confir-

---

[40] Article 2.17 PICC:
'(1) Where one party or both parties use standard terms in concluding a contract, the general rules on formation apply, subject to Articles 2.18–2.20.
(2) Standard terms are provisions which are prepared in advance for general and repeated use by one party and which are actually used without negotiation with the other party.'
Article 2.19 PICC:
'No provision contained in standard terms which by virtue of its content, language or presentation is of such a character that the other party could not reasonably have expected it, shall be effective, unless it has been expressly accepted by that party.'
[41] *Filanto S.p.A.* v. *Chilewich Int. Corp.*, 789 F. Supp. 1229, United States District Court S.D. New York, Decision of 14 April 1992.

[42] Consumer contracts, however, will almost never be governed by CISG, see Art. 2(a).
[43] Article 2.18 PICC:
'If both parties use standard terms and they reach an agreement except on those terms, a contract is concluded on the basis of the agreed terms and any standard terms which are common in substance unless one party clearly indicates in advance or later, without undue delay, informs the other that he does not intend to be bound by such a contract.'
Article 2.20 PICC:
'If there is a conflict between a standard term and another term [which is not a standard term] the other term prevails.'

mation. Again, UNIDROIT's draft is more progressive, providing for the contract shaping effects of letters of confirmation that were not answered by the recipient,[44] Article 2.11 PICC.

6. Validity of contracts

Article 4 sentence 2 (a) CISG expressly leaves to domestic law 'the validity of the contract or any of its provisions'. The only exception to this principle is Article 11 CISG, which provides that a contract of sale is not subject to any requirements as to form.[45] To this extent, the Uniform Sales Law does address one aspect of the validity of the contract, contrary to what is indicated in Article 4 sent. 2 (a) CISG.

(a) The principle of freedom of form was extremely controversial in Vienna, so that—once again—a compromise was agreed upon in the form of a reservation clause. According to Article 96 CISG, Contracting States can declare, at the time they deposit their documents of ratification or accession, that they will not be bound by Article 11 CISG. Examples of states which have made Article 96 reservations are: Argentina, the People's Republic of China (PRC), Chile, the former USSR, the Ukraine, Hungary and Byelorus. The result is that when any party to a contract has its place of business in a state which has made this reservation, the principle of freedom of form does not apply. Instead, domestic provisions governing the form of the contract are to be observed. It is, however, a matter of dispute as to whether the private international law of the forum state should select the domestic law governing the form, or whether the formal requirements of the reservation state in which one party has its place of business should always prevail.[46]

(b) Apart from the principle of freedom of form and agreement of the parties, which is evidenced by congruency of offer and acceptance, the determination of the validity of the

contract is still made according to the domestic law referred to by the private international law of the forum. This rule has extraordinarily far reaching consequences and could prove to be a nightmare for the application of the Uniform Sales Law and could frustrate legal harmonisation. A similar rule existed in Article 8 sentence 2 of the ULIS. Issues concerning the actual agreement (for example, the problems of lack of intent, legal capacity and agency) or issues concerning the validity of the content (as determined by legal prohibitions, public policy and general customs) should not and could not be unified. Therefore, according to Article 4 sent. 2 (a) CISG, legal capacity, the rules of agency and invalidity or avoidability as a consequence of lack of legal intent, mistake, illegality or violation of public policy are still governed by domestic law. Domestic laws which define prerequisites for the validity of a contract, for example a licence or authorization, will also lead to invalidity if not complied with. Laws designed to regulate the economy (for example, those controlling the import or export of certain goods) and which prohibit contracts of sale or require an official authorization, fall under Article 4 sent. 2 (a) CISG, as do consumer protection laws which invalidate certain forms of contracts.[47]

II. Rights and obligations of the parties and remedies in case of breach

The provisions on rights and remedies of the parties in CISG are less complicated and better organized than in ULIS because they follow a simple pattern: After provisions common for seller and buyer in chapter I of part 3, chapter II defines the obligation of the seller and the remedies of the buyer in case of breach of the seller's obligation, followed by chapter III with the obligations of the buyer and the seller's remedies in case of breach. After chapter IV on risk

---

[44] Article 2.11 PICC:
'If a writing which is sent within a reasonable time after the conclusion of the contract and which purports to be a confirmation of the contract contains additional or different terms, such terms will become part of the contract, unless they materially alter the contract or the recipient, without undue delay, orally objects to the discrepancy or dispatches a notice to that effect.'

[45] This principle also applies in the Swiss code of obligations (OR) and in the German civil code (BGB), while the French *code civile* and the Anglo–American law do not lay down fundamental principles concerning freedom of form, see *Bucher*, Schweizerisches Obligationenrecht–Allgemeiner Teil, 2nd edn., Zürich 1988, § 11/I/1, p. 160 and note 1.

[46] For a discussion of both sides of the issue, see *Huber*, Der UNCITRAL-Entwurf eines Übereinkommens über interna-

tionale Warenkaufverträge, RabelsZ 43 (1979), 413, 434; *Czerwenka*, *Drobnig* (contributions to discussion), in: *Schlechtriem* (note 8), pp. 170 et seq., 175 et seq.; *Rehbinder*, Vertragsschluß nach UN–Kaufrecht im Vergleich zu EAG und BGB, in: *Schlechtriem* (note 8), pp. 149, 154 et seq.; *Stoffel*, Formation du contrat, in: Schweizerisches Institut für Rechtsvergleichung (ed.), Wiener Übereinkommen von 1980 über den internationalen /Warenkauf, Zürich 1985, pp. 55, 60.

[47] This is the starting point for an additional problem that is being debated. Do the provisions of the law of the contract govern its validity exclusively? Suppose, for example, that the law of Germany would apply to a seller from Germany. Are relevant norms which concern the validity of the contract from other States to which the contract has some relations—so-called *Eingriffsnormen* (intervening rules)—to be applied?

of loss, there is a chapter with common provisions for the obligations of seller and buyer with such important topics as the uncertainty defense, avoidance of contract in case of anticipatory breach and instalment contracts and, especially, the provision on damages (Articles 74 et seq.) and on the responsibility of the parties in case of breach of their respective obligations.

Despite the symmetrical regulation in chapter II and chapter III for seller and buyer, there are fundamental differences: While the main obligation of the seller to deliver in time could be compared to the buyer's obligations to pay and to accept goods, there is the additional obligation of the seller to deliver goods conforming to the contract, in other words, goods free of defects and third party rights.

1. Obligations to deliver and to pay: Respective remedies

The remedies of the Convention are specific performance, avoidance of the contract, damages and retention of the obligee's own performance.

(a) Specific performance

The remedy of specific performance is regarded by continental lawyers as the backbone of an obligation. The Principles of European Contract Law, too, state that the aggrieved party generally 'is entitled to specific performance', but regulates some exceptions.[48] This looks dramatically different from common law and was one of the topics, where a special compromise had to be found between the common law system and the rest of the world. The compromise is now embodied in Article 28 CISG and contains two rules: First of all, Article 28 is a conflict of law provision allowing the courts of the forum state to apply their own domestic law in regard to claims for specific performance. But Article 28 is also a substantive norm of CISG restricting the general remedy of specific performance in cases where the domestic law of the forum does not grant this remedy.

It is obvious from the history of this provision—

and its predecessor Article 16 ULIS and Article VII of the Hague Convention—that these provisions should preserve only the common law rules in regard to specific performance. But there is now a lively discussion in the German legal literature whether Article 28 CISG could also be applied if the non-performance of a party could be excused under national legal rules such as those on impossibility or supervening events. These proposals were provoked by the peculiar provision of Article 79 (5) CISG which says that even in case that a non-performance of a party can be excused because of force majeure or similar circumstances there could still be a claim for specific performance, something rather senseless in case of absolute impossibility. Since some legal systems, however, know the instrument of a court penalty (astreinte) which could be levied by a court in case that a party condemned to perform does not obey the judgement, it is feared that thereby the excuse of an obligor under Article 79 (1) in case of force majeure or the like could be circumvented. I do hope that this is a rather theoretical problem, and that, anyway, the claim for specific performance in the international trade of goods is rare, if not absent altogether.

(b) Avoidance of the contract

Avoidance of the contract in case of non-delivery or late delivery requires a fundamental breach or an additional period of time set by the obligee and not used by the obligor to perform. The remedy of contract avoidance is based on the principle that only a very severe breach of obligation justifies an exception from the rule that contracts must be kept (*pacta sunt servanda*). That this is an approach to be found in most legal systems, was convincingly elaborated by Prof. *Treitel* in the Encyclopedia of Comparative Law:[49] The most important principle is that the default attains a certain minimum degree of seriousness.[50] The Principles of European Contract Law and UNIDROIT's Principles for International Commercial Contracts confirm this analysis.[51]

---

[48] Article 4.102 PECL:
'(1) The aggrieved party is entitled to specific performance of an obligation other than to pay money, including the remedying of a defective performance.
(2) Specific performance cannot, however, be obtained where:
    (a) performance would be unlawful or impossible; or
    (b) performance would involve the non-performing party in unreasonable effort or expense; or
    (c) the performance consists in the provision of services or work of a personal character or depends upon a personal relationship; or
    (d) the aggrieved party may reasonably obtain performance from another source.'
[49] Encyclopedia of Comparative Law, Vol. VII, Chapter 16, Remedies for Breach of Contract, no. 147, 155 et seq.

[50] *Id.* no. 161.
[51] Article 4.301 PECL:
'(1) A party may terminate the contract if the other party's non-performance is fundamental.
(2) In the case of delay the aggrieved party may also terminate the contract under Article 3.106 (3).'
Article 3.106 PECL:
'(1) In any case of non-performance the aggrieved party may by notice to the other party allow an additional period of time for performance.
(2) During the additional period the aggrieved party may withhold performance of his own reciprocal obligations and may claim damages, but he may not resort to any other remedy. If he receives notice from the other party that the latter will not perform within that period, or if upon expiry of that period due performance has not been

The seriousness of the breach of obligation is circumscribed in CISG in the concept of fundamental breach defined in Article 25 CISG, and its function as threshold for avoidance is regulated by Articles 49 (1) (1), 64 (1) (a) CISG. In case of non-delivery by the seller or non-payment or non-acceptance of the buyer, the other party can set an additional period of time for performance and declare the contract avoided, when the obligor lets this additional period for performance pass without result. The idea of this 'additional period of time' scheme, which is said to be influenced by a provision in the German Civil Code, § 326 BGB, and therefore was dubbed during the preparation of the Hague Uniform Sales Law as '*le nachfrist allemand*', is easy to understand: If the obligor does not perform during this 'second chance', his breach of obligation is now qualified as fundamental, even if it was not yet fundamental before, or if there were doubts as to the seriousness of the breach. This is, of course, a rather dogmatic rationalisation of the '*Nachfrist*' principle; a better reason for the obligee's right to avoid the contract is that after such an additional period of time for performance it is clear that the contract is gravely in danger and there has to be, therefore, a way for the obligee to get

out. The PECL and the PICC follow the same pattern.[52]

The interplay of fundamental breach and additional period of time should cover most situations, where a termination of the contract seems to be the adequate solution. The immediate avoidance for fundamental breach covers situations such as impossibility or refusal to perform because of impracticability, but also the breach of contract terms stating that time or some other modality of the obligation and its performance is of the essence of the contract. Thus, it is up to the parties to make clear in their contract what they value as fundamental for their respective expectations. This is, in my opinion, the core of Article 25 CISG and its definition of fundamental breach, which was the object of lengthy discussions and many modifications during the drafting of the UN-Convention.

While in most contracts there should be no problem to know whether and when there is a fundamental breach of the main obligations to deliver, to pay and to accept the goods, questions can be more difficult in regard to ancillary obligations, because there is no 'Nachfrist' instrument to get rid of a contract breached by the other party, unless the violation of

made, the aggrieved party may resort to any of the remedies that may be available under Chapter 4.
(3) If in a case of delay in performance which is not fundamental to the aggrieved party has given notice fixing an additional period of time of reasonable length, he may terminate the contract at the end of that period if the other party has not by then performed. The aggrieved party may in his notice provide that if the other party does not perform within the period fixed by the notice the contract shall terminate automatically. If the period stated is too short, the aggrieved party may terminate or, as the case may be, the contract shall terminate automatically, after a reasonable period from the time of the notice.'
Article 3.103 PECL:
'A non-performance of an obligation is fundamental to the contract if:
(a) strict compliance with the obligation is of the essence of the contract; or
(b) the non-performance substantially deprives the aggrieved party of what he was entitled to expect under the contract, unless the other party did not foresee and could not reasonably have foreseen that result; or
(c) the non-performance is intentional and gives the aggrieved party reason to believe that he cannot rely on the other party's future performance.'
Article 6.3.1 PICC:
'(1) A party may terminate the contract if the failure of the other party to perform an obligation under the contract amounts to a fundamental non-performance.'
(2) In determining whether a failure to perform an obligation amounts to a fundamental non-performance the following circumstances are significant.
(a) whether the non-performance substantially deprives the aggrieved party of what he was entitled to expect under the contract unless the other party did not foresee and could not reasonably have foreseen such result;
(b) whether strict compliance with the obligation which

has not been performed is of essence under the contract;
(c) whether the non-performance is intentional or reckless;
(d) whether the non-performance gives the aggrieved party reason to believe that he cannot rely on the other party's future performance;
(e) whether the defaulting party will suffer disproportionate loss as a result of the preparation or performance if the contract is terminated.
(3) In the case of delay the aggrieved party may also terminate the contract if the other party fails to perform before the time allowed him under Article 6.1.4 has expired.'
Article 6.1.4 PICC:
'(1) In any case of non-performance the aggrieved party may by notice to the other party allow an additional period of time for performance.
(2) During the additional period the aggrieved party may withhold performance of his own reciprocal obligations and may claim damages but he may not resort to any other remedy. If he receives notice from the other party that the latter will not perform within that period, or if upon expiry of that period due performance has not been made, the aggrieved party may resort to any of the remedies that may be available under this chapter.
(3) If in a case of delay in performance which is not fundamental the aggrieved party has given notice allowing an additional period of time of reasonable length, he may terminate the contract at the end of that period. If the additional period allowed is not of reasonable length it shall be extended to a reasonable length. The aggrieved party may in his notice provide that if the other party fails to perform within the period allowed by the notice the contract shall automatically terminate.
(4) Paragraph (3) does not apply when the obligation which has not been performed is only a minor party of the defaulting party's contractual obligation.'
[52] See note 51; as to the definition of fundamental breach, see Articles 6.3.1 (2) PICC and 3.103 PECL.

41

such an ancillary obligation is fundamental. A German case may illustrate the problem: A shoe dealer had ordered shoes to be manufactured by an Italian producer. The contract stated that the shoes should bear the trademark 'Marlboro' to which the German dealer had an exclusive right. It further stated that the Italian manufacturer was prohibited to use this trademark for his own line of shoes. The seller/manufacturer nevertheless exhibited shoes bearing the German buyer's trademark at an Italian fair indicating that he could deliver shoes with this trademark to anyone who ordered them. The Frankfurt court of appeal allowed the German buyer to avoid the contract because of a fundamental breach. Examination of witnesses had made it clear that the agreement regarding the protection of German buyer's trademark was of the 'essence of the contract' so that the breach of this condition was on a par with non-delivery and the Italian sellers offering shoes bearing this trademark at a trade fair amounted to a fundamental breach.[53]

Some provisions deal with the problem of breaches affecting only part of the contract, e.g. if the seller delivers only a part of the goods—Article 51— or fails to deliver one or several instalments of an instalment contract—Article 73. The question in these cases is whether the obligee can avoid the whole contract or only part of it. In general, avoidance can be declared only to that part of the contract which is violated. But the party may declare the contract avoided in its entirety, if the breach of a part of its obligation(s) amounts to a fundamental breach of the whole contract, Article 51 (2) CISG or—in case of instalment contracts—if the failure to perform the obligation in respect of one instalment 'give the other party good grounds to conclude that a fundamental breach of contract will occur with respect to future instalments', Article 73 (29) CISG. In regard to past deliveries, the instalment contract can be avoided only if the deliveries already made are so interdependent with the missing or non-conforming instalment that they could not be used for the purpose contemplated by the parties while concluding the contract, Article 73 (3) CISG. The underlying principle seems to me that it is—again—the impact of the breach directly affecting only part of the contract on the whole contract, which determines the reach of the remedy of avoidance. The PICC, therefore, makes do with the general provisions on fundamental breach,[54] while Article 4.302 contains a rule similar to Article 51 CISG.[55]

Finally, the provision for anticipatory breach has to be mentioned allowing avoidance of a contract before performance became due, if it is clear that the obligor will commit a fundamental breach, Article 72 CISG. There are some safeguards against immediate declaration of avoidance in para. 2 of Article 72 (notice of the intention to avoid), but in case of a preliminary declaration of the obligor that he will not perform at the time of maturity of his obligation—which probably is the most frequent case of anticipatory breach—no notice of the obligee that he is going to avoid the contract is necessary, Article 72 (3) CISG. The PECL and the PICC are more concise in the regulation of this issue, stating: 'Where prior to the time for performance by a party it is clear that there will be a fundamental non-performance by him the other party may terminate the contract' (Article 4.304 PECL); 'Where prior to the date for performance by one of the parties it is clear that there will be a fundamental non-performance by him, the other party may terminate the contract' (Article 6.3.3 PICC).

In dealing with the prerequisites for avoidance one must not overlook an important restriction of the remedy of avoidance even if there is a fundamental breach: Under Article 82 (1) CISG a buyer cannot declare the contract avoided if it is impossible for him to restitute goods substantially in the condition in which he received them. There are, however, important exceptions from this loss of the remedy of avoidance in Article 82 (2) CISG. Nevertheless, the Uniform Sales Law—and the PICC, Article 6.3.6, too—here follows a path probably influenced by the German Civil Code and highly controversial in Germany nowadays. There are good reasons to advocate an entirely different solution for the problem of restitution or inability of the avoiding party to restitute, namely, treating this as a problem of responsibility of the parties for performance of their obligation to restitute and not as one of a bar to avoidance.

(c) Damages

By far the most important remedy is the claim for damages. The provisions in the Uniform Sales Law, based on the rule of *Hadley* v. *Baxendale*, should be more familiar with English lawyers than with German jurists who still have sometimes problems in dealing with consequential damages and to draw a line of limitation for their recovery. PECL and PICC

---

[53] OLG Frankfurt a.M., NJW 1992, 633; see also note 22.
[54] See note 49.
[55] Article 4.302.
'If the contract is to be performed in separate parts and in relation to a part to which the counter-performance can

be apportioned there is a fundamental non-performance, the aggrieved party may exercise his right to terminate under this Section in relation to the part concerned. He may terminate the contract as a whole only if the non-performance is fundamental to the contract as a whole.'

use a similar formula, Article 4.503 PECL[56] and Article 6.4.4 PICC.[57]

The rule in Article 77 CISG on mitigation of damages and in Article 80 CISG on the loss of remedies in case of contributory behaviour of the obligee to the breach of the obligor should also be more familiar with English jurists than with continental lawyers, who are already beginning to interpret these provisions as an expression of the continental rules on contributory negligence, therefore allowing for partition of damages not only in case of Article 77 but also in case of a contributory causation of the obligee to the obligor's failure to perform.

2. Conformity of Goods

The seller has not only to transfer possession and title but also and above all to deliver goods which are conforming to the contract and free from any right or claim of a third party, Articles 35 et seq. CISG. The respective provisions are, as the court decisions show, the centre piece of both the Uniform Sales Laws, i.e. ULIS and CISG. Especially the restrictions on the buyer's remedies have to be mentioned.

(a) Examination and notice

Amongst the issues most heavily debated at the Vienna Conference and during the preliminary work of UNCITRAL were the requirements to examine the goods and to give notice of any lack of conformity within a reasonable time (Articles 38, 39 CISG), as well as the excuse for failure to give the required notice (Article 44 CISG).[58] As is well known, most of the delegates from the developed countries insisted on the requirement of notice and, above all, on the absolute loss of all remedies in the case of failure to give notice. The third world countries, however, complained that the notice requirement would be foreign to their traders, or at least difficult to comply with, so that the hardship of losing all remedies was not acceptable. Concessions to these views were made. Thus, the time limit for notice was more flexibly formulated, as 'reasonable time', and the buyer who has a reasonable excuse for failing to give notice was given the benefit of certain remedies detailed in Article 44 CISG. From the positions adopted by the two sides in this discussion, it might be assumed

that the notice requirement is familiar to traders in developed countries and presents them with no difficulties. The cases, however, present another picture. It was clear from our collection of judgments involving the Hague Sales Laws (ULIS and ULFIS) that about 1/5 of all the cases concerned questions of correct and timely notice and the consequences of failure to give notice. Obviously even merchants in the developed countries have problems with the requirements of examination and notice.[59] This proposition is confirmed by the cases which have so far been collected concerning the CISG. In a case decided in 1989 by a district court in Munich, an Italian seller had delivered fashion goods to a German buyer. The German buyer did not want to pay for them because they were said to be defective. The German buyer presented documents to the court indicating that he had asserted that the goods completely failed to conform, approximately four weeks after they had been delivered.[60] The court held that notice was not given correctly. The buyer could not, therefore, avoid the contract and was obliged to pay the purchase price. Irrespective of any question of timeliness, the documents which were presented were incapable of constituting effective notice because they failed to provide a precise description of the non-conformity; they merely referred in general to the goods' poor quality and fit.

In a similar case decided by the district court in Stuttgart, the German buyer's reliance on the non-conformity of the delivered shoes failed. The shoes were delivered on 25 May 1988, but notice was not given until 10 June 1988 and was therefore not timely.[61] The court rejected the German buyer's argument that he had been unaware of the non-conformity which was first brought to his attention by his customers' complaints. The court stated that the buyer had failed to fulfil his obligations of care, which had required a proper examination of the goods. The notice had concerned obvious defects— tears in the shoes, untidy seamwork, varying sized uppers—which were evident before the shoes were worn. The buyer, on the basis of his expertise in the subject, should have performed an expert and thorough examination of the goods—particularly since defects had already appeared in a prior delivery. If

---

[56] Article 4.503 PECL:
'The non-performing party is liable only for loss which he foresaw or could reasonably have foreseen at the time of conclusion of the contract as a likely result of his non-performance, unless the non-performance was intentional or grossly negligent.'

[57] Article 6.4.4 PICC:
'The defaulting party is liable only for loss which he foresaw or could reasonably have foreseen at the time of the conclusion of the contract would be likely to result from

his non-performance.'

[58] See *Schlechtriem*, Uniform Sales Law, Wien 1986, pp. 70 et seq.

[59] It is therefore correct to point out, as does the German commentator *Huber* (in *v. Caemmerer/Schlechtriem* (note 20), Article 44 CISG Rn. 9), that the possibility for excuse under Article 44 CISG will also be relied upon frequently by European merchants.

[60] LG München, I, IPRax 1990, 316.

[61] LG Stuttgart, RIW 1989, 984.

this had been done, he would have discovered the defects and the delay in giving notice was therefore not justifiable.

In a case decided by the district court of Baden-Baden in 1991, tiles had been delivered by an Italian seller to a German buyer.[62] One delivery had been made before October 1988, although the notice of non-conformity had not been given until April 1989. A further delivery was invoiced on 7 June 1990 but written notice of non-conformity was only given on 10 December 1990. The unusual feature of the case was that the seller's standard terms provided for a notice period for complaints of 30 days from the invoice date. The court first explained why this clause in the delivery conditions did not materially alter the offer (Article 19 (2) CISG) and that, as a result of the buyer's silence, it had become a term of the contract. According to this unobjectionable clause, the buyer had, in any case, missed the period in which to complain and therefore had no right to claim for the non-conformity of the goods.

A judgement of the district court in Aachen from 1990 was also concerned with non-conforming shoes delivered to Germany from Italy.[63] The German buyer claimed for a reduction of the price because the shoes had silver rivets at the toe. According to the order, shoes without rivets should have been delivered. The buyer discovered this non-conformity on the day the shoes were delivered and gave notice the next day—clearly within the required time. This German buyer was obviously one of the merchants for whom the notice requirement was intended since he complied with the letter of the law—and not only the letter of the CISG, but also of the German Commercial Code.

(b) Remedies of the buyer

Compared with the breach of the seller's obligation by non- or late delivery, the remedies of the buyer in case of non-conformity are somewhat different.

(1) Claim for performance

While in case of third party rights to the goods the buyer can demand that the seller 'performs' by defending the buyer against these third party rights or by discharging debts on which third party rights to the goods are based, in case of non-performing quality of the goods the remedies of the buyer to this kind of performance are restricted. Performance in case of defective goods would mean either cure or replacement. The obligation of the seller to cure defects is, however, restricted by Article 46 (3) CISG if such a claim is 'unreasonable having regard to all the circumstances'. The remedy of replacement by

delivery of substitute goods is even more restricted, for it requires that the non-conformity amounts to a fundamental breach. The underlying rationale is, of course, that delivery of substitute goods is costly and risky in many cases, and since the defective goods have to be restituted, similar to an avoidance of the breached contract and the conclusion of a new on. Therefore it makes sense to put the threshold for the claim to substitute goods as high as the threshold for avoidance.

(2) Avoidance

While in cases of non-delivery or late delivery, if it is doubtful whether they amount to a fundamental breach, the buyer can secure his right to avoidance by setting an additional period of time, this way is not open to him in case of non-conformity of goods under CISG while it was possible under ULIS. Since in many cases it will be controversial whether non-conformity amounts to a fundamental breach, this results in a restriction of the buyer's remedy of avoidance in most cases. This is at least new to legal systems based on Roman law, where buyers were used to the Roman heritage of *actio redhibitoria* in cases of any defects of the goods, allowing for an easy way to avoidance.

(3) Consequential damages

As mentioned before, recovery of consequential damages is limited by the contemplation rule in Article 74 sent. 2 CISG. There is at least one case by the German Supreme Court decided under the similar rule of Article 82 ULIS: A German importer had purchased cheese from a Netherland seller. It turned out that a small fraction of the delivered cheese was inedible, and the German buyer claimed to have lost customers. While the German Supreme Court generally regarded the loss of customers by a retailer/purchaser as damages within the contemplation of the parties, the fact that only a tiny fraction of 3% of the cheese was non-conforming turned out to be a problem. Was it within the contemplation of the parties that the buyer would lose customers even if only a small fraction of the goods delivered were non-conforming? The court regarded this not as a matter of law but as a matter of fact to be evaluated by experts. It overturned the judgement of the court of appeals because the expert opinion heard by this court was regarded as insufficient.

(4) Price reduction

While the avoidance of the contract in case of minor defects is not allowed, another part of the Roman heritage could be salvaged, the *actio quanti minoris*,

[62] LG Baden-Baden, RIW 1992, 62.

[63] LG Aachen, RIW 1990, 491.

Article 50 CISG. The remedy of price reduction, although ridiculed by some common law delegates during the Vienna Conference because of the availability of damages for the buyer, is of some importance in cases, where the buyer can excuse himself for the non-conformity under Article 79 CISG. In these cases, it preserves the parity of performances as agreed upon by the parties. It is my conviction that this remedy of the buyer, if it were not inherited from the Romans, would have to be invented nowadays, because otherwise the courts would use concepts such as '*Geschäftsgrundlage*' or '*clausula rebus sic stantibus*' to adjust contracts in cases of disturbed balance of parity.

Conclusions

Only a few aspects of the Uniform Sales Law could be reported here. Many more details are worth considering and discussing, and without doubt, many more problems will come up if more courts have to apply the Uniform Sales Law. Therefore, it is still too early to give an evaluation. I can only summarize that in comparison to the German sales law, the main solutions of the CISG to me seem to be superior and better suited not only to transnational dealings but to internal sales, too. It is, therefore, not surprising that some of the prominent features of CISG could also be found now in the draft of a reform proposal for the provisions on breach of obligations, submitted by a Law Reform Commission in 1992. And the comparison with the PICC and PECL could be evidence that the main solutions of the CISG are consistent with what some leading scholars of contract law regarded as the common core of solutions for issues of contract law.

PART II

THE CONDITION OF THE LAW OF TORT

4. The Condition of the Law of Tort

SIR ROBIN COOKE

S IR John Salmond—piety dictates that those be the opening words of a paper requisitioned from a New Zealand lawyer on the condition of the law of tort—wrote the preface to the sixth edition of his *The Law of Torts* in May 1923. It was the last edition published in his lifetime. He began by saying that 'For the most part the law of Torts is well settled, and such questions as arise relate in general to matters of supplementary detail'. Then he went on to outline 'some unsolved problems of far-reaching significance . . .' Some of these are hardly any nearer solution seventy years later. Their number has been much augmented by the work of the generations after Salmond. A diagnosis of the condition of the subject cannot be reassuring.

Structures, Chattels and Economic Loss

One of Salmond's unsolved problems, responsibility for harm done by dangerous premises or dangerous chattels, was partly taken in hand by Parliament in the Occupiers Liability legislation.[1] This was virtually forced on the legislature by the failure of the courts, largely after Salmond's time, to produce a just and satisfactory body of law in what began as and, if judicial performance had been adequate, would have remained a common law field. There was no political content, but the courts vacillated in working out principles.

Thus the Privy Council in a judgment delivered by Lord Radcliffe in *Commissioner for Railways* v. *Quinlan*[2] held that an occupier's duty to trespassers depended on whether their presence was known to be extremely likely; whereas in the judgment delivered a decade later by Lord Reid in *Southern Portland Cement* v. *Cooper*[3] it had to be pointed out that the nature and extent of the duty were determined by considerations of humanity, these being less rigorous. In that era it was well known in legal circles in Australasia that in *Quinlan* the Commissioner had gone to the Privy Council on appeal, rather than to the High Court of Australia as was then only an alternative, because he rightly expected a more restrictive approach on the other side of the world. Some English courts even displayed something like enthusiasm for extending refined doctrines against liability. In *Perkowski* v. *Wellington Corporation*[4] the plaintiff's husband had broken his neck through diving into the sea at low tide from a diving board installed by the local authority. The jury found that both parties were negligent but that the diving board was not a hidden trap. The point that the board was a misrepresentation of conditions *outside* the defendant's premises, leading the deceased to think it safe to dive into the sea, was rejected by the Privy Council by invoking as an alleged obvious analogy the owner of unfenced cliffs. Reflection in more maturity on one's own unsuccessful arguments does bring one to see often enough that they were rejected rightly; but *Perkowski* has not turned out to be such a case, and it is not surprising that Lord Denning formally recorded his dissent from the judgment at a time when reasoned dissenting judgments were not allowed to be delivered in the Privy Council. Reading again, after many years, the reasons given by Lord Somervell of Harrow on behalf of himself and Viscount Simonds, Lord Morton of Henryton and Lord Keith of Avonholm, I cannot avoid the suspicion that their Lordships preferred to gloss over an awkward point by ignoring an available distinction. By owning a cliff one does not encourage visitors to jump off it. Afterwards Lord Morton was so gracious as to write inviting me to lunch in the House of Lords, but by then I had flown away.

Salmond's unsolved problems have been only partly resolved by legislative intervention. A new range of problems, relating to liability to persons outside the premises occupied by the defendant, have been judicially created or exposed by the conflicting decisions of the English courts in the *Dutton–Anns* line of cases on the one hand[5] and the *Murphy* group of cases on the other.[6] One of these new problems concerns remedial expenditure. At the highest English judicial level it has been recently said[7] that if a building stands so close to the boundary of the

---

[1] Occupiers Liability Acts 1957 and 1984 (U.K.); Occupiers Liability Act 1962 (N.Z.).

[2] [1964] 1 All E.R. 897; [1964] A.C. 1054.

[3] [1974] 1 All E.R. 87.

[4] [1958] 1 All E.R. 368; [1959] A.C. 53.

[5] *Dutton* v. *Bognor Regis U.D.C.* [1972] 1 All E.R. 462; [1973] 1 Q.B. 373. *Anns* v. *London Merton Borough Council* [1977] 2 All E.R. 492; [1978] A.C. 728.

[6] *Murphy* v. *Brentwood D.C.* [1990] 2 All E.R. 908; [1991] 1 A.C. 398. *D. & F. Estates Ltd.* v. *Church Commissioners for England* [1988] 2 All E.R. 992; [1989] A.C. 177. *Department of the Environment* v. *Thomas Bates & Son* [1990] 2 All E.R. 943; [1991] 1 A.C. 499.

[7] *Murphy* [1990] 2 All E.R. at 926; [1991] 1 A.C. at 475, per Lord Bridge of Harwich.

owner's land that after discovery of a dangerous defect it remains a potential source of injury to persons or property on neighbouring land or on the highway, the building owner ought, in principle, to be entitled to recover in tort from the negligent builder the cost of obviating the danger, so far as that cost is necessarily incurred in order to protect him from potential liability to third parties. But at the same level, and in the same case, even this was doubted by another Law Lord.[8] And the actual holding, as is well known, was that repair costs cannot be recovered in tort in such a case from either a negligent builder or a negligent local authority, notwithstanding that the costs are necessary to meet an imminent risk to the health and safety of the occupants of the house.

The *Murphy* group of cases were contrary to many decisions in Canada, the United States and New Zealand[9] and represented what has been described judicially in England as 'a considerable upheaval'[10] of the English law of negligence. There would appear to be no doubt that a leap backwards was deliberately taken for policy reasons. Those reasons themselves are perhaps less easy to identify but may ultimately reduce to the floodgates factor. With great respect, the doctrine that a dangerous defect once known becomes merely a defect in quality seems to propound a dogma rather than a lesson of experience. Before long the English Court of Appeal declined to apply it, holding in *Targett* v. *Torfaen Borough Council*[11] that a landlord responsible for the design and construction of a house was liable in common law negligence to the plaintiff who knowingly used steps not provided with a handrail and inadequately lighted. The decision was expressly based on *Donoghue* v. *Stevenson*,[12] not on contractual liability, and the damages were reduced by 25 per cent for contributory negligence. In the field of *Donoghue* v. *Stevenson* liability for dangerous premises or chattels it is not easy to see any distinction in principle between a landlord and a vendor when each is responsible for negligent construction.

A related doctrine enunciated in *Murphy* is that

economic losses are recoverable if they flow from breach of a relevant contractual duty but, in the absence of a special relationship of proximity, are not recoverable in tort.[13] The reference to a special relationship of proximity may seem question-begging, but it is also revealing. Implicit in it is an acknowledgment that if there is sufficient 'proximity'—a term which is a label, not a test—there is no reason in principle why a careless contractor, manufacturer or controlling authority should not be liable in the tort of negligence for a defect of quality. If Mrs Donoghue had been the purchaser, no eyebrow would have been lifted at the inclusion in her special damages of the wasted price of the bottle of ginger beer.

Many torts entail liability for economic loss. Familiar examples are deceit, malicious falsehood, defamation, trespass to land or goods, nuisance, *Rylands* v. *Fletcher* (assuming it to be different from nuisance[14]), all the intellectual property torts, and all torts of wrongful interference with contractual or other economic relations. That truth comes home particularly clearly if one works in a jurisdiction where actions for damages for personal injury by accident are not allowed. Broadly that is still the effect of the New Zealand legislation, although because of cost the accident compensation scheme has now been made less comprehensive.[15] So the legislature has prohibited claims which in other common law jurisdictions are often seen as the paradigm of tort litigation. But we have found that there is a lot of tort left. It would be no exaggeration to say that our tort law is *concerned mainly* with liability for economic loss.

Of course it is accepted in *Murphy* that 'pure' economic loss is redressible when there has been reliance on representations made negligently in breach of a duty of care, as in *Hedley Byrne*[16] and perhaps *Junior Books*[17] and *Pirelli*.[18] But that too is revealing. It brings out that no inexorable logic compels the conclusion that a defect in quality is not redressible in negligence. The fact that the detriment is recoverable in contract, if there is a contract, has

[8] *Ib.* 936; 489, per Lord Oliver of Aylmerton.
[9] See 106 L.Q.R. 525; 107 L.Q.R. 46.
[10] *Nitrigin Eireann Teoiranta* v. *Inco Alloys Ltd.* [1992] 1 All E.R. 854, 857, per May J.
[11] [1992] 3 All E.R. 27, following *Rimmer* v. *Liverpool City Council* [1984] 1 All E.R. 930; [1985] Q.B. 1.
[12] [1932] A.C. 562.
[13] Per Lord Bridge of Harwich in [1990] 2 All E.R. at 926; [1991] 1 A.C. at 475.
[14] For the argument that it was intended to be the same, see the chapter by R. S. Chambers Q.C., D.Phil., on *The Rule in Rylands* v. *Fletcher* in Todd and others *The Law of Torts in New Zealand*, The Law Book Company Ltd., Sydney (1991), 399. Since this seminar Lord Goff of Chieveley (whose attendance at the seminar is gratefully noted by the author) has accepted for the House of Lords the view of Professor Newark

that *Rylands* v. *Fletcher* was essentially concerned with an extension of nuisance to isolated escapes: *Cambridge Water Co. Ltd.* v. *Eastern Counties Leather PLC* [1994] 1 All ER 53, 75.
[15] See now the Accident Rehabilitation and Compensation Insurance Act 1992, s.14, and for the earlier Acts and their interpretation *Willis* v. *Attorney-General* [1989] 3 N.Z.L.R. 574; *McKenzie* v. *Attorney-General* [1992] 2 N.Z.L.R. 14, 21.
[16] *Hedley Byrne & Co. Ltd.* v. *Heller & Partners Ltd.* [1963] 2 All E.R. 575; [1964] A.C. 565.
[17] *Junior Books Ltd.* v. *Veitchi Co. Ltd.* [1982] 3 All E.R. 201; [1983] 1 A.C. 520. See *Murphy* [1990] 2 All E.R. at 919 and 930; [1991] 1 A.C. at 466 and 481.
[18] Note 53 *infra.* See again *Murphy* at the pages last cited. When *Junior Books* and *Pirelli* were decided, they do not appear to have been seen by the House of Lords in the way explained in *Murphy*.

no necessary connection with the tort issue. Salmond defined a tort as *a civil wrong for which the remedy is an action for damages, and which is not exclusively the breach of a contract or the breach of a trust or other merely equitable obligation.* Most textbooks contain similar definitions.[19] The 'exclusively' underlines the formalism of the definition. As often as reasons of policy—or, I should prefer to say, the dictates of common justice—require the recognition of a tort duty in addition to some contractual one, so often the definition of tort will naturally be satisfied. For some sixteen years I have been submitting that the law of tort need not stop short of recognising a duty not to put out carelessly a defective thing, nor are the courts compelled to withhold relief in tort from a plaintiff misled by the appearance of the thing from paying too much for it.[20]

No doubt, so far as the submission has been considered at all, it has been dismissed as too *outré* to call for express demolition. But, in New Zealand at least, whatever outrageousness attaches to it may not now matter very much. Parliament has come to the rescue again by enacting in the Fair Trading Act 1986, s.9, that 'No person shall, in trade, engage in conduct that is misleading or deceptive or is likely to mislead or deceive'. Pecuniary relief is available under the statute; and commentators point out that this can extend to indemnity.[21]

What the courts do by failing to achieve justice in fields where it is open to them is to force the legislature to intrude. For constitutional reasons concerning the separation of powers, as well as professional reasons concerning the competence of the legal profession, that can hardly be healthy. The debilitated condition of the law of tort may be seen as partly due to judicial failure to take sufficient exercise in discharging the judicial responsibility for looking after the development of the common law. These are quite strong words, but a pattern of quite strong language has been set in this field in *Murphy*[22] and on other occasions.

To avoid a charge of obsession, I should not linger over *Murphy*, but one further point should not go without mention. In the Defective Premises Act 1972 the United Kingdom Parliament recognised the justice of imposing on house builders a transmissible warranty of quality, actionable in tort and expressed

to be in addition to any duty a person may owe apart from that provision. In *Murphy* the fact that the legislature had adopted this policy was treated as a reason *against* the courts doing so in cases not covered by the Act.[23] A rather different approach appears to have been adopted in the Court of Appeal and the High Court to the Congenital Disabilities (Civil Liability) Act 1976, an Act declared to apply in respect of births after (but not before) its passing. In *Burton* v. *Islington Health Authority*[24] it was held that at common law a child born suffering from disabilities caused as a result of medical negligence before birth could maintain an action. Dillon, Balcombe and Leggatt L. JJ. in the Court of Appeal and Phillips J. in the High Court treated the statute as in no way discouraging judicial recognition of a common law duty of care in pre-Act cases. That approach does not seem heterodox and is one to which we are accustomed in New Zealand.[25] Indeed the use made in *Burton* of the maxim of civil law that an unborn child shall be deemed to be born whenever its interests require it adds a satisfying flavour of traditional legalism.

Wider Horizons

Salmond subtitled his work *A Treatise on the English Law of Liability for Civil Injuries.* Discarded by his editors, it was never a happy subtitle, being inconsistent with his own acceptance in his definition of tort that breaches of contract or trust are also civil wrongs. In addition it has become steadily less appropriate as the general common law of torts has become steadily less English. Salmond himself would of course have been well aware that there was a vast sea of United States case law in which it would be imprudent and beyond the compass of his work to dip. It remains striking that even he, a New Zealand Judge by the time of his last two editions, did not think of the courts of the Dominions (the word that he would have used) as trying to do more than faithfully to apply English precedents as best they could. The evolution of the Commonwealth has made a sea change. Among the leading textbooks today are those especially valued for their breadth, such as Fleming[26] and Linden.[27] It has to be said that the richer present-day tort jurisprudence is found

[19] A well-known collection is in Prosser and Keeton on *Torts*, 5th ed. (1984), ch. 1.

[20] *Bowen* v. *Paramount Builders (Hamilton) Ltd.* [1977] 1 N.Z.L.R. 394, 423.

[21] Todd, op. cit., n. 14 supr, 165; Hill and Jones *Fair Trading in New Zealand*, Butterworths, Wellington (1989), pp. 167–9. In England the Consumer Protection Act 1987, s.5(2), is more restrictive, so the tort issue could be more important.

[22] Some of the epithets used in *Murphy* in criticising the reasoning of earlier very distinguished Judges are collected in 107 L.Q.R. at 56.

[23] See [1990] 2 All E.R. at 912, 930, 938 and 942–3; [1991] 1 A.C. at 457, 480, 491, and 498.

[24] [1992] 3 All E.R. at 833.

[25] As to the bearing of statutes on the existence of common law duties, see *South Pacific Manufacturing Co. Ltd.* v. *New Zealand Security Consultants and Investigators Ltd.* [1992] 2 N.Z.L.R. 282, 297–8, 307, 313, 318, 325.

[26] John G. Fleming, *The Law of Torts*, The Law Book Company Ltd., Sydney, 8th ed. (1992).

[27] Allen M. Linden, *Canadian Tort Law*, Butterworths, Toronto and Vancouver, 4th ed. (1987).

outside England, perhaps most rewardingly in Canada. In 1992 alone, the Supreme Court of Canada produced at least three tort decisions outstanding for their sensitivity to and in-depth consideration of basic issues: *Canadian National Railways Co.* v. *Norsk Pacific Steamship Co. Ltd.*[28] (economic loss); *Norberg* v. *Wynrib*[29] (battery, negligence and medical fiduciary duty); and *K.M.* v. *H.M.*[30] (incest).

The second and third cases should be dealt with a little later. The first is in context here. *Norsk* was a case of negligent navigation of a barge, causing damage to a bridge of which the plaintiff, C.N.R., was to the knowledge of the defendant the primary user. The issue was whether re-routing expenses were recoverable. There is a distinct similarity with the Australian case of *Caltex Oil (Australia) Pty Ltd.* v. *The Dredge 'Willemstad'*,[31] well-known for (*inter alia*) its subtle variety of judicial reasoning and the decisive significance given to knowledge of likely economic loss to a particular person, not merely to a member of an unascertained class. Despite differences in reasoning, it is a striking fact that the final courts of appeal in both Canada and Australia have found liability in the circumstances of these two cases.

To English readers it may also be striking that, although the Supreme Court of Canada was divided as to the result in *Norsk*, the seven members of the Court were unanimous that *Murphy* does not represent the law of Canada. It was seen as laying down 'an indefensible general rule.'[32] In New Zealand, where the courts are still subject to the Privy Council, we may have thought much the same, possibly without expressing our judgments so bluntly. It is recognised that the fact that damage may be classified as purely economic may tell against liability, but is no more than one factor to be weighed in the task of judicial judgment.[33] And it is considered that the task is neither much helped nor well avoided by solutions falling back on verbal formulae.

Certainly there was no glossing over of the issues in *Norsk*. Judgments occupying one hundred pages of a law report cannot adequately be analysed in one brief paper. It will have to suffice to say that McLachlin J. and the two Judges who agreed with her held

that pure economic loss was *prima facie* recoverable when, in addition to negligence and foreseeable loss, there was sufficient proximity: here that was supplied by the close alliance of the plaintiff's operations with those of the owner of the damaged bridge: in effect they were joint venturers. Stevenson J., concurring in the result, did so on the *Caltex* ground of foreseeability of loss to a specific individual. In dissent La Forest J. and the two Judges agreeing with him thought that, *prima facie*, relational economic loss, such as that suffered by a party having a contract with the owner of a property damaged physically, should not be recoverable; and that here there was no joint venture. They also thought that the deterrent purpose of tort law was sufficiently served by liability to the bridge owner; while, as to loss-spreading, the plaintiff was in a better position than the defendant to predict and bear the loss. All stressed that on these various approaches there was no danger of indefinite liability.

Glad that I had no part of the responsibility of deciding either *Norsk* or *Caltex*, and conscious that a first impression can readily be changed by the facing of that responsibility, I must admit to some attraction, not for the first time, for the La Forest result. Sometimes it has been suggested that 'the New Zealand approach' is generally in favour of liability whenever foreseeable loss can be linked to carelessness. Such suggestions would not be made by those who have had time to read the New Zealand judgments. Obviously liability for the consequences of carelessness must stop somewhere. In each *class of* situation (not in each situation, because in the interests of certainty the law cannot be reduced to a wilderness of factual decisions) a range of factors will have to be weighed in determining whether an actionable duty of care exists.

A factor to which Salmond might have given much weight, in the light of his dislike of absolute liability and his emphasis on the fault principle, is moral culpability. McLachlin J. does appear to give much weight to this, indeed more than La Forest J.[34] In her words 'The fact is that situations arise, other than those falling within the old exclusionary rule, where

---

[28] 91 D.L.R. (4th) 289.

[29] 92 D.L.R. (4th) 449.

[30] 96 D.L.R. (4th) 289.

[31] (1976) 136 C.L.R. 529.

[32] 91 D.L.R. (4th) at 380 per Stevenson J. La Forest J. at 303 and McLachlin J. at 362, 366-7 and 371 spoke to the same effect.

[33] See for example the *South Pacific* case, n. 24 supra, throughout. In that case investigators for the insurer were held not to owe a duty of care to the insured where suggestions of arson arose, but the decision was based on factors much wider than the mere economic loss point. *Connell* v. *Odlum* (1993) 2 N.Z.L.R. 257 and *Comptroller of Customs* v. *Martin Square*

Motors Limited [1993] 3 N.Z.L.R. 289 are recent Court of Appeal cases in which duties of care to prevent economic loss or detriment have been accepted. They concern respectively a solicitor's certificate that he had explained to the prospective wife of the plaintiff the effect of a proposed settlement on her matrimonial property rights, and information about concessions, given by the Customs Department to a prospective importer. Both can be categorised as reliance cases, but so, directly or indirectly, are many cases of economic damage, including such damage caused or contributed to by vendors, builders and controlling authorities.

[34] Compare 91 D.L.R. (4th) at 344 with the same report at 365, 372 and 374.

it is manifestly fair and just that recovery of economic loss be permitted'. The qualification *manifestly* must be important. It is no part of the business of the courts to impose a code of ethics. Yet there are situations where any person of goodwill, the reasonable man or woman, the man on the Clapham omnibus, right-thinking members of society generally would almost certainly say that the defendant should be answerable. Loose though these tests may seem, they underlie much of the common law and pragmatically have been found capable of judicial management. If a court can identify a new situation as meeting such tests, liability should follow in the absence of compelling reasons to the contrary. It is because, bearing in mind the indirectness of the economic damage, I seriously doubt that contemporary and responsible community opinion would hold Norsk liable to C.N.R. that I provisionally lean to the minority Canadian result. Once that serious doubt exists, but not in my view until then, economic considerations such as comparative cost, insurance and loss-spreading come into play. They have some role in tort law, but it is a secondary one.

A final point about *Norsk*. The text 'direct' has been out of favour in English common law since *Polemis*[35] was disapproved of by the Privy Council in the first *Wagon Mound*[36] case. The latter has always seemed a rather unconvincing decision,[37] not to be compared favourably with *The Wagon Mound* (No. 2)[38] six years and a different Board later. As a matter of common sense, whether harm to the plaintiff is caused directly by the defendant's careless conduct or only indirectly should be a significant factor. It is therefore heartening to see 'directness' surfacing again as an important consideration in the judgment of McLachlin J. in *Norsk*.[39]

Escapes

It may be superfluous to remind this seminar of the learned that in his preface Salmond said of the decision of the House of Lords in *Rylands* v. *Fletcher*[40] 'No decision in the law of Torts has done more to prevent the establishment of a simple, uniform, and intelligible system of civil responsibility'. For more reasons than one Sir John would now have to reconsider that verdict. In such preventive tendencies *Rylands* v. *Fletcher* has been eclipsed. And there has

probably been a move away from absolute liability (which *Rylands* v. *Fletcher* never was, because of the act of God and act of a stranger defences) or even from strict liability independent of any negligence on the part of anyone for whom the defendant is responsible. *Rylands* v. *Fletcher* itself has been reduced to a precedent of obscure scope by the speeches in the House of Lords in *Read* v. *J. Lyons & Co. Ltd.*[41] In the result there is relatively little *Rylands* v. *Fletcher* litigation today.[40a]

Let us remind ourselves yet again of the words of Blackburn J. in the Court of Exchequer Chamber with which Lord Cairns L. C. and Lord Cranworth in the House of Lords expressed entire concurrence:

We think that the true rule of law is, that the person who, for his own purposes, brings on his land and collects and keeps there anything likely to do mischief it if escapes, must keep it in at his peril; and if he does not do so, is *prima facie* answerable for all the damage which is the natural consequence of its escape. He can excuse himself by shewing that the escape was owing to the Plaintiff's default; or, perhaps, that the escape was the consequence of *vis major*, or the act of God; but as nothing of this sort exists here, it is unnecessary to inquire what excuse would be sufficient. The general rule, as above stated, seems on principle just. The person whose grass or corn is eaten down by the escaping cattle of his neighbour, or whose mind is flooded by the water from his neighbourhood's reservoir, or whose cellar is invaded by the filth of his neighbour's privy, or whose habitation is made unhealthy by the fumes and noisome vapours of his neighbour's alkali works, is damnified without any fault of his own; and it seems but reasonable and just that the neighbour who has brought something on his own property (which was not naturally there), harmless of others so long as it is confined to his own property, but which he knows will be mischievous if it gets on his neighbour's, should be obliged to make good the damage which ensues if he does not succeed in confining it to his own property. But for his act in bringing it there no mischief could have accrued, and it seems but just that he should at his peril keep it there, so that no mischief may accrue, or answer for the natural and anticipated consequence. And upon authority this we think is established to be the law, whether the things so brought be beasts or water, or filth, or stenches.

Lord Cairns, not in a way that could easily be called judicially responsible, introduced the requirement of non-natural use of land, in language full of obscurity, with the result that in *Read* v. *Lyons*, apart from the simple ground of decision that there was no

Rylands v. *Fletcher* one stage towards Salmond's position, by holding that, although the storage of substantial quantities of chemicals on industrial premises is an almost classic case of non-natural use, foreseeability of damage in the event of escape is a prerequisite of liability. It was found that, at the time of the use of the chemical solvent, damage at the plaintiff's borehole could not reasonably have been foreseen.

[35] *Re Polemis* [1921] 3 K.B. 560.
[36] *Overseas Tankship (U.K.) Ltd.* v. *Morts Dock & Engineering Co. Ltd.* [1961] 1 All E.R. 404; [1961] A.C. 388.
[37] See (1978) 37 C.L.J. 288–93.
[38] [1966] 2 All E.R. 709; [1967] 1 A.C. 617.
[39] 91 D.L.R. (4th) at 363, 365, 366, 369 and 371.
[40] (1868) L.R. 3 H.L. 330.
[40a] In *Cambridge Water*, n. 14 supra, Lord Goff has moved
[41] [1946] 2 All E.R. 471; [1947] A.C. 156.

escape from the defendant's premises, two members of the House of Lords cast doubt on whether the making of munitions in wartime could be held a non-natural use. In the light of values presently prevailing it now seems strange that their Lordships apparently treated, or were at least not unwilling to treat, injury to adjoining land as more serious than injury to persons on that land, property as more deserving of protection than life.[42]

It is interesting that the most definite statements to that effect were made by Lord Macmillan, whose contribution to what has been widely seen as enlightened tort law throughout the common law world has been re-emphasised by Lord Rodger of Earlsferry's research into the history of his *Donoghue* v. *Stevenson* speech.[43] Of *Rylands* v. *Fletcher*, Lord Macmillan said in *Read* v. *Lyons* 'The duty is to refrain from injuring not alium but alienum'. He began his speech by observing that nothing could be more far-reaching than the discussion of fundamental principles to which the case gave rise. He ended with remarks about the perilous field of rationalising the law of England (not mentioning Scotland) not being the function of the House of Lords and 'may well be left to other hands to cultivate'. One wonders what solid justification exists for a third-tier appeal unless it be rationalisation and leadership in matters of principle. Lord Macmillan's *A Man of Law's Tale*,[44] a most readable book of reminiscences, seems to give few clues to his legal philosophy, though that may well emerge more from other writings or papers of his. Perhaps in the end the most valuable insight in *Read* v. *Lyons* is Lord Uthwatt's concise remark '. . . the law, whose function it is to give effect to reasonable expectations . . .'[45]

In *Attorney-General* v. *Geothermal Produce NZ Ltd.*,[46] where roses in the plaintiff's greenhouse had been killed by hormone spray used by the defendant's independent contractor across the road to kill broom, there arose the question whether toxic spraying was a natural use of rural land. In the light of post-Blackburn case law the question could not be answered confidently, and liability was in fact founded on negligence. The research occasioned by the argument forced me to say that, although Salmond's editors understandably claim that Blackburn's judgment has always been recognised as one

of the masterpieces of the Law Reports,[47] it has hardly been taken seriously by modern English courts.[47a]

In that fate it has become part of a possibly distinctive common law tradition. Great generalisations are made, receive some lip service, and are then quietly ignored in the practical business of judgment. As well as Blackburn J.'s 'master-mind' judgment in *Rylands* v. *Fletcher*, examples are Alderson B.'s statements in *Hadley* v. *Baxendale*[48] that damages in contract are those that *would* happen in the usual course of things or in special circumstances communicated to the defendant; Lord Atkin's neighbour principle in *Donoghue* v. *Stevenson*, now said to have suffered 'relegation to a footnote';[49] and Lord Wilberforce's *Anns* propositions. The latter are replaced by an overt preference for 'incrementalism', a term which describes how the common law has always advanced in fact but fails to rise to the level of a principle, or an outline of considerations, guiding future advances.[50]

Contributory Negligence

After his assault on *Rylands* v. *Fletcher* Salmond went on in his preface to his last edition to point out that the common law about contributory negligence was essentially unsound:

Another fundamental question which is still unsettled is that of the true nature of the rule as to contributory negligence. No more baffling and elusive problem exists in the law of Torts. It is true that since the publication of the last Edition the question has been the subject of consideration in the House of Lords in the case of the *S.S. Volute* [1922] 1 A.C. 129. That case, however, is affected by special considerations relative to maritime collisions and the exceptional rules in force as to contributory negligence in the Admiralty jurisdiction. It does not clearly appear that the observations of the House of Lords are to be accepted as an exposition of the law in its general application. An endeavour to solve the difficulties inherent in this problem leads to the conclusion that the common law rule of contributory negligence is essentially unsound. It seems impossible to establish any satisfactory doctrine whereby, in cases where an accident happens through the combined negligence of two persons, the total liability is nevertheless cast on one or the other of them exclusively according to the circumstances. It would seem that the only satisfactory rule is that

---

[42] [1946] 2 All E.R. at 474–5, 476, 478, 479, 481, 484; [1947] A.C. at 168–9, 172, 174, 178, 181, 186.
[43] (1992) 108 L.Q.R. 236.
[44] Macmillan & Co. Ltd., London, 1952.
[45] [1946] 2 All E.R. at 454; [1947] A.C. at 186.
[46] [1987] 2 N.Z.L.R. 348.
[47] In Salmond & Heuston, *The Law of Torts*, Sweet & Maxwell, London, 20th ed. (1992), the encomium appears at 314.

[47a] *Cambridge Water*, decided after this seminar (see note 14 supra) perhaps marks a return to Lord Blackburn.
[48] (1854) 9 Ex. 341; the point about *Hadley* v. *Baxendale* is developed in the article mentioned in n. 37 supra and *McElroy Milne* v. *Commercial Electronics Ltd.* [1993] 1 N.Z.L.R. 39, 42 et seq.
[49] Salmond & Heuston, op. cit., n. 47, 19th ed. (1987) viii.
[50] Some further discussion of the unhelpfulness of the term may be found in *Connell* v. *Odlum*, [1993] 2 N.Z.L.R. at 259–60.

which is adopted in the Admiralty jurisdiction, and in those systems which are derived from the Civil Law, namely that of dividing the loss between the persons who are responsible for it, either equally or in proportion to the degree of their fault.

As far as is known, neither in Salmond's time, nor in the preceding half century or more, nor at any subsequent time has there existed any significant body of legal opinion contrary to his on this subject. It appears to have been virtually the universal view that the common law rules were unsatisfactory. In a 1950 article,[51] Lord Wright described the common law as 'defaced', adding that 'As long ago as 1887 Fry L. J., a great judge, demanded why the court should not be empowered to divide the loss.' Having regard to the willingness of the courts from time to time to make radical changes in the common law, as evidenced in different directions by *Donogue* v. *Stevenson*, *Hedley Byrne* and *Murphy*, it is difficult to understand the failure to work out something better. Again there was no political content. Indeed there was scarcely even any controversial content. It was a field which the courts should have been able to manage for themselves.

But the initiative was left to the legislature. Even since the legislature has responded by the Law Reform (Contributory Negligence) Act 1945 and the equivalent Acts in other countries, difficulties have been allowed to have play. In particular the scope of the Act, in providing for apportionment of damage in accordance with shares of responsibility, has been threatened by a restrictive interpretation of the statutory definition of fault.

Grammatically, and as a beneficial interpretation to advance the remedy, it seems perfectly possible to read the definition as follows:

'fault' means
negligence,
breach of statutory duty,
or other act or omission which gives rise to a liability in tort or would, apart from this Act, give rise to the defence of contributory negligence.

There have been arguments, however, that the third limb should be treated as cutting down the meaning of the first limb, so confining the Act to negligence in breach of tort duty only and excluding negligence in breach of contractual duty. Up to a point those arguments may have prevailed so far in England. In a case concerning insurance brokers, *Forsikringsaktieselskapet Vesta* v. *Butcher*,[52] while accepting that the Act applies to breaches of duty arising from both contract and tort (as is commonly the case with professional duties[53]), the Court of Appeal apparently considered, *obiter*, that it would not apply if the defendant's duty of care arose from contract only. The view has been ventured, with the powerful support of the conclusions of Professor Glanville Williams, that the courts are not compelled to that interpretation. The Act can be held to apply to all cases of negligence, irrespective of the source of the duty of care.[54] But one of the cases in which that has been ventured is under further appeal and the New Zealand Courts are at the mercy of the Privy Council.[54a] Their Lordships have it in their power to impose their view of English common law on New Zealand common law, although they have not always regarded that as their function.[55]

The view has also been taken in a number of Canadian and New Zealand judgments that, whether or not the Contributory Negligence Act applies, there is now a general jurisdiction to reduce damages for contributory negligence or other contributing fault in at least all cases where the defendant's breach of duty stems from negligence, no matter whether historically the duty arises from tort or contract or fiduciary relationship or trust. Even if regarded as not strictly applicable, the Contributory Negligence Act is an analogy. It supports a wider development with deeper and, as far as courts of equity are concerned, older roots in the manifest requirements of fairness and justice. This approach is set out more fully in reported judgments. For the purposes of the kind of a survey of tort law required for the present paper, it will have to be enough to give some references.[56] Let it be stressed that no dilution of the fiduciary duties is involved. The high standards required of fiduciaries will be reflected in any apportionment of responsibility.

---

[51] 13 M.L.R. 2.

[52] [1988] 2 All E.R. 43, 46–9, 59, 61–2; [1989] 1 A.C. 852, 858–62, 875, 879, C.A.

[53] The concurrence of tort and contract duties was accepted by the English Court of Appeal throughout the *Vesta* judgments and appears to have been accepted by the present-day House of Lords in other cases: *Pirelli General Cable Works Ltd.* v. *Oscar Faber & Partners* [1983] 1 All E.R. 65, 67; [1983] 2 A.C. 1, 12; *Murphy* [1990] 2 All E.R. at 919; [1991] 1 A.C. at 466, per Lord Keith of Kinkel. It was accepted by the House of Lords in the past in *Brown* v. *Boorman* (1844) 11 Cl. & Fin. 1 and *Nocton* v. *Ashburton* [1914] A.C. 932. See further *Day* v. *Mead* [1987] 2 N.Z.L.R. 443, 449–50.

[54] *Mouat* v. *Clark Boyce* [1992] 2 N.Z.L.R. 559, 564 et seq.

[54a] In the event their Lordships did not find it necessary to consider the contributory negligence point: [1993] 4 All E.R. 268.

[55] See *Australian Consolidated Press Ltd.* v. *Uren* [1967] 3 All E.R. 523; [1969] 1 A.C. 590, where Sir Alfred North of New Zealand was a member of the Board. See now also *Attorney-General for Hong Kong* v. *Reid* [1994] 1 All E.R. 1.

[56] *Doiron* v. *Caisse Populaire D'Inkerman Ltee* (1985) 17 D.L.R. (4th) 660; *Coopers & Lybrand* v. *H. E. Kane Agencies Ltd.* (1985) 17 D.L.R. (4th) 695; *Canson Enterprises Ltd.* v. *Boughton & Co.* (1991) 85 D.L.R. (4th) 129, 148–52; cf. 154–62; 165–6; *Day* v. *Mead* and *Mouat* v. *Clark Boyce*, notes 53 and 54 supra; *Malhotra* v. *Choudhury* [1979] 1 All E.R. 186, 207; [1980] Ch. 52, 81; I.C.F. Spry Q.C., LL.D. *Equitable Remedies*, The Law Book Co. Ltd., Sydney, 4th ed. (1990), 632.

Vicarious Liability

The only other subject singled out in the Salmond preface taken as the starting point of this paper was 'the comparatively new and still undeveloped cause of action for intimidation, coercion, boycotting, conspiracy and other forms of oppressive interference with liberty of action'. Sir John described the authorities as 'in a state of chaotic confusion'. Whether or not chaos has been reduced to some form of order would be a large inquiry, taking us into the depths of industrial relations law. It is a tract of the law of great importance in the work of the courts and much affected by statutes. Such an inquiry cannot be contemplated here. But in relation to the law of employment there is one fundamental principle of the common law on the recent treatment of which several things fall to be said. They may be put under three headings.

(i) A principle of ancient lineage is that an employer or other principal is liable for the torts of his employee or other agent committed in the course or scope of the employment. It is immaterial that the employer obtains no benefit. As Earl Loreburn L. C. put it in the case of the solicitor's fraudulent managing clerk, *Lloyd* v. *Grace, Smith & Co.*,[57] 'It was a breach by the defendant's agent of a contract made by him as defendant's agent to apply diligence and honesty in carrying through a business within his delegated powers and entrusted to him in that capacity. It was also a tortious act committed by the clerk in conducting business which he had a right to conduct honestly, and was instructed to conduct, on behalf of his principal'. The House of Lords treated the case as a simple one, vouched for by authority going back to Sir John Holt, and did not suggest that the fact that the clerk owed a fiduciary duty to the defrauded client made any difference. Modern recognitions of the principle in the House of Lords and the Privy Council include *Heatons Transport (St. Helens) Ltd.* v. *Transport & General Workers Union*[58] and *Kooragang Investments Pty Ltd.* v. *Richardson & Wrench Ltd.*[59]

Attention is now drawn to an apparent departure from this principle, radical and of potentially profound importance in commercial law, although as yet perhaps not widely appreciated. In *Kuwait Asia Bank Ltd.* v. *National Mutual Life Nominees Ltd.*[60] one of the issues was whether company directors who gave to a trustee for depositors certificates as to the financial position of the company owed a duty of

care to the trustee. Another issue was whether the appointor of two of the directors, an overseas bank holding 40 per cent of the share capital, was vicariously liable for any breach of that duty by two directors whom it had appointed. There were procedural issues as well, and much of the judgment of the Privy Council, delivered in the name of Lord Lowry, is concerned with these. Only the vicarious liability issue is here relevant. The New Zealand Court of Appeal had refrained from expressing an opinion on it, as the case was at the pre-trial stage and major issues of fact remained to be determined. In so refraining we were, as I now acknowledge, unwise. For the Privy Council held while the trial was actually in progress that the bank could not be liable on any view of the facts. The reasons for the holding were given some six months later.

It was said *inter alia* that an employer who as a shareholder of a company nominates an employee to be a director does not owe a duty to the company unless the employer interferes with affairs of the company. It was accepted that there was an arguable case against the directors personally. Notwithstanding that the two directors in question were full-time employees of the bank in Bahrain, sent down to New Zealand from time to time to perform their function as directors of the company, it was held that the bank could not be responsible for their actions.

Insofar as it rests on the concept that, in performing their duties as directors, the appointees were bound to ignore the interests and wishes of their employing bank—which seems to be the main ground of the holding—the decision is at odds with commercial reality, as recognised in other contexts. Thus in *Bartlett* v. *Barclays Bank Trust Co. Ltd.*[61] Brightman J. (as he then was), a Chancery Judge of acknowledged learning and experience, decided that a professional corporate trustee holding a controlling interest in a company had failed in its duty of care to the beneficiaries; and in doing so he attached weight to the circumstance that there was no director who regarded himself as the bank's representative or nominee. It is everyday knowledge that nominee directors are there to safeguard the interests of their nominator. The law is losing touch with commercial reality if it shuts its eyes to that fact.

Be that as it may, what seems more pertinent here is that the existence of a duty to a third party, overriding any duty to the employer, does not normally emancipate the employer from vicarious liability for a breach of the employee's duty to that third party.

---

[57] [1912] A.C. 716, 724–5.
[58] [1972] 3 All E.R. 101; [1973] A.C. 15.
[59] [1981] 3 All E.R. 64; [1982] A.C. 462.
[60] [1990] 3 All E.R. 404, 424; [1991] 1 A.C. 187, 222–3.

[61] [1980] 3 All E.R. 139, 143; [1980] Ch. 515, 519 et seq. On this case, see Professor P. B. H. Birks, *Civil Wrongs: A New World*, the Butterworth Lectures 1990–91, 107–8.

The Kuwait Bank's nominee directors were acting in the course of their employment by the bank in making decisions regarding the company's affairs. It was exactly as if the bank itself were at the board table. Indeed under English law a company may be a director of another private company.[62] The *Kuwait Bank* case has been thought to need reconsideration on this point at least.[63] Whether their Lordships budge is perhaps some sort of a test of devotion to both principle and realism.

(ii) Corporate business activity also provides the converse question. Can a company be liable in tort if no individual shareholder or director or employee is liable? In particular, it is not in doubt that a duty of care in the giving of advice arises in some cases of known or expected reliance.[64] When the party relied upon is a company, does a duty of care to the plaintiff fall also on individuals within the corporate structure or shield? At first sight it might be thought that the answer lies in the conventional approach that liability always begins with a negligent human, the further question then arising whether his or her wrong is to be attributed to the company.[65] But cases where the employee is personally immune from suit yet the employer liable show that the rule is not unqualified.[66] The respondent in *Hedley Byrne*[67] was Heller & Partners Limited. It does not seem to go without saying that, had there been no disclaimer, Mr L. Heller would have been held personally liable.

The problem arises in a stark form in the case of a one-man company. In *Trevor Ivory Ltd.* v. *Anderson*[68] Mr Ivory had incorporated with the usual limited liability his horticultural advisory business. The company had a long-term contract to advise the plaintiffs. Acting under the contract Mr Ivory told the plaintiffs that they could kill the couch grass in the vicinity of their raspberry plants by spraying a powerful herbicide. He did not explain that they should ensure that any of the foliage of the plants near the ground was removed first or not sprayed. The plaintiffs followed his instructions to the letter, thus killing both the couch grass and the raspberry plants. The Privy Council might regard this as further evidence that the danger of overkill is not

understood in New Zealand.[69] The company was clearly liable in negligence. The more difficult issue was whether Mr Ivory was personally liable. We answered No.[70]

There can be no advantage in trying to put into other words the reasoning stated in *Trevor Ivory Ltd.*, so the following extract[71] is convenient:

Perhaps the contrary result reached in the High Court reflects partly the inculcated belief of many present-day lawyers that there is a clear and water-tight division between contract and tort, and that the two heads of liability should be considered quite separately. *Hedley Byrne*, now a quarter of a century old, may be cited to show that it can be a simplistic belief.

Without venturing further into what some would see as unduly theoretical, if not heterodox, I commit myself to the opinion that, when he formed this company, Mr Ivory made it plain to all the world that limited liability was intended. Possibly the plaintiffs gave little thought to that in entering into the consultancy contract; but such a limitation is a common fact of business and, in relation to economic loss and duties of care, the consequences should in my view be accepted in the absence of special circumstances. It is not to be doubted that, in relation to an obligation to give careful and skilful advice, the owner of a one-man company may assume personal responsibility. *Fairline*[72] is an analogy. But it seems to me that something special is required to justify putting a case in that class. To attempt to define in advance what might be sufficiently special would be a contradiction in terms. What can be said is that there is nothing out of the ordinary here.

To soften the austerity of the discussion something anecdotal may be intruded. Sir Alexander Turner has given me a copy of Broom's *Legal Maxims*[73] which belonged initially to my grandfather, then to my father, and passed to Sir Alexander on my father's death. In due course this heirloom should go to my own son in the law. The following maxim taken by Dr Broom from Coke on Littleton may be seen as summing up *Trevor Ivory Ltd.* in peculiarly happy language:

BENIGNAE FACIENDAE SUNT INTERPRETATIONES PROPTER SIMPLICITATEM LAICORUM UT RES MAGIS VALEAT QUAM PEREAT; ET VERBA INTENTIONI, NON E CONTRA, DEBENT INSERVIRE.

[62] *In re Bulawayo Market & Offices Co. Ltd.* [1970] 2 Ch. 458; 7(1) *Halsbury's Laws of England*, 4th ed. Reissue (1988), para. 557, n. 6.
[63] *ANZ Banking Group (New Zealand) Ltd.* v. *Dairy Containers Ltd.* N.Z.C.A., judgment 17 December 1992.
[64] Supra, pp. 6 and 10.
[65] D. A. Wishart so argues in [1993] N.Z.L.J. 175.
[66] *Broom* v. *Morgan* [1953] 1 All E.R. 849; [1953] 1 Q.B. 597; Salmond & Heuston, op. cit. 20th ed., 446. Consider also *Rainham Chemical Works Ltd.* v. *Belvedere Fish Guano Co. Ltd.* [1921] 2 A.C. 465, discussed by Lord Goff in *Cambridge Water* (n. 14 supra) [1994] 1 All E.R. at 74–5..
[67] Supra, n. 16.
[68] [1992] 2 N.Z.L.R. 517.
[69] *Rowling* v. *Takaro Properties Ltd.* [1988] 1 All E.R. 163, 173; [1988] A.C. 473, 502.
[70] Authorities from England and other jurisdictions are collected in the judgments. The closest was *Sealand of the Pacific* v. *Robert C. McHaffie Ltd.* (1974) 51 D.L.R. (3d) 702, which decision was followed.
[71] [1992] 2 N.Z.L.R. at 524; cf. Hardie Boys J. at 528 and McGechan J. at 532.
[72] *Fairline Shipping Corporation* v. *Adamson* [1974] 2 All E.R. 967; [1975] Q.B. 180.
[73] Sweet & Maxwell Ltd., Chancery Lane, 8th ed. (1911), 410.

What created and governed the proximity between Mr Ivory and the plaintiffs was the contract made by his company. To effectuate to the fullest extent the intention of the parties, the contract may be seen as an assumption of a duty of care by the company only, a standing disclaimer of personal liability by its major shareholder and managing director. In determining whether a duty of care exists all the circumstances have to be weighed. They include any relevant contract and the parties to it.

(iii) Salmond thought that the tendency of legal development was in the direction of extending rather than restricting the vicarious liability of employers of independent contractors, and that it was impossible therefore to state with any confidence the exact scope and limits of this form of responsibility.[74] His editors note[75] that sub-contracting in the building industry 'has given rise to great problems: financially irresponsible contractors, and their employers, may leave an injured person without remedy. So there was a distinct tendency to hold that the developer of a housing estate cannot delegate his duties to men of straw or shell companies, but this is now doubtful'.

Those last words refer explicitly to the speech of Lord Bridge of Harwich in *D. & F. Estates Ltd.* v. *Church Commissioners for England.*[76] The earlier 'distinct tendency' may allude to *Mount Albert Borough Council* v. *Johnson,*[77] one of the many New Zealand decisions which to our great regret have failed to appeal to Lord Bridge. In that case the so-called construction company, Sydney Construction Company Limited, had as its three directors an ex restaurateur, an insurance salesman and an accountant, and it employed no staff at all. It delegated all the construction work to a partnership of builders, who proved not worth suing. There appeared to be no authority directly in point. After reviewing such decisions as might provide any guidance the Court of Appeal had little difficulty in concluding that the company was liable for negligent construction by the builders. As a developer the company was causing to be put up buildings intended to house people for many years and was responsible for extensive and abiding changes in the landscape.

Lord Bridge said that as a matter of social policy this might be entirely admirable, but that as a matter of legal principle he could discover no basis on which it was open to the court to embody this policy

in the law without the assistance of the legislature; and that it was, in his opinion, a dangerous course for the common law to embark on the adoption of novel policies which it sees as instruments of social justice but to which, unlike the legislature, it was unable to set carefully defined limitations. With great respect for the opinion of my Privy Council colleague, these words seem more emotive than in accordance with sound legal tradition.

The *Mount Albert* decision was not reached before thought had been given to high United Kingdom and Australian authority bringing out the difficulty of drawing the line as to liability or not for independent contractors. For example, some observations of Lord Reid to that effect[78] were expressly cited. The point concerning developer's liability apparently not having been decided before by any court, it was necessary to come down one way or the other. The entire law of vicarious liability has been evolved by the courts without the assistance of the legislature. Salmond & Heuston bring this out,[79] citing *inter alia* House of Lords authority that the doctrine depends on 'social convenience and rough justice'.[80] The latter ideas are the reverse of novel. 'Carefully defined limitations' may be an allusion to the statutes of limitation. Their general scheme is to date the running of time from the accrual of the cause of action, a date left to the common law to define. The result of the recent case law since Salmond is to leave the condition of the law of tort in this field still less possible to state with confidence than it was in his day.

The Inevitability of Judicial Legislation

The point just touched on goes much further. A decade ago the authentic spirit of English tort law seemed to be maintained in such statements as the following from a case about nervous shock:[81]

To attempt to draw a line at the furthest point which any of the decided cases happen to have reached, and to say that it is for the legislature, not the courts, to extend the limits of liability any further, would be, to my mind, an unwarranted abdication of the court's function of developing and adapting principles of the common law to changing conditions, in a particular corner of the common law which exemplifies, par excellence, the important and indeed necessary part which that function has to play. In the end I believe that the policy question depends on weighing against each other two conflicting considerations.

[74] *Torts*, 6th ed. 119.
[75] Salmond & Heuston, op. cit. 20th ed. 475.
[76] Supra, n. 6, All E.R. at 1009; A.C. at 209.
[77] [1979] 2 N.Z.L.R. 234.
[78] *Davie* v. *New Merton Bond Mills Ltd.* [1959] 1 All E.R. 346, 367–8; [1959] A.C. 604, 646.

[79] 20th ed. 444–5.
[80] *I.C.I. Ltd.* v. *Shatwell* [1964] 2 All E.R. 999, 1012; [1965] A.C. 656, 686, per Lord Pearce.
[81] *McLoughlin* v. *O'Brian* [1982] 2 All E.R. 298; [1983] 1 A.C. 410, 441–2, 443, per Lord Bridge.

...

My Lords, I have no doubt that this is an area of the law of negligence where we should resist the temptation to try yet once more to freeze the law in a rigid posture which would deny justice to some who, in the application of the classic principles of negligence derived from *Donoghue* v. *Stevenson* [1932] A.C. 562, ought to succeed, in the interests of certainty, where the very subject matter is uncertain and continuously developing, or in the interests of saving defendants and their insurers from the burden of having sometimes to resist doubtful claims.

Decisions in grey area cases were thus acknowledged as depending on justice and 'the policy of the law'. At times the same acknowledgment remains apparent. Thus in the latest major case on nervous shock, *Alcock* v. *Chief Constable of South Yorkshire*,[82] it was held that close relatives suffering shock from seeing a disaster on live television had no cause of action. Although some of the speeches include apparently artificial presumptions,[83] the essence of the decision seems to be stated by Lord Oliver of Aylmerton:

The failure of the law in general to compensate for injuries sustained by persons unconnected with the event precipitated by a defendant's negligence must necessarily import the lack of any legal duty owed by the defendant to such persons. That cannot, I think, be attributable to some arbitrary but unenunciated rule of 'policy' which draws a line as the outer boundary of the area of duty. Nor can it rationally be made to rest upon such injury being without the area of reasonable foreseeability. It must, as it seems to me, be attributable simply to the fact that such persons are not, in contemplation of law, in a relationship of sufficient proximity to or directness with the tortfeasor as to give rise to a duty of care, though no doubt 'policy', if that is the right word, or perhaps more properly, the impracticability or unreasonableness of entertaining claims to the ultimate limits of the consequences of human activity, necessarily plays a part in the court's perception of what is sufficiently proximate.

The term 'policy' there questioned by Lord Oliver is perhaps a substitute for judgment, a slightly uncandid or anodyne term serving to paper over the fact that negligence liability cases may not be solved by logic or formulae but by judicial assessment or discretion. In short by judicial legislation.[84] At other times, as in the *D. & F. Estates* case, this is repudiated.

One cannot but agree with a passage in the speech of Lord Goff of Chieveley in *Woolwich Building Society* v. *Inland Revenue Commissioners* (No. 2).[85] It is a passage destined for quotation down the generations since it expresses what so many lawyers in various parts of the world have said for so long and what all lawyers know to be true. Three sentences from it say almost everything:

I feel bound, however, to say that, although I am well aware of the existence of the boundary, I am never quite sure where to find it. Its position seems to vary from case to case. Indeed, if it were to be as firmly and clearly drawn as some of our mentors would wish, I cannot help feeling that a number of leading cases in your Lordships' House would never have been decided the way they were.

The process of deciding cases not clearly covered by established precedent degenerates into a pseudo-science as often the result is said to depend solely on deduction.

Towards Synthesis

Professor P. B. H. Birks is conditioning us to thinking in terms of an integrated law of civil wrongs, rather than sharply compartmentalised laws of tort, contract, fiduciary relationship and trust.[86] I respectfully believe that this is a valuable insight by the Honorary Secretary, for it can help to simplify problems; and simplicity, fairness and correspondence with reasonable expectations are presumably in the forefront of the purposes of the common law.

The most obvious field in which this approach may be useful is negligence, liability for which is found under all the four rubrics. A single example may be given to illustrate the point. In *Hedley Byrne*,[87] liability in the absence of disclaimer was founded on a tort duty of care in responding to an enquiry. Basically, however, it can be said to have arisen from carrying out an agreement to respond. The law was willing to require reasonable care in carrying out the agreement, and would have done so by affixing the label of contract if only the smallest and most adventitious of considerations had passed between the parties. The fineness of the line and the technicality of the distinction is evidenced by the doubt of textbook writers as to whether in *De la Bere* v. *Pearson Ltd.*[88] consideration was present and

---

[82] [1991] 4 All E.R. 907, 914–5, 920, 925; [1992] 1 A.C. 310, 397–8, 404, 410. Applied in *Ravenscroft* v. *Rederiaktiebolaget Transatlantic* [1992] 2 All E.R. 470.

[83] For example 'In my opinion the mere fact of the particular relationship was insufficient to place the plaintiff within the class of persons to whom a duty of care could be owed by the defendant as being reasonably foreseeably at risk of psychiatric illness by reason of injury or peril to the individuals concerned'. Supra, n. 82, All E.R. at 915; A.C. at 398.

[84] This point is developed in the *South Pacific* case [1992] 2 N.Z.L.R. at 295 and in *Tort Illusions*, a chapter in *Essays on Torts*, edited by Professor P. D. Finn, The Law Book Company Ltd., Sydney, 1989.

[85] [1992] 3 All E.R. 737, 760–1; [1993] A.C. 70, 173.

[86] See his lectures delivered at Queen Mary and Westfield College included in the booklet cited in n. 61 supra.

[87] Supra, n. 16.

[88] [1908] 1 K.B. 280.

whether liability should have been founded on contract or tort.[89]

Not much of the twentieth century is left. For most of the century the common law of England, despite some glaring inadequacies, moved on the whole forwards and 'incrementally', affording redress in no situation where it was not demanded by justice. More latterly there has been some faltering, but *Woolwich*[90] and *Lipkin Gorman*[91] are widely hoped to promise a renewal of progress. At this time, perhaps four major breakthrough cases during the century can be identified. They are *Nocton* v. *Ashburton*,[92] where it was held that a solicitor's fiduciary duty of care to his client could be founded on equity, contract or tort, and its breach redressed by an award of monetary compensation;[93] *Donoghue* v. *Stevenson*[94] on the duty of care owed by a manufacturer to a consumer; *Home Office* v. *Dorset Yacht Co. Ltd.*,[95] where negligence principles were extended to government departments acting under statutory powers but failing by their employees to exercise due care for the interests of persons suffering foreseeable economic loss in the form of property damage;[96] and *United Scientific Holdings Ltd.* v. *Burnley Borough Council*,[97] where Lord Diplock, Lord Simon of Glaisdale and Lord Fraser of Tullybelton determined, in the now famous words of the first-named:[98]

Your Lordships have been referred to the vivid phrase traceable to the first edition of *Ashburner, Principles of Equity* where, in speaking in 1902 of the effect of the Supreme Court of Judicature Act he says (p. 23) 'the two streams of jurisdiction' (sc. law and equity)—'though they run in the same channel, run side by side and do not mingle their waters'. My Lords, by 1977 this metaphor has in my view become both mischievous and deceptive. The innate conservatism of English lawyers may have made them slow to recognise that by the Supreme Court of Judicature Act 1873 the two systems of substantive and adjectival law formerly administered by courts of law and Courts of Chancery (as well as those administered by courts of admiralty, probate and matrimonial causes), were fused. As at the confluence of the Rhône and Saône, it may be possible for a short distance to discern the source from which each part of the combined stream came, but there comes a point at which this ceases to be possible. If Professor Ashburner's fluvial metaphor is to be retained at all, the waters

of the confluent streams of law and equity have surely now mingled.

One is aware that those words are quite commonly not taken seriously and that fine discriminations can be made between 'fusing' and 'mingling'. The fact is that the House of Lords so decided, by a majority perhaps, and as far as I know the House of Lords as subsequently composed have not repudiated the decision. By now it would surely be hopeless to contend that it can make any difference that one member of the majority was a Scottish Law Lord who adopted the views of two English Law Lords on the concept of merger into a single stream. Scottish Law Lords have laid down much of the law of England, and, more curiously perhaps, New Zealand also.

Advantages of the Confluence

Two useful consequences can follow from the recognition that there has been merger, mingling or fusion. They relate both to the substantive law of rights and duties and to remedies. As to the substantive law it may be more helpful to concentrate on defining the true nature of an obligation and the basic reason for it, rather than becoming immersed in one or other of the separate streams of the past.[99] Much of the law of civil duties, whatever the sources from which it has drawn, is about the assumption of responsibilities. One puts oneself in a position of responsibility to others by making a contract, accepting a trust or a position of confidence, making or proffering something for the use of someone else or a group or succession of people. If the link is sufficiently strong, close or direct, it will be natural for the law to uphold a duty of care. Patently the civil law includes much more than duties of care: there are many strict contractual duties: but duties of care are a large and unifying part of the civil law. It would perhaps be a step forward to acknowledge that wherever they exist they should *prima facie* have the same incidents.

It is received doctrine that a cause of action arises in contract on breach, but in tort on the commission of the tort, which is quite commonly not complete until damage has been caused. This leads to conces-

---

[89] Cheshire, Fifoot & Furmston *Law of Contract*, Butterworths, London, 12th ed. (1991) 87; Butterworths, Wellington, 8th N.Z. ed. (1992) 102; G. H. Treitel *Law of Contract*, Sweet & Maxwell/Stevens & Sons, London, 8th ed. (1991) 143.

[90] Supra, n. 85.

[91] *Lipkin Gorman* v. *Karpnale Ltd.* [1991] 2 A.C. 548, [1992] 4 All E.R. 512.

[92] Supra, n. 53.

[93] Viscount Haldane L.C., with the concurrence of Lord Atkinson, at 945–7; Lord Dunedin at 962–4; Lord Shaw of Dunfermline at 967–72; Lord Parmoor at 977–8.

[94] Supra, n. 12.

[95] [1970] 2 All E.R. 294; [1970] A.C. 1004.

[96] It is believed that this decision is considered bad law by some eminent subsequent holders of judicial office.

[97] [1977] 2 All E.R. 62; [1978] A.C. 904.

[98] [1977] 2 All E.R. at 68; [1978] A.C. at 924–5. Lord Simon's observations to the same effect are at 83–4 and 944–5 of the respective reports; those of Lord Fraser are at 94 and 957–8.

[99] This section is partly a development of views outlined in *Aquaculture Corporation* v. *New Zealand Green Mussel Co. Ltd.* [1990] 3 N.Z.L.R. 399, earlier cases there collected, and other cases already cited in footnotes in the present paper.

sions or assumptions, such as have been made in *Pirelli*[100] and many other cases, that a cause of action based on the same negligence may be barred in contract but not in tort. The complication disappears if it is accepted that there is only one substantive duty, a duty to exercise reasonable care, albeit arising from two sources; and that there are not two breaches of that duty but only one. Even seen purely from the point of view of contract law, negligence in the abstract should not matter. If a physician carelessly fails to advise an X-ray but in fact no bones are broken and the patient suffers in no way from the failure, the law need not insist on the existence of a cause of action. Nor must it do so when the taxi-driver goes too fast but there is no accident. The duty of care, however arising, can be seen as a duty not to cause damage by negligence. Otherwise our lives are full of countless causes of action for nominal damages.

In *Midland Bank Trust Co. Ltd.* v. *Hett, Stubbs & Kemp*,[101] Oliver J. suggested that this kind of difficulty could be circumvented by striking out actions for abuse of process. Any abuse, however, would lie in bringing an action although no damage had been suffered. It is more straightforward to say frankly that there is no cause of action,[102] while allowing a *quia timet* remedy when required and accepting that necessary remedial expenditure is recoverable damage. Further, the problem of undiscovered damage can be met by similar frankness. It can be said that as a matter of ordinary common sense no one has a cause of action until he or she knows or ought to know of it. Causes of action in negligence arise when substantial detrimental consequences of a failure to take reasonable care become reasonably manifest. Successive actions will lie for truly distinct damage not reason-

ably discoverable or predictable earlier. On this approach the unfortunate English decisions in *Cartledge* v. *E. Jopling & Sons Ltd.*[103] and *Pirelli*,[104] which had to be rectified by legislation, could have been avoided.[105]

Fiduciaries

Fiduciary duty is as great a transcendent concept of the civil law as negligence, which it overlaps. While the content of fiduciary duties varies, as some fiduciaries are free to pursue their own interests so far as is no true conflict with the interests of the principal, they all stem from the idea that the parties have come into a relationship where one has accepted a responsibility for looking after some interest of the other and where the other necessarily depends on the fidelity with which the responsibility is carried out.[106] Since the Judicature Acts it will often be more helpful to define the substance of the alleged fiduciary's duty than to allot it to any one single historical source. Instances of it may be found between professional adviser and client,[107] parties negotiating a contract,[108] employer and employee,[109] owners of intellectual property and their licensees,[110] probably husband and wife,[111] possibly *de facto* spouses,[112] close relatives,[113] trustee and beneficiary of course, company director and company,[114] and so on. The categories are not closed, the cases are legion, and the compartments traditionally found convenient for expounding the civil law are crossed. So powerful and far-reaching is the idea that an adaptation of it has penetrated constitutional law in the major field of duties owed by Governments to indigenous peoples.[115]

Where this crossing of the lines or synthesis can

---

[100] Supra, n. 53.
[101] [1978] 3 All E.R. 571, 611–2; [1979] Ch. 384, 435.
[102] The points here made are dealt with more fully in some respects in *Tort and Contract*, a chapter contributed to *Essays on Contract*, edited by Dr P. D. Finn, the Law Book Company Ltd., Sydney, 1987.
[103] [1963] 1 All E.R. 341; [1963] A.C. 758.
[104] Supra, n. 53.
[105] New Zealand common law is not necessarily the same as that laid down in *Cartledge* and *Pirelli*: *Mount Albert Borough Council* v. *Johnson*, op. cit. n. 77 supra, at 239, not cited in *Pirelli*; Todd, op. cit. n. 14 supra, at 908–15. The author of the chapter, Stephen Todd, expresses the unequivocal opinion that it is clear beyond peradventure that the correct test is discoverability and that *Pirelli* was wrongly decided, as 'is implicit in *Murphy*'s case itself'.
[106] In arms-length commercial relationships the courts are slow to inject fiduciary notions, but they can arise of course in commercial dealings as in others. For contrasting reactions to a commercial situation of factual dependence, see *Liggett* v. *Kensington* [1993] 1 N.Z.L.R. 257, 267, 298–300.
[107] *Nocton* v. *Ashburton*, n. 53 supra; *Canson Enterprises Ltd.* v. *Boughton & Co.*, n. 56 supra.

[108] *LAC Minerals Ltd.* v. *International Corona Resources Ltd.* (1989) 61 D.L.R. (4th) 14. In that particular case the Court was divided on the fiduciary question, but, as a majority held in favour of a restitutionary constructive trust on the ground of breach of confidence, the label was not seem to matter in the result. For the concerns of Professor Birks but the support of Mr J. D. Davies, see the lecture cited in n. 61 supra at 90–3.
[109] *Schilling* v. *Kidd Garrett Ltd.* [1977] 1 N.Z.L.R. 243; *Reading* v. *R.* [1951] 1 All E.R. 617; [1951] A.C. 507; *Dowson & Mason Ltd.* v. *Potter* [1986] 2 All E.R. 418.
[110] *Watson* v. *Dolmark Industries Ltd.* [1992] 3 N.Z.L.R. 311.
[111] *Duchess of Argyll* v. *Duke of Argyll* [1965] 1 All E.R. 611; [1967] Ch. 302; *Barclays Bank plc* v. *O'Brien* [1992] 4 All E.R. 983.
[112] *Phillips* v. *Phillips* [1993] 3 N.Z.L.R. 159, 167..
[113] *Coleman* v. *Myers* [1977] 2 N.Z.L.R. 225.
[114] *Guinness plc* v. *Saunders* [1990] 1 All E.R. 652; [1990] 2 A.C. 663.
[115] *R.* v. *Sparrow* (1990) 70 D.L.R. (4th) 385, 406–9; *Mabo* v. *State of Queensland* (1992) 107 A.L.R. 1, 85–6, 157–60; *Te Runanga O Wharekauri Rekohu Inc.* v. *Attorney-General* [1993] 2 N.Z.L.R. 301.

lead is vividly illustrated by the judgments in the Supreme Court of Canada in the two 1992 cases[116] of *Norberg* v. *Wynrib* and *K.M.* v. *H.M.* In the first a physician had prescribed a drug to an addict in return for sexual favours. She sued for battery, negligence and breach of fiduciary duty. In the lower courts she failed on a range of grounds: consent, no physical injury, her own illegal and immoral acts. The Supreme Court unanimously found liability, with differences of opinion as to quantum. The inequality of power and the fiduciary duty overcame the objections to allowing a remedy. The award of the majority of the Judges, whose reasons were delivered by La Forest J., was aggravated damages of $20,000 and punitive damages of $10,000. Of the minority Sopinka J. would have given less and McLachlin J. more.

In the second case the appellant suffered incest from her father when she was aged from eight to seventeen. As an adult she developed psychological problems and underwent therapy, thereby learning that the father's conduct was the cause. Regrettably it is a known syndrome. At the age of 28 she brought action against him for damages for assault, battery and breach of fiduciary duty. The jury awarded $50,000, but the action was dismissed as barred by the Limitation Act. The Supreme Court restored the verdict, holding *inter alia* that the relationship of parent and child is fiduciary, and that incest is a breach of the parent's fiduciary duty to protect the child's well-being and health. It had been conceded that the Ontario Limitation Act did not bar actions for breach of fiduciary obligations, although the equitable defence of laches was available. The position would appear to be the same in England[117] and New Zealand.[118]

The approach of the Supreme Court of Canada in *K.M.* v. *H.M.* is obviously in the sharpest of contrasts to that of the House of Lords in *Stubbings* v. *Webb*,[119] where a similar action, against a stepfather and stepbrother, was held statute-barred without even a mention of fiduciary duty. Presumably neither any of the counsel nor any of the Judges thought of

the point. On the narrower matters of statutory interpretation which were the focus of *Stubbings* v. *Webb*, the reasoning is encapsulated in the memorable sentence of Lord Griffiths:[120] 'If I invite a lady to my house one would naturally think of a duty to take care that the house is safe but would one really be thinking of a duty not to rape her'.

I am not obliged to take sides on this particular issue. It is more complicated than can be suitably set out here. My point is rather that there has been a wider and perhaps deeper perception of the ends and possibilities of the common law in Canada. Occasionally a similar note has been struck in recent times in England.[121] But it has not been as frequent as in the days when the senior English and Scottish Judges were automatically seen as indisputably among the pre-eminent leaders of the common law world. We have huge debts to the English Courts; any attempt to repay them cannot be in kind, but only in such advantages as can flow from a different perspective.

In the field of this paper much more could be said on the themes outlined. For example, some practical experience of the alternatives suggests that since the Judicature Acts there exists, on the one hand, a more beneficial scope for exemplary damages than is currently accorded in England[122] under the confessedly restrictive judicial legislation in *Rookes* v. *Barnard*[123] and *Cassell & Co. Ltd.* v. *Broome*;[124] and, on the other, a greater scope for guiding and controlling awards of exemplary and aggravated damages than is accepted in *Sutcliffe* v. *Pressdram Ltd.*[125] In New Zealand there is both more breadth and more control. Partly this is because it has been necessary for the purposes of the Accident Compensation legislation to distinguish carefully between compensatory damages (barred by the legislation) and punitive damages (held to be left recoverable).[126]

Thus in the British Government's *Spycatcher* case in New Zealand[127] the Court of Appeal would have considered an award of exemplary damages for aiding Wright's breach of fiduciary duty. But any award of damages was ruled out by the newspaper's suc-

[116] Supra, n. 29 and n. 30.
[117] Limitation Act 1980, s. 36.
[118] Limitation Act 1950, s. 4(9).
[119] [1993] 1 All E.R. 322. Judgment was given on 16 December 1992, The Canadian decision had been given on 29 October 1992 and was apparently not drawn to the attention of their Lordships.
[120] Ib. 329.
[121] As by Bingham J. in *Neste Oy* v. *Lloyds Bank* [1983] 2 Lloyd's Rep. 658, 665–6, a passage which has helped us more than once in New Zealand (e.g. *Elders Pastoral Ltd.* v. *Bank of New Zealand* [1989] 2 N.Z.L.R. 180; *Liggett* v. *Kensington* n. 106 supra, where it was accepted as authoritative even in the dissenting judgment) and which may be said to have indicated the appointment of the Master of the Rolls.

[122] One would not at all query the refusal of exemplary damages for public nuisance on the facts in *AB* v. *South West Water Services Ltd.* [1993] 1 All E.R. 609, having regard particularly to the multitude of potential claimants. The jurisdictional disclaimer to which the Court of Appeal felt constrained is another matter.
[123] [1964] 1 All E.R. 367; [1964] A.C. 1129.
[124] [1972] 1 All E.R. 801; [1972] A.C. 1027.
[125] [1990] 1 All E.R. 269; [1991] 1 Q.B. 153. Now, up to a point, rectified by legislation: Courts and Legal Services Act 1990, s. 8; *Gorman* v. *Mudd* C.A. 15 October 1992.
[126] Supra, n. 15. The basic case is *Donselaar* v. *Donselaar* [1982] 1 N.Z.L.R. 97.
[127] *Attorney-General* v. *Wellington Newspapers Ltd.* [1988] 1 N.Z.L.R. 129, 165, 172.

cessful defences that the information was already in the public domain and that publication was in the public interest, the book having been admitted for the purposes of the New Zealand proceedings to be a true account of the facts. It was not thought material to label the cause of action in question as arising exclusively in tort or exclusively in equity or from both sources concurrently: it was simply an action for breach of a fiduciary duty of confidence.[128]

A great deal of the foregoing might have been foreign to the thinking of Sir John Salmond, who did not even cite *Nocton* v. *Ashburton*[129] or *Brown* v. *Boorman*.[130] We may be sure that his analytical powers would have assimilated and illumined the deci-

sions rendered by the courts in the work required of them since his time. Whether even his capacity could have guided the common law world into the issues of the twenty-first century is a more open question. Old arbitrary lines of demarcation are crumbling. Travel along new avenues of practical and just juristic thought is increasingly sensed to be inevitable. A cautious creativity going beyond analysis is called for. Even fifty years hence, much of the law of civil wrongs as now articulated will in all likelihood seem superficial. More and more, tort law may come to be regarded as a loose description of a form of civil liability not clearly discrete and not developed from distinctive principles of its own.

[128] For an example of an award of moderate exemplary damages ($5000) in addition to compensatory damages ($65,000) for breach of an employee's fiduciary duty, see *SSC & B: Lintas* v. *Murphy* [1986] 2 N.Z.L.R. 436.

[129] Supra, n. 53.
[130] Supra, n. 53. An oil broker was held by the House of Lords liable to his client in tort for not exercising reasonable care and diligence.

5. Some Reflections on *Junior Books*

ALAN RODGER

FOR anyone who has been involved in a well-known case it is interesting to see how it is handled subsequently by the courts and by commentators. Of no case can that be more true perhaps than of *Junior Books Ltd.* v. *Veitchi Co. Ltd.* [1983] 1 A.C. 520, the speeches in which caused an uproar when they were handed down in late July 1982. The effect on practitioners in England and the Commonwealth was all the more dramatic since they had previously been unaware of the existence of the case. When the speeches appeared in the following Saturday's *Times* there was consternation over the toast and coffee in many a barrister's household, for the decision seemed to herald the end of much which was received and familiar. Eleven years later we know better, and the picture has been redrawn by the House of Lords along more familiar lines. Still *Junior Books* is worth at least another glance, not only because it has not yet been over-ruled (perhaps because their Lordships are waiting for a Scottish appeal) but also because it still features in discussions of some of the issues in the law of torts. Having been junior counsel for the unsuccessful appellants in the case, I would not feel free to criticise the decision. None the less I believe that I can properly comment on certain matters of fact and on the way in which the decision has been treated since 1982.

Mr. Ken Livingstone

I start with Mr. Ken Livingstone. His role in the history of negligence is not perhaps well known, but readers may recall that, in the words of Lord Denning, 'in 7 May 1981 there was an election for the Greater London Council. In advance of the election, the Labour Party issued a manifesto' promising to cut fares on the 'buses and tubes by 25%. In due course fares were cut and in September of that year the London Borough of Bromley applied for judicial review of the new Council's policy. The G.L.C. won in the Divisional Court, but lost in the Court of Appeal early in November. The matter seemed to be urgent and so the House of Lords agreed to give priority to the G.L.C.'s appeal by awarding it the slot which began on 24 November: *Bromley L.B.C.* v. *Greater London Council* [1983] 1 A.C. 768. Of course, this meant clearing a space in the lists: the appeal which was removed was *Junior Books*. So it was not heard until the following April. By then the significance of

the postponement was not lost on counsel for the appellants at least: Lord Wilberforce, who chaired the judicial committee which heard the Fares Fair appeal, and who would probably therefore have presided over the committee if it had heard *Junior Books* in November, had retired on 1 March 1982. Had he presided in the *Junior Books* appeal, it seems quite likely that their Lordships' speeches would have been rather different. The subsequent history of the law of negligence might well have been different too.

This is not to assume that with Lord Wilberforce the appellants would have won the case. Far from it. At the time indeed we thought that, even though our argument depended not on challenging *Anns* but on putting bounds on it, we might have difficulty in persuading Lord Wilberforce to accept a somewhat narrow interpretation of his speech. So his retirement seemed on balance to be a good thing from the appellants' point of view. The point which I make is rather that, if Lord Wilberforce had presided and had written the leading speech dismissing the appeal, the reasoning in it would have been different and would almost certainly have been more persuasive. Certainly the legal reasoning of the majority opinions of Lord Fraser and Lord Roskill has been severely criticised, perhaps most notably by Robert Goff L. J. in *Muirhead* v. *Industrial Tank Specialities* [1986] Q.B. 507, a passage whose force is only enhanced by the courteous terms in which it is couched. The criticisms of the reasoning made it much harder for supporters of wider liability in negligence—which was the substantive issue in the appeal—to defend the newly-won territory. With better argued speeches the position might well have been very different. As it was, Lord Wilberforce never had an opportunity to reinforce or refine *Anns* in a building context and Lord Roskill's use of his test in *Junior Books* came to cast doubt on *Anns* itself. This led inexorably to *Murphy*. The importance of the standard of formal legal reasoning in determining the fate of issues of substance should not be underestimated. The point is of significance in relation to *Murphy*. Whatever critics may think of the policy underlying the decision in *Murphy*, the formal legal reasoning in their Lordships' speeches is on a quite different plane of sophistication from that in the speeches in *Junior Books*—doubtless because counsel's arguments were superior too. So, whereas *Junior Books* was an easy target for commentators and judges, *Murphy* will not be—and the policy which it enshrines will be that much harder to attack in the courts than the policy enshrined in *Junior Books*.

The Anns Test

What qualifications, if any, Lord Wilberforce would have made to his two-stage test beyond those in *McLoughlin* v. *O'Brian* [1983] A.C. 410 we shall never know. From my own experience in practice I must say that I found that the two-stage test did indeed put an enormous burden on defenders. In *South Pacific Manufacturing Co. Ltd.* v. *New Zealand Security Consultations and Investigations Ltd.* [1992] 2 N.Z.L.R. 282 Cooke P. refers, not for the first time, to the suggestion that Lord Wilberforce's test creates a prima facie presumption of a duty based on reasonable foresight and says 'I am of the school of thought that has never subscribed to that view, largely because of Lord Wilberforce's reference to a *sufficient* relationship of proximity or neighbourhood. It would be naive, and I believe absurd and dangerous, to assert that a duty of care prima facie arises whenever harm is reasonably foreseeable.' At the risk of being condemned as naive, I must confess that this was precisely how I interpreted Lord Wilberforce's words: 'First one has to ask whether, as between the alleged wrongdoer and the person who has suffered damage there is a sufficient relationship of proximity or neighbourhood such that, in the reasonable contemplation of the former, carelessness on his part may be likely to cause damage to the latter, in which case a prima facie duty of care arises.' I construed 'sufficient' along with 'such that' so that the test was satisfied if there was such a degree of proximity or neighbourhood (whatever that term or those terms might mean) that the defendant could reasonably foresee that carelessness on his part was likely to cause damage to the plaintiff. I felt unable to interpret the test otherwise when arguing *Twomax* 1982 S.C. 113 and can only take comfort in the fact that others appear to have been as naive as I: see e.g. the discussion in *Sutherland Shire Council* v. *Heyman* (1985) 157 C.L.R. 424 per Gibbs C. J. On that approach, in nearly all cases where there was a real issue to determine, the defender began with a severe handicap which it was difficult to overcome. So, while I agree, of course, that there is no particular magic in adopting an incremental approach, I do believe that the House of Lords performed an invaluable service when they first qualified and then cut out Lord Wilberforce's two-stage test. By removing it, the House of Lords have made it much easier for the courts to apply what everyone agrees is the correct approach, viz. to

weigh all the factors in order to decide whether to impose a duty of care. That process was much more difficult to perform properly when likelihood of damage seemed somehow to tilt the scales, and there was no indication of what weight of countervailing factors was required to displace the prima facie duty of care.

Proximity in *Junior Books*

It was my naive approach to the two-stage test in *Anns*, shared by my senior, which led us to concede at all stages in *Junior Books* that in one sense the pursuers' case passed the first stage of that test. It seemed to us that we could not deny that if the floor were carelessly laid to a sufficient degree the defenders could foresee that the pursuers would be likely to suffer damage. Our point was rather that, however foreseeable such damage might have been, in actual fact, to judge by their averments (the only possible test), the pursuers had not suffered any 'damage' at all. What they were averring rather was that their building had a defective floor, and while the defenders could of course have foreseen that if they laid a defective floor the pursuers would become owners of it, that did not amount to foreseeing the pursuers suffering 'damage' in any legally relevant sense. Given then that no issue was ever taken on the first stage of the test, it is all the stranger to find that Lord Roskill seems to have found it necessary to set out eight factors which pointed to the existence of the requisite degree of proximity ([1983] A.C. at 546). Having done so, he refers to Lord Devlin's speech in *Hedley Byrne* and adds that 'all the conditions existed which give rise to the relevant duty of care by the appellants to the respondents.' It is in this way that Lord Roskill introduces the concept of reliance and seems somehow to be tying the *Junior Books* liability into the *Hedley Byrne* family of cases. Lord Fraser says that the pursuers nominated the defenders as specialist sub-contractors and 'must therefore have relied upon their skill and knowledge' ([1983] A.C. at 533).

Reliance

These references to reliance have come to assume considerable importance since they constitute the basis on which *Junior Books* has been allowed to survive the chopping-down of the *Anns* tree of which it had previously appeared to be a branch. While five of their Lordships in *Murphy* maintained a discreet silence about *Junior Books*, Lord Keith and Lord Bridge mentioned it, both justifying it by reference to the concept of reliance—though Lord Keith had not founded on reliance in his own speech in *Junior Books*. In *Murphy* Lord Keith said that in a case such as *Pirelli* [1983] 2 A.C. 1 'where the tortious liability arose out of a contractual relationship with professional people, the duty extended to take reasonable care not to cause economic loss to the client by the advice given. The plaintiffs built the chimney as they did in reliance on that advice. The case would accordingly fall with the principle of *Hedley Byrne & Co*. I regard *Junior Books* as being an application of that principle' (citations omitted). Lord Bridge said 'There may, of course, be situations where, even in the absence of contract, there is a special relationship of proximity between builder and building owner which is sufficiently akin to contract to introduce the element of reliance so that the scope of the duty of care owed by the builder to the owner is wide enough to embrace purely economic loss. The decision in *Junior Books* can, I believe, only be understood on this basis.'

It is fair, I think, to say that Lord Bridge at least is hardly enthusiastic about this way of looking at *Junior Books*, but I believe in any event that one must ask whether such a rationalisation of *Junior Books* is really possible, given what the facts and arguments in that case were. The use of the concept of reliance by Lord Fraser and Lord Roskill in *Junior Books* was subjected to a powerful, not to say devastating, analysis by Robert Goff L. J. in *Muirhead*. I merely add one or two footnotes to what he said there.

First, it may be useful to draw attention to the averments which were before the House in *Junior Books*. They are not printed in the Law Reports but can be found conveniently in 1982 S.L.T. 333. This is what was said about nomination: 'Messrs. Wilson & Wilson . . ., the architects employed by the pursuers, asked the defenders for a quotation for flooring work at the factory . . .' After that the averments on reliance were as follows: 'The architects relied on the defenders as flooring specialists to recommend a suitable material for the production area floor . . . No instructions were given as to the actual mix of magnesium oxychloride composition used, or the procedure to be followed, since the architects relied on the defenders as specialist sub-contractors to ensure that the correct mix was used and that the correct procedure was followed.' The first of these averments is not relevant, since the pursuers' case was not based on any allegation that the material chosen was unsuitable: it was based on allegations of fault in using an excessively wet mix, in applying too thin a top coat of magnesium oxychloride composition and in allowing inadequate curing of the magnesium oxychloride composition. So the only averment which could be relevant was the second.

In *Muirhead* Robert Goff L. J., while generously trying to discover what Lord Fraser meant by proximity and Lord Roskill by the very close 'relationship' between the parties, said that they must 'have had in mind the dealings between the parties which led to the pursuers nominating the defenders, who were specialists in flooring, as sub-contractors to lay the flooring in their factory.' As can be seen, however, the pursuers did not aver that they themselves had nominated the defenders as sub-contractors, nor that they had had any kind of dealings with the sub-contractors at all. Rather, according to the averments it was the architects who nominated the defenders as specialist sub-contractors. The general understanding is that in nominating sub-contractors architects do not act as the agents of the employers. (Cf. Keating on Building Contracts,[5] 287 and Hudson on Building Contracts,[10] 111 and 742 et seq.) So one should perhaps be cautious in explaining their Lordships' approach in this way.

On a related matter, while Robert Goff L. J. points out that Lord Fraser said that the pursuers 'had full knowledge of the appellants' contractual duties', it is not actually clear why Lord Fraser thought this since the pleadings contained no averment to that effect and the system of nomination is indeed used in part to distance employers from the sub-contract.

It is also noteworthy, I believe, that the reliance averment does not say that the pursuers, the building owners, relied on the defenders' expertise. Rather, apparently in order to negative any suggestion that the architects who had designed the project were responsible for specifying the mix etc. of the composition floor, the averment says the *the architects* relied on the defenders as specialist sub-contractors. While such an averment may be a basis for leading evidence to negative any suggestion that the architects should be blamed for what went wrong, and may indeed also be a good basis for leading evidence to show that any blame should rest with the defenders, for the reasons already given it does not seem altogether an adequate basis for saying that the pursuers were relying on the defenders' skill and expertise.

Jane Stapleton has remarked that 'reliance proves to be a particularly slippery concept' (107 L.Q.R. 284) and Robert Goff L. J. showed just how nebulous the idea seemed to be in *Junior Books*. I also have difficulty with Lord Keith's use of it in *Murphy*. One can, of course, see that *Pirelli* can be attached to the *Hedley Byrne* set of reliance cases, since there the plaintiffs alleged that they had built a chimney on the basis of design advice given by the defendants and had suffered loss when the chimney proved to be defective. There the plaintiffs acted in reliance upon the advice. By contrast in *Junior Books* the pursuers did not aver that they had acted in reliance on the defenders' skill and expertise in laying the floor: they merely said that the defenders had laid a defective floor and they asked for damages to put it right. It was as though the plaintiffs in *Hedley Byrne* had simply said that they had been given defective advice by the defendants and had asked for damages to put the advice right. If those had been the facts of *Hedley Byrne*, surely no-one would have said that the plaintiffs had suffered loss by relying on the defendants and I see no more reason to say so in *Junior Books*. I very much doubt therefore whether their Lordships' decision can properly be defended on the basis of *Hedley Byrne* reliance.

The Damages Sought

The claim in *Junior Books* has been described as a claim for 'quality complaints' without any added claim for profits lost as a consequence of the defect and hence as not being indeterminate in the *Ultramares* floodgate sense (Stapleton, 107 L.Q.R. 256 and 267). But there was in fact a profit element involved. Admittedly the pursuers did not specifically aver that they had already suffered any loss of profits, but they said that the floor required to be replaced to avoid continual maintenance 'which would be more expensive than immediate replacement or treatment' and added inter alia that 'The pursuers' business will be partially closed during the period of treatment. They will accordingly lose profits as a result of such closure. They estimate that said loss of profits to be [sic] £45,000'. The averments about maintenance turned out to be important since, by construing them to mean that the pursuers were suffering higher maintenance costs than with a sound floor, Lord Keith was able to conclude that the pursuers' manufacturing operations were being 'carried on at a less profitable level than would otherwise have been the case, and that they are therefore suffering economic loss' ([1983] A.C. at 536). This was precisely the narrow basis upon which he decided that the pursuers' case was relevant. On the broader front one can see that the claim was really of a rather indeterminate kind if one compares the original sub-contract price for laying the floor (just over £17,000) with the pursuers' claim for damages (£206,000). As we saw, the make-up of the claim included damages for relaying the floor, rather than simply for loss caused by the defect in the floor. This was suspiciously like a claim for damages measured according to the contractual standard and that again suggested that the pursuers' case did not really fall within the usually understood limits of a claim in delict or tort.

The Standard of Quality

At the end of his speech Lord Brandon drew attention to the difficulty which a court would have in determining 'by what standard or standards of quality' the question of defectiveness would fall to be decided ([1983] A.C. at 551–2). Lord Fraser also recognized the point, though he felt able to overcome it on the averments in the case ([1983] A.C. at 533–4). Referring to the passage in Lord Brandon's speech, Jane Stapleton has called this a 'dubious justification' which courts no longer seem to stress. As for the British courts, they may not have stressed this particular matter since it really arises sharply as an issue only in pure cases of defective quality such as *Junior Books*. But in fact we may notice that Lord Prosser was not unsympathetic to the point in *Parkhead Housing Association* v. *Phoenix Preservation Ltd.* 1990 S.L.T. 812 at 816. So it may not yet be extinct even here. It is noteworthy also that the passage in Lord Brandon's speech was cited by Grosskopff A. J. A. in the South African Appellate Divison in *Lillicrap, Wassenaar and Partners* v. *Pilkington Brothers* 1985 (1) S.A. 475 at 501 as part of his reasoning that delictal liability did not fit comfortably into a contractual setting.

Stapleton says that the issue of the standard of quality does not 'need to be more of a problem than the issue of, say, merchantability is in the law of sales. This, like the standard of care in physical damage cases and negligent misstatement cases, can be influenced by surrounding circumstances such as price (if any)' (107 L.Q.R. 270 n. 92). Perhaps because we thought that this was one of our better arguments in *Junior Books*, I am not yet entirely convinced that it can be so easily brushed aside. I would make two points.

In the first place it is not perhaps the best recommendation for a new concept that it need be no more of a problem than merchantability. A glance at the current edition of Benjamin confirms that few concepts have proved more elusive, and for present purposes it is enough to note the editors' conclusion that 'The standard required has proved difficult to define' (*Benjamin on Sale,* 11–026 et seq. and 11–047 n. 17).

Secondly, in physical damage and negligent misstatement cases the defendant is required to take reasonable care to avoid causing physical damage to the plaintiff or to avoid causing loss to the plaintiff who acts on the statement. What is to be avoided is easily determined, and then the court has to look at all the surrounding circumstances and decide what constitutes reasonable care to avoid it in the circumstances. So equally if the Veitchi company had been sued by someone who had fallen on a piece of defective flooring or by Junior Books, one of whose fork-lift trucks had been damaged by a defect in the floor, a court would have had little difficulty in deciding what the defenders should have done by way of mixing the chemicals or laying the surface to avoid such injury or damage. But Junior Books made and could make no such averments: all they said was that there was cracking on the floor and that 'the entire floor surface requires replacement at as early a date as possible to avoid the necessity of continual maintenance, which would be more expensive than immediate replacement or treatment.' In other words they had a defective floor which would need continual maintenance. Relaying the floor would be cheaper than maintaining it and they wanted the defenders to pay for relaying it. In that situation the question was: what was the target standard of flooring which the defenders should have achieved? Presumably not a floor which required no maintenance. Moreover, given that the floor was laid in 1970, had not begun to crack until 1972 and was still in everyday use when the action began in 1977, it was certainly very far from a useless floor. In those circumstances I confess that I see great force in Lord Brandon's conclusion that the question of the standard by which the alleged defects are to be judged either 'remains entirely at large and cannot be given any just or satisfactory answer' or else is determined by the provisions of the contract under which the work is done. If, as Stapleton suggests, the price would be a relevant factor, then that is simply one element taken at random from the contract. It would hardly be justifiable to look at the price in isolation from the other terms of the contract which must have been relevant to determining the price. But once a court gets drawn into considering various aspects of the contract, would it really be right to pick the parts which favoured the plaintiff and to ignore, say, the exclusion provisions which favour the defendant? To approbate and reprobate in this way is hard to justify.

The strength of *Donoghue* v. *Stevenson* [1932] A.C. 562 and the line of cases which descend from it is precisely that they proceed wholly on the duty of care not to injure the plaintiff and ignore any contract with someone else under which the defendant may have acted. By contrast if, to establish the standard of liability, a court used any part of the contract under which the defendant was operating, it would be very hard to justify not using the whole of the contract to determine the scope of the duty in tort. And that is just to allow the contracting parties' arrangements to determine the scope of the duty which one of them owes to a third party in tort. This seems at least unusual since one of the characteristics of tort liability is generally thought to be that it is determined by the law independently of any agree-

ment to which the plaintiff is not a party. In cases where the plaintiff and defendant are parties to a contract it is of course now well established that the plaintiff cannot invoke the law of tort in order to obtain an advantage which would not be available under the contract: *Tai Hing* v. *Liu Chong Hing Bank* [1986] A.C. 80.

In the South African case of *Lillicrap, supra* Grosskopf A. J. A. put the matter in this way: '. . . in general, contracting parties contemplate that their contract should lay down the ambit of their reciprocal rights and obligations. To that end they would define, expressly or tacitly, the nature and quality of the performance required from each party. If the Aquilian action were generally available for defective performance of contractual obligations, a party's performance would presumably have to be tested not only against the definition of his duties in the contract but also by applying the standard of the *bonus paterfamilias*. How is the latter standard to be determined? Could it conceivably be higher or lower than the contractual one? If the standard imposed by law differed in theory from the contractual one, the result must surely be that the parties agreed to be bound by a particular standard of care and thereby excluded any standard other than the contractual one. If, on the other hand, it were to be argued that the *bonus paterfamilias* would always comply with the standards laid down by a contract to which he is a party, one would in effect be saying that the law of delict can be invoked to reinforce the law of contract.' Having pointed out the emphasis which the plaintiffs placed on the detailed requirements laid down in the contract as determining the standard by which negligence fell to be determined Grosskopf A. J. A. concluded 'It seems anomalous that the delictual standard of *culpa* or fault should be governed by what was contractually agreed upon by the parties.' The general thrust of the learned judge of appeal's remarks seems to be applicable in our law also.

Having looked back to *Junior Books*, I now make a few remarks on the position after *Murphy*.

Defective Premises Act 1972

In *Murphy* a certain amount is made of the significance of the Defective Premises Act 1972, and in his well-known article Sir Robin Cooke has noted the suggestion that this may prove a relevant distinction when the application of *Murphy* comes to be considered in New Zealand where there is no equivalent statute (107 L.Q.R. 69). The point is of interest nearer home too, since the 1972 Act does not apply to Scotland. In any Scottish case raising the same point there could therefore be an argument that *Murphy* should not apply because the 1972 Act does not apply. For my own part I very much doubt whether such a contention would prevail. Given the formidable analytical arguments which are marshalled in *Murphy* and which are quite untouched by this particular point, I cannot envisage the House of Lords reviving *Anns* or any close relative of *Anns* and allowing it to develop north of the Border. This suggests to me at least that the 1972 Act point is at best a makeweight in their Lordships' reasoning.

Defective Dwellings

In suggesting the way forward for the law of torts relating to buildings, Sir Robin Cooke has suggested that a distinction could be drawn by the courts between dwellings and commercial buildings, and he points out that all the New Zealand cases have related to dwellings (107 L.Q.R. 67). There seem to me to be difficulties with this suggestion, at least for us in Britain. Perhaps because I come from Scotland where we have many blocks of flats—I noted a preponderance of single-storey houses in my one brief visit to New Zealand—the separation between the two categories strikes me as being far from clear-cut.

Leaving on one side the point that blocks of flats may be built as a commercial venture, there remains the fact that many blocks of flats will be built with commercial premises such as shops on the ground floor. In that situation, if the proposed distinction were applied, a court would surely be faced with one of two alternatives. The court could hold that the purchaser of a flat could sue for defects in construction, while the purchaser of a shop in the same block could not. This does not look like an easily defended distinction for the common law, especially if it came up in proceedings where both the owner of a flat and the owner of a shop were suing for the same defect in construction. Worst of all, of course, would be where the owner of the shop lived in a flat which he owned in the same block. The court might then be faced with allowing his claim for the flat, but denying his claim for the shop. What would happen if, like many advocates in Scotland, the purchaser bought a house with the aim of using part for conducting his business also seems unclear. As an alternative approach, the court might hold that the presence of the shops made the whole building commercial in nature and so took the owners of the flats out of the category of residential proprietors favoured by the law. That seems to be equally unattractive. In any event, the suggested rationale for the distinction—that home owners should be protected, while purchasers of commercial buildings can look after themselves—works only so long as one sees them as very distinct categories. I have suggested that the distinction is not clear-cut. But even where it is, I have difficulty in seeing on what policy grounds a court should decide, say, that the purchaser of a luxury flat in a splendid development requires more protection than a struggling businessman who buys a modest commercial unit in a poor neighbourhood. One might reasonably expect the former to commission much more elaborate structural reports than the latter. Of course, the fact that the flat was in a luxury development or the shop in a poor neighbourhood might form part of that 'most careful analysis' which is now required (*Rowling* v. *Takaro Properties* [1988] A.C. 473) but, if pragmatism extends this far, then advising clients on their prospects of success is going to be difficult indeed.

Jus Quaesitum Tertio

Finally, it has been said that the decision in *Junior Books* to extend the scope of tort liability really arose because of the strictures put on contract remedies in English law by the doctrine of consideration and the resulting rules on privity. (See for example Dias and Markesinis, *Tort Law*,[2] 12 et seq.) That is, however, not an entirely fair reading of the case. It has to be remembered that *Junior Books* was a Scottish appeal and in Scots law, unlike in English law, there is a doctrine of jus quaesitum tertio. The House of Lords were indeed well aware of this, for at one point during the hearing Lord Keith remarked that on one view the pursuers' argument was tantamount to introducing a jus quaesitum by the back door—the point being that it might seem to give the benefits of a jus quaesitum tertio to a party who had not fulfilled the usual requirements for such a right in Scots law.

The matter arose expressly in the Outer House of the Court of Session in *Scott Lithgow Ltd.* v. *G.E.C. Electrical Projects Ltd.* 1992 S.L.T. 244 at 259 et seq. The case concerned events during the construction of the submarine H.M.S. Challenger for the Ministry of Defence. The facts are somewhat complicated and many points were argued, including the scope of a sub-contractor's duty of care in delict or tort. (The decision antedates *Murphy*.) For present purposes, however, we can concentrate on the fact that the shipbuilders, apparently in more than one sub-contract, sub-contracted the design and provision of the propulsion and surveillance system of the submarine to G.E.C. who in turn sub-contracted various aspects to other companies. Certain defects were discovered in the electrical wiring of that system and these had to be put right. This caused delay and certain consequential losses to the Ministry of Defence who then sought to recover them inter alia on the basis that according to the Scots law of jus quaesitum tertio the Ministry had a right to sue G.E.C. for G.E.C.'s failure to perform their duties under their sub-contract with the shipbuilders.

G.E.C. argued that the Ministry's case on jus quaesitum tertio should be dismissed without any inquiry into the facts. In the event Lord Clyde expressed grave doubts about the sufficiency of the Ministry's averments under this head, but somewhat reluctantly allowed the matter to go to proof so that the facts could be determined. (The case actually settled before any appeal could be heard and before proof.) What Lord Clyde's judgment shows is that a jus quaesitum tertio does not fit at all easily into this kind of situation. His Lordship was prepared to accept that the fact that the Ministry was mentioned in some unspecified way in the sub-contract carried them some distance in arguing for a right to sue, but he had more difficulty with the requirement that for the Ministry to be able to sue it should have been the intention of the parties to the sub-contract to benefit the Ministry. Cf. *Finnie* v. *Glasgow & South Western Railway Co.* (1857) 3 Macq. 75.

The greatest difficulty in inferring an intention to benefit the Ministry arose perhaps out of the point that the Ministry itself was a party to a contract with the shipbuilders who had in their turn been a party to a sub-contract with G.E.C. The terms of the respective contracts were not before the judge and so he was unable to see what similarities, if any, there were between the sub-contracts and the main contract. But obviously the terms of the contracts must have been different to some extent at least. In that situation there was well-established authority in *Blumer & Co.* v. *Scott & Sons* (1874) 1 R. 379 which suggested that no jus quaesitum tertio arose. In *Blumer* the pursuers had contracted for the supply of a steamer. The shipbuilders entered into a separate contract with the defenders for the supply of the engines. Lord President Inglis held that since the terms of, and obligations under, the two contracts

were different, the pursuers who had a right to demand performance of their contract with the shipbuilders, had no right to sue on the entirely separate sub-contract between the shipbuilders and the engine suppliers. Lord Clyde took the view that the existence or not of a jus quaesitum tertio might therefore depend on the terms of the main contract and sub-contracts. While he accepted the general proposition that the existence of a chain of contracts did not preclude the possible inference of an intention in the sub-contracts to benefit the eventual recipient of the goods 'the fact of the existence of the main contracts and the relationship between the terms of the main and the subcontracts may have a bearing on the issue before me. Indeed the conclusion to be drawn in relation to one of the subcontracts on the matter of a jus quaesitum tertio may not necessarily be the same as that to be drawn in respect of the other.'

The discussion in *Scott Lithgow* does indeed suggest that for Scots Law at least the doctrine of jus quaesitum tertio would not have assisted the pursuers in the kind of situation which arose in *Junior Books*. Plainly the terms of Junior Books' contract with the main contractor were different from the terms of the main contractor's sub-contract with Veitchi. So *Blumer* would suggest that Junior Books should have had no right to sue on the sub-contract. Not only would that conclusion be in line with well-established authority, but in addition that authority springs from a sound acknowledgment of the principle that, where the parties have deliberately chosen to arrange their affairs by separate contracts with the very object of not creating direct relations between the employer and the supplier of specialist services, the law should be slow to frustrate that choice by holding that the employer can directly sue on the sub-contract. The argument applies just as much in the field of jus quaesitum tertio as it does in the field of delict or tort. (For a particularly forceful discussion of the point in tort see J. Blom, in *The Paisley Papers*, 139, at 161 et seq.)

6. Tort Law in the Contract State[1]

BOB HEPPLE

A New Dimension

THIS paper raises some questions about the role of tort law in regulating the provision of public services[2] in the context of privatisation, market-testing and contracting-out. The subject is one of general interest because it exposes many of the current concerns about the condition of the law of tort, and the ways in which it could be improved.

Any discussion of the 'frontiers of liability' in tort has to take account of major changes which are occurring in the provision of public services. The 1980s were marked by the privatisation of a number of public authorities and utilities. In the 1990s 'market-testing', the creation of 'internal markets', and contracting-out to private entrepreneurs, are features of central and local government, and the National Health Service. We may be some way yet from the 'contract State', in which government is simply a 'series of contracts',[3] but the growing shift from direct provision by the state has obvious ideological and political significance with its legitimation of market choice and the suggested empowerment of 'citizens' and 'consumers'. It also has legal significance because it involves the use of the mechanisms of private law by public authorities to secure the provision of services to the public.

The use of contract in the provision of public services is not new, but in the past its main application has been indirect, namely in the procurement of goods and services to support government which was both procurer and provider. Since the mid-1980s the emphasis of government policy has been on separating the procurement and the provision of services. Under the Local Government Act 1988,[4] local authorities and certain other public authorities are allowed to undertake specified activities 'in-house' through their own direct service organisation (DSO) only if they have first satisfied themselves by a process of compulsory competitive tendering (CCT) that the activity could not be more economically performed by using external contractors. The activities in question include refuse collection, cleaning buildings, catering, managing sports and leisure facilities, and maintenance of grounds and vehicles.[5] Market-testing is now also widespread in central government departments, with the award of contracts to private contractors where this is more economical than in-house delivery of services.[6] The fundamental feature of market-testing is the separation of the roles of purchaser (or 'client') and provider (or 'contractor'), whether the work is performed in-house or by a private body. In central government, the aim of separating responsibility for deciding the nature and standard of the service, from delivery of that service cost-effectively is reflected in the creation of Next Steps Agencies.[7] The Framework Documents (CD) for each Agency are not legally binding contracts, and the Agencies themselves are not independent statutory corporations, but the White Paper on their financing and accountability refers to 'the Department as "owner" and where appropriate customer of the Agency.'[8] In the National Health Service (NHS), the aim of the National Health Service and Community Care Act 1990, was to separate the roles of District Health Authorities (DHAs) as purchaser and provider of health services. The basic idea of the internal market is that of a contractual relationship between the provider (whether a directly managed unit (DMU) or an NHS Trust) and the purchaser

---

[1] I am grateful to Professors Carol Harlow, Jeffrey Jowell, and Gillian Morris, and Tony Weir, for their helpful comments on an earlier draft.

[2] For purposes of this paper 'public service' is defined in the sense used by Ian Harden, *The Contracting State*, Buckingham, Open University Press, 1992, pp. 8–9, namely a service whose 'existence is currently mandated by public authority', so bringing into consideration: '(a) services provided by a public body directly; (b) services purchased by a public body through contract; and (c) services which a private body has a public law duty to provide.'

[3] As suggested by Graham Mather, *Government by Contract*, London: Institute of Economic Affairs, 1991.

[4] This was preceded by the Local Government Planning and Land Act 1980, Part III, which required compulsory competitive tendering for construction and maintenance work. The

extension was envisaged in a Green Paper, *Competition in the Provision of Local Authority Services* (1985).

[5] Local Government Act 1988, s.2 and sched. 1.

[6] For the background see Treasury, *Using Private Enterprise in Government: report of a multi-department review of competitive tendering and contracting for services in government departments*, London: HMSO, 1986; and *Competing for Quality*, 1991, Cm. 1730.

[7] D. Goldsworthy, *Setting up Next Steps: a short account of the origins, launch and implementation of the Next Steps Project in the British Civil Service*, London, HMSO, 1991.

[8] *The Financing and Accountability of Next Steps Agencies*, Cm. 914, 1989, para. 2.7.; see too, *Developments in the Next Steps Programme*, Cm. 841, 1989; *Progress in the Next Steps Initiative*, Cm. 1263, 1990.

(DHA or GP fund holder). The contract specifies the agreed quantity, quality and cost of the services to be provided.[9]

The legal issues which arise under these new contractual or semi-contractual arrangement have so far been almost exclusively the concern of public law,[10] and of specialists in government contracts.[11] There is an important question which needs to be addressed by tort lawyers. What are to be the rights and remedies of the ultimate 'consumers', 'customers' or other recipients of the public goods and services provided under these new arrangements? One needs little imagination to envisage claims by mistreated inmates of contracted-out prisons,[12] or by those who suffer through negligent certification of building plans by an 'approved' person under contract to a local authority,[13] or by 'consumers' who fail to receive expected benefits either from in-house or contracted-out providers.

The Government puts its faith in competition and in the implementation of the non-statutory Citizen's Charter, which promises 'quality', 'choice' and 'standards' and redress for the citizen 'when services go badly wrong.'[14] The methods of implementation include fixed levels of compensation for failure to meet prescribed performance targets and quality standards,[15] and more effective complaints procedures.[16] Mr William Waldegrave, the Public Service and Science Minister, believes that the Citizen's Charter should 'not aim to establish a spider's web of new justiciable rights' because the 'lethal combination of litigation and pressure groups can kill innovation and introduce a desperate timidity into decision making.[17] His critics[18] claim that privatisation and government by contract could lead to corruption, fraud and mismanagement on a massive scale—one might think a fertile field for tort lawyers.

The primary aims of market-testing and CCT have been seen by the Treasury as 'value for money'. If 'value' denotes not simply the lowest price, but also optimal quality then acceptable standards may have to be determined through the mechanism of tort law as well as by public regulators. As Harden says, 'failure to meet the promised standard provides a legitimate basis for criticism and complaint. However, to create individual rights analogous to those enjoyed under a contract, there must be a means for individuals to enforce performance of the service, to obtain damages.'[19] Individual rights in relation to public services have been variously described as the 'new property',[20] and a 'new contract'.[21] The lawyer might more appropriately describe individual rights to claim damages for failure to confer the benefits created by contract between public authorities and providers as 'new torts'. 'Reinventing government'[22] will almost certainly require us to reinvent torts.

The present structure of the law of tort places at least four major obstacles[23] in the path of individual legal rights to public services in contracting-out situations:

(1) the limited, uncertain and irrational scope of the action for damages for breach of statutory duty;

(2) the principle of immunity of public authorities from liability for negligence in the exercise of certain discretionary decisions;

(3) the principle of non-liability for the acts or omissions of independent contractors; and

(4) the absence of enforceable rights under contracts for third party beneficiaries.

Before considering these issues, it is necessary to say something about the relationship between public law and private rights.

Public law and private rights

Tort law is 'private' law. The new regulatory and contracting regimes have been created within the province of 'public' law. The tension between the

---

[9] Department of Health, *Contracts for Health Services; operational principles*, London: HMSO, 1990; Department of Health, *Funding and Contracts for Hospital Services*, Working Paper 2, London: HMSO, 1989.

[10] The leading study is by Ian Harden, *The Contracting State*, Buckingham: Open University Press, 1992.

[11] Colin Turpin, *Government Procurement and Contracts*, Harlow, Longman, 1989; Sue Arrowsmith, *Civil Liability and Public Authorities*, Humberside, Earlsgate Press, 1992, esp. at pp. 96–102.

[12] The Criminal Justice Act 1991, ss. 76–86, allows the contracting-out of court security officers, prison escort arrangements and new remand prisons.

[13] Building Act 1984, s. 16.

[14] *The Citizens Charter: Raising the Standard*, Cm. 1599, July 1991, p. 5; for an analysis see G. Drewry [1993], P.L. 248.

[15] Cm. 1599, p. 48 (British Rail); and see below regarding compensation schemes in the utilities.

[16] Cm. 1599, pp. 42–6.

[17] *The Times*, 26 April 1993, p. 9, and see generally, W. Waldegrave, *Public Service and the Future: Reforming Britain's Bureaucracies*, Conservative Political Centre, February 1993.

[18] E.g. John Sheldon (General Secretary of the National Union of Public Employees), *The Times*, 14 May 1993, p. 15; and see Radford (1988), 51 M.L.R. 747 at p. 749.

[19] Harden, op. cit., p. 60,

[20] Charles Reich, 'The New Property', (1964), 73 Yale, L. J. 773.

[21] M. Pirie, *The Citizens' Charter*, London: Adam Smith Institute, 1991, p. 8.

[22] The phrase made famous (or notorious for some) by David Osborne and Ted Gaebler, *Reinventing Government*, Reading, Mass.: Addison-Wesley, 1992.

[23] Other obstacles, not discussed in this paper, include the inadequacy of the tort of misfeasance in public office, and the absence of an action for damages for ultra vires action.

two, and the potential of tort law to undermine the Government's grand scheme, are obvious. The question is how they should relate to each other.

The problem is that the legal relationships arising from market-testing and contracting-out are neither exclusively 'public' nor 'private', but involve a complex mixture of public regulation and private rights. The range of relationships includes the following:

(1) Between the consumer and the public authority which provides the service through an in-house provider: since Next Step Agencies, local authority DSOs and Health Service DMUs have no separate legal identity the legal relationships between these providers and their respective public authorities are not contractual; individual rights must derive either from public law or action in tort against the public authority itself.

(2) Between the consumer and the public authority which procures the service from a private body by contract: the Crown has the same common law capacity as private individuals to make contracts, although some special public law rules apply, such as that against fettering the exercise of public powers; local and other public authorities are subject to the public law principles of ultra vires.

(3) Between the consumer and a private body with a public law duty to provide the service: examples include the statutory duties to supply gas, water, and electricity, to consumers.[24]

(4) Between the consumer and a private body which is under a contractual duty to a public authority to provide the service: here the consumer's rights appear to arise only in private law.

In this classification the word 'consumer' has been used to describe those (usually individuals) for whom a particular public service is provided. Like 'customer', this is a 'slippery term'.[25] In the tort context, it may refer not only to the identifiable recipient but also to a wider range of persons who suffer damage or loss as a result of the breach of duty by the provider or by the public authority procuring the service.

The complex interaction of public law and private rights in these relationships makes it difficult to uphold the principle of procedural exclusivity established in *O'Reilly* v. *Mackman*.[26] This appeared to entrench a rigid classification of public and private law, and seems to have influenced the failure of the application for judicial review of the allegedly unfair way in which the Lord Chancellor's Department processed tenders for the provision of court transcripts, on the grounds that neither the pre-contractual negotiations nor the contracts themselves had a sufficient public law element.[27] Here procedural law is like a dog chasing its own tail. It was the extraordinary extension of civil liability in *Thornton* v. *Kirklees District Council*[28] for breach of a statutory duty to provide accommodation for a homeless person, that led the House of Lords in *Cocks* v. *Thanet District Council*,[29] another homeless persons case decided at the same time as *O'Reilly*, to suggest that a discretionary decision had first to be challenged by way of judicial review. This case has since been distinguished,[30] and it has been suggested by Lord Bridge that the incidental involvement of a public law issue in private law claims cannot debar the plaintiff from taking civil proceedings.[31] The Court of Appeal in *Lonrho plc* v. *Tebbit*[32] has now held there is no need to apply for judicial review before asserting a private law right arising out of a statutory background. Sir Michael Kerr echoed the academic commentators when he remarked that our law 'has already suffered too much from the undesirable complexities of this overlegalistic procedural dichotomy' between public and private law.[33] The argument that because Parliament has chosen to allow regulation by contract, it has adopted a private law mechanism, and so precluded a supervisory jurisdiction seems to involve just such a legalistic approach. In contracting-out situations, the flaws of the exclusivity principle are apparent.[34] There are cases of *ultra vires* contracting-out by public authorities,[35] and cases where public authorities create legitimate expectations to certain

---

[24] See below, under 'Action for breach of statutory duty'.
[25] Harden, op. cit., p. 11.
[26] [1983] 2 A.C. 237, H.L.
[27] *R.* v. *Lord Chancellor, ex parte Hibbit and Saunders (a firm)*, *The Times*, 12 March 1993; [1993] Crown Office Digest 326; comment by D. Oliver [1993] P.L. 214.
[28] [1979] Q.B. 626, C.A.
[29] [1983] 2 A.C. 286.
[30] E.g. in *Davy* v. *Spelthorne B.C.* [1984] A.C. 262; *Wandsworth LBC* v. *Winder* [1985] A.C. 461; *Roy* v. *Kensington and Chelsea and Westminster FPC* [1992] 1 A.C. 624, at p. 628–9 per Lord Bridge; cf. in the context of homeless persons

legislation, *Ali* v. *Tower Hamlets LBC* [1992] 3 All E.R. 512 and *Tower Hamlets LBC* v. *Abdi*, (1992) 91 L.G.R. 300.
[31] *Roy* v. *Kensington and Chelsea and Westminster LBC*, above, at p. 628–9.
[32] [1992] 4 All E.R. 280.
[33] At p. 288.
[34] See e.g. *R.* v. *IBA, ex parte Rank organisation plc*, *The Times*, 14 March 1986; *R* v. *East Berkshire HA, ex parte Walsh* [1985], Q.B. 152; and generally J. Beatson (1987), 103 L.Q.R. 34, at pp. 53–9.
[35] E.g. *R.* v. *London Borough of Islington, ex parte Building Employers' Confederation* [1989] I.R.L.R. 382.

services,[36] where judicial review is obviously appropriate. It would be mistaken to exclude all cases involving contractual relationships from judicial review, where public law functions are being exercised. If a public body exercises either common law or statutory powers which affect the public interest or the rights or vital interests of individuals or organisations, then the exercise of those powers ought to be subject to judicial review.[37]

Equally, in civil proceedings, no sharp distinction should be drawn between the relevant public law issues and private law rights. However, in *Swain* v. *Law Society*[38] Lord Diplock, in one of the idiosyncratic restatements of the law which characterised his later years,[39] concluded that private law remedies (in this case for breach of trust and equitable account) were not available to make the Law Society accountable to solicitors for the money it received under commission-sharing arrangements, because in exercising its statutory power to make rules regarding solicitors' compulsory insurance, and in discharging its functions under those rules, the Law Society was acting in a public capacity and was governed solely by public law. He made the distinction even more difficult to comprehend by also expressing the view that although the legal consequences of exercising their powers might be to create rights enforceable by private law, 'these rights are not necessarily the same as those that would flow in private law from doing a similar act otherwise than in the exercise of statutory powers.'[40] The desire to protect public bodies from vexatious litigation and to expedite disputes about their powers, which motivated the public/private distinction in judicial review cases, should not also be used as a restriction on civil liability. It is the substance of the rights rather than the forms of action which should govern our law on market-testing and contracting-out.[41]

Action for Breach of Statutory Duty

In the 'difficult and developing' field of law[42] relating to the tortious liability of public authorities, the 'missing link', as Harlow has pointed out,[43] is the action for breach of statutory duty. This is true, as well, in relation to the statutory duties imposed on various public authorities, and sometimes on some private providers, in contracting-out situations.

Occasionally, a right to claim damages is expressly created by the statute. Here we may distinguish between those statutes which confer rights of action primarily for the benefit of competitive bidders to provide the services, and those which create rights of action for consumers of those services. An example in the first category is section 19(7) of the Local Government Act 1988. This gives a right of action to any person who suffers damage in consequence of a breach by the public authority of its duty, under section 17(1) of the Act, not to have regard to 'non-commercial matters'[44] when exercising its functions. The Act does not in terms limit the class of persons who may sue, but the indications are that this is a charter for bidders and not citizens. The Act specifies that the amount of damages which can be claimed by a party who has submitted a tender is limited to 'damages in respect of expenditure reasonably incurred by him for the purpose of submitting a tender.'[45] This limit applies only where a tender has been submitted and, apparently, not where the contract has been awarded on the basis of 'non-commercial' considerations after informal negotiations with two or more parties. In that situation, it is arguable that the damages should be assessed on a 'reliance' basis as in analogous common law claims.[46] Even if consumers do fall within the class protected by the statute, it is difficult to see how they could prove that but for the breach of duty they would have received the benefit in question.

An even more important example of express statutory torts in relation to public procurement is to be found in EC law. Under the EC Treaty, and a series of Directives, a wide range of contracts for works, supplies, services and utilities, have to be awarded by competitive procedures in such a manner as to afford equal opportunities to bidders from all Member States.[47] The Remedies Directive[48] places an express

---

[36] As suggested by Harden, op. cit., p. 45.
[37] D. Oliver [1993] P.L. at p. 215.
[38] [1983] 1 A.C. 598. (I am grateful to Tony Weir for drawing my attention to this case.)
[39] See the comments by Sir William Wade, *Administrative Law*, 6th ed., Oxford, 1988, p. viii.
[40] At p. 608.
[41] See generally, the review of the general issue by the Law Commission, Consultation Paper No. 126, *Administrative Law: Judicial Review and Statutory Appeals*, HMSO, 1993, paras. 3.1–3.26.
[42] Per Dillon, L. J. in *Lonrho plc.* v. *Tebbit* [1992] 4 All E.R. 280, C.A., at p. 286.
[43] C. Harlow, *Compensation and Government Torts*, London: Sweet & Maxwell, 1982, p. 68.

[44] These include the terms on which contractors employ their workers, the conduct of contractors in industrial disputes, the country of origin of supplies, political, industrial or sectarian affiliations: Local Government Act 1988, ss. 17 (5) (7) (8). One of the curiosities of this prohibition is that while the authority may stipulate for compliance with general health and safety laws, this may not include requirements on the contractor in relation to the terms of employment of its own workers: *R.* v. *London Borough of Islington, ex parte Building Employers' Confederation* [1989] I.R.L.R. 382.
[45] s. 19 (8); see Arrowsmith, op. cit., p. 100.
[46] *Anglia Television* v. *Reed* [1972] 1 Q.B. 60.
[47] For a summary see Arrowsmith, op. cit., pp. 103–7.
[48] Directive 89/665/EEC, and see too Directive 92/50/EEC.

obligation on Member States to provide certain remedies for breach of the procurement rules, and this includes damages for persons harmed by an infringement.[49] Here the potential claimants appear to be limited to aggrieved contractors who, given the inability of the EC Commission itself in practice to ensure compliance, are likely to be the main initiators of remedial action, with damages being assessed on a tortious basis. Although the Directive refers to 'persons harmed by an infringement' it is once again difficult to envisage a case in which a customer in Britain, deprived of cheaper Continental goods because of a breach of the EC rules, would be able to succeed in an action for damages under the Directive.

In the second category, express statutory torts creating remedies in damages for consumers, the best examples are to be found in the Acts privatising the utilities. Here the duties in tort are closely allied to administrative enforcement. For example, the Telecommunications Act 1984, most recently amended by the Competition and Service (Utilities) Act 1992, imposes general duties on the Secretary of State and the Director-General of Telecommunications to secure telecommunication services and to promote the interests of consumers, purchasers and other users. No one may run a telecommunication system without a licence which contains conditions and a duty to comply with the Director's directions. The Director is empowered to make an order for the purpose of securing compliance with a condition.[50] The order is deemed to create a duty towards 'any person who may be affected by a contravention of it,'[51] and is actionable at the suit or instance of that person if it causes him or her loss or damage.[52] Added to this is an express right of action—aimed at the organisers of industrial action—in respect of any act which by inducing a breach of the duty or interfering with its performance, causes loss or damage and which is done wholly or partly for the purpose of achieving that result.[53]

The Competition and Service (Utilities) Act 1992, confers a new power on the Director to make regulations setting standards of performance for relevant services provided by a designated operator. Failure by an operator to comply with the specified level of performance will result in liability to pay a predetermined amount of compensation 'to any person affected by the failure.'[54] The making of such compensation does not prejudice any other remedy available to the consumer.[55]

The notion of statutory duties to provide a prescribed standard of service, enforced by financial compensation paid to the consumer in most cases automatically either by way of credit to the customer's account or a refund, is not new. The model is the Electricity Act 1989, s.39, and regulations made thereunder.[56] Similar provisions have been introduced in respect of water and sewerage services (where the customer has to make a claim),[57] and gas supply.[58] The important change made by the 1992 Act is that instead of standards being set by the utility companies themselves, with voluntary compensation schemes, the standards are now set by an external agency with prescribed penalties, with requirements for publishing information about levels of performance and with mechanisms for determining disputes. The right to statutory compensation exists alongside the actions for damages for breach of statutory duty.[59] The actions for damages are subject to certain statutory defences. In the case of electricity supply, there is also the possibility for the public electricity supplier to require the consumer to accept in respect of the supply a reasonable restriction in liability for economic loss resulting from negligence.[60] No similar restriction is mentioned in respect of the action for breach of statutory duty.

In the absence of express statutory torts, it seems unlikely that the courts will imply an action for damages in relation to contracting-out. At first glance, this may seem surprising because for nearly 100 years the relationship between public authority and

[49] Mention may also be made of the right of the individual to sue the Member State itself for damages, if the Community obligation is not implemented, where the conditions set out in *Frankovich* v. *Italian Republic*, Cases C6/90 and C9/90 [1992], I.R.L.R. 84, are satisfied; see Szyszczak (1992) 55 MLR 690; Ross (1993) 56 MLR 55; Lewis and Moore [1993], P.L. 151.
[50] Telecommunications Act 1984, s. 16 (1); see s. 16 (2) (3) regarding provisional orders.
[51] S. 18 (5).
[52] S. 18 (6). The Director may also enforce the order by civil proceedings for an injunction or interdict: s. 18 (8). The Director may give assistance in relation to certain proceedings: s. 52.
[53] S. 18 (6) (b); see Gillian Morris, *Strikes in Essential Services*, London: Mansell, 1986, pp. 20–1; (1991) 20 I.L.J. 89.
[54] Telecommunications Act 1984, s. 27A, as inserted by Competition and Services (Utilities) Act 1992, s. 1.

[55] S. 27A (5). This still leaves the court with the problem whether the availability of statutory compensation indicates a parliamentary intention not to create civil liability: see generally, K. Stanton, *Breach of Statutory Duty in Tort*, London, Sweet & Maxwell, 1986, pp. 38–40.
[56] Electricity (Standards of Performance) Regulations 1991, S.I. 1991 No. 1344.
[57] Water Industry Act 1991, s. 38; Water Supply and Sewerage Services (Customer Service Standards) Regulations 1989, S.I. 1989 No. 1159.
[58] Gas Act 1986, s. 33A, inserted by Competition and Service (Utilities) Act 1992, s. 11.
[59] Electricity Act 1989, s. 27A (5); Gas Act 1986, s. 33A (5); cf. Water Industry Act 1991, 38 (2).
[60] Electricity Act 1989, s. 21 (b).

consumer has usually been classified as statutory rather than contractual.[61] The courts could follow the 'simply principle that the breach of a duty created by a statute, if it results in damage to an individual, is a tort for which an action for damages will lie at his suit.'[62] Arrowsmith suggests that it may be 'the fear of imposing widespread liability on utilities, particularly for economic losses, which has led the courts to the conclusion that there is no contract.'[63] She adds that for the same reasons the courts have circumscribed carefully any cause of action against utilities for negligence, and for breach of statutory duty. Wills J. gave the classic explanation when denying an action for damages for failure to supply gas:

'When large numbers of people are supplied with gas, the undertakers may be speedily ruined if any one could bring an action of this kind against them ... Where there is an obligation created by statute to do something for the benefit of the public generally, or of such a large body of persons that they can only be dealt with, practically, en masse, as it were, and whether the failure to comply with the statutory obligation is liable to affect all such persons in the like manner though not necessarily in the same degree, there is no separate right of action to every person injured, by breach of that obligation, in no other manner than the rest of the public.'[64]

Harding argues that this kind of reasoning would make the possibility of an action for damages for failure to perform a statutory duty virtually an academic one, but he demonstrates that it has not been applied consistently so as to deny a remedy in all cases.[65] The courts have also been inconsistent in the importance they have attached to the existence in the statute of an alternative remedy, whether criminal or administrative.[66]

Despite Lord Simonds' dictum in *Cutler* v.

Wandsworth Stadium Ltd.,[67] that 'if a statutory duty is prescribed but no remedy by way of penalty or otherwise for its breach is imposed, it can be assumed that a right of action accrues to the person who is damnified by the breach,' it seems unlikely that the courts will allow such actions to consumers of contracted-out services. In the past, even in cases where civil liberties have been infringed, for example through a breach of prison rules, the courts have been reluctant to countenance actions for breach of statutory duty.[68] There is no reason to suppose that the courts will adopt a different attitude in contracting-out situations, such as a breach by a contracted-out prisoner custody officer of the duty to 'attend to the well-being' of those in his custody'.[69] Moreover, there has been a disinclination to find a breach of the duty of care owed by prison authorities to prisoners: contracted-out custodians will not face any higher duty of care than public authorities have in the past.[70]

Negligence: The Immunity Principle

In market-testing and contracting-out situations, the issue will usually relate to the exercise of a discretion by the authority rather than to the performance of a statutory duty. For example, the duty of a local authority to satisfy itself that the activity could not be more economically carried out by the private sector arises only if the authority is considering performing the function in-house. The immunity principle protects public authorities from the tort of negligence in respect of 'policy' decisions, but not from liability for 'operational' negligence, or for acts or omissions which are outwith a discretion bona fide exercised.[71]

The justification for this principle is the unique

---

[61] *Clegg, Parkinson & Co.* v. *Earby Gas Co.* [1986] 1 Q.B. 592 (gas supply); *Read* v. *Croydon Corporation* [1938] 3 All E.R. 631 (water); *Willmore* v. *S.E. Electricity Board* [1957] 2 Lloyds Rep. 355 (electricity). The privatisation statutes still treat the supplier as being under a statutory duty: Gas Act 1986, s. 9; Electricity Act 1989, s. 16; Water Industry Act 1991, s. 37; cf. Telecommunications Act 1984, sched. 5, para. 12 which treats provision of telephone services as contractual, but the Conditions for Telephone Service (1991) paras. 21.3.2 and 21.4, expressly limit damages for economic losses. There is statutory duty, and not a contractual one, between patients and the NHS: *Pfizer Corporation* v. *Ministry of Health* [1965] A.C. 512.

[62] *Salmond and Heuston on the Law of Torts*, 20th ed. by R. F. V. Heuston and R. A. Buckley, London: Sweet & Maxwell, 1992, p. 251. For early cases taking this approach, see K. M. Stanton, *Breach of Statutory Duty in Tort*, London: Sweet & Maxwell, 1986, pp. 2–4, and for public law cases, P. P. Craig, *Administrative Law*, 2nd ed., London, 1989, p. 455.

[63] Sue Arrowsmith, op. cit., p. 50.

[64] *Clegg, Parkinson & Co.* v. *Earby Gas Co.* [1896] 1 Q.B. at pp. 594–5; see too Wright, J. at p. 595, who also doubted whether any action would lie for a nuisance.

[65] A. J. Harding, *Public Duties and Public Law*, Oxford: Clarendon Press, 1989, p. 237; R. A. Buckley (1984), 100 L.Q.R. 204 at pp. 210–13; and see the reasoning of Lord Diplock in *Lonrho Ltd.* v. *Shell Petroleum Co. Ltd.* [1982] A.C. 173 at pp. 185–8.

[66] Compare *Groves* v. *Lord Wimborne* [1898] 2 Q.B. 402, where there was held to be a private right of action because it was uncertain whether the 'inadequate' statutory penalty would be awarded to the plaintiff, with *Cutler* v. *Wandsworth Stadium Ltd.* [1949] A.C. 398, where the creation of a criminal offence was regarded as a reason for non-liability.

[67] [1949] A.C. 398 at p. 407.

[68] *R.* v. *Deputy Governor of Parkhurst Prison, ex parte Hague* [1992] 1 A.C. 58, following *Becker* v. *Home Office* [1972] 2 Q.B. 407.

[69] Criminal Justice Act 1991, ss. 82 (3) (d), 86 (3) (d). On the effects of privatisation of prisons see generally Rod Morgan, 'Prisons Accountability Revisited,' [1933] P.L. 314 at pp. 320–6.

[70] See Rod Morgan, loc. cit. (note 69).

[71] Feldthusen, op. cit., p. 293.

character of public authority liability in negligence. This, as Cohen and Smith say,[72] is that claims are made by individuals who allege 'that they are entitled to certain benefits from the state which they have not received, or that they have been injured as a result of not receiving those benefits.' These claims are to be distinguished from 'ordinary' negligence claims, for example arising from traffic and employment accidents, or cases of private nuisance, where an employee or agent of the public authority interferes with an established individual right. For example, where the driver of a police vehicle causes an injury while pursuing another vehicle at high speed, we are able assess the exercise of judgment by the public officer at the standard of care stage.[73] It is where discretionary decisions are taken about the provision of benefits to individuals that the immunity principle operates.

In order to determine the circumstances when such discretionary decisions in respect of contracting-out may give rise to liability, it is useful to classify the relationships in a functional way:

(a) 'Policy' functions as to the benefits to be provided, at what level, by whom and to what class of persons;

(b) 'Procurement' functions as to the conduct of the tendering process, the selection of providers, and the monitoring of results;

(c) 'Provision' or delivery/performance functions (carried out either by in-house teams or Agencies or by private licensees, undertakers or contractors);

(d) 'Consumption' by those for whom the benefits are intended.

The distinction between category (a), 'policy', and categories (b), 'procurement', and (c), 'provision', does not directly correspond to the 'policy/operational' dichotomy that featured in Lord Wilberforce's speech in *Anns*, and, which despite judicial doubts[74] and academic criticisms,[75] continues to influence arguments about the liability of public authorities.[76] Where services are provided in terms of a contract with a public authority, it is not only the 'policy' decisions (category (a)) but also many of the 'pro-

curement' decisions (category (b)) which have in them some element of discretion as to the selection of the contractor, the standards to be required and subsequent monitoring etc. If the courts take the immunity principle seriously in relation to contracting-out they will have to scrutinise closely the scope of the 'policy/operational' dichotomy.

Their starting point might be the one which Weir has made in relation to the building cases.[77] This is that the liability of the authority will normally be secondary. The primary tortfeasor will be the provider of the service who causes harm to the consumer; the public authority, if directly liable at all, must incur responsibility on the basis of a failure to avert harm to the consumer. Although the linkage of liability of the public authority and the negligent builders, in *Anns*[78] and in *Murphy*,[79] has been much-criticised,[80] the essential point in our context is that one would not normally expect a consumer to look to a public authority for damages for failure to avert harm where there is a suitably insured and solvent tortfeasor available. If a contracted-out prison mistreats a prisoner it is the tort of the contractor which would normally be the primary focus of legal concern. If the Home Office can be made vicariously liable for the wrongdoer—a point to be discussed later—all the better, but any common law duty of the Home Office to avert harm is secondary. That analogous actions have been attempted in relation to local authorities is, as Weir trenchantly observes,[81] the result of our law as to subrogation which means that in such cases 'the public must bail out private insurers.' It is a matter of obvious concern if private contractors who have successfully bid to be allowed to provide services to the public are being subsidised out of the public purse.

A second point is that the courts are unlikely to abandon the immunity principle altogether in defining the common law duty of care owed by public authorities in contracting-out situations. Although the Diceyian constitutional ideal of applying the ordinary private law to public authorities 'still provides the basis of a rational, workable and acceptable theory of governmental liability,'[82] the ordinary law is in a state of unprincipled disarray. The

[72] Cohen and Smith (1986), 64 Can. B.R. 1 at p. 16.

[73] E.g. *Marshall* v. *Osmond* [1983] Q.B. 1034; *Watt* v. *Hertfordshire County Council* [1954] 2 All E.R. 368.

[74] *Rowling* v. *Takaro Properties Ltd.* [1988] A.C. 473 at p. 501.

[75] S. H. Bailey and M. J. Bowman [1986], C.L.J. 430; P. Craig (1978), 94 L.Q.R. 428; C. Harlow, *Compensation and Government Torts*, London: Sweet & Maxwell, 1982, pp. 54–7; A. J. Harding, *Public Duties and Public Law*, Oxford: Clarendon Press, 1989, pp. 259–72; B. Feldthusen, *Economic Negligence*, Toronto: Carswell, 1989, pp. 293–310; R. A. Buckley, *Modern Law of Negligence*, London, 1991, pp. 217–22.

[76] See e.g. *Lonrho plc.* v. *Tebbit* [1992], 4 All E.R. 280, at p. 287.

[77] Tony Weir [1989], Public Law 40 at p. 45.

[78] [1978] A.C. 728.

[79] [1991] 1 A.C. 378.

[80] Peter Cane, *Tort Law and Economic Interests*, Oxford: Clarendon Press, 1992, p. 513; Markesinis and Deakin (1992), 55 M.L.R. at p. 622; cf. Weir, op. cit., at p. 45.

[81] Op. cit., at p. 43.

[82] Harlow, op. cit., p. 80, agreeing with Hogg, *The Liability of the Crown in Australia, New Zealand and the United Kingdom*, 1971, p. 2.

pragmatism or 'incremental approach' favoured by the House of Lords in the context of the duty of care,[83] stands in marked contrast to their recent development of the law of restitution. Negligence law may, hopefully, follow the lead given in *Woolwich Building Society* v. *IRC*.[84] it is for the courts to formulate general common law principles, and then to leave it to Parliament to limit or reverse those principles on grounds of policy or good administration. The 'unsystematic and not fully thought out series of shifts'[85] of the House of Lords in relation to economic loss, and their 'all-or-nothing' approach, stands in marked contrast to the way in which principles were formulated in the *Woolwich* case. Although many of the contracting-out cases may involve claims for economic loss, rigid distinctions between physical and economic loss are unhelpful.[86] Stapleton contends that the courts should adopt a 'policy' approach to economic loss, in which one of the pre-conditions for liability would be 'that the area is not one more appropriate for Parliamentary action.'[87] However, when one examines the current patchwork of statutes, 'framework documents', contracts and informal practices relating to market-testing and contracting-out the inadequacies of a purely 'policy' approach are apparent. A series of general principles, themselves informed by policy, needs to be developed.

On of these is the immunity principle, redefined in a way that is consistent with the rule of law principle. Public authorities owe the same duty of care as private individuals, and the immunity principle could be reformulated to state that they owe no duty of care in respect of those discretionary policy decisions which are unique to their special character as public authority. The extent of the duty is therefore the same as that owed by the private employer of an independent contractor, which is discussed below. There is no duty of positive action to avert harm or to confer a benefit unless a private individual would be liable. So where the public authority is making a discretionary choice as to whether a particular service should be undertaken in-house or contracted-out, and as to the standards to be required, the court should not substitute its 'policy' view (category (a) above) for that of the legislature.[88]

If the courts accept this limitation, the 'politics' of

contracting-out would properly remain largely outside the system of civil liability, but procurement and performance functions would not. Tort law is not a substitute for judicial review in controlling abuses of power; it provides a means of obtaining compensation from public authorities only where private individuals would be held liable. Negligence law is an inadequate vehicle for regulating the exercise of power by public authorities, and attempts to use it for this purpose can only result in the kind of distortions of negligence law which have occured in economic loss cases over the past fifteen years. If Parliament considers this common law principle to be inadequate it could legislate in various ways, for example by improving statutory compensation schemes and complaints mechanisms of the kind found in the privatisation statutes.[89]

Liability for independent contractors

The extent to which employers are liable for the acts of independent contractors is critical to the liability of public authorities for defective delivery of public goods and the performance of public services by their contractors. So far as the Crown is concerned, the aim of the Crown Proceedings Act 1947 was broadly speaking to make the Crown liable in respect of torts committed by its servants or 'agents' in the same way as any other person of full age and capacity. Section 38 (2) defines an 'agent' to include an independent contractor, and section 40 (2) (d) provides that nothing in the Act is to impose a greater liability on the Crown in respect of the torts of independent contractors than would attach at common law to any other employer of an independent contractor.

No question of vicarious liability will arise where the performance function is undertaken in-house. As already indicated, the Next Step Agencies, local authority DSOs and Health Service DMUs have no separate legal identity. The government department, local authority or health authority remains responsible. The problem arise where there is a contracting-out to a private contractor.

The general principle is that the employer of an independent contractor is responsible only if in breach of a personal non-delegable duty, a concept

---

[83] *Rowling* v. *Takaro Properties Ltd.* [1988] A.C. 473, at p. 501, followed in *Lonrho plc.* v. *Tebbit* [1992] 4 All E.R. 280 at p. 287.
[84] [1992] 3 All E.R. 737, esp. per Lord Slynn at p. 783 and Lord Goff pp. 757–8.
[85] Markesinis and Deakin, op. cit., at p. 620.
[86] See, for general critique B. S. Markesinis and Simon Deakin (1992), 55 M.L.R. 619; Sir Robin Cooke (1991), 107

L.Q.R. 47; I. N. Duncan Wallace (1991), 107 L.Q.R. 229; Jane Stapleton (1991), 107 L.Q.R. 249.
[87] (1991) 107 L.Q.R. at pp. 286, 295.
[88] Feldthusen, op. cit., p. 306.
[89] See D. Cohen and J. C. Smith (1986), 64 Can B.R. 1 for a more ambitious 'theory of entitlement' allowing individuals to claim benefits or damages in lieu thereof.

which has expanded in recent years.[90] One such case is where a statutory duty is imposed directly on the public authority. In the *Murphy* case,[91] the House of Lords did not find it necessary to decide whether or not the local authority was responsible for the negligence of consulting engineers who were independent contractors, because of its ruling against liability for economic loss. The trial judge, and the Court of Appeal, held that the local authority's duty to take reasonable care had not been discharged by acting on the independent contractor's advice. This was based on the provisions of section 64 of the Public Health Act 1936 which imposed a duty on the authority itself to pass or reject plans. Ralph Gibson LJ characterised this as a 'public law duty', and the 'private law duty' to take reasonable care could not be avoided by delegation[92] Nicholls L. J. said that 'the common law duty of care would be in danger of being emasculated and its purpose partly defeated, if the local authority's liability for the negligence of those advising it were to depend upon whether the authority had decided to go outside for advice rather than dealing with the matter in-house.'[93] It is to be noted that the specific statutory duty under section 64 of the 1936 Act has now been repealed by the Building Act 1984, which envisages certification by private persons or bodies 'approved' by the Secretary of State. In any event, the *Murphy* decision severely restricts the possibilities for superadding common law duties to statutory ones.[94] The question also arises whether the element of compulsion in CCT, under the Local Government Act 1988, has the consequence of discharging the local authority from any further duty in relation to the contracted-out service. In each case, it will depend upon the precise statutory duty in question whether or not the duty can be delegated.[95]

In cases where there is no statutory duty laid upon the public authority, general principles apply.[96] Usually, the employer is liable only for care in selection of a competent contractor,[97] unless the activity is classified as 'extra-hazardous', or constitutes a public or possibly even a private nuisance. There are a few dicta which suggest that there is liability for independent contractors where a person employs a contractor for the performance of a statutory power.[98] In *Darling* v. *Attorney-General*[99] contractors employed by the Ministry of Fuel and Power were authorised by the Minister under statutory powers to enter the plaintiff's field to drill boreholes. Owing to the negligence of the contractors in leaving a heap of timber lying on the field, a horse was injured. Morris J. held that the Minister had a duty to the occupier not to cause unnecessary damage and this duty was non-delegable. Although no adequate reasons were given for this conclusion, it could be explained on the basis of a principle that where an authority is authorised by statute to do certain work, an individual whose private law rights are infringed should be entitled to look to the authority, and not only the tortious contractor, for damages. Such a principle is, however, dubious because it would be inconsistent with the general considerations, discussed earlier, which militate against state liability.

McKendrick,[100] has suggested that the proper approach, in the context of atypical employments, is to abandon the 'fruitless search for a non-existent unifying principle' of vicarious liability and to concentrate instead on the particular statutory or common law context of the dispute. It does seem unlikely that the English courts could be persuaded one day to accept the broad principle of 'assumption of responsibility' suggested by Mason J. in the High Court of Australia.[101] This is said to arise where the person 'has undertaken the care, supervision or control of the person or property of another or is to placed in relation to that person or his property as to assume a particular responsibility for his or its safety, in circumstances where the person affected might reasonably expect that due care will be exercised.' The power of a public authority to exercise 'care, supervision and control' through its contractual arrangements with the provider might form the basis of an assumption of responsibility. This would be the tort of the public authority, a next cousin of *Hedley Byrne & Co. Ltd.* v. *Heller and Partners Ltd.*[102] But, despite the attempted resuscitation of the

---

[90] Ewan McKendrick (1990), 53 M.L.R. 770, for a discussion of the recent cases; and see *Alcock* v. *Wraith The Times*, 23 December 1991, for a statement of principles.

[91] [1991] 1 A.C. 378.

[92] [1991] 1 A.C. at pp. 412–13.

[93] At p. 436.

[94] [1991] 1 A.C. at p. 457 (Lord Mackay), p. 463 (Lord Keither), p. 479 (Lord Bridge), pp. 491–92 (Lord Oliver).

[95] Cf. the Criminal Justice Act 1991, s. 85, under which a contracted-out prison must have a 'controller' who is a Crown servant appointed by the Secretary of State, and for whom the Crown would apparently be responsible under s. 2 (1) of the Crown Proceedings Act 1947.

[96] See Atiyah, *Vicarious Liability in the Law of Tort*, London: Butterworths, 1967, pp. 327–49; McKendrick, op. cit.

[97] E.g. *Rivers* v. *Cutting* [1982] 1 W.L.R. 1146 (constable who engaged contractor to tow away a car not liable for contractor's negligence).

[98] *Hardaker* v. *Idle DC* [1986] 1 Q.B. 335; Atiyah, op. cit., pp. 358–9.

[99] [1950] 2 All E.R. 793.

[100] (1990) 53 M.L.R. 770 at p. 784.

[101] *Kondis* v. *State Transport Authority* (1984) 154 C.L.R. 672 at p. 687.

[102] [1964] A.C. 465.

'reliance principle' in *Murphy*,[103] it has too insecure a foothold in tort theory to become the basis for consumer rights against public authorities.

Third Party Rights

The English law doctrine of privity of contract, or, as some would prefer, the principle that consideration must move from the promisee,[104] prevents the consumer from acquiring rights under a contract in which the contractor promises the purchasing public authority that it will provide services to a particular person or class of persons. This may not only affect private law rights, but may also be used by a public authority as a reason for denying the existence of any 'legitimate expectations' of a kind which could give rise to judicial review.[105]

This problem does not arise in those common law jurisdictions where the doctrine of privity has been abolished or modified. Examples from United States case law show just how important third party rights can be in enforcing government contracts. For example, in one case, the owner of a car which was towed away by the defendant, pursuant to a contract with the City of New York for towing away abandoned cars, successfully sued the defendant as a third party beneficiary to that contract. Under the contract the defendant was required to hold the car for five days before destroying it. In breach of the contract, the defendant cannabilised the car after three days.[106] In another case, a sewer tunnel construction contract between the City of St Joseph and the contractor provided that the contractor would 'protect, repair and restore property and structures from damage.' The plaintiff (power) company's buildings were damaged in the course of construction of the sewer and it successfully sued the contractor for damages as a third party beneficiary under the contract.[107] These cases show how third parties can rely on a contract in contracting-out situations.[108]

In England, the question of third party beneficiaries is under consideration by the Law Commission.[109] Until such time as the law is altered, consumers of public services provided under contract will be limited to tort claims in which all the usual objections to principles such as that of transferred loss,[110] will be raised. For example, will the standard and ambit of the duty of care be determined by the contract between contractor and public authority, or be derived from published performance targets or non-statutory charters?

Perhaps it was the difficulties of creating new torts to benefit third parties, which led the Government to create a unique remedy for citizens against whom no tort has been committed but whose services are interrupted by unlawful industrial action. Section 22 of the Trade Union Reform and Employment Rights Act 1993, implements a Citizens' Charter promise,[111] so as to allow any individual who claims that the effect of unlawful industrial action[112] will be to prevent the supply of goods or services, or to reduce their quality, to seek an injunction (but not damages) against the trade union or other organisers.[113] This is not limited, as the Citizens' Charter had envisaged, to public services. The citizen, who may seek assistance from a Commissioner for Protection Against Unlawful Industrial Action, even if not eligible for legal aid, may obtain an injunction although no tort has been committed against herself. This solicitude for the victims of industrial action has not been extended to the victims of contractors who run bad or disruptive public services, even where they have a virtual monopoly. But could the new remedy without a right be the thin edge of a wedge for consumer power?

Summary and Questions

This paper has given a preliminary sketch of the problems which market-testing and contracting-out may pose for the law of tort. The conclusions may be summarised as follows.

---

[103] [1991] 1 A.C. 398, at p. 427 (Lord Keith), p. 441 (Lord Bridge); see too *D. & F. Estates Ltd.* v. *Church Commissioners* [1989] A.C. 177 at p. 215 (Lord Oliver).

[104] J. C. Smith, *The Law of Contract*, London: Sweet & Maxwell, 1989, p. 85.

[105] See Harden, op. cit., p. 45.

[106] *Turkel* v. *Fiore* 308 N.Y.S. 2d 432.

[107] *St Joseph Light & Power Co.* v. *Kew Valley Tunnelling Inc.* 589 S.W. 2d 260.

[108] Compare the New Zealand Contracts Privity Act 1982, s. 4 of which creates a presumption that where a promise contained in a contract confers, or purports to confer, a benefit on a designated third party, the promisor will be under an obligation, enforceable at the suit of that third party, to perform the contract. The presumption can be rebutted only if it can be shown, on the proper construction of the contract, that the promise was not intended to create, in respect of that benefit, an obligation enforceable by that party. Query whether the requirement of 'intention' to benefit, might lead to different results to those in the American cases cited.

[109] Law Commission, Consultation paper No. 122 (1993).

[110] As suggested by Goff L. J. (as he then was), and rejected by the House of Lords, in *Leigh and Sillavan Ltd.* v. *Aliakmon Shipping Co. Ltd.* [1986] A.C. 785; see B. S. Markesinis (1987), 103 L.Q.R. 354.

[111] Cm. 1599, p. 46.

[112] The action is unlawful where either (1) the statutory requirements for ballots have not been complied with, or (2) there is a tort which is not protected by the immunities in s. 219 of the Trade Union and Labour Relations (Consolidation) Act 1992. The latter could include inducing a breach of statutory duty.

[113] Trade Union Reform and Employment Rights Act 1993, s. 22, on which see Gillian Morris (1993), 22 I.L.J. 194.

(1) The rights of consumers of public services provided under contracts between public authorities and in-house providers or private contractors, involve a complex mixture or public regulation and private rights. The issues cannot be dealt with exclusively by either judicial review or by civil proceedings.

(2) The right to claim damages for breach of statutory duty has been expressly recognised by the legislature (a) for the benefit of competitive bidders who suffer loss as a result of discriminatory or non-commercial considerations, and (b) for the benefit of some consumers of services provided by privatised utilities. However, public regulation (e.g. by the Directors-General of utilities) and statutory compensation schemes, have been the preferred means of control. In the absence of express statutory torts, it is unlikely that the courts will develop private law rights to claim damages particularly in cases of nonfeasance or economic loss.

(3) The immunity principle protects public authorities from liability in negligence in respect of 'policy' decisions. This can be justified by the fact that public authorities have the unique characteristic of being able to decide the level and standard of the benefits individuals should receive and the most cost-effective way of delivering those benefits. In contracting-out situations, governmental liability will normally be secondary and is based on the failure to avert harm to the customer. The courts could develop common law principles, one of these being a modified immunity principle. This would exclude a duty of care in respect of those policy decisions which are unique to a public authority. The courts should not substitute their policy view for that of the legislature in these situations. If Parliament wishes to alter this principle, it could develop new public law rights and rights to statutory compensation.

(4) Public authorities are responsible for torts in the same way as private individuals where services are provided by in-house organisations. Where provision of services is contracted-out, three general principles of responsibility could be developed by the courts: (a) for the performance of statutory duties imposed on the public authority; (b) for the performance of statutory powers granted to the public authority; and (c) where the public authority has assumed care, supervision and control through contractual arrangements with the provider and the person affected might reasonably expect that due care will be exercised.

(5) In English law consumers cannot enforce rights as third party beneficiaries under contracts. Where the ambit and standard of the duty of care has to be decided this will be on the pragmatic, incremental, basis of negligence law, with all the problems this poses of inconsistent contractual and tortious duties.

These conclusions may stimulate a number of questions about the future development of the law of tort. One could simply leave the issues in contracting-out situations to be resolved on a case by case basis. Or one could begin now to develop general principles. An implicit theme of this paper is that the problems of market-testing and contracting out cannot be resolved in isolation from the condition of the law of tort as a whole, and that in this area, tort law and administrative law are intertwined in a way which makes the traditional classifications, and in particular the procedural rules, a barrier to the rational development of the law. If principles are to be developed, the following are among the questions which need to be addressed.

(1) Do we need a law of public torts? Harden,[114] suggests a 'public law contract' to remedy the defects of ordinary contract law, and the weaknesses of tort law in the context of contracting-out might suggest a regime of administrative liability. One of the gravest weaknesses of administrative law is the relative absence of effective remedies. A right to 'damages' for *unlawful* administrative action would, however, do little for consumer and citizens' rights because most of the complaints relate to harm done within the legitimate exercise of discretion. One might usefully examine the principle of compensation or 'liability without fault' developed in French administrative law, and accepted in EC law.[115] Without declaring the administrative action illegal, the loss caused may become a public charge. A clearer and more satisfactory principle could be developed that once public authorities have decided what benefits a class of individuals should receive, the members of that class have an entitlement to receive those benefits, or to compensation in lieu thereof.[116]

(2) Can statutory compensation schemes be improved? The privatisation statutes provide an example. They may be criticised for inadequacy,

---

[114] Op. cit., p. 75.
[115] See Harlow, op. cit., p. 102.

[116] See David Cohen and J. C. Smith (1986), 64 Can. B.R. 1.

even after recent improvements, but these compensation schemes have several advantages over tort law, including the reduction of transaction costs by operating a fixed tariff, the ability of the provider to capture the costs in the contract price because of levels of compensation which are known in advance, and the avoidance of crushing liability which would reduce or destroy the provision of the service.

(3) *What should be the role of tort law where there are statutory schemes of regulation?* Cane,[117] and Stapleton[118] have pointed out the inconsistency of the House of Lords when using the existence of statutory regulation as a reason for not imposing a common law duty of care, and in suggesting that consumer protection is a matter for Parliament not the courts.[119] Conagahan and Mansell,[120] argue that it is disingenuous for the courts to pretend that they are not themselves taking political decisions when they decide that the shoulders of a local authority are not broad enough to carry civil liability. They also remind us that the tort system may appear to be an attractive mechanism for allocating losses at a time when the dominant philosophy is against reliance on the state and wishes to facilitate individual resolution of disputes, but they argue that this is no reason for denying broader community goals or a concept of entitlement to benefits based on citizenship.

It may be suggested that the relationship between tort and regulation is more complex than this. Following Shavell,[121] one might postulate the following

criteria: (1) regulation is to be preferred when the harm is so diffuse that individual consumers have little incentive to sue and cannot effectively sue as a group; (2) if the contractors providing services are poorly resourced, a system of ex post facto tort damages will not effectively deter them from harmful conduct; (3) statutory regulation or taxes can more effectively improve the standard of services than individual tort actions because they do not rest on proving a causal link between the particular parties; (4) statutory regulation can impose uniform rules on similarly situated contractors without the need to consider the costs and benefits in individual cases; only if each situation has unique cost and benefit features and the individuals are best able to balance these factors, should tort (and contract) law have a role; and (5) the costs of operating a tort system for individual cases should be compared with those of regulatory schemes.

These considerations point to tort law as no more than a stopgap which may complement statutory regulation until such time as an adequate system of administrative regulation and statutory compensation has been established.[122] However, in reality, compensation schemes are rarely adequate,[123] particularly where economic loss has been suffered, and we can therefore expect consumers of contracted-out public services to try to stretch the frontiers of tort liability.

---

[117] Peter Cane, *Tort Law and Economic Interests*, Oxford: OUP, 1991, p. 515.

[118] Jane Stapleton (1991), 107 L.Q.R. 249 at pp. 253, 268–9.

[119] E.g. in *Murphy* v. *Brentwood District Council* [1991] 1 A.C. 378, at p. 457 (Lord Mackay), p. 463 (Lord Keith), p. 479 (Lord Bridge) p. 491 (Lord Oliver).

[120] Joanne Conaghan and Wade Mansell, *The Wrongs of Tort*, London: Pluto Press, 1993, pp. 35, 95.

[121] S. Shavell, *Economic Analysis of Accident Law*, Cambridge, Mass.: Harvard UP, 1987, pp. 277–90.

[122] Susan Rose-Ackerman, 'Tort Law in the Regulatory State', in *Tort Law and the Public Interest*, (Peter H. Schuck, ed.). New York: Norton & Co., 1991, p. 87.

[123] C. Harlow and R. Rawlings, *Law and Administration*, London, Weidenfeld & Nicolson, 1984, at p. 371

7. In Restraint of Tort[1]

JANE STAPLETON

ONE approach to the task implied by the daunting title of this seminar is to try to prophesy in which areas tort liability will contract or atrophy and in which areas it may develop substantially. Another strategy, and the one which commends itself to me, is to examine some of the analytical processes by which liability issues are now handled with a view to suggesting how they may be improved so that real concerns already imbedded in the law may be made manifest and outcomes may be made less anomalous than at present. An attempt is also made to tease out some of these concerns although a full exposition of them must be left to another time.

1. Problems With the Position We Are Now In

The collapse twenty years ago of confidence in tort law had little to do with the state of formal doctrine. Rather it concerned the large gap between the apparent promise of tort law and its reality. The promise that a wide range of causes of action is available to all suitably aggrieved citizens was seen to be betrayed by the operation of non-legal barriers to claiming[2] which prevented all but a very few claims by those technically entitled to sue. These claims were almost wholly confined to one tort—that of negligence—and to the two types of defendants who happened to be subject to compulsory insurance (employers and motorists). The presence of insurance behind virtually all defendants was seen as undermining the deterrence claims of the new economic theorists and the corrective justice claims of moral defenders of tort, while resolution of the suits of plaintiffs was often found to hinge in practice so much on the vagaries of evidence that they became a 'forensic lottery'.[3]

These structural challenges to the respectability of tort still exist but excite less interest nowadays, no doubt partly due to the recessionary times which force expensive reform programmes of comprehensive compensation for, say, personal injuries a long way down the political agenda. It is on other features of tort law that the current wave of anxiety is focused, namely the reach of liability and the coherence of liability rules specifically in the tort of negligence.

It may seem ironic that, having learnt how irrelevant tort law is to most people, lawyers have become even more troubled by its appearance of intellectual incoherence and anomaly. But even if tort law remains in practice erratic in outcome and the preserve only of the very rich or very poor plaintiff, it may still be important in its symbolic role as vindicating certain values for society. And in *that* role the success of tort law will still depend on its appearance of being fair, sensible and focused. In other words, even those of us who think that any 'compensation for disability' goal should be pursued by no-fault social security mechanisms and who do not see tort as having much more than an important symbolic role in society as the law's most patent experiment in 'applied morality',[4] should share the current concern with the application and direction of some areas of tort doctrine. In particular, it is a useful corrective for those tempted by the idea of 'money for everyone, regardless of everything'[5] to investigate the reasons why tort should *refuse* a remedy to a plaintiff who has been injured by the defendant.

(a) The working out of established doctrine

A minor thread of current concern with the condition of tort is an uneasiness about the working through of tortious principles (usually negligence) into areas which previously had not produced claims. It is one thing to claim that a manufacturer must take care not to have snails in its ginger beer but it may seem quite another to claim that those involved in making goods and buildings should involve themselves in expensive post-supply surveillance of their safety.[6] Such claims are now being made and with some success but they are not the only examples of the pressures the negligence idea is putting on the perceived ambit of tort law. We are

---

[1] I would like to thank Peter Cane, the participants in the SPTL seminar and members of the Sydney University Law Faculty for comments on the text of this paper.

[2] Of which some, including the availability of legal aid, have now become even more of a problem.

[3] T. Ison, *The Forensic Lottery* (Staples Press, London, 1967). See also P. S. Atiyah, *Accidents, Compensation and the Law*, 1st ed. (London, Weidenfeld & Nicolson, 1970); The Report of the Royal Commission on Civil Liability and Com-

pensation for Personal Injury (Cmnd 7054, 1978).

[4] S. Stoljar, 'Concerning Strict Liability' in *Essays on Torts*, ed. P. Finn (Sydney, Law Book Co., 1989), 267.

[5] T. Weir [1992] C.L.J. 375, 376.

[6] e.g. *Walton* v. *British Leyland*, The Times, 13.7.78; *Eckersley & Others* v. *Binney & Partners* (the Abbeystead pumping station disaster), leave to appeal refusal of House of Lords 9.6.88, see *Independent*, 10.6.88.

now seeing whole new types of claim which were simply not considered by practitioners twenty or thirty years ago. For example, some victims of crime are now suing their assailants in tort.[7] More unusually, a local education authority was recently sued in negligence by children who had been sexually assaulted by a headmaster in one of its schools;[8] earlier this year newspapers reported that people who believed their health was damaged in childhood by passive smoking have begun to take legal advice about suing their parents;[9] and just recently a man won legal aid to sue for 'personal injury and loss' a council he claims negligently failed to have him adopted when a child.[10]

Violence and accidents within families and homes are noticeably now giving rise to tort claims. In recent years appellate courts have been faced with claims by, for example, a woman who alleged she had suffered mental illness as a result of childhood sexual abuse by her adoptive father and rape by her adoptive brother;[11] and a claim by a person against her foster mother and local authority for alleged negligence in leaving her as a two-year old (1966) near a source of scalding hot water while the mother fetched a towel.[12]

Particularly noteworthy is the rise in the past twenty years in claims alleging negligent failure by one party to control another. Usually it is alleged that a third party should have been controlled: local authorities allegedly failing to control builders;[13] occupiers failing to control hooligans and vandals;[14] police failing to control criminals.[15] But in one extraordinary case the plaintiff was the party who, it was alleged, ought to have been controlled. It must be quite a sight to the ordinary citizen to see a man securing a £45,000 out-of-court settlement from the Trafford Health Authority on the basis that one of the causes of his killing his mother was the Health Authority's negligent discharge of him from hospital.[16]

The incidence of extraordinary applications of the negligence principle seem to be increasing. They not only surprise some observers but they must bewilder those to whom the protection of tort law is refused, especially when the refusal is based on grounds which are patently unconvincing. The parent who comes across her child's bloodied corpse just a little too late for the current rules on recovery for nervous shock to apply to her might wonder why the law rules her child's blood too dry to found an action while allowing the matricide to sue.

The dilemma these cases throw up is that there is a lot of conduct in modern life which can be implicated in the occasioning of injury and much of this can plausibly be described as negligent.[17] The penetration into non-traditional areas of claims for recovery in tort was an inevitable consequence of the formulation of negligence liability in terms of fairly general principle, at least so long as restraining principles were regarded as peripheral subsidiary considerations. The challenge this phenomenon clearly now presents is that we may not be willing to accept a tort system which seeks to provide compensation (and deterrence) in this vast array of situations.[18] If not, we need to eschew that old confusing cliché that tort law is about compensation and loss—spreading, and to focus in a detailed way on those concerns which provide reasons for denying recovery to those who have admittedly been injured by the negligent conduct of the defendant. Only in that way will we be able to restrict the overall ambit of tort law to broadly familiar bounds without resort to artificial devices which appear so manifestly unjust to the non-lawyer.

The nature of the concern with these cases is in striking contrast to the nature of the dominant con-

---

[7] See e.g., the claims by Meah's victims which formed the background to *Meah* v. *McCreamer No. 2* [1986] 1 All E.R. 943. Not surprisingly the phenomenon is even more widespread in the US where, e.g., at least 200 lawsuits have been filed by HIV-positive people against the person, who it is claimed, infected them: *Independent*, 18.2.93. See also the *Halford* v. *Brookes* litigation (*The Times*, 22.7.91) in which the mother of Lynn Siddons sued her alleged murderer for damages after the relevant authorities declined to prosecute.

[8] P. v. *Harrow London Borough Council*, *The Times*, 22.4.92 (the claim failed). The Catholic Church in the UK is currently facing similar claims with respect to sexual abuse by its priests: the *Guardian*, 24.5.93.

[9] *Independent on Sunday*, 31.1.93.

[10] *Independent on Sunday*, 9.5.93.

[11] *Stubbings* v. *Webb* [1993] 2 W.L.R. 120 (H.L.) (held statute barred).

[12] *The Independent*, 27.3.91, p. 26 (the claim failed). In 1990 a girl was awarded £35,000 damages (for burns) against a friend's mother who had given the 9 year olds candles to play with in a 4 foot square tree house: *The Independent*, 3.10.90.

Injured wife recovered £0.5m from (the household insurer of) husband for his failure to repair window: *The Times* 26/4/94.

[13] *Anns* v. *Merton London borough Council* [1978] A.C. 728.

[14] *Cunningham* v. *Reading Football Club Ltd.* (Q.B.D.) *Independent*, 20.3.91.

[15] *Hill* v. *C.C. of South Yorks.* [1990] 1 All E.R. 1046.

[16] *The Independent*, 18.6.91. Compare *Meah* v. *McCreamer* [1985] 1 All E.R. 367 and *Meah* v. *McCreamer No. 2* [1986] 1 All E.R. 943.

[17] Moreover, there is arguably also a modern tendency to debase the standard against which conduct is judged: without the benefit of hindsight would the police behaviour at Hillsborough look so self-evidently negligent? To what degree was admission of liability the less damaging alternative to police public image given that the particular circumstances of death in that case were so public and distressing?

[18] Which even Schwartz, who seems to support this view, concedes is 'a very large responsibility': G. Schwartz, 'The Beginning and the Possible End of the Rise of Modern American Tort Law' (1992) 26 Georgia L.R. 601, 608.

cern of lawyers in the area of tort. On the one hand these unusual claims and the anomalies they may present can be seen as the worrying result of the development and application of broad principles of negligence—for example, liability for failure to control another party. Yet for lawyers the principal current concern with the condition of tort law, again centering on the law of negligence, relates to the retreat by appellate courts from broad principle to timid pragmatism. *McGhee* is overtaken by *Wilsher*, *McLoughlin* by *Alcock*, *Hedley Byrne* by *Caparo*, and most famously *Anns* by *Murphy*.[19] Dealing with this complaint requires, however, the same agenda for future action as does the concern with the potentially vast new liabilities generated by broad principles: an explicit focus on those policy concerns which militate against the protection by tort of everyone who has been injured by the carelessness of the defendant.

(b) The retreat to incrementalism

The debate concerning the retreat to incrementalism has been focused on the duty of care in negligence. This is not the place to rehearse the origin of this retreat but it is fairly clear that it was motivated principally by concern that recovery in negligence for economic loss was threatening to get out of hand. In the decade since *Junior Books*[20] appellate judges have succeeded in substantially tightening up liability in this area. Had this strategy been accompanied by careful and open explanation, no doubt much later criticism would have been avoided. But the intellectual tactics used were unconvincing. In attacking the earlier broad approach to the duty question as enunciated in *Dorset Yacht*[21] and *Anns*,[22] the House of Lords focused on the open-ended and vague terms in which it was couched. The complaint seemed to be that if the analysis of duty was generalised in this way into some sort of simple principle or 'test' it was doomed to generate far too much liability in the hands of lower courts who needed more restraining guidelines. Better to eschew this 'modern' approach and return to an incremental approach.

The first difficulty which emerged with the new

incremental approach was that the terms in which it was itself originally couched proved to be virtually empty concepts which gave litigants and lower courts no better guidance than the rejected approach as to the direction, if any, in which the law could legitimately develop. Not surprisingly most lower courts began to 'play safe', refusing the economically damaged plaintiff's claim for the protection of a tort obligation in novel circumstances but only being able to justify this result in obscure and virtually meaningless terms. It took most of the late 1980s and early 1990s before terms such as 'special relationship', 'just and reasonable', 'voluntary assumption of responsibility', 'reasonable reliance' and 'proximity' were finally revealed as little more than labels in which a court wrapped up the conclusion it had already reached on other (often unenunciated) grounds.

Next, the House of Lords' attempt[23] to state in more detail analytical steps for the new incremental approach in a way which would prevent the generation of too much new liability by any single new case, revealed further problems. The lower court faced with a novel claim for the protection of a tort obligation was, in effect, told first to blinker its eyes so that it only considered the relevant 'pocket' of caselaw dealing with the relevant features of the case at hand. Sometimes this would be a pocket of liability, sometimes a pocket of no liability. Yet for this to produce stability and coherent outcomes two fairly obvious conditions must be satisfied. First, it must be clear what it is about the new case which characterises it and which indicates the relevant earlier caselaw 'pocket' within which it needs to be judged. But how are we to know this? Why is it that what is important about the facts of *Smith* v. *Bush* is the form of the defendant's carelessness (negligent professional advice) so that it can be associated with earlier caselaw allowing a duty of care (*Hedley Byrne*)?[24] Why was not the relevant fact that the plaintiff suffered the economic loss through the acquisition of defective property so that the case would be placed in the *D & F Estates/Murphy* 'pocket' of caselaw with the result that a duty of care would be denied?[25]

---

[19] *McGhee* v. *National Coal Board* [1972] 3 All E.R. 1008; *Wilsher* v. *Essex Area Health Authority* [1986] 3 All E.R. 801; *McLoughlin* v. *O'Brien* [1982] 2 All E.R. 298; *Alcock* v. *Chief Constable of the South Yorkshire Police* [1991] 4 All E.R. 907; *Hedley Byrne & Co. Ltd.* v. *Heller & Partners Ltd.* [1964] A.C. 465; *Caparo Industries plc.* v. *Dickman* [1989] 1 All E.R. 798; *Anns* v. *Merton London Borough Council* [1978] A.C. 728; *Murphy* v. *Brentwood District Council* [1990] 2 All E.R. 908.

[20] *Junior Books Ltd.* v. *Veitchi Co. Ltd.* [1983] 1 A.C. 520.

[21] *Dorset Yacht Co. Ltd.* v. *Home Office* [1969] 2 Q.B. 412.

[22] *Anns* v. *Merton London Borough Council* [1978] A.C. 728.

[23] In *Caparo Industries plc.* v. *Dickman* [1989] 1 All E.R. 798.

[24] *Smith* v. *Bush [1989] 2 W.L.R. 790*; Hedley Byrne & Co. Ltd. v. *Heller & Partners* [1964] A.C. 465.

[25] *D. & F. Estates Ltd.* v. *Church Commissioners for England* [1988] 2 All E.R. 992; *Murphy* v. *Brentwood District Council* [1990] 2 All E.R. 908. In general, see J. Stapleton, *'Duty of Care and Economic Loss: A Wider Agenda'* (1991) 107 L.Q.R. 249 in particular the uncertainties as to whether cases such as *Junior Books* fall into the same pocket as the *Hedley Byrne* 'reliance' case (see p. 283). The facts of *Lancashire and Cheshire Assoc. of Baptist Churches Inc.* v. *Howard & Seddon Partnership* [1993] 3 All E.R. 467 (Q.B.D.) also seem to straddle the two pockets described in the text.

The second and associated condition which needs to be satisfied if the incremental approach is to produce stability and coherence using a pocket of caselaw as its starting point is that the boundaries of existing pockets, must make sense. One reason why the current state of the law relating to economic loss is so unsatisfactory and unstable is that at present cases are not grouped into pockets in a way which makes sense. The pockets overlap. As we have just seen, a particular fact situation could plausibly fit into both of two pockets enunciated by the courts, even though one is associated with recognition of a duty of care and the other with its denial. To some extent this has been because, in defining pockets, courts have often been beguiled by the superficial similarity of facts rather than being concerned to focus on what, if any, policy concern cases had in common. Even if the approach of starting within a pocket of caselaw was otherwise workable, then, these boundaries would have to be rethought and yet this would require the very sort of broad consideration of principles from which the incrementalists are trying to distance the analysis.

In any case, the fundamental flaw in the 'prejudged pockets' approach which makes it unsatisfactory is that any case may have more than one factor which is juridically significant. The case may involve a local authority defendant, a problematic kind of loss, conduct consisting of an omission, an under-age plaintiff and so on. By focusing without explanation on only one of them—so that, for example, the case is designated *at the outset* as one 'about negligent misstatements'—courts de-emphasize and run the risk of ignoring other factors to which in other contexts they do give considerable attention. Analytical method needs to be richer than this. It needs to consider each factor in turn—some factors weighing in favour of liability, and some countervailing factors tilting the balance the other way. This needs to happen without any pre-judging of what the eventual point of balance might be by the characterization of the case, *at the outset*, as belonging to a particular set of past cases. Of course, across many fact situations this balancing process will *produce* 'pockets' of like outcomes— for example there would be a pocket of liability for much physical damage caused by the direct act of a negligent defendant and a pocket of no-liability for the negligent omission to rescue a stranger—so principles would emerge on which practitioners could often confidently advise clients. But hard cases will always arise which do not fit smoothly into settled areas of principle.

Indeed these are the ones most likely to be litigated. The flaw in the *Caparo* approach is that it suggests a court will be able to determine *at the outset of its analysis* in these hard cases which of the existing clusters of cases the hard case in hand is best associated with.

(c) What might be done

What any court needs to consider in the duty analysis are all the reasons for helping the plaintiff and all those against doing so: a difficult and complex balancing of the arguments 'for' and 'against'. On its face the Wilberforce test in *Anns* was simply one attempt to reflect this truism. There were, however, problems with that particular statement of the balancing process. For a start, the first limb skirts over the major problem for any general statement of a negligence principle, namely that there are large areas in which careless conduct causing injury to innocent parties is not actionable.[26] Even if there *is* one strong general principle to be found at this stage—and I doubt it—its application across different types of plaintiff, of loss, of defendant and of form of casual connection[27] is extremely variable and complex. Judicial manipulation of the 'foreseeability' concept did not convincingly provide an understanding of this complexity, while the 'proximity' notion scarcely hinted at it. As more unconventional, 'not obvious'[28] plaintiffs bring their unusual claims to court the inadequate fleshing out of this first limb, of the 'why should the law help this plaintiff' arguments, begins to prove more problematic. This half of the equation needs attention and may prove just as useful in controlling the widening and dilution of tort principles as the more obvious role of arguments directly against liability in the case.

Here, in this paper, however, I want to concentrate on the latter arguments. It seems widely believed that under the modern Wilberforce test of duty of care insufficient weight was given to those concerns which militate against extending the protection of tort to the plaintiff and that now in order to restore coherent and symbolically convincing boundaries to tort the balance needs to be reset by a firmer emphasis on these countervailing factors. To do this courts should abandon the strategy of searching at the outset for the 'relevant' pocket of caselaw and replace it with one focused, inter alia, on these factors. Courts should identify reasons why negligently caused loss should not be compensated (the 'countervailing agenda'), identify in any particular case, which of those reasons apply and which do not, and decide,

---

[26] Consider the negligent/intentional infliction of economic loss by successful parties on their competitors in a free market.
[27] Including failure to control a third party or providing an opportunity for a negligent third party.
[28] As Lord Goff described them at this Seminar.

on balance with the pro-liability argument(s), whether the weight of countervailing concerns should lead to a denial of liability.

Sometimes the plaintiff's claim might cause concern on a number of fronts, sometimes just one, sometimes it would be found to clear all the existing countervailing objections to the protection of tort. If the threshold search for a relevant pocket of caselaw was replaced by this analysis it would release lower courts from the problem of identifying with which earlier cases to associate the current complex case. As the court considered each in turn the earlier caselaw relevant to *that* particular objection to the recognition of the duty of care would be come relevant. Moreover the conservatism of the current House of Lords can be accommodated: the degree to which the court needs to be satisfied that the plaintiff's case did overcome these concerns might be set very high. Indeed, this approach might be a more successful vehicle for the conservatism of the House of Lords, because although it might involve more detailed analysis in some cases it would produce results which openly tallied with rational policy concerns and were therefore more convincing than the somewhat mysterious threshold selection of 'relevant caselaw' based on a received but not explained wisdom.

Clearly the first step on an approach which seeks to re-emphasize the law's countervailing concerns about the imposition of tort liability must be a stronger identification of what these factors are. Ironically, incrementalism has recently worked to hinder just such a development. One result has been that appellate courts have delivered some confusing and awkward dicta on what the concerns of tort law should be. Thus in the two very similar cases mentioned above (*Smith* v. *Bush* and *D & F Estates*) the House of Lords not only reached opposite results but called upon the concept of 'consumer protection' to support respectively the recognition of a duty of care and its denial.[29] Another result is that courts have failed to draw out of earlier cases and develop a policy of not assisting with the protection of a tort obligation those plaintiffs who had an appropriate avenue of alternative protection (on which see below) has made tort law appear (apparently, at least) more protective of business interests than arguably it should be, especially given that the severe and increasing problem of access to justice faced by private plaintiffs has become more widely appreciated. A third inadequacy of the current incre-

mental approach is that it has failed to provide a doctrinal basis for understanding cases such as *Ross* v. *Caunters*[30] where recovery was, until recently at least, widely agreed as justified but the facts of which fell into no recognised pocket of cases let alone one which sanctioned recovery for economic loss.

Finally the current incremental approach provides no satisfying answer to the question of the relationship of one cause of action to another. It is obvious that, once the law has taken a wrong turning or otherwise fallen into an unsatisfactory internal state in relation to a particular cause of action, incrementalism cannot provide the answer: it will not, for example, be able to rectify the ludicrous position the rules governing recovery for nervous shock have now reached (see below). But it also does not begin to answer the more common problems which arise where, for example, the behaviour of a particular defendant may support allegations of more than one tort. In such cases the claim of the plaintiff may call for the resolution of the question of how the torts interact—specifically the question of whether the fact that the defendant can claim a defence to one tort should influence that defendant's exposure to liability under the other. This problem, recently exposed in two cases before the Court of Appeal (see below), can only be satisfactorily resolved on the basis of broad principles, and, like the problem of the duty of care in negligence, what is needed here are not crude aphorisms: defamation trumps negligence; natural rights trump nuisance; negligent professional advice trumps acquisition of defective property.[31] What is needed and what is still compatible with the general conservative approach preferred by the House of Lords is sharp identification of those underlying concerns/policies/principles on which the law's caution in recognising the plaintiff's cause of action under each tort is based. This could provide lower courts with substantive arguments (as well as conservative arguments if desired) for analyzing new cases and could provide disappointed plaintiffs with explanations for their fate which are more convincing than the simple assertion that it was not just and reasonable to help them.

2. Some Misconceived Countervailing Concerns

Most physical loss cases in the tort of negligence raise sufficiently few concerns that a duty of care is

[29] *Smith* v. *Bush* [1989] 2 W.L.R. 790; *D. & F. Estates Ltd.* v. *Church Commissioners for England* [1988] 2 All E.R. 992, 1007 (per Lord Bridge).
[30] *Ross* v. *Caunters* [1980] Ch. 297. But see *White* v. *Jones* [1993] 3 All E.R. 481 (C.A.), HL appeal heard 7.3.94—14.3.94..

[31] See respectively, *Spring* v. *Guardian Assurance plc.* [1993] 2 All E.R. 273 (C.A.), HL appeal heard 29.11.93—30.11.93, *Cambridge Water Co.* v. *Eastern Counties Leather plc.* (C.A.), [1994] 1 All E.R. 53 but see 63 (reversal by HL); *Smith* v. *Bush* [1989] 2 W.L.R. 790.

either 'self-evident'[32] or militated against only by a couple of concerns. At its simplest such cases merely require a balance to be struck between the two countervailing freedoms, one person's freedom of action and another's freedom from injury, although this can involve profound questions about legitimate expectations and the trade-off between autonomy and prevention.[33] Even so, in some cases special concern can arise with regard to issues as diverse as the impact of liability on industrial relations or on social benevolence.[34]

The area in which replacement of 'pockets' with an emphasis on countervailing concerns against liability would have most impact is the field of economic loss.[35] Although it was anxiety about such claims which produced the current retreat to incrementalism in general and tightening of economic loss recovery in particular there are three misunderstandings underlying that anxiety which will need to be resolved before a coherent agenda of countervailing factors can be defined for that and other areas of law.

Originally the problem with allowing liability for economic loss had been thought to be the unfairness on defendants of indeterminate liability the so-called 'opening of the floodgates' problem. So it seemed odd that the context in which the House of Lords' hostility to recovery in tort for economic loss first arose was not those cases in which the ripple effect of negligent conduct raised the floodgates problem most acutely (for example, bad investment advice) but in the area of claims for economic loss where it was patently absent: claims by owners for the economic loss suffered in acquiring property of defective quality. Factors other than floodgates were clearly fuelling judicial disquiet. Three different concerns can be identified.

(a) Socio-economic impact of the common law; separation of powers

A system which allows law to be made or 'developed' by common law judges and by a supreme legislature has at its heart a dilemma which the separation of powers doctrine is inadequate to resolve. On the one hand, looking back in time it is those judgments which cut through the minutiae of legal precedents to draw from them and establish a bold new principle which are regarded as the finest pillars of the common law and which back its claim to be a vital and responsive source of law. Often such cases can be seen with hindsight to have produced, sometimes gradually (*Donoghue* v. *Stevenson*) sometimes rapidly (*Hedley Byrne*), a large rearrangement of socio-economic relationships. In confident times this is seen as an acceptable even desirable consequence of the flexibility and power of the common law. *Donoghue* v. *Stevenson* is a notable example from tort law,[36] but one of the best illustrations comes from contract: the paternalistic implication of warranties into commercial dealings in goods in the 19th century which, although having substantial impact on those sellers who had hitherto relied on the caveat emptor principle is now regarded as the 'very heart' of the modern law of sale.[37]

Periodically, however, it is to be expected that the judiciary will be daunted by the power at its disposal to disrupt expectations and generate powerful new economic forces.[38] Nor is it unexpected that even when there is a wave of restraint affecting a much broader field, it will be felt most strongly in the relatively unstructured field of tort law, especially negligence law. The most powerful catalyst of the recent swing back to fettering the discretion of judges to develop the law of tort was the controversial and almost immediately apparent impact on local government finances of the decision in *Anns*. Of course there is a real problem for the law when a deep pocket defendant (such as a local authority) is held jointly and severally liable with a class of defendants (for example builders) who often turn out to be judgment-proof. De facto a disproportionate burden of the liability will fall on the former, a particularly problematic result if it has public duties to perform. But it is not a convincing argument simply to deride

---

[32] See e.g., the comment of Lord Brandon in *Mobil Oil Hong Kong Ltd. and Dow Chemical (Hong Kong) Ltd.* v. *Hong Kong United Dockyards Ltd.*, The 'Hua Lien' [1991] 1 Lloyds L.R. 309, 329 (P.C.).

[33] For example, by staying awake and keeping a lookout a car passenger may have been able to help avoid the accident which injures her but respect for her autonomy is here held to outweigh the concern with deterrence so she is not held contributorily negligent. Contrast the question of what obligation if any a pregnant woman owes her unborn child, see *Re S* [1992] 3 W.L.R. 806, casenote at [1993] C.L.J. 21.

[34] See respectively *Morris* v. *Ford Motor Co. Ltd.* [1973] Q.B. 792 and the rescue cases.

[35] J. Stapleton, op. cit.

[36] A decision praised by Mr Justice Evatt in a letter to Lord

Atkin on the grounds that 'the common law is again shown to be capable of striking through the forms of legal separateness to reality': G. Lewis, *Lord Atkin* (London, Butterworths, 1983) 67.

[37] P. Atiyah, *The Sale of Goods*, 8th ed. (London, Pitman, 1990) 142.

[38] There is, for example, recent evidence of a widespread judicial concern on this point in the US leading to a significant retrenchment of tort liability: J. Henderson and T. Eisenberg, 'The Quiet Revolution in Products Liability: An Empirical Study of Legal Change' (1990) 37 U.C.L.A. 479. Note also the dramatic shift in emphasis of Lord Bridge who as recently as 1982 had been opposed to an 'unwarranted abdication of the courts function of developing and adapting principles of the common law to changing conditions': *McLoughlin* v. *O'Brien* [1982] 2 All E.R. 298, 319.

Anns as the sort of 'judicial legislation'[39] which offends the separation of powers doctrine, as this could be said of those other admired landmarks in the law which had comparable effects. There may be special problems with the *Anns* decision but the fact that it produced a significant socio-economic impact does not distinguish it from other settled cases.

Nor was it convincing to attack *Anns* on the basis that before that case Parliament had in some way attempted to 'cover the field' by enacting the Defective Premises Act 1972. Ironically the history of that piece of legislation shows rather that it was the culmination of Parliamentary frustration at the timidity of judges unwilling to *extend* the broad principle of *Donoghue* v. *Stevenson* to builder/vendors.[40] If anything, that Act shows how important Parliament is as a corrective when the complex activities of the common law go badly wrong. If matters in the economic loss field continue to lurch along in the way they have done, perhaps the future will again see Parliament intervening to correct the anomalies the current blinkered incremental approach is producing.

But the concern with socio-economic impact and the separation of powers is not a specious one. Even if the role of tort law is principally a symbolic one, it must take care not to appear to usurp the regulatory role of Parliament across large fields—a criticism to which the considerably more activist US judiciary is exposed. Perhaps the non-lawyer is better at seeing the intuitive difference between a court declaring the design of a chimney or car negligent, and a court holding that given its health risks the marketing of tobacco is negligent: the former holding has relatively isolated impact, the latter threatens to destroy an industry,[41] put thousands out of work and have significant tax revenue implications. The implied 'separation of powers' argument in the rhetoric of judges recognises the fact that those adversely affected by the wide ranging redistributional effects of such cases may legitimately prefer to see these grave matters in the hands of elected representatives. The problem for the law is that so far no legitimate doctrinal technique has been found to distinguish claims by individuals injured by the negligent design or marketing of dangerous products according to the size of the market for the particular product.

There are techniques by which litigants and courts can mask the problem. Negligent design cases for

example can be couched as failure to warn claims; but sometimes this is not feasible. Applying joint and several liability to deep pocketed authorities for their failure to control the conduct of third parties in a major area of their activity is one such case. Where the third party is often not good for judgment the impact on taxpayers is large, obvious and direct. But as New Zealand law shows, courts do still have a choice when faced with cases with large socio-economic implications, such as building inspection cases. Courts can choose to make a bold application of general principle to the relevant activity thereby indirectly applying pressure on Parliament to regulate the activity. The alternative is to make a reasoned case for exempting local authorities from liability for their carelessness. Underlying this choice is a tradeoff between different goals. The advantage of the New Zealand approach is that it ensures the individual plaintiff has someone worthwhile to sue. Its disadvantage, as in all cases of liability for the conduct of third parties, is that it deflects attention from the party directly responsible for the damage, and this undermines the deterrent and moral symbolism of liability (a point I will return to later). The strength of the approach of the current House of Lords is that it avoids this deflection of attention. Unhappily, however, it has also thrown up a protective wall around negligent subcontractors who are responsible for much of the creation of defective property and with respect to whom the imposition of liability would not create a disturbing socio-economic impact.

To sum up: in *D & F Estates/Murphy* the references to Parliament were ill-thought out. Except in rare cases (such as the Occupiers' Liability Act 1957) there is no evidence that Parliament has or wants impliedly to cover a field of civil obligation. Moreover, unless the common law is to become moribund, bold decisions which result in major rearrangement of socio-economic relationships are inevitable. Such rearrangements *per se* are not a reason for concern: cases such as *Walton* (the manufacturer's duty to recall certain dangerous products) and *Smith* v. *Bush* had substantial effects but are not regarded as results of improper 'judicial legislation'. That is not to say that we cannot extract from *Murphy* a sound countervailing factor to include on any agenda of concerns militating against tort liability,

---

[39] *Murphy* v. *Brentwood District Council* [1990] 2 All E.R. 908, 923 (per Lord Keith).
[40] Stapleton, op. cit., 268–9 (see also 278). See Law Commission Report No. 40 (1970) para. 73 and the speech of Mr Ivor Richard, Parl Debates, Vol. [830] col. 1821 (11.2.72), a relevant 'promotor' of the legislation for the purposes of *Pepper* (*Inspector of Taxes*) v. *Hart* [1993] 1 All E.R. 42 (H.L.). The Occupiers

Liability Act 1957 was similarly a response by a legislature frustrated by the failure of judges to extend the simple *Donoghue* v. *Stevenson* principle to the occupiers' liability field. See also n. 111 below.
[41] As has been the fate of the intra-uterine device industry and most of the asbestos industry.

but it has nothing to do with Parliament or large socio-economic impact *per se*. The concern is and should be defined more specifically, namely that the relevant liability had a particular socio-economic effect—a substantially damaging impact on local government finances—which attracted concern. In failing to separate out this specific concern, the House of Lords has confused the reasons for shielding local authorities from liability with the quite separate reasons for shielding private contractors.

(b) Insurance

Recently I have heard appellate judges informally describe the current incremental approach to tort claims as a reaction to the insurance background of such claims. One impression given is that in certain cases, denying a duty of care is justified because it will not leave future victims uncompensated because they have or could have insured the particular loss. But this argument is as flawed as the earlier reliance by some advocates of *expansion* of liability on the argument that future defendants will not be crippled by the relevant liability because they are or could be insured against that loss. If tort law is to retain an appearance of coherence as a private law mechanism for the vindication of an individual plaintiff's rights against an individual defendant it must be that, as Justice Stephen of the Australian High Court implied, insurance may follow liability but liability need not follow insurance.[42]

Any intended moral or economic incentives of liability are already weakened where insurance exists[43] but predicating the existence of liability on the existence or availability of insurance cuts away any grounds for such incentives. The concept of negligence liability is posited on the defendant's conduct being wrong, a 'wrong', and it is morally incoherent for such a judgement to hinge on the availability of first party insurance to his victim. Just as if liability is treated simply as a gateway to an insurance pool,[44] it fails to provide a reason why anyone ever should

lose a tort claim. If liability is denied because the plaintiff could get first party insurance it penalises the cautious and would severely limit the scope of tort recovery since such insurance is available against many forms of actionable loss. The liability of one particular individual to another must be based on reasons other than insurance.

The presence or absence of insurance certainly affects who sues and is sued,[45] but it should not determine who is liable to whom, any more than the wealth or poverty of the parties does.[46] It is certainly not a legitimate factor for inclusion in any agenda of countervailing concerns militating against tort liability.

(c) The 'correct' spheres of tort and contract: linear liability

Underlying the reining in of liability in negligence seems to be a concern that it had begun to encroach on the legitimate sphere of contract. Thus to grant protection to the plaintiff in *Junior Books* was seen as tantamount to providing it with a warranty of quality for which it had not paid the defendant.[47] The most obvious objection to this is that the *very nature* of tort protection is that it is awarded even where the plaintiff had not paid the defendant for it. Mrs Donoghue was in effect given the protection of a warranty of safety without paying for it. Moreover, in the context of *Junior Books* to say that warranties of quality are the province of contract is mere assertion. A better reason for opposition to that decision needs to be found.

In fact there is, underlying the 'warranty' argument against *Junior Books*, a much stronger and far more general dichotomy, one which does not correspond with the line of privity but is often confused with it, and one which provides a more convincing basis for criticism of that and other expansionary cases. This is the choice the law of obligations has when faced with a sequence of dealings or potential dealings. On the one hand, the law might prefer to simplify the

---

[42] *Caltex Oil* v. *The Willemstad* (1976) 136 C.L.R. 529, 580: 'the task of the court remains that of loss-fixing rather than loss-spreading'.

[43] J. Stapleton, *Product Liability* (London, Butterworths, 1994), 6.05 (i).

[44] D. Harris, 'Evaluating the Goals of Personal Injury Law: Some Empirical Evidence' in *Essays for Patrick Atiyah*, ed. P. Cane and J. Stapleton (Oxford, Clarendon Press, 1991) 289.

[45] For example, house insurance was the motivation for the girl and wife's claims in n. 12.

[46] Contrast T. Weir describing s. 2 of the Defective Premises Act 1972 as a 'striking and admirable instance of the ouster of tort law where the plaintiff has adequate insurance cover against the risk in question': *Casebook on Tort*, 6th ed. (London, Sweet & Maxwell, 1988) 66. The preferable interpretation is that while the D.P.A. creates a cause of action for owners of the defective premises, it excludes from such protection those

owners who have been able to secure from an appropriate party alternative (warranty) protection in their bargain (*and price*). More generally: even if a plaintiff can get first-party insurance for the risk, the question is, *should* the plaintiff have to pay for such cover or should he/she be *entitled* in law to that protection. (The question is important because the wealth distribution consequences are quite different in the 2 cases.) If a plaintiff is held to be entitled to the protection in law *and* he can bargain with the obliged party he may freely choose to sell it (by accepting an exclusion clause in return for a monetary advantage). One piece of evidence that he did so freely would be that he had the back-up of freely available first party insurance for that type of risk, but here insurance is relevant only to the genuineness of the bargaining around the legal entitlement not to its initial allocation.

[47] See discussion of the warranty point in Stapleton op. cit. (1991) 268 et seq.

relevant obligations of the parties by imposing them in a linear form. The first party would owe an obligation only to the party next in sequence and that party's obligations in turn would only be owed to the next and so on. In other words, the eventual victim, the plaintiff, would be prevented from leapfrogging a party with whom it had had dealings or could have had dealings in order to sue a distant party. This form of liability is most well known in contract where it is secured by the doctrine of privity. However it is a major and widespread misconception to see this form of liability arrangement as synonymous with a contractual vision of law. It is a form of arrangement also available in tort law: a tort plaintiff may be refused a claim against a distant party even though the plaintiff does not have (nor reasonably could have had) a contract with another intermediate party so that any protection the plaintiff could fall back on when faced with this refusal is at most a *tort* obligation owed by, say, that intermediate party.[48] Although not yet explicitly recognised in UK law,[49] the 'learned intermediary' doctrine in the US is a good example of this. This doctrine states that so long as the drug manufacturer adequately warns the GP of the product's risks, it has discharged its duty to warn and is not liable to a patient injured by the product, who is therefore forced to concentrate his claim, be it in tort or contract, against the GP. The deployment by US *tort* law of this linear form of liability rests on the wholly tenable assumption that patients are far more likely to have been influenced by GP advice than by package inserts from manufacturers.[50] In other product contexts where this assumption about the intermediary's role fails, the law may then revert to the alternative strategy of imposing obligations on manufacturers to distant victims regardless of whether, for example, the manufacturer had adequately warned the intermediary.

Intermediary not a co-tortfeasor

The preferable basis of the criticism of *Junior Books*, then, is that sometimes a linear arrangement of liability may be justified and that, on the facts of that case, this was the situation there. Such a linear arrangement may be justified even where the intermediary is not negligent. In *Junior Books* the argument would be

that given the circumstances it was not unfair to require the commercial plaintiff to seek protection from the party with which it had directly dealt, that is, the main contractor. Instead of relying on bald and unconvincing assertions that warranties of quality are the province of contract not tort, appellate court would be better advised to defend their criticism of *Junior Books* by explaining why, in certain circumstances, it is preferable to channel liability through the sequence of dealings of the parties than to allow the victim to leapfrog the party it had or could have dealt with and sue the negligent creator of the defective property directly. Care would have to be taken here. The 'explanation' cannot simply be the assertion that it is unfair for the defendant subcontractor to have to face obligations other than those owed to parties in privity with him, for this is the privity fallacy.[51]

But reasons can be found here, just as they could in the learned intermediary context. The most convincing reason in the circumstances of *Junior Books* is that the plaintiff had had an *appropriate* opportunity to protect itself, either in its dealings with the main contractor or by dealing directly with the subcontractor.[52] Instead, then, of deriving from the opposition to *Junior Books* a denial of *all* claims against the creator of defective acquired property with respect to its quality, the more convincing deduction is a countervailing factor to liability which refers to the adequacy of the appropriate alternative means of protection available to the plaintiff. Not all avenues of protection are 'appropriate' in this sense. First party insurance, for example, is not. In *Junior Books* the alternative means of protection of bargaining with the contractors were 'appropriate' because this (unlike insurance) would have been likely to generate adequate deterrence incentives on sub-contractors.[53]

Distinct advantages would follow if appellate courts abandoned their reliance on assertions that certain types of obligation are the province of contract and determined whether a plaintiff should be granted the protection of a tort obligation from a distant defendant on the basis of whether the plaintiff had had an appropriate opportunity to protect itself in its dealings, or potential dealings, with another suitable party. First, some case law would be more

---

[48] For example, if for some reason local authorities were held not to owe pedestrians a duty of care with respect to the maintenance of roads, the injured pedestrian would have to look to the vehicle driver for protection.
[49] A fact clearly related to the remarkable paucity of judgments relating to pharmaceuticals in the UK.
[50] Stapleton, *Product Liability*, op. cit. 10.07 (ii), The vendor's immunity from suit, which is another example of a form of linear arrangement of obligations, rests on more controver-

sial assumptions.
[51] Which is antithetical to the existence of independent tort obligations, see Stapleton (1991), op. at 251–2.
[52] Among other reasons for channelling obligations is easing proof problems of plaintiffs—the probable basis of the channelled form of liability in the Consumer Protection Act 1987.
[53] A later article will give a more detailed explanation of these deterrence-based ideas.

intelligible: for example the decision in *Smith* v. *Bush* would be compatible with opposition to the decision in *Junior Books*. Secondly, there would be no risk of the reasoning collapsing into some version of the privity fallacy. Thirdly, adequacy of appropriate alternative means of protection is part of a much bigger picture. It is relevant in all situations not just in cases where there is a sequence of parties; and it is an important and effective constraint on the growth of tort law. In particular it would help us to find the demarcation line between plaintiffs to whom the law grants protection not bargained for, and plaintiffs to whom no such help is to be given. It is now appreciated that in many areas this line does not correspond with the no privity/privity line. Plaintiffs technically linked by privity with the defendant may still be given protection while plaintiffs who are strangers to the defendant may yet be refused tort protection. Privity is not the appropriate organising principle here.

Appropriate Alternative Means of Protection

Elsewhere I have noted that imbedded in past caselaw on economic loss there is a concern not to assist plaintiffs who had *certain* alternative means of protection[54] and some recent dicta and caselaw have confirmed the importance of this particular hurdle in both tripartite and bilateral cases. Thus in the recent Canadian case of *Norsk*[55] the powerful dissent of La Forest et al. used this argument to find against the plaintiff in a situation analogous to that of the *Mineral Transporter* case: the plaintiff, who relied on the integrity of the property of a party with whom it had a contractual relationship, suffered economic loss as the result of physical damage caused to that property by the negligence of the defendant. The plaintiff is regarded as having in its contractual relationship with the property owner, real (not just nominal) and adequate means of protecting itself from the relevant risk, while appropriately feeding back into a relevant

chain of dealings adequate deterrence incentives. Its claim, if any, should therefore be against that party who in turn has a claim against the negligent injurer of the property.

Closer to home, the availability of *certain* alternative means of protection has been used in judicial reasoning across a wide range of issues.[56] In recent personal injury cases involving the discretion under section 33 of the Limitation Act, for example, the Court of Appeal has held that one factor relevant to the exercise of that discretion is whether the plaintiff has an alternative means of protection in the form of a claim against his or her solicitor for negligence.[57] In another important Court of Appeal case the alternative means of protection argument was used to support a decision that a local authority could not sue for libel in respect of its governing or administrative reputation when no actual financial loss was alleged.[58] Similarly the argument is becoming more explicit in advice cases. For example the more powerful reason used to defeat the plaintiff's claim in tort in *Gran Geltao*[59] was that the plaintiff's claim directly against the landlord was sufficient protection, and a duplicate claim in tort against the landlord's solicitor was not necessary. Similarly the reasonableness of reliance is now being seen to hinge, inter alia, on the advisee's ability to obtain independent advice. In *James McNaughton*[60] (in the context of a friendly takeover) it was stressed that a relevant factor in denying an advisee-bidder a claim against the advisor (the auditor of the target company) was that the advisee should have sought independent advice, and it was noted that in business transactions conducted at arms length it would be difficult to rebut the view that advisees should take independent advice even where the advisor-defendant had dealt directly with them. Of course, in this light the recognition of a duty of care in *Hedley Byrne* itself is open to serious question (and rightly so) because the plaintiffs in that case could either have obtained independent advice or paid for the

---

[54] Stapleton (1991) op. cit.

[55] *Canadian National Railway Co.* v. *Norsk Pacific Steamship Co.* (1992) 91 D.L.R. (4th) 289, 346 (La Forest J. with whom Sopinka and Iacobucci J. J. concurred). On which see casenotes by J. Fleming (1993) 1 Tort Law Rev. 68; M. McInnes [1993] Camb. L.J. 12; B. Markesinis (1993) 109 L.Q.R. 5. See also the discussion in Stapleton (1991) op. cit. 263–4 of the *Mineral Transporter* case [1986] 1 A.C.1.

[56] See e.g., *Wentworth* v. *Wiltshire County Council* [1993] 2 All E.R. 256 (C.A.) and *Wood* v. *The Law Society*, *The Times*, 30.7.93 (Q.B.D.). Some of the reasoning in these cases, especially in the advice cases, is problematic because it does not address the issue of when the alternative means of protection may be 'inappropriate' because, for example, their use encourages wasteful duplication of effort and actual *dilution* of deterrence incentives. Nevertheless, there is clearly an important restraining principle to be developed here.

[57] *Hartley* v. *Birmingham City District Council* [1992] 2 All E.R. 213 (C.A.). *Ramsden* v. *Lee* [1992] 2 All E.R. 204 (C.A.), although in both cases s. 33 was exercised in the plaintiff's favour.

[58] *Derbyshire County Council* v. *Time Newspapers Ltd.* [1992] 3 All E.R. 65, 81 (Balcombe L. J.).

[59] *Gran Gelato Ltd.* v. *Richcliff (Group) Ltd.* [1992] 1 All E.R. 865 (Ch.). For criticisms of the other reasons (and outcome) see P. Cane, 'Negligent Solicitor Escapes Liability' (1992) 109 L.Q.R. 539; A. Tettenborn, 'Enquiries before Contract—The Wrong Answer?' [1992] Camb. L.J. 415. Also, what about the potential claim by the plaintiff against his or her own solicitors?

[60] *James McNaughton Papers Group Ltd.* v. *Hicks Anderson & Co. (a firm)* [1991] 1 All E.R. 134, 144–6. See also: *Ultramares Corp.* v. *Touche, Niven & Co.* (1931) 174 N.E. 441.

information, thus securing contractual protection. But it is a good explanation for *Smith* v. *Bush* and provides a clear justification for shifting the protection of tort towards private plaintiffs and away from commercial plaintiffs.

Multiple Causes

The more courts are willing to adopt a linear arrangement of obligations in tort—refusing to allow plaintiffs to leapfrog a party the plaintiff had or could have dealt with in order to sue a distant tortfeasor—the more manageable becomes the problem of multiple causation. In the modern world, as it has become more feasible to implicate the 'carelessness' of many parties in a deleterious outcome plaintiffs often appear to be in a position to choose randomly between defendants. Short of abandoning joint and several liability—itself an interesting option—the control of this problem and the associated de facto channelling of liability burdens to deep pocket defendants is best helped by the use of linear obligations to shield the more peripheral parties.

One objection to linear liability here is that it may force the plaintiff to sue a party other than the one whose careless conduct directly created the dangerous situation. In most cases it will force the plaintiff to rely on suing an intermediate party usually in contract, and to rely on a chain of litigation to ensure the loss is ultimately distributed to the correct parties. This may not only appear odd but unjust if the intermediate party is not good for judgment;[61] and these are both factors against which the original reason for channelling must be weighed.

Where the intermediary is a co-tortfeasor

Ironically though, unless we are solely committed to making life easier for plaintiffs, the phenomenon of a party not being good for judgment can cut the other way and in favour of linear liability where the intermediate party is a co-tortfeasor. We have already seen in the context of the liability of local authorities for negligent inspection of buildings that the likelihood of the intermediary in such cases (a builder) not being good for judgment proved a positive reason *for* channelling liability and preventing the plaintiff leapfrogging the builder to sue the local authority

(because otherwise a disproportionate amount of overall liability with respect to defective buildings would end up on the shoulders of local taxpayers rather than on careless builders).

But there are other fields in which reasons exist for preventing plaintiffs leapfrogging another party who is most directly responsible for their injury. Take, for example, the area of liability for the criminal acts of third parties. Violent criminals are very often not themselves good for judgment.[62] Was it really such a self-evidently good idea to make the Home Office liable for the property damage caused by escaping Borstal boys?[63] Why is it right that a football club should be held liable when hooligans break off concrete parts of the premises and hurl them at other entrants?[64] Isn't it stretching the reach of a respectable tort law too much for a rape victim to be able to sue the local authority employer of her attacker?[65] From the area of products liability; when and why should the law of tort require manufacturers to render their products resistant to criminal tampering?; and should a lock or burglar alarm manufacturer be liable for personal injury damages when its defective product fails and someone is attacked by a burglar?

Given that the criminal is usually judgment proof, is it a sensible outcome for the full load of liability to end on the shoulders of a party whose negligence is really peripheral? Of course, if we believe tort is or should become a conduit for substantial compensation we might be tempted to say yes, because allowing plaintiffs to sue many different parties increases the chances of recovering from at least one. But if we believe this is not the case, and that the role of tort law is really a symbolic one of maintaining balance and justice then we might regard it as unfortunate that such defendants end up with all the liability burden and accompanying stigma. Moreover, already in the Criminal Injuries Compensation Scheme society seems to have acknowledged that such injuries are a group risk with group responsibility. In as much as the impetus for the expansion of tort law in the field of obligations to control third parties is generated by a hope that substantial numbers of plaintiffs will use tort as a gateway to compensation, it is a false basis for expansion. To the extent that tort is really about the symbolism of moral and deterrence values, we should be taking a much harder look at

[61] As in *Gran Gelato Ltd.* v. *Richcliff (Group) Ltd.* [1992] 1 All E.R. 865. Compare *Junior Books*.
[62] Although see cases noted earlier where the criminal is sued directly.
[63] *Dorset Yacht Co. Ltd.* v. *Home Office* [1969] 2 Q.B. 412. Compare, attitudes to the police: footnote 71 below.
[64] *Cunningham* v. *Reading Football Club* (Q.B.D.) *Independent*, 20.3.91. Compare the preferable approach to liability in *Topp* v. *London County Bus (South West) Ltd.* (C.A.) [1993] 1 W.L.R. 976 (defendant's highjacked bus causing injury to plaintiff).
[65] F. Bawdon, 'Putting a Price on Rape: increasing compensation awards', N.L.J., 12.3.93, 371, 372.

such liability and deploying linear arrangements of obligations where possible without necessarily denying plaintiffs any claim at all.[66]

3. Teasing out some countervailing concerns from existing caselaw

(a) Is the plaintiff using tort to circumvent an understanding of where the loss should fall?

There needs to be a more tightly developed *tortious* notion which denies protection to plaintiffs who are seeking to use tort to evade a prior understanding (to which the plaintiff was party) of how obligations are arranged. This is another and again a better reason on which to attack *Junior Books*[67] than that given by judicial critics. It is also a further reason in support of the dissentients' denial of a duty of care in *Norsk* where the plaintiff had chosen not to extract contractual protection with the property owner (the licence agreement explicitly provided the plaintiff could not claim damages from the latter in the event of closure of the bridge in an emergency[68]) and had presumably gained a financial advantage in doing so.

In bipartite situations where a defendant injured a plaintiff directly by positive conduct the issue is handled moderately well by a variable standard of care and very occasionally by the defence of *volenti*. But if we hope to restrain tort by an increased emphasis on linear liability (and we recognise that this does not necessarily mean that the protection to which plaintiffs will have to resort need be in contract) the position is more complex: the courts must be sensitive to arguments by distant tortfeasors that the understanding between the parties was that the plaintiff would seek protection/redress against another party (perhaps an intermediary) rather than directly against the distant party himself. In accepting this argument courts must feel confident that they know what it is that the plaintiff had accepted. In contract, express terms are a useful starting point for the same restraining pre-condition on protec-

tion.[69] But outside that, courts are not yet sufficiently scrupulous in policing this pre-condition to protection. In contract this does not matter so much given the need for plaintiffs positively to establish an implied term for protection—and the unduly restrictive attitude English courts take to terms implied by law. But in tort there is as yet insufficient development of the idea and its associated problems, for example of how a distant but known exclusion clause affects a plaintiff's claim in tort.

(b) Dignity of the law

Another partly-submerged consideration relevant to the protection by the law of a plaintiff by, say, the recognition of a new duty of care is whether such a move would bring the law into disrepute or maintain it in that state. Defining this countervailing factor can be tricky. Even though it is well known for example that the occasions on which courts are moved to deploy the defences of *volenti* and especially illegality are best explained on this concern rather than other grounds,[70] the formulation of a predictive test of these occasions has proved elusive. Even so the concern is a real one. It implicitly bolsters for example the protection from suit afforded to much police action.[71] But it is a factor that can cut both ways. The pro-plaintiff decision in *Baker* v. *Willoughby*[72] (where the plaintiff succeeded even though he could not establish the but-for connection between the defendant's fault and the damage complained about) was clearly influenced by the embarrassment it would be to the law that the victim of one tort would have been better off than the victim of two torts.

The dignity of the law is a concern which deserves re-emphasis in the future not least because doctrinal developments have now produced areas of intolerable embarrassment with which incrementalism—in particular, incrementalism of the 'pre-judged pockets' form—is inadequate to deal. P. R. Glazebrook has already eloquently attacked the 'affront to public decency' represented by awards of damages for the

---

[66] Compare caveat emptor and J. Gordley's argument that it was used to protect innocent middle-parties in a chain of sales: *Philosophical Origins of Modern Contract Doctrine* (Oxford, Clarendon Press, 1991) 159.

[67] See Stapleton (1991) op. cit. 287.

[68] *Canadian National Railway Co.* v. *Norsk Pacific Steamship Co.* (1992), 91 D.L.R. (4th) 289, 296 (per La Forest, J.).

[69] For if they are freely agreed to by the plaintiff, he or she is denied any claim for an inconsistent implied term: *Johnstone* v. *Bloomsbury Health Authority* [1991] 2 W.L.R. 1362 (here the term contended for was held to be not inconsistent with the express term). The problem also arises in chains of contracts, see e.g., P. Atiyah, op. cit., 148–9.

[70] K. Williams, 'Defences for drunken drivers: Public Policy on the roads and in the air' (1991) 54 M.L.R. 745, 751. See, on

illegality, *Pitts* v. *Hunt* [1990] 3 W.L.R. 542 and on volenti see *Morris* v. *Morris* [1990] 3 All E.R. 801.

[71] *Hill* v. *Chief Constable of West Yorkshire* [1988] 2 All E.R. 238 (H.L.); *Ancell* v. *McDermott* N.L.J., 12.3.93 (C.A.); *Osman's* case *Independent*, 8.10.92 (C.A.), although see *Kirkham* v. *Anderton, Independent*, 16.1.90 (C.A.) (damages against police with respect to a suicide would *not* affront the public conscience or shock the ordinary citizen so the defence of ex turpi causa failed), and the (surely borderline) case of *Welsh* v. *Chief Constable of the Merseyside Police* [1993] 1 All E.R. 692, concerning the Crown Prosecution Service.

[72] *Baker* v. *Willoughby* [1970] A.C. 467 (H.C.). In the causation field, see also *Cook* v. *Lewis* [1952] 1 D.L.R. 1; *Summers* v. *Tice* (1948) 199 P. 2d 1; *McGhee* v. *National Coal Board* [1972] 3 All E.R. 1008 (H.C.). Is the loss of amenities head of damages in personal injuries claims motivated by a related concern?

upkeep of 'unwanted' children.[73] But a class of claims which even more obviously offends this principle is that concerning nervous shock. It is no small irony that the area of nervous shock is both the best historical example of incremental development and yet also the area where the silliest rules now exist and where criticism is almost universal. Even Lord Oliver does not think the law here is 'logically defensible'.[74] A popular but obvious criticism of the relational, spatial and sensory requirements for the existence of a duty of care with respect to nervous shock is that they do not represent sine-qua-non factors to the causation of the actionable damage. Nervous shock, pathological grief, psychiatric illness or however this damage is best described does not *only* occur to those with tight ties of affection to the victim who see with unaided sense the injured victim at the time of injury or near enough thereafter.[75] Nervous shock can afflict other sorts of people in other circumstances and can do so foreseeably. Drawing a line between the cases of pathological grief now recoverable and pathological grief caused by, say, the sudden shock of being told of a brother's grisly death and then dwelling upon it, has nothing to do with foreseeability. A brother may foreseeably suffer such a fate even though he has no special or indeed *any* particular tie of affection to his deceased brother. What is going on in these rules is simply a line-drawing exercise.

The first question is why is it thought that a line must be drawn more tightly than the class of foreseeable victims? In the past there was a fear that approximating nervous shock to other forms of physical loss so that the duty was 'self evident' if the loss was foreseeable would generate far too many claims. This is now unpopular as a modern rationale of nervous shock limitations.[76] This is because, inter alia, it is thought that medical data on the condition suggests it is not common.[77] But the real root of concern may be that appellate courts suspect, and with reason it seems to me, that once a general duty to avoid nervous shock was recognised, many more individuals would be recognised as presenting the relevant symptoms to their GPs. Recovery from grief is a com-

plex and mysterious process. May it not be a major concern of judges that while the prospect of compensation for, say, a broken leg may inhibit recuperation to a minor degree, the prospect of compensation for grief would have a much more powerful disincentive to rehabilitation and one which medical evidence would find extremely difficult to unravel from the original condition?[78] If a central factor in grief and depression is anger, might not the adversarial nature of legal process be especially counter-productive? Associated with this concern is the very real one of characterising the relevant actionable damage. We are told that pathological grief is compensatable (so long as it satisfies the above artificial relational etc. requirements) but not normal grief. Leaving aside the perplexing question of why this is so, we are still confronted by the possibility that with hindsight and in the context of a civil claim, medical opinion may define 'pathological grief' much more loosely than the law would find tolerable. After all, the boundary between normal and pathological grief is of virtually no significance for medical treatment.

So the corners about recovery for nervous shock are real, but the available techniques for controlling it are not only artificial but bring the law into disrepute. That at present claims can turn on the requirement of 'close ties of love and affection' is guaranteed to produce outrage. Is it not a disreputable sight to see brothers of Hillsborough victims turned away because they had *no more* than brotherly love towards the victim? In future cases will it not be a grotesque sight to see relatives scrabbling to prove their especial love for the deceased in order to win money damages and for the defendant to have to attack that argument? Moreover, most other feasible control devices which might be used instead of 'ties of love' would still turn on the status of the plaintiff and so produce the same unseemly arguments over meaningless boundaries.

Some US jurisdictions who had once recognised a tort relating to privacy have now abolished it because it was felt that no reasonable boundaries for the cause of action could be found, and this was an embarrassment to the law.[79] Should not our courts

---

[73] P. Glazebrook, 'Unseemliness Compounded by Injustice' [1992] Camb. C.J. 226. The reformulation of the damage as economic loss rather than of life (as in *McKay* v. *Essex Area Health Authority* [1982] Q.B. 1166) does little to mask the problem.

[74] *Alcock* v. *Chief Constable of the South Yorkshire Police* [1991] 4 All E.R. 907,932 (H.L.). Other critics include, S. Hedley, 'Hillborough—Morbid Musings of a Reasonable Chief Constable' [1992] Camb. L.J. 16; B. Lynch, 'A Victory for Pragmatism? Nervous Shock Reconsidered' (1992) 108 L.Q.R. 367, 370; H. Teff, 'Liability for Psychiatric Illness After Hillsborough' (1992) 12 O.J.L.S. 440, 441.

[75] Teff, op. cit.

[76] See e.g., the speeches in *McLoughin* v. *O'Brien* [1982] 2 All E.R. 298 (H.L.).

[77] Teff, op. cit.

[78] Note that (1) this argument is not the same as a fear of fraudulent claims, and (2) that Lord Bridge noted that the logical deduction from this concern was to wipe out liability for pure nervous shock—the reform argued for here.

[79] D. Bedingfield, 'Privacy or Publicity? The Enduring Confusion Surrounding the American Tort of Invasion of Privacy' (1992) 55 M.L.R. 111, 112.

wipe out recovery for pure nervous shock on the same basis?[80]

4. A Few Ideas for Future Movement of Doctrine

(a) When should anticipatory claims be allowed?

The plaintiff suing in defamation does not have to prove any actual damage to reputation: the plaintiff need not find a friend who will testify that he now thinks less of the plaintiff. One way of looking at this fact is that the law is seeking to avoid just the sort of humiliating forensic spectacle it is at present ensuring in nervous shock cases. But another way of seeing the absence of a damage-to-reputation requirement in defamation is that the law regards the interest threatened by the defendant's conduct as so precious that it penalises even mere threats to its integrity for the sake of deterrence. Yet another reason the law might choose to allow claims before any conventional type of damage has been suffered is in order to allow the plaintiff to mitigate his loss. This was the quite rational driving force behind the liability on builders for property which presented 'an imminent threat to health and safety'.[81] It also would support claims in the future by, for example, those exposed to excessive radiation in hospitals. The categories of actionable damage are not closed.[82] Just as we may choose in future to wipe out recovery for nervous shock, courts may choose to recognise certain categories of exposure to risk as actionable per se (i.e. recognition that the 'loss of the chance' of avoiding the threatened outcome was actionable 'damage'). Of course an unbridled recognition of such a form of 'damage' as actionable has overwhelming arguments against it. Some sort of qualification is needed otherwise everyone living near Sellafield could sue for their increased risk of leukemia, bringing the whole system of civil obligations into public ridicule.[83] But in some cases the mitigation argument is very strong. In the US, those

negligently exposed to x-rays can sometimes recover damages under the label of 'damages for the cost of medical surveillance' where the surveillance will pick up cancers early enough to limit their impact. Moreover in the current dramatic situation involving defective Bjork-Shiley heart valves (a quarter of which are defective and will fail catastrophically without warning[84]), the law might be brought into considerable disrepute were it to insist that the recipients 'wait and see' before they (or rather their estates) could sue. In other words there may be some class of anticipatory claims which, although speculative (not all recipients of such damages would eventually suffer the deleterious outcome), may be justified, and to this extent the future may see a re-embrace of the broad concern underlying the decision in *Anns*.

(b) Ranking types of loss; private profit

A vigorous common law might also in the future draw out distinctions within certain categories of actionable damage. In the twentieth century, Parliament has been sensitive to the greater social concern generated by personal injuries relative to property damage,[85] and within property damage to the greater concern where a person's dwelling is affected.[86] Might not these sorts of considerations be given more prominence and definition in future common law doctrine?

Similarly there is in both parliamentary enactments and certain areas of the common law a distinction drawn between defendants who act in the course of a business and others.[87] A common law which seeks to be responsive to social concerns and distinctions may choose to develop this idea more explicitly. In the future, therefore, we might want to see such a factor enter into the determination of whether a particular plaintiff should be able to sue a particular defendant and on what basis. This is not simply the issue of protecting certain public activities such as those of the police and local authorities

---

[80] If in a case where statute barred room for manoeuvre Lord Reid was moved to complain that 'the common law ought never to produce a wholly unreasonable result . . .', *Cartledge* v. *E. Jopling & Sons Ltd.* [1963] A.C. 758, 772), how much more forceful is that complaint here where no statute obstructs rational reform.

[81] *Anns* v. *Merton London Borough Council* [1978] A.C. 728.

[82] *Hotson* v. *East Berkshire Area Health Authority* [1987] 1 All E.R. 210, 217 (per Sir John Donaldson M.R.): 'I can see no reason why the categories of loss should be closed either'.

[83] As well as having dramatic side-effects in limitation law—potentially barring claims later brought when a person did actually contract leukemia. This has a parallel in the recognition that 'acquisition of defective property' claims are really ones concerning economic loss—the defendant can use this characterization of what is the actionable 'damage' to argue that the claim is statute barred. See J. Stapleton, 'The Gist of

Negligence, Part 1' (1988) 104 L.Q.R. 213, 236 and *Nitrigin Eireann Teoranta* v. *Inco Alloys Ltd.* [1992] 1 W.L.R. 498. The same construction is probably true of a claim that a defective herbicide was ineffective so that the crop is more vulnerable to weeds.

[84] By 1992 there had been 470 recorded failures of this heart valve (43 in the UK) with fatal results in two-thirds of cases (33 in the UK): *Prob. Liab. Internat.* [March 1992] 38. See also *The Guardian*, 3.12.92.

[85] e.g. Limitation Act 1980, s. 33; Occupiers' Liability Act 1984 sl. (9); Unfair Contract Terms Act 1977 s. 2 (1).

[86] e.g. Defective Premises Act 1972.

[87] See e.g., Sale of Goods Act 1979; Unfair Contract Terms Act 1977; Consumer Protection Act 1987. This argument is developed in detail under the term 'moral enterprise liability' in Stapleton, *Product Liability*, op. cit., Chapter 8.

(see above), but of developing a distinction between, say, one who advises, feeds or carries another in pursuit of financial gain and one who does so without that motivation. It might be, for example, that sometime in the future the vicarious liability of employers for the acts of employees in the course of employment will evolve into a personal but strict liability of employers for injuries caused in this way. Certainly UK courts are hostile to employers relying on their former common law entitlement to seek an indemnity from the tortfeasor-employee, and such reliance is now rare. Indeed, so settled in some countries is the consensus that this is a just arrangement that there is a growing momentum to remove formally the personal liability of the employee in line with this practice.[88] One relevant application of this idea might resolve the problematic basis of Richcliff's liability in *Gran Gelato*[89] because Richcliff's 'vicarious liability' would be replaced by a personal strict liability imposed on defendants for acts done by their employees and agents acting in pursuit of the defendant's profit.[90]

5. Interaction of torts inter se and with other causes of action; recourse actions

In the recognition of a tort obligation it can be relevant to consider issues of the maintenance of the integrity of another area of the law and the availability in another area of law of a preferable technique of protection. Both these issues are present for example in the recent cases involving negligent solicitors and wills. The rule that a testator's clear changed wishes cannot override an existing valid will means that the newly favoured parties will lose out unless a new will is executed (and even then they will only have an expectation not an entitlement). When the execution is delayed by the negligence of the testator's solicitor and the testator dies, there is a problem for the law.[91] The victim of the negligence is clearly the favoured party, but he or she is a stranger to the relevant dealings and may be completely oblivious of them. Fashioning protection for the victim *in tort* while also allowing the solicitor and client to be free to fashion their own relationship is therefore tricky. A less tricky alternative is relaxing the privity

requirement for suing on the solicitor/client contract on the ground that it was clearly for the benefit of the third party favoured beneficiary.[92] For example, the solicitor and client might agree that the solicitor would assign the work to an inexperienced articled clerk who would take considerably longer to process the work than would be reasonable for an ordinary solicitor. The client may have secured a considerable reduction in fee as a result. It is clear that when faced with a claim by the newly favoured party after the testator dies the law would not want to ignore this fact. Yet how can this best be done? If the claim is brought in tort how could the concern about the client–solicitor agreement be taken into account given that the plaintiff may be a stranger to it? Already we have seen that the agenda of countervailing factors against tort protection should include hostility to a plaintiff who is trying to use tort to evade an arrangement he or she had agreed to, but that factor would not be an adequate control here because the plaintiff may have been a stranger to the client–solicitor arrangement. Similarly trying to fashion the control in terms of what the defendant had expected his obligations to the testator to be smacks of the privity fallacy. It is hard to see how a suitable countervailing factor *could* be constructed in *tort* to handle this situation, short of an awkward special exception.[93] A much more satisfactory technique would be to fashion the relevant protection of the newly favoured party out of the client's contractual entitlement which would not only enable the reason for protection of an apparently unconnected plaintiff to be evident but would also bring with it the required limitations of that protection, including the common sense decision by Judge Moseley Q.C. to deny a duty of care to a disappointed beneficiary under a negligently drafted inter vivos transaction (where the settlor had subsequently changed his mind).[94] In short, these wills cases suggest a further countervailing factor against tort liability: would a non-tort avenue of protection be more suitable.

Next, the current keenness of appellate courts to confine negligence liability has had the disturbing side-effect of subordinating and hence distorting its principles in relation to other causes of action. Thus the Court of Appeal has asserted[95] that a referee has

[88] J. Fleming, *The Law of Torts*, 8th ed. (Sydney, Law Book Co. 1992) 367–8.
[89] Cane, op. cit. On the other hand, on reading this draft paper Cane asks could the 'learned intermediary' analysis be applied to the solicitor?
[90] A rationale which would not then apply to the conduct of the independent contractor (the surveyor) in *Smith* v. *Bush*.
[91] *White* v. *Jones* [1993] 3 All E.R. 481 (C.A.); (1993) 109 L.Q.R. 344 (casenote by J. G. Fleming); HL appeal heard 7.3.94—14.3.94. See also *Ross* v. *Counters* [1980] Ch. 297.
[92] On which see The Law Commission, *Privity of Contract:*

Contracts for the Benefit of Third Parties, Consultative Paper No. 12 (London, HMSO, 1991).
[93] The position is different if the plaintiff had had dealings with a relevant party (see above discussion of linear liability in tort).
[94] *Hemmens* v. *Wilson Brown*, The Times, 30.6.93.
[95] *Spring* v. *Guardian Assurance plc.* [1993] 2 All E.R. 273 (C.A.); HL appeal heard 29.11.93—30.11.93. See also *Petch* v. *Comrs of Customs and Excise* (C.A.), The Times, 4.3.93 and compare *Lonrho plc.* v. *Fayed* (No. 5), The Times, 27.7.93 (C.A.).

no duty in negligence to the subject of the reference because defamation (and specifically the defence of qualified privilege) covers the field. That is, a negligence claim is denied on the ground that otherwise a defence available in another tort would be 'bypassed'. Yet at almost the same time the Court of Appeal in the *Cambridge Water*[96] case held that another claim (for physical loss) can succeed even though the defendant had acted with reasonable care and so had a complete answer to a claim in the tort of negligence.

Spring imperils many of the professional misstatement precedents[97] and is almost certainly wrongly decided. The idea of a defence covering the field is bizarre if we see different civil obligations as responding to different and perhaps overlapping interests of the plaintiff. Moreover, in *Spring* there was no attempt to argue that the defendant in a defamation suit should be able to resist it by claiming he had acted carefully (and so would have an answer to a negligence claim which answer would be bypassed by the imposition of strict liability in defamation). To judge a plaintiff's claim against the defendant by whether the defendant has an answer to a different claim is to fall into the same trap as those who championed the privity fallacy: that we must not in determining causes of action disturb the expectations of security a defendant may have acquired from his being safe from a claim under a different cause of action. As we have seen, there may be legitimate reasons why we might choose to channel civil obligations, but protecting defendant's expectations is not one of them.

The Court of Appeal decision in *Spring* was an ill-thought out attempt to rein in *one* tort, that is negligence, and subordinate it to another, that is defamation. It may well be desirable that negligence (or tort as a whole or perhaps like equity[98]) be kept in reserve—and the recognition of the requirement that plaintiffs have no other feasible appropriate means of protection as a precondition of tort's assistance is a reflection of this. But that does not imply that its form should be distorted by the outlines of alternative claims for protection which have been *unsuccessful* because the defendant had an answer to them.

Cambridge Water involved a claim about contaminated ground water. Whether the plaintiff's claim was seen as one of nuisance or *Rylands* v. *Fletcher*,[99] the Court of Appeal decision seemed clearly wrong. This was not because the defendant had a defence in a different tort (negligence), but because the parallel defence (of due care) should have been accorded to the defendant in those causes of action on which the plaintiff was relying.[100] But this is not the limit of the interest in the case. If we do not intend to irradicate strict liability completely from the law of obligations[101] (and the strict nature of many contractual obligations makes this unlikely) cases such as *Cambridge Water* raise a much more fundamental question. Let us suppose that a plaintiff in a particular cause of action is unequivocally entitled to the protection of a strict obligation. Because the interconnectedness of much human activity has become apparent and the duty of care in negligence has come to be applied to many more types of conduct than previously, it is now much more likely that there is some other party whose conduct may be implicated in the causation of the relevant injury and whose conduct may be regarded as careless. This means it is now more likely that the strictly obliged defendant will have some 'careless' party against whom to seek recourse.

A plaintiff is usually interested in pursuing compensation in the easiest and most secure way, and not interested in ensuring that the liability costs eventually land on the party or parties which the law may regard as most appropriate. One feature of a system of joint and several liability, itself designed to ease the plaintiff's pursuit of compensation, is that the preferred target of the plaintiff's claim is often the wrongdoer with the deepest pocket. But the fact that the law holds some parties to strict obligations and some only to obligations of care suggests that there are different moral and/or economic norms at work. This would seem to necessitate in any system of joint and several liability that a defendant should, prima facie, have access to a recourse action against other wrongdoers.[102] In other words the very phenomenon of strict and fault based liabilities which are joint and several suggests that the law has more than an interest in compensating plaintiffs in certain circumstances—it seems also to be interested in

---

[96] *Cambridge Water Co.* v. *Eastern Counties Leather plc.* (C.A.), [1994] 1 All E.R. 53 but see 63 (reversal by HL)..

[97] Starting with the recognition of a duty of care in the context of a financial reference in *Hedley Byrne* (which may be wrong on other grounds—see earlier text).

[98] *Chandler* v. *Kerley* [1978] 2 All E.R. 942, 945: 'the role of equity is supplementary and supportive', per Lord Scarman. See also *Simaan General Contracting Co.* v. *Pilkington Glass Ltd.* (*No. 2*) [1988] 1 All E.R. 791, 804: 'Just as equity remedied the inadequacies of the common law, so has the law of torts

filled the gaps left by other cases of action where the interests of justice so required' per Bingham, L.J.

[99] *Rylands* v. *Fletcher* (1866) L.R. 1 Ex. 265; (1868) L.R. 3 H.L. 330 (H.L.).

[100] In accordance with modern attitudes to such claims: T. Weir, 'The Polluter Must Pay—Regardless' [1993] C.L.J. 17, 19.

[101] The origin of the strictness of contractual obligations is, to some extent, obscure—see Stapleton, *Product*, op. cit., 2.02.

[102] Contrast T. Weir, Torts, Vol. XI of *International Encyclopedia of Comparative Law* (Mouton, The Hague, 1976), 58–9.

ranking the behaviour of defendants. To allow the whole liability load to rest on one party by virtue of a factor (the whim of the plaintiff's choice, the deep pocket of certain defendants) which is not built into the basis of liability seems inconsistent with such a ranking. The law seems to have an interest, not only in compensating suitable plaintiffs but also, once this is accomplished, in enabling the liability costs to be allocated between all those liable to the plaintiff in a way which reflects some moral or economic pecking order of liabilities inter se.

The theoretical and notorious problem[103] here is what should the rules governing recourse look like? In every likelihood the concerns of the law will be different in respect of the claim by the plaintiff from its concerns in relation to recourse claims between liable parties. For example, any pragmatic argument of easing plaintiff's proof problems disappears at the recourse stage. The Civil Liability (Contribution) Act 1978 contemplates contribution/indemnity between parties whose liability with respect to the damage is based on breaches of different duties (see s. 6(1)), for example, negligence, breach of contract and breach of statutory duties. But how should apportionment proceed in such cases—causation, blameworthiness, a combination of both these and/or other factors? Does the negligence principle, for example, swamp whatever basis and goals lie beneath the other liability rules under which non-negligent parties have been held liable, so that the latter are justified in claiming a full indemnity from the former?[104] While this accords with the formal attitude to the vicariously liable employer (who is technically entitled to a full indemnity from the negligent tortfeasor-employee), there is no general clear authority for the proposition that the negligent party should indemnity the strictly liable party. Indeed, many commentators argue that there is caselaw running the other way showing that blameworthiness in not the sole criterion under the 1978 Act.[105] Of course, the courts' decree of apportionment (not indemnity) in such caselaw might be rationalized by an implicit finding of some sort of fault or carelessness on the part of the 'strictly liable' party; but it may not be.

The courts may be attempting to give weight to the bases of the relevant strict liability, including the relative causal potency of those liable.[106] In other words, the task of apportionment here inevitably requires the court to elaborate on the notion of 'responsibility' in the apportionment legislation and, in so doing, to speculate about and rank the policy objectives thought to underlie the different legal rules.[107]

It may be, or course, that in recourse actions most courts *would* simply always give sole weight to the negligence principle allowing full indemnity against the negligent party. But if so, this would have profound implications for the theoretical basis of civil obligations. It would mean that whatever mix of elegant moral, economic or pragmatic ideas was used to justify the initial strict liability of parties *to victims*, they would be eclipsed at the recourse stage by the negligence paradigm. Thus, whatever the *given* rationale of a strict liability may be, it would amount to no more in *practice* than a facade for the real basis of the strict liability—the pragmatic one of facilitating the plaintiff's suit—because this defendant would eventually be entitled to shift all responsibility on to the negligent party. The phenomenon of strict liability would support no more than this pragmatic rationale save in those very rare cases where no human negligence could, by any device, be said to have been involved in the relevant injury. Modern theories of civil obligation have yet to tackle this fundamental problem, which has implications for the hierarchy of norms reflected in different causes of action not only in the area of multiple wrongdoers but also in cases such as *Spring* and *Cambridge Water*.

The problem *for theory* is exacerbated by two factors in practice. First, as we have seen, the more the inter-connectedness of conduct is perceived and the wider the reach of negligence law becomes (especially its expansion in the area of failure to control third parties), the more parties become potential targets for claims and thereby involved in recourse determinations. Secondly, lawyers acting for plaintiffs seem to be becoming (perhaps due to the increased fear of malpractice claims) more assiduous

---

[103] T. Hervey, ' "Responsibility" under the Civil Liability (Contribution) Act 1978' [1979] New Law J. 509; G. Williams, *Joint Torts and Contributory Negligence* (London, Stevens & Sons, 1951) 160.
[104] Certainly Glanville Williams thought this should be the case, op. cit. 160. See also W. Landes and R. Posner, 'Joint and Multiple Tortfeasors: An Economic Analysis' (1980) 9 J. Leg. Studs, 517 553, but contrast J. Phillips, 'Contribution and Indemnity in Products Liability' (1974) 42 Tenn. L.R. 85, 102–3.
[105] Hervey (1979) op. cit., 510; M. Brazier, *Street on Torts*,

8th ed. (London, Butterworths, 1988) 532, citing cases which appear to hold that the negligence of a co-tortfeasor does not necessarily relieve a strictly liable defendant completely. Compare *Tennant Radiant Heat Ltd.* v. *Warrington Devel Corp.* [1988] 1 E.G.L.R. 41 (C.A.), see below.
[106] e.g. *Morris* v. *Ford Motor Co.* [1973] Q.B. 792.
[107] Certainly, as between a strictly liable landlord and careless tenant, the Court of Appeal recently preferred to deal with their claim and counterclaim (not a recourse claim) as 'a problem of causation' alone: *Tennant Radiant Heat Ltd.* v. *Warrington Devel Corp.* [1988] 1 E.G.L.R. 41 (C.A.), 44 (Dillon, L.J.).

in pleading an exhaustive list of possible alternative causes of action;[108] so the list of causes of action per defendant which need to be considered at the recourse stage can be considerable. Of course we could mask the problem which arises at the recourse stage if we abolish joint and several liability, as some jurisdictions in the United States have partially done in order to protect 'deep pocket' defendants, in particular public authorities. But this would have clear disadvantages for plaintiffs. Alternatively even more favour could be shown to plaintiffs than joint and several liability affords them, for example, as in the Netherlands where in a recent case the Supreme Court held that a plaintiff injured by a generic product (diethylstilbestrol) can sue any or all manufacturers of such a product jointly and severally, and only at the recourse stage can the individual manufacturer argue the market share doctrine to reduce liability to its proportion of the market in that generic product.[109]

In *practice* however, the whole field of contribution and indemnity is conveniently shrouded in mystery because of the tendency for out-of-court settlements on the issue to be subject to secrecy clauses—as in the Hillsborough football disaster;[110] by the failure of past courts to attempt to address these issues; their omission to set out clear reasons for their decisions; and the virtual absence of appellate litigation on the issues. Ideally, law should illuminate not only who the plaintiff can sue under a rule and why, but who should ultimately bear the relevant loss and why. That the basis of civil liabilities and their relative ranking in importance can be buried in recourse actions so successfully without comment by most observers supports the allegation that it is law's facade which is important, not its final allocation of loss.

5. Conclusion

Current criticism of the state of tort law can be resolved into two forms: that which takes a political line and boils down simply to a complaint about the House of Lord's conservative vision for the overall reach of tort protection; and that which concerns the processes by which decisions are taken. I have concentrated here on the latter. Just as, in Lord Goff's words 'piecemeal legislation may exercise a distorting effect on the law'[111] so too can the ad hockery implicit in the *Caparo* 'pre-judged pocket' approach to new cases. Very recently we have seen courts struggling to rationalise quite sensible outcomes within the constraints of this type of thinking.[112] Now a clearer approach is needed.

We might at first be tempted to rely on the fashionable new theories of tort liability developed (nearly all in the US) to combat the collectivist arguments of the late 1960s.[113] But these new theories do not help. Nearly all only focus on two of the complex constituents of any cause of action: the standard of the defendant's behaviour (fault or strict liability); and causation. No analysis here of why the law does or should have a different attitude to economic loss; how to rank different bases of liability; or whether legislative emphasis in certain areas (personal injuries, dwellings, conduct in the course of a business etc.) should legitimately be reflected in the direction to be taken in the common law.[114] Moreover, there is a substantial amount of terminological confusion in this theoretical debate. Key language is used in quite different ways—particularly the idea of 'strict liability'. The effects of a law (for example, compensation, self-insurance) are often elided with its goals. An ideological bias is also not uncommon: this is exemplified by the assertion of 'back to contract' theorists, that virtually all important transactions are consensual (or potentially consensual).

Next we might be persuaded to rely heavily on a study of comparative law. Recently there has been much criticism of the alleged 'parochialism'[115] of the current British judicial scene. In recent commentaries on both *Murphy* and *Norsk* sharp criticism has been made of the Law Lords' failure to analyse the comparative precedents from other jurisdictions. At its most diplomatic this criticism takes the form of bemoaning the limitations on the House of Lords working in 'physically crammed conditions with minimal library facilities and non-existent research assistance'.[116] I have no doubt appellate judges are overworked and need more time to read and reflect

---

[108] Even where liability is admitted as in *A.B. and Others* v. *South West Water Services Ltd.* [1993] 1 All E.R. 609. (A case which shows the naivety of the argument that the E.C. Directive on Products Liability would make life simpler for plaintiffs.)

[109] H.R. 9.10.92, Rwd. W. 219 (compare *Sindell* v. *Abbott Laboratories* (*1980*) 607 P. 2d. 924). On the argument that a defendant should only be allowed recourse against another party if they had been acting in the course of a business, see Stapleton, *Product Liability*, op. cit., Chapter 11.

[110] *The Independent*, 9.10.90.

[111] Lord Goff of Chieveley, *Judge, Jurist and Legislature* (The Child & Co., Oxford Lecture, 1986) 11.

[112] *Cook* v. *Square D. Ltd.* [1992] I.C.R. 262 (C.A.); *Khorasandjian* v. *Bush* [1993] 3 All E.R. 669 (C.A.).

[113] I. England, 'The System Builders: A Critical Appraisal of Modern Tort Theory' (1980) 9 J.L.S. 27. To the economic theories (by Calabresi, Posner and Alan Schwartz) and ethical theories (of Weinrib, Epstein and Honoré) should now be added books by J. Coleman, *Risks and Wrongs* (Cambridge, Cambridge Univ. Press, 1992); and I. England, *The Philosophy of Tort Law* (Aldershot, Dartmouth, 1993).

[114] For other examples, see T. Weir [1992] C.L.J. 388, 389.

[115] See e.g., Fleming (1993) op. cit. 74.

[116] B. Markesinis, 109 L.Q.R. 5, 6.

on the complex matters which come before them. But the strength of judicial reasoning comes not from the citation and analysis, thesis-like, of a range of responses from other jurisdictions to the issue at hand. The most powerful and convincing judgments are those which spell out basic principles and explain their application to the specific case in a clear manner.

The way forward lies in thinking clearly about the reasons both for and against helping the plaintiff. Here I concentrated on the latter, the separate consideration of the countervailing factors which militate against the imposition of tort liability. This may require, at the most abstract level, a rethinking of our basic ideas of what tort law is for and some of these will certainly be found wanting. Take for example the common cliché that the tort of negligence is about compensation. Quite apart from the *fact* that only a tiny fraction of those many people injured by negligence sue and recover in tort, this description is simply inadequate to convey what is the 'meat' of negligence law, which is the analysis of the *boundaries* of the tort which explain why only *some* victims of negligence are allowed to recover compensation. In this sense, a re-emphasis on the countervailing factors which weigh against the protection of tort is at least as appropriate and useful as the *Anns* strategy which in effect, was interpreted as asking 'why not' as a peripheral afterthought to the duty analysis.

In rethinking what tort law should be for in this broad sense we may choose in future to shift emphasis in a major way, for example by putting greater weight on prevention and on preventative remedies. In the future perhaps tort law should develop greater use of injunctive relief. We have already seen this recently in the novel case of *Khorasandjian* v. *Bush*[117] which may and should herald, not the fatal unravelling of the property requirement in private nuisance, but the long overdue (albeit covert) birth of new tort of harrassment. But we might also want to see injunctive relief developed in other areas, for example, to give those threatened with personal injuries by the continuing conduct of defendants (for example, their employer) some effective remedy. There may, of course, be some areas in which tort will only rarely be able to operate successfully, even symbolically. One such field is that of toxic torts: the embarrassing sight of the Sellafield litigants squabbling over the meaning of 'soft' statistics is the best current example of how tort law is inadequate here, even as a symbol of justice. Nevertheless in many

other areas the potential role of tort for signalling important social values remains substantial.

This paper's main suggestions as to how tort law might be restrained within coherent boundaries may be summarised as follows:

1. The strategy of searching for a relevant 'pocket' of caselaw *at the outset* of the duty analysis should be replaced with an analysis based on arguments for liability and on an agenda of countervailing factors to the imposition of tort liability which have been explicitly constructed from policy concerns.

2. More attention needs to be paid to understanding the complexity of and limitations to the pro-liability side of the duty equation.

3. With regard to the no-liability side of the equation, the following are *not* convincing countervailing arguments to the imposition of tort liability:
   (a) that the imposition of tort liability might have a large socio-economic and redistributive impact;
   (b) that the plaintiff or defendant has or could have obtained insurance;
   (c) that 'warranties of quality' are necessarily the province of contract;
   (d) that the defendant has a defence to a different cause of action;
   (e) that to impost tort liability would disturb the defendant's expectations.

4. The agenda of countervailing concerns should include:
   (a) that the imposition of liability might produce a specific unattractive socio-economic impact (such as severely depleting local government finances[118]);
   (b) that a linear arrangement of obligations is preferable in the area in order, for example, to shield peripheral deep-pocketed parties and/or to control the problem of multiple causation;
   (c) that the plaintiff had adequate and *appropriate* alternative means of protection;
   (d) that the plaintiff may be seeking to use tort as a means to evade an understanding as to where the risk would fall;
   (e) that to assist the plaintiff would bring the law into disrepute and injure its dignity;

---

[117] *Khorasandjian* v. *Bush* [1993] 3 All E.R. 669 (C.A.).
[118] See e.g., T. Weir, 'Governmental Liability' [1989] Public Law 40. On the general point, note that H. L. A. Hart includes

in his version of an agenda of countervailing factors that the imposition of liability might 'unduly hamper enterprise'. *The Concept of Law* (Oxford, Clarendon Press, 1961) 162.

(f)   that a more convincing and doctrinally convenient form in which to deliver protection to the plaintiff exists in another field of law.

4.   The following issues may play a role in the future direction of tort and so deserve more consideration:

(a)   the accommodation within the tort analysis of the phenomenon of a plaintiff's prior acceptance of where the risk would lie;

(b)   the degree to which tort law in future should provide incentives to prevent or mitigate harm;

(c)   the degree to which tort law should distinguish types of physical harm

(d)   the degree to which tort law should distinguish conduct in pursuit of financial profit and other forms of conduct.

(e)   the interaction of torts inter se and of tort with other causes of action, both in claims by plaintiffs and in recourse claims.

8. Errare Humanum Est

TONY WEIR

WHEN Lord Agamemnon and King Menelaus and even the wily Odysseus had had their say, before the captains and the kings departed, a lowly commentator stood up. He made some disobliging observations and was soundly thrashed for it. Thersites got what he deserved. He spoke out of turn. By contrast (I hope) the role of commentator is one for which I have been fingered by our genial animator: it is not a responsibility voluntarily assumed, though whether that makes much difference these days is perhaps not very clear.

Jane Stapleton set the tone of the day with the acute observation that whereas twenty years ago we would have been agonising over why there was no liability without fault, we are now asking why, given harm, there is ever fault without liability. In both cases, let it be noted, we are doing the same thing—looking at one side of the picture only. Twenty years ago people kept saying that the plaintiff's hurt was just the same whether or not the defendant was negligent, so why should it matter whether he was or not? Now we are saying 'The consequences may differ, but the defendant was just as much at fault in either case, so why should it matter what kind of harm it is?' For instance, we ask why, if a careless manufacturer is liable for personal injury due to his defective product, he should not equally be liable for the cost of repairing or replacing it, or for any foreseeable consequential loss. We seem forever to be concentrating on one side of the picture, the harm or the conduct, whereas we really know that both count, both conduct and consequence. The judge, after all, sits in the middle, with an eye to either side, and supposedly an equal eye. The interrelation of conduct and consequence emerges from Robin Cooke's recalling that purely economic harm is clearly compensable by a defendant who was very much to blame for causing it, whether by deceit or inducing breach of contract or whatever. We may fuss about whether and when a merely negligent person should have to pay for the economic harm he causes, but if he is fraudulent or otherwise wicked, we have no problem. The principle is a simple one: 'bad people pay more'. 'Fraud unravels all', as Lord Denning once said: not that all fraud gets unravelled, least of all by the SFO. The moral aspect is alluded to by both Jane Stapleton and Robin Cooke, and I shall return to it.

However delighted one may be by what one has seen in an art gallery, on leaving it one should nevertheless ask what one has *not* seen. Not 'where's the beef?' but 'where was the Poussin? Were the expressionists not in short supply?' (they usually are!). What have we not heard about today, or not heard enough about? Defamation is the obvious case. A tort which has been held substantively unconstitutional by the Supreme Court of the United States, reprobated, *quoad* damages, by the European Commission of Human Rights, and described by a judge as having passed redemption by the courts is a part of tort law which is in lamentable condition, if ever there were one. But we heard nothing of it, though Jane Stapleton did mention the dubious decision in which defamation was allowed to paralyse the law of negligence.[1] Nor did we hear much of nuisance, where the Court of Appeal has recently imposed the strictest of liabilities for what is not very attractively named 'historical pollution'—a decision whose economic impact far outweighs that of *Anns*.[2] The Court also used the occasion to doubt the existence, after a century of recognition, of the defence of 'natural user' in *Rylands* v. *Fletcher*, but that did receive a mention today, when Robin Cooke described Lord Cairns's introduction of it as 'judicially irresponsible'. Causation—an area where another decision of Lord Wilberforce might have proved revolutionary had it not been reinterpreted out of existence[3]—is another subject we didn't hear much of today.

But the really curious incident, the subject that didn't bark, was Europe. Bob Hepple alluded to it in his paper, and Ross Cranston mentioned it in the discussion, but otherwise it was silence. English courts have been charged with parochialism—by John Fleming, as Jane Stapleton reminds us—and there were hints of that charge, too, in Robin Cooke's paper. In both cases the grief is that English courts insufficiently attend to the decisions of other Commonwealth courts. Today we have heard a good deal about cases from Canada and the Antipodes, but we have still been parochial. Those cases are quite interesting, but they are increasingly *nil ad rem*. The fact is that our House of Lords is no longer our supreme court, that statutes of the United Kingdom now not

---

[1] *Spring* v. *Guardian Assurance* [1993] 2 All E.R. 273.
[2] *Cambridge Water Co.* v. *Eastern Counties Leather* now reversed at [1994] 1 All E.R. 53.

[3] *McGhee* v. *National Coal Board* [1973] 1 W.L.R. 1, gutted by *Wilsher* v. *Essex A.H.A.* [1988] A.C. 1074.

only may, but sometimes must, be disregarded (and Ministers enjoined from applying them), and that from now on the state may be sued for not legislating *pro bono privato*. For all we heard today, these might not be facts, or critical facts. But they are. For example, Bob Hepple couldn't have done a better job of describing how, with our traditional legal baggage, we might deal with problems arising from the contracting-out of public services. But the ECJ has put the kybosh on the whole proceeding of privatisation by extending the reach of the Transfer of Undertakings rules,[4] and the Commission has a Directive on Liability for Services in the pipeline, fortunately stuck there for the minute. This will cover public services (except those directed to public safety) and may have the effect of rendering the supplier of a service liable (though admittedly only for personal injury or personal property damage) even if it is provided through another.

Even if it were not for Europe, the common law would, as appeared during the discussion, be becoming increasingly fissiparous. Just as the *ius commune* of Europe broke up as a result of particularist legislation like the Prussian Code of 1794, the French Code of 1804 and the Austrian one of 1811, so with the Commonwealth. We learnt (we should, I suppose, have known) that the Defective Premises Act 1972 doesn't apply in Scotland, and I guess we did know that the New Zealand Fair Trading Act 1986 and their Contracts (Privity) Act 1982 don't apply here. Legislation greatly alters the legal context in which courts decide even common law cases not directly affected by any enactment: the impact of legislation is greater than its scope. English may well remain a common language for a long time yet, but law common to the English-speaking peoples is certainly on the way out, almost through the door of history already. England must be like the 'fashionable host, That slightly shakes his parting guest by th' hand, And with his arm outstretch'd, as he would fly, Grasps in the comer.'[5] To discuss tort law in England in the light of Commonwealth decisions is almost anachronistic today;[6] to ignore the European dimension is certainly unrealistic.

Just as Europe will certainly alter our law itself, it should (and will) alter our realisation of our law and

its supposed problems. Take (as we have taken, almost all day) the case of economic loss caused to a non-contractor by negligent conduct. France, on the one hand, makes no overt distinction between different kinds of damage: *any* certain damage directly resulting from fault (omission or commission) calls for reparation, a word surely dear to the heart of Alan Rodger. This equiparation of physical and non-physical as 'material harm' (the ambiguous term used so misleadingly by Lord Wilberforce in *Anns*) is a tenet, so much so that the distinction drawn in the EC Products Liability Directive between physical harm and non-physical economic harm is regarded as an outrage.[7] Germany, by contrast, almost specifically excludes merely economic interests from protection against negligence not criminal, though of course (as we do, though less elegantly) they protect such interests against conduct which is disgusting to the right-thinking person (recalling Robin Cooke's 'man of good-will', whose judgment determines liability).

It follows that we needn't be embarrassed about having a problem with economic loss in negligence. I sometimes had the feeling today that people were almost ashamed and angry that we have such a problem. I tell my freshmen that they will often be miserable during the next three years, but they are not to feel miserable about what is only natural, given their youth: there is no call for meta-misery. If everyone has problems, having a problem isn't an extra problem. Today we have been behaving as if it were, as if there were something wrong and shameful in our having this problem. But there is nothing surprising about it: *in medio* of two jurisdictions which have opposing views on the matter, we neither wholly exclude it as Germany does (and can afford to)[8] nor wholly admit it, as France seems to (but really doesn't).[9] Far from being ashamed of our position, we are actually doing quite well in saying that 'something special'[10] is required to render a merely negligent person liable for the merely economic harm he causes to a non-contractor, even if, as Robin Cooke says in a slightly different context, 'to attempt to define in advance what will be sufficiently special would be a contradiction in terms.'

Europe might give us a hint on another matter which has been much ventilated today—the relation

---

[4] *D'Urso* v. *Ercole Martelli* [1992] I.R.L.R. 136 (E.C.J.), and see H. McLean [1993] Camb. L.J. 214.

[5] Shakespeare, *Troilus and Cressida*, III. 3, 165.

[6] It is therefore perplexing that our law reviews contain increasing numbers of comments on decisions and events from the old Commonwealth. It may be because of the gratifying but very marked increase of law teachers from those places.

[7] Indeed, the French have not yet implemented the Directive, five years after the final date, and have been sued for it.

[8] Germany is able to deal with the *Hedley Byrne* situation in

terms of contract, since lack of consideration is no problem, and anyway they have the 'relationship equivalent to contract' which is perfectly reflected by those very words in the speech of Lord Devlin in *Hedley Byrne*.

[9] See *C.N.R.* v. *Norsk Pacific Steamship Co.* 91 D.L.R. 4th 289, 320–3 (1992).

[10] But the 'something special' must be between plaintiff and defendant, not between plaintiff and third party, as in *Norsk*. After all, we do not give the parents of an injured child a claim in their own right for wages lost in looking after the victim.

between judge and legislator.[11] Portalis was quite clear on their respective roles: it was for the legislator to lay down general principles and for the judge to fill in the detail in application. To go by today's discussion, we have got it marvellously bassackwards. Bob Hepple says 'it is for the courts to formulate general common law principles, and then to leave it to Parliament to limit or reverse those principles on grounds of policy or good administration.' Instead of thanking Parliament for the Occupiers Liability Acts, Robin Cooke blames the judges for the vacillation which rendered them necessary. Those Acts may not be apostolic, but they are surely not anathema. He also believes that 'rationalisation and leadership in matters of principle' is the task of the House of Lords and deprecates what I most admire, viz. that 'Great generalisations are made, receive some lip service, and are then quietly ignored in the practical business of judgment.' This is exactly as it should be. People need an outing every now and again, trumpets, *Land of Hope and Glory* and so on, perhaps even a Lord Chancellor's breakfast, and then back to business as usual, the knotty nitty-gritty.[12] Principle is an indulgence, leading to victories of that purely moral variety so familiar to England in the sports arena.

Today there has been much talk of the two-stage test of duty, perhaps most illuminatingly from Robert Goff, who said that he believed other judges were like him in asking both 'Why?' and 'Why not?'. He suggested that too much can be made of the *Anns* approach, but Alan Rodger was surely right to say that in fact the *Anns* test was taken to be taking the answer to the first stage for granted whenever the harm was just what you would expect. We had no mention of the alarming views of Lord Scarman and Lord Bridge in *McLoughlin* v. *O'Brian*,[13] that matters of policy were not for the judiciary at all, thereby reducing the number of stages from two to one, and

that one virtually taken for granted. To this we must surely prefer the 'incrementalism' now endorsed: even in doing a jig-saw—where, after all, unlike law, there is a pre-existing Grand Design and Whole Picture—you put in only the next piece, and then only if it fits (as *Anns* most certainly did not, imposing liability for mere failure to guard a stranger from a bad bargain). *Pedetemptim* is Lucretius's good description of the way to proceed, one step at a time, testing the ground—much better than adopting a principle and thereby committing oneself to all its unseen and possibly disgratifying implications.

As Jane Stapleton indicates, one can learn from the U.S.A., where quite often the courts have, in the name of principle lightly assumed and then devoutly believed, gone too far—much too far—so that the unruly horse had to be reined in by the legislature. A good instance is the problem of the social host: if you unreasonably make someone drunk do you have to pay his victims? The Supreme Court of California[14] held that if you gave too good a party you had to pay the unfortunates your drunken guest ran over on the way home: the better the party the greater the liability.[15] The politicians (of both parties) were understandably unkeen on this, since the better the party, the better the chance of election. So they passed an Act reversing this doctrine,[16] and it fell to the Supreme Court to decide whether this Act were constitutional: reluctantly so held.[17] More familiar, perhaps, is the case of the Good Samaritan, the doctor who stops to help the highway victim in the ditch. Of course the victim's lawyer sued the doctor just to show his gratitude and advance the cause of principle without exception; the courts acceded and the legislatures had to intervene, starting in California.[18]

This is not really a proper method of proceeding. Lord Wilberforce himself, whose daemon has hovered over this meeting to an extraordinary extent,[19]

---

[11] Much was said about *Anns* and the Defective Premises Act 1972. I have a mild personal interest in the matter. Before the hearing in the House of Lords, where he led for the appellant, Keith Goodfellow sought my views. When I suggested he should argue that there was no need for development at common law since the legislature had dealt with the problem in issue he said 'I'm afraid that's an argument I cannot make.' I never understood why he couldn't make it.

[12] Never has there been such a judicial jamboree as *Hedley Byrne*, [1964] A.C. 465, where one almost has the feeling that their Lordships had been on a trip to Mount Olympus and perhaps smoked a joint on the bus. *Something* certainly went to their heads, presumably not the merits of the claim, which they dismissed.

[13] [1983] 1 A.C. 410 (a decision I was astonished to hear mentioned with approbation).

[14] Which has had to backtrack, in *Thing* v. *La Chusa* 771 P.2d 814 (1989) from its extensive views about liability for nervous shock in *Dillon* v. *Legg* 441 P.2d 912 (1968), much praised in *McLoughlin*.

[15] *Coulter* v. *Superior Court* 577 P.2d 669 (1978), 'relying on

traditional common law negligence principles' as the court said in the later case.

[16] And doing it in a most peculiar way, by ordaining that it is not the provision of drink which is the proximate cause of injuries inflicted by a drunk but rather its consumption: 1978 amendments to s. 1714 Civil Code.

[17] *Cory* v. *Shierloh* 629 P.2d 8 (1981). The facts (the first problem I set my freshmen), have not yet reached the courts in England. I expect that, in Jane Stapleton's terms, English courts would not leap-frog the drunken motorist so as to reach the publican or feckless friend, and rightly so. But the question might well be raised by the drunk driver's insurer, invoking that horrid Contribution Act, so beloved of equity lawyers.

[18] 3 Harper, James & Gray, The Law of Torts 718–19 (1986).

[19] Given that not only *Anns* but also *McGhee* has had to be dismantled, that *Baker* v. *Willoughby* [1970] A.C. 467 narrowly escaped overruling, that *Goldman* v. *Hargrave* [1967] 1 A.C. 645 has, predictably, led to the injustice of *Leakey* [1980] Q.B. 485; it is only a wonder that *Dorset Yacht* [1970] A.C. 467, which I am glad to see from Robin Cooke's paper is now doubted, was decided in his absence.

implied as much in reversing a decision in which Lord Denning had held that the owner of a car was liable for bad driving by anyone permitted to use it or in whose use the owner had an interest. Lord Wilberforce was ready to allow that 'some adaptation of the common rules to meet these new problems of degree' might be possible, but declined to effect any such adaptation because 'Any new direction, and it may be one of many alternatives, must be set by Parliament.'[20] This is quite in line with the views of Lord Bridge (rather deprecated by Robin Cooke) when he said 'that as a matter of social policy this might be entirely admirable, but that as a matter of legal principle he could discover no basis on which it was open to the court to embody this policy in the law without the assistance of the legislature.'[21]

Now it is true that the creative activity of judges is constrained by the peculiarity that the judicial vocabulary is extremely limited: they have very few terms, concepts and categories at their disposal. Not only can the courts not lay down, for example, a rule that something is valid if in writing but otherwise not, much less fix a definite time-within-which, but they cannot even lay down a rule applicable to motor-vehicles and not other chattels, nor one (*pace* Robin Cooke) applicable to dwellings and not to commercial premises. The legislator, by contrast, has a very fat dictionary (up to and including 'immobilisation device') and doubtless a thesaurus as well, so it can prescribe in adequate appropriate and adjusted detail. But this does not at all mean that courts must fumble for the sort of simple principle you find in fortune-cookies or do in poker-work and place above the mantle, such as *neminem laedere* or *pacta sunt servanda*, both of which seem to have mesmerised the Court of Appeal in recent cases.[22] Since it is certain that more and more cases will turn on legislation, including foreign legislation more principled than we are used to, this talk of judicial law-making being important or essential seems to me a bit like whistling in the gloaming.

Even if this were not so, one might apply the saying 'by their fruits shall ye know them' and test these principles not in the echo-chamber of the class-room but in actual practice. In *D. & F. Estates*, for example, the plaintiffs, who, as it appeared, had got their Lon-

don flat gratuitously from a property company in which they were interested, and were now living in the South of France, were complaining that the plaster was starting to fall off the walls to the risk of their persons (!) only fifteen years after the flat was completed. The trial judge awarded them a sum of over £89,000 plus interest. The principle which led to this was surely ripe for lopping. *Acrecrest* v. *Hattrell*[23] is another case to test the allegiance of the proponents of principle. Admittedly negligent architects, having settled with the developer who had retained them, claimed contribution from the local authority, i.e. the ratepayers. In allowing the claim for 25% of the payout, Lord Donaldson realised that it would be odd to make the local authority indemnify the architects for the consequences of their own negligence, but did not think it odd that it should indemnify the developer for the consequences of his architects' negligence, and held that the local authority must therefore make payment to the negligent architects. Huh! In *Murphy* itself,[24] if we dare to look at the facts, cracks appeared in the house eleven years after the nominal plaintiff bought it, and he sold it five years later for a sum which, when added to what he got from his insurance company, amounted to the full value of the house had it been in good condition. The buyer, a builder, undertook no repairs and was still living in it at the time of the trial, although the courts, knowing better than the builder, were satisfied that the house had been an 'imminent risk' to the health of the occupants, and gave judgment for the plaintiff until the House of Lords was reached.

I am delighted that all three of these cases have been overruled or reversed. If such decisions result from principle, we would be better without it, though teaching and learning the law may be a mite more difficult. I am reminded of a story of Lord Rutherford. An assistant came to him in the laboratory one day with a very long face, and said 'Sir, I'm afraid that we have run out of money.' 'Oh dear' said Rutherford, 'then we'll just have to *think*, won't we?'

There is another side to the dialectic between principle and practice. The aim of the law may well be to meet people's reasonable expectations, but its most urgent duty is to make it possible for lawyers to give clear advice to their clients; it is much less important

---

[20] *Morgans* v. *Launchbury* [1973] A.C. 127, 136–7. He also said this ... 'Liability and insurance are so intermixed that judicially to alter the basis of liability without adequate knowledge (which we have not the means to obtain) as to the impact this might make on the insurance system would be dangerous and, in my opinion, irresponsible.' This theme was ventilated at the meeting, in particular as regards Jane Stapleton's view that, whereas a plaintiff's ability to obtain protection from elsewhere might be a factor militating against imposing liability on someone else, this did not apply to the plaintiff's being able to obtain (first-party) insurance or actually having it. Note that in

both *Dorset Yacht* and *Murphy* the claim on public funds was brought by an insurance company, paid to take the risk of which it was complaining. Another instance of the deplorable effect of equity on the law of tort.

[21] *D. & F. Estates* v. *Church Comm'rs.* [1989] A.C. 177, 209.

[22] *Cambridge Water Co.* v. *Eastern Counties Leather*; *Williams* v. *Roffey Bros.* [1990] 1 All E.R. 512, where the Court not only condoned but actually rewarded sloppy and dilatory workmanship of the kind for which the country is renowned.

[23] [1983] Q.B. 260.

[24] [1991] 1 A.C. 398.

whether or not they can set such advice in a larger justificatory context, as a teacher might like to be able to do. Alan Rodger makes the point in connection with dwellings: 'if pragmatism extends this far, then advising clients is going to be difficult indeed.' Throughout the day we have sensed assumptions (heard assumptions are strong, but those unheard are stronger) that results are easier to predict if courts operate on principle rather than by 'pockets' of facts. I don't believe this to be at all true. A French lawyer who advised on the basis of the text of the very general principle of art. 1382 Code civil without adverting to the pockets into which the courts have discerpted it would be very negligent indeed (though his liability would be contractual only).

Jane Stapleton seems more concerned with providing consolation after the event than advice about how to avoid it: the law should be such that one can 'provide the disappointed plaintiffs with explanations for their fate which are more convincing than the simple assertion that it was not just and reasonable to help them.' I leave aside the point that it seems quite fair to tell a disappointed plaintiff that his expectations were objectively unreasonable and that the function of the law is to meet only reasonable expectations. I note simply that like doctors, lawyers tend to spend more time with their clients before the fatal event than after it: application comes before explication. From this point of view the decision of the Court of Appeal in the *Hillsborough* cases[25] was superior to that of the House of Lords.[26] The Court of Appeal would allow claims by shocked victims (not otherwise implicated in the affair) only if they were spouse or parent of the party primarily endangered. For the solicitor, this is just dandy: when the client comes in all jittering with the hee-bie-jeebies, the solicitor asks for the marriage lines or the certificate of m/paternity and then says either 'Well, I think we have a case here' or 'Gosh, I'm really sorry, but the thing is that with the law as it is at present there isn't anything we can do.' Now Jane Stapleton apparently regards paternity and matrimony as 'meaningless boundaries', and that this is 'just line-drawing', though what is wrong with just line-drawing, or even slightly unjust line-drawing, when a line has to be drawn somewhere, is quite beyond me.[27] Her refusal to compromise on this issue leads her to throw in the sponge or throw out the water, baby and all. I think this a pity, especially

as Parliament has decided, I suppose deliberately, that the only persons who can claim bereavement damages are parent and spouse.[28] Is there anything wrong with such a rule? It is arbitrary, of course (from *arbiter* = a judge), but not irrational: the present status of the family in Britain may well be such that one is, at best, indifferent to the fate of one's spouse or kids, but most people do, I believe, think that among chosen and unchosen relationships, these are really the most important, even if only in a 'these you have loved' sense, and the law should not be castigated for reflecting this fact. If perfection is unattainable, we should not let the unattainable best be the enemy of the attainable good.

We have heard much praise of the judgment in the *Norsk* case in Canada.[29] To me it seems to be an outstanding example of exactly what courts should *not* be doing. It is fortunate that there are, or were, so many trees in that ex-dominion, for otherwise one might wonder at spending over 100 pages on futile exercises in comparative law and juvenile law-and-economics. On internal evidence I would suppose that Canadian judges have research assistants/law clerks, and that bilingualism is limited to the franco-phone. What is quite clear is that no practitioner is aided in the slightest by these contradictory disquisitions, more suitable to a law review—if one could get them published—than the law reports. If, as Robin Cooke suggests, decisions like this make Canada a leader, I have to say that the lead is one without a master at one end or a dog at the other. We look to the courts for advice, or the basis for giving advice, and here abstraction, principle is not at all helpful: nor, actually, is the identification of various policy considerations working one way or another: what the practitioner needs (I suppose) is to be told that cases with these characteristics go one way, cases with other features in another. There will be borderline cases, of course, but I do not suppose that the advising of commercial clients was rendered any easier when the Court of Appeal in *Hong Kong Fir*[30] decided that the question, when considering whether a contractor had the right to 'sail away' on the other party's breach, depended not on whether the term broken was a condition or a warranty but on whether the consequences of the breach were such as to deprive the innocent party of virtually the whole benefit of the transaction.

The lawyer's (and hence the client's) difficulty

---

[25] *Jones* v. *Wright* [1991] 3 Al E.R. 88.
[26] *Alcock* v. *Chief Constable* [1992] 1 A.C. 310.
[27] Of course one should draw only lines one can *hold*. Before *McLoughlin* the shocked victim had to be *there*. *McLoughlin* substituted *nearly there*, and in *Alcock* Lord Oliver was right to doubt the wisdom of this. If 'immediate

aftermath' is a bad line to hold, the same is true of 'immediate vicinity', applied in *Dorset Yacht* and rightly dissented from as impractical by Viscount Dilhorne.
[28] Now Fatal Accidents Act 1976, s. 1A (2).
[29] 91 D.L.R. (4th) 289 (1992).
[30] [1962] 2 Q.B. 26.

may be seen in a Scottish case very like *Norsk*, namely *Wimpey Construction* v. *Martin Black*.[31] A vast engineering project in the Firth of Forth depended on the functioning of a crane-barge. One member of the consortium of which Wimpey was a lead member hired the barge and got the slings supplied by the defender. A sling snapped one day when one of Wimpey's concrete beams was being lifted; the barge was destroyed by the strain, and the three months delay to the work cost Wimpey a huge sum of money. Lord Maxwell sensibly gave judgment for the defender, the sling-manufacturer, but then *Junior Books* hit the breakfast table.[32] The pursuer proposed to appeal. The defender settled for £1m. This was wrong as well as costly, yet in the muddy wake of *Junior Books* quite reasonable. The House of Lords in that case did not make life any easier for lawyers or their clients.

Morality surfaced in the papers and discussion more than economics. I am glad of this, since it is much the more interesting of the two. If you doubt it, just consider what a symposium such as today's would have been like in the United States. Robin Cooke says that if most everyone would feel that the defendant should pay, then pay he must; but in the absence of any such general feeling, then there should be a discussion and then a decision about whether he should pay or not, taking into account loss-spreading, insurance and so on. I have no quarrel with that, really, especially as I believe that there would no general agreement that the Tillmans, sojourning in Provence, should get nearly £100K because the plaster on the walls of their free flat in London is falling off after fifteen years; or that ratepayers should compensate the developer's architects for carelessly reducing his profits from blotting the landscape; or that Brentwood should indemnify Norwich Union Insurance Co., or whatever it is called, presenting itself in the mask of Murphy, who is off rejoicing elsewhere with compensation already received.

Now this view of Robin Cooke's leads inevitably to incrementalism, because the general morality (except in the U.S.A., where it changes overnight, depending on the weather or the television) moves rather slowly. Daily commuters to Damascus do not frequently have blinding visions. Needless to say, I do not disapprove of the gradualness implicit in such an approach. In this connection, however, it should not

be forgotten that the law not only meets expectations, if reasonable, but also engenders them, and should see to it that the expectations it engenders are also reasonable. I take two examples. First, until 1982, the law used to be that the bereaved parent could claim nothing for the loss of the infant child negligently killed.[33] Then bereavement damages were introduced at £3,500. Parents were outraged to be offered so little in lieu of nothing. Defendants were constrained to pay more than the fixed sum ordained by statute. The Lord Chancellor had the sum raised to £7,500.[34] Still not enough. Claimants demand more, and get more, more than the defendants know they need pay. There is no satisfaction here. German law gives nothing. What Germans expect, I don't know. Second example, time-bar. Until the implications of *Hedley Byrne* were recognised, the victims of professional negligence with only economic consequences lost their claim once six years had expired from the defendant's last breach of contract. This, of course, could be well before they knew they had any claim at all, well before any damage had manifested itself. Comes *Hedley Byrne* and the realisation of its supposed implications. Now the architect is guilty of a *tort* (Shriek!!) as well as a breach of contract, though he hasn't done anything different or extra or worse than before. This being now a tort, time does not start to run till the damage occurs. But suppose the plaintiff didn't know that the damage had occurred, couldn't know? Is his claim to be barred, poor pet, because he couldn't know he had one? Outrage!!! The courts did their best to bring the date of the damage forward, so that the old law wasn't wholly sidelined[35] but the legislature moved in, wetly, so as to delay the starting point of limitation in these cases which are for the most part fake-tort, real-contract cases.

With this qualification, I do not at all dissent from Jane Stapleton's view that tort has 'a symbolic role in vindicating certain values in society', as 'applied morality.' As she herself says in relation to contribution claims between tortfeasors, the law must make a ranking between claims, which must mean a ranking between kinds of damage, *inter alia*. So it should. So it does. Lord Oliver makes the point with characteristic clarity, that the causing of physical damage universally requires justification, while the causing of merely economic harm does not. The reason is not far to seek, unless one looks in the books. It is that

---

[31] 1982 S.L.T. 239.

[32] [1983] 1 A.C. 520.

[33] Fatal Accidents Act 1976, s. 1A, introduced by Administration of Justice Act 1982. Previously, of course, at any rate after 1934, the child could rise from the grave and claim a sum for having been killed, which would ineluctably go to the parents. In Scotland children as well as parents and spouses can

claim for grief, no amounts being fixed: Damages (Scotland) Act 1993.

[34] Damages for Bereavement (Variation of Sum) Order, S.I. 1990, no. 2575.

[35] *Pirelli* [1982] 2 A.C. 1; *Bell* v. *Peter Browne* [1990] 2 Q.B. 495. This is another area where concern has focussed on plaintiffs' interests and ignored those of defendants.

money is less important than other things, that is, *things*, and *a fortiori* people, neither of which should be regarded solely, or even mainly, as units of active or passive consumption and production. Perhaps it is because the point is so obvious that it is not often mentioned, but—to take but one example—we are inured to the government's taking money away from us in the form of tax, if not fine, but only rarely does the government confiscate our property (with compensation), and it is really quite strongly disinclined to chop off our hands or other parts.

In connection with this prioritisation, as some people might be tempted to call it, I draw attention to a serious blot on our present law of negligence, namely, the practice of making the health service pay the parents of an unwanted but healthy child resulting from failed sterilisation and continued sexual congress.[36] Jane Stapleton mentions that the immorality of a plaintiff's conduct may lead to the dismissal of his claim.[37] So it should. So also should the immoral greed of the plaintiff's claim, even if his conduct is irreprehensible.

After morality, of course we come to reason. There was little risk of our passing the day without hearing of the 'rational development of the law'. Bob Hepple used the phrase. It doesn't mean nothing, but it doesn't mean much. Alan Rodger tells us that *Junior Books* was effectively decided by Ken Livingstone, the newt-keeping politico. And I remind you that had Bognor Regis U.D.C. either been insured by the late lamented Municipal Mutual or been less noxious in the eyes of other local authorities, *Dutton*'s case[38] would have been appealed to the House of Lords and quickly aborted (I say that with the confidence of one whose assertion cannot be disproved). Is it rational development that *Hedley Byrne* (which, I must recall, was a case of an advertising agent complaining about misrepresentation—from their roots shall ye know them also) should have the effect that architects and solicitors are liable for damage which occurs umpty years after their last act of negligence?

Let us not pay ourselves with words; as Hobbes tells us, they are the wise man's counters but the money of fools. The development of the law is not rational, except in the most superficial way. It reacts as best it can to the chaotic and unpredictable anfrac-

tuosities of life, lurching and staggering to maintain its balance in the wake of social, political and economic disturbances of one kind or another and in the face of the individual personal problems which come—also quite unpredictably—before the courts. A thin gloss of rationality comes in at two points. First, before the decision, in the terms and tenor of the advocate's argument. Alan Rodger rightly says 'The importance of the standard of formal reasoning in determining the fate of issues of substance should not be underestimated.' No, indeed, for it led to *Acrecrest* v. *Hattrell*.[39] Progress in the wrong direction is likely to lead you far afield. Judges, we are told, are not bound by the arguments they diligently listen to, for Lord Wilberforce once said: 'Judges are more than mere selectors between rival views: they are entitled to and do think for themselves.'[40] But the fact that he had to say so is significant.

Secondly, rationality, or rather rationalisation, comes in also once the decision has been rendered, for then it is grist for the academic mill, and it is the function of the academic to incorporate it into his theory or spew it out as an abomination if it fit not. Much of today's irritation seems to me to come from the difficulty of rationalising recent decisions. Well, it doesn't matter if one can't, so long as people know where they stand. Thus I wholly approve of the view of the Court of Appeal that *if* the claim by the legatee bereft of his legacy through the negligence of the solicitor retained by the testator is to be allowed, it may be allowed even if it cannot be fitted in with other types of case.[41] If the academics cannot make it fit, *tant pis*. If you haven't got a pocket, use a sporran.

The legal scholar is rather like the historian. We have heard plangent complaints today that the scholar in the study cannot get at the real reasons which actuate the judge in making his decision. Since, as we have seen, the giving of reasons is no basis for prediction of future results, there must be some other reason why academics want the 'true' reasons, perhaps to save themselves the problem of the historian in determining what Bismarck or Lenin 'really' meant, as if there were a pattern into which it might be fitted if only one could come to the psychological or intellectual or REAL reasons. Well, in my

---

[36] *Emeh* v. *Kensington A.H.H.* [1985] Q.B. 1012, an unreserved opinion (!), taken as conclusive where the child is healthy, in *Gold* v. *Haringey H.A.* [1988] Q.B. 481.

[37] I am sorry that in *Tinsley* v. *Milligan* [1993] 3 All E.R. 65 the House of Lords has upheld the majority of the Court of Appeal, holding that a person who had effected a legal transfer of property in order to defraud the state was permitted to recover it on *equitable* grounds. The iniquitous and dysfunctional role of equity in the law of tort (subrogation, contribution) ought to be stressed whenever there is talk of fusion.

Equity just *loves* money, possibly because it never deals with anything important such as personal injury—it is like Mrs. Bourhill, and rather faints at the sight of blood. As to property, it disclaims interest in goods and has managed magnificently to etiolate land into a series of abstractions.

[38] [1972] 1 Q.B. 373.
[39] [1983] 2 Q.B. 260.
[40] *Saif Ali* v. *Sydney Mitchell* [1978] 3 All E.R. 1033.
[41] *White* v. *Jones* [1993] 3 All E.R. 481.

view the legal scholar must make the best of it. He is the least significant member of the legal corps (not wholly insignificant, since he has time to think, if he has the capacity): he writes up the battle once it is over, providing only doubtful help for the next one.

Finally, the condition of the law of tort. Robin Cooke describes it as 'debilitated', but detects signs (in restitution, that South Sea Bubble of the Nineties) of a 'renewal of progress'. Jane Stapleton sees the present 'ludicrous' situation as to nervous shock as 'bringing the law into disrepute'. More alarmingly, she speaks of a 'current wave of anxiety'. Anxiety is fear without an object. I am not myself washed by this wave of anxiety. Nor, I apprehend, is Alan Rodger, who thinks things are better than they were. Nor are those who wrote the report for the Likierman Committee on Professional Liability so far as professionals in the construction business are concerned: they refrained from proposing radical law reform because 'judge-made law is more settled than in the past two decades.'[42] The reports were in before *Caparo*,[43] or the auditors would have expressed themselves likewise.

But whether we think it good or bad, better or worse than it was, let us stand back a little, and remember that having problems isn't a problem in itself. The condition of the law of tort isn't as bad as, say, criminal procedure: after all, no one complains very loudly when a civil defendant is held unjustly liable in damages, or when the prosecution fails to obtain a proper conviction. But the question is what you can expect. Robin Cooke quotes Lord Uthwatt, saying that the law is there to meet people's reasonable expectations.[44] So be it. But we should have only reasonable expectations of the law. After all, it is made, manned and manipulated by people, *nos semblables, nos frères*. We should remember that the leading human characteristic is to err. Those who man the law have to use words, which slip and slide and slither, and if they deploy policies, they are inevitably, whether made manifest or not, vague and nebulous and unagreed. And we expect them to be both sensible and intelligent, when sense and intelligence go hand in hand as rarely as the queen of spades and the jack of diamonds in bezique.

In this sublunary sphere we cannot wisely expect too much. I think that in this area we should be grateful for what we have, and not howl or moan and groan in a culture of complaint.

[42] Professional Liability: The Report of the Study Teams (H.M.S.O., 1989).

[43] [1990] 2 A.C. 605, as to which I cannot understand the doubts expressed as to its meaning during the discussion. Does it not decide that a company's auditor reporting to shareholders is not liable to them if, in reliance on the report, they buy more shares and regret it?

[44] *Read* v. *Lyons* [1947] A.C. 156, 186.

PART III

INNOVATIONS IN CONTRACT

9. Innovations in Contract: An Australian Analysis

A.M. GLEESON*

I N recent years, in certain common law jurisdictions, the law relating to contracts has been affected by substantial change. At the risk of disturbing the previous level of certainty in the law, judges have set out to identify and develop principles capable of making the law more responsive to what they see as the requirements of justice. Whilst there is still a strong reluctance on the part of the courts to introduce the intricacies of trusts and fiduciary obligations into ordinary commercial transactions,[1] there has been an increasing willingness to invoke principles of equity to modify what has been regarded as the inflexibility of the common law. The concepts of unconscionability and unjust enrichment have been of central importance in this process.

This judicial activism has been taking place against a background of legislation which has made extensive changes to the law governing dealings in trade and commerce. The rise of consumerism has brought legislation, with effects extending well beyond the field of consumer protection, that has substantially altered the rights of contracting parties.

A striking feature of some recent case law has been an emphasis upon the formulation and application of general principles, which have displaced more specific rules and have overridden some particular precedents. Those principles have a good deal in common with what have been described as the 'overriding and super-eminent principles enunciated by civil codes'.[2] It may be that some of the judicial method currently at work in the High Court of Australia reflects civilian influences. It is also likely that another influence has been the tendency, in recent years, of Australian legislatures to lay down general norms of commercial behaviour. These have had a great deal of practical significance for the law of contract, and are regularly invoked by litigants. For example, for almost 20 years the *Trade Practices Act 1974 (Cth.)* has prohibited, and provided sanctions in the case of, misleading and deceptive conduct in trade or commerce. More recently it has prohibited unconscionable conduct. This legislation will be referred to in more detail below.

There are two different levels at which these general principles, or general standards of behaviour, operate.

The first level relates to the work of the High Court, as an ultimate appellate court, in developing the common law for Australia. In *Dietrich* v. *The Queen*[3], Brennan, J. referred to the role of the High Court in creating new rules of common law. His Honour spoke of moulding the law to correspond with the contemporary values of society. Legislation of the kind mentioned above is an expression of such contemporary values, and this is why it is likely to have some influence on judicial law-making. However, there is a distinction between the High Court, on the one hand, and first instance courts and intermediate courts of appeal, on the other hand, which are constrained by precedent. The use of general principle by an ultimate court of appeal, to modify existing rules and, on occasion, to replace a number of particular rules with one that is more general and perhaps more flexible, is in line with the way the common law has grown over time.

At another level, however, the change is more radical. When, either as a result of a change of law made by the High Court, or as a result of legislation, there is established a general standard, such as unconscionability, which is to be applied by first instance courts and intermediate courts of appeal, to conduct relating to contracts, then there must come about a substantial alteration in the extent to which the law is certain, and the outcome of cases predictable. This is in aid of what is seen as greater flexibility and a form of justice more responsive to the needs of the individual case.

One of the virtues of the common law's reliance upon precedent, and upon relatively specific rules, has been that, generally speaking, people do not have to go to court to ascertain their rights and obligations. By reason of the trends mentioned above, and to be examined in this paper, there has been a significant alteration in the balance previously struck between the requirements of certainty and of individual justice.

---

* Chief Justice of New South Wales.
[1] cf. *Hospital Products Ltd.* v. *United States Surgical Corporation* (1984–1985) 156 C.L.R. 41 at 97, *Liggett* v. *Kensington* [1993] 1 N.Z.L.R. 257 at 267, *Neste Oy* v. *Lloyd's Bank P.L.C.* [1983] 2 Lloyd's Rep. 658 at 665.

[2] Gutteridge, *Comparative Law—An Introduction to the Comparative Method of Legal Study and Research*, 2nd ed., 1949, p. 94.
[3] (1992) 67 A.L.J.R. 1 at 13–14.

Common Law—Unconsionability and Estoppel

During the last ten years the High Court of Australia has delivered a number of challenging decisions concerning the law of contract. Whether the challenge is to orthodoxy, or merely to uncritical formalism, may be a matter of opinion. What is notable, however, is the juristic basis upon which the decisions rest. It is equity's jurisdiction to grant relief against unconscientious conduct; a refusal to permit a party to insist upon strict legal rights that would otherwise exist under, or in relation to a matter concerning, a contract.[4]

The risks involved have been acknowledged. Lord Radcliffe's warning against using equity to adjust contracts between competent persons when they have shown a rough edge to one side or the other[5] has been noted.[6] The danger of equating unconscionability with idiosyncratic notions of unfairness has been stressed.[7] Much effort has been directed to answering criticisms that the High Court has embarked upon the destruction of basic principles of contract law.[8]

An examination of these decisions may usefully commence with a case that, in its actual result, could be explained as an example of an incremental approach to legal development, but which was decided by reference to principles with wider implications. It is the operation of those principles in other contexts that will be of greater interest, but this case contains both a clear statement of the principles and an illustration of an aspect of them which is of concern, that is to say, their capacity to produce differences of judicial opinion as to their practical application.

Stern v. *McArthur*[9] was a case about relief against forfeiture under a terms contract for the sale of vacant land. The purchase price was payable in instalments over several years. The purchasers went into possession immediately and, with the vendors' knowledge, built a house on the land. Some years later they defaulted in the payment of instalments and, after showing a deal of patience, the vendors terminated the contract, offering to refund to the purchasers the value of the improvements. By majority (Deane, Dawson and Gaudron, J. J., Mason, C. J. and Brennan, J. dissenting), the High Court decided that

the purchasers were entitled to relief against forfeiture of their interest in the land. The majority regarded the transaction as one in which, in substance, the purchasers were borrowers from the vendor, the form of the contract being chosen to achieve the commercial object of securing a loan. They considered that the case was analogous to that of a mortgage. In those circumstances, insistence by the vendors upon their strict legal rights was unconsionable. Deane and Dawson, J. J. identified the basis of relief as follows:

'The general underlying notion is that which has long been identified as underlying much of equity's traditional jurisdiction to grant relief against unconscientious conduct, namely, that a person should not be permitted to use or insist upon his legal rights to take advantage of another's special vulnerability or misadventure for the unjust enrichment of himself'.[10]

They regarded the case as falling within the first of the two heads of jurisdiction to grant relief against forfeiture identified by Lord Wilberforce in *Shiloh Spinners Ltd.* v. *Harding*,[11] that is to say, where the object of the transaction and the granting of the right to forfeit is essentially to secure the payment of money.

The division in the Court exemplifies a practical difficulty with the notion of unconscionability. One particular aspect of the case that was regarded by the majority as involving unconscionability in the forfeiture of the purchasers' interest (or unjust enrichment of the vendors) was that, over the years since the contract was entered into, the value of the land had increased substantially. The minority saw nothing unjust in this increase in value resulting in a benefit to the vendors. They accepted that, as the High Court had earlier decided in *Legione* v. *Hateley*,[12] equity would relieve against an unconscionable exercise of legal rights where what was involved was the rescission of a contract for the sale and purchase of land. However, they insisted that it would only be in exceptional circumstances that such relief would be granted; to hold otherwise *'would be to eviscerate unconscionabilty of its meaning'*.[13] Such circumstances would have to be found in conduct of the vendor which caused or contributed to the alleged unconscionability. Mason, C. J.[14] denied that the

---

[4] It has been observed that, in Australia, the concept of unconscionable conduct has captured the legal imagination—P. D. Finn, *Equity, Commerce & Remedy*, N.Z. Law Society Conference, Auckland, Jan. 1993. For a discussion of similar developments in New Zealand see D. W. McLaughlan, *The 'New' Law of Contract in New Zealand* [1992] N.Z. Recent Law Review 436.

[5] *Campbell Discount Co. Ltd.* v. *Bridge* [1962] A.C. 600 at 626.

[6] *Stern* v. *McArthur* (1988) 165 C.L.R. 489 at 514 per Brennan, J.

[7] e.g. *The Commonwealth* v. *Verwayen* (1990) 170 C.L.R. 394 at 443 per Deane, J.

[8] At 439–40 per Deane, J.

[9] (1988) 165 C.L.R. 489.

[10] (1988) 165 C.L.R. at 526–7.

[11] [1973] A.C. at 722.

[12] (1983) 152 C.L.R. 406.

[13] (1985) 165 C.L.R. at 503 per Mason, C. J.

[14] Ibid.

jurisdiction to grant relief against forfeiture authorised a court to reshape contractual relations into a form the court thinks more reasonable or fair where subsequent events have rendered one side's situation more favourable. Brennan, J.[15] observed that the concept of unconscionability is not a charter for judicial reformation of contracts and that it is not to be regarded as synonymous with the judge's sense of what is fair between the parties. He identified as the essence of the unconscionability, founding relief against forfeiture in such a case, the insistence upon a stipulation which was merely designed to secure performance of a purchaser's covenants, where relief could be granted to the purchaser upon terms which would achieve the same result. Here there was no reliance on any such stipulation. Rather, there was reliance upon a right of rescission which the general law gave in the event of repudiation of the contract.

The division within the Court as to the reach of the concept of unconscionability, in the context of relief against forfeiture, is significant.[16] Of greater significance, however, is the use that has been made of that concept, and the disagreements as to its practical operation, in a series of decisions in which the principles of estoppel have been applied to resolve contractual disputes. Part of the significance lies in the potential for estoppel to undermine the doctrine of consideration.

The corollary of the rule that a promise made in consideration for an act or promise on the part of the promisee will be enforced is that a gratuitous promise will not be enforced. However, as Robert Goff, J. observed in *Amalgamated Investment & Property Co. Limited (in Liquidation)* v. *Texas Commerce International Bank Limited*,[17] the general principle that a purely gratuitous promise is unenforceable at law or in equity, and that neither law nor equity will perfect an imperfect gift, requires qualification by reference to the circumstances in which a court will conclude that conduct has given rise to an estoppel. His Lordship identified three such groups of cases and said that they all proceeded upon a common principle, which was that, despite the general rule, it would be unconscionable in the circumstances for a representor not to give effect to a representation. Because of those qualifications he

said that the proposition that no cause of action in contract could be created by an estoppel was too sweeping, and that the three groups of cases were cases where estoppels may be enforced despite infringement of the general rule earlier mentioned. (It was stressed that the list was not exhaustive.)

The tension between certain aspects of the rules relating to estoppel by representation and fundamental principles of the law of contract has long been recognised.

Holmes, J. in *Commonwealth* v. *Scituate Savings Bank*[18] said:

'It would cut up the doctrine of consideration by the roots, if a promisee could make a gratuitous promise binding by subsequently acting in reliance of it'.

The English solution to the problem, exemplified in *Jorden* v. *Money*[19] and *Maddison* v. *Alderson*,[20] involved confining the representations that could give rise to an estoppel and also limiting the use that could be made of an estoppel. Even as Lord Denning in developing the law of promissory estoppel was relaxing the first of these restrictions,[21] he was insisting upon the second.[22] As recently as 1981 the Australian edition of Cheshire and Fifoot's *Law of Contract* asserted that the doctrine of estoppel was restricted to representations of fact and did not extend to representations of future intention, and that estoppel was a rule of evidence which would not found a cause of action.[23] Thus was preserved the integrity of the doctrine of consideration. Equity's refusal to permit unconscientious departure from representations was limited to representations of fact, representations of future intention being left to be governed by the law of contract; and estoppel could be used as a shield but not as a sword,[24] (or, to take up another metaphor, as a minesweeper but not a capital unit[25]).

In the United States the law took a different course. In the *First Restatement of Contracts*, s. 90, in the form it took in 1932, it was stated:

'A promise which the promisor should reasonably expect to induce action or forbearance of a definite and substantial character on the part of the promisee and which does induce such action or forbearance is binding if injustice can be avoided only by enforcement of the promise'.[26]

---

[15] (1988) 165 C.L.R. at 514.
[16] The decision may be contrasted with that of the House of Lords in *Scandanavian Trading Tanker Co. A.B.* v. *Flota Petrolera Ecuatoriana* [1983] 2 A.C. 694 where it was held that the exercise of a withdrawal clause in a time charter did not attract the jurisdiction to relieve against forfeiture.
[17] (1982) 1 Q.B. 85 at 106.
[18] (1884) 137 Mass 301 at 302.
[19] (1854) 5 H.L. Cas. 185, 10 E.R. 868.
[20] (1883) 8 App. Cas. 467.
[21] *Central London Property Trust Ltd.* v. *High Trees House*

Ltd. (1947) K.B. 180.
[22] *Combe* v. *Combe* [1951] 2 K.B. 215.
[23] Fourth Edition p. 604.
[24] *New South Wales Rutile Mining* v. *Eagle Metal and Industrial Products* (1960) S.R. (N.S.W.) 495.
[25] Spencer Bower, *The Law Relating to Estoppel by Representation*, 1923, p. 12.
[26] In *Restatement (Second) of Contracts*, 1979, s. 90(1) it is stated as follows:
'A promise which the promisor should reasonably expect to induce action or forbearance on the part of the promisee or a

Here is a substantial intermingling of estoppel and contract. There is no reference to consideration; reliance is the key. Justice is secured, if necessary, by enforcing the promise. Note, however, the word *'promise'*, which is not a synonym for representation.

Recent developments in Australia concerning the principles of estoppel have, inevitably, involved the High Court in the need to address the relationship between those principles and the doctrine of consideration.

In a series of cases members of the High Court have expressed opinions about the law of estoppel which have involved significant developments of the position as it was previously understood in Australia. The principle cases involved are *Legione* v. *Hateley*,[27] *Waltons Stores (Interstate Ltd.)* v. *Maher*,[28] *Foran* v. *Wight*,[29] and *The Commonwealth of Australia* v. *Verwayen*.[30]

It is convenient to look in some detail at the latest of those cases, *Verwayen*. First, however, two points about the earlier cases should be mentioned. *Legione* v. *Hateley* was the first case in which the High Court expressly accepted the doctrine of promissory estoppel; it was a case where the parties were in a pre-existing contractual relationship. In *Waltons Stores* v. *Maher* a further step was taken. Promissory estoppel was invoked where the parties were merely intending to enter into future contractual relations. In *Verwayen* there was no question of either an existing or an intended contractual relationship; the parties were tortfeasor and victim. The court bound the tortfeasor to a representation of future intention which was made to the victim, and which concerned the conduct of litigation between them.

The issue in *Verwayen* was, from one point of view, simple. The plaintiff, whilst a member of the Royal Australian Navy, was injured in the Voyager disaster in 1964. At the time, the common law as it was understood in Australia precluded him from suing for damages, the prevailing view being that the Commonwealth did not owe to persons in his position a duty of care. The law in that respect was changed by the High Court, and in 1984 the plaintiff sued the Commonwealth for damages for negligence.

A number of others did the same. The Commonwealth Government announced, as a matter of general policy, that in relation to actions by survivors of the Voyager disaster it would admit liability, and would not plead the Statute of Limitations. After the plaintiff's proceedings had been on foot for a substantial time, but before they had come to trial, the Commonwealth reversed its policy and sought leave to amend its pleadings by raising, amongst other things, a defence under the Statute of Limitations. At first sight this might look like an application to be determined according to the ordinary principles relating to leave to amend pleadings. Indeed, after all that was said in the case about estoppel, the decision ultimately turned upon an issue very similar to that which determines, in an ordinary case, applications to amend pleadings. The court asked whether the plaintiff had, by reason of the conduct of the Commonwealth, suffered prejudice which could not adequately be compensated for by an order for costs. However, in coming to that point, there was a good deal said about the principles of estoppel, and the relationship of those principles to the doctrine of consideration. (Waiver also was in issue, but it is not material to this paper.)

There is no novelty about invoking estoppel to resolve issues concerning the conduct of litigation which, at another level, could be viewed as issues to be resolved by the exercise of the discretionary powers of a court in controlling proceedings before it. Defendants have been held to be estopped from pursuing claims to have actions dismissed for want of prosecution on the ground that they by their conduct induced a belief that the action would be allowed to proceed and the plaintiffs acted to their detriment by incurring further costs.[31] In such cases the matter is taken beyond the exercise of judicial discretion and into the area of binding legal consequence. However, there may then arise the very question that arose in *Verwayen*: can the estopped party *'buy out the estoppel'*[32] by reimbursing the costs thrown away? The latter became the critical question in *Verwayen*, but the way in which it was approached is interesting.

Mason, C. J. and Brennan, Deane and Dawson, J. J., concluded that the conduct of the Commonwealth,

---

third person and which does induce such action or forbearance is binding if injustice can be avoided only by enforcement of the promise. The remedy granted for breach may be limited as justice requires'.

A detailed examination of the development of United States doctrine in comparison with Australian doctrine appears in *Estoppel—Liability and Remedy* a paper delivered by Priestley, J. A. of the Court of Appeal of New South Wales in Victoria, British Columbia, January 1993, which appears in Waters (ed.), *Equity, Fiduciaries and Trusts* published by Carswall Thompson Professional Publishing Company, Scarsborough, Ontario, Canada.

[27] (1983) 152 C.L.R. 426.
[28] (1988) 164 C.L.R. 387.
[29] (1989) 168 C.L.R. 385.
[30] (1990) 170 C.L.R. 394.
[31] e.g. *County & District Properties Limited* v. *Lyall* [1991] 1 W.L.R. 683 (Note).
[32] The expression was used by Balcombe, L. J. in an unreported case decided on 4 December 1992, which raised just such a question: *Roche* v. *Church & Anor*, *The Times*, 23 December 1992.

in representing to the plaintiff that it would not rely on the limitation point, created an estoppel. They were, however, divided upon the manner in which the court should give effect to the estoppel. Mason, C. J. and Brennan, J. considered that the only remedy to which the plaintiff was entitled was an order for costs, or, to put the matter differently, they were of the view that, provided an appropriate order for costs to date was made in the plaintiff's favour, the Commonwealth was entitled to raise the limitation point. Deane, J. and Dawson, J., on the other hand, held that the Commonwealth was not entitled to rely on the limitation point or, to put the matter differently, they were of the view that the court should bind the Commonwealth to its representation that it would not rely upon that point. In other words, Deane, J. and Dawson, J. applied the estoppel to enforce what was in substance a gratuitous promise, whereas Mason, C. J. and Brennan, J. applied it to force the Commonwealth to compensate the plaintiff for what they regarded as the only detriment the plaintiff had suffered by reliance upon the representation, that is to say, costs.

It may be commented that a principle that can yield such different conclusions when applied to an uncomplicated set of facts requires scrutiny on that account alone.

All four agreed that where estoppel operates in order to prevent unconscionable conduct on the part of a person who, having made a representation to another who acts on the faith of it, seeks to resile, the appropriate remedy is to effect the minimum equity necessary to do justice. The remedy is not primarily designed to force the person to make good the representation, although, in some circumstances the minimum equity will not be satisfied by anything short of that.[33] This was the point of departure on the facts of the case.

It does not seem to have been doubted that, in principle, where someone has been induced to expend money on the faith of a representation, the resulting equity may, in appropriate circumstances, be satisfied by covering the expenditure. If the same problem were considered in terms of enforcing a promise, the difference would be between fulfilling the expectation (by an order for specific performance or expectation damages) and compensating for the reliance. The central problem of whether to satisfy an expectation or compensate for reliance is inherent in a principle which makes reliance, rather than con-

sideration, the critical factor. The difference can be of great importance, as the respective conclusions in *Verwayen* demonstrate. It is not that Deane and Dawson, J. J. took the view that one can never 'buy out' an estoppel. They simply considered that, on the facts, it could not be done in that case. One of the issues the High Court will have to address in the future is that of identifying the discrimen by which one is to distinguish between cases where reimbursement of expenditure will satisfy the requirements of equity and cases where it will not.

On the question of the nature of estoppel, Mason, C. J. took the broadest view. He referred to the labels that were applied in the past to various categories of estoppel, such as promissory estoppel, proprietary estoppel, estoppel by acquiescence, common law and equitable estoppel, estoppel by conduct and estoppel by representation. However, he said, these were all intended to serve the same fundamental purpose, that is to say, protection from the detriment which would flow from a party's change of position in certain circumstances.

Mason, C. J. pointed out that some of the distinctions which had been emphasised in previous cases, and in particular the distinctions between representations of law and representations of fact, or representations of fact and representations as to future conduct, were difficult to sustain in practice. The same point had been made by Oliver, J. in *Taylors Fashions Limited* v. *Liverpool Trustees Co. Limited*,[34] where his Lordship said that the line between representations of law and representations of fact is very narrow, and that in a sense most representations of law can be approached on the footing that, whatever the law may be, it is the existing intention of the party making the representation to treat the law as it is represented to be as the conventional basis for the particular transaction in mind.[35] Mason, C. J. said that there had been a strong trend towards an underlying unity in the various categories of estoppel, and that modern decisions pointed towards the emergence of one overarching doctrine of estoppel rather than a series of independent rules. This he described as estoppel by conduct. In this connection, it is interesting to recall the observation made by Scarman, L. J. in *Crabb* v. *Arun District Council*[36] following a discussion of the circumstances in which proprietary estoppel would be found. His Lordship observed that *'the plaintiff has to establish as a fact that the defendant, by setting up his right, is taking advantage of*

---

[33] (1990) 170 C.L.R. at 429.
[34] (1982) 1 Q.B. 133 at 151.
[35] The facts in *Walton* v. *Maher* provide a very good illustration of the same point. It is interesting to consider the ways in which the various judges who decided that case characterised

a representation by a solicitor in a conveyancing transaction that, although contracts had not been formally exchanged, the other party could safety proceed upon the basis that the solicitor's client would exchange contracts in due course.
[36] [1976] Ch. 179 at 195.

him in a way which is unconscionable, inequitable or unjust'. The trend in Australia is towards a general principle that if the setting up against the plaintiff of a right claimed by the defendant is unconscionable, then equity will afford a remedy.[37]

Mason, C.J. declared[38] that the decision in *Jorden* v. *Money* no longer represented the law in Australia. Promissory estoppel, he said, had undermined the idea that voluntary promises can never be enforced in the absence of consideration; the doctrine is not now confined to pre-existing contractual relationships (*Waltons* v. *Maher*) and there is now a recognition that the distinction between present and future fact is unsatisfactory and produces arbitrary results instead of serving any useful purpose.

One of the problems involved in enforcing representations as to future conduct must be emphasised. Although it is true to say that there is often only a semantic distinction involved, nevertheless there is in principle a substantial difference between a statement of present intention as to future conduct, and a promise. The former is sometimes accompanied by a clear indication that the latter is not involved, and would on that account not found an estoppel. However, the position is often less simple. Although the facts found in the case are a little unclear, all three Law Lords in *Jorden* v. Money appear to have agreed that when Mrs Jorden declared to Mr Money that she intended not to enforce her rights under the bond she was acting honestly and not misrepresenting her intention. The issue was whether she could be prevented from later changing her mind, in the absence of a binding contract. In expressing what he described as the central principle of the doctrine of estoppel by conduct, Deane, J. used terms that focus on the position of the representee rather than the representor.[39] What is prevented is an unconscionable departure by one party from an assumption that has been adopted by the other party in defined circumstances. One such circumstances involves an assumption induced by express or implied representation. However, the question of when a representation of present intention as to future conduct, as distinct from a promise, would reasonably induce an assumption as to future conduct is one that is, in practice, capable of giving rise to difficulty. If the question is considered in terms of the reasonable or legitimate expectations of the representee, why should not one start from the point that, as a general rule, people who have honestly stated their future intentions may change their intentions unless they have made a binding promise? After all, people often

have good reasons for changing their minds. Suppose, for example, that it had appeared in *Verwayen* that the Government changed its policy for compelling budgetary reasons. Would that have been relevant? When is it reasonable to give a statement of future intention the same force as a promise? This will be a fruitful source of disputation, and potential uncertainty, as these principles are worked out in lower courts. Departure from *Jorden* v. *Money* makes it necessary to face up to the question of deciding when it is just to hold a person to a representation that does not amount to a promise. It may be that, in practice, by reason of this kind of problem, the role of estoppel will continue to be more important in the area of modification of existing contractual rights than in the area of pre-contractual or extra-contractual communications.

The operation of unconscionability as a controlling factor or mechanism, and the question of what will be regarded as amounting to unconscionability, is also a point of potential uncertainty. The members of the High Court have been at pains to reject the notion that unconscionability is a concept of such breadth and flexibility that its employment is capable of overturning the fundamental principles of the law of contract and of creating uncertainty where there was previously reasonable certainty.

Brennan, J., in *Waltons Stores* v. *Maher*,[40] explained the essence of the principle in this way:

'It is essential to the existence of an equity created by estoppel that the party who induces the adoption of the assumption or expectation knows or intends that the party who adopts it will act or abstain from acting in reliance on the assumption or expectation . . . When the adoption of an assumption or expectation is induced by the making of a promise, the knowledge or intention that the assumption or expectation will be acted upon may be easily inferred. But if a party encourages another to adhere to an assumption or expectation already formed or acquiesces in the making of an assumption or the entertainment of an expectation when he ought to object to the assumption or expectation—steps which are tantamount to inducing the other to adopt the assumption or expectation—the inference of knowledge or intention that the assumption or expectation will be acted on may be more difficult to draw.

The unconscionable conduct which it is the object of equity to prevent is the failure of a party, who has induced the adoption of the assumption or expectation and who knew or intended that it would be relied on, to fulfil the assumption or expectation or otherwise to avoid the detriment which that failure would occasion. The object of the equity is not to compel the party bound to fulfil the assumption or expectation; it is to avoid the detriment

---

[37] This view had been expressed by Powell, J. at first instance in a case reported as *Silovi Pty. Ltd.* v. *Barbaro* (1988) 13 N.S.W.L.R. 416.

[38] (1990) 170 C.L.R. at 410.

[39] (1990) 170 C.L.R. at 444.

[40] (1988) 164 C.L.R. at 422–3.

which, if the assumption or expectation goes unfulfilled, will be suffered by the party who has been induced to act or to abstain from acting thereon'.

It has been suggested[41] that the general rule that the law will not enforce gratuitous promises is so well entrenched and widely understood that the proposition itself has a major bearing on the content of the concept of unconscionability in this context. The essence of the majority opinion in *Jorden* v. *Money* was that everybody knows, or ought to know, that the way to bind a person to a statement of future intention is to make a contract. That involves providing consideration. Encouraging or inducing a person to accept a certain assumption can, of course, be done by representations falling short of promises, but it can also, and often most effectively, be done by making a promise. It may be doubted whether, at least in the case of parties who are not legally represented, confidence can be placed in a general appreciation of the doctrine of consideration. In *Verwayen* the relevant representation was made to, and acted on, by the plaintiff's solicitor. However, if the law is developing to the stage where a promise seriously made and intended to be relied upon by the promisee can become a foundation of a cause of action, then there has indeed been a significant reshaping of the law relating to contractual obligations.

It was this problem that was addressed in detail by Deane, J. in *Verwayen*.

Deane, J. also assimilated promissory estoppel to a general, overarching, principle of estoppel by conduct. However, in explaining[42] why estoppel, especially of the kind earlier described as promissory estoppel, did not confound the doctrine of consideration, he returned to the theme of Lord Denning in *Combe* v. *Combe*; estoppel does not of itself constitute an independent cause of action. Whilst the assumed fact or state of affairs (present or future, legal or otherwise) which one party is estopped from denying may be relied upon defensively or aggressively, the nature of such reliance is limited by the nature of estoppel itself. Deane, J. gave a series of practical examples, some taken from earlier authorities, to demonstrate the differences between using estoppel in aid of a cause of action and attempting to use it as an independent cause of action.

The members of the High Court in *Verwayen* who relied upon estoppel to bring about the result that the Commonwealth was bound to its gratuitous statement that it would not raise the limitation point were at pains to explain that they were not treating

reliance and unconscionability as being, in every case, available substitutes for consideration. In that particular case it had that practical result. However, even accepting the existence of a general doctrine of estoppel by conduct of which promissory estoppel is one instance, they insisted on two qualifications, both seen as of importance in preserving the integrity of the doctrine of consideration: estoppel does not provide an independent cause of action; and the relief that will flow in a case of estoppel is governed by the equitable principle of granting the minimum relief necessary to do justice in the circumstances.

One of the earlier cases in the group mentioned above, *Foran* v. *Wright*, provides an interesting illustration of another use of estoppel in a contractual context. That was a case of anticipatory breach, which took the form of an intimation by one party to a contract to the other of the former's unwillingness or inability to perform an obligation which was interdependent with an obligation of the latter. The consequences were analysed in terms of estoppel. The latter was induced to refrain from tendering performance and the former was estopped from relying upon such failure in working out the consequences of what had occurred.[43]

The direction in which the High Court is moving may be summarised as follows. Promissory estoppel is recognised as part of the law of Australia and is not confined in its operation to cases involving pre-existing contractual relations. Some of the members of the court now identify one overarching principle of estoppel by conduct. Promissory estoppel is one aspect of this, but the working out of the consequences of all kinds of estoppel will be strongly influenced by equitable principles as to remedies. The distinction between representations of existing fact and representations as to future conduct is no longer decisive; *Jorden* v. *Money* is not the law in Australia. An estoppel may be used defensively or aggressively, in aid of a cause of action; but it cannot on its own constitute a cause of action. The central principle is that '*the law will not permit an unconscionable departure by one party from the subject matter of an assumption which has been adopted by the other party as the basis of some relationship, course of conduct, act or omission which would operate to that other party's detriment if the assumption be not adhered to for the purposes of the litigation*'.[44]

Now that, at least in certain circumstances, estoppel can produce the practical result that a court will

---

[41] e.g. Robert Goff, J. in *Amalgamated Property Co.* v. *Texas Bank*, op. cit. at 107.
[42] (1990) 170 C.L.R. at 434–7.
[43] See also *Peter Turnbull & Co. Ltd. Ltd.* v. *Mundus Trading*

Co. (Aust.) Pty. Ltd. (1953–1954) 90 C.L.R. 235 at 246–7 per Dixon, C. J.
[44] (1990) 170 C.L.R. at 444 per Deane, J.

hold a party to a gratuitous promise, it will become necessary to consider how the defences that may operate to defeat reliance upon a promise for consideration (a contract) compare with the factors that may operate to preclude reliance upon what would otherwise amount to an estoppel.

If a representor can show that, for some reason, it is not unconscionable to fail to honour or adhere to the representation, then there will be no estoppel. Consider, for example, fraud by the representee. It is categorically asserted in *Spencer Bower and Turner*, '*Estoppel by Representation*'[45] that if a representation was made as a result of fraud by the representee, there will be no resulting estoppel.[46] This, if the rule is as inflexible as stated, produces a stricter result than exists in the law of contract. A contract induced by fraud is voidable, not void, and there can exist various circumstances in which a person who has been guilty of fraudulent misrepresentation can nevertheless hold the other party bound. Again, is the principle limited to misrepresentations that are fraudulent?

Insofar as an estoppel is raised in aid of equitable relief, maxims such as he who seeks equity must do equity, and he who comes to equity with clean hands, may also have a role to play.[47]

In the light of the flexibility which is claimed for equitable estoppel, it would be surprising if there were more rigidity at the level of defences than exists in relation to the law of contract.

Other issues as to the conduct of the party asserting an estoppel, including, for example, what in another context might be called contributory negligence, will arise for determination. To what extent will equity permit parties to avoid responsibility for their own errors, or for imprudent reliance on another?[48] As was noted above, inducement and unconscionability necessarily give rise, on occasion, to questions as to the legitimacy of expectations which the law is asked to fulfil.

Problems will also arise as to the possible relevance of changes in circumstances affecting the position of a party making a representation or a promise. The common law takes a rather strict view of the obligation of a party to a contract to perform it, notwithstanding that altered circumstances may have made performance onerous or even ruinous. Subject to the law of frustration, it is left to the contracting parties to stipulate, in their contract, for the way in which relief may become available. To what

extent do the equitable principles invoked to oblige performance of gratuitous promises, or fulfilment of gratuitous representations, allow for hardship occasioned to the representor?

As a general observation it may be said that many of the considerations of justice, commonsense and even practical expediency that have informed the rules of contract law would also be relevant to the practical application of principles of estoppel. However, as estoppel is given a larger role there will inevitably follow a need to relate such consideration to a new context.

Before leaving this topic, it may be useful to formulate certain issues which are raised by the developments in the law considered above. They are as follows:

1. How satisfactory is the concept of unconscionability as a test for enabling courts, or legal advisers, to identify the circumstances in which assurances, representations of future intention or gratuitous promises will be treated as binding?

2. What is the criterion by which courts, or legal advisers, distinguish between those estoppels which result in satisfaction of expectations and those which lead to compensation for reliance loss?

3. What principles can be applied, with reasonable predictability of outcome, to ensure proportionality between the conduct of the representor and the relief granted to the representee?

4. What principles determine the circumstances in which what would otherwise be an estoppel may be lost or defeated?

5. Do the current developments alter the balance between the requirements of certainty and individual justice too much in favour of the latter?

Legislation—Misleading and Deceptive Conduct: Unconscionability

It is not intended to attempt any comprehensive review of legislation which has significantly affected the common law of contract. Rather, it is intended to focus upon particular legislative provisions that have become of large practical importance in Australia.

Section 52 of the *Trade Practices Act 1974 (Cth.)*

---

[45] Third Edition, p. 137.
[46] See also *Geo. Whitechurch Ltd.* v. *Cavanagh Co.* [1902] A.C. 117 at 145; *Porter* v. *Moore* [1904] 2 Ch. 367; *National Westminster Bank* v. *Barclays Bank International Ltd.* [1974] 3 All E.R. 834 at 852; *Official Trustee in Bankruptcy* v. *Tooheys Ltd.* (1993) 29 N.S.W.L.R. 641.

[47] cf. *Texas Commerce International Bank Ltd.* v. *Amalgamated Investment & Property Co. Ltd.* [1982] Q.B. 84 at 109.
[48] See the discussion in P. D. Finn, *Australian Developments in Common and Commercial Law* [1990] Journal of Business Law, 265 at 270.

provides that a corporation shall not, in trade or commerce, engage in conduct that is misleading or deceptive, or is likely to mislead or deceive. The practical importance of that provision is related in large part to the presence in the same Act of s. 82, which empowers courts to award damages for contraventions of the Act, and s. 80 which provides for injunctive relief. By reason of other legislation that need not be examined in detail, State courts have jurisdiction to apply the above provisions. Moreover, they are mirrored by provisions of State legislation such as s. 42 of the *Fair Trading Act 1987* (*NSW*), which is in the same terms as s. 52 of the *Trade Practices Act*, except that it refers to persons and not merely to corporations.

A number of principles relating to the operation of this legislation have been settled. Although the legislative context is referred to as '*consumer protection*' the courts have rejected any attempt to read the provisions down to apply only to transactions between a trader and a consumer. Nor are the provisions only available to be relied upon by consumers. They are frequently invoked, in practice, by trading corporations alleging that their competitors are engaging in conduct which is misleading or deceptive. Actions for passing off are ordinarily accompanied by allegations of a breach of s. 52, and, although there is no tort of unfair competition, this legislation goes a good way towards serving a similar purpose. In relation to the measure of damages for contravention of these provisions, the courts have preferred the analogy of damages in actions for deceit.[49] There is an unresolved problem as to the way in which damages are to be awarded when the loss suffered by a complaining party is partly the result of that party's own fault.

For there to be a contravention of s. 52 it is not necessary that there be an intention to mislead or deceive. Nor is it necessary that there be proof that someone has actually been misled or deceived; it is the tendency of conduct to mislead or deceive that matters. Where there is an issue concerning the capacity of conduct to mislead or deceive, questions can arise as to the level of astuteness or intelligence to be attributed to members of the public exposed to the conduct in question. Obviously, circumstances alter cases. If what is in question is a form of advertising, the nature of the target audience is important. However, the test is whether a significant number of people would be deceived; not whether all people, or even an average person, would be deceived.

The statute is easy enough to apply to conduct such as advertising. It can be more difficult to apply to other conduct, and some more extravagant uses of the provision have been rejected. For example, an unsuccessful attempt was made to rely on the section in the context of personal injuries litigation, where it was argued that an employer had misled an employee in relation to the safety of certain work practices.[50]

Where conduct involves making representations, s. 52 extends beyond representations as to existing fact. However, there is a separate provision, s. 51A, which deals particularly with what are referred to as representations with respect to a future matter, including the doing of, or the refusing to do, any act. That provision expands, and does not limit, the operation of s. 52. Expressions of opinion, or the making of predictions, or the conveying of information provided by third parties can in some circumstances give rise to a breach of s. 52, but usually only where accompanied by some false representation of fact. Disclaimers, and exclusion of liability clauses, are not determinative of whether there has been a breach of s. 52, but they may be of factual relevance. There may be circumstances where silence involves a breach. Cases where part only of the truth has been told are usually easier, but where it is alleged that silence constitutes misleading or deceptive conduct it will ordinarily be necessary to show, on some grounds, a duty to reveal the truth. The general law may be important in deciding whether, in the circumstances of the case, there is such a duty.

New Zealand has virtually identical legislation.[51]

In appropriate circumstances, the legislation operates to provide an action for damages for innocent misrepresentation. This in itself is no novelty. Section 2 of the *Misrepresentation Act* (*United Kingdom*) *1967* has the same effect in certain circumstances. In Canada, the British Columbia Court of Appeal expressed the view that in some cases a money award may be given instead of rescission as a remedy for misrepresentation, even though it was not fraudulent.[52]

Just as judicial development of the law relating to negligent misrepresentation has had important practical consequences in relation to pre-contractual representations so have the above statutory provisions.

One interesting feature of these legislative developments is that although they are not confined in their operation to the area that is sometimes described as '*consumer protection*', they are largely

---

[49] *Gates* v. *City Mutual Life Assurance Society* (1985–86) 160 C.L.R. 1.
[50] *Concrete Constructions* (*N.S.W.*) *Pty. Ltd.* v. *Nelson* (1990) 169 C.L.R. 594.

[51] Fair Trading Act (1986), s. 9.
[52] *Bank of Montreal* v. *Murphy* [1986] 6 W.W.R. 610 at 615–16 per Lambert, J.

inspired, at least in part, by dissatisfaction with the common law approach that appeared to treat arm's length commercial transactions between parties of equal bargaining power, and a comparable capacity to protect their individual interests, as the paradigm of contract. This is an abiding source of contention. Courts frequently express a disinclination to import fiduciary duties, and to introduce the complexities of equity, into ordinary, arm's length commercial transactions.[53] However, the law relating to contracts has to deal with many other situations as well and, at the other extreme, the courts have developed principles which in a number of respects anticipated modern consumer protection legislation. One of the difficulties is that ordinary arm's length commercial transactions do not constitute a clearly defined category. Nor, for that matter, do transactions in which one of the parties might appropriately be described as a consumer. It is easy enough to identify some cases which clearly fall within one or other of those two categories, but they are blurred at the margin.

As from 1 January 1993 the *Trade Practices Act* has included a new Part IVA dealing with the subject of unconscionable conduct. The conduct in trade or commerce that is prohibited is described as '*conduct that is unconscionable within the meaning of the unwritten law*'.[54] Although the meaning of the term is deliberately left at large, and the legislation is not limited to consumer transactions, there is a particular provision dealing with consumer transactions where the emphasis is upon taking improper advantage of unequal bargaining power.[55] Contraventions of these provisions do not attract criminal sanctions or give rise to a right to damages; nevertheless a number of remedies, including injunctive relief and compensation (as distinct from damages) are provided.

Since 1980 New South Wales has had a *Contracts Review Act*[56] which empowers courts to grant relief where a contract or a provision in a contract is found to have been unjust in the circumstances relating to the contract at the time it was made.[57] The term '*unjust*' is defined to include '*unconscionable, harsh or oppressive*'.[58]

One of the most striking features of a general statutory rule of behaviour, such as that laid down by s. 52 of the *Trade Practices Act*, is the way in which it can cut across common law principles or other statutory provisions which represent a careful and some-

times complex balancing of competing considerations. The common law relating to negligent misstatement, or the law of defamation (where in various States of Australia the common law has been modified by statute) provide examples. Consider, for example, the relationship between a general prohibition against misleading conduct, on the one hand, and the law of defamation on the other hand, when applied to the publication of defamatory matter which is untrue, but which is published reasonably and in good faith. Again, the careful qualifications that were drawn around the law concerning tortious liability for negligent misstatements are in some circumstances rendered irrelevant by s. 52.

If one comes to consider the effect such legislation might have on the attitude of the courts towards the common law, there are two possible, and quite different, consequences that might be postulated. On the one hand the courts might (as, for example, in *Photo Production Ltd. v. Securior Transport Ltd.*)[59] treat the enactment of legislation as a form of relief from the necessity to bend the common law to achieve justice in individual cases, and revert to true doctrine. Some courts, on the other hand, might regard the legislature as giving a lead, and feel encouraged to develop and change the common law accordingly. It seems to be the latter, rather than the former, effect that has occurred in Australia. Legislation of the kind described has become such a well-established part of the background against which litigation is now conducted that it has inevitably influenced the way in which advocates, and judges, approach the law, including the common law.

Modifying Consideration—Existing Duty to Promisee

Stilk v. *Myrick*[60] was cited by text books as authority for the proposition that where A owed an existing contractual duty to B, performance of, or a promise to perform, that duty could not amount to consideration for a promise by B to A. Thus if A were obliged by contract under B to perform certain work for B, a mere affirmation of a willingness to perform that work could not support, as a binding variation of that contract, an agreement by B to pay more for the same work.

In *Williams* v. *Roffey Bros. & Nichols (Contractors) Ltd.*[61] the English Court of Appeal said, in effect, that

[53] cf. William Goodhart & Gareth Jones, 'The Infiltration of Equitable Doctrines into English Commercial Law' (1980) 43 Modern Law Review, 489.

[54] Section 51AA.

[55] Section 51AB. See *Commercial Bank of Australia Ltd.* v. *Amadio* (1983) 151 C.L.R. 447; *Bromley* v. *Ryan* (1956) 99 C.L.R. 362.

[56] Contracts Review Act, 1980, N.S.W.

[57] Section 7 (1). The provisions were partly inspired by the U.C.C. Art. 2–302.

[58] Section 4 (1).

[59] [1980] A.C. 827.

[60] (1809) 2 Camp. 317.

[61] [1991] Q.B. 1.

might be so if that is all there is to it, but there will often be more to it than that. There the court was willing to find consideration in the obtaining of a practical benefit (or avoidance of a disbenefit) by B. What is significant is the ease with which the benefit to B was found. It is rarely to the advantage of one party to a contract to force the other party, by insistence on strict contractual right, into insolvency.

At one level, the decision may be regarded as exposing the undue rigidity of the exchange theory of consideration, in much the same way as modern methods of dealing often require a more flexible approach to the analysis of contractual formation by reference to offer and acceptance.[62] Indeed, the unreality of distinctions previously drawn between cases where there was, and was not, found to be consideration (or benefit or detriment) in contractual renegotiations had resulted in questioning of the usefulness of the doctrine of consideration in this area.[63] A possible point of view (though hardly one available to an intermediate appellate court) might have been that consideration need have nothing to do with variations of contract.

The case also raises questions as to estoppel and economic duress.

As to estoppel, Russell, J. J.[64] referred to the possibility, not made the subject of argument, that in the circumstances B.'s agreement to pay the extra money to A might have given rise to an estoppel. It is perhaps surprising that estoppel was not argued. After all, promissory estoppel had its modern revitalisation in the context of compromising contractual rights.

As to economic duress, the Court of Appeal recognised that, on the facts of *Stilk* v. *Myrick* (a ship's crew striking for better pay), or at least on the facts of similar cases which would then have been regarded as quite likely to arise, there could well be overtones of duress. Their Lordships were concerned, therefore, whilst modifying the requirements of the doctrine of consideration, to emphasise the need for the absence of economic or other duress, or fraud, in a case where B is to be held to the promise to pay the greater sum.

When contractual arrangements are being renegotiated against the background of an unwillingness or inability of one party to honour the existing contract (and, in practice, unwillingness and inability may

often amount to the same thing)[65] there may well be a strong flavour of economic pressure. This decision will make it important to define the limits of the concept of economic duress.[66] What constitutes '*illegitimate pressure*' in such circumstances can be difficult to define, especially in a context of hard commercial bargaining.[67]

In practice it may also prove a fertile field for dispute about misrepresentation.

Other systems of law (e.g. Japan) recognise the significance of changed economic circumstances in ways quite different from the common law. The common law of frustration has a much more limited operation and does not cover some unexpected turn of events which merely renders a contract more onerous than had been contemplated.[68] Subject to the qualifications concerning duress and fraud, this case may go some distance towards treating changed economic circumstances as a significant factor in finding consideration.

Unjust Enrichment and Restitution

During 1992, two decisions of the House of Lords and the High court of Australia marked major developments, in England and Australia respectively, in what might once have been described as an area of the law concerned with the action for money had and received.

The circumstances in which a person might wish to recover money paid to another on the ground that it was not due are various. The payment might have been made voluntarily or under some form of compulsion; if it were made with compulsion, that may have come from the payee, or a third party, or from some set of circumstances; it may have been the result of mistake and, if so, the mistake may have been one of different kinds.

The irrecoverability of voluntary payments is not a matter of contention, although difficult questions can arise as to whether it is appropriate to characterise certain payments in that way.[69] People often make payments which they would prefer not to make, and which they believe they are not obliged to make, to avoid what they regard as a greater evil. That does not of itself make the payments involuntary. It is not only cheerful givers who are denied restitution.

[62] cf. *New Zealand Shipping Co. Ltd.* v. *Satterthwaite & Co. Ltd.* [1975] A.C. 154 at 167 per Lord Wilberforce.
[63] Treitel, *The Law of Contract*, Seventh Edition, p. 74.
[64] [1991] Q.B. at 17.
[65] *Universal Cargo Carriers Corporation* v. *Citati* [1957] 2 Q.B. 401 at 437.
[66] cf. *Pao On* v. *Lan Yiu Long* [1980] A.C. 614, *Barton* v. *Armstrong* [1976] A.C. 104, P. B. H. Birks, *The Travails of Duress* (1990), Lloyd's M.C.L.Q. 342.

[67] cf. *Shivas* v. *Bank of NZ* [1990] 2 N.Z.L.R. 327 at 345.
[68] *Davis Contractors Ltd.* v. *Fareham Urban District Council* [1956] A.C. 696.
[69] As to the difficulties occasioned by the concept of voluntariness, see P. B. H. Birks, 109 L.Q.R. 164–8. The High Court in *David Securities Pty. Ltd.* v. *Commonwealth bank of Australia* (below) remitted the matter to the Federal Court for further consideration of the facts, in order to decide whether the payment was voluntary.

The issue which confronted the House of Lords in *Woolwich Equitable Building Society* v. *Inland Revenue Commissioners*,[70] the right of recovery of monies paid pursuant to an unlawful demand by a public authority, was resolved by reference to principles closely related to those which underlay the decision of the High Court in *David Securities Pty. Ltd.* v. *Commonwealth Bank of Australia*.[71] The High Court was concerned with the case of a payment by one contracting party to another of monies owing under a contractual stipulation that was later found to be illegal and void; that is to say, money paid under what was treated by the court as a mistake of law.

There are many instances in which a taxpayer could characterise an exaction made by a public authority as involving duress or wrongful extortion of such a kind as would have justified recovery under well-established principles.[72] However, to make that form of compulsion the necessary basis of an entitlement to recover taxes unlawfully demanded and paid is unsatisfactory. The distinction between a taxpayer who pays under protest and a taxpayer who also pays under such form of compulsion as would support an action for recovery under the law as it previously stood was often blurred. Many forms of exaction by public authorities are reinforced by sanctions which most taxpayers prefer to avoid.

The distinction which had previously been regarded as critical in a case of the kind confronting the High Court was also one that was notoriously unsatisfactory. The distinction between mistakes of fact and mistakes of law had been trenchantly criticised.[73]

In both cases the previously determinative distinctions were put aside, and the issues were resolved on the basis of principles concerning the law of restitution.

In both cases the right of recovery that was accepted (the right to recover overpaid taxes, or money paid under a mistake of law) was prima facie only, and was subject to the defendant's entitlement to show circumstances that might render it unjust to prevent recovery. An obvious example of the latter

would be a voluntary payment. The High Court also appeared to accept the qualification, based on a defendant's change of position, recognised in *Lipkin Gorman* v. *Karpnale Ltd.*[74] The nature and scope of the qualifications grow out of the principle giving the prima facie rights.[75]

In *Woolwich Building Society*, Lord Goff of Chieveley[76] referred to the *'formidable argument'* developed by leading academic lawyers[77] to the effect that money paid to a public authority pursuant to an ultra vires demand should be repayable simply on the ground that there was no consideration for the payment. The unjust entitlement of the recipient of the payment is the key to the right of recovery. Lord Browne-Wilkinson, who was also in the majority, referred to the case[78] as '*the paradigm of a case of unjust enrichment'*.

In *David Securities* the High Court went a step further in the same direction. Referring to what was said in *Woolwich Building Society* the majority declared that, in the context of payments under a mistake, the distinction between mistakes of law and mistakes of fact, was, in Australia, no longer determinative of a right to recover. *Bilbie* v. *Lumley*[79] no longer represents the law in Australia. Some cases that had been explained on the basis of the distinction are now to be explained on the basis that the law enforces compromises freely entered into (i.e. that the payments in question were voluntary). The reason in principle for the rejection of the distinction was expressed as follows:[80]

'If the ground for ordinary recovery is that the defendant has been unjustly enriched, there is no justification for drawing distinctions on the basis of how the enrichment was gained, except in so far as the manner of gaining the enrichment bears upon the justice of the case'.

The question of the way in which the conduct, or state of mind, of the recipient of the payment bears upon the justice of the case is one that will require further examination in future cases. This is another area where a general test of unconscientiousness is sometimes applied, but more specific principles may need to be formulated.[81]

The High Court also closely examined the issues

---

[70] [1993] 1 A.C. 70.

[71] (1992) 175 C.L.R. 353.

[72] e.g. *Mason* v. *New South Wales* (1959) 102 C.L.R. 108.

[73] e.g. by Dickson, J. in *Hydro Electric Commission of Township of Nepean* v. *Ontario Hydro* (1982) 132 D.L.R. 193 at 201–11. See also *Air Canada* v. *British Columbia* (1989) 59 D.L.R. (4th) 161 at 191 per La Forest, J.

[74] [1991] 2 A.C. 549. See also *Strang Patrick Stevedoring Pty. Ltd.* v. *The Owners of MV 'Sletter'* (1992) 38 F.C.R. 501.

[75] As to the problems concerning the boundaries of the concept of change in circumstances, see Prof. Gareth Jones, in P. D. Finn (ed.), *Essays in Restitution*, p. 15.

[76] [1993] 1 A.C. at 166.

[77] e.g. Professor P. B. H. Birks, in P. D. Finn, *Essays in Restitution*, p. 164 et seq.

[78] [1992] 1 A.C. at 197.

[79] (1802) 2 East 409, 102 E.R. 448.

[80] (1992) 175 C.L.R. at 375.

[81] In Story, *Commentaries on Equity Jurisprudence*, 2nd Ed. 1830, para. 1255 the central question is expressed as whether the recipient of the payment in question can conscientiously retain it. In *Neste Oy* v. *Lloyd's Bank PLC.* [1983] 2 L.L.R. 658 at 666, Bingham, J. concluded that in the circumstances it would have seemed contrary to any notion of fairness that the

that arise in determining whether a payment has been made without consideration. It was held that, to resist restitution on the ground of good consideration, the payee had to show that the payer received at least part of the benefit bargained for, being a benefit that was consideration for the payment sought to be recovered.[82]

One further observation concerning unjust enrichment, which is perhaps of some wider significance, may be made. This is not the occasion to examine recent developments in the law relating to constructive trusts, but underlying a good deal of what is written about that subject is the notion of the justice of satisfying reasonable and legitimate expectations created in certain circumstances. If consideration is a particular feature of the law of contract that is threatened by development of equitable principles, it is worth considering the role that will be played by the idea of contract itself with the expansion of the means of fulfilling expectations created otherwise than by contractually binding promises.

Future Possibilities

So far, this paper has been confined to a consideration of developments that, at least in some jurisdictions, have actually taken place, either as a result of decisions of courts of ultimate authority or through legislation. It would be inappropriate to leave the subject of innovations in the law of contract without making brief reference to possible future changes that have attracted some judicial interest and support but have not yet commanded majority approval.

(a) Privity of Contract

The rules that only a party to a contract can sue on it, and that consideration must move from the promisee, are said to be fundamental to the common law of contract.[83] They have, however, provoked criticism at the highest level. In 1968 Lord Reid said that if Parliament did not deal with the question the House of Lords might find it necessary to do so.[84] A similar view was expressed by Lord Scarman in 1980[85] and by Lord Diplock in 1983.[86] Lord Diplock referred to the 'juristic subterfuges' to which courts have resorted to mitigate the effect of an anachronistic shortcoming that is a reproach to English private law.

The problems that are involved in any proposed modification of the existing rules are well known, and it is unnecessary to rehearse them. The same applies to the judicial techniques that have been adopted over the years to mitigate their consequences.

In *Trident General Insurance Co. Ltd.* v. *McNiece Bros. Pty. Ltd.*,[87] the High Court of Australia was confronted with a classic example of the injustice of the strict rules: a policy of insurance which was expressed to provide cover for persons who were not parties to the contract of insurance and who paid none of the premium. In the intermediate appellate court, McHugh, J. A., who has since gone to the High Court, took the bold course of rejecting the continued operation of the traditional rules at least in their application to policies of insurance. A majority of the High Court found in favour of the insured, but the differing reasons of the majority yield no single ratio for the decision. Only two members of the majority, Mason, C. J. and Wilson, J., adopted the approach of McHugh, J. A., and it was expressly rejected by Brennan, Deane and Dawson, J. J.

Trident is not a case that marks the demise in Australia of these fundamental principles, but it casts doubt on their state of health.

One interesting feature of *Trident*, which relates to a subject discussed earlier in this paper, is what was said by Deane, J. about possible solutions to the perceived injustice, consistently with the maintenance of what he regarded as the fundamental principle of privity of contract. *Trident* preceded *Verwayen*, and a deal of what Deane, J. said in the latter case, concerning the need to protect the doctrine of consideration from being overrun by promissory estoppel, is connected to what he had said in *Trident*. Deane, J. took the view that in a case such as that before the court, if a stranger to a policy of insurance had a right to indemnity under it, then it must be because there had been created a trust of the benefit of the insurer's promise. In the course of his judgment, however, he raised the possibility that an insurer may, by conduct, induce a third party to act to his detriment on the assumption that he is effectively indemnified under the policy with the result that the insurer will, in an appropriate case, be estopped from denying the enforceability of such indemnity. Clearly enough, such an approach raises for

agent in question should retain a certain payment. P. D. Finn, *Equity, Commerce—Remedy*, N.Z. Law Society Conference, Auckland, Jan. 1993 treats the case and *Liggett* v. *Kensington* [1993] 1 N.Z.L.R. 257 as cases where an innocent party has made a contractually required transfer of property or payment of money in circumstances where, unknown to that party but to the knowledge of the other, reciprocal performance would not be provided.

[82] (1992) 175 C.L.R. at 382–4.

[83] *Dunlop Pneumatic Tyre Co. Ltd.* v. *Selfridge & Co. Ltd.* [1915] A.C. 847; *Wilson* v. *Darling Island Stevedoring & Lighterage Co. Ltd.* (1956) 95 C.L.R. 43; *Midland Silicones Ltd.* v. *Scruttons Ltd.* [1962] A.C. 446.

[84] *Beswick* v. *Beswick* [1968] A.C. 58 at 72.

[85] *Woodan Investment Ltd.* v. *Wimpey Ltd.* [1980] 1 W.L.R. 277 at 300.

[86] *Swain* v. *Law Society* [1983] 1 A.C. 598 at 611.

[87] (1988) 165 C.L.R. 107.

consideration the issues, earlier discussed, about the relationship between estoppel and the doctrine of consideration.

Since *Trident* there has come the decision of the Supreme Court of Canada in *London Drugs Ltd.* v. *Kuehne & Nagel International Ltd.*[88] The majority in that case decided upon what was described as a relaxation of the doctrine of privity to give a third party the benefit of a limitation of liability provision. They created what was referred to as a specific and limited exception to the requirement of privity which permitted employees who qualify as third party beneficiaries to use their employer's limitation of liability clauses as shields in actions brought against them.

(b) Good Faith

Concepts of good faith and fair dealing are clearly at work in many well established principles of contract law. The law relating to penalties, or implication of contractual terms, and certain rules of construction may be regarded as manifestations of such concepts.[89] However, a New Zealand High Court judge, Thomas, J., in *Livingstone* v. *Roskilly*[90] invoked a principle that *'in general, the parties to a contract must act in good faith in making and carrying out the contract'*. He cited Lord Mansfield's statement[91] that good faith was *'the governing principle ... applicable to all contracts and dealings'*.[92]

There is a difference between applying a requirement of good faith to making a contract and applying it to at least some aspects of performing a contract. In *Walford* v. *Miles*[93] Lord Ackner observed that parties involved in pre-contract negotiations are in an adversarial position, each being entitled to pursue a policy of self-interest so long as there are no misrepresentations. His Lordship regarded the concept of a duty to carry on negotiations in good faith as repugnant to this adversarial position. The room for notions of good faith is greater in the area of contractual implication and interpretation and performance than in the area of formation.

The civil law principle of good faith is attracting the interest of some judges and learned commentators in common law jurisdictions, although of course, there has been nothing like the developments that have

occurred in the United States.[94] The judgment of Priestley, J. A. of the New South Wales Court of Appeal in *Renard Constructions (M.E.) Pty. Ltd.* v. *Minister for Public Works*[95] contains a detailed discussion of what his Honour called *'the notions of good faith which are regarded in many of the civil law systems of Europe and in all States in the United States as necessarily implied in many kinds of contract'*.

Judicial responses to this topic have so far been very cautious in Australia,[96] and I believe the same applies to England and New Zealand. The principles of *'laissez-faire'* which contributed to the growth of much of the common law of contract are not easily reconciled with what some regard as an invitation to judicial paternalism. The assumption that the pursuit of enlightened self-interest, within proper bounds, is likely to promote the general welfare, is deeply ingrained. Subject to fairly clearly defined and reasonably specific qualifications, individuals are not only entitled, but are positively encouraged, to pursue their own interests in making and giving effect to contracts.

However, it is now common for commercial codes[97] to invoke standards of good faith and fair dealing, and legislation in various common law jurisdictions enables courts to intervene in the case of unfair contracts. This background of legislation and commercial practice, and the pressures of increasing internationalisation, may be expected to encourage further exploration of the idea, expressed in *Restatement of the Law (Second) Contracts, s. 205*, that every contract imposes upon each party a duty of good faith and fair dealing in its performance and its enforcement.

It may be that some of the arguments both for and against more extensive use of the idea of good faith are based upon an exaggerated apprehension of its possible role. Professor Farnsworth[98] pointed out that the chief utility of the concept of good faith performance of a contract is as a rationale in the process of implying contract terms. To that might be added its use in the process of the interpretation of contractual provisions. An examination of the judgment of Lord Mansfield cited in the New Zealand case mentioned above, shows that his Lordship was dealing with a contract of insurance, and whilst he said that it was a principle applying to all contracts

---

[88] (1992) 97 D.L.R. (4th) 261.

[89] P. D. Finn, *Australian Developments in Common and Commercial Law* [1990] Journal of Business Law, 265.

[90] [1992] 3 N.Z.L.R. 230 at 237.

[91] *Carter* v. *Boehm* (1766) 3 Burr. 1905.

[92] See also the judgment of Bingham, L. J. in *Interfoto Picture Library Ltd.* v. *Stiletto Visual Programmes Ltd.* [1989] Q.B. 433 at 439.

[93] [1992] 2 A.C. 128 at 138.

[94] e.g. the paper delivered on 16 May 1990 by Steyn, L. J., entitled, The Role of Good Faith Dealing in Contract Law.

[95] (1992) 26 N.S.W.L.R. 234.

[96] e.g. Beaumont, J. in *Amann Aviation Pty. Ltd.* v. *Commonwealth* (1988) 80 A.L.R. 35. The same does not apply in Canada; see *L.A.C. Minerals Ltd.* v. *International Corona Resources Ltd.* (1989) 61 D.L.R. (4th) 14 at 47 per La Forest, J.

[97] cf. Uniform Commercial Code, U.S.A., Art. 1–201; United Nations Convention on Contracts for the International Sale of Goods Art. 7 (1).

[98] *Good Faith Performance and Commercial Reasonableness under the Uniform Commercial Code* (1963) 30 University of Chicago Law Review 666 at 672.

and dealings that good faith forbids either party, by concealing what he privately knows, to draw the other into a bargain, he went on immediately to say that either party may be innocently silent as to grounds open to both to exercise their judgment upon, and that the concept of concealment must be restrained to the precise subject of any contract.

An example of the use by the common law of the concept of good faith in a manner that modern lawyers would identify as an unexceptionable approach to the construction of a contract is to be found in the judgment of Lord Kenyon in *Mellish* v. *Motteux*.[99] That was a case in which the buyer of a ship sued a seller for failing to disclose latent defects known to the seller. Lord Kenyon's judgment, as reported in its entirety, was as follows:

[99] (1792) Peake 156 at 157; 170 E.R. 113 at 113–14.

'There are certain moral duties which philosophers have called of imperfect obligation, such as benevolence to the poor, and many others, which courts of law do not enforce. But in contracts of all kinds it is of the highest importance that courts of law should compel the observation of honesty and good faith. This was a latent defect which the plaintiffs could not, by any fashion whatever, possibly discover, and which the defendants knowing of ought to have disclosed to the plaintiffs. The terms to which the plaintiffs acceded, of taking the ship with all faults and without warranty, must be understood to relate only to those faults which the plaintiffs could have discovered, or which the defendants were unacquainted with'.

For more than one reason, that is a model judgment.

10. Innovations in Contract: An English Perspective

J. BEATSON

'A theme that runs through our law is that the reasonable expectations of honest men must be protected. It is not a rule or a principle of law. It is the objective which has been and still is the principal moulding force of our law of contract. it affords no licence to a judge to depart from binding precedent. On the other hand if the prima facie solution to a problem runs counter to the reasonable expectations of honest men, this criterion sometimes requires a rigorous re-examination of the problem to ascertain whether the law does indeed compel demonstrable unfairness.'[1]

I N 1983, in his Maccabean Lecture, Lord Goff said that the process of legal development should be a gradual development from the identification of specific heads of recovery to the identification and closer definition of the limits to a generalised right of recovery; a search for principle.[2] This paper seeks to consider how well the English law of contract has been served by the incremental approach taken, in particular by the House of Lords. Although there are, as will be seen, notable counter examples, a case can be made for saying that the overall trend in the contract law of the 1980's has been to move towards greater certainty. The late Professor Corbin, who stated that 'certainty in the law is largely an illusion at best and altogether too high a price may be paid in the efforts to attain it",[3] would not have approved. The question is whether English law has achieved a reasonable balance between certainty and predictability and fairness in individual cases. Has English law's tradition of providing practical solutions to demonstrated problems meant that, on occasion, it has lost sight of the goal of a general principle?[4] Is it willing rigorously to re-examine its rules when it appears that the reasonable expectations of honest people are not being protected? Is it sufficiently concerned with ensuring that the law reflects the standards of behaviour expected by the public in the modern world; standards that are expected to be in a number of respects higher than in the past? What follows is not intended to be an exhaustive exposition and it may raise more questions than it answers.

The extent to which common law and equitable contract doctrine has developed over the last two decades and the relationship of contract with other branches of the law of obligations will be considered. The relationship between common law and statute and in particular the influence and likely influence of European civil law jurisdictions in view of recent developments in E.C. law, will also be touched on. The two are connected and we shall consider the extent to which refusal to develop and generalise doctrine, for example the refusal in *National Westminster Bank plc.* v. *Morgan*[5] to adopt a general principle of inequality of bargaining, has resulted from a particular view about the respective province of judges and legislators.

A number of introductory comments can be made. First, while some scholars such as Patrick Atiyah have argued that the development of non-contractual obligations in both pre-contractual bargaining situations and completed contracts put into question the separation and integrity of the law of contract, it is also arguable that the development of these remedies removes the pressure to stretch 'classical' contractual doctrines to deal with particular problems. For example, it may be easier for courts to adhere strictly to the rules governing formation of contracts when they know that tortious, reliance based, and restitutionary remedies may arise in a pre-contractual situation to deal with potential injustice. It is thus arguable that innovations outside the law of contract have meant that in certain areas there is perceived to be less need for innovation within contract. It is also arguable, however, that even if the non-contractual possibilities are appreciated (and they are not always), the risk is that certain problems will be left unsolved.

For instance, in the context of carriage of goods by sea, the fact that the Court of Appeal took a strict view of the requirements of offer, acceptance and contractual intention to limit the situations in which an implied contract between a bill of lading holder and a carrier could be found,[6] meant that it was left to the legislature to provide a new commercially workable solution.[7] Secondly, there is the case of

---

[1] *First Energy (U.K.) Ltd.* v. *Hungarian International Bank Ltd.* [1993] 2 Lloyd's R. 194, 196 (per Steyn, L. J.).

[2] (1983) 59 Proc. Brit. Acadm. 169, 179–82.

[3] *Contracts,*)1960 ed.) §609.

[4] Thus Bingham, L. J. pointed out in *Interfoto Ltd.* v. *Stiletto Ltd.* [1988] 1 All E.R. 348, 353–3 that English law has committed itself to no overriding principle of good faith, contenting itself with piecemeal solutions to demonstrated problems of unfairness.

[5] [1985] A.C. 686. Cf. developments in Australia; *Legione* v. *Hateley* (1982/83) 152 C.L.R. 406; *Commercial Bank of Australia* v. *Amadio* (1982/83) 46 A.L.R. 402.

[6] *The Aramis* [1989] 1 Lloyd's Rep. 213. Cf. *The Captain Gregos (No. 2)* [1990] 2 Lloyd's Rep. 395. See Law Com. No. 196 'Rights of Suit in respect of Carriage of Goods by Sea' (1991) paras. 2.11–2.12.

[7] Carriage of Goods by Sea Act 1992.

stale arbitrations. Commercial and legal opinion were of the view that a party who had commenced an arbitration but had then been guilty of prolonged and inexcusable delay should not be able to proceed. Arbitration, however, is a contractual institution and adherence to the traditional rules of offer and acceptance (and the inability to accept by silence) and treatment of contractual rights as only subject to implied qualification in exceptional circumstances meant that the law of contract was unable to reflect their views.[8] Again legislation was needed to deal with the problem.[9] Thirdly, as will be seen serious and arguably unnecessary limitations have been placed on the ability of parties to undertake to negotiate with each other and not to negotiate with third parties. The story is not, however, all one of missed opportunities. In the context of the effect of breach, the move away from the *Hong Kong Fir* approach, exemplified in *Tradax Export SA* v. *Bunge Corpn.*[10] represents an adjustment of the balance between the requirements of flexibility and *ex post facto* fairness and certainty, which balance had arguably swung too much in the direction of flexibility.

(I) Doctrinal Innovation and Relationship with Other Categories

This section considers three areas in which there has been doctrinal innovation; pre-contractual duties, variation and renegotiation of contracts, and illegal contracts. It also considers two areas where English judges have stated that major developments should be achieved by legislation rather than the common law; rights of third-party beneficiaries to contracts, and a general principle of unconscionability or inequality of bargaining. This is not to say that other areas, such as the position of remedies for breach of contract[11] or the general position of implied terms[12] do not deserve examination.

(a) Pre-contractual duties

The various techniques used to deal with the situation where, during the course of or following con-

tractual negotiations (involving tendering, letters of intent, or a 'battle of the forms') one of the parties takes action, for instance, by manufacturing or delivering goods, rendering services, or expanding money to prepare himself for performance, are familiar. The techniques that have been used to protect the interests of the party who has taken action include estoppel, reliance, restitution, and that work-horse of the common law of contract, the implied contract.

Although English law has not yet moved to a position in which it can be said, as it can in Australia[13] and the United States, that the doctrine of promissory estoppel is no longer confined to pre-existing contractual relationships it seems clear that it is moving in this direction. Lord Oliver, in an address to Australian lawyers,[14] thought so and the decision in *Attorney General of Hong Kong* v. *Humphrey's Estate* points in the same direction.[15] In that case the Judicial Committee of the Privy Council was willing to conceive of circumstances in which a party to negotiations expressly stated to be 'subject to contract' would nevertheless be able to show that some form of estoppel had arisen. If that is even conceivable in negotiations expressly stated to be 'subject to contract', there is surely much less distance to be travelled where the negotiations are not so limited. Apart from the instances in which it is generally accepted that estoppel can found a cause of action, proprietary estoppel[16] and estoppel by convention,[17] one can point to cases in which a negotiating party's reliance has given rise to a remedy although no contract has resulted. The clearest example is provided by the decision of the Court of Appeal in 1954 giving recompense to a property owner in respect of alterations made to his property at the request of prospective tenants during the course of the negotiations for a lease.[18] This case, commonly explained as an example of a restitutionary quantum meruit, is, it is submitted, better explained as a case in which directly induced reliance was protected, as occurs in cases of estoppel.

Why then is there still no clear decision by an English court taking the step taken in other jurisdic-

---

[8] E.g. *The Leonidas D* [1985] 2 Lloyd's R. 18. For a full discussion of the many cases and commentaries see Sir Thomas Bingham, 'The Problem of Delay in Arbitration' (1985) 5 Arb. Int. 333.
[9] Courts and Legal Services Act 1990, s. 102.
[10] [1981] 1 W.L.R. 711.
[11] In that area new interests deserving the protection of the law by an award of money damages have been identified, specific remedies have been extended (in part because of this identification) and, there has been a greater willingness to permit recourse to non-compensatory measures where an independent restitutionary claim can be established (*Rover International Ltd.* v. *Cannon Film Sales Ltd.* (*No. 3*) [1989] 1 W.L.R. 912) although not simply as an alternative contractual

measure (*Surrey C.C.* v. *Brodero* [1993] 1 W.L.R. 1361 C.A.).
[12] See in particular *Scally* v. *Southern Health & Social Services Bd.* [1992] 1 AC 294 (H.L.), discussed by Phang, [1992] J.B.L. 242.
[13] *Waltons Stores (Interstate) Ltd.* v. *Maher* (1988) 164 C.L.R. 387.
[14] (1993) 67 A.L.J. 675.
[15] [1987] 1 A.C. 114, 127–8.
[16] *Crabb* v. *Arun DC* [1976] Ch. 179.
[17] *Amalgamated Investments* v. *Texas Commerce International Bank* [1982] Q.B. 84.
[18] *Brewer St. Investments* v. *Barclays Woollen Co. Ltd.* [1954] Q.B. 428.

tions? There are dicta in support and cases in which the point has been ignored, but no authoritative holding[19] such as that in *Waltons Stores (Interstate) Ltd.* v. *Maher*.[20] It may simply be that it has not been *necessary* to do so in the cases that have come before the courts either because a contract or a restitutionary remedy could be found or invented. Alternatively, Lord Hailsham L.C. pointed out in *Woodhouse Ltd.* v. *Nigerian Product Ltd.*[21] that the cases of contractual modification based on promissory estoppel raised problems of coherent exposition which have never been systematically explored. The apparent difficulty of reducing estoppels arising out of contractual modifications to a coherent body of doctrine may have meant that the courts were disinclined to take this further step.

The growing recognition that a non-contractual remedy will be available in respect of benefits conferred or detriment suffered during the negotiating process[22] means that courts are less likely to be driven artificially to construct a contract, as happened in the well known case of *Upton R.D.C.* v. *Powell*[23] where a person who called the police to call 'the fire brigade' was held to be liable *in contract* to a fire brigade which came under the mistaken belief that the fire was in its area and the service would be gratuitous. The controversy (alluded to above) as to whether all such cases should truly be seen as examples of restitutionary liability should not deflect attention from the fact that what has been developed and is increasingly recognised are remedies which cannot be accommodated within the 'bargain' model of contract and which are, accordingly, best seen (as they clearly are in the case of restitutionary remedies) as non-contractual.

Objections have, however, been put to non-contractual (in particular restitutionary) analysis in such cases.[24] It is said that non-contractual approaches are inconsistent with the intention of the parties to enter into a legally binding contract, that they do not protect the interests of a party where no action has been taken and no benefit conferred (i.e. the transaction is purely executory) or where, although a benefit has been conferred, the person who has received the benefit or the one who has conferred the benefit has suffered a greater loss. Thus, it is argued that while a restitutionary or reliance analysis may protect the expectations or reliance interest of the supplier of goods or services, the correlative expectations in the counterparty (in respect of time of delivery, quality, etc.) can only be protected by contractual analysis. Finally, there are said to be difficulties in determining the extent of the remedy which either turns on the value of the benefit,[25] or determining the appropriate discretionary equitable relief. These objections are not, it is submitted, compelling.[26] It is for the court to decide whether the requisite intention exists for the creation of a contract. If it does not, pure expectations should not be protected and it is submitted that restitutionary and reliance based remedies represent an appropriate balance between the interests of the parties.

This activity does not mean that courts do not still have recourse to the traditional approach of implying a term or a contract. A recent example of this is *Blackpool and Fylde Aero Club* v. *Blackpool Borough Council*[27] where the Court of Appeal considered a tendering process for the concession to operate pleasure flights from a municipally owned airport and implied a contract to open and consider all tenders submitted before the specified deadline. A tenderer which posted its tender into the defendant's letter box in due time, but whose tender was not considered because the defendant's staff did not clear the box as they were supposed to have done,[28] was held to be contractually entitled to have its tender opened and considered after the deadline in conjunction with all other conforming tenders.[29] Questions of quantum were postponed but, in principle, the successful plaintiff should have been entitled to expectation damages, perhaps reduced on the *Chaplin* v. *Hicks* 'loss of a chance' principle.[30] Even a supporter of the decision has commented that 'it almost seems that the reasoning process of the court was that the implied term was necessary to give business efficacy to the relationship between the parties:

---

[19] Treitel, *The Law of Contract*, 8th ed. (1991) p. 108.
[20] (1988) 164 C.L.R. 387.
[21] [1972] A.C. 741 at 758.
[22] *British Steel Corporation* v. *Cleveland Bridge and Engineering Co. ltd.* [1984] 1 All E.R. 504 (*quantum meruit* for nodes made and delivered for use in the construction of a building which was to have a steel latticework frame).
[23] [1942] 1 All E.R. 220.
[24] See especially Ball, 'Work carried out in pursuance of letters of intent—Contract or Restitution?' (1983) 99 L.Q.R. 572.
[25] This might be either the market value or the cost of the provider (either with or without an allowance for profit).
[26] For fuller discussion, see McKendrick, 'The Battle of the

Forms and the Law of Restitution' (1988) 8 O.J.L.S. 197, 208–19.
[27] [1990] 1 W.L.R. 1195 (C.A.) the technique used in this case has attracted adverse comment, see Adams and Brownsword (1991), 54 M.L.R. 281, 287; Phang (1991), 1 J.C.L. 46 but also support, Davenport (1991), 107 L.Q.R. 201.
[28] Nothing seems to have turned on this and it would seem that even if the letter box would not in the ordinary course of events have been cleared between the time the tender was placed in it and the deadline, the result would have been the same. Or would it?
[29] [1990] 1 W.L.R. at 1202 (Bingham, L. J.).
[30] [1911] 2 K.B. 786.

the term needed a contract into which it could be implied: therefore the contract must exist.'[31] Bingham, L. J. refused to accept the argument that there was no legal obligation to consider a conforming tender because to so hold would be to create 'an unacceptable discrepancy between the law of contract and the confident assumptions of commercial parties'. The only two bases of liability considered by the court were contract and tort, and Bingham, L. J. was tentatively of the opinion that the tort claim was ill founded.[32] In this case it is arguable that neither a remedy based on restitution nor one based on the protection of the reliance interest would have protected the plaintiff's expectation of getting a chance to be awarded the concession if the tender was submitted in time.

The acceptance in the *Blackpool* case that, although a tendering process is in many respects heavily weighted in favour of the invitor, where the invitation 'prescribes a clear, orderly and familiar procedure'[33] the submission of a conforming tender creates a contractual right to be considered, means that it will be difficult to confine the decision to the special facts of the case. It is likely to apply to all formalised tendering processes. Therefore, even where the E.C. Directives do not apply so that the tenderer has no statutory remedy, he will be protected.[34] The question, however, is whether this expectation *should* be protected or whether it is sufficient to recompense the plaintiff in respect of the cost of submitting the tender or any benefit conferred on the defendant. The answer may depend on the effect a given remedy has on the incentives to participate in a tender. Given the known risks of tendering, it is possible that reliance or restitutionary remedies will suffice. It is possible, however, to conceive of a situation in which they would not. Take for example a person who approaches the government with an idea he has developed for a new 'private' toll road or bridge to be constructed on a particular route and persuades the government to take it forward reasonably expecting to be able to participate in the tendering process to construct and operate the road or bridge. In such a case the possibility of reimbursement if he is not able to participate might not suffice to encourage the initial investment and development of the idea.[35]

The willingness of the Court of Appeal in the *Blackpool* case to ensure that the law supports and reflects the confident assumptions of commercial parties (and others conducting negotiations) can, however, be contrasted with the decision of the House of Lords in *Walford* v. *Miles*.[36] It was held that undertakings for good consideration to negotiate in good faith to reach an agreement with a stipulated party or not to negotiate with any person other than that party (for an unspecified or a reasonable period of time) are unenforceable. To hold such undertakings as giving rise to contractual liability was, according to Lord Ackner 'inherently repugnant to the adversarial position of the parties when involved in negotiations.' It also lacked the necessary certainty for a legally enforceable contract since courts would be unable to police performance and determine whether there was breach because the House considered that while negotiations are in existence either party is entitled to withdraw at any time and for any reason. There could accordingly be no obligation to continue to negotiate until there was a 'proper reason' to withdraw with the result that an agreement to negotiate could have no legal content. The defendants, who broke their undertaking to 'terminate negotiations with any third party or consideration of any alternative with a view to concluding agreements' for the sale of their photographic processing business if the plaintiffs obtained a letter of comfort from their bankers, were not accordingly liable in contract. However, the House left undisturbed an award of £700 damages which the trial judge had awarded for misrepresentation by the defendants' that they were not in negotiation with third parties including the persons to whom they sold their business.

The case throws up difficult distinctions between these ineffective undertakings and similar undertakings 'to use best endeavours to agree' or 'not to negotiate for a fixed period of time', both of which are enforceable.[37] It in effect requires a higher degree of certainty and a more complete form of agreement than Lord Wright required in *Hillas* v. *Arcos*[38] and does not, as he did in *Way* v. *Latilla*,[39] consider alternatives to contract and tort. In *Way* v. *Latilla* although it was held there was no concluded contract because the parties had failed to reach agreement about an essential term, a *quantum meruit* was

---

[31] Davenport, 'Obligation to consider Tenders', (1991) 107 L.Q.R. 201, 202.

[32] See *Holman Construction Ltd.* v. *Delta Timber Ltd.* [1972] N.Z.L.R. 1081.

[33] [1990] 3 All E.R. 25, 30 (Bingham, L. J.).

[34] *R.* v. *Lord Chancellor, ex. p. Hibbert* [1993] C.O.D. 326 (tendering for court reporting services).

[35] Such a tendering process would probably be subject to the E.C. Directives and this breach of the procedures would

give rise to a damages remedy: see S.I. 1992, No. 3279; Arrowsmith (1992), 1 Pub. Procurement Law Review 28.

[36] [1992] 2 A.C. 128. See Neill, 'A Key to Lock-Out Agreements?' (1992) 108 L.Q.R. 404. See also Brown, 'The Contract to Negotiate: a Thing Writ in Water' [1992] J.B.L. 353.

[37] *Pitt* v. *P.H.H. Asset Management Ltd.* [1993] N.L.J.R. 1187 (C.A.).

[38] [1932] 147 L.T. 503.

[39] [1937] 3 All E.R. 759.

awarded to the appellant gold prospector. In *Courtney and Fairbairn Ltd.* v. *Tolaini*,[40] in which it was held that an agreement to negotiate was too uncertain to amount to a contract, the possibility of non-contractual analysis was not considered. In *Courtney and Fairbairn* the failure to consider non-contractual alternatives was probably not important because there was nothing to indicate that the defendant had not negotiated in good faith with the plaintiff and only turned elsewhere when he concluded that there were good reasons for not entering into a contract with the plaintiff. In *Walford* v. *Miles* on the other hand, it was clear the defendants had, contrary to their undertaking, continued to negotiate with a third party to whom they eventually sold when he matched the plaintiff's offer. Whether, however, contractual damages would have been substantial or even more than the £700 reliance damages awarded for misrepresentation is questionable.[41]

An objection which is perhaps more fundamental is that it assumes a paradigm of contract in which as one commentator put it, contracts 'spring, full-blown, from the collective brows of the parties or their attorneys'.[42] But that is not how many agreements, in particular complex agreements negotiated over a protracted period, are made. Although it is often difficult to say at what point each party regards himself or the other party bound, as the same commentator concluded:

'the evidence of case and our own experience is that parties do often wish to register in an effective way their common commitment to an agreement, while reserving the privilege of differing over points not yet settled. If they have made such an agreement, the law has no business telling them their act of agreement was devoid of legal significance. Nor is the court, in characterising that agreement, obliged to choose between only two labels, 'complete contract' or 'mere negotiation', neither of which accurately describes the case.'

Although these comments were made in the context of contracts to bargain rather than lock out agreements, they appear equally relevant to the latter. Commercial parties and their lawyers regard *Walford* v. *Miles* as placing an unhelpful obstacle in the path of those engaged in negotiations. It is to be hoped that when the matter comes before the House of Lords again, it will be re-examined.

In conclusion, the discussion above asks whether it is better to solve problems that arise in negotia-

tions by the law of contract or outside it. An important consequence of not using contract is said to be that the remedy is different; only contract will protect expectations. But courts have not, it is submitted, paid sufficient attention to remedial issues when deciding questions of liability. It is a well known criticism of many promissory estoppel cases (including *High Trees*) that they in fact do just this. For instance, in *Attorney-General of Hong Kong* v. *Humphrey's Estate*[43] the Judicial Committee of the Privy Council envisaged that, if an estoppel had arisen, it would have prevented both parties from refusing to proceed with the transaction. This may reflect the equitable nature of the doctrine which gives specific rather than monetary relief. If so, it is to be questioned whether this is not anachronistic and needs reconsideration. There is a similar failure to consider remedial implications alongside liability in common law cases. In the *Blackpool* case the court did not consider the practical consequences of deciding that there was a contract to consider conforming tenders. It is arguable that where all that a person has lost is the chance of contracting, there may be little difference in practice between expectation and reliance. Would the House of Lords have shown less hostility to the lock-out agreement in *Walton* v. *Miles* if the remedial implications of finding that it was enforceable had not been envisaged in terms of protecting the loss of bargain in not being sold the business (an alleged £1 million)?

(b) The renegotiation of contracts

The tension between the commercial desire to facilitate reasonable renegotiation of contracts and the lawyer's fear that the legal enforceability of renegotiations may lead to extortion and unconscionable conduct is well known. In *Foakes* v. *Beer*[44] Lord Blackburn recognised the factual benefit of a bird in the hand. Although devices such as peppercorn and invented consideration were used to render renegotiations legally binding, these were not directly aimed at and did not therefore prevent extortion. As the pre-existing rule invalidated non-extortive as well as extortive renegotiations, the result was an unsatisfactory body of law. hence the development of the doctrine of promissory estoppel which, although controversial was perceived as much needed. Its overall effect was to facilitate and even encourage renegotiation.

---

[40] [1975] 1 W.L.R. 297.

[41] The claim was for £1 million which it was claimed would have been made had the business been sold to the plaintiffs. But all the lock-out agreement would have given them was a period in which there would be no dealings with rivals. At the end of that the defendants would, on any view, have been free to sell to whoever they wished. See N. Cohen, 'Two Freedoms

and the Contract to Negotiate', (Contract Symposium, Oxford, September 1993), pp. 14–16.

[42] Charles Knapp, 'Enforcing the Contract to Bargain (1969), 44 N.Y.U.L.R. 673, 727.

[43] [1987] 1 A.C. 114, 127–8.

[44] (1894) 9 App. Cas. 605, 602 on which see *Re Selectmove Ltd. The Times,* 13 January 1994 (CA).

However, as has been mentioned, in the 48 years since the decision in *High Trees*, the broad statements of principle used to describe the situations which will give rise to an estoppel and the limits to such estoppels have not been reduced to a coherent body of law. Thus, for instance, although in general the effect of an estoppel is 'suspensory', it can extinguish rights. However, the textbook treatment (reflecting the cases) of the situations in which an estoppel will be held to extinguish rights and a person who has made a promissory representation will not be permitted to go back on it, goes little further than to say that this will be so when it is no longer possible for the representee to resume his original position and it is inequitable to require him to do so or be liable to the other party under the contract.[45] Questions such as whether account should be taken of the fact that the event making it impossible to resume the original position was one which under the contract was at the representee's risk or of the fact that the impossibility was the fault of the representee remain largely unanswered. Again it is, for instance, not yet clear whether the fact that there has been detrimental reliance by the promisee means, as statements in one case suggest,[46] that prima facie the right is extinguished. Similarly, although there is clear authority that an estoppel will not arise where the representee has acted 'inequitably',[47] there has been relatively little development of the concept by discussion of what conduct by a contracting party seeking renegotiation constitutes 'inequitable' conduct. Some of the responsibility for this lies with the jurists who have preferred the high ground of fundamental principle and may have neglected the need to move from principle to developed doctrine.

The doctrinal tendency of estoppel to encourage recognition by making many renegotiations enforceable may have appeared satisfactory in the relatively stable times of the 1950s and early 1960s. However, higher rates of inflation and sharp fall in oil and other markets following the Arab–Israeli wars of 1967 and 1973 meant that, from the point of view of one of the contracting parties, many contracts went wrong. The commercial pressures to renegotiate were accordingly great. It is not, therefore, surprising that one of the most important innovations in the modern law of English contract, the development of economic duress, occurred shortly afterwards in 1976.

For the first time a doctrine primarily and directly concerned with the question of extortion and unconscientious conduct was available to control renegotiations. However, the overall effect was to move the balance of doctrine in the direction of the sanctity of the initial contract for a renegotiation could now be vitiated by reason of economic duress even if supported by consideration. It is interesting to note that the tools used both by courts and commentators to develop this new vitiating factor in contract came from the law of tort (intimidation) and restitution rather than from equity. Although, not surprisingly, many questions concerning economic duress have yet to be decided, the indications are that the courts are seized of the need to develop a set of principles that will guide contracting parties seeking renegotiation as to what they can and they cannot do.

The most difficult situations concern threats to break contracts.[48] The line between (a) threats to break a contract unless its terms are varied; (b) warnings of likely inability to perform as a result of, for instance, extreme cash flow problems, market fluctuations, or inflation, and (c) simple pre-intimations of proposed action[49] can be a fine one. However, it appears from the cases that the degree of control that the party making the statements have over the events is important in determining whether a renegotiation will be vitiated by duress. So is whether, when the pressure for renegotiation has come from the actions of third parties, the party who has indicated that he will not perform (or not be able to perform) the contract without extra payment has made any reasonable effort to deal with the third parties.[50] Again, where the renegotiation is in fact prompted by circumstances that existed at the time of the contract but which were not appreciated because of an erroneous assessment of the risks or a misunderstanding as to the effect of the contract, it is likely to be easier to establish duress.[51] It also seems possible that courts will have regard to whether the original bargain was a hard one, at any rate where renegotiation was initiated by the beneficiary of the original bargain who feared that the financial difficulties of his counterparty would lead to non-performance.[52]

The courts appear to be moving to a position in which they will consider whether it is commercially reasonable for the person seeking to renegotiate the

---

[45] Anson's *Law of Contract* (26th ed. 1984), pp. 104–5; Cheshire, Fifoot and Furmston's *Law of Contract* (12th ed. 1991), pp. 101–3; Koffman and MacDonald, *The Law of Contract* (1992), 68–70; Treitel, op. cit., pp. 107.
[46] *The Post Chaser* [1982] 1 All E.R. 19, 27 (Robert Goff, J.).
[47] *D. and C. Builders* v. *Rees* [1966] 2 Q.B. 617.
[48] For fuller (perhaps over-sceptical) treatment see Beatson, *The Use and Abuse of Restitution* (1991), pp. 117–29.

[49] These do not constitute a 'threat' in the context of the economic torts *Hodges* v. *Webb* [1920] 2 Ch. 70, 87.
[50] *B. and S. Contracts* v. *Victor Green Publications* [1984] I.C.R. 419.
[51] *Atlas Express Ltd.* v. *Kafco* [1989] Q.B. 833.
[52] *Williams* v. *Roffey Brothers & Nichollas (Contractors) Ltd.* [1990] 2 W.L.R. 1153.

contract to do so.[53] If it is and if the renegotiation does no more than is necessary to meet the changed circumstances it is possible that the court will consider that the party seeking renegotiation had no practical alternative. This ties in with policies favouring finality which favour compromises. Where there is a threat not to perform which involves pressure beyond the threat to sue the other party, the court, in considering whether a compromise should be upheld, appears to take account of the objective reasonableness of the claim as well as the good faith of the claimant.[54] This movement is similar to that which has occurred in the United States between the first and the second Restatement of Contracts. Under §176 (2) of the *Restatement of Contracts 2d* the binding nature of a renegotiation will depend on whether it is commercially reasonable to seek renegotiation and whether the renegotiated terms are 'fair and equitable'. In short, the tendency of a doctrine of economic duress appears to be to develop into a method of monitoring good faith and fairness in contract renegotiation. It might be said that this removes one of the advantages claimed for duress over the promissory estoppel as a monitor of renegotiations. While there is truth in this, there may nevertheless be advantages in a doctrine which is structured to go from the particular to the general as economic duress seems to be doing.

Professor Simpson's important article on innovation in nineteenth century contract law[55] showed clearly how the many functions performed by consideration were separated out and supplemented by new, more targeted, doctrines of offer and acceptance and intention to create legal relations. Economic duress is the latest example of this. It is not surprising that, while the new doctrines started out as supplementary, their existence has led to a re-evaluation of consideration, and the conclusion that some of its sub-rules may have been rendered redundant. So the existence of economic duress, a doctrine directly dealing with improper pressure, enabled further dilution of the consideration requirement in *Williams* v. *Roffey Brothers & Nicholls (Contractors) Ltd.*[56] In that case a promise by a carpentry sub-

contractor to perform his contractual obligation was held binding because the head contractor to whom the promise was made enjoyed a practical benefit in ensuring that work continued, that the trouble and expense of engaging new sub-contractors was avoided, and that any penalty for delay under the head contract would be avoided. This decision of the Court of Appeal has attracted much comment.[57] It potentially has great impact on the 'bargain' model of contract. There are difficult questions as to what constitutes practical benefit. It is also arguable that, in adopting a contractual solution, it provides an inappropriate remedy.[58] It certainly increases the need to have a clear and predictable law of duress. There are a number of statements indicating that *in practice* the requirement of consideration does not operate as an impediment to the enforceability of contracts.[59] The overall effect of *Williams* v. *Roffey* may be that as a matter of *law* consideration is no longer required for modifications to obligations to supply goods and services. It should not, however, be seen as either illogical or unprincipled to require consideration for the creation of a contract but not for contractual modifications. Sir Frederick Pollock (in the pre *High Trees* era) stated that

'The doctrine of consideration, especially . . . [the pre-existing duty rule] . . . has been extended with not very happy results beyond its proper scope, which is to govern the formation of contracts, and has been made to regulate and restrain the discharge of contracts.'[60]

Although, therefore, the role of consideration could be restricted in this way in order to deal with the problem of renegotiations and contract modification, it is not obvious that practical benefit will only be regarded as consideration in cases of modification.[61]

The question raised by the discussion in this section concerns the relative merits of the common law and equitable routes. Some might ask why the result in *Williams* v. *Roffey* could not have been achieved by using promissory estoppel. They might point to the remedial appropriateness of a reliance based remedy and it has indeed been suggested that the

---

[53] Goff and Jones, *The Law of Restitution* (4th ed.) pp. 251, 265–6.

[54] Where the only pressure is an explicit or implicit threat to sue, only the good faith of the claimant is taken account of.

[55] (1975) 91 L.Q.R. 247, 263.

[56] [1990] 2 W.L.R. 1153.

[57] Including Adams & Brownsword (1990), 53 M.L.R. 536; Coote (1991), J.C.L. 23; Halson (1990), 106 L.Q.R. 184, (1991) [1990] C.L.P. 111, 107 L.Q.R. 649; Hooley [1991], J.B.L. 19. It does not apply to obligations to pay money: *Re Selectmove Ltd. The Times*, 13 January 1994 (CA).

[58] Chen-Wishart, 'Consideration for Contract after *Williams* v. *Roffey Brothers*' (Oxford Contract Symposium, September 1993).

[59] See, e.g., *Thorenson Car Ferries* v. *Weymouth B.C.* [1977]

2 Lloyd's R. 614 (per Donaldson, J.); *The Eurymedon* [1974] A.C. 154, 167 (per Lord Wilberforce).

[60] This is to be found in all editions of his *Principles of Contracts* from the first in 1876 (p. 160), to the twelfth by P. H. Winfield in 1946 (p. 147).

[61] In *Pitt* v. *P.H.H. Asset Management Ltd.* [1993] N.L.J.R. 1187 (C.A.) three items were regarded as valuable consideration for a 'lock-out' agreement; (a) desisting from seeking an injunction proceedings, (b) not causing trouble with the third party who had made a higher offer, and (c) the promise to exchange contracts in two weeks. If the first sufficed, it appears it could only do so on the basis of practical benefit because the claim for an injunction was hopeless and the threat to seek one was 'vapid' and only of nuisance value.

remedy in fact given in the case may have been so restricted.[62] However, one advantage of the use of the common law rather than estoppel is that the courts have directly to confront the difficulties with consideration and to re-evaluate the purposes of that doctrine. Much ink has been spilt over the relationship between promissory estoppel and consideration, and there is no need to tread over familiar ground. However, the co-existence of promissory estoppel with 'strict' requirements of consideration with the two often seen to be operating in separate spheres means that they can appear to be like ships passing in the night. This can mean that the use of estoppel makes it easier to avoid addressing the difficult questions than it is if the approach (economic duress and practical benefit) in *Williams* v. *Roffey* is developed. It is to be hoped that the *Williams* v. *Roffey* approach will provide a firmer basis for rational development.

(c) Illegality

The recent decision of the House of Lords in *Tinsley* v. *Milligan*[63] provides an interesting illustration of the way difficulties and possible defects of contract law can be avoided by recourse to a non-contractual solution, here based on property. Again, however, the risk is that it is possible to sidestep difficult issues of policy. In that case two women jointly bought a house. All the money provided by them for the purchase came ultimately from their joint business. It was, however, registered in the name of *T.* so as to enable *M.* to make (with *T.*'s knowledge) fraudulent claims for social security benefits. The transaction between *T.* and *M.* was therefore an illegal contract and when they fell out the question arose as to whether the court could give effect to their intention that it be owned jointly by declaring that it was held by *T.* on trust for the parties in equal shares.

The declaration was given and appeals to the Court of Appeal and House of Lords were dismissed but on very different grounds. A majority of the Court of Appeal held that when confronted with a defence of illegality,

'. . . the underlying principle is the so-called public conscience test. The court must weigh, or balance, the adverse

consequences of granting relief against the adverse consequences of refusing relief. The ultimate decision calls for a value judgment.'[64]

The House of Lords unanimously rejected this broad discretionary test in which recovery ultimately depended on whether the court considered that the ordinary citizen would be shocked by a court making the order sought. Lord Browne-Wilkinson considered the test to be 'imponderable' and Lord Goff thought it was inconsistent with the authorities. However, a bare majority (Lord Goff and Lord Keith dissenting) considered that the rule that the court will enforce property interests acquired in pursuance of an illegal transaction if, but only if, he can establish his title without relying on his own illegality, the *Bowmakers* rule,[65] applied to equitable as well as to legal property interests.[66] As the creation of *M.*'s equitable interest did not depend upon a contractual obligation but on a common intention acted on by the parties to their detriment, *M.* was entitled to the declaration she sought.[67]

Although in *Bowmakers* v. *Barnet* the illegality was regarded as 'technical' and in *Tinsley* v. *Milligan* the fraud was (perhaps surprisingly) regarded as 'relatively minor',[68] the 'recognition of property' approach enables the court to avoid any consideration of the gravity of the illegality. Thus, as Lord Goff feared, even terrorists who acquire a house in the names of a third party would appear to be able to invoke the assistance of the court.[69] More seriously, given that property can generally pass by delivery or intention, this approach may mean that the person who knowingly enters into an illegal transaction will be in a better position than an innocent person. For the person who does so knowing of its illegality can structure the transaction to enable him to avoid the *ex turpi causa* and *in pari delicto* rules. He can ensure that any property is transferred to or remains with him and enforce his property rights. It is to be regretted that the majority speeches did not address this question which is well aired in the academic commentary.[70]

The case also provides some insight as to the current approach to innovation. The majority, having decided the case by either an incremental extension

---

[62] Chen-Wishart, op. cit., suggests that expectation damages would have been more than the £3,500 awarded which represented recompense for the sub-contractor's performance at the data he accepted a breach by the head-contractor as discharging the contract.

[63] [1993] 3 All E.R. 65.

[64] [1992] Ch. 310, 319 (Nicholls, L. J.).

[65] [1993] 3 All E.R. 65, 90, referring to *Bowmakers Ltd.* v. *Barnet Instruments Ltd.* [1945] K.B. 65.

[66] '. . . in 1993, English law has one single law of property made up of legal and equitable interests.': [1993] 3 All E.R. at 86 (Lord Browne-Wilkinson).

[67] [1993] 3 All E.R. 65, 90.

[68] [1993] 3 All E.R. 65, 70f–g, 79a–b (apparently because of its prevalence and because *M.* had confessed).

[69] Note that in *Bowmakers* the principle was said not to extend to 'that class of cases in which the goods claimed are of such a kind that it is unlawful to deal in them at all, as for example, obscene books'. Is this, however, a serious limitation: leaving aside sawn-off shotguns, even guns can be licenced, and prohibited drugs may be prescribed to registered addicts.

[70] See especially Coote, 'Another Look at *Bowmakers* v. *Barnet Instruments*' (1972) 35 M.L.R. 38, 50.

to or a broad application of an established exception to the *in pari delicto* rule, had no need to look further. However, Lord Goff, having concluded that equitable relief could not be given to one who does not come to equity with clean hands, considered whether it would be appropriate to develop the law by qualifying the equitable principle. He thought it would not.[71] First, it would be difficult to distinguish between degrees of iniquity: the *Bowmakers* principle could be invoked by outrageously guilty parties as well as the innocent and the relatively innocent. Secondly, the adoption of the public conscience test meant replacing a system of rules ultimately derived from a principle of public policy with a discretionary balancing process.

The implication is that, while judicial innovation by the identification of a new principle underlying the authorities, as occurred in *Woolwich Equitable B.S.* v. *Inland Revenue Commissioners*,[72] is legitimate, the creation of a policy-based discretion is not.[73] Lord Goff considered innovation of this sort to be a task for legislation following a full inquiry into the perceived advantages and disadvantages of both the present law and a system of discretionary relief. While we shall return to this question when considering statute law and common law, at this stage it may be worth noting that even where there is statutory guidance, difficulties have arisen. For instance, the Insurance Companies Act 1974 prohibited unauthorised persons from 'effecting and carrying out contracts of insurance'. The purpose of the statute was to protect insured parties against misconduct and insolvency by insurers and it was generally accepted that good public policy and common sense required that contracts of insurance, even if made by unauthorised insurers, should not be invalidated.[74] However, the courts (albeit reluctantly) decided that the prohibition on 'carrying out contracts of insurance' meant that the payment of claims was expressly prohibited by the statute and that insurers

could not accordingly be required to do so.[75] Section 132 of the Financial Services Act 1986 changed this and gives the insured the option of enforcing the contract or claiming the return of money paid under it and also gives a discretion to permit an innocent insurer to enforce the contract or to retain money paid under it.

(d) Contracts for the benefit of third parties

The reluctance of English judges to reconsider the doctrine of privity of contract which prevents third party beneficiaries from suing on contracts which were explicitly made for their benefit is perhaps the best example of a consensus that major developments, even in areas hitherto the preserve of common law doctrine, should in the future, be achieved by legislation.[76] This was perhaps to be expected in the 1960s and 1970s given the newly established Law Commission and the fact that many of its recommendations were implemented *by government*. It was not surprising that Lord Scarman, the first Chairman of the Law Commission was a leading exponent of this view,[77] but it was widely held by the senior judiciary. But even Lord Scarman recognised that the courts may be forced to act if there were to be a further prolonged period of legislative inactivity. There are signs that as appellate courts confront the fact that in the pressure for space in a crowded legislative timetable the reform of private law, and in particular contract and tort law, loses out to legislative initiatives with a higher political profile they will be more willing to innovate. The first cracks in the old consensus are already visible.[78]

Should the courts of this country reconsider their attitude and follow those common law jurisdictions—from New York in 1859 to Australia in 1988—in which third party rights were recognised in a decision of the courts? I have set out my reasons for believing that this would be a second-best solution elsewhere.[79] At bottom they rest on the fact that the

---

[71] [1993] 3 All E.R. 65, 79.

[72] [1993] 1 A.C. 70.

[73] For this reason, it appears unlikely that the House of Lords would recognise a power to apportion damages for breach of contract where the plaintiff has contributed to his loss: this sort of innovation, although based on the principle of relative fault, would be left to the legislature. The Law Commission has recommended this in respect of contractual duties to take care but not in respect of strict contractual duties: Law Com. No. 219, 'Contributory Negligence as a Defence in Contract' (1993).

[74] *Phoenix General Insurance* v. *Adas* [1987] 2 All E.R. 152, 175 (Kerr, L. J.).

[75] As well as *Phoenix* v. *Adas*, see *Bedford Insurance* v. *Instito de Resseguros do Brazil* [1985] 1 Q.B. 966; *Re Cavalier Insurance* [1989] 2 Lloyd's Rep. 430. Cf. *Stewart* v. *Oriental Fire and Marine Insurance* [1985] 1 Q.B. 988. See also Treitel, op. cit., p. 433.

[76] *Beswick* v. *Beswick* [1968] A.C. 58, 72; *Woodar* v. *Wimpey*

Construction U.K. Ltd. [1980] 1 W.L.R. 291, 297–8, 300; *Swain* v. *Law Society* [1983] 1 A.C. 598, 611.

[77] As well as *Woodar* v. *Wimpey Construction U.K. Ltd.* above, see *National Westminster Bank plc.* v. *Morgan* [1985] A.C. 686, 708.

[78] *Woolwich Building Society* v. *I.R.C.* [1993] 1 A.C. 70 (Lord Goff, deciding to recognise a new right to restitution of ultra vires tax payments, said 'This opportunity will never come again. If we do not take it now it will be gone forever. . . . [H]owever, compelling the principle of justice may be, it would never be sufficient to persuade a government to propose its legislative recognition . . .'). See also *R.* v. *R.* (*Rape: Marital Exemption*) [1991] 4 All E.R. 481; *R.* v. *Kearley* [1992] 2 All E.R. 245 (reform of the hearsay rule in criminal proceedings).

[79] 'Reforming the Law of Contracts for the Benefit of Third Parties: A Second Bite at the Cherry' (1992) 45 C.L.P. 1, esp. 15–18, 20–2. For judicial discussion, see the minority judgments (Brennan, Dawson and Dean, J. J.) in the *Trident* case, below.

abolition of the privity rule throws up a number of difficult problems that cannot be isolated and which are unlikely to be dealt with on a case by case basis without undue loss of certainty and without making choices of policy rather than of principle. The choices include the test of enforceable benefit, revocability or variability by the parties, the defences to an action by a third party and, whether the third party should be bound by obligations imposed on him by the contract. Common law as opposed to statutory development may also lead to (unanticipated and undesired) knock-on effects on rules developed on the assumption that third parties could not sue on contracts, for instance the rules of trusts, agency, and estoppel.

The experience of the jurisdictions which have introduced it judicially is not encouraging. Francis Reynolds has pointed out[80] that the variety of approaches in the majority judgments in High Court of Australia's decision in *Trident General Insurance Co. Ltd.* v. *McNeice Bros. Pty. Ltd.*[81] leaves the law there in a state of considerable uncertainty. There is clarity neither as to the scope of the new rule nor the subsidiary but vitally important questions of defences, revocability, and double recovery. As far as scope is concerned, is it confined to liability insurance (Toohey, J.) or all insurance (the decision of Mason, C. J. and Wilson, J.), or to all contracts where a firm intention to benefit the third party can be shown (the reasoning of Mason, C. J. and Wilson, J., and the fears of the minority who thought that it was not possible to make a distinction between different kinds of contract by reference to any coherent principle). While it may be thought unfair to point to the uncertainty that inevitably results from the introduction of a new common law doctrine, over a century after the recognition of third party rights in the United States there is still uncertainty as to the test of enforceable benefit and the time revocation or variation by the parties is no longer possible. Although Professor T. B. Smith has stated that the *ius quaesitum tertio* has been well established in Scotland since the sixteenth century,[82] it appears that many of the major issues remain unresolved.

One should not underestimate the difficulties of reforming a deeply embedded, although not funda-

mental,[83] common law rule by legislation.[84] However, the Law Commission's provisional proposals[85] for the recognition of third party rights of suit on contracts if that is what the contracting parties intended were, with one exception,[86] enthusiastically supported on consultation both by lawyers and commercial concerns. The desire for reform stems from the view that the present law necessitates elaborate arrangements to achieve the parties intentions in a complex multi-party transactions. Even then it may require several trips to the House of Lords to find out exactly how to structure contractual arrangements. In the case of well established commercial relationships this may be tolerable, but it leaves our law ill-equipped to deal with new forms of transactions. If, once the Commission reports, it becomes clear that legislation is not forthcoming, I believe that it will not only be desirable but will be *necessary* for the House of Lords to take the initiative.

In the present context, however, the case of contracts for the benefit of a third party suggests that even Lord Goff's ideal method of legal development has its limits and that one such limit may be reached when it is asked to consider a development raising polycentric issues.

(d) A General Doctrine of Inequality of Bargaining Power or Unconscionability

In *National Westminster Bank plc.* v. *Morgan* Lord Scarman ruled out a general doctrine of inequality of bargaining power on the ground that the task of limiting freedom of contract so as to relieve against such inequality was essentially a legislative task for Parliament. This argument is one of policy and institutional appropriateness, not one based (as were the minority judgments in the *Trident* case) on the nature of the judicial process. A general doctrine could, however, have been rejected on less policy-oriented grounds.

The authors of a leading text on the Uniform Commercial Code state of its main unconscionability provision, §2–302, that 'It is not possible to *define* unconscionability. It is *not a concept, but a determination* to be made in the light of a variety of factors not unifiable into a formula.'[87] A general doctrine of this sort is likely to be elusive, with uncertainty as

---

[80] 'Privity of Contract, the Boundaries of Categories and the limits of the Judicial Function' (1989) 105 L.Q.R. 1.

[81] (1988) 62 A.L.J.R. 508, discussed by Reynolds (1989), 105 L.Q.R. 1. See also Edgell [1989], L.M.C.L.Q. 139; Kincaid [1989], C.L.J. 243, 250–1; Jackman (1989), 63 A.L.J. 368; Soh (1989), 105 L.Q.R. 4; Sutton (1988), 16 A.B.L.R. 475; Finn (ed.), *Essays in Restitution* (1990), 32–6 (Mason), 58 (Gummow).

[82] *Studies Critical and Comparative* (1962), 92.

[83] *Tomlinson (Hauliers) Ltd.* v. *Hepburn* [1966] A.C. 451, 470–1.

[84] The New Zealand Law Commission's *Contract Statutes Review* (1993), however, concluded that the Contracts (Privity) Act 1982 only required one, relatively minor, amendment.

[85] Law Com. C.P. No. 121 (1991).

[86] Certain sectors of the construction industry (main contractors).

[87] White & Summers, *Uniform Commercial Code* (3rd ed., 1988), pp. 203–4, citing *Mieske* v. *Bartell Drug Co.* 593 P.2d 1308 (1979) Wash.

an inherent feature of it rather than something that only affects it in the period immediately after it is introduced. It remains to be seen whether when fully developed the High Court of Australia's doctrine of unconscionability is open to this criticism. Commentators have pointed to the concern of that court with 'basal' principles,[88] and suggested that this produces a simpler, more principled body of law. However, the variety of different approaches used in the High Court of Australia's judgments[89] on unconscionability prompts the comment that the variety of ways of formulating the 'basal' principle means that it is questionable whether the law in fact appears simple to the users of legal services and those advising them.

An example of the sort of issue which needs to be addressed by a general doctrine of unconscionability is the relationship between substantive and procedural unconscionability. Substantive unconscionability is solely concerned with the outcome of the bargaining process, i.e. with price in the broadest sense of that word while procedural unconscionability concerns the process itself. A general doctrine, not working through smaller factually based categories, is often criticised for failing to make a sharp distinction or indeed any distinction between these. Even when stated in a general way rather than more particularly (fraud, misrepresentation, duress and other forms of unlawful pressure), rules preventing procedural unconscionability can be justified as protecting the integrity of the bargaining process and parties' freedom of choice. But, since legal principles do not give courts the means of making a sophisticated determination of value, substantive unconscionability is seen by many as an elegant *ex post facto* justification for covertly and arbitrarily interfering with price. It is therefore less easy to justify than procedural unconscionability. Courts have, however, struggled to do so by reference to factors such as public policy (in the salvage cases)[90] and that the plaintiff is a member of a vulnerable class of persons, sometimes coupled with a requirement of exploitation by the defendant (at present reflected in the 'manifest disadvantage' requirement).

However, whatever one's views about a general principle of unconscionability, *National Westminster Bank plc* v. *Morgan* shows that there are dangers in too particular a view of doctrine and a reluctance to look to principle. For that case turned equitable undue influence in upon itself and appeared to subject the cases of pressure and the cases of a dominant or vulnerable relationship without actual pressure to the same regime, without having considered the common law on unlawful pressure—duress. The possibility was left open that some cases of pressure would be treated separately and arguably inappropriately within the equitable category. This was what in fact happened when, in *BCCI* v. *Aboody*,[91] the requirement of 'manifest disadvantage', perhaps suitable to a case of presumed or relational undue influence, was applied to a case where pressure had in fact been used.

We now have the decisions of the House of Lords in *Barclays Bank* v. *O'Brien* and *CIBC Mortgages plc.* v. *Pitt*,[92] two cases involving, as did *National Westminster Bank plc.* v. *Morgan*, wives who provided security for their husband's debts, usually in the form of a mortgage or re-mortgage of the family home. The choice of rule, was between treating married women like all other sureties and regarding them as members of a vulnerable class (perhaps together with elderly parents) which needs special protection when providing security. The first approach would only preclude the creditor from enforcing its security where there had, *to its knowledge*,[93] been misconduct (i.e. misrepresentation, duress or undue influence). The second approach (the 'special equity') would preclude enforcement if the creditor knew the surety was within the protected class, there had been misconduct by the debtor or lack of understanding by the surety, and the creditor had not taken reasonable steps to try to ensure that the surety had an adequate understanding of the nature of the transaction. The Court of Appeal chose the second route.

The House of Lords rejected the 'special equity'.[94] However, it reconsidered the requirement of notice and held that a third party who knows of facts which put him on inquiry as to the possible existence of rights and fails to make such inquiry or to take such other steps as are reasonable to verify whether such a right does or does not exist will have constructive

[88] E.g. Finn [1990], J.B.L. 265, 269.
[89] For example, compare Deane and Dawson, J. J. and Gaudron, J. in *Stern* v. *McArthur* (1988) 62 A.L.J.R. 588, 604–5, and 609–10.
[90] Although here the jurisdiction developed at a time the court was assisted by expert maritime assessors.
[91] [1990] 1 Q.B. 923.
[92] [1993] 3 W.L.R. 786 and 802. For the Court of Appeal decisions, see [1993] Q.B. 109 and *The Times*, 7 April 1993 respectively.
[93] Or imputed knowledge if the debtor (husband) had been acting as the agent of the creditor (bank) in dealing with the surety (wife).
[94] [1993] 3 W.L.R. 786, 797. One important reason for this was that it would in effect reintroduce a presumption of undue influence arising as a matter of law in the husband–wife relationship although this had been decisively rejected in the case law. This presumption should be distinguished from the tone that arises where it is shown (as it often can be between husband and wife) that in the *particular* relationship the complainant generally reposed trust and confidence in the other party. See ibid., p. 792.

notice of the earlier rights. Lord Browne-Wilkinson said that creditors are put on inquiry when a wife offers to guarantee her husband's debts 'by the combination of two factors: (a) the transaction is on its fact not to the financial advantage of the wife; and (b) there is a substantial risk in transactions of that kind that, in procuring the wife to act as surety, the husband has committed a legal or equitable wrong that entitles the wife to set aside the transaction.[95] What steps should the creditor take to ensure that it does not have such constructive notice of the wife's rights? It was said that in the case of guarantees by spouses or cohabitees, the creditor will, as a general rule, have taken reasonable steps if he warns the surety at a meeting not attended by the principal debtor of the amount of her potential liability and of the risks involved and advises her to take independent legal advice.[96] The House of Lords did not need to use a general doctrine of unconscionability to set the appropriate standards.[97] In *CIBC Mortgages plc.* v. *Pitt* the House did, however, reconsider the 'manifest disadvantage' rule, introduced in *National Westminster Bank plc.* v. *Morgan*, restricted its application to cases of presumed undue influence and stated that even in such cases it was difficult to see how the rule fitted with the long standing principle that requires those in a fiduciary position who enter into transactions with those to whom they are fiduciary duties to establish affirmatively that the transaction was a fair one.[98] It is, however, not altogether clear whether the approach of their Lordships will draw a clearer line between cases in which the protection is given because of the incapacity or vulnerability of the plaintiff and cases in which it is given because of the misconduct of the defendant is sufficiently sharply drawn.[99] Although both will be present in many fact situations it is important to keep them separate. One disadvantage of a general doctrine of unconscionability or inequality of bargaining power is that it may not be capable of doing so. The identification of the categories of presumed undue influence—presumed in law and presumed because of general trust in the particular relationship—should assist in keeping the

two separate. In both the protection is given irrespective of wrongdoing.

(II) Notes on the Role of Statute Law and European Community Law

Are we moving from a common law system of contract to a statutory system? New Zealand, for instance, has since 1969, enacted five statutes which deal with general principles of contract; the Minors Contracts Act 1969, the Illegal Contracts Act 1970, The Contractual Mistakes Act 1977, the Contractual Remedies Act 1979 and the Contracts (Privity) Act 1982. Although the current climate may not favour legislation, in the same period England has enacted the Misrepresentation Act 1967, the Unfair Contract Terms Act 1977, the Civil Liability (Contribution) Act 1978, and the Minors Contracts Act 1987.[100] The New Zealand Law Commission has recently reviewed the operation of the New Zealand statutes and the extent to which they had fulfilled their purpose of 'strengthen[ing] the institution of contract by liberalising the effect of the law in a limited number of areas where it could operate unfairly.'[101] The Commission concluded that by and large the statutes had achieved their purpose and that 'fears which might have been entertained for "sanctity of contract' because discretions were conferred on the courts have proved to have little if any foundation'. It recognised that there had been some difficulties but found very few points on which it could recommend amendments to improve the legislation: for the most part its recommendations involve only a fine tuning.[102] Sir Robin Cooke, while an advocate of bold common law development of the law, points out one powerful advantage of statute. If courts are reluctant to discover and articulate the general principle upon which discrete categories of case rest as he suggests English courts are), development is unlikely to be in the direction favoured by Lord Goff but towards an increasing number of small, factually based categories, in other words to greater complexity and obscurity and less flexibility. A statute can have a

---

[95] Ibid. at 798. In *C.I.B.I.C. Mortgages plc.* v. *Pitt* [1993] 3 W.L.R. 802 where the mortgage company was told that the loan was to be used to purchase a second property, it was not put on inquiry; there was no indication that the transaction was anything other than a normal advance to husband and wife for their joint benefit.

[96] Where this advice is declined see *Clark* v. *Mouatt* [1993] 3 W.L.R. 1021 (P.C.).

[97] Though cf. the Privy Council decision in *Boustani* v. *Pigot* [1993] E.G.C.S. 85 (Antigua & Barbuda).

[98] [1993] 3 W.L.R. 802, 807–9. The abuse of confidence cases establishing this had not been considered in *Morgan*'s case.

[99] For a powerful argument to this effect, see Birks and

Chin, 'On the Nature of Undue Influence' (Oxford Contract Symposium, September 1993).

[100] I exclude the Supply of Goods and Services Act 1982 and the Law of Property (Miscellaneous Provisions) Act 1989 since, although of great importance, these were concerned with particular types of contract rather than with contracts in general. The Sale of Goods Act 1979 was, of course, a consolidation.

[101] B. Coote, 'The Contracts and Commercial Law Reform Committee and the Contract Statutes' (1988) 13 N.Z.V.L.R. 160, 188.

[102] New Zealand Law Commission No. 25 (1993), 'Contract Statutes Review', pp. 1–2.

general cleansing effect, as Sir Robin suggests the Unfair Contract Terms Act 1977 has had, in giving back to the courts the power to control contract so as to do reasonable justice between consumers and suppliers, a control which he considered they had abandoned by self-imposed doctrine.[103]

Even if we do not go as far as New Zealand, the discussion in part I and the examples at notes 6–9 suggest that innovation in contract will often have to be achieved legislatively. How, given the difficulties of introducing legislation, will contract law adapt to new commercial and societal needs? Secondly, how will contract law adapt to the injection into it of European Community legislative norms derived from civil law systems and expressed in terms of greater generality than either English legislation or in our mature common law system as worked out through thousands of decisions? In the period after the United Kingdom joined the European Communities in 1972, a series of decisions established that the traditional approach to statutory interpretation could not apply without modification to the interpretation of European Community legislation, couched as it was in broad language. Will the same process start to happen as the impact of the E.C. Directives and the legislation implementing them are considered by English courts? This seems probable, particularly since there is an increasing tendency for the U.K.'s implementing secondary legislation simply to track the language of the Directive (the technique is described as 'copy out') and hence be less detailed than domestic legislation.[104] Underlying these preliminary points is a concern that the common law lacks a theory enabling the judges to use principles embodied in statutes as guides or analogues when considering common law doctrine and the limits of such use. One question which I believe needs to be discussed—but to which I do not have an answer—is how the common law, and in the context of our discussion the common law of contract, can exist and develop in an age of statutes.[105]

In England there has been relatively little work of a more theoretical nature on the relationship of common law and statute.[106] It has two aspects. First there is the question of whether the existence of a statute

has a direct effect on the common law. In some situations, for instance, it seems clear that the existence of a statute covering part of the ground has led to the re-evaluation of a common law not within its scope. The two best examples of this are the effect of the Law Reform (Contributory Negligence) Act 1945 on causation (in contract where there is concurrent liability with tortious liability) and of the Unfair Contract Terms Act 1977 on the construction of exemption clauses. In the former the possibility of apportionment of fault meant that courts were less willing to say that the chain of causation had been broken.[107] In the latter, the fact that exemption clauses in standard form and consumer contracts were subject to a statutory reasonableness test meant that courts were less inclined to construe them strictly so as to cut down their width.[108] The second aspect, which cannot conveniently be considered here, concerns the more indirect effect of statutes and regulations. Does the fact that a sphere of contractual activity is regulated affect the content of the contract through the medium of implied terms, or custom, or in some other way.[109] For instance, are even general legislative provisions likely to lead to a less cohesive law of contract? The reluctance of appellate courts to interfere with the decision of trial judges on what constitutes 'reasonableness' under the Unfair Contract Terms Act 1977 means that a decision on this issue has some similarities to an exercise of discretion.[110] This means that the jurisprudence is more likely to be developed at the trial than the appellate level and for different patterns to emerge in different transaction types.

In the context of the issues of good faith and disclosure that are of current concern, the statutory duties of good faith and disclosure in the Consumer Credit Act 1974 and the Financial Services Act 1986 have had less influence. The statutes reflected a legislative decision that consumers buying on credit and the purchasers of the products of the financial services industry (insurance policies, investments, and advice) required protection. This was to be achieved by a licensing system and by close control of the way those licensed conduct their businesses. The former only applies to consumers and, in the

---

[103] 'Dynamics of the Common Law', Address to the 9th Commonwealth Law Conference, Auckland, 1990.

[104] See *Times* Leader, 15 November 1993.

[105] Cf. Calabresi, *A Common Law for the Age of Statutes* (Yale) and Eisenberg, *The Nature of the Common Law* (Harv. 1988), the latter taking the view that there is greater value in separating analysis of the common law from that of statute law.

[106] For important exceptions, see Cross, *Statutory Interpretation* (2nd ed.), pp. 44 ff.; Atiyah (1985), 48 M.L.R.F. 1. Both rely on Roscoe Pound's important Harv. L. Rev. article on statutes and the common law.

[107] For a recent example of the overt recognition of this see *Schering Agrochemicals Ltd.* v. *Resibel N.V.S.A.* (C.A., 26 November 1992). See further Law Com. No. 219, 'Contributory Negligence as a Defence in Contract' (1993) para. 3.11.

[108] *Photo Productions* v. *Securicor* [1980] A.C. 827; *Ailsa Craig* v. *Malvern Fishing Ltd.* [1983] 1 W.L.R. 964 (H.L.).

[109] This issue is considered in Law Commission C.P. No. 124, *Fiduciary Duties and Regulatory Rules* 1992), Part III.

[110] *George Mitchell (Chesterhall) Ltd.* v. *Finney Lock Seeds Ltd.* [1983] 2 A.C. 803, 810 (Lord Bridge).

case of financial services, private investors have a higher degree of protection than others.[111] It is required that financial services practitioners subordinate their own interests to those of their clients and make proper provision for disclosure of interests in and facts material to transactions entered into or advice given.[112] Unless they are transacting business on an 'execution-only' basis, practitioners are under an obligation to 'know' their customers so they can give appropriate advice, and they must explain the risks of a particular investment. Particularly detailed disclosure is required in the case of long term contracts such as those for life assurance.

Although there are many differences between the financial services and the consumer credit regimes, they have similar disclosure provisions. Both regimes also exercise close control over the content of advertisements. The fact that the legislative schemes are so detailed means that it is not unreasonable to see them as self-contained codes. However, that part of the regimes which relates to disclosure might arguably be of wider significance. In both contexts the relationship is one of inequality; in financial services (and probably in consumer credit) there is also imbalance of information in the sense that the professional has information that the client cannot acquire from any other source—or cannot do so without incurring considerable expense. This imbalance can also be seen at the root of the equitable doctrine of undue influence, and the duty of disclosure in contracts *uberrimae fidei*.

It is accordingly arguable that the fact that the legislature has imposed a duty of disclosure in one such case, can be seen, alongside the cases in which a duty exists at common law, as an indication of the underlying rationale and principle of such a duty, and therefore as a guide to a court which is considering the extension of the duty to a new fact situation.[113] If one is considering whether exceptions to a rule have become so extensive as to undermine that rule, as has happened in the case of the parol evidence rule, which has been said not to exist,[114] it would be odd to consider only the common law exceptions. However, in the absence of an adequate theoretical framework for considering such statutory modifications, until recently the more likely approach would be for

a court to conclude that the necessity for statutory intervention showed the limits of any common law duty of disclosure and also precluded further common law development. Although, in discussing whether all the rules of English law to control unfairness yield an overall result that is different from the civil law principle of good faith, Bingham, L. J. in *Interphoto Ltd.* v. *Stiletto Ltd.*,[115] looked at statute as well as common law, this was as part of a description rather than an analysis.

At one time it was thought that European Community law would not impinge on national contract systems. This is no longer true. Large areas of contracting have been affected by E.C. law. Only two are mentioned here: Public procurement and unfair terms in consumer contracts. However, particular types of contract, for example banking and insurance, are regulated by E.C. Directives *inter alia* to prevent discrimination against non-nationals and other barriers to free trade. There are also negotiations for common standards on electronic documentary interchange, including contract formation.

We have seen that English law has developed to provide a remedy to a tenderer whose conforming tender is not considered. It remains to be seen how this remedy compares with those available where the European Community's Directives on public procurement apply. These seek to ensure that there is no discrimination (on national lines) in tendering procedures for major contracts for public works, supplies and services[116] and utilities contracts. All national, regional and local government authorities are subject to these as well as bodies governed by public law which are financed or controlled by the state and are not of an industrial or commercial nature, and projects relating to building work for hospitals, sport and leisure, schools and universities where more than half the funding is provided by government. Contracting by authorities in energy, water, transport, and telecommunications utilities are subject to a separate directive.

Co-ordinated and fairly elaborate procedures (including Community wide advertisements and time limits to afford those in other member states the opportunity to participate) now apply to the award of such contracts. The Directives leave the fate of a

---

[111] In particular they are given a right to civil damages for contravention of regulatory rules: F.S.A. 1986, s. 62A. Private investor is defined by S.I. 1991, No. 489.

[112] F.S.A. 1986, Schedule 8, paras. 3, 5–8.

[113] Cf. the different approach in *Banque Financiere de la Cite S.A.* v. *Westgate Insurance Co. Ltd.* [1990] 2 All E.R. 947, 954 (H.L.) where the only policy issues relevant to the imposition of a duty of disclosure addressed in the leading speech by Lord Templeman were that the information which had to be disclosed may be unreliable or doubtful or inconclusive, and that disclosure may expose the informer to criticism or litiga-

tion: 'A professional should wear a halo but need not wear a hairshirt.'

[114] See Law Com. No. 154 (1986), 'The Parol Evidence Rule'.

[115] [1988] 1 All E.R. 348, 353, 357.

[116] Directives 71/305/E.E.C. (1971 O.J. L.185/5); 77/62/E.E.C. (1977 O.J. L.215/1); 92/50/E.E.C.; 90/531/E.E.C. (1990 O.J. L.297/1). These have respectively been implemented in the U.K. by S.I. 1991 No. 2680; S.I. 1991, No. 2679; S.I. 1992, No. 3279. See Arrowsmith (1992), 1 Public Procurement Law Review 28; Weiss, *Public Procurement in European Community Law* (1993).

contract made in breach of the rules to national law,[117] and the United Kingdom's implementing regulations provide that concluded contracts are not to be set aside on the application of a third party (normally a disappointed tenderer).[118] Therefore, the reviewing remedies of public law such as certiorari and mandamus will not be of much assistance unless a person complaining of breach can invoke the assistance of the court before the award of the contract *and persuade the court to grant interim relief.* In other cases the only remedy will be monetary compensation; the Directives require there to be a damages remedy.[119] The remedies may be sui generis, and there is some debate as to whether damages for the 'loss of a chance' are available under the regulations implementing the directives as they are for breach of contract.[120] However, for a very large class of public contracts there is now a formalised pre-contractual process backed by legal remedies. Given the size of the contracts and the fact that tenderers are likely to have incurred substantial expenses in preparing their bid and ensuring that it satisfies the rules, it is, moreover, likely that disappointed parties will seek to use these remedies.

Will the experience of the courts in developing the statutory remedies in respect of tendering subject to the E.C. requirements have any influence on tendering processes that are not so subject but which are conducted according to settled rules and procedures? For instance, will a party who becomes aware of the fact that the tenderee does not propose to consider his conforming tender seek injunctive relief? This seems unlikely. We have seen, however, that the remedy for breach of the implied contract has not yet been worked out and it does seem reasonable to suppose that the courts will try to ensure that the damages remedy under the Directives is based on the same principle as the remedy arising from the *Blackpool Aero Club* implied contract. Perhaps more significantly, the Directives are likely to affect attitudes to whether there should be a remedy at all in a tendering situation. The existence of a very large number of tenders which give rise to legal obligations under the Directives, is surely likely to affect the expectations of those who participate in formal tendering processes, whether or not the Directives apply. The factual expectations raised by such tendering processes may differ in degree but they do not differ in kind. As a matter of policy, it does not seem satisfactory for similar processes giving rise to similar expectations to have sharply different legal effects.

The Directive on Unfair Terms in Consumer Contracts[121] must be implemented by 31 December 1994. Its structure is clearly civilian and indeed seems to be based on the German Standard Contract Terms Act 1976. It is accordingly arguable that, especially as the Directive is to be implemented by statutory instrument rather than by an amendment of the Unfair Contract Terms Act, the jurisprudence developed in those countries will be of relevance in the interpretation of the implementing regulations. Secondly, it uses concepts which are not used in English law, in particular 'good faith' and 'significant imbalance'.

Article 3.1 states that a term is to be regarded as unfair if, judged to be the circumstances at the time the contract was concluded, it is:

'contrary to the requirement of good faith, it causes a significant imbalance in the parties' rights and obligations arising under the contract, to the detriment of the consumer.'

By Article 4.1 the unfairness of a term is to be assessed by taking account of the nature of the goods or services, all the circumstances attending the contract, all the other terms of the contract (or of any other contract on which it is dependent. The Recitals to the Directive state that:

'Whereas the assessment, according to the general criteria chosen, of the unfair collective services which take account of solidarity among users, must be supplemented by a means of making an overall evaluation of the different interests involved; whereas this constitutes the requirement of good faith; whereas, in making an assessment of good faith, particular regard shall be had to the strength of the bargaining positions of the parties, whether the consumer had an inducement to agree to the term and whether the goods or services were sold or supplied to the special order of the consumer; whereas the requirement of good faith may be satisfied by the seller or supplier where he deals fairly and equitably with the other party *whose legitimate interests he takes into account . . .'*

The Directive is wider that U.C.T.A. in applying to all terms and not only terms excluding or limiting liability. It also extends control to contracts of insurance and contracts for the sale of land. It attempts to

---

[117] Compliance Directive 21 December 1989, O.J. L.395/33, Art. 2 (6). See Gilliams (1992), 1 Public Procurement Law Review 292.

[118] S.I. 1991, No. 2679, r. 26 (b); S.I. 1991, No. 2680, r. 31 (7); S.I. 1992, No. 3279, r. 30 (6).

[119] Ibid. Art. 2 (1) (c). For the U.K. provisions, see S.I. 1991, No. 2679, r. 26 (2), 26 (5) (b); S.I. 1991, No. 2680, r. 31 (3), 31 (6) (b); S.I. 1992, No. 3279, r. 30(1), 30 (5) (b) (ii).

[120] *Chaplin* v. *Hicks* [1911] 2 K.B. 786.

[121] Council Directive 93/13/E.E.C. of 5 April 1993; O.J. L. 95/29, 21 April 1993. See the Report of and Evidence to the Select Committee on the European Communities on the Draft Directive 1991/92 6th Rep. (H.L. 28), 21 January 1992. See Beale, paper given at Oxford Contract Symposium (September 1993).

give guidance as to fairness by 'an indicative and non-exhaustive list of terms which may be regarded as unfair' in an Annex. However, the adequacy of the price as against the services or goods supplied is not subject to control on the ground of unfairness if the terms are in plain intelligible language. It also seems from the recitals that terms which *clearly define* the main subject matter of the contract will not be subject to control of the ground of fairness. The Department of Trade and Industry's Consultation Document[122] on the proposed regulations to implement the Directive states that the main effect of the Directive will be to introduce for the first time a general concept of fairness into the U.K. law of contract. It does so not by replacing or amending the Unfair Contract Terms Act but by providing a separate regime with a different definition of 'consumer' and the possibility of different approaches to 'fairness' under the Directive and 'reasonableness' under the 1977 Act. Although the Directive applies to all terms in consumer contracts and not only to exemption clauses, this is unfortunate. The duplication will add

to the complexity of the law and to the costs of compliance. It will also make the law less transparent from the point of view of the consumer. This is, however, not the place for detailed consideration of the Directive's provisions, of the draft regulations by which the Department of Trade and Industry proposes to implement it, or of the question whether the draft regulations do in fact implement the Directive. There does not, for instance, appear to be any implementation of Article 7 on the need for effective means to prevent the *continued* use of unfair terms.[123] In the present context what is important is the width and approach of the Directive, particularly its direct use of the concept of good faith. It is arguable that this will have profound effects on the English law of contract. At first, no doubt, these will be confined to those contracts which are directly subject to the Directive. Can they, however, be confined to that? Whether or not it will be so confined, English contract law will be under great pressure to move from its incremental approach based on relatively specific rules rather than general principles.

[122] October 1993.

[123] See Reynolds, (19994) 110 L.Q.R. 1.

11. Scots and English Contract Laws

W.W. McBRYDE

Introduction

THERE has often been a tension between Scots and English law, although any discomfort has tended to be on the side of the smaller partner. The Union of 1707 occasionally gives rise to arguments, but one suspects in Scotland more than in England. I do not know the extent to which English lawyers contemplate the Acts of Union but Scots lawyers have from time to time argued about whether the Queen is Elizabeth the Second or the First[1] or whether or not it was 'for the evident utility of the subjects within Scotland' and a contravention of an Act of Union to have the Community Charge or E.E.C. rules on fishing.[2]

Part of the feeling is political or patriotic, but also there has, from time to time, been concern that the interests of Scots law have been damaged by an ignorant House of Lords or a less than perfect legislature. On the former a reading of *Law From Over The Border* by Professor Gibb[3] will reveal why the neutral Scots lawyer may feel anxious about the influence of English law on our jurisprudence. It was surely illogical to have the possibility, which existed for a time, that the decision of the 15 judges of the Court of Session could be overturned by English judges who knew very little about Scots law and who could refuse to recognise their own ignorance. Nor have all the problems disappeared with the maturity of the Union. The Scottish citizen may be startled to discover, as the late Professor Wilson has observed, that under the scheme introduced by the Child Support Act 1991 the appeal from the child support commissioner may be to the English Court of Appeal unless the comissioner thinks the Court of Session appropriate.[4]

If it were now to be asked what lasting harm has come to the Scots law of contract it is a difficult question to answer. Contract law does not have a scandal like the doctrine of common employment imposed on the Scots law of delict on the grounds that:

'. . . if such be the law of England, on what ground can it be argued not to be the law of Scotland? The law, as established in England, is founded on principles of universal application, not on any peculiarities of English jurisprudence; and unless, therefore, there has been a settled course of decision in Scotland to the contrary, I think it would be most inexpedient to sanction a different rule to the north of the Tweed from that which prevails to the south.'[5]

This is as dubious in law as it is misleading in geography.[6]

There are areas of confusion in Scots contract law—like error (mistake)—and many of these problems are not the fault of English judges. Scottish judges, and examples are hinted at later, are perfectly capable of making a mess of Scots law and, some would argue, of English law also when sitting in the highest courts.[7] The problem is not so much judicial, or Parliamentary, mistakes, or claims that there have been blunders, but the attitude that English law is superior and that existing Scots law can be ignored.

I will confine myself to two examples of unfortunate influence (often assisted by Scots lawyers), although others could be chosen. Of some commercial importance is the right to interest on sums unpaid. The present law is dominated by an *obiter dictum* of Lord Westbury which is so incomplete and obscure that his Lordship must have temporarily forgotten that he was sitting in a court of last resort.[8] The Sale of Goods Acts 1893 and 1979, based on English rules adapted to Scotland, are a muddle in their treatment of remedies so far as Scots law is concerned.[9]

But these and some other areas of doubtful law

---

[1] *MacCormick* v. *The Lord Advocate*, 1953 S.C. 396.

[2] *Gibson* v. *Lord Advocate*, 1975 S.C. 136; *Stewart* v. *Henry*, 1989 S.L.T. (Sh. Ct.) 34; *Fraser* v. *MacCorquodale*, 1989 S.L.T. (Sh. Ct.) 39, 1992 S.L.T. 229; *Murray* v. *Rogers*, 1992 S.L.T. 221.

[3] A. D. Gibb, *Law From Over the Border* (Edinburgh, 1950).

[4] Child Support Act 1991, s. 25 (4); W. A. Wilson, 'The Bairns of Falkirk,' 1991 S.L.T. (News) 417.

[5] *Bartonshill Coal Co.* v. *Reid* (1858) 3 Macq. 266 at p. 285 per Lord Chancellor Cranworth; see the views of the Court of Session judges at (1852) 15 D. 135; the law was changed by the Law Reform (Personal Injuries) Act 1948.

[6] The medium filum of the Tweed divides the two countries for about 17 miles only and even then the position is complicated; W. A. Wilson, *Introductory Essays on Scots Law* (Edinburgh, 2nd ed. 1984), p. 35.

[7] An example sometimes given is *Murphy* v. *Brentwood D.C.* [1991] 1 A.C. 398 although in that case the three Scottish judges were not in a majority.

[8] *Carmichael* v. *Caledonian Ry. Co.* (1870) 8 M. (H.L.) 119 at p. 131; 'Interest can be demanded only in virtue of a contract, express or implied, or by virtue of the principal sum of money having been wrongfully withheld, and not paid on the day when it ought to have been paid.'; part of the problem may be the unnecessary respect shown to the views of a former Lord Chancellor in a case which did not involve a normal contract of sale; nevertheless the dictum has been often quoted.

[9] This is a good example of legislative ignorance of Scots law; a story is told *inter alia* in T. B. Smith, *Property Problems in Sale* (London, 1978), although his treatment ignores the Scottish pressure for the legislation to apply to Scotland—A. Rodger, 'The Codification of Commercial Law in Victorian

may not be as strident a condemnation of the results of a system as at one time I was lead to believe. Professor Sir T. B. Smith was an exponent of the 'crisis' caused by mixing civil and common law principles.[10] A comprehensive view may be obtained in his major work, *A Short Commentary on the Law of Scotland*,[11] which in a text of over 900 pages had an index entry, 'English law, influence on Scots law, *passim.*' The subject is ingrained with passion and subjective judgment,[12] which has added zest to the study of Scots law.[13] As a counter it is useful to remind ourselves of how the English writers on contract of the 19th century borrowed from Roman law, Domat, Grotius, Pufendorf, Pothier and Savigny.[14]

All this is a background to the relationship between the Scots and the English law of contract. I am sometimes asked, usually by English lawyers, what the differences are. There is not a simple answer but there are many similarities in the two laws. Variations in concepts and terminology exist as do different statutory provisions.[15] Sometimes the differences are subtle which is a trap for the unwary. What is remarkable is how much English case law is used in Scotland both in the lecture hall and in the court room. For present purposes I leave aside the debate about the extent to which this corrupts native Scottish doctrine. My hypothesis is that (1) in so far as the laws are the same or similar, Scots authority has been a source neglected by the English academic and practitioner; (2) Scots law cannot afford to be regarded as a quaint or obscure system, but should

be a modern law with which any contracting party from anywhere can be comfortable; and (3) some of the distinctive features of Scots law may be of interest to law reformers in England and elsewhere.

Scots authority in England

An instance, perhaps a rare instance, of the dangers in ignoring Scots authority is an English tax appeal *Winter* v. *Inland Revenue Comrs.*[16] The case concerned the meaning of 'contingent liability'. The construction of a Finance Act was in issue, which is a speciality, but it allowed Lord Reid to decide the case on the basis of extensive quotation from Erskine, a retired Professor of Scots law of the middle 18th century, whose posthumous *Institute of the Law of Scotland* is of high authority.[17] Lord Guest quoted Erskine and cited Gloag on Contract, the classic work on the Scots law of Contract although dated 1929.[18] Lord Birkett approved of the citations from Scots law by the two Scottish judges and so, by a majority, the Scots view prevailed, the Court of Appeal was reversed, and the only English dictum on the subject was disapproved. I would have been surprised if both parties had been previously told by their legal advisers about the texts of the two Professors of Scots Law whose views determined the case. These authorities do not appear to have been cited to the court.[19] It may also be that only some writers on English law would search north of the border for authority which might influence the supreme civil court in England.

Britain,' (1992) 108 L.Q.R. 570; while it is almost impossible to defend the present state of the law there is a remarkable dearth of reported case law which indicates a serious problem in practice—see *Millars of Falkirk Ltd.* v. *Turpie*, 1976 S.L.T. (Notes) 66; M. G. Clarke, 'The Buyer's Right of Rejection', 1978 S.L.T. (News) 1; Anon. 'The Buyer's Right of Rejection', 1978 S.L.T. (News) 61; see also the Law Commission and the Scottish Law Commission, 'Report on Sale and Supply of Goods,' (Law Com. No. 160, Scot. Law Com. No. 104, Cmnd. 137, 1987) esp. at paras. 2.27–2.31.

[10] See T. B. Smith, *Studies Critical and Comparative* (Edinburgh, 1962).

[11] Edinburgh, 1962; one of the last expressions of his views is in 'The interaction of Scots law and English law in historical perspective,' in *Essays in Memory of Professor F. H. Lawson* (ed. P. Wallington and R. M. Markin, London, 1986).

[12] E.g. D. M. Walker, *The Scottish Legal System* (Edinburgh, 6th ed. 1992), at p. 157: 'Since 1800 English law has been a most powerful factor, not so often imported on its merits as taken over and applied by mistake, in ignorance, through reliance on English books or cases, frequently without appreciation of the subtle differences between the two systems of law, and by subordination to a single Parliament often ignorant and careless of Scottish conditions, traditions and sentiment, composed of men sometimes more concerned with party than with country, and by the existence of an ultimate appeal in civil causes to a court composed as to a majority of English lawyers with no necessary knowledge of, qualification in, or sympathy with, the principles of Scots law.' The writer continues in similar vein at p. 158.

[13] As did the style of the comments; see Professor W. A. Wilson in an obituary referring to T. B. Smith's Scottish volume in the 'British Commonwealth' series: 'a work which had a considerable impact on academic law; to those who had been brought up on the arid prose of Gloag and Henderson a book which treated Scots law in an urbane, discursive style was a revelation.'; 1989 J.R. 1 at p. 2.

[14] R. Zimmermann, *The Law of Obligations* (Cape Town, 1990, pp. 569–71; P. S. Atiyah, *the Rise and Fall of Freedom of Contract* (Oxford, 1979), pp. 399–400; J. Gordley, *The Philosophical Origins of Modern Contract Doctrine* (Oxford, 1991), p. 134; A. W. B. Simpson, 'Innovation in Nineteenth Century Contract Law', (1975) 91 L.Q.R. 247.

[15] See, e.g. the Unfair Contract Terms Act, 1977; a brief and inadequate summary is in W. W. McBryde, *The Law of Contract in Scotland* (Edinburgh, 1987), paras. 1–19 to 1–22.

[16] [1963] A.C. 235; followed on a point of company law in *S.B.A. Properties Ltd.* [1967] 1 W.L.R. 799.

[17] First published in 1773, the edition now usually cited is the eighth by J. B. Nicolson (Edinburgh, 1871), recently reprinted by Butterworths (Edinburgh, 1989), with a mistake in the title on the spine.

[18] W. M. Gloag, *The Law of Contract* (Edinburgh, 2nd ed. 1929).

[19] In a court in Scotland it is improper for a judge to use a case without an opportunity for parties to address the court on its effect—*Lees* v. *North East Fife D.C.* 1987 S.L.T. 769; *Brebner* v. *British Coal Corp.*, 1988 S.L.T. 736; presumably the same rule should apply to the writings of academics.

Other instances may be found where a Scottish judge in the House of Lords has mentioned Scots contract law in deciding an English appeal.[20] There is even the occasional incidental reference by an English judge to a Scottish case.[21] If a Scottish reference appears in a case reported in English reports, it may enter the stream of English thought, of which a good example is a sciolistic quotation from Gloag about construction of contracts by Lord Reid in *McCutcheon* v. *MacBrayne Ltd.*[22]

Using Scots cases

For various reasons the Scots law student acquires a familiarity with the hierarchy of English courts and many of the main English text books. The converse is probably not true of most English law students. Ignorance may inhibit the reference to another system. It may also produce strange results.

I remember a visiting English lawyer, of some seniority, addressing a Scottish audience on the demerits of *Duke* v. *Jackson*[23] as an example of the poverty of thinking of Scots law on consumer issues. *Duke* is a decision of the Second Division of the Court of Session in 1921 in which it was held that household coal which was supplied with a detonator was not supplied in breach of a warranty under the Sale of Goods Act because there was nothing wrong with the coal. This case must be in that sad collection of daft decisions which, if the judges were still alive, would be referred to 'with the greatest respect.' *Duke* was distinguished by Sheriff Substitutes in two later decisions, although *Duke* was binding on them.[24] *Duke* is so notorious that it is treated in a student's text book as a case which should not be followed[25] and its reasoning was not adopted by the English Court of Appeal in 1954.[26] It is highly unlikely that

Duke would ever now be followed in Scotland. Is it not true that with any legal system there are strange decisions; that the fate of a decision must be traced in subsequent case law, articles and textbooks?

In Scots law there has been an explosion of publication in recent years and a good, unfortunately outside Scotland it may have to be a very good, law library will supply several up to date texts on most areas of the law.[27] As my earlier example of *Winter* demonstrates it may be necessary to refer to old authority although this does require some expertise. The novice should start with cases and text books in the last thirty years or so and for the law of contract there is plenty of material. Finding cases is not so easy as in England but the position is improving.[28]

Recent case law on contract

What might the curious find if there is a look at the recent case law on contract? In reality it is the reported law which might be exported, even although it does not reflect the daily grind of the practitioner in the sheriff courts.

A guide may be the recently published index of Scots Law Times cases for 1961–1990 plus subsequent indices in annual volumes and weekly parts. As a matter of impression the content is what might be expected in any advanced contract system. There is much concerned with remedies, with construction of terms and with contract formation. What is hidden by an index is that most of this case law applies the same rules as English law and the terms of the judges' opinions would be as easily understood, or not as the case may be, by an English lawyer as by a Scots lawyer. Also once the significance of 'Sheriff Court', 'Outer House' and 'Inner House' are realised, which is not difficult to follow,[29] the hierarchy of

---

[20] E.g. *The Aello* [1961] A.C. 135 at pp. 188–98 per Lord Keith; *Moschi* v. *Lep Air Services Ltd.* [1973] A.C. 331 at p. 359 per Lord Kilbrandon.

[21] *Bank of Nova Scotia* v. *Hellenic Mutual Ltd.* [1992] 1 A.C. 233 at p. 262 per Lord Goff; *Kelly* v. *Cooper* [1993] A.C. 205 at p. 215 (Privy Council appeal from Bermuda).

[22] 1964 S.C. (H.L.) 28, also reported in [1964] 1 W.L.R. 125, [1964] 1 All E.R. 430, [1964] 1 Lloyd's Rep. 16; Lord Reid's citation from Gloag was repeated in *British Crane Hire* v. *Ipswich Plant Hire* [1975] Q.B. 303 at p. 311 per Lord Denning; *The 'Santa Carina'* [1977] 1 Lloyd's Rep. 478 at p. 483 per L. J. Roskill, *The 'T.S. Havprins'* [1983] 2 Lloyd's Rep. 356 at p. 362 per Staughton, J., *The 'Chevalier Roze'* [1983] 2 Lloyd's Rep. 438 at p. 443 per Parker, J., *The 'Antclizo'* [1987] 2 Lloyd's Rep. 130 at p. 146 per Nicholls, L. J. on appeal [1988] 1 W.L.R. 603; and in a Canadian case *Atomic Interprovincial Transport (Eastern) Ltd.* v. *Geiger*, Manitoba Court of Appeal (1988), 45 D.L.R. (4th) 312 at p. 316.

[23] 1921 S.C. 362.

[24] *Fitzpatrick* v. *Barr*, 1948 S.L.T. (Sh. Ct.) 5; *Lusk* v. *Barclay*, 1953 S.L.T. (Sh. Ct.) 23.

[25] D. M. Walker, *The Scottish Legal System* (Edinburgh, 6th

ed. 1992), p. 499; see also 'The Sale of Coal', 1954 S.L.T. (News) 97.

[26] *Wilson* v. *Rickett, Cockerell & Co. Ltd.* [1954] 1 Q.B. 598.

[27] As an absolute minimum a library should contain the series of standard texts produced by the Scottish Universities Law Institute ('SULI'), published by W. Green & Son Ltd., Edinburgh (a subsidiary of Sweet & Maxwell) and the *Stair Memorial Encyclopaedia* published by Butterworths. The Scots Law Times contains cases and articles. The Scottish Civil Law Reports commenced in 1987. The official series—Session Cases—has been erratic in appearance in recent decades.The Juridical Review is the major periodical.

[28] For recent case law the usual sources are Current Law, the Scots Law Times Index, 1961–1990 and subsequent yearly volumes and monthly parts, and Scottish Civil Law Reports Index 1987–1991 and subsequent volume and parts; in certain circumstances LEXIS has transformed research on Scottish cases and has the advantage of availability outside Scotland.

[29] See, e.g. Walker, sup. cit. Chap. 8; for a simpler and more readable account see H. L. MacQueen, *Studying Scots Law* (Edinburgh, 1993), pp. 8–14.

precedent becomes obvious and a wealth of material is available on the development of English rules of contract.

The trap is that some areas are different from English law e.g. error (mistake), force and fear (extortion or duress), other cases which involve factors which invalidate consent, and rules on written pleadings and evidence. This is one reason for reference to textbooks.

Offer and acceptance

Most law students tend to start to think of contracts in terms of offer and acceptance. Although this model of contract formation can be shown to be inappropriate to all commercial contracts, there is a tenacious attraction in its apparent simplicity, its detailed rules and its occasional obscurities. Both Scots and English law have their different uncertainties, but in substance the law is, or should be, the same.

It may be that for the future Scots lawyers will look to European and international sources. The Scottish Law Commission has considered recently the reform of rules on contract formation particularly in the light of the provisions of the Vienna Convention. Their recommendation is to adopt the rules of that Convention, with some modification, as part of the general law of Scotland.[30] The proposals, which are not limited to sale of goods, include the abolition of the 'posting rule' and a slight extension of the law on 'battle of the forms.' The aim is to have a modern and internationally recognised set of rules which will have advantages for Scottish traders, lawyers and arbiters.

One area of current concern is the effect of a qualified acceptance and much may be learned about how not to approach the problems from recent decisions of the Court of Session.[31]

Course of dealing

The incorporation of terms by a course of dealing, an issue which remains to be analysed properly,[32] relies on both English and Scots authority. At the least the English law teacher looking for examples may delight students with the tale of how Mr McSporran contracted with MacBraynes for the carriage of a Ford Popular motor car which was immersed in the sea when the ship struck a rock due to negligent navigation[33] or the case of the supply of allegedly defective tyres for civilian use in Saudi Arabia[34] or the consignment of whisky which went missing whilst in the hands of carriers.[35] In all these cases you will find English case law analysed and commented upon.

Construction of contracts

In practice many of the problems which practitioners have with contracts arise from problems of construction or interpretation. The principles of English law tend not to be explained in English text books by reference to recent dicta in the House of Lords. Nevertheless these dicta, mainly in English appeals, are applied in Scots law. In the specialised area of exclusion and indemnity clauses Scots law in 1956[36] adopted the dictum of Lord Morton in the Privy Council case of *Canada Steamships Lines Ltd. v. R.*[37] and this has been followed in many cases including two decisions of the House of Lords in Scottish appeals.[38] Likewise issues of implied terms often rely on English authority.[39]

Restraint of trade

On restrictive covenants there are enough Scottish cases, both reported and unreported, for the cynical observer to suggest that in Scotland there is a problem with a tendency to wish to work for a competitor. The principles of the law can largely be derived

[30] Report on Formation of Contact: Scottish Law and the United Nations Convention on Contracts for the International Sale of Goods (Scot. Law Com. No. 144, 1993).

[31] *Wolf and Wolf v. Forfar Potato Co.*, 1984 S.L.T. 100; *Rutterford Ltd. v. Allied Breweries Ltd.*, 1990 S.L.T. 249; *Findlater v. Maan*, 1990 S.C. 150; the problems are discussed in D. J. Cusine and R. Rennie, *Missives* (Edinburgh, 1993), paras. 3.18 to 3.32.

[32] There may be a difference between (1) a series of contracts concluded using a form followed by a contract without the standard form; and (2) contracts consistently followed by the issue of a form with conditions. (1) is represented by the arguments in *McCutcheon v. David MacBrayne Ltd.* sup. cit.; and *Hollier v. Rambler Motors* [1972] 2 Q.B. 71. (2) is illustrated by most of the other cases e.g. *Grayston Plant v. Plean Precast Ltd.*, 1976 S.C. 206; *Continental Tyre & Rubber Co. Ltd. v. Trunk Trailer Co.* 1987 S.L.T. 58; *J. Spurling Ltd. v. Bradshaw* [1956] 1 W.L.R. 461; *Hardwick Game Farm v. Suffolk*

Agricultural Poultry Prod. Assoc. [1969] 2 A.C. 31; *British Crane Hire v. Ipswich Plant Hire* [1975] Q.B. 303.

[33] *McCutcheon v. David MacBrayne Ltd.*, sup. cit.

[34] *Continental Tyre & Rubber Co. Ltd. v. Trunk Trailer Co. ltd.*, 1987 S.L.T. 58.

[35] *William Teacher & Sons Ltd. v. Bell Lines Ltd.*, 1991 S.L.T. 876.

[36] *North of Scotland Hydro Electric Board v. D. & R. Taylor*, 1956 S.C. 1.

[37] [1952] A.C. 192 at p. 208.

[38] *Smith v. U.M.B. Chrysler (Scotland) Ltd.*, 1978 S.C. (H.L.) 1; *Ailsa Craig Fishing Co. Ltd. v. Malvern Fishing Co. Ltd.*, 1982 S.C. (H.L.) 14.

[39] As examples see the authorities referred to in three recent decisions in the Inner House—*Prestwick Circuits Ltd. v. M. Andrew*, 1990 S.L.T. 654; *G. M. Shepherd Ltd. v. North West Securities*, 1991 S.L.T. 499; *Crawford v. Bruce*, 1992 S.L.T. 524.

from five decisions of the House of Lords in English appeals.[40] The 1980's saw an increase in the number of reported cases in Scotland, for reasons which some day someone may examine.

Remedies

Procedure may be different, but there is a similarity in the remedy of damages.[41] The Scots will claim that they invented the rule in *Hadley* v. *Basendale* before that case.[42] Nevertheless it is *Hadley* and its English successors which would be cited in a Scottish court. Indeed in a very recent case, now on appeal to the House of Lords, Lord Justice Clerk Ross commented on developments, or 'glosses' as he referred to them, upon the law stated in *Hadley* v. *Baxendale* and concluded:

'With all respect to the distinguished judges who have done so, it appears to me that little advantage is gained from altering the language used in *Hadley* v. *Baxendale* and that the law to be applied is as stated by Alderson, B. in *Hadley* v. *Baxendale*.'[43]

Recovery of damages for injured feelings following a breach of contract, i.e. damages for solatium, might be thought a peculiarly Scottish remedy but this is one instance where the principles of Scottish authority have been applied in England, although the source has not always been acknowledged. The decision in *Diesen* v. *Samson*[44] was an award of damages for injured feeling to a bride arising from the failure of a photographer to appear at a wedding. The photographer engaged by the bride failed to appear because he had forgotten about the booking. Some of the guests were wearing Norwegian national costume which attracted a press photographer who took the only successful photograph of the wedding, attempts to use flash at the reception having failed. The decision to award damages was at the lowest level in the sheriff court and the case is not binding on any other Scottish judge. Nevertheless the result has been followed in England,[45] Northern Ireland,[46] Canada[47] and Scotland.[48]

Important differences arise with the concept of breach of contract where there may be a reflection of

the Scottish tendency to think in general terms and to try to avoid categories. A Scots lawyer asks, 'Was a breach of contract material?' He or she does not, at least in the first instance, look at the nature of the term breached and try to classify it as a warranty or a condition or intermediate term or something else. Our concentration is on the breach and not on what we would regard as an artificial approach to the nature of terms. It is this which gave rise to some of the problems with the Sale of Goods Act 1893 and 1979 mentioned earlier. The words 'condition' and 'warranty' do not mean the same in the two systems[49]—which is a snare for those who use styles of English contracts which will be governed by Scots law.

The Scottish approach to breach has much to recommend it, a fact occasionally appreciated by English lawyers. In the fifth edition of Cheshire and Fifoot's *The Law of Contract*, it was stated:[50]

'In the Scots law the very distinction is unknown between conditions and warranties, and the draftsman of the Sale of Goods Act was careful to provide that this native virtue should not be corrupted by loose Southron ways. It would surely be both simpler and more sensible to abandon the distinction in the English law as well: to rule that for any breach of contract the injured party can obtain damages and that it shall be for the court in its discretion to award or to refuse the additional remedy of rescission.'

This criticism of English law and praise of Scots law has proved too strong for subsequent editors and the passage no longer appears.

In case you think I am hinting that Scots law is always superior, that would be dangerous because it would be like the jingoistic arrogance shown by Lord Chancellors in Scottish appeals in the 18th and 19th centuries. There is one area you should avert your eyes from. I would like to keep secret the difficulties which arise in contracts of sale to which the 1979 Act does not apply—mainly sales of heritage—about the extent to which we do, or do not, recognise an *actio quanti minoris*. Various writers discuss the problems and I am sure if you read their words, through no fault of the commentators, you may receive an unfavourable impression of the Scots law

---

[40] See McBryde on *Contract*, para. 25–55 et. seq.

[41] Other remedies include interdict and specific implement; it would be a bold person who would assert that they were the same as injunction or specific performance; cf. *Freevale Ltd.* v. *Metrostore (Holdings) Ltd.* [1984] 1 Ch. 199.

[42] McBryde on *Contract*, paras. 20–01 to 20–02.

[43] *Balfour Beatty Construction (Scotland) Ltd.* v. *Scottish Power plc.*, 1993 S.L.T. 1005 at p. 1009.

[44] 1971 S.L.T. (Sh. Ct.) 49.

[45] See McGregory on *Damages* (London, 15th e.d. 1988) para. 98—'The new view was heralded by a Scots case.'; A. I. Ogus, *The Law of Damages* (London, 1973), p. 309; *Jarvis* v. *Swans Tours Ltd.* [1973] Q.B. 233; *Jackson* v. *Horizon Holidays*

[1975] 1 W.L.R. 1468; *Heywood* v. *Wellers* [1976] Q.B. 446; *Warren* v. *Truprint* [1986] B.T.L.C. 344.

[46] For which the evidence is unsatisfactory in that it is an undated transcript of the decision of the Queen's Bench Division in *Northern Bank Ltd.* v. *McKeown* available on LEXIS.

[47] *Wilson* v. *Sooter Studios Ltd.*, British Columbia Court of Appeal (1988), 55 D.L.R. (4th) 303.

[48] *Fleming* v. *Strathclyde R.C.*, 1992 S.L.T. 161; *Colston* v. *Marshall*, 1993 S.C.L.R. 43.

[49] See J. J. Gow, *The Mercantile and Industrial Law of Scotland* (Edinburgh, 1964), pp. 203, 209.

[50] At p. 120.

of contract. I hope I never have to explain to a person wishing to contract under Scots law that there is this *actio* which may or may not reflect Roman law, which we may or may not have in certain circumstance, and which cannot be explained in terms which would with reasonable certainty be followed in any sheriff court.[51] The problem is one of some importance, often now avoided by terms in the contract,[52] and it illustrates the difficulties of judge made law in the way that the Sale of Goods Act shows the obscurities which can be produced by Parliament.

Specialities of Scots Contract Law

I have mentioned already that factors affecting consent to contract have specialities in Scots law, which is largely for historical reasons. I would not expect these areas to have much interest to those outside Scotland apart, perhaps, from recent consideration of the capacity of children.[53] Scots law has been reformed by legislation which sweeps away ancient distinctions between pupils and minors which Stair traced in the 17th century to Aristotle and Grotius.[54] This necessary modernness has not been opposed by many on the grounds that it is evidence of the decline and fall of traditional Scottish principles and a betrayal of our ancestors' wisdom.

Major features which may be of interest are that Scots law (1) does not have a doctrine of consideration; (2) does have a concept of unilateral promise; and (3) recognises third party rights through the doctrine of *jus quaesitum tertio*.

Consideration

Scots law does not have the doctrine of consideration. The absence of a doctrine makes it difficult to find authority. The point may have been argued in 1623[55] and there is not much case law since.

There are no plans for reform. I suggest that there

are areas of Scots law which no one would adopt; conversely if there are areas of English law which no one would wish to copy there may be doubt about the value of the concepts. At any rate the argument that '(t)he law as established in England is founded on principles of universal application not on any peculiarities of English jurisprudence'[56] appears to be weak in this context. As Professor Zimmermann has observed; 'The continental lawyer usually perceives [the doctrine of consideration] as one of the strange and idiosyncratic features which have the effect of turning the English common law into such an ungodly and impenetrable jumble.'[57] On the other hand, as the author points out, there is a similarity to the medieval doctrine of causa, and civil law systems do have methods to indicate the seriousness of a bargain.

Promises

I do not wish to repeat much of what I have written elsewhere on the development of the Scots law of promises.[58] A unilateral promise is binding in Scots law if it can be proved in the appropriate way. The promise is binding without acceptance. This makes it necessary to distinguish between a promise and a contract, and, largely because of the absence of a need for acceptance of a promise, renders much of the theoretical Anglo–American discussion on promises, and promise as the basis of contract, of limited application. Scots law may be unusual in its general recognition of the unilateral promise. German law and Austrian law recognise a unilateral binding promise but only in the context of an offer of reward,[59] which is also one of the few examples of the idea in Italian law.[60] In English law there may be a promise in a deed but for reasons I do not understand this does not feature large in discussions of the theory of the English law of contract.

There is no need in Scots law for consideration or promissory estoppel. Nor is it necessary to distort the rules on acceptance of offers in cases where it is

---

[51] The most recent consideration in the sheriff court, which has an unusually full reference to the authorities and writings on the subject, is *Fortune* v. *Fraser*, 1993 S.C.L.R. 470, a case which comes to an unexpected result and on which Sheriff Stewart in his commentary expects 'more ink will be spilt.'

[52] e.g. *The House Purchase and Sale Guideline and Standard Clauses*, revised version issued by the Law Society of Scotland, April 1992, clause B12.

[53] Scottish Law Commission Report on the Legal Capacity and Responsibility of Minors and Pupils (1987, Scot. Law Com. No. 110); Age of Legal Capacity (Scotland) Act 1991; the Act abolishes the two tier system of pupillarity and minority with its distinctions between pupils (girls aged under 12 or a boys under 14) and minors (girls aged 12–18 or boys aged 14–18) which had existed for a very long time, with a reduction from the age of 21 to 18 by the Age of Majority (Scotland) Act 1969.

The new system introduces a single tier of children under 16 who have no legal capacity, with some exceptions, and children aged 16–18 who have full legal capacity with the possibility, in certain circumstances, of challenge of the transaction.

[54] Stair, *The Institutions of the Law of Scotland* (1693, 2nd ed.; 1832, 5th ed.), 1.5.2. There are sometimes differences between the text of the 2nd ed. on which Stair worked and the commonly cited 5th ed.

[55] *Kintore* v. *Sinclair* (1623) Mor. 9425.

[56] sup. cit.

[57] R. Zimmermann, *The Law of Obligations* (Cape Town, 1990), p. 505.

[58] W. McBryde, 'Promises in Scots Law,' 1993 I.C.L.Q. 48.

[59] B.G.B. para. 657; A.B.G.B., arts. 860, 861; Zimmermann, op. cit., pp. 574–6.

[60] Italian Civil Code, paras. 1988, 1989.

difficult to show acceptance as in 'offers' of reward.[61] The concept of promise may develop in practice if certain unnecessary rules on constitution and proof of promises are reformed as the Scottish Law Commission have proposed.[62] Writing will not be required for a promise except in the case of a non-business gratuitous obligation.[63]

A promise may be either gratuitous or onerous in its motive.[64] Much of the discussion of this area of law has been bedevilled by examples of the gratuitous promise, as Dr MacQueen has observed.[65] There is actually a body of case law arising out of promises to pay sums for family, personal or charitable reasons.[66] Of future interest might be the development of promises made in the commercial context, particularly if the Scottish Law Commission reforms are enacted. Examples of these promises are:

(1) The promise to keep an offer open. This appears in almost every offer for the purchase of heritage, usually with a provision for withdrawal of the offer, e.g. 'This offer, unless sooner withdrawn, will remain open for acceptance by letter reaching us not later than 31st October . . .'[67] Without the provision for withdrawal, however, there would be an obligation to keep the offer open.[68]

(2) An obligation to grant an option.[69]

(3) An obligation to buy shares.[70]

(4) A unilateral undertaking to pay sums, which might include promissory notes,[71] bills of exchange, or a promise to accept a bill or honour the drafts of another or letters of credit.[72] The theory has not been fully evolved but at least there is a possible basis in promises, while for English law Professor Goode has

observed in the context of payment undertakings: 'The mysteries of a promise which defies all known rules of contract formation remain to tantalize us for the foreseeable future.'[73]

(5) A promise or 'offer' or 'guarantee' by a manufacturer or distributor in the event of purchase from a retailer.[74]

(6) A promise to accept the highest or lowest offer or to increase an offer.[75]

(7) A promise made in negotiation or renegotiation of contracts and which might, or might not, be considered under English law as an example of promissory estoppel; but in Scots law the promise would be enforced without consideration, without acceptance and without actions in reliance on it.

Jus quaesitum tertio

The phrase 'jus quaesitum tertio' is liable to provoke worry in any initiate to the study of Scots law. Partly this is because of the Latin; also because the Latin is incomplete. To recognise that there could be a right sought for a third party is a concept of some antiquity, which makes it more or less appealing according to your inclinations. There may be attractions to academics and some practitioners, but less so to the business person or consumer who cannot understand why a concept several hundred years old should be relevant to a modern legal system. As has been said: 'the conservative attachment of lawyers to the learning of past generations is not readily comprehended by the layman, who would never put his trust in a

---

[61] Examples of cases treated as offer and acceptance which might with more theoretical coherence have been classified as promise would be *Hunter* v. *Hunter* (1904) 7 F. 136 discussed in McBryde, 'Promises in Scots Law,' sup. cit. pp. 63–46, where native Scots concepts were not used and *Carlill* v. *Carbolic Smoke Ball Co.* [1983] 1 Q.B. 256 where, of course, the unilateral promise was absent from the jurisprudential armoury.

[62] McBryde, 'Promises in Scots Law,' sup. cit. pp. 65–6.

[63] Scottish Law Commission, *Report on Requirements of Writing* (Scot. Law. Com. No. 112), pp. 10–11.

[64] Which does *not* mean that we have the English doctrine of consideration; the distinction between gratuitous and onerous obligations has had a significance in the context of constitution and proof of obligations.

[65] H. MacQueen, 'Constitution and Proof of Gratuitous Obligations,' 1986 S.L.T. (News) 1, at p. 3.

[66] McBryde on *Contract*, paras. 2–01 to 2–51.

[67] See *The House Purchase and Sale Guideline and Standard Clauses*, sup. cit. Appendix 1.

[68] *Littlejohn* v. *Hadwen* (1882) 20 S.L.R. 5 at p. 7 per Lord Fraser; *A. & G. Paterson* v. *Highland Ry. Co.*, 1927 S.C. (H.L.) 32 at p. 38 per Viscount Dunedin; cf. The Law Commission, Working Paper No. 60, Firm Offers)1975) on which consultation revealed 'no great dissatisfaction with the existing law' according to the Scottish Law Commission Report on Forma-

tion of Contract, sup. cit. para. 1.5.; the Ontario Law Reform Commission has recommended that firm offers in the course of business should be binding without consideration—*Report on Amendment of the Law of Contract* (1987) 20–5.

[69] *Sichi* v. *Biaqi*, 1946 S.N. 66.

[70] *Beardmore & Co.* v. *Barry*, 1928 S.C. 101; affd. 1928 S.C. (H.L.) 47.

[71] *McTaggart* v. *MacEachern's J.F.*, 1949 S.C. 503.

[72] *Hunt* v. *Waugh* (1808) Hume 58; *Sir William Forbes & Co.* v. *McNab*, 29 May 1816 F.C.; *Shepherd* v. *Campbell Frazer & Co.* (1823) 2 S. 346 (n.e. 304); *Smyth* v. *Hunter* (1830) 9 S. 76; *National Bank of Scotland* v. *Robertson* (1836) 14 S. 402.

[73] R. Goode, 'Abstract Payment Undertakings,' in P. Cane and J. Stapleton (eds), *Essays for Patrick Atiyah* (Oxford, 1991), p. 209 at p. 235.

[74] Various 'offers' are made in the commercial world for serious and deliberate purposes; if only two parties are involved any promise can be treated as part of a contract, but if a third party makes a promise this might be enforceable, e.g. if a petrol company promises goods to those who buy certain quantities of petrol from petrol retailers; cf. *Esso Petroleum Ltd.* v. *Commrs. of Customs and Excise* [1976] 1 W.L.R. 1.

[75] cf. *Harvela Investments Ltd.* v. *Royal Trust Co. of Canada Ltd.* [1986] A.C. 207; and a Canadian case, *Gilbert Steel Ltd.* v. *University Construction Ltd.*. (1976) 67 D.L.R. (3d) 606.

doctor who adhered to medical theories in vogue before the days of Lister, Simpson or Fleming.'[76]

In *Wood* v. *Moncur* in 1591[77] a tenant had right under a contract between a liferenter and a fiar[78] which was intended to benefit tenants in general. The problem of tenants' rights continues to arise 400 years later. For a third party to have a right under a contract several conditions have to be satisfied and merely to have an interest in the performance of the contract is not enough. So a tenant cannot normally sue under contracts entered into by a landlord and contractor to repair the ceiling of a kitchen[79] or claim against a feudal superior under a feu disposition to a vassal,[80] or claim under a contract between buyer and seller.[81] Scots law does recognise privity of contract, although this must be a different doctrine from English law, or from classical Roman law.[82] In any event 'privity' itself can be an elusive and varying concept with a circular argument, and, for these reasons, the phrase 'privity of contract' is best avoided in Scots law.[83]

The essentials of a *jus quaesitum tertio* are (1) there must be a contract between A and B; (2) A and B must intend to benefit C;[84] (3) the third party C must be identified but need not be named; (4) there must be some intimation to C of his or her rights, but the form of this, or even in some cases the need for this, is controversial; and (5) C must have not only a title to sue but also an interest to sue.

There is continued reference in Scottish courts to *jus quaesitum*, in many contexts, not confined to personal contracts; and sometimes the right of the third party is sustained and sometimes not. It is relatively easy for Scots law to recognise third party rights because of the doctrine of unilateral promise[85] and the lack of a need for consideration. If A may

promise to pay £X to B, it is not of great significance whether the promise is in a unilateral document by A or the promise is in a contract between A and C. If promises should be enforced, so should promises to third parties.

The concept of *jus quaesitum tertio* has been relied on in relation to titles to land, which might be thought a rather specialised use, but the cases illustrate two principles: (1) the benefit to the third party need not be the primary purpose of the relationship between the other parties; and (2) the third party's rights can be express or implied.

A neighbour may, in certain circumstances found on a restriction contained in your title which arose from the conditions of the grant of a title to you or your predecessor in title. The neighbour is a third party to the agreement but the neighbour might prevent breach of a condition of the title and control the size and sub division into houses of proposed buildings[86] or object to the building of a stable and garage instead of a green house[87] or prevent a car park instead of a swimming pool[88] or object to the extension of an amusement arcade[89] or stop the installation and operation of a sawmill[90] or prevent detriment to amenity by the siting of a cocktail bar, ball room and kitchens.[91] This control on development by neighbours, quite separate from the law of servitudes, has been argued to be one reason for the preservation of the New Town of Edinburgh.[92] This system of privatised planning control may have sometimes been more effective than a public system of planning permission which, in any event, did not exist in a really substantial form until 1947.

Because a Scots lawyer tends to think in terms of principles, as well as detailed rules, there is not an objection to the use of cases on leases and feudal

---

[76] T. B. Smith, *Studies Critical and Comparative*, sup. cit. p. 229.

[77] (1591) Mor. 7719; said to be followed in *Irving* v. *Forbes* (1676) Mor. 7722; see also other cases from Mor. 7720–45.

[78] In broad terms a fiar has a fee which is a full and unlimited right to capital or a subject; a liferenter has a right to use and enjoy a subject during lifetime; thus a farm could be 'owned' by a fiar but occupied by a liferenter.

[79] *Collins* v. *William Graydon & Co.*, 1951 S.L.T. (Sh. Ct.) 100 where the point seemed so obvious it probably was not argued.

[80] *Eagle Lodge Ltd.* v. *Keir & Cawder Estates Ltd.*, 1964 S.C. 30.

[81] *Mann* v. *Houston*, 1957 S.L.T. 89 at p. 95 per Lord Sorn; *Wallace* v. *Simmers*, 1960 S.C. 255; it is arguable that some of these restrictions are unfortunate—see the position of tenants in German law—K. Zweigert and H. Kotz, *Introduction to Comparative Law* (2nd ed. trans. T. Weir, Oxford, 1987), vol. II, pp. 146–7.

[82] On which see Zimmermann, op. cit. pp. 34–9.

[83] On some of the difficulties see A. L. Corbin on *Contracts* (St. Paul, Minn., 1951), para. 778; the argument is circular when it is in the form that privity of contract prevents third parties having rights under contracts, and third parties do not

have rights because of privity of contract.

[84] In an advanced discussion this reference to 'intention' would be scrutinised because of the usual problems of imputing intention to contracting parties; the problem is one of construction or interpretation; see on 'intention', A. de Moor, 'Intention in the Law of Contract,' (1990) 106 L.Q.R. 632.

[85] The context in which Stair mentioned *jus quaesitum*—see Stair, sup. cit. 1.10.5.

[86] *Nicholson* v. *Glasgow Asylum for the Blind*, 1911 S.C. 391.

[87] *Braid Hills Hotel Co.* v. *Manuels*, 1909 S.C. 120.

[88] *Lees* v. *North East Fife D.C.*, 1987 S.L.T. 769.

[89] *Lawrence* v. *Scott*, 1965 S.C. 403.

[90] *Fergusson* v. *McCulloch*, 1953 S.L.T. (Sh. Ct.) 113.

[91] *Macdonald* v. *Douglas*, 1963 S.C. 374.

[92] E.g. *Main* v. *Lord Doune*, 1972 S.L.T. (Lands Tr.) 14 at p. 16 'By means of land obligations imposed on separate proprietors and designed to carry out the plan and elevations of a leading architect of the day there duly arose throughout the Moray Feu one of the finest townscapes in the United Kingdom.' See also one of the first cases in which an implied *jus quaesitum* was upheld—*Mags. of Edinburgh* v. *Macfarlane* (1857) 20 D. 156.

property as examples of a principle which applies to contracts or conversely, while recognising that specialities may arise.[93] Third party rights can be created in many types of contracts, e.g. a nominee who has rights under a partnership agreement,[94] a son who is covered under a contract of motor insurance between his father and an insurer[95] or a policy of life insurance,[96] a pension scheme which confers rights on relatives,[97] or a contract for the purchase of a coffee set and entré dish on which the donee had a title to sue.[98] Indeed the use of the term *jus quaesitum* can be pervasive and applied to circumstances which might be better viewed as the rights of a promisee under a promise[99] or of a beneficiary under a trust.[100]

While English law considers whether or not to have third party rights[101] and some may argue for the preservation of the English concept of privity of contract, few Scots lawyers, I suggest, would wish to depart from our traditional ideas, except to clarify some obscurities. To the extent that English lawyers have used devices like trust or agency to overcome the barrier to third party rights there may be a recognition of the practical need for third parties to be able to sue: a need which has been recognised, to varying degrees, in common law jurisdictions such as California,[102] New Zealand,[103] and Ontario.[104]

Scots law has a problem in certain circumstances about the method of creation of the third party's right and the requirement, or otherwise, for the right to be irrevocable. So much has been written on this it

would be superfluous for me to add now to the controversy.[105] My view is that a revocable right can be conferred, but not everyone would agree. It is difficult to state the present law with certainty. Part of the problem hinges around the circumstances in which delivery of a document is necessary and what constitutes delivery. It would be a relief if Scots law could adapt the approach of English law that a deed is delivered if words or acts sufficiently show that a document was intended to be finally executed.[106] There is also a potential problem in Scotland with the rights of the third party in the event of defective performance.[107] We may sometimes have lost our way but that should not deter others from following the route with map and compass. A careful analysis of our case law, which can be mentioned only briefly in this paper, would enable others to produce a better system with the benefit of our sometimes unfortunate experience.

The challenge for future generations of Scots lawyers is whether the concept of *jus quaesitum* will develop in practice into new areas. The prospects are not good. There is a tendency for judicial restraint; a reluctance to take principle and expand or up date it. This is in contrast to the attitude of Australian and Canadian courts whose recent approach to entrenched doctrines of privity of contract could be a revelation to Scottish lawyers.[108]

I wish to examine briefly the scope for expansion in three areas: (1) contracts for the sale of goods and supply of services; (2) exclusion and indemnity

---

[93] A speciality with feudal rights arises from the circumstances in which the rights of third parties might be inferred, in the absence of an express right—*Hislop* v. *MacRitchie's Trs.* (1881) 8 R. (H.L.) 95.

[94] *Thomson* v. *Thomson*, 1962 S.C. (H.L.) 28.

[95] *Kelly* v. *Cornhill Insurance Co.*, 1964 S.C. (H.L.) 46 at p. 67 per Lord Hodson, p. 69 per Lord Guest; the point was so obvious it was admitted.

[96] *Carmichael* v. *Carmichael's Ex.*, 1920 S.C. (H.L.) 195, which is the source of much of the debate about irrevocability; it is interesting that in French law insurance contracts appear to be responsible for much of the early development of the *stipulation pour autrui*—B. Nicholas, *The French Law of Contract* (Oxford, 2nd ed. 1992), pp. 184–7.

[97] *Love* v. *Amalgamated Society of Lithographic Printers*, 1912 S.C. 1078.

[98] *Cullen* v. *McMenamin Ltd.*, 1928 S.L.T. (Sh. Ct.) 2.

[99] *Denny Trs.* v. *Dumbarton Mags.*, 1945 S.C. 147 at p. 151 per L. J. C. Cooper.

[100] The use of the concept in trust requires a reconsideration which is not possible here; see, however, *Muir's Trs.* v. *Williams*, 1943 S.C. (H.L.) 47; *Parker* v. *Lord Advocate*, 1958 S.C. 426 at p. 437 per Lord Mackintosh; *Dunnett* v. *Dunnett's Trs.*, 1985 S.L.T. 382.

[101] The Law Commission, Consultation Paper No. 121, 'Privity of Contract: Contracts for the Benefit of Third Parties,' (London, 1991).

[102] The Californian Civil Code para. 1559 has since 1872 provided that '(a) contract, made expressly for the benefit of a third person, may be enforced by him at any time before the

parties thereto rescind it.'

[103] The Contracts (Privity) Act 1982 followed on the Contracts and Commercial Law Reform Committee, *Report on Privity of Contract* (1981), and a minor amendment to the Act is suggested in the New Zealand Law Commission Report on *Contract Statutes Review*, sup. cit.

[104] Ontario Law Reform Commission, *Report on Amendment of the Law of Contract* (1987), pp. 49–71; see also Law Reform Commission of Victoria, Discussion Paper No. 27, *An Australian Contract Code* (1992), art. 9.

[105] To avoid a very large footnote I refer to McBryde on *Contract*, p. 408, note 2 and pp. 412–19.

[106] *Xenos* v. *Wickham* (1867) L.R. 2 H.L. 296 at p. 312 per Blackburn, J.; *Macedo* v. *Stroud* [1922] 2 A.C. 330 at p. 337 per Viscount Haldane; of course we would not want to inherit specialities of sealing and deeds; see also Report No. 10 of the Law Reform Commissioner, Victoria, *Delivery of Deeds* (Melbourne, 1980).

[107] Discussed in T. B. Smith, *Short Commentary*, sup. cit. at pp. 782–4; *Scott Lithgow Ltd.* v. *G.E.C. Electrical Properties Ltd.*, 1992 S.L.T. 244 at pp. 260–1 per Lord Clyde.

[108] *Trident General Insurance Co.* v. *McNeice Bros. Pty. Ltd.* (1988) 165 C.L.R. (High Ct. of Australia); *London Drugs Ltd.* v. *Kuehne & Nagel International Ltd.* (1992) 97 D.L.R. 261 (Supreme Ct. of Canada); it is a matter for speculation whether abolition of an appeal to the House of Lords would liberate the Inner House of the Court of Session and promote the development of Scots law in the way which is now possible in Australia or Canada with the removal of a right of recourse to the Privy Council.

clauses; and (3) claims against solicitors. In some cases change might need legislation and, in the absence of that, it is possible that the Scottish system of third party rights will lack sophistication when compared to other legal systems.

(1) Contracts for the sale of goods and supply of services. One of the effects of a strict division of rights into contractual rights, on the one hand, and delictual or tortious rights, on the other hand, is that a third party may have no rights under a contract between A and B but might be better advised to sue in delict or tort in an appropriate case. This was the problem underlying the Scottish case of *Donoghue* v. *Stevenson*.[109]

If A sells a defective product to B knowing that the product will be used or consumed by C, why cannot C sue A *under the contract*? Obviously C may have delictual rights against A and conversely a case based simply on C's interest in the contract will fail (as in *Donoghue's* case where the action at one point was against Minghella—usually wrongly referred to as 'Minchella'—but this case was abandoned).[110] Why should C not have rights as a tertius against A if it were to be averred and proved that, say, B bought ginger beer from A in the presence of C with the knowledge of all present that the beer was to be consumed by C? There is a clear intention to benefit the third party, and any doubt about that, for the purposes of initial analysis, can be removed by express statements by B to A and by A to B that the purchase is for consumption by C. B is a contracting party, and liable for the price. B is not the agent of C who never acquires any liability under the contract. That a donee could acquire rights under a contract was decided in a sheriff court case.[111]

Of course, it is insufficient to say that a third party has rights. The further question has to be asked—what rights? But is it really a great extension of the law to argue that in a contract for sale of goods these

rights would include an action for breach of implied warranties or conditions? What other right against the seller is really worth having when your friend buys you a beer? A problem would be the present law in the Sale of Goods Act which concentrates on the relationship of buyer and seller. Although the Act does not expressly prevent someone other than the buyer having a remedy, there are difficulties with the argument in favour of the third party which might require amending legislation.[112]

Jus quaesitum could also solve some problems of title to sue when various third parties are affected by a breach of contract, e.g. when a holiday firm disappoints a family, or a restaurant turns away guests, or a coach strands a choir, being examples given in another context by Lord Denning.[113]

It is also for consideration as to whether or not a manufacturer who contracts with a wholesaler should be liable to the ultimate consumer for express or implied warranties about the goods, with such contractual restrictions on liability as the law allows. An interesting proposal of this nature has been made by the Ontario Law Reform Commission.[114] Using contract law overcomes some of the difficulties with recovery of economic loss which are presented by delict and tort, given the present attitude of the House of Lords. Recovery under the Consumer Protection Act 1987 is limited to death or personal injury or loss or damage to property and also to defects in products.[115] Delictual liability is not always an adequate substitute for contractual liability.[116]

An obstacle to much of this development in Scots law on the present state of the authorities might be *Cameron* v. *Young*[117] in which the wife and children of a tenant contracted typhoid because of the insanitary condition of a house let by a firm of Stirling bakers. It was held that the tenant's family did not have a title to sue. *Jus quaesitum tertio* does not appear to

---

[109] 1932 S.C. (H.L.) 31; incidentally, a Scottish lawyer should refer to the case as Donoghue against Stevenson; a lawyer trained in an English or English based system usually betrays his or her origins by an incorrect reference to Donoghue and Stevenson. It has to be admitted, however, that with this case the Scots are not always consistent, although the use of 'against' is the normal rule.

[110] It is a tragedy that this famous case has not been fully reported; its background and more of the detail of the pleadings and procedure are discussed in the writer's 'Donoghue v. Stevenson: The Story of the "Snail in The Bottle" Case', *Obligations in Context* (Essays in Honour of Prof. D. M. Walker; ed. A. J. Gamble), (Edinburgh, 1990) p. 13; reprinted with revisions in *Donoghue* v. *Stevenson and the Modern Law of Negligence*; *The Paisley Papers*, ed. P. T. Burns and S. J. Lyons (British Columbia, 1991), p. 25.

[111] *Cullen* v. *McMenamin* sup. cit.

[112] There may also be difficulty at common law unless there

is a very clear expression of an intention to confer rights on the third party—*Blumer & Co.* v. *Scott & Sons* (1874) 1 R. 379 where the contracting parties appear to have known well of the third party's interest but the third party was not named in the contract (see at p. 387 per Lord Ardmillan); Lord Deas dissented using an agency argument to overcome the third party's lack of a title to sue; also the presence of a reference to a third party does not by itself create a right—*Scott Lithgow Ltd.* v. *G.E.C. Electrical Projects Ltd.* sup. cit. at p. 261.

[113] In *Jackson* v. *Horizon Holidays* [1975] 1 W.L.R. 1468 at p. 1473.

[114] *Report on Consumer Warranties and Guarantees in the Sale of Goods* (1972), pp. 65–77.

[115] s. 2 (1) and 5 (1).

[116] See, e.g. B. S. Markesinis, 'An Expanding Tort Law—The Price of A Rigid Contract Law' (1987), 103 L.Q.R. 354 and *White* v. *Jones* [1993] 3 All E.R. 481 at p. 501 per Steyn, L. J.

[117] 1907 S.C. 475; 1908 S.C. (H.L.) 7.

have been in issue and, indeed, Lord Kinnear thought that there was no ground for the plea.[118] A court might feel bound to follow *Cameron* v. *Young*, unless it could be distinguished by clear averments about the contract conferring rights on the tenant's family. Nevertheless in reality, if not in law, when a man lets a house for himself, his wife and three sons, the purpose of the contract is to provide a home for the family. The presence of poisonous sewer gases, in breach of express or implied terms of the lease, will affect all who occupy under the lease.[119] Scots law needs a Lord Denning who can ignore past confusion and inhibition. Only in that way, or by legislation, can *jus quaesitum* develop.

(2) The draftsman of an exclusion or indemnity clause will sometimes wish to protect those close to his client, e.g. associated, parent or holding companies, employees, agents or independent contractors. May these third parties have rights under a contract to the effect of limiting or excluding liability or seeking indemnity from another party? In principle there is no reason why not. In so far as there is indemnity there is a similarity to insurance. In any event the requirements for *jus quaesitum tertio* can be satisfied, certainly if there is intimation of the rights to the third parties, which may, however, not often be done.[120] Allowing a third party defences to an action, rather than contemplating the third party as the pursuer and claimant of a right, is a departure from traditional examples, but it is not a breach of principle.

It would not be essential, nor always desirable, in Scots law to make one of the contracting parties agent of the third parties.[122] The difference between third party rights and the modern concept of agency is important; apart from questions of authority to act, a principle can be under obligations to perform while a *tertius* cannot have obligations imposed.

Another difference arises if the beneficiary does not exist, e.g. a contract for a company not yet formed. There are problems with binding a non-existence principal which should not arise with conferring rights on a third party, who need not exist at the time of the contract. Although a Scottish decision rejected this approach in the context of pre-incorporation contracts, Dr MacQueen has pointed out the defects in the court's analysis.[123]

The issue of limitation of a third party's liability has arisen in argument about the contract between a building society and a prospective borrower for the provision to the borrower of the valuer's report obtained by the society. There may be a disclaimer of liability in favour of the valuer. This disclaimer might be unenforceable because of the Unfair Contract Terms Act 1977.[124] The right of the valuer, as a third party, to a restriction of liability could exist, however, if the terms could be shown to be fair and reasonable.[125]

(3) On one view a clear instance of a contract which has an intention to benefit a third party is the contract between solicitor and client for preparation of the client's will. If the solicitor prepares the will negligently, the beneficiaries, in certain circumstances, may have an action in delict.[126] The question is whether they have an action in contract.

The right of the beneficiaries to sue under the contract to which they were not a party appears to fulfil at least some of the requirements of Scots law. The main purpose of the testator in obtaining the services of the solicitor is to benefit those named in the will. Those who claim third party rights must be identified, but need not be named or even be born at the time of the contract.[127] An obstacle is the uncertainty in Scots law over whether a revocable right can be a *jus quaesitum tertio* and whether some form of intimation to the third parties would be necessary in the

---

[118] At p. 483.

[119] See opinion of Sheriff Principal Lees at (1907) 44 S.L.R. 344 at p. 346.

[120] And how should you intimate to a class such as employees?; the requirement for delivery or an equivalent could limit the practical application of *jus quaesitum tertio*; see the Canadian approach in *London Drugs Ltd.* v. *Kuehne & Nagel International Ltd.* sup. cit.

[121] See S. Todd, 'The Contract (Privity) Act 1982' in New Zealand Law Commission, Report No. 25, *Contract Statutes Review* (1993), p. 219.

[122] Cf. *New Zealand Shipping Co. Ltd.* v. *A. M. Satterthwaite & Co. Ltd.* [1975] A.C. 154; *Port Jackson Stevedoring Pty. Ltd.* v. *Salmond & Spraggon (Australia) Pty. Ltd.* [1981] 1 W.L.R. 138.

[123] *Cumming* v. *Quartzag Ltd.*, 1980 S.C. 276; H.L. MacQueen, 'Promoters' Contracts, Agency and the Jus Quaesitum Tertio,' 1982 S.L.T. (News) 257; for a guide to other problems see A. Griffiths, 'Agents without principals: pre-incorporation contracts and section 36C of the Companies Act 1985,' (1993) 13 Legal Studies, p. 241.

[124] *Smith* v. *Eric S. Bush*; *Harris* v. *Wyre Forest D.C.* [1990] 1 A.C. 831.

[125] *Melrose* v. *Davidson and Robertson*, 1993 S.L.T. 611 at p. 614 per L. P. Hope; the effect of disclaimers by surveyors has featured in a number of other cases—*Hadden* v. *City of Glasgow D.C.*, 1986 S.L.T. 557; *Martin* v. *Bell-Ingram*, 1986 S.C. 208; *Commercial Financial Services Ltd.* v. *McBeth & Co.*, 1988 S.L.T. 528; *Robbie* v. *Graham & Sibbald*, 1989 S.L.T. 870; as a result of *Robbie*, the Unfair Contract Terms Act was amended by the Law Reform (Miscellaneous Provisions) (Scotland) Act 1990, s. 68, but as *Melrose* shows *Robbie* might have proceeded on the basis of an unwise concession by counsel that no contract existed.

[126] *Ross* v. *Caunters* [1980] Ch. 297; *Gartside* v. *Sheffield, Young and Ellis* [1983] N.Z.L.R. 37; *Clarke* v. *Bruce Lance & Co.* [1988] 1 W.L.R. 881; *White* v. *Jones* [1993] 3 All E.R. 481; W. Lorenz and B. Markesinis, 'Solicitors' Liability Toward Third Parties: Back Into the Troubled Waters of the Contract/Tort Divide,' (1993) 56 M.L.R. 558.

[127] See McBryde on *Contract*, paras. 18–04 to 18–09.

case of a will. There are ways in which the courts could prevent an indeterminate liability arising in favour of an indeterminate number of people.

Another problem is that the House of Lords decided in 1861 that the disappointed legatee cannot sue,[128] although *jus quaesitum* was not argued. This area of law is confused because of the changing nature of thought in the last 150 years on the relationship between contract and delict.[129] It has also been said that '(t)he distinction between contract and tort in England has never found its full counterpart in Scotland.'[130] Whether or not this is true it would be a failure if Scots law ceased to develop. Californian law, for example, recognises the right of the disappointed legatee in certain circumstances.[131] The problem, as often, is imperfect judicial expression of the concepts involved plus a rigid doctrine of precedent which is English in origin, and which may be the most unfortunate influence on Scots law.[132]

In *Weir* v. *J. M. Hodge & Son*,[133] the Lord Ordinary held that he was bound by the decision of the House of Lords in *Robertson* v. *Fleming* notwithstanding subsequent developments of the common law. This is an understandable view for a judge of first instance, but if the result is injustice to one party it is a high price to pay for the advantage of certainty which following precedent is said to confer.

Conclusion

Scots law has had a tradition of adopting rules from other countries. Its contract law combines civil and common law rules which is, in my view, a strength rather than the weakness some have perceived. It enables a Scots lawyer to move on an international stage whether as a practitioner or a law reformer. An example is the ease with which the Scottish Law Commission were able to accept the rules of the Vienna Convention which were similar to Scots law and in some cases an improvement.[134] Another instance is in arbitration where the English have declined to adopt the UNCITRAL rules which are now part of Scots law as a result of the Law Reform (Miscellaneous Provisions) (Scotland) Act 1990.[135]

It may be that consideration of international codes and European Directives[136] will be the basis for future major reform of Scots law. Too much of the academic analysis of Scots contract law has been backward looking and bemoaning the mistakes of the past. Having engaged in that activity I know its interest. But the oil executive who arrives in Aberdeen, or the insurance company who sell their services, or the manufacturer buying from a supplier, all should easily be persuaded that their contracts are to be governed by Scots law; a system with modern and internationally recognised rules. To the extent that this is not so the Scots lawyers have work to do; to the extent that English law has helped us on the way we should be grateful.[137]

William W. McBryde

---

[128] *Robertson* v. *Fleming* (1861) 4 Macq. 167; see also *Tully* v. *Ingram* (1891) 19 R. 65.
[129] On *Robertson* v. *Fleming* see *Ross* v. *Caunters* and *White* v. *Jones* sup. cit.
[130] *Robertson* v. *Bannigan*, 1965 S.C. 20 at p. 30 per Lord Wheatley (dissenting); see the point elaborated in Professor D. M. Walker's Introduction to the reprint of Stair's *Institutions* (Edinburgh and Glasgow, 1981), p. 39; to the writer it is surprising that there is argument about whether an action in negligence arises when there is a contract, cf. *Lancashire and Cheshire Assoc. of Baptist Churches Inc.* v. *Howard & Seldon Partnership* [1993] 3 All E.R. 467.
[131] *Lucas* v. *Hamm* (1961) 56 Cal. 2d. 583, 364 P. 2d. 685; see also *Stowe* v. *Smith* (1981) 184 Conn. 194, 441 A.2d 81, 83; an attorney's primary duty is to the client and that may negative a duty to a certain class of beneficiary when questions arise as to how a will should be framed and what options are open to the client—*Krawczyk* v. Stingle (1988) 208 Conn. 239, 543 A.2d. 733; see also Lorenz and Markesinis, sup. cit. at p. 559.
[132] T. B. Smith, *Doctrines of Judicial Precedent in Scots Law* (Edinburgh, 1952); an intriguing, although unlikely solution at present, is the suggestion of the Law Reform Commission of Victoria, sup. cit., reminiscent of French law, that a contract code should be authoritative and self contained and that judicial decisions are illustrative but not rules; art. 3 of the Draft Code provides—'neither past nor future decisions govern the application of the Code.'

[133] 1990 S.L.T. 266; despite my earlier promotion of the Scots Law Times Index 1961–1990 it provides a trap in trying to discovery this case which is indexed under 'Stare Decisis' and 'Process' only; no entry appears under the expected heading of 'Reparation—Solicitor'.
[134] See the Report on Formation of Contract, sup. cit., para. 1.7.
[135] Sched. 7; this followed on a Report from the Lord Advocate's Scottish Advisory Committee on Arbitration Law dated 11 May 1989; the work of the English Departmental Advisory Committee on Arbitration Law chaired by Lord Justice Mustill did not reach the same conclusions about the UNCITRAL Model Law—*A Report on the UNCITRAL Model Law on International Commercial Arbitration* (Department of Trade and Industry, 1989) esp. at paras. 89–91, where the conceptual and philosophical similarity is noted between Scots law and the Model Law of the United Nations Commission; C. Reymond, 'The Report of the Mustill Committee: A Foreign View,' (1990) 106 L.Q.R. 431.
[136] E.g. the E.C. Directive on Unfair Terms in Consumer Contracts, Directive 93/13 E.E.C., O.J. L.95/29, 21/4/93; M. Dean, 'Unfair Contract Terms: The European Approach,' (1993) 56 M.L.R. 581.
[137] I would like to thank Lord Rodger of Earlsferry, and Professors Aubrey Diamond and Francis Reynolds for their helpful comments at the seminar which enabled me to correct some of my infelicities.

12. Drawing the Strings Together

F. M. B. REYNOLDS, Q.C.

O F the jurisdictions whose law was discussed at the seminar, the most striking developments have occurred in Australia and New Zealand. Australia is the subject of a thorough survey in the first paper by Chief Justice Gleeson, and it seems appropriate therefore to start with that country. As anyone who has a minimal familiarity with the Australian legal scene—at least as in the High Court of Australia and New South Wales—would expect, the paper largely concentrates on the influence of equity on contract law. This is a very prominent feature of much Australian contract law and gives a special appearance to some of the cases. Some of these have recourse to a wide and diffused notion of unconscionability. The most extreme example of this is the Discussion Paper[1] of the late Law Reform Commission of Victoria, which sought to reduce contract law to a small number of codified propositions, of which one of the more dramatic was Article 27:

'A person may not assert a right or deny an obligation to the extent that it would be unconscionable to do so.'

Most lawyers would think that this goes rather too far, though the case law under section 52 of the Trade Practices Act, referred to below, can be described as coming quite near to such a result. Other cases, more practically, employ a set of more focused equitable notions. Whether the doctrines are wide or narrow, however, some of the commentators posit a dramatic change in attitudes. Thus Professor Paul Finn quotes William Butler Yeats on the aftermath of the Irish Easter Rising:

'All changed, changed utterly:
A terrible beauty is born.'[2]

Whether the attitude of lawyers to contract disputes is now so completely different in Australia from that to be found in England is something which only a person with practical experience in both countries could properly judge. There are dangers in assessing other legal systems by merely reading their law reports, and I do not wish to run the risk of seeking to make such an assessment. But some general observations, suggesting caution as regards the making of sweeping judgments, may be advanced.

First, the most noticeable changes in Australia appear not in decisions but in the (often lengthy and far from univocal) judicial discussion of doctrine which accompanies them. *Waltons Stores (Interstate) Ltd.* v. *Maher*[3] is certainly an important decision, but the importance lies mostly in what is said rather than what is done. The actual decision, I would suggest, is not surprising and could be reached by an English court: there are some low-profile decisions which get quite close. In particular, the actual decision requires but a small advance from what the English Court of Appeal decided in *Amalgamated Investment & Property Co. Ltd.* v. *Texas Commerce International Bank Ltd.*[4] and hardly any advance from what Robert Goff J. said at first instance in that case. The topic of whether one can sue upon a relied-on promise has been a staple of contract teachers ever since I started teaching: various cases have from time to time been used to trigger off consideration of the point.[5] It is not difficult nor very revolutionary to posit a technique supplementary to the doctrine of consideration which, like section 90 of the *Restatement*, makes actionable a few promises without consideration in fringe situations, on the basis of estoppel. It should be noted that it is not clear from *Waltons Stores* how damages are to be calculated in such a situation. That is where *Commonwealth* v. *Verwayen*[6] comes in. However much one may disapprove of the actions of the Commonwealth Government, the actual decision is surprising. But on the analysis preferred by the minority the case could almost be regarded as one on costs. All in all, as a supplement to but not as a substitute for consideration, the notion of reliance is not difficult to accept. But it was suggested at the meeting by way of warning that 'a principle which can yield so many results in different hands requires scrutiny.'

For an English lawyer, the significant distinction is in fact probably not that, much discussed in Australia, between common law and equitable estoppel, nor notions of 'overarching estoppel', none of which have attracted much interest in England, but rather that between estoppel in the making of contract and in the alteration of contract. Estoppel in the making of contract is, as above suggested, probably accept-

---

[1] No. 27 (1992).
[2] 'Commerce, the Common Law and Morality' (1989) 17 Melbourne U.L. Rev. 87, 92. But Brennan, J. did not entirely agree: 'Commercial Law and Morality', ibid., 100.
[3] (1988) 164 C.L.R. 387.
[4] [1982] Q.B. 85.
[5] E.g., *Evenden* v. *Guildford City Assoc. Football Club Ltd.* [1975] Q.B. 917.
[6] (1990) 170 C.L.R. 394.

able in a limited group of cases, but not yet fully established. Estoppel, or some doctrine that is related even if it has another name such a waiver or forbearance, has however long been accepted in England as relevant to the modification or discharge of contract, and as a way round the requirement of consideration for modifications of contract established in *Foakes* v. *Beer*.[7] It is an incomplete solution to the problem however: even if it can be extended to the 'upwards' modification in cases like *Stilk* v. *Myrick*[8] it creates an undesirable discretionary element in a situation that should not by modern (or indeed Roman) ideas require consideration at all, but depend simply on agreement, controlled by better targeted notions of duress and coercion rather than by the mysteries of estoppel and 'inequitability'. This is what Lord Denning was after in *D. & C. Builders Ltd.* v. *Rees*;[9] but his approach did not quite work. Thus, whatever may be thought of the reasoning, the decision in *Williams* v. *Roffey Bros. & Nicholls (Contractors) Ltd.*[10] is surely to be welcomed as reducing the role of consideration in the modification of contract by what is apparently a more acceptable route from that tried by Lord Denning. It is worth remembering that Lord Blackburn came near to dissenting in *Foakes* v. *Beer*.

It should next be noted that the law to some extent takes its flavour from the type of dispute litigated to the highest tribunal. In England since the war the big contract cases such as *Hong Kong Fir*,[11] *Bunge* v. *Tradax*,[12] *Suisse Atlantique*[13] and *The Heron II*[14] have concerned shipping operations and international commodity sales (or both). The decisions of such cases, involving planned commercial situations, is obviously affected by a sentiment that certainty is more important than an absolutely fair result in every case. In Australia the leading cases seem to me mostly to concern land, and chattel financing.[15] On these topics there have been few English leading cases in the last sixty years. This type of case more readily attracts the operation of equity. How far equitable reasoning should affect the result of the first type of case is more problematical:

a leading flashpoint for this is *The Scaptrade*,[16] which might be decided differently in Australia. Assuming the distinction between types of case is a valid one, a major problem is how to tell one from the other. Another distinction that can be made in this context is between cases where the court upholds the results of the planning, especially by allowing one party to terminate the contract, and those where the court is clearing up unexpected results by way of a damages award, as if in a tort case—as in *H. Parsons & Co. (Livestock) Ltd.* v. *Uttley Ingham & Co. Ltd.*,[17] which could indeed have been a tort case. Here again there may be difficulty in telling one from the other.

It was suggested however that this concentration on equitable techniques may lead to a new legal method whereby guidelines are laid down and the court then reaches a conclusion by balancing these rather than by purporting to apply rules—by exercising a 'structured discretion'. There are certainly areas where this is appropriate, such as relief in the case of unfair exclusion clauses, or transactions alleged concluded under duress, undue influence, or by taking advantage of the known weakness of an other in a unconscionable way.[18] But it seems doubtful whether such a method is suitable for all disputes, and least of all for those relating to planned transactions.

For common lawyers, the notion of good faith is a new offspring of the equitable approach, though its true origin lies of course in Roman law. It is becoming fashionable at present even in England. Partly it is seen as having a potential role as a new rubric for implementing aspects of an equity-dominated approach.[19] It can also, however, be described, as it was orally by Chief Justice Gleeson, as 'an answer waiting for a question.' It can certainly explain some of the results we now reach by other means, for example, some of the rules of formation of contract and implied warranties. As such it can be said to be a fifth column waiting for its moment. But it will only become significant if it actually dictates new results, for example, a general duty of disclosure, or a requirement of good faith in the exercise of

[7] (1884) 9 App. Cas. 605.
[8] (1809) 2 Camp. 317.
[9] [1966] 2 Q.B. 617.
[10] [1991] 1 Q.B. 1. But cf. now *Re Selectmove*, C.A., 21 December 1993.
[11] *Hong Kong Fir Shipping Co. Ltd.* v. *Kawasaki Kisen Kaisha* [1962] 2 Q.B. 26.
[12] *Bunge Corporation* v. *Tradax Export S.A.* [1981] 1 W.L.R. 711.
[13] *Suisse Atlantique Société d'Armement Maritime S.A.* v. *N.V. Rotterdamsche Kolen Centrale* [1967] 1 A.C. 361.
[14] *C. Czarnikow Ltd.* v. *Koufos (The Heron II)* [1969] 1 A.C. 350.
[15] An estimate was made in 1989 that sale of land had featured in 68% of the contract cases coming before the High

Court: Ellinghaus (1989) 2 J. Contract Law 13, 19. Construction cases do not feature prominently in either jurisdiction.
[16] *Scandinavian Trading Tanker Co. A.B.* v. *Flota Petrolera Ecuatoriana (The Scaptrade)* [1983] 2 A.C. 694.
[17] [1978] Q.B. 791; a decision which sparked off the article by Sir Robin Cooke in [1978] C.L.J. 288, expressing views which he repeated judicially some years later in *McElroy Milne* v. *Commercial Electronics Ltd.* [1993] 1 N.Z.L.R. 39, referred to below.
[18] E.g. *Commercial Bank of Australia* v. *Amadio* (1983) 151 C.L.R. 447.
[19] See Finn, 'The Fiduciary Principle', in *Equity, Fiduciaries and Trusts*, ed. Youdan (1989), Ch. 1, esp. at pp. 10 et seq.; Lücke, 'Good Faith and Contractual Performance' in *Essays on Contract*, ed. Finn (1987), Ch. 5.

remedy—an idea which the common law has not so far accepted.[20]

Another topic which arises from Australian developments is that of the extent to which reforms and developments can come from judicial action and when it is appropriate that the change should be made by statute. In England the courts have talked about altering the rule of privity of contract by judicial decision,[21] but have not done so: it seems now accepted that a statute is appropriate, at least where it is desired to confer a right on a third party to sue. In Australia the *Trident*[22] case develops the law so as to give the same effect as a statute which had come into effect but did not cover the actual facts because of the date at which they occurred. The decision is not however based on the idea that policy can be derived from statute: on the whole common lawyers, unlike civil lawyers, are unfamiliar with this idea. The signals given by the decision are more general; but they are far from clear and it remains to be seen whether the law can be developed from this starting point and if so, how. The dominant English view is probably that to allow a third party to sue on a contract presents too many side issues for resolution to be achieved by judicial decision, and needs a statute.[23]

The application of exclusion clauses to third parties is however a problem more easily dealt with by judicial decision: there are less points to settle. For this reason the English Law Commission[24] may be wrong in trying to solve it by the same method as that which they suggest for third party rights. Thus it is not difficult to absorb the decision of the Supreme Court of Canada in the recent *London Drugs*[25] case (though it is in one sense a surprising decision in that the persons held to benefit were not mentioned in the clause itself). Something like this was thought to be the law in England till the intervention of Lord Simonds in 1961;[26] it would not be that difficult to return to it. However, it must be pointed out that both the Australian and the Canadian courts in their 'great leaps forward' were profoundly divided in their reasoning (quite apart, in the Australian case, from actual dissents); and this does not assist development. To argue for a new application of the *Trident* case in Canberra will be a formidable task.

Multiple judgments are beneficial only if they do not become too diffuse.

There is also however a quite different movement in Australian law which is not so well known from outside, but is arguably more significant. This stems from the Trade Practices Act, section 52 of which provides that a corporation shall not, in trade or commerce, engage in conduct that is misleading or deceptive, or is likely to mislead or deceive. This provision, together with various related provisions added later, seem to be moving towards the offer of a new perception of how contractual disputes should be solved. It originated at a time when there were very limited remedies indeed for representations in the sphere of negotiations which were not contractual promises, and can be said to have been largely directed at this problem. But this full potential of the breadth of the wording is now being realised. The recent *Comalco* case[27] provides a striking example. In this case freight forwarders advertised themselves as a careful packers,[28] and this impression was reinforced by representations by one of their employees as to the methods of packing to be employed, made near the time of formation of the contract. The goods were damaged because of bad packing. The contract itself limited the forwarder's liability in respect of packing so that he could not be held liable for breach of contract: and such limitation, operating outside the period of carriage, is accepted by international conventions. The forwarder was however held liable on the basis that he had represented himself as a careful packer. Most contractors can be regarded as representing themselves as competent to do what they undertake to do: to concentrate on the conduct rather than the undertaking opens new vistas. The new approach, which overrides what would elsewhere be regarded as contractual allocations of responsibility, obviously has great potential; and this is perhaps more remarkable than the developments of equitable doctrine. It is worth noting that very similar legislation is now applicable in New Zealand:[29] but the practitioners and courts seem at present to have their heads turned to a different direction.

This is a striking change: but there is also a general knock-on effect. It is said also that in Australia

---

[20] See *White & Carter (Councils) Ltd. v. McGregor* [1962] A.C. 413, 430 per Lord Reid; cf. *Sunbird Plaza Pty. Ltd. v. Maloney* (1988) 166 C.L.R. 245, 263 per Mason, C. J.; and see *Service Station Association Ltd. v. Berg Bennett & Associates*, (1993) 117 A.L.R. 393.

[21] *Woodar Investment Development Ltd. v. Wimpey Construction U.K. Ltd.* [1980] 1 W.L.R. 277, 300 per Lord Scarman.

[22] *Trident General Insurance Co. Ltd. v. McNiece Bros. Pty. Ltd.* (1988) 165 C.L.R. 107.

[23] See Law Com. C.P. No. 121 (1991).

[24] Op. cit. supra.

[25] *London Drugs Ltd. v. Kuehne & Nagel (International) Ltd.* [1992] 3 S.C.R. 299.

[26] *Midland Silicones Ltd. v. Scruttons Ltd.* [1962] A.C. 446.

[27] *Comalco Aluminium Ltd. v. Mogal Freight Services Pty. Ltd. (The Oceania Trader)* (1993) 113 A.L.R. 677; affd. 1 October 1993.

[28] There had been advertising 18 months prior to the event in which they described themselves as 'specialists in the trade' and 'ideally positioned to provide the complete door to door service.'

[29] Fair Trading Act 1986, s. 9.

judges become used to exercising the wide powers conferred by the Trade Practices Act, and, in New South Wales, the Contracts Review Act; and that this affects judicial decisions in general. This prompts the more general suggestion that the use of powers under statutes may accustom judges to taking a broader view of their powers when statutes are not applicable.

Moving away from Australia, the use of statutes to change contract law has in fact its most remarkable example in New Zealand, a jurisdiction to which none of these papers is directed, but which repays nevertheless careful attention.[30] A sequence of statutes have conferred discretions on the courts: the Illegal Contracts Act 1970, the Contractual Mistakes Act 1977, and the Contractual Remedies Act 1979; and the rights of third parties to sue on contracts has been conferred by the Contracts (Privity) Act 1982. To take the last first, this seems to be regarded as successful in New Zealand even though there is virtually no litigation on it. In fact, of course, the absence of litigation may show that a statute is working rather than the reverse; and this seems to be the case. Argument may be possible about the extent to which the Act should be regarded as allowing third parties who are not specifically designated in the contract as intended to have the right to sue to do so. But it appears that the main virtue of the Act is so far perceived as facilitating the drafting of and reliance on documents which specifically designate third parties as intended beneficiaries of the relevant promises.

The Illegal Contracts Act confers a discretion as to remedies on the courts in cases where a party to a contract is affected in some way by illegality (a situation usually carelessly referred to, as in the drafting of this Act, as one raising an 'illegal *contract*'). As the recent case of *Tinsley* v. *Milligan*[31] shows, English courts at least are reluctant to appear to exercise a discretion unless this power has been conferred *ab extra*; yet the cases on illegal contracts do not easily yield the impression of the application of more than the vaguest sort of principle. This Act is obviously beneficial. The Contractual Mistakes Act has been more controversial by virtue of cases in which, where the court has exercised a discretion where the contract would (or at least might) have been valid at common law, a result which does not appear to have been the intention of those responsible for the Act. The Contractual Remedies Act confers limited discretions on the court when a contract is 'cancelled', i.e., in old-fashioned terminology,

treated as discharged for breach. A recent case[32] however, extends considerably the effect of section 9 of the Act, which confers the power to grant 'relief' in such situations, but which is thought to have been intended to cover interim relief and the like only. It has been treated as empowering the court to make general monetary awards on principles not limited by, even though they remain in the case itself analogous to, the established principles of damages. However, it is worth noting also that the Court of Appeal of New Zealand has itself made advances in respect of the common law and equity: in *McElroy Milne* v. *Commercial Electronics*[33] Sir Robin Cooke, P. says:

'I must respectfully continue to demur to suggestions that *Hadley* v. *Baxendale* (1854) 9 Exch. 341 is a classic authority on remoteness of damage, except in the sense of being a ritual incantation in discussions of the subject . . . Precisely how the test in contract should be formulated, and whether there is any true difference in this respect between negligence in breach of contract and negligence in breach of a tort duty, remains obscure.'

It may be that here again the freedom conferred by a statute encourages a more liberal approach elsewhere.

We now move nearer home. Professor McBryde's paper draws attention to the potential of Scots law. His reference to the sometimes unsatisfactory influences of English law and lawyers on Scots law is doubtless justified, though it is worth noting that the Scottish law lords have had a considerable influence on English law (including equity) and indeed, via the Privy Council, on the law of distant common law territories not part of the United Kingdom at all (e.g. New Zealand[34]); and obviously not everyone agrees with all of the results. The general points made—the advantages of not having a doctrine of consideration and not requiring estoppel as an extra way to make a promise actionable; the fact that third parties can sue on contracts—are known in principle south of the border. What English lawyers do not know and would like to know is how these things actually work. In a sense the doctrine of consideration distinguishes between onerous and gratuitous contracts: one wonders in what way the results of disputes turning on this issue would differ in Scotland, what proof is needed for unilateral obligations, the extent to which a gratuitous promise must still be performed despite a change of circumstances, and above all when third parties can sue on contracts. One would also like to know what influence the Romanistic notion of good faith has in the Scottish law of

---

[30] See 'Contract Statutes Review', Report No. 25 of the New Zealand Law Commission (1993).
[31] [1993] 3 W.L.R. 126.
[32] *Coxhead* v. *Newmans Tours Ltd.*, C.A., April 7, 1993.
[33] [1993] 1 N.Z.L.R. 39, 42.
[34] See, e.g. *Clark Boyce* v. *Mouat* [1993] 3 W.L.R. 1021.

contract: it is said that instead of this a wide doctrine of fraud was developed, but cut down, as for English law, by *Derry* v. *Peek*.[35] A detailed comparison of the way in which Scots law would solve some English cases, and English law some Scots cases, would be of great interest.

The impression one has as an outsider is that Scots law is a vehicle which could carry developments of great international interest, but that, unlike the laws of Australia and New Zealand, perhaps it has not yet started to do so. The most interesting law reform seems usually to be accomplished in small jurisdictions. New Zealand is a case in point; others are Ireland and Sweden (and the Scandinavian countries in general). Australia is a larger country than these, but is a federation, and within federations individual states are able to alter private law in ways that would be almost impossible to achieve in a jurisdiction of 50 million, where someone will have cause to object to almost anything. Perhaps the future for Scots private law is to free itself from any connection with English law and develop freely in accordance with its own genius. This is what Commonwealth countries have done, and are doing; though with them of course the similarities of concept and technique with English law make comparisons and connections easier—not, however, always that much easier, as the Australian Trade Practices Act and the New Zealand legislation shows.

What of the English law of contract? I have suggested that some of the equitable techniques deployed in Australia could apply here also, should the right litigation present itself. A block to development of the jurisdiction in respect of undue influence and other situations of unconscionability was imposed by Lord Scarman in *National Westminster Bank Plc.* v. *Morgan*,[36] and extended further than it need have been by the Court of Appeal in *Bank of Credit and Commerce International* v. *Aboody*.[37] This has been partly loosed, with the prospect of further relaxation, by the House of Lords in *C.I.B.C. Mortgages Plc.* v. *Pitt*.[38] The problems of precontractual negotiations were solved here in a less dramatic manner than was found appropriate in the Antipodes. In Australia they were picked up in wide words by the Trade Practices Act. In New Zealand they were actually the cause of the original report of

1967 which led several years later to the Contractual Remedies Act: and indeed, however it appears now, it can be said that the main purpose of the legislation was to apply the remedies for breach of contract to pre-contractual representations. This is done in section 6, the full effect of which, as Sir Robin Cooke has said, may not have been appreciated by the profession in New Zealand.[39] A difficulty was also perceived in the parol evidence rule, and was dealt with in section 4. In England the problems were dealt with less conspicuously, by a virtual disregard of the parol evidence rule, an extension of the tort of negligence and of collateral warranties, and by the curiously drafted but ultimately, it seems, quite successful section 2 of the Misrepresentation Act 1967. Other developments in the area of contract formation are discussed by Mr Beatson: some decisions, like *Walford* v. *Miles*,[40] seem too narrow.

It does not appear that serious concern as to the state of contract law has been voiced by practitioners, and the assumption seems to be that reform should be effected by statute: hence the Law Commission's proposals on privity of contract.[41] It is also an article of faith among commercial judges and perhaps practitioners, first, that certainty is a value much prized by commercial persons, and secondly, that the method of the English law of contract (for example, by its notion of conditions and warranties) provides that certainty.[42] It remains to be seen what legal trends, if any, will emerge from the present and forthcoming spate of insurance litigation, which seems to be superseding some of the shipping and commodity cases. It must also be remembered that some significant doctrinal differences with other systems are simply due, as Mr Beatson points out, to differing answers as to whether particular situations are best picked up by contract, estoppel, tort, or restitution. But in some parts of the law of contract at least, significant changes of attitude may be triggered off by Europe. The English preoccupation with international commercial litigation has never been appreciated there. The detailed and intricate provisions of the Unfair Contract Terms Act 1977 (which has not, surprisingly, generated much interesting law and in any case rarely applies in international contracts) are now about to be supplemented by the much wider and more general terminology of the E.C. Directive

---

[35] (1889) 14 App. Cas. 337.
[36] [1985] A.C. 686.
[37] [1990] 1 Q.B. 923.
[38] [1993] 3 W.L.R. 802, 808–9. See Lehane (1994) 110 L.Q.R. 167.
[39] *Walsh* v. *Kerr* [1989] 1 N.Z.L.R. 490, 493.
[40] [1992] 2 A.C. 128; cf. *Coal Cliff Collieries Pty. Ltd.* v. *Sijehama Pty. Ltd.* (1991) 24 N.S.W.L.R. 1.

[41] Law Com. C.P. No. 121 (1991).
[42] See Sir Robert Goff (as he then was), [1984] L.M.C.L.Q. 382. But cf. Dr. F. A. Mann (1980) 97 L.Q.R. 382: 'What is the value of such words in a case in which it is plain that both parties would have received a "clear and confident answer" in opposite senses, and that they would not have received the same "clear and confident answer" even if they had consulted every available commercial lawyer?'

on Unfair Terms in Consumer Contracts,[43] which actually deploys the 'requirement of good faith'. In that it applies to consumer only, this is limited. But if a liberating influence for the English judges is needed, and some obviously think it is, perhaps this, like legislation in other common law countries, may provide it.

---

[43] 93/13 of 5 April 1993: O.J. 1993 L. 95/29, 21 April 1993. See also Commercial Agents (Council Directive) Regulations 1993 (S.I. 1993, No. 3053) implementing Council Directive 86/653 of 18 December 1986, O.J. 1986 L. 382/17.

PART IV

THE REMEDIAL CONSTRUCTIVE TRUST

13. The Nature of the Remedial Constructive Trust

DONOVAN W. M. WATERS, Q.C.

1. Introduction

IN 1941 Dr E. I. Sykes[1] described the doctrine of the Anglo–Commonwealth constructive trust as 'a vague dust-heap for the reception of relationships which are difficult to classify or which are unwanted in other branches of the law.' In 1992 Mr Justice E. W. Thomas[2] of the New Zealand Supreme Court declared that 'the case law is in chaotic disarray, and attempts to clarify the essential principles by reference to past authorities are destined to disappoint the investigator.' He points to the occurrence of 'seemingly learned decisions adding to the general confusion.' In the previous year in this city Sir Peter Millett was of the view that at least for some circumstances' the use of the language of constructive trust has become such a fertile source of confusion that it would be better if it were abandoned.'[3]

Indeed within the Commonwealth countries (and I essentially have in mind New Zealand, Australia, England and Wales, and common law Canada) debate since the 1960s has been constant and sometimes quite heated. There has been volumes of it. Much of it does not so much enquire, but take the position of convinced advocacy. Some of it attempts to do both. Academics of all backgrounds—jurists, property lawyers, family law, 'equity', and commercial law specialists, to name but the most familiar—have come forward on the subject, and practitioners at Bar and Law Society meetings throughout the Commonwealth have taken the occasion of professional legal gatherings to speak on the subject from the perspective of one expertise or another across a similar range of legal interests and background. Family lawyers have had much to say; commercial and corporate lawyers are maybe a little apprehensive and less forthcoming, but litigators evidently enjoy the search for the furthest reach of constructive trust application. In some jurisdictions imaginative pleadings have become a frequent experience. Reactions indeed are very different. Solicitors on behalf of their clients, joined in this opinion by members of the judiciary, may well have a prime concern for certainty and predictability, while the litigator and other judges welcome a perceived new flexibility with enthusiasm. 'Equity' specialists divide into those who mean by 'equitable principles' the received doctrinal inheritance from the nineteenth century and those who envisage a return to the concerns with unconscionable conduct of a yet earlier age. Some of this difference of approach is associated with another debate over what it was that happened when the Judicature Acts redrew the map. Was it nothing, 'mingling', or one doctrinal pot, that came about or at least was meant to come about?

The countries of the Commonwealth also take different positions, as all of us are aware. Canada and England (with Wales) probably represent the two poles, New Zealand being nearer the Canadian position and Australia poised somewhere in the centre. There is also change everywhere in the Commonwealth, but it is different in speed and often in character as between the jurisdictions, and in my opinion the differences between us are beginning to reflect the distinct social, economic, and political backgrounds. There are different emphases reflecting local values[4] as between the countries of the Commonwealth. As a result in my opinion there is neither right nor wrong in the sense that an 'age of faith' would have had it. The senior appellate courts in each of the major Commonwealth common law countries are also beginning to assume distinct characteristic ways of thinking of their own. This can only become more apparent as the influence of the Judicial Committee of the Privy Council recedes yet further into history. To take an analogy from the kitchen, that curious mix of doctrinal consistency and of pragmatism that is the common law simmers differently on different stoves, and moreover each set of cooks answers its critics in terms of those cooks' conception of what is to be, or should be, the ultimate dish. The cooks in no camp, I suspect, can be quite sure how the dish will turn out.

In this paper I intend to argue that what is the

---

[1] 'The Doctrine of Constructive Trust' (1941), 15 Aust. L.J. 171, 175.

[2] A paper presented to the Ninth Annual Banking Law and Practice Conference, Queensland, Australia, on 1 May 1992.

[3] *Commercial Aspects of Trusts and Fiduciary Obligations*, ed. E. McKendrick, Clarendon Press, 1992, at p. 3. Sir Peter continued, 'Sometimes it is the necessary foundation for a proprietary claim, sometimes for a purely personal claim': *ibid.*

[4] E.g., as to matrimony and quasi-matrimony, and what the parties in such a relationship may expect of the courts. The courts' concern in Canada with community-accepted standards of conduct is another example.

remedial constructive trust[5] cannot be answered without the distinction first being made between liability (or obligation) and remedy. The nature of the liability (or obligation) can be and is expressed in any one of a number of ways. However, that, I will argue, has nothing to do with the constructive trust when it is conceived as a remedy. It is only when liability (or breach of the obligation) has been established, that the question arises as to the appropriate remedy. The desirable outcome of breach of obligation, I would argue, is a monetary payment or the requirement or cessation of certain conduct. However, in some circumstances the claimant may be more appropriately awarded specific assets in the defendant's name. The constructive trust is such a proprietary remedy. It affords the claimant specific property (or assets), and any increase of value inherent in that property over the period of wrongful withholding by the owner/defendant. Other proprietary remedies which may be more appropriate in the particular circumstances are lien and subrogation.

Framed as wholly a remedy, the constructive trust gives rise to a series of questions, not unfamiliar in connection with the traditional account of the constructive trust as an institution, but now to be seen in terms of *what* redress the claimant can obtain in the court's order. When is it appropriate, as between claimant and defendant, to award the claimant specific assets (as opposed to damages or other compensation or personal relief)? The language of trust concentrates the mind on property, and the recovery or acquisition by the plaintiff of property. But in order to localise redress and its effects personal remedies are favoured over proprietary remedies. If we have isolated the obligation latent in the traditional constructive trusts, how do we rationalise those occasions when personal remedy for breach of the obligation should be enough? If the defendant is insolvent or bankrupt, is a proprietary remedy appropriate when its effect is as between the claimant and the unsecured creditors of the defendant?[6] Similarly, is a proprietary remedy to be awarded when the spe-

cific assets in question are in the hands of a third party (or a yet more subsequent transferee)? Is the decision to award a proprietary remedy to be based on a consideration of the merits of the claimant's position alone or on that of the comparative merits of the respective positions of the claimant and the affected third parties, be they creditors of the claimant or other persons with the title to, or control and possession of, the specific assets? For instance, is it clear why the uninsured corporation that negligently and mistakenly pays an insolvent debtor twice should prevail over the insolvent's unsecured creditors at 100 cents in the dollar? If it is, I continue to doubt that many courts would wish to operate with that proposition as a general rule.

With these considerations in mind, and also the family property division problem as between persons for whom statute makes no provision, an observer might ask whether a court order can, or the law should, provide that in certain circumstances a proprietary remedy may be awarded only when the claimant is solvent at the date of trial. Should a proprietary remedy carry no ability of the claimant to trace into the hands of others unless the tracing right has also been awarded by the court?

The date from which the constructive trust is to operate is another issue. Can, and, if so, should the moment of the occurrence of the injury to the claimant itself determine the date on which the remedial constructive trust order takes effect, or does the decision of the court decide that date, when it may be retroactive to a particular date, effective on issue date, or effective at a specified future date?

These questions, as yet unanswered *in toto* in any Commonwealth jurisdiction, at least become crisp and unambiguous, as I would suggest, once the context is undeniably and solely remedial.

It is unfortunate that in a seminar concerned disinterestedly with common law jurisdictions at large this paper is so heavily oriented around Canadian case law. As a presenter from Canada I would have had it otherwise. However, it is in common law Canada, as I believe, that within the Commonwealth

---

[5] The meaning of the word, remedial, in this description has been questioned. In Canada the broad meaning is that of the *Restatement* (American Law Institute, *Restatement of the Law of Restitution: Quasi-Contracts and Constructive Trusts*, 1937); the constructive trust is a remedy imposed to prevent unjust enrichment. Professor Roy Goode's distinction between the 'institutional' and the 'remedial', i.e., between the term, constructive trust, as it is used in 'Anglo–Australian jurisprudence', and the same term as used in the United States and Canada, is precise. See 'Property and Unjust Enrichment', *Essays on the Law of Restitution*, ed. Andrew Burrows, 1991, at pp. 216–17. Describing the remedial, he writes, 'the function of the court is not to recognise a pre-existing proprietary right but rather to impose a trust on [the defendant] whenever and on

such conditions as the justice of the case may require. . . . the division of ownership . . . results from the court order itself.' This description might usefully be regarded as the starting point of this paper. See in furtherance the text to note 65, *post*. My position is that the judgments of La Forest and McLachlin, JJ. in the Supreme Court of Canada accept that the exact meaning of 'remedial constructive trust' in Canada is as I suggest it to be in the text to that note.

[6] Without legislative provision, and absent a bona fide purchaser for value without notice defence, it is possible also for there to be a contest between the claimant and a secured creditor; each party is asserting a prevailing proprietary interest in a specific asset. See further, *post*, pp. 31–4.

the remedial constructive trust has really taken hold and is now most firmly established. This paper may serve to give a Canadian perspective on what this trust means, how in Canada it has operated to date, and the issues that we are aware remain.

2. Liability and Remedy

Since the beginnings of the Equity jurisdiction, the purpose of equity has been to offer remedy where the unconscionable has occurred and no other remedy is available. The trust is but the principal instance of this intervention into the processes of the common law. However, the trust intentionally created became an institutional concept—an alternative mode of property management for the benefit of others—that the person with assets was free to choose instead of agency, and ultimately of incorporation. The constructive trust in its seventeenth century origins was a descriptive term. It described the duty of the express trustee to account for or deliver up the trust assets with which he had been vested on assuming office, or which later had been transferred to him as additional trust property. The person who assumed without authority to act as an appointed trustee fitted into this same description. It was a description because the obligation to account or deliver was created by the express trust. It also came to describe those situations where because of the nature of the parties' property transaction (e.g., sale or mortgage of realty), Equity's response to the nature of the relationship between parties (e.g., fiduciary relationships involving property), or a party's undertaking to another upon which that other had relied (e.g., fraud and secret trust), Equity had imposed upon the person vested with the property in question an obligation to account or to deliver the specific property to another. In each instance, however, an obligation created by the law over specific assets of the transaction, or arising out of a non-trust relationship comparable in character to the trust relationship or equitable fraud, gave rise to the duties of one and the enforcement rights of another. That obligation imposed by the law and the enforcement right were compared with the express trust; the party made subject to the obligation was a trustee, and the person with the enforcement right was a beneficiary. That is, no obligation was created by the constructive trust. The term recognised a proprietary right or interest

raised by Equity. It described a relationship that was similar to the obligations and enforcement rights of the express trust. This was not to be misunderstood, however. The extent of the obligation and the nature of the enforcement right of the particular constructive trust would depend upon the particular relationship (i.e., transaction, fiduciary relationship, or fraud) under consideration.

This institutional constructive trust—the adjective, institutional, coined in the twentieth century only—remained the law of constructive trusts for three hundred years. It was with the *Restatement of Restitution* in 1937[7] that this remote and, frankly, unimportant term came out of the shadows. For the first time another thesis was abroad; the constructive trust was a remedy, and it was invoked in circumstances of unjust enrichment. It compelled 'restitution' in the form of the delivery of the disputed property to the claimant. In 1939 the distinguished Austin Scott was to describe[8] the constructive trust's effects in this way, a sentence which over the intervening years has caught the imagination of so many other writers:

'[The constructive trustee] is not compelled to convey the property because he is a constructive trustee; it is because he can be compelled to convey it that he is a constructive trustee.'

What Scott meant by the first part of that sentence is that the term, 'constructive trustee', had hitherto been used descriptively of an obligation that arose independently of any trust or the constructive trust in question itself. But what he meant by the second half of the sentence is less clear. Did he mean that because a person has been unjustly enriched by the acquisition of title to property and is therefore obligated, apparently in consequence, to deliver that property to the claimant, the defendant (as I will call the unjustly enriched person) *is* a constructive trustee? Or did he mean that because the defendant is unjustly enriched the defendant is subject to personal and proprietary remedy which awards the claimant specific property together with all its increment of growth and the fruits, namely, the constructive trust?

The first of those explanations appears to have become the widely accepted meaning. The *Restatement* provides, for instance, that a constructive trust may arise where rectification or recission is the appropriate remedy. I have previously written on this subject,[9] and the argument I made should not be

---

[7] Supra, note 5.

[8] *Scott on Trusts*, 4th ed. by W. F. Fratcher, para. 462 (vol. V, p. 306). 'The court does not give relief because a constructive trust has been created; but the court gives relief because otherwise the defendant would be unjustly enriched; and because the court gives this relief it declares that the defendant

is chargeable as a constructive trustee': Scott, A. W., 'Constructive Trusts' (1955), 71 L.Q.R. 39, 41.

[9] *Equity and Contemporary Legal Developments*, ed. Stephen Goldstein, Hebrew University of Jerusalem, 1992, at p. 457.

repeated here. Suffice it to say on this occasion that in my opinion all that that statement about the constructive trust achieves is to lay stress on a unifying principle (an unjust enrichment) said to explain all the circumstances where *liability* would arise. If that liability is established, says *Scott*, then the defendant is compelled to convey the property in question. That compulsion makes him a constructive trustee. If a personal remedy, e.g., *quantum meruit*, or an action for money had and received, is adequate, continues *Scott*, then the court may not actually impose *in rem* restitution,[10] and clearly *Scott* is conceiving of this constructive trust as a term describing a proprietary obligation. But *Scott's* constructive trust remains institutional, in my opinion, because the occurrence of a breach of the obligation (e.g., unjust enrichment) thereupon causes the enriched party to become a constructive trustee. He is a constructive trustee whose breach may be adequately redressed with an award against him of damages. The trust merely *looks* more remedial because of the proprietary restitution that it is said to bring about in the case of land and unique chattels, and whenever the enriched person is insolvent at the time of trial.

In the 1940s in England, and throughout the Commonwealth of the time, when English case law was uniformly applied and appeals could be taken to the Judicial Committee of the Privy Council from every jurisdiction, the unjust enrichment principle was rejected. And so nothing changed in the Commonwealth. The constructive trust continued to be compared and contrasted with the express trust, and the thinking of Diplock, J., as he then was, in *Port Line Ltd.* v. *Ben Line Steamers Ltd.*[11] in 1958, odd as it seems today to many observers in the Commonwealth, very much represented traditional institutional analysis of the constructive trust of this epoch.

It was the confusion caused by *Pettitt* v. *Pettitt*[12] and *Gissing* v. *Gissing*,[13] to be seen in the light of the increasing anger of large parts of the Canadian population over the failure of the appellate courts (as it was seen) to recognize the property expectations of

women in marriage breakdown situations, that in large part led Laskin, J., as he then was, to dissent in *Murdoch* v. *Murdoch*.[14] His judgment in the Supreme Court of Canada, handed down in 1973, reached out to the U.S. law of unjust enrichment and the constructive trust. The 1937 *Restatement of Restitution* was by now in the United States courts a well-entrenched and developed body of law. Quoting *Scott*,[15] but not the passage given above, he said,[16] '... a constructive trust is imposed where a person holding title to property is subject to an equitable duty to convey it to another on the ground that he would be unjustly enriched if he were permitted to retain it.'

The matrimonial and quasi-matrimonial cases, which I will call the 'family property' cases, have dominated the years of development of the remedial constructive trust, and the shortcoming they have is that the almost invariable facts do not test the limits of the law. One party has assets in his or her name, and the other is claiming that a share, or some of those assets, should be transferred to the claimant. Despite there being a series of such disputes in the Supreme Court of Canada,[17] Laskin, J.'s passage, above, from *Scott* was not developed. Development was not required. If there was unjust enrichment, then a constructive trust was imposed. That was the remedy the non-titled spouse (or cohabitee) sought. It was only in *Sorochan* v. *Sorochan*,[18] another family property dispute, that the Court for the first time referred to the possibility of alternative remedies for unjust enrichment. 'The constructive trust', said Dickson, C. J. C., giving the judgment of the Court,[19]

'constitutes one important judicial means of remedying unjust enrichment. Other remedies, such as monetary damages, may also be available to rectify situations of unjust enrichment. We must, therefore, ask when and under what circumstances it is appropriate for a court to impose a constructive trust.'

The clear distinction between liability and remedy, only latent in the previous case law,[20] was not made before 1986, and in my opinion no discussion

---

[10] Supra, note 8, para. 462.3.
[11] [1958] 2 Q.B. 146, [1958] 1 All E.R. 787.
[12] [1970] A.C. 777, [1969] 2 All E.R. 385.
[13] [1971] A.C. 886, [1970] 2 All E.R. 780.
[14] [1975] 1 S.C.R. 423, (1974) 41 D.L.R. (3d) 367.
[15] Ibid. at p. 455 (S.C.R.), p. 388 (D.L.R.). *Scott on Trusts*, 3rd ed., 1967, para. 404.2 (Vol. V, p. 3215).
[16] Supra, note 14, at p. 455 (S.C.R.); p. 388 (D.L.R.).
[17] *Rathwell* v. *Rathwell*, [1978] 2 S.C.R. 436, 71 D.L.R. (3d) 509; *Pettkus* v. *Becker*, [1980] 2 S.C.R. 834, 117 D.L.R. (3d) 257; *Palachik* v. *Kiss*, [1983] 1 S.C.R. 623, 146 D.L.R. (3d) 385.
[18] [1986] 2 S.C.R. 38, 29 D.L.R. (4th) 1. The court ordered part of the disputed land to be transferred to the claimant, and granted additionally an award of damages. The basis on which the Court upheld the trial judge's award of damages is not

apparent. Was it a 'topping up' measure of the value of the claimant's *contribution* to the defendant's enrichment (the land he in fact owned prior to the marriage), or of the claimant's services rendered (*quantum meruit*—a claim *in personam*)?
[19] Ibid., at p. 47 (S.C.R), 7 (D.L.R.).
[20] 'The principle of unjust enrichment lies at the heart of the constructive trust'; *Pettkus* v. *Becker*, supra, note 17, at p. 847 (S.C.R.), p. 273 (D.L.R.), per Dickson, J., as he then was, for the Court. Cf. *Restatement of Restitution*, section 160 (the rule). 'The constructive trust does not lie at the heart of unjust enrichment. It is but one remedy, and will only be imposed in appropriate circumstances', *per* La Forest, J. in *Lac Minerals Ltd.* v. *International Corona Resources Ltd.*, [1989] 2 S.C.R. 574, 674, 61 D.L.R. (4th) 14, 48.

of the remedial constructive trust can effectively be had without that distinction being made at the very beginning. There are two issues in each case; (1) is the defendant obligated to the claimant because of property the defendant is withholding from the claimant? (2) if so, should the claimant receive the value of that which he claims or some other *in personam* remedy, or should the specific assets be the subject of an order for transfer to the claimant?

(1) The Liability Issue

As I read the situation, the first question is interpreted in England, as involving a preliminary consideration of whether the facts of the instant claim fall within one of several historic and enumerated 'constructive trust' situations. Family property distribution is the only new situation to have been added to that traditional list, and it is possible that in that context the elements of common intention and reliance to detriment may ultimately be expressed in the form of a general principle of liability covering all family property cases. It is not envisaged that fiduciary relationship will be applied in a more expansive manner, as has happened elsewhere in the Commonwealth, there is little or no enthusiasm for carrying the received constructive trust thinking into the world of contract, especially commercial contracts, and the search elsewhere in the Commonwealth for a general principle to express the nature of liability in all constructive trust situations, established and to come, is felt as a consequence to be rather an academic exercise without much, if any, practical significance. In short, the liability issue, save within the context of family property cases, is for all practical purposes, a non-issue. It may be that the recent judicial interest in unjust enrichment will bring about some changes of perspective, but as we see it from the other side of the Atlantic any suggested generalization of 'constructive trust' liability would be resisted still by a significant body of legal opinion. Even as to the family property cases, taken on their own in isolation from other 'constructive trust' situations, Chief Justice Mason of Australia recently said[21] of the law in England:

'This approach rests on a combination of intention and equitable estoppel, and involves a rejection of unconscionable conduct and unjust enrichment as sufficient bases for the relevant relief.'

In Australia there is both liberalism and the traditional conservatism in terms of whether one can speak of any unified principle of liability. The High Court in two leading judgments of 1984[22] and 1987[23] has expressed a favouring of 'unconscionable conduct' as an appropriate equitable principle to express the reason for judicial intervention in the family property cases, and possibly more broadly among the so-called constructive trust situations. It may be that as further cases come before the Australian courts criteria may emerge that bring further into focus this very broad notion, seemingly as wide as 'good conscience' and the *raison d'être* of Equity itself. Perhaps it is its novelty as of 1984, and the absence as yet of very much conceptual infrastructure, that has recently caused more conservative Australian opinion to consider 'further evolution of equitable doctrines' to have been held back 'by vigorous, but somewhat incoherent, invocations of 'unconscionability' as the equitable *grundnorm*.'[24]

The New Zealand courts are among the most reform minded, and indeed interventionist, in the Commonwealth. The thrust of the case law is perhaps summed up in Thomas, J.'s remark in *Powell* v. *Thompson*[25] that 'in New Zealand the constructive trust has become a broad equitable remedy for reversing that which is inequitable or unconscionable.'[26] Again, 'a constructive trust is one of the most productive concepts by which equity reverses the unconscionable.' It is 'a device for imposing a liability to account.'[27] In a dispute on that occasion involving the rule in *Barnes* v. *Addy*,[28] he was of the view that in 'knowing receipt' cases, where property has passed, the claim is based upon 'the material advantage'[29] gained at the claimant's expense. Here the principle of unjust enrichment is therefore the underlying principle, he adds. In the 'knowing assistance' cases, where property may or may not have passed, he saw the basic principle as being 'unconscionable behaviour'. Both the unjust enrichment principle and the unconscionable conduct he brought under the umbrella of the 'inequitable or unconscionable.'[30]

In Canada, even more clearly than in New Zealand, a unifying principle is recognized. Thirteen years ago in 1980 the break with the *Pettitt* and *Gissing* thinking was finally taken in the Supreme Court of Canada, and since then the Canadian courts have uniformly applied and developed the principle of

---

[21] *Equity, Fiduciaries and Trusts, 1993*, ed. Waters, D. W. M., Carswell, Toronto, 1993. 'The Place of Equity and Equitable Doctrines in the Contemporary Common Law World: An Australian Perspective', ch. 1, p. 16. Also (1994), 110 L.Q.R. 238.
[22] *Muschinski* v. *Dodds* (1984), 160 C.L.R. 583.
[23] *Baumgartner* v. *Baumgartner* (1987), 164 C.L.R. 137.
[24] Meagher, R. P., Gummow, W. M. C., Lehane, J. R. F.,

Equity: Doctrines and Remedies, 3rd ed., 1992, Preface, xi.
[25] [1991] 1 N.Z.L.R. 597, 615.
[26] Ibid., at p. 605.
[27] Ibid., at p. 615.
[28] (1874) 9 Ch. App. 244.
[29] Supra, note 24, at p. 607.
[30] Ibid., at p. 615.

unjust enrichment. Any later notion of unconscionability has therefore not been canvassed as an alternative; Australian and New Zealand adoption of that principle came only during the 1980s.[31] The English concern and apparent preference for an estoppel approach (reliance to detriment) has also not been commented upon in Canada. Curiously enough, to date Canadians have given very little consideration to proprietary estoppel, and have not struck out in any adventurous manner with promissory estoppel. The sole consideration has been the ramifications of the unjust enrichment principle, and the correct manner of interpretation and application of the three-part test for the determination in any particular case of whether unjust enrichment exists.

Does it make any difference which principle of liability is adopted? Giving judgment in a family property dispute, *Gillies* v. *Keogh*,[32] the President of the New Zealand Court of Appeal, Sir Robin Cooke, thought not, at least in terms of the result. 'Normally', he said,[33] 'it makes no practical difference in the result whether one talks of constructive trust, unjust enrichment, imputed common intention or estoppel. In deciding whether any of these are established it is necessary to take into account the same factors.' He himself spoke of the 'reasonable expectations' of the parties, and went on to speak of each of his *Gillies* v. *Keogh* descriptions of the principle as a 'legal label or rubric'.[34] He observed that each of them, including unconscionability, was 'but [an] application in a particular field of the equitable jurisdiction to interfere where the assertion of strict legal rights is found by the Court to be unconscionable.'[35]

Recently Chief Justice Mason, in the paper earlier mentioned,[36] has expressed the view that unconscionability and unjust enrichment may be interchangeable rationalisations in some circumstances, and that, unjust enrichment now being recognised in Australia, it may come to play the part of a unifying concept. 'In appropriate circumstances', he has said, the constructive trust may come to be based upon unjust enrichment. 'It may be that this concept is capable of providing greater assistance, at any rate in

some cases, in resolving the issues which usually arise.' The qualifications in these remarks are more than evident, but it is interesting that the Chief Justice should see some ultimate convergence in the Australian and Canadian directions. On the other hand, as the Chief Justice acknowledges, the view has been expressed in the N.S.W. Court of Appeal that, where the claim is not for unjust enrichment by subtraction[37] but the breakdown of a quasi-matrimonial relationship during which time the parties have pooled their resources in order to acquire assets, unconscionability is a better foundation for liability than unjust enrichment. In *Bryson* v. *Bryant*[38] one member of the majority in the Court, Sheller, J. A., suggested that it may be preferable to ask whether in the circumstances the titled party's denial of the property interest of the non-titled party is unconscionable rather than, as unjust enrichment requires, determine whether the contribution of the non-titled party was non-voluntary. The judge was inclined to conclude that unjust enrichment is a more narrow ground 'for imposing a constructive trust' than unconscionability.

The two approaches have been compared. It has been said that unjust enrichment looks to the expectations of the parties, and enquires into the circumstances of one party's enrichment, while unconscionability directs attention to the conduct of that party, a person who has taken advantage. 'But that', comments the Chief Justice of Australia,[39] 'is not to say that the expectations of the parties are irrelevant to the concept of unconscionable conduct.' Nor, of course, as one should add, is the defendant's conduct irrelevant to the decision of whether there has been an unjust enrichment. In *Pettkus* v. *Becker*[40] the Supreme Court of Canada spoke of expectations of which during the time of the contributions the consequently enriched party was, or ought to have been, aware. However, let it be said that the embrace of a conduct assessment may indeed be wider than that of an enrichment (or outcome) assessment.[41] The following, previously mentioned, appears in terms of accepted current

---

[31] I am not referring here, of course, to the unconscionable transaction doctrine exemplified in *Blomley* v. *Ryan* (1956), 99 C.L.R. 362 (High Court, Australia), and in Canada in *Morrison* v. *Coast Finance Ltd.* (1965), 55 D.L.R. (2d) 710 (B.C.C.A.)

[32] [1989] 2 N.Z.L.R. 327 (C.A.)

[33] Ibid., at p. 330.

[34] Ibid., at p. 331.

[35] Ibid.

[36] Supra, note 21.

[37] E.g., disposition by mistake or compulsion, or accompanied by a total failure of consideration. In each instance the non-voluntary act of the deprived party has conferred benefit on the other party.

[38] (1992), 29 N.S.W.L.R. 188, 222–3.

[39] Supra, note 21.

[40] Supra, note 17.

[41] Professor P. D. Finn argues for this position most cogently in his recent paper, 'Constructive Trusts—A New Era', 1993 New Zealand Law Conference, 203. He writes (at p. 216), 'There are few equitable doctrines that have the prevention of unjust enrichment as their sole or principal purpose, though a possible (often usual) remedy for their breach can have the effect of denying such an enrichment.' See also Cope, M., *Constructive Trusts*, Law Book Co., 1992, at pp. 37–9.

It is valuable to be reminded that by adopting the one general principle of unjust enrichment the Canadian courts may in fact be producing for themselves a distorted approach to more than one form of transgressive conduct whose character is more significant than the effect of that conduct. The defendant may have disappointed the plaintiff's expectations of perfor-

terminology to be one such instance. In *Powell* v. *Thompson*[42] Thomas, J. of the New Zealand High Court pointed to the instance of 'knowing assistance' to the fiduciary's dishonest or fraudulent breach of trust, where the third party (the so-called 'constructive trustee') had at no time title to or control over the fiduciary property. This, he said, is an occurrence of unconscionable conduct.[43]

However, I would have to say that to the best of my knowledge the difficulties Mr Justice Sheller foresees with a principle of liability rationalised as the prevention of unjust enrichment have not been experienced in Canada. Patrick Parkinson of the University of Sydney, Australia, for a recent stimulating article on the quantification of relief in Canada for *Pettkus* v. *Becker* unjust enrichment,[44] examined hundreds of family property cases. In his conclusion to that article he pointed to certain dominant elements. There is the *intention* of the parties through their attitude towards, or clear adoption of, joint enterprise so far as property in either name is concerned. In an environment of partnership between them the lifestyle of one has been adopted to *detriment* at the encouragement of the other. He concluded from his study that these are the circumstances in which Canadian courts have awarded specific property to the non-titled party.[45] If no joint enterprise or partnership can be discerned, then *in personam* restitution relief (*quantum meruit*) is available to compensate for money provided or services rendered that were not intended to be gratuitous. If one recalls, I would add, (1) that for the past thirteen years the Canadian courts have found liability to exist, or otherwise, with the aid of an objective assessment of what is a reasonable result, given all the evidence, (2) that this is an assessment couched within the established taxonomy of the *Restate-*

ment's unjust enrichment, and (3) that liability based on unjust enrichment does not necessarily exclude any other complementary ground of liability, should unjust enrichment prove to be too narrow a principle or inapplicable to the circumstances, it is not easy to see where practical problems are likely to arise.

It is also a factor that Canadian courts, unlike English courts, are very deliberately not concerned with whether the claimant had any pre-existing property right in the asset or assets he or she claims. 'The imposition of a constructive trust can both recognize and create a right of property', said La Forest, J. in *Lac Minerals Ltd.* v. *International Corona Resources Ltd.*[46] I shall have need to return to this fundamental proposition later, but my present point is to emphasize that, in framing the nature of the liability imposed upon the defendant, the courts are not limited in any way by the form of relief, personal or proprietary, that they can grant the claimant who is able to establish that the obligation has been breached.

The debate over the most appropriate description of the liability (or obligation) the Commonwealth courts are imposing has been confined, as I have previously suggested, by the fact that since the 1960s it is essentially the family cases and their attendant property dispute issues that have occupied the court's attention when considering liability. In this context I am inclined to agree from all the evidence with Sir Robin Cooke's opinion in *Gillies* v. *Keogh*[47] that 'normally it makes no practical difference in the result' what rationale one gives to the basis of the judicial intervention. Indeed, the leading cases involving the liability issue are family property cases, whether we look to Australia, England, or even New Zealand. The issue of the appropriate description or rationale of liability becomes more

mance or caused the plaintiff loss through the latter's reliance or the defendant's interference. Restitution, even for the enthusiast, does have its confines. However, the North American experience since 1937 suggests that the courts have found the law of restitution at least a workable basis upon which to proceed in terms of a general principle. In reviewing the reasons for the injustice of an enrichment the courts are clearly examining the particular conduct of the alleged transgressor as part of all the circumstances, and where the limits of restitution, as then understood, become apparent the courts are always free to formulate a wider or additional principle. My own view is that the necessity for a broader base of liability has yet to become apparent, and I am mindful that the more diffuse the theme of liability becomes the more we risk in the lower courts a return to the confusion from which most common law systems are trying to escape. However, which direction Canadian appellate courts take depends in some measure on future development of the law of restitution in Canada, and whether those courts are convinced that there is sufficient practical gain in a judicial departure from the sole general principle of unjust enrichment.

[42] Supra, note 25.

[43] 'Knowing assistance' is also an instance where there is solely a personal liability to account. The remedy in our courts

would probably be damages. In the absence of any proprietary claim or remedy, a Canadian court would not be expected to employ the term 'constructive trust'. See, however, *Air Canada* v. *M. & L. Travel Ltd.* (1993), 159 N.R. 1, 67 O.A.C. 1 (S.C.C.), where, surprisingly, both the majority judgment (at pp. 24, 25, 45) and the minority judgment (at p. 47) chose to retain the terminology of English law, and to describe the 'knowing assistant' or 'participant' as a constructive trustee. No reason was given for this in either judgment. See also the text to note 86, post.

[44] 'Beyond *Pettkus* v. *Becker*: Quantifying Relief for Unjust Enrichment' (1993), 43 Univ. of Toronto L.J. 217.

[45] For a subsequent recent instance of this thinking, *quantum meruit* being also not available in this instance, see *Coddington* v. *Hubert Estate* (1993), 49 E.T.R. 9 (B.C.S.C.).

[46] Supra, note 20, at p. 676 (S.C.R.), p. 50 (D.L.R.). La Forest, J. prefaced this remark by saying, 'it is not the case that a constructive trust should be reserved for situations where a right of property is recognised. That would limit the constructive trust to its institutional function, and deny to it the status of a remedy, its more important role.'

[47] Supra, note 32.

complex, however, once one moves to commerce, because there the courts are, or would be, concerned with policy considerations different from those that arise in connection with family property disputes. And with these disputes it is interesting that there is a not dissimilar pattern of contemporary attitudes and values in each of these liberal, Western, largely secular, and economically developed countries. The question in commercial matters is the extent to which the courts should impose liability of any kind as between opposing business interests who have reached an agreement as to the terms upon which they wish or are content to be obligated to each other.[48] Though Canadian courts have been prepared to describe relationships as fiduciary with noticeably greater willingness than has been the case in England, and more so, I think, than in Australia, courts in all Commonwealth countries have drawn back from readily imposing extra-contractual fiduciary obligations upon one commercial party in favour of the other. Also in the commercial context the rationale of liability can be observed to change. Commonwealth courts have described the assertion of a constructive trust in a situation involving a claim to take ahead of a bankrupt's creditors as based on 'good conscience',[49] and on applicable 'equitable principle or doctrine' influenced by 'the traditional equitable notice of unconscionable conduct.'[50] In New Zealand, where there has been a markedly greater willingness 'to do equity'[51] in commercial matters as in family property matters, the need for 'fair commercial dealing' has caused money to be held 'on constructive trust' because that is 'in conscience'[52] or it defeats unconscionable conduct. In other words the nature of the general principle of the liability appears less certain once the family property cases are left behind.

In Canada, however, the Supreme Court of Canada has shown no hesitation in applying the rubric of unjust enrichment and restitution in those commercial cases where it has concluded the circumstances may exist for the finding of liability (or a cause of action, as Professor Rickett has described it).[53] In *Hunter Engineering Co.* v. *Syncrude Canada Ltd.*[54] Dickson, C. J. C. observed that 'in *Pettkus* v. *Becker*, the Court moved to an approach more in line with restitutionary principles by explicitly recognising constructive trust as one of the remedies for unjust enrichment', and he applied the 'three criteria' of *Pettkus* v. *Becker*, as did the two dissenting members of the Court. In *Lac Minerals Ltd.* v. *International Corona Resources Ltd.*[55] the issues were (1) fiduciary relationship and breach, and (2) breach of confidence. Two members of the Court found a fiduciary relationship and breach; three found no such relationship. All five found breach of confidence, and three agreed that the appropriate remedy was proprietary rather than personal. The judgment of La Forest, J. for the majority opinion as to the appropriate remedy remains to this day in my opinion a classic statement of the Canadian position on *Pettkus* v. *Becker* restitutionary claims.[56] And, though a member of the minority that was of the view that there also existed a fiduciary relationship and breach in the particular commercial circumstances under consideration, La Forest, J. observed that, while a finding of 'a fiduciary relationship is not precluded by the fact that the parties were involved in pre-contractual negotiations',[57] 'it is almost trite to say that a fiduciary relationship does not normally arise between arm's length commercial parties'.[58]

Reflections on Liability

If it does not normally matter which description is given to the nature of the liability, so far as the results in the domestic cases are concerned, and if with regard to the rationale for liability in commercial situations there is no real consensus in any Commonwealth country, other than Canada, one has to ask what has been achieved to date. Will 'uncon-

---

[48] E.g., *Re Australian Elizabethan Theatre Trust* (1991), 102 A.L.R. 681, 698–700 (Fed. Ct.).

[49] *Neste Oy* v. *Lloyds Bank PLC.*, [1983] 2 Lloyd's Law Reports 658, 666 (England). See further, 'Recovery of Advance Payments', S. R. Scott (1991), 14 N.Z.U.L.R. 375, 395.

[50] *Re Stephenson Nominees Pty. Ltd.* v. *Official Receiver* (1987), 76 A.L.R. 485, 506, 507, *per* Gummow, J., diss. (Fed. Ct.) (Australia).

[51] *Elders Pastoral Ltd.* v. *Bank of New Zealand*, [1989] 2 N.Z.L.R. 180, 186 (C.A.), *per* Cooke, P. (New Zealand), upheld on other grounds, [1991] 1 N.Z.L.R. 385 (P.C.). See 'The Remedial Constructive Trust in Commercial Transactions', S. R. Scott, [1993] L.M.C.L.Q. 330, for support of the N.Z.C.A. in the much debated *Liggett* case. Sir Robin Cooke has described and commented upon this case ([1993] 1 N.Z.L.R. 257 (C.A.)) in his paper, *supra*, note 21, 'The Place of Equity and Equitable Doctrines: A New Zealand Perspective', ch. 2, at pp. 33–4.

[52] *Ibid.* See also p. 193 (Somers, J.).

[53] *Supra*, note 21, 'Trusts and Insolvency: The Nature and Place of the *Quistclose* Trust', ch. 15, at p. 342.Professor Waddam's conclusions as to the part that restitution plays in the subject of contract should also be noted: *Essays on the Law of Restitution*, *supra*, note 5, pp. 197–213.
The line between a general principle of liability and an independent cause of action is a fine one, but the Court has not overtly made that move as yet. See Maddaugh, P. D., and McCamus, J. D., *The Law of Restitution*, Canada Law Book, 1990, pp. 21–7.

[54] [1989] 1 S.C.R. 426, 471; 57 D.L.R. (4th) 321, 349. The majority in this case found no unjust enrichment, however.

[55] *Supra*, note 20.

[56] *Ibid.*, at pp. 668–80 (S.C.R.), pp. 44–52 (D.L.R.).

[57] *Ibid.*, at p. 667 (S.C.R.), p. 43 (D.L.R.).

[58] *Ibid.*, at p. 655 (S.C.R.), p. 34 (D.L.R.). However, La Forest, J. for the minority on this subject did conclude that such a relationship existed in this case.

scionability' prove to be too amorphous a description, as the circumstances calling for remedy move beyond the novel terrain of domestic relationship breakdown and the associated property disputes? I would prefer not to answer that question, because I think it is a subject upon which Australians and New Zealanders will have a better sense of future directions in their own countries. However, should a generalization of liability in family cases be accepted in Australia and in England, and the implications of the free extension of liability into commercial matters be judicially explored in New Zealand, I suspect that an increasing volume of case law will lead to the development of a taxonomy of unconscionability as it did in the case of unjust enrichment and restitution in North America after 1937.[59] I presume to say 'North America' because Canada adopted the *Restatement's* rubric of unjust enrichment and restitution as early as 1954 when the constructive trust, outside the U.S.A., was 'a vague dust-heap', as Dr. Sykes called it.[60] But until that taxonomy begins to form—as surely it must in an inductive system—it is not easy to judge the utility of that particular legal label. Especially is this so, given that for some lawyers 'unconscionable' outcome or conduct is sufficient description, while others—and I have Australia in mind—will concede significance to that word only as an umbrella for 'equitable principles or doctrines'. There are those for whom established, in-depth doctrines of the equity jurisdiction are the indispensable foundation of any understanding of this liability, and one wonders whether the apparent English preference to remain with the traditional fiduciary relationships and the family property situations as the confined area of significant constructive trust activity is not motivated in large part by the same concerns. It has been suggested that in England the proprietary estoppel approach to these family property cases has 'stunted' the potential growth of a remedial constructive trust.[61] So far as the family property cases are concerned, it certainly seems it is a matter for conjecture as to when the reliance to detriment factor leads to the personal remedy of estoppel and when on the other hand it will lead to the proprietary consequences of a constructive trust.

However, I think there is something else that is holding back the clarification of this liability (or cause of action) everywhere in the Commonwealth save for Canada, which country is excluded only because it has made the distinction. And that is the clear separation of liability and remedy. 'Constructive trust' as a term is consistently used to refer to liability; the remedial consequence that flows therefrom is thereby assumed to be recognised and identified. That is my quarrel with *Scott*. The phrase is familiar in every form of writing—judgments, *ex cathedra* papers, and academic articles—that breach of fiduciary relationship, or the overall principle of unjust enrichment or unconscionability, 'gives rise to a constructive trust'. I need here to say only that in my opinion much of the prolonged debate over the constructive trust, a process which began in the early 1960s, stems from this usage. Some have found the distinguishing between substance and remedy to be an arid exercise, and a mere semantic quibble it may appear, but in my submission we do not move away from the continuous debate about the meaning and purpose of the 'constructive trust' to assistance of the courts, especially first instance courts, until liability and remedy are distinguished.[62]

The institutional constructive trust looks to the express trust; it is compared with the trusteeship, the trust property, the obligations of trusteeship and the rights of action, plus the obligations, of the express trust beneficiary. Those rights of action are to secure an accounting by the trustee, and at the appropriate time a delivery up of legal title to the qualified beneficiary. The express trust beneficiary may also invoke the equitable right to trace; armed with an equitable proprietary interest, he thereby takes the trust property from the trustee in breach or, if it has been transferred to another and subject to certain qualifications,[63] from that other or from successive transferees. The property is then held once again for the trust beneficiaries. The rights of the express trust beneficiary therefore include a personal action and a real action, the second of which, but not the first, will afford the beneficiary the means of going ahead of all the trustee's personal creditors. However, as a result of Equity's intervention, the claimant traditionally has an equitable right or interest in the assets in question. It follows that by implication the institutional constructive trust recognises its beneficiary to have the same two-fold right of action.[64] If we say then that the person who has acquired an asset in breach of a nominate 'constructive trust', or has acquired it 'unconscionably', has thereby become 'a constructive trustee' of the asset in question, we say nothing about the appropriate right of action. Most writing assumes that this 'constructive trust' means a real action, and

[59] 'The Notion of Unconscionability' appears as ch. 5 in *Unfair Dealing*, P. Clarke and P. Parkinson (eds), which is contained in Vol. 35, *Laws of Australia*, Law Book Co., 1993, at pp. 1–42.
[60] Supra, p. 1.
[61] Supra, note 21, and note 53, C. E. R. Rickett, at p. 341.
[62] See further, supra, note 21.
[63] Notice or gratuitous transfer.
[64] See, e.g., supra, note 3.

those who see at once the consequences of this for the law of bankruptcy and insolvency naturally draw back. But what can they draw back from? Only, in my view, from whether there exists 'a constructive trust' at all, that is, from there being *any* available remedy.

The traditionalist will also challenge that there can be any generalised principle of liability, such as unconscionability or unjust enrichment, fearing as some do, no doubt remembering Lord Denning's interventions on the subject, that any such concession of general principle opens up a non-doctrinal future with the whims of an unpredictable judicial discretion. Others, less apprehensive, would prefer rules to determine liability if the nominate 'constructive trusts' are to go, but would tolerate a measure of judicial discretion, perhaps as to the actual redress the successful claimant may obtain. The most traditional position is taken by those who advocate a steady-as-she-goes policy of recognising new nominate 'constructive trusts', if at all, only when it is known in advance precisely what equitable right or interest in an asset the new 'trust' will recognise and with what calculable result. This last position regards rules and predictability as much preferable to the consequences of any judicial discretion; at the same time such an argument unsettles those who favour a generalised principle such as 'unconscionability'. The latter, now apprehensive of the volume of *in rem* redress that may be awarded successful claimants, sense a compulsion that they be tentative about whether after all a generalised principle of liability is practicable. Yet others, enthusiastically supporting the idea of a principle, react to the contrary by asserting such a principle with even more vigour.

This, as it seems to me, and I speak with respect, has produced some individually fine judgments and excellent writing, but essentially a tale of confusion that need not have arisen or continue. Difficulties to be overcome and questions to be answered there are in plenty, nor can there be an absence of differences of opinion, but in my view there must be an initial abandonment of familiar terminology. I agree with Sir Peter Millett, and would go further than he in my discarding of 'constructive trust'. The issue as it seems to me is the nature of the liability or obligation for which we are proposing remedy, and then, liability or obligation being established, what redress the claimant shall have. If we *must* employ the term, constructive trust, I understand the remedial constructive trust as a name for the redress that takes the

form of awarding specific assets to the successful claimant.[65]

It follows that the liability I have been discussing at considerable length in this paper is irrelevant to the title to which I was asked to speak. What I should have been discussing from the beginning are the forms of redress that the courts can award the claimant who is able to establish that liability has occurred. The difference in the Supreme Court of Canada between La Forest, J. and Sopinka, J. in *Lac Minerals Ltd.* v. *International Corona Resources Ltd.*[66] was as to whether the successful respondent should have title to the mine and an ownership subject to a lien for the appellant's purchase costs and later development expenditures, or have damages compensating the respondent for the loss of the mine consequent upon the appellant's conduct, leaving title to the mine in the appellant. This gold field was perhaps the most substantial find in North America for some time; it certainly had all the financial pages agog, awaiting the Court's long delayed judgment. *Lac Minerals* was compelled by the majority, for whom La Forest, J. spoke, to give up title and ownership in the mind to International Corona. The reasoning behind this discretionary award of what the court considers the appropriate remedy is in truth central to my paper, and it is also of central importance that *Lac Minerals* resulted in the remedial constructive trust giving proprietary redress, not for breach of fiduciary relationship, but for breach of confidence.

However, I have discussed liability because that, I have assumed, is the primary concern of this seminar. The conclusion I reach as to liability (or obligation, or cause of action) is that whether it is to take the form of nominate heads of obligation, or the obligation is to be generalised under the one head, as 'unconscionability' or 'unjust enrichment' or other nomenclature, is largely determined by the ethos of the particular jurisdiction. In my observation the goals of the Australian, New Zealand and Canadian societies of today may be different from those of the United Kingdom, and they may differ to some degree from each other. In each of these overseas countries, from Europe's perspective, there is and has been for some years—going back in Canada's case to the later 1960s—an increasing sense of movement and change, both social and economic, and this has caused the courts to re-assess several doctrines from the standpoint of first principles. In Canada also the *Charter of Rights and Freedoms*, which came into

---

[65] See further, supra, note 5. I see little gain in developing independently this clear dichotomy, and by-passing traditional 'constructive trust' doctrine, which is thereby left in place. Confusion will remain also; in Canada the legacy of the past continues to haunt us. In my opinion we either use the term as here suggested, or we do not use it at all.

[66] Supra, note 20.

force in 1982, has put the courts into the front line of what in my opinion can only be described as policy-making. I cannot over-emphasize the impact this constitutional change has increasingly had on judicial attitudes throughout the country, and at all levels of courts. So far as private law is concerned, the fresh winds of a novel kind that were generated by Lord Denning's period of judicial office were received with particular welcome in Canada, and they are welcome still. As one might expect, then, there is an open attitude towards generalised principle that to all appearances was not in existence a quarter of a century ago.

The generalisation of liability also came about in Canada, it will be recalled, because society in that country looked to the courts for a solution to the matrimonial property controversy. What is clear is that throughout the 1970s Laskin, C. J. C., Spence, J., and Dickson, J. were consistently drawn to the established and developed doctrine of *Restitution* in the United States. It was not new to Canada as a head of liability, as previously noted; it had been adopted by the Supreme Court of Canada in *Deglman* v. *Guarantee Trust Co. and Constantineau*[67] many years before, and unjust enrichment afforded the courts, as they may well have seen it, an opportunity both of looking at the family property cases from a more realistic viewpoint, and of introducing into Canada the total scope of Restitution learning in the United States. That is, a vehicle would be adopted that allowed the Court to design empirically a Canadian doctrinal infrastructure—with the aid of American and English restitution scholarship—as future litigation ensued.

There has been a tendency since *Pettkus* v. *Becker* in 1980 for courts at first instance to invoke that judgment, quote a passage or two, and then move to a solution of the particular family property dispute without very much, if any, doctrinal association of the authorities with the factual resolution.[68] But the Supreme Court of Canada, in all but two instances, has kept a firm hand on the tiller, and in my opinion the in-depth meaning and applicability of unjust enrichment has been steadily developed. There may be some way to go before it can be said that the circumstances have largely been isolated in which the courts are willing to find an unjust enrichment, but I find myself in agreement with Peter Maddaugh and John McCamus[69] as to the manner in which this particular corner of Restitution is working out in Canada. These authors have isolated three 'kinds of

cases' where a discretionary proprietary relief might be awarded.[70] They concern the involuntary creditor (mistake, duress), the recovery of the profits of wrongdoing (whether of fiduciary, tortious, or possibly contractual obligation), and contribution to the acquisition, maintenance or improvement of property. The progression of the development of the remedial constructive trust has also been measured, as can be seen in my opinion from three events. The first was the nature of the reasoning in *Hunter Engineering Co.* v. *Syncrude Canada Ltd.*[71] where in a contractual setting the Supreme Court, by a majority, concluded there was no unjust enrichment. Then there was *Lac Minerals* which has proved to have stopped in its tracks what appeared in some lower courts and at the Bar to be a gathering enthusiasm for a largescale introduction of fiduciary relationships into business and commerce, and finally, the Court has said on several occasions that it is anxious that liability shall be considered in the lower courts on the basis of established jurisprudence, not any vague notion of fairness. La Forest, J. put it this way in *Lac Minerals*:[72]

'The determination that the enrichment is "unjust" does not refer to abstract notions of morality and justice, but flows directly from the finding that there was a breach of a legally recognised duty for which the courts will grant relief. Restitution is a distinct body of law governed by its own developing system of rules.'

I would suggest that, once liability and remedy are clearly distinguished, 'constructive trust' having no part in the nature or description of liability, the essential issue emerges for the first time, and that is the pragmatic one of whether there is need of such a liability. Is there any would-be plaintiff who has been injured by another so that the law might well have given remedy—whether the injury is viewed initially in terms of the conduct which caused it, or the effect which that conduct had—but to whom the private law in fact affords no remedy? For this purpose—I go no further—law and equity constitute one landscape; the substantive law that has emerged from the forms of action, and the equitable doctrines that came from the distinct and remedial court of conscience, do not constitute a dichotomy that must necessarily be perpetuated. There is little or no value in duplicating obligations. If remedy is needed, the question becomes—what is the obligation that the defendant has breached, and for which the private law gives no remedy?

[67] [1954] S.C.R. 725, [1954] 3 D.L.R. 785. The context then was *quantum meruit.*
[68] See further, Parkinson, supra, note 44.
[69] Supra, note 53.

[70] Ibid., at pp. 94–100.
[71] Supra, note 54.
[72] Supra, note 20, at p. 670 (S.C.R.), p. 45 (D.L.R.).

(2) The Remedy Issue

Once liability is established, the court then considers what remedy is appropriate, and it is evident that, given the potential impact upon third parties of proprietary redress, both personal and proprietary remedies should be available for breaches of the obligation. Unjust enrichment liability is the head of obligation with which in this paper we are primarily concerned, but there is no reason why the remedies under consideration here should not provide appropriate redress for other heads of obligation. That is, I do not see why unjust enrichment alone should lead to compensatory damages or the remedial constructive trust. In *Lac Minerals*[73] the Supreme Court of Canada awarded proprietary relief in the form of constructive trust subject to a lien[74] for the enriched party's material contribution. The unjust enrichment obligation was breached by breach of confidence, not fiduciary relationship. It may well be that courts in future will choose to go further and adopt another head of obligation that concerns unconscionable conduct, where that is needed.

It is interesting in the *Lac Minerals* judgments that no member of the Court denies constructive trust is *available* as a remedy for breach of confidence. The remedy is recognised to be independent of the cause of action. The only issue is the appropriateness of this particular remedy.[75] Lac sought to have damages awarded against itself, if liability on either ground were established. International Corona argued for the imposition of a proprietary remedy, and constructive trust was the particular remedy that met International's object. International was successful, and that can be traced to a consideration that can arise whatever the obligation that has been breached. In this instance, as the majority underlined, the award of damages had no deterrent effect. If the defendant uses confidential information obtained from a prospective joint venturer and gets away with it, it obtains the desired asset. If the defendant is successfully challenged, it pleads the position that the plaintiff has been deprived of, and is entitled to compensation for, the joint venture share it would have had if there had been no breach and the venture had gone ahead to fruition. Compensation by way of damages was therefore ruled by the majority to be inappropriate. The constructive trust on the other hand produced justice and fairness—the property at

issue was unique, International Corona would have acquired it but for Lac's interception, and it was virtually impossible accurately to value such a property as an undeveloped mine.

As a remedy, and here again *Lac Minerals* covers the matter, the constructive trust can be awarded whether or not the claimant had previously or at the time of trial any proprietary interest in the disputed asset.[76] Moreover, the remedial constructive trust, as defined in Canada, means solely a proprietary remedy. There is no suggestion that, like the institutional trust, it can mean either an accounting or an *in rem* recovery. In this lack of ambiguity the Canadian remedial constructive trust in my opinion is unique in the Commonwealth, and again in my opinion a sole meaning of *in rem* recovery is indispensable to the dichotomy of liability and disassociated remedy. The proprietary remedy that includes all incremental value must be as distinct a remedy as lien and subrogation, as account and damages.

The freedom of the court to consider the remedy appropriate to the circumstances means that it can consider whether priority should be given over unsecured, and even secured, creditors in the defendant's bankruptcy or simply a personal remedy permitting the claimant to rank equally with them. The increase in value of the disputed asset while in the defendant's name, the asset's specificity and uniqueness, and the moral wrongness of the defendant's act (e.g. conscious wrongdoing), are other factors that the court will take into account.[77] Limitation periods usually differ as between the availability of personal and proprietary remedies, and this can be another consideration in the claimant's mind.

However, the singular value of the proprietary remedy to the claimant, as we all know, is the priority it confers in insolvency and bankruptcy. At the beginning of this paper I posed a number of questions concerning the circumstances in which the remedial constructive trust might be awarded, and the manner in which it might be awarded, when the defendant is insolvent at the time of trial. The issue is whether the existence of specific property as the subject-matter of the dispute should invariably lead to the priority of the plaintiff's claim. Should it be possible for the courts to award a constructive trust effective against the defendant alone? For instance, a woman who has lived with a man, and can link the acquisition, improvement or maintenance of specific

---

[73] Supra, note 20.

[74] See further, supra, note 69, at pp. 100–2.

[75] Sopinka, J., supra, note 20, at p. 618 (S.C.R.), pp. 76–7 (D.L.R.), was of the opinion for the minority on this point that 'in a breach of confidence case the focus is on the loss to the plaintiff and, as in tort actions, the particular position of the plaintiff must be examined. The object is to restore the plaintiff

monetarily to the position he would have been in if no wrong had been committed.' He considered the 'restitutionary remedy' to be appropriate for fiduciary breach because there the issue is the disgorging of benefits.

[76] Supra, note. 46.

[77] Ibid., at pp. 678–9 (S.C.R.), pp. 51–2 (D.L.R.).

assets in his name with her contributions to the association, may seek those specific assets. One can contemplate an order that would give her a constructive trust remedy with regard to those assets that at trial remain in the man's name free of any security burden, but deny other than a compensatory (or *in personam*) remedy with regard to such of those specific assets that are in the hands of, or constitute security for, third parties. One would assume that the position of third parties with a security interest in the disputed property would always be a relevant consideration, as the circumstances of the creditors of a man should be an appropriate factor in consideration in the event of his being insolvent at the time of trial.[78] Once the injustice of the enrichment, or the unconscionability of conduct or outcome, is the basis of the liability, the claimant who seeks proprietary redress should always have to justify his going ahead of creditors.

I can offer you my reflections, but I confess I have no answer to those questions. No Commonwealth court of which I am aware has yet had reason to consider them.[79] All I can say is that I hope when the time eventually comes, at least in common law Canada, for such questions to be answered, the courts will be prepared to limit the effect of a proprietary remedy where such a remedy and such a limitation are appropriate. In the redress it gives, the court should be able to make any order which is appropriate as between all affected parties. There is no need for all the connotations of property to flow from a court order if neither a personal remedy, nor a proprietary remedy in the conventional sense, is appropriate. It will be evident that I look forward to a distinction between the proprietary remedy and the opportunity to trace; I can see no reason in a remedial context why the one would automatically imply the other. Again I have to underline that I am not thinking of a constructive trust as the assertion of the plaintiff's equitable proprietary interest; that is a concept associated with the institutional constructive trust.[80]

3. Liability, and Breach of Express Trust

Reference to the equitable proprietary interest takes one inevitably to the question of whether the general principle of liability, be it unconscionability, unjust enrichment, or any other 'legal label or rubric', embraces or is able to embrace all those situations that I have called the nominative constructive trusts, traditionally recognised in English law. In *Rawluk* v. *Rawluk*[81] the question of the scope of applicability of the unjust enrichment principle was referred to by McLachlin, J., and she drew attention to a marked difference of academic opinion in Canada. Since this was a family property case, however, she could expressly restrict what she had to say to case law that has unquestionably been associated with unjust enrichment. She noted that she did not have to decide the matter of how the unjust enrichment case law was related to the traditional constructive trusts of English law, and passed on to other issues.

For the purposes of this paper I will draw upon the list of nominate constructive trusts existent in English law as they are described in *Underhill and Hayton*.[82] If one imagines a dart board with a bull's eye and a series of outer concentric circles, breach of an express trust, and in my analysis trusteeship *de son tort*,[83] lie at the centre in the bull's eye. The express trust beneficiary asserts his equitable proprietary interest by an action for account or recovery of the trust property against the express trustee or the trustee *de son tort*, as the case may be. In the next circle, concentric to the bull's eye, are the fiduciary relationships other than that arising out of an express trust. The next circle includes fraudulent acquisitions or retentions, and gain by unconscionable conduct, including retention of assets mistakenly transferred. The next circle includes strangers receiving or dealing with trust property,[84] and this is where *Underhill and Hayton* brings in the trustee *de son tort*. The next circle includes the vendor under a specifically enforceable contract, and the outermost circle the mortgagee. The last two circles (the vendor/purchaser, mortgagor/mortgagee situations) are somewhat anomalous, and for present purposes will not be considered further.[85]

---

[78] This aspect of the subject has been considered by a number of writers. See for recent references and consideration, C. E. F. Rickett, [1991] Conv. 125, at p. 132, note 32, and 'The Precise Effect of the Imposition of a Constructive Trust', A. J. Oakley, supra, note 9, at p. 427.

[79] A clear concern with the impact of the institutional constructive trust upon the position of unsecured creditors was expressed by Gummow, J. in the *Elizabethan Theatre Trust* case, supra, note 48.

[80] See further, however, on the 'equitable right to trace', *Underhill and Hayton, Law Relating to Trusts and Trustees*, 14th ed., 1987, at p. 764.

[81] [1990] 1 S.C.R. 70, 102–3; 65 D.L.R. (4th) 161, 184–5.

[82] Op. cit., supra, note 80, at p. 301 et seq.

[83] Under this term I include for the purposes of this analysis the stranger who knowingly receives express trust property, or who knowingly assists the express trustee in a dishonest breach of trust.

[84] For present purposes I restrict this stranger liability to those involved with the breach of a fiduciary relationship other than an express trust.

[85] The vendor/purchaser constructive trust arises from the principle that equity regards that as done which ought to be done—it notionally converts personal into proprietary rights. The mortgagor/mortgagee situation can only be described today as a constructive trust as to any surplus moneys left in the mortgagee's hands following a foreclosure and sale.

The Nature of the Remedial Constructive Trust

It will be evident from what has gone before in this paper that the subject-matter of all the circles, save the bull's eye (breach of express trust and trusteeship *de son tort*), are brought in Canada within the general principle of unjust enrichment. I suspect this may also be true of unconscionability, but since the Australian and New Zealand cases have been concerned so heavily to date with the application of that principle to the family property disputes, it seems only fair to say that this remains to be confirmed. What then of breach of express trust and in my view trusteeship *de son tort*? Does the institutional constructive trust, available to the express trust beneficiary against the express trustee, the trustee *de son tort* and the *Barnes* v. *Addy*[86] stranger, continue to be a feature of Canadian law? Does this express trust enforcement area remain a precinct where the equitable proprietary interest is protected?

In the first place I do not think it matters, certainly for the purposes of the validity and applicability of the remedial constructive trust. Once liability is severed from remedy, we are not concerned, when thinking of remedies and the action brought by the beneficiary of the express trust, whether one head of obligation is restitution (or unjust enrichment) and another is the liability of the express trustee, or of the person who intermeddles in the trust or assumes without authorization the office of trustee.[87] Secondly, the express trust beneficiary derives his remedy from the concept of express trust; the institutional constructive trust merely describes an obligation otherwise in existence. In my view this constructive trust that attaches to the express trustee is solely of semantic interest, and it could safely be abandoned at any time. However, it does reflect the equitable proprietary interest of the express trust beneficiary resulting from the fact of the express trust, and the question is as to whether a Canadian court would classify the express trust and its remedies as a different head of obligation from that of unjust enrichment (and the restitution remedies, personal and proprietary, legal and equitable in origin).

The majority judgment in *Canson Enterprises Ltd.* v. *Boughton & Co.*[88] suggests that the Supreme Court of Canada sees the sphere of the express trust (the obligations of the trustee and the rights of the benefi-

ciary) as distinct from the sphere of fiduciary relationships other than the express trust, and subject to different considerations. That is one solution, namely, that if we must go on using the term, constructive trust, to describe the chose in action of the express trust beneficiary as against the trustee, and that beneficiary's right to recover *in specie* and to trace, we acknowledge that this is the institutional and not the remedial constructive trust.

As I have said elsewhere,[89] however, it is my view that Dickson, C. J. C. for the majority in *Hunter Engineering*[90] intended to include the express trust situations within the unjust enrichment rubric. Indeed, in my opinion it would be preferable that the restitution obligation in circumstances of unjust enrichment be extended to cover the express trust, and that for the purpose of, but only of, securing restitution when unjust enrichment has occurred, the connotations of the equitable proprietary interest not follow. The express trust concept is a very much more flexible and flexibly applied notion than it was even in the 1960s. The three certainties have been significantly relaxed and so have lost much of their formerly central importance; the emphasis now is upon whether the particular trust will work, as drafted, rather than whether it meets the nineteenth century rule requirements. *McPhail* v. *Doulton*[91] is typical of the winds of change. These developments encourage one to think of improper conduct and unjust enrichment within the trust fiduciary relationship rather than concentrate solely upon the property aspects of the trust. In the presence of unjust enrichment it is arguable that the range of available remedies should be the same, whether the particular fiduciary relationship is classified as trust or non-trust. Moreover, it has been said[92] that the rule in *Barnes* v. *Addy*[93] should be reconsidered, given the draconian way it can draw within the net of an express trust level of liability the third party who becomes involved with a breaching trustee or other fiduciary. If this is to be done, then perhaps for this reason too it would be preferable to bring the express trust breach itself, together with trusteeship *de son tort*, within the sphere of unjust enrichment and the range of restitution remedies.

Such an inclusion would mean that the express trust beneficiary would retain his personal right of

---

[86] Supra, note 28. See now *Air Canada* v. *M. & L. Travel Ltd.*, supra, note 43.

[87] Professor Roy Goode also thinks it does not matter, but that is because he is of the view that the institutional (property based) and remedial (wrong based) constructive trusts are mutually exclusive, and can both exist in the same legal system: 'Property and Unjust Enrichment', *Essays on the Law of Restitution*, supra, note 5, p. 215, at 218. I find much that is attractive about that analysis, but I hesitate markedly as to its effects in practice. See, post, note 94 and note 122, and the text to the latter note.

[88] [1991] 3 S.C.R. 534, 85 D.L.R. (4th) 129. There is something of this also in *Guerin* v. *The Queen*, [1984] 2 S.C.R. 335, 13 D.L.R. (4th) 321, though the facts there perhaps constituted a very particular situation.

[89] Supra, note 9, at pp. 506–14.

[90] Supra, note 54.

[91] [1971] A.C. 424, [1970] 2 All E.R. 228.

[92] Supra, note 21, 'The Liability of Third Parties for Knowing Receipt or Assistance', Paul D. Finn; ch. 10, p. 195.

[93] Supra, note 28.

action to sue the trustee for due and proper administration of the trust, but that where misappropriation of trust property is concerned, or acquisition of unapproved gain by the trustee has occurred while that trustee was acting in the role of trustee, the range of personal and proprietary restitution remedies would be available to that beneficiary.[94]

However, I hasten to say that no conceivable hint of any such thinking can be discovered in the judgments of the Court. I am pursuing a thought of my own, realising that one day the question will arise in the Court and call for an answer.

4. Getting to the Remedial Constructive Trust

The distinction between constructive trust as institution and constructive trust as remedy is markedly easier to draw if one ignores the terminology, and observes that, while an institution comes into existence when the legally required elements creating an equitable proprietary interest or right are in place, a remedy can only exist from the moment of the court order. Of course, what the terms of that order may be is a different matter.

Shortly after *Pettkus* v. *Becker*[95] was reported, a percipient commentator on the judgment picked up this point. What is the significance of saying that a constructive trust 'arises' to remedy unjust enrichment? 'The consensus of opinion', wrote Professor McClean[96] in 1982, 'is that [the constructive trust] comes into existence on the date an order could first have been made, and is not postponed until the date on which an order actually is made.' He went on to observe that if the court order is simply recognising 'an already existing proprietary right, that conclusion is obvious'. But it is not so obvious, he concluded, if the trust is seen as a discretionary remedial device, 'for it may then be argued that no trust can arise until it is known if a court is prepared to act.' Professor McClean ruminated that perhaps it is justifiable that the constructive trust come into existence as of the date an order could first have been made, because the deprived claimant would then be protected in the interval before any order is given. Moreover, he added, 'the courts will generally have sufficient discretion to ensure that [the order's] retrospective operation does not unfairly affect the [constructive] trustee or third parties.'[97]

Unfortunately, as I read the Court's decisions down to *Sorochan* v. *Sorochan*[98] in 1986, the fact that other remedies beside constructive trust are available to remedy a finding of unjust enrichment concerning specific property was not until that time made clear. Until *Sorochan* it could well have seemed the case, whatever the talk of remedy, that the remedy for unjust enrichment of that kind *is* constructive trust. However, I do not think any Canadian court ever entertained the view that the constructive trust is a mode of saying that the claimant owns an equitable proprietary interest or right (whether existing or arising out of the circumstances), and that therefore a principle of liability based on ownership is appropriate. This, as I have earlier said, would be more of an institutional trust, and one therefore which directs the claimant both to a personal remedy in account and to a proprietary remedy for *in specie* restitution. Though an advocate of the institutional trust today might find it hard to locate any remark from the Court prior to *Sorochan* which can be construed as referring to a property interest created at the moment of the unjust enrichment, the ambiguity, I think, was there.

Nor do I criticise others by saying this. As I have said too often, the family property cases are not the ready vehicle for highlighting this problem. In almost all instances one party has assets in his or her name at the date of trial and the other party is claiming part of those assets. Almost always there has been an appreciation of value while the disputed assets were in the titled party's name, and, if unjust enrichment liability is established, with proprietary redress as the appropriate remedy, the date of the taking effect of the order is not called in question. Secondly, it is clear that the Supreme Court was thinking and developing the doctrine of the law as cases came before it, and understandably it continues to do this.

Rawluk v. *Rawluk*[99] in 1990 brought the issue of when the remedial constructive trust 'arises' directly before the Court. A classic exposition of the theory of a property interest *recognised* by the order can be found in just three paragraphs of Cory, J.'s judgment for the majority. He concludes that, 'as Professor Scott makes clear, the fact that the proprietary interest is deemed to have arisen before the remedy was granted is not inconsistent with the remedial

[94] The immediate response to this suggestion might be. 'Well, does the express trust beneficiary have an equitable proprietary interest, or doesn't he?'. As I shall argue later, I believe we have to soften here, as elsewhere, the rigid lines between property and obligation, and I foresee a time when the courts— and ultimately perhaps, newly fashioned rules— will determine whether the plaintiff may pursue a property or an obligation (unjust enrichment or unconscionability) claim.

[95] Supra, note 17.
[96] 'Constructive and Resulting Trusts—Unjust Enrichment in a Common Law Relationship', A. J. McClean (1982), 16 U.B.C. Law Review 155, 174.
[97] Ibid.
[98] Supra, note 18.
[99] Supra, note 81.

The Nature of the Remedial Constructive Trust

characteristics of the doctrine'.[100] The Court divided 4:3, and McLachlin, J. for the minority argued vigorously that, very much to the contrary, the remedial constructive trust 'cannot be regarded as arising automatically when the three conditions set out in *Pettkus* v. *Becker* are established'.[101] The court has to consider what is the appropriate remedy, she said; first, the personal remedies will be examined, and then the proprietary remedies. Finally the court makes a decision, and then grants the order. 'When the Court declares a constructive trust, at that point the beneficiary obtains an interest in the property subject to the trust.'[102]

Elsewhere I have considered at length the merits of the two judgments delivered in the *Rawluk* case.[103] On this occasion I will concern myself with how we might in Canada deal with the situation that now exists, an unfortunate legacy of our reception of the letter of the *Restatement of Restitution*. It is possible that the ultimate reconciliation of these two schools of thought will be found in the terms of the order that is given. While I find it impossible to conceive how a *remedy* in awarding compensation or in this instance specific property can also recognise and thereby give legal effect to a property interest created by the unjust enrichment, it may be that Cory, J. and McLachlin, J. have suggested how, while adopting the position that the claimant obtains redress only when the court order is made, the concerns of both are met. The object is to achieve an outcome where the disputed asset is protected, between the enrichment and trial, from the activities of the enriched party, and from third parties claiming through him. Cory, J. notes[104] Lord Denning's words in *Hussey* v. *Palmer*[105] that a constructive trust 'may arise at the outset when the property is acquired, or later on, as the circumstances may require'. Cory, J. continues,[106] 'As a result, even if it is declared by a court after the parties have already separated, a constructive trust *can be deemed to have arisen* when the duty to make restitution arose.'

Speaking of the property interest that is obtained

by the judicial award of a constructive trust, McLachlin, J. said this:[107] 'it appears [it] may be taken as extending back to the date when the trust was "earned" or perfected.' Here she too referred to Lord Denning's words in *Hussey* v. *Palmer*. It seems to me that, though this involves a departure from the theories put forward by *Scott* and probably also by *Bogert*,[108] Canadian courts should routinely state in the order the date from which the judicially-created property interest is to run. If the order is to be retrospective to any earlier date and thereby have any degree of retroactive operation, then, reasons having been given for this, the court order should state against whom the proprietary order is to operate. The recognition and enforcement of an existing equitable proprietary interest under the traditional constructive trust doctrine already produces an upheaval for third parties who were unaware of, but affected by, the constructive trust circumstances prior to the order. And if it is the case[109] that when the law imposes an institutional constructive trust an equitable proprietary interest or right is thereby *recognised*, I suggest—particularly in the volatile doctrinal area of family property disputes—that decisions of a creative kind are already being made.[110] So nothing is significantly changed in that respect; the change is that, instead of a rule of the constructive trust 'arising' out of unjust enrichment circumstances or of automatic retroactivity to those circumstances, we have discretion. And a discretionary award of retroactivity, by contrast, means that the court can have regard as to who is to be affected by it, why, and to what extent. Again I am looking at unjust enrichment and the remedies to correct it as an issue primarily concerned with people, conduct, expectations and relationships rather than the assertion or denial of rights to property. It is with this primary concern in mind that I put forward these ideas as a possible solution to our problem.

However, as Professor Paciocco has explained,[111] there is an argument to be made on the basis of judgments in our appellate courts that the remedial con-

---

[100] Ibid., at p. 92 (S.C.R.), p. 177 (D.L.R.). Scott's explanation for his remark would be that the constructive trust is imposed to *remedy unjust enrichment* (see, supra, note 5).

[101] Ibid., at p. 107 (S.C.R.), p. 188 (D.L.R.).

[102] Ibid., at p. 103 (S.C.R.), p. 185 (D.L.R.).

[103] Supra, note 9. My opinion was that *Scott*'s position (supra, note 47, para. 462.4) should not be adopted in Canada, and that Bogert's automatically retroactive effect of the court order to the date of the unjust enrichment (*The Law of Trusts and Trustees*, 2nd ed. rev., para. 472) in large part meets the criticism of *Scott*'s position, but is too inflexible. I preferred Professor Palmer's arguments (*Law of Restitution*, 1978, Supp. 1982, vol. 1, p. 6).

[104] Supra, note 81, at p. 92 (S.C.R.), p. 176 (D.L.R.)

[105] [1972] 1 W.L.R. 1286, 1290, [1972] 3 All E.R. 744, 747 (C.A.).

[106] Supra, note 81, at p. 92 (S.C.R.), p. 176 (D.L.R.). Emphasis added.

[107] Ibid., at p. 103 (S.C.R.), p. 185 (D.L.R.).

[108] I.e., arising at the date of the unjust enrichment (*Scott*), retroactive to the same date from the moment of issue of the court order (Bogert).

[109] I have in mind the implications of the finding of a fiduciary obligation in *Chase Manhattan Bank N.A.* v. *Israel–British Bank* (*London*) *Ltd.*, [1981] Ch. 105, [1979] 3 All E.R. 1025.

[110] See the range of cases, other than family property disputes, assembled by Lord Goff and Jones, G. H., *Law of Restitution*, 3rd ed., 1986, at p. 61.

[111] 'The Remedial Constructive Trust: A Principled Basis for Priorities over Creditors', D. M. Paciocco (1989), 68 Can. Bar Rev. 315.

structive trust does indeed 'arise' when the unjust enrichment occurs. In my view it is most unfortunate if this support exists, because I think that in the context of the dichotomy of liability and remedy the argument is totally misconceived. I believe Canadian law must now move beyond *Scott*'s conception of the constructive trust and *Bogert*'s apparently automatic retroactivity, and that the Court must deliberately and expressly make that move. Nevertheless, I have to admit that clearly this remains an area where there are two opinions, and that the present law in Canada may be the majority opinion in *Rawluk*. I doubt we have heard the last of this unfortunate decision.

5. Family Property Cases and Commercial Cases

It comes to this, then, that the majority judgment in *Rawluk*[112] has introduced the doctrine into common law Canada that, though in earlier words of the Court a remedial constructive trust may recognise and also create an entitlement to specific property, in either manifestation the entitlement arises on the day the unjust enrichment took place or commenced. Though Cory, J. made no reference to the matter, the question has been raised as to the circumstances in which this new analysis is to be applied. Is this approach to be taken in commercial cases, for instance, as well as in family property cases?

My own conclusion is that the *Rawluk* majority would have envisaged that approach being taken in all cases where a remedial constructive trust is being imposed. In all cases the court *recognises* an accomplished fact. However, it appears I may be wrong, and that *Rawluk* is concerned with family property cases only. In *Peter* v. *Beblow*[113] Cory, J., this time for the minority, appears to condone for family property cases a less demanding test of the link between the contribution(s) of the deprived party on the one hand, and specific property of the enriched party on the other hand, than would be permitted in a commercial case. Of this most recent pronouncement McLachlin, J., in my respectful opinion correctly, speaking for the majority, would have none. Indeed, the majority judgment in *Peter* v. *Beblow* reiterates the thesis of the minority judgment in *Rawluk* v. *Rawluk*. The constructive trust is a remedy; it requires the existence neither of a fiduciary relationship nor of an equitable proprietary interest or right. It does not 'recognise' at all; the court order is the sole source of the redress the claimant obtains. In the

Peter case the point is emphasized by the majority that a proprietary remedy is justified as against a damages award only when there is a clear and convincing link between the contribution the claimant made and a specific asset in the name of the enriched party. The manner of determination of the existence of this link must be the same and as rigorous in all cases. Otherwise, we slip away from criteria and doctrinal structure to individual moral judgments. The structure has itself been kept so far to a minimum, surely in order to balance the twin desires for certainty and judicial freedom to respond appropriately to the infinite variation of fact situations.

On the other hand it could be said that with any general principle of liability applied directly to fact situations—that is, without more interposed doctrine or deduced rules than are contained in *Pettkus* v. *Becker*—there is bound to be an inclination for the courts to approach family property cases and commercial cases differently. In the circumstances of what may be called family property there is an evident readiness in society to see a man and a woman who are living together in a matrimonial manner, and acquiring or working upon assets they then use in common, as intending to share the ownership of those assets. In the commercial setting, where business and arm's length attitudes prevail, that readiness is absent. I think any Canadian observer of the scene would concede that there is this readiness and there is this absence. It may be that in practice it is much harder to deny a proprietary remedy in the family property cases than in the commercial cases, whatever is said about the primacy of personal remedies.

Once unjust enrichment is found to have occurred—that there was in the particular case a 'causal connection' between the enrichment of one and the deprivation of another[114]—that issue is concluded. It is a successive and separate matter as to which remedy (or what redress) is most appropriate. A proprietary remedy must be justified on some other basis than that the enriched party should account or compensate. That the contribution made by the deprived party is clearly and convincingly linked to the form of the enrichment appears to me to be the only possible justification. 'You would not have had this asset but for what I did to help you acquire it' is extended to 'You would not have had this asset as it now is in its transformed state but for my work on it (or financial assistance to its extensive improvement),' It is evident that with such a question of fact—just how clear and convincingly linked

---

[112] Supra, note 81.
[113] [1993] 1 S.C.R. 980, 101 D.L.R. (4th) 621.
[114] And an absence of 'juristic reason' for the enrichment.

McLachlin, J. for the majority discusses this criterion in the family property cases at some length.

was the contribution?—different minds may come to different conclusions, especially in the area of family property disputes and after three decades of concerned controversy. With the rising incidence in our societies of a preference for quasi-matrimonial relationships, it is more than likely that each of the Commonwealth jurisdictions will ultimately extend matrimonial property legislation to these presently extramural relationships. The problem, I perceive, is not a principle, of desiring to exclude, but in what manner the inclusion is to be made. However, the likelihood of ultimate statutory provision for cohabitees is no answer to the majority judgment in *Rawluk* and its repetition in the minority judgment in *Peter* v. *Beblow*, and until there is legislation in all our nine common law provinces and the two territories we in Canada will have a problem with how direct a contribution of the non-titled party has to be.

In my opinion McLachlin, J.'s approach for herself and others in both cases is right because we cannot have a link *doctrine*—and this, I think, is what we are after—which is loosely or strictly applied according to the court's reaction to the facts. Either we have a rule or we do not. For one thing, on the practical level, there is no neat dividing line between the facts of family property cases and the commercial cases.[115] The observation is commonplace that often family homes are mortgaged, he or she has worked in or contributed significantly to the other's business, or assets in the name of one have been used to secure loans for the other's, or a joint, enterprise. Relaxation of the linkage required assumes a very different perspective once the third party is introduced, whether that party is unsecured or secured. The facts in *Rawluk* and in the *Peter* case happened not to concern such elements. Nobody other than the disputing couple was involved. But one does not need to rely on the observation that family and commercial considerations may be intertwined. The concept of clear and convincing link is only worth anything, and can only be developed in subsequent case law, if it means the same thing in every case of unjust enrichment. What we are discussing in any event is not an all or nothing outcome; the issue is whether the deprived spouse shall have compensation or specific assets. Compensation does not have to be solely or strictly for the value of services or goods supplied. It can at least be generous, as it was in *Boardman* v. *Phipps*,[116] but there is no reason why the measure of

compensation should not be the value of a disputed asset. If market increase of value of an asset is what the deprived person is after, surely he or she will lean over backwards to show a clear and convincing link between the contribution and that asset.

The problem, I suggest, is the tendency for Canadian courts to fuse the law and their response to the facts in these family property cases. In *Peter* v. *Beblow*, despite the difference of opinion about the application of the link test, the Court was unanimous in holding, thereby reversing the lower appeal court, that the woman's care and upbringing of the minor children, both hers and his, and her housekeeping and landscaping, entitled her to have the house outright. But at the end of the day the majority came to this conclusion because, the woman having contributed substantially to *all* the assets of "the family enterprise', 'the house reflects a fair approximation of the value of the [woman's] efforts as reflected in the family assets'.[117] The trial court's judgment, in which the Supreme Court majority considered the right answer had been reached but link had not been made, was thus upheld. And here one may have cause for some puzzlement. Is the route taken to awarding the woman the house to be described as a *linking* of the house and her contributions, or was it another approach to the manner of granting compensation for services rendered? The answer to that question is masked because the increased value of the house at trial happily reflected the value of her contribution to the then value of all the assets of the family.

I confess that for my part I think we still have a way to go on the justification for the award of a proprietary remedy. In my opinion cases like *Lac Minerals* are clear enough; the continuing difficulty is how to rationalise the award of what the court determines to be appropriate in the highly sensitive arena of the personal relationship breakdown cases. Patrick Parkinson, it will be recalled,[118] has concluded from empirical research that the line between proprietary and personal relief in the family property cases is drawn in Canada between the presence or absence of joint enterprise or partnership. This may constitute yet another approach, or prove to be the required evidence of linkage. That is something more that has to be thought out.[119] However, I am persuaded we will get there; it merely takes time and occasion.

---

[115] Having adopted a general principle of liability, Canadian courts in my opinion should be very reluctant to resign themselves to distinct doctrinal treatment of different factual situations, even situations as distinguishable as family property disputes and the commercial contract or joint venture cases.
[116] [1967] A.C. 46, [1966] 3 All E.R. 721 (H.L.).
[117] Supra, note 113, at p. 1003 (S.C.R.), p. 654 (D.L.R.).

[118] Supra, note 44.
[119] Those who would have the courts handle differently the family cases and the commercial contract (or joint venture) cases can effectively make the point that many distinct factors exercise influence on the outcome of the family property disputes. This is not true of the average commercial case (e.g. the *Lac Minerals* litigation).

6. Conclusions

The remedial constructive trust, as I envisage it, connotes the type of redress which a claimant receives by way of court order, and in the manner decreed by that order, when the claimant is successful in establishing that the defendant to the claim has breached an obligation owed to the claimant. In Canada that obligation is that the defendant shall not be unjustly enriched, i.e., at the expense of the claimant. The constructive trust is the terminological vehicle for conferring specific property upon the claimant. It matters not whether the claimant has a pre-existing legal or equitable right of a proprietary nature in the specific property awarded; 'the imposition of a constructive trust can both recognise and create a right of property.'[120] Nor in my respectful opinion should the law in common law Canada stipulate that the grant of a constructive trust by a court *recognises* in that property an interest of the claimant that arose at the time when the unjust enrichment, so found, took place or commenced. Were the law so to provide, the claimant might effectively demand the recognition of the property interest when the court is of the view that the appropriate remedy would be damages or some other form of personal relief. Were that to be possible, the law would have found its way back to what Canadians see for their purposes as the barren state of the institutional constructive trust.

Little has been said in this paper, though much has been written, on the subject of the meaning and application of the three criteria—enrichment, corresponding deprivation, and an absence of juristic reason for the enrichment—set out in the leading case of *Pettkus* v. *Becker* for the determination of whether unjust enrichment has occurred. Canadian courts see these criteria as invaluable touchstones in the approach to each set of litigated facts. Some critics on other shores regard them as mere statements of the obvious, doctrinal in no meaningful sense, and still after thirteen years undeveloped by our courts. However, this is a topic concerning liability that must be for another occasion. What I have tried to emphasize is that, though in some quarters in the early 1980s the three criteria were conceived as the test for determining whether *a remedial constructive trust* should be imposed by the court, it has been apparent since *Sorochan* v. *Sorochan* in 1986 that, far from being the only possible response to unjust enrichment when specific assets are claimed, the constructive trust is only one possible award. The

Court there referred expressly to the alternative remedy of damages. Subsequent judgments from the Court have added the proprietary remedies of lien and subrogation, and the personal remedies of account and injunction. When courts also speak of the availability of *quantum meruit*, *quantum valebat*, and the action for money had and received in the context of restitutionary theory, it is recognisable that quasi-contractual and equitable restitutional remedies, personal and real, constitute the range of potential relief that the post-*Sorochan* courts have in mind. And personal remedies are identified as being primary, because of the far-reaching consequences— as the case law now stands—of the award of proprietary remedies.[121] One can foresee increasing pressures from within the Court for the requirement of a direct and very obvious link between contribution and the property claimed, so emphasized in *Peter* v. *Beblow*. Though the nature of that link will continue to be the subject-matter of argument in future litigation, linkage will be *the* criterion for the award of a remedial constructive trust.

On the whole wherever it can the Court has avoided lines between distinct, or allegedly distinct, theoretical or factual circumstances. A distinction between family property cases and commercial cases, for the purposes of remedying the presence of unjust enrichment, is strongly resisted by the four members of the Court who constituted the majority in *Peter* v. *Beblow*, the latest authority from the Court. Nor in my opinion, though I do not think it matters once a principle of liability (or obligation) is adopted for all future 'constructive trust' cases, is it necessarily advisable for the Court at a future date—unless it is to be done with a totally different nomenclature—to recognise any doctrinal distinction between the remedying of unjust enrichment on the one hand and breach of *express* trusts. I speak here of express trust beneficiary actions, where restitution is sought of trust assets or of assets acquired by the fiduciary at the expense of the trust. In the last twenty years the trust concept has become noticeably much more flexible both as to theory and in its application. The drawing of lines between trust and powers, and between the trust and common law concepts like debt, agency and contracts for the benefit of third parties, has become increasingly more difficult to make and to defend when made. In Canada today whether parties, usually in commerce, have brought into existence, or are otherwise in, a trust relationship, or on the other

---

[120] Supra, note 46.
[121] Canadian courts are not likely to feel themselves hampered by the jurisdictional distinction that led to the dichotomy of personal restitution remedies at law and in equity. However, the rationalisation of restitution remedies for

the contemporary scene—a process on the part of the courts which would clarify where personal and proprietary remedies are appropriate, and would cause their origins in the nineteenth century or earlier to fade from significance—has yet in my view to have been seriously commenced.

hand in a debt, agency, deposit or third party contract relationship, is one of the most frequently litigated or otherwise contended trust issues.[122] Often they are to be found in both trust and contractual relations, and the issue—as in a 'trusteed' pension plan, for instance—is when the relationship is contractual and when it has trust characteristics.

In these borderline areas, as well as the family property dispute area, the emphasis today in Canada appears to be upon the nature of the relationship of parties rather than property and apposing property rights and the duties of others with regard to that property. But if relationship is the emphasis, then perhaps the Court should pause before it draws the line, as the majority did in *Canson Enterprises Ltd. v. Boughton & Co.*,[123] between the trust and other fiduciary relationships. The trust relationship is but one, if at the top, of a range of fiduciary relationships that moves from those that are the most intense to those that are slight and are little more demanding overall than relationships at law.

Finally, there is the question of judicial discretion. The scope of the courts in determining how the three-part *Pettkus v. Becker* test shall apply to the instant case, and, if liability exists, whether remedy shall be personal or proprietary, is considerable. Discretion is a powerful weapon in the hands of the judiciary whereby to advance policies of its choosing, and in the exercise of discretion the responsibility for self-restraint imposed upon the courts, especially in such sensitive fields as family property disputes and intervention in commercial contractual and pre-contractual relationships, is consequently equally considerable. Nothing can or should disguise this fact. However, apprehension need not be one's inevitable reaction.

First I turn to liability. Speaking in 1982 of the *Pettkus v. Becker* decision,[124] Professor McClean wrote, 'There is no doubt a risk of uncertainty and of inconsistency of decision involved in proceeding by reference to either unjust enrichment or good conscience, but the risk may be exaggerated.' He noted the 'already well-established restitutionary claims', and

he concluded that the case law, inductive by nature, was likely to develop much as it has always done.[125] I think the Canadian courts would agree that this is the way things have gone in the last thirteen years. Certainly the Supreme Court is well aware of the risks, and of the slips from grace that have occurred. It has spoken with regard to both liability and to remedy. 'There is a tendency on the part of some', writes McLachlin, J. for the majority in *Peter v. Beblow*,[126] 'to view the action for unjust enrichment as a device for doing whatever may seem fair between the parties. In the rush to substantive justice, the principles are sometimes forgotten. . . . On the remedies side, the requirements of the special proprietary remedy of constructive trust are sometimes minimized.'

I conclude that, while the shoals are there in plenty, the Court in what is now a long series of judgments has kept a steady and sensitive hand on the direction of the case law. The decisions of the Court have remained within a range of content and outcome that has disturbed no Canadian of whom I am aware, and, when they have discerned error or excess in lower courts, members of the Court have not hesitated to speak their minds, albeit tactfully and appreciating the formative stage in which this branch of the law remains. In my opinion the occasional rhetoric of judgments proclaiming with some fanfare the existence of judicial discretion does not necessarily reflect anything more than the desire that formulae and rules shall not settle upon the law before the formative age is clearly over. Nor in making that comment do I wish to be understood as implicitly preferring rules to discretion. On the other hand there will be unfortunate rulings, a telescoping of liability and remedy considerations by busy lower courts, and a continuing need for the appellate courts in our eleven common law jurisdictions to see that 'the middle course between the extremes of inflexible rules and case-by-case "palm-tree" justice', as McLachlin, J. put it in *Peel (Regional Municipality) v. Canada*,[127] is maintained. The doctrinal development is evidently at an early stage, for

---

[122] This is my personal reason for being hesitant regarding Professor Goode's otherwise clarifying distinction between the property-based and the wrong-based constructive trust (supra, note 87). While I realize that for many the notion of property and the distinction between ownership and obligation are inviolable, I do not think the drawing of such lines is reflective of present trends of doctrine, and therefore, whatever else it accomplishes, I fear it will create its own particular brand of tortuous case law attempting to avoid those rigid lines.

Once a principle is isolated and accepted as an explanation of what the courts are doing with constructive trusts, an obligation comes into existence which can be applied creatively by the courts to circumstances other than the historic constructive trust situations. Equitable ownership is then seen, not as some-

thing existent in definitive circumstances determined by case law, but as the outcome of the breach of that obligation and a judicially chosen remedy with regard to specific assets. The prevention of unjust enrichment in this context operates as a principle in that grey border country (as I believe it to be) between property and obligation.

[123] Supra, note 88.

[124] Supra, note 95, at p. 169.

[125] It will be recalled that this is the analysis of the present state of the law and the expectation of Maddaugh, P. D., and McCamus, J. D., *The Law of Restitution*, 1990, supra, the text to note 70.

[126] Supra, note 113, at p. 988 (S.C.R.), pp. 643–4 (D.L.R.).

[127] [1992] 3 S.C.R. 762, 802, 98 D.L.R. (4th) 140, 164

there is much yet to be decided, issues of considerable policy implication as well as of doctrinal challenge. The 'middle course' will be difficult to determine, and then to hold. But in my view—a future I could hardly imagine when writing 'The Constructive Trust' in the early 1960s—the remedial constructive trust in Canada today is both doctrinally and empirically a legacy for the future which has promise and potential. The way ahead may be treacherous, but the direction is sure.

14. The Element of Discretion

SIMON GARDNER*

T HIS paper begins by noting the essential characteristics of remedial constructive trusts, as they are used by the Canadian and also the Australian[1] courts. It finds that one of these characteristics (the one which ostensibly differentiates them from institutional constructive trusts) is the fact that their incidence lies in the discretion of the court. To date, the discussion of remedial constructive trusts, whether judicial or academic, has not given much focused thought to this feature of them. This paper aims to make a start in this direction. It therefore continues by developing some perceptions about the phenomenon of discretion in general. Armed with these perceptions, it finally returns to consider whether the reliance upon discretion in remedial constructive trusts is wholesome.

I. The Characteristics of Remedial Constructive Trusts

What are remedial constructive trusts? We shall begin this enquiry by seeing, briefly, why they are 'constructive trusts' at all. This part of the exercise is important, but relatively uncontentious. Then we shall look at the more troubled question of what differentiates them from institutional constructive trusts.

Remedial constructive trusts . . . and personal obligations

Let us begin with a broad focus. The first characteristic of remedial constructive trusts is that, like all trusts, they have proprietary effect. They are thus to be differentiated from any legal phenomenon having only personal effect. In particular, they can affect third parties, such as recipients of the subject-matter in question, and they will take priority in the

trustee's bankruptcy. It is true that some decisions may be found which seem to incline to the opposite view,[2] but the proprietary position has been asserted with authority on several occasions.[3]

. . . and non-trust proprietary obligations

Narrowing the focus somewhat, the second point is that (it has been said) remedial constructive trusts must have subject-matter, a trustee, and a beneficiary.[4] If this proposition is right, remedial constructive trusts share this ground with other (express and institutional constructive) trusts, but stand apart from other proprietary phenomena which may lack these characteristics. The proposition would probably command general assent, but there are a few difficulties about it. Some authorities might comment that the terminology of this statement is too reminiscent of express or institutional constructive trusts. Their point would be that, as will be seen in a moment, the function of a remedial constructive trust is to compel a defendant to disgorge some property to a plaintiff, rather than to constitute an enduring relationship of 'trustee' and 'beneficiary' between them. But even if we accept this, the quarrel is with the flavour of the words, rather than with the requirement of two legal persons as the subject and object of the obligations.[5] The requirement of subject-matter is perhaps more contentious. Some decisions, dealing with the liability of non-trustees for breaches of trustees' obligations, claim to concern (remedial?) constructive trusts but appear to dispense with subject-matter. But the appearance is conventionally regarded as deceptive. The decisions in question hold that the non-trustee is liable 'under a constructive trust' even if she does not hold any relevant property.[6] It has become usual to say that what is involved here is not really a (constructive) *trust* at all, but rather the (constructive) imposition of a trustee's personal liabilities.[7] It is hard to fault this

* Lincoln College, Oxford.

[1] See *Muschinski* v. *Dodds* (1986) 160 C.L.R. 583 at 612–17, per Deane, J.; *Baumgartner* v. *Baumgartner* (1987) 164 C.L.R. 137 at 147–9, per Mason, C. J. Wilson and Deane, JJ, 152, per Toohey, J., 156, per Gaudron, J.

[2] See especially *Palachik* v. *Kiss* (1983) 146 D.L.R. (3d) 385.

[3] In particular, the point is at the heart of *Rawluk* v. *Rawluk* (1990) 65 D.L.R. (4th) 161: see especially at 176–7, per Cory, J., 185–8, per McLachlin, J.

[4] See *Muschinski* v. *Dodds* (1986) 160 C.L.R. 583 at 614, per Deane, J.

[5] Deane, J., loc. cit., also mentions the possibility that instead of a beneficiary there might be a purpose. That is of course true so far as express trusts go, but remedial constructive trusts rem-

edy the defendant's enrichment at the beneficiary's expense. Does it make sense to substitute 'purpose' for 'beneficiary' here?

[6] The concept of *relevant* property is of course not an easy one. The tracing cases discuss how far it can be extended. The furthest stretch in the English (more exactly, Privy Council) authorities is Lord Templeman's dictum in *Space Investments Ltd.* v. *Canadian Imperial Bank of Commerce Trust Co. (Bahamas) Ltd.* [1986] 1 W.L.R. 1072.

[7] See especially *Selangor United Rubber Estates Ltd.* v. *Cradock (No. 3)* [1968] 2 All E.R. 1073 at 1097; *Karak Rubber Co. Ltd.* v. *Burden* [1972] 1 W.L.R. 602 at 632; H. G. Hanbury and J. E. Martin, *Modern Equity* (14th ed., 1993), 298; A. Underhill and D. J. Hayton, *Law Relating to Trusts and Trustees* (14th ed., 1987), 350.

recharacterisation, and seen thus, the decisions in question pose no threat to the requirement of subject-matter.

In the foregoing respects, then, remedial constructive trusts may be recognised as different from many other legal phenomena, though not from other types of trust. It should occasion no surprise that remedial constructive trusts have common features with other kinds of trust: it would be linguistically unsatisfactory if it were otherwise. Narrowing the focus once more, however, we now examine the matters which are said to differentiate remedial constructive trusts from other types of trust.

. . . and express trusts

The genus 'trusts' has a major division into express and constructive trusts, and it is evident that remedial constructive trusts lie on the constructive side of that divide. That is, although (as we have just seen) there are the ingredients of a trust, that trust arises for a reason other than that a settlor wants it to: which is the conventional distinction between constructive and express trusts. This distinction, however, has difficulties. It is certainly naïve to think that all express trusts are products of a settlor's intention; and on the other hand it seems too that some constructive trusts are such products.[8] But we can pass over this problem quickly. The distinction between express and constructive trusts is of practical significance only for such matters as formalities and limitation, and those issues are in practice approached teleologically.[9] Certainly, to the extent that the distinction represents any recognisable reality, remedial constructive trusts have as good a claim to be termed constructive as institutional constructive trusts do.

. . . and institutional constructive trusts

Then, finally, there is the demarcation of remedial constructive trusts from institutional constructive trusts. The focus is now narrowest of all.

As to this, one sometimes encounters a suggestion that remedial constructive trusts are different from institutional constructive trusts in that they can arise where there is no fiduciary relationship, whilst institutional constructive trusts cannot.[10] It is certainly true that those who become the trustee and beneficiary of a remedial constructive trust may have no prior fiduciary relationship—or, indeed, any prior legal relationship at all. Classically, they will be respectively the recipient and the mover of an unjust enrichment, and that may very well be their only connection. What is not clear is the foundation for the view that institutional constructive trusts arise only where there is a prior fiduciary relationship. Probably the confusion has arisen from the rule, in English law, that equitable tracing is possible only where the property in question originally emanated from a fiduciary relationship.[11] But it is surely by now commonplace that the fiduciary relationship can perfectly well take the form of a constructive trust, which need not itself have arisen in a fiduciary context at all.[12] Constructive trusts are also found as between parties who are not otherwise fiduciaries in contexts not involving tracing, such as between grantor and grantee of an interest pending execution of the legal transfer, and between a testator's killer who inherits under the will and the testator's residuaries or intestate successors.[13] So let us leave this suggestion to one side.

Two characteristics remain which have been said to differentiate remedial constructive trusts from their institutional counterparts.[14] They are: first, that, unlike institutional constructive trusts, remedial constructive trusts exist as a reaction to unjust enrichment; and second, that, again unlike institutional constructive trusts, remedial constructive trusts are a mechanism for disgorging property from a defendant, rather than for establishing an enduring trustee–beneficiary relationship. These characteristics must detain us.

A response to unjust enrichment

It is clear that in the law of Canada, remedial constructive trusts are seen primarily, or even exclusively, as a means of redressing unjust enrichment.[15]

---

[8] See S. Gardner, *An Introduction to the Law of Trusts* (1990), 225.

[9] See, e.g. *Oughtred* v. *I.R.C.* [1960] A.C. 206; *Soar* v. *Ashwell* [1893] 2 Q.B. 390.

[10] See, e.g. *Hunter Engineering Co.* v. *Syncrude Canada Ltd.* (1989) 57 D.L.R. (4th) 321 at 349, per Dickson, C.J.: 'Until the decision of this court in *Pettkus* v. *Becker* (1980) 117 D.L.R. (3d) 257, the constructive trust was viewed largely in terms of the law of trusts, hence the need for the existence of a fiduciary relationship.'

[11] *Re Diplock's Estate* [1948] Ch. 465 at 521.

[12] *Sinclair* v. *Brougham* [1914] A.C. 398; *Lake* v. *Bayliss* [1974] 1 W.L.R. 1073; *Chase Manhattan Bank N.A.* v. *Israel–British Bank (London) Ltd.* [1981] Ch. 105. These author-

ities do not, however, show that equitable tracing will operate where the legal as well as the equitable title remains with the plaintiff, as in an ordinary case of theft (though cf. P. Millett (1991), 107 L.Q.R. 71 at 76).

[13] For these two areas, see A. Underhill and D. J. Hayton, *Law Relating to Trusts and Trustees* (14th ed., 1987), 368–72 and 347.

[14] See *Rawluk* v. *Rawluk* (1990) 65 D.L.R. (4th) 161 at 184, 187, per McLachlin, J.

[15] See e.g. D. W. M. Waters, *Law of Trusts in Canada* (2nd ed., 1984), 390: 'The American Law Institute in 1937 seriously considered putting the whole subject of constructive trusts into the *Restatement of Restitution*, where in terms of nature and function it properly belongs.'

As a characteristic differentiating such trusts from (especially) their institutional counterparts, however, there are difficulties about this.

On the one hand, there seems in principle no reason why remedial constructive trusts should not perform other types of legal work besides the redress of unjust enrichment.[16,17] For example, it is possible to envisage them as a proprietary remedy for a cause of action founded on expectation. Indeed, it could be argued that the remedy of specific performance for the sale of land is an instance of this;[18] and the transfer of a promised interest under the doctrine of proprietary estoppel seems to be as well.[19]

On the other hand, it is unclear why unjust enrichment should not equally underlie an institutional constructive trust. It is certainly possible to imagine an enduring trustee-beneficiary relationship, rather than a disgorgement, being the appropriate response to some situations of unjust enrichment. Say a house is bought as premises for two business partners, with money provided by each but with title going into the name of one alone. Here is a situation of unjust enrichment demanding a proprietary response—i.e. a constructive trust[20]—but it is unnecessary, perhaps even inappropriate, to make the title-owner transfer anything to the other: what is needed is that she should hold the property on trust for the two of them. Similarly with family property, where the issue is not the division of the parties' property upon their separation, but the non-title-owner's rights in opposition to, say, a mortgagee.[21]

On the face of it, then, remedial constructive trusts should not be seen as wedded exclusively to unjust enrichment, rather than other bases of obligation; and unjust enrichment should not be seen as wedded

exclusively to remedial, rather than institutional, constructive trusts. So why should the association with unjust enrichment be perceived as so important? The key seems to lie in an accompanying perception of the contrast between unjust enrichment and the situations in which traditional, institutional constructive trusts arise. The situations in which institutional constructive trusts arise are perceived as probably heterogeneous, and sharply defined: whilst unjust enrichment is seen as a single, generic, less precisely defined notion.[22]

That unjust enrichment is seen in this imprecise way in the jurisdictions linking it with remedial constructive trusts is easily evidenced from the Canadian material. Dickson, J.'s classic discussion in *Pettkus* v. *Becker*[23] is illustrative. It is true that Dickson, J. apparently demands a degree of precision when he notes that unjust enrichment comprises three matters: 'an enrichment, a corresponding deprivation and absence of any juristic reason for the enrichment.'[24] But by itself, this explication is little more than a paraphrase of the expression 'unjust enrichment'. To reduce the flexibility of the notion in a substantial way, a good deal more would need to be spelt out: as to what exactly counts as an enrichment, and as a juristic reason for it. As to that, Dickson, J. comments: 'It would be undesirable, and indeed impossible, to attempt to define all the circumstances in which an unjust enrichment might arise. . . . The great advantage of ancient principles of equity is their flexibility: the judiciary is thus able to shape these malleable principles so as to accommodate the changing needs and mores of society, in order to achieve justice.'[25] And in a later decision, Dickson, J. adds: 'Unjust enrichment is no formula

---

[16] It might be thought that *L.A.C. Minerals Ltd.* v. *International Corona Resources Ltd.* (1989) 61 D.L.R. (4th) 14 shows Canadian law using remedial constructive trusts to react also to breach of confidence, and (per Wilson and La Forest, JJ.) to breach of fiduciary obligation. But closer reading suggests that unjust enrichment has not been displaced; the breach of confidence or of fiduciary obligation was seen as the ground on which the defendant's enrichment at the plaintiff's expense was unjust. See per Wilson, J. at 17, La Forest, J. at 44–6; semble, without disagreement from Sopinka, J. at 75–7.

[17] For development of this point, though without particular reference to *remedial* constructive trusts, see G. Elias, *Explaining Constructive Trusts* (1990).

[18] See S. Gardner (1987), 7 O.J.L.S. 60 at 74, citing *Atcherley* v. *Vernon* (1725) 10 Mod. 519 at 528; *Beckford* v. *Wade* (1805) 17 Ves. 87 at 96; *Crofton* v. *Ormsby* (1806) 2 Sch. & Lef. 583 at 603; *Clarke* v. *Moore* (1844) 1 Jo. & Lat. 723.

[19] It is controversial whether proprietary estoppel is quite about expectations, though a strong case can be made to that effect (see the discussion by C. Davis (1993), 13 O.J.L.S. 99 at 111–15); but it is entirely clear that it is about something other than the redress of unjust enrichment.

[20] The established law gives a presumed resulting trust, but this can be seen as essentially the same thing; if there was no such doctrine, there can be little doubt that a constructive trust

would be found.

[21] H. G. Hanbury and J. E. Martin, *Modern Equity* (14th ed., 1993), 296 makes a similar point about the situation where the beneficiary of the constructive trust is an infant; if the subject-matter is land, it could not be simply conveyed to her.

[22] *Rawluk* v. *Rawluk* (1990) 65 D.L.R. (4th) 161 at 183–4, per McLachlin, J.: 'In Canada, we have not followed the traditional English view of the constructive trust as a limited doctrine applying in limited, clearly defined cases. . . . The new concept of constructive trust now prevailing in Canada . . . eliminates the need to find recognizable categories in which the constructive trust can be applied, relying instead on the more general concept of unjust enrichment. . . .'

[23] (1980) 117 D.L.R. (3d) 257.

[24] *Pettkus* v. *Becker* (1980) 117 D.L.R. (3d) 257 at 274; also *Sorochan* v. *Sorochan* (1986) 29 D.L.R. (4th) 1 at 5.

[25] (1980) 117 D.L.R. (3d) 257 at 273. References to unjust enrichment as an *equitable* doctrine are not uncommon. They are, of course, historically inaccurate: unjust enrichment is as much a creature of the common law as of equity. The idea is presumably to lend additional force to the view that unjust enrichment is flexible. (Though why should it be assumed that equity is flexible? Many who profess themselves equity lawyers would say otherwise.)

for easy decisions. But it does ... provide a useful framework in which to strike the necessary balance.'[26] Although the word is not commonly used, what is envisaged is in reality a discretion: whereby, perhaps within certain broad bounds,[27] the judges can declare situations to involve unjust enrichment on a case-by-case basis, rather than the characterisation being determined by a set of firm rules.[28,29]

In Australia, remedial constructive trusts are imposed on a slightly different basis. Unjust enrichment is seen as an 'informative generic label for purposes of classification', as opposed to a 'general principle ... as a basis for decision'.[30] Remedial constructive trusts are founded instead on the 'narrower and more specific basis'[31] (which may, of course, fall within that generic label) of 'the general equitable principle which restores to a party contributions which he or she has made to a joint endeavour which fails in circumstances in which it was not intended that the other party should enjoy them'.[32] The apparent message of these remarks is a perceived contrast with the Canadian idea of a wide discretion: in Australian law, remedial constructive trusts are predicated upon much more sharply defined situations. This may, however, be deceptive. Some Australian decisions, ostensibly founded on this basis, in reality give themselves discretion by taking a creative approach to the finding of the relevant facts.[33] Signs can also be seen of a tendency to ignore the specific meaning of the governing formulæ altogether, treating them as conferring a broad discretion after all.[34]

A mechanism for disgorging property

Canadian and Australian law agree upon the second characteristic differentiating remedial constructive trusts from their institutional counterparts. Remedial constructive trusts are viewed as a mechanism for effecting a disgorgement: a tool which a court can use to make a defendant hand over property to a plaintiff, once this property has been seen to constitute an unjust enrichment or a contribution to a failed joint endeavour. Institutional constructive trusts, by contrast, are seen as static phenomena, in which the trustee is to hold the property in question enduringly for the beneficiary.[35]

The remedial constructive trust may be a tool for disgorgement, but it comes with the rider, noted earlier, of proprietary effect. This is what differentiates it from remedies by way of personal restitution, such as account. But what, in concrete terms, is this 'proprietary effect'? In principle, it might just be a matter of the defendant being ordered to transfer a particular item of property, rather than a sum of money. Or it might additionally be a matter of the item (or indeed sum) in question being given priority in the

---

[26] *Nepean Hydro-Electric Commission* v. *Ontario Hydro* (1982) 132 D.L.R. (3d) 193 at 205 (citing from S. M. Waddams, *The Law of Contracts* (1977), 213). Flexibility is claimed also as regards the quantification of the defendant's enrichment, central to the idea of unjust enrichment: see *Peter* v. *Beblow* (1993) 101 D.L.R. (4th) 621 at 635, 641–2, *per* Cory, J.; cf., however, McLachlin, J. at 643–4.

[27] Even this degree of constraint was rejected by Waite, J. in *Herman* v. *Smith* (1984) 42 R.F.L. (2d) 154 at 160, saying of Dickson, J.'s three-fold analysis: 'I am not satisfied that, as a matter of modern principle, that type of pigeon-holing ought to be required'.

[28] From a Canadian viewpoint, therefore, S. Gardner (1993), 109 L.Q.R. 263 at 269–74 is arguably wrong in assessing the Canadian family property decisions by reference to an analysis of unjust enrichment taking the rigorous lines advocated by P. B. H. Birks, *An Introduction to the Law of Restitution* (revised ed., 1989). However, even if the judgments in question would insist on retaining flexibility over unjust enrichment, they do claim to found their conclusions upon certain identified points in their facts: and it is observable that these points are in truth fabricated, which is Gardner's main point. See also A. J. McClean (1982), 16 U.B.C.L.R. 155 at 163–4, 170; B. Hovius and T. G. Youdan, *The Law of Family Property* (1991), 123–4.

[29] That unjust enrichment rests in the eye of the beholder is well illustrated by *Hunter Engineering Co. Inc.* v. *Syncrude Canada Ltd.* (1989) 57 D.L.R. 321 and *Atlas Cabinets and Furniture Ltd.* v. *National Trust Co. Ltd.* (1990) 68 D.L.R. 161. At bottom, these cases concern the issue whether, 'so as to accommodate the changing needs and mores of society', the doctrine of unjust enrichment should be used to, in effect, impose contracts on commercial parties which they might have made for themselves but did not. By their majorities, the two cases take fundamentally opposite positions regarding this issue. (The same issue also underlies the discussion regarding exclusion

clauses in *Hunter Engineering*. See also *Waselenko* v. *Touche Ross Ltd.* [1983] 2 W.W.R. 352; and G. H. L. Fridman (1991), 11 L.S. 304.) The case of judicial opinion on this issue is not necessarily clearer in England; cf. *The Scaptrade* [1983] 2 A.C. 694 and *Interfoto Picture Library Ltd.* v. *Stiletto Visual Programmes Ltd.* [1989] Q.B. 433.

[30] *Muschinski* v. *Dodds* (1986) 160 C.L.R. 583 at 617, per Deane, J. See now *David Securities Pty. Ltd.* v. *Commonwealth Bank of Australia* (1992) 109 A.L.R. 57.

[31] Ibid. At 615–16, Deane, J. also rejects any idea of remedial constructive trusts arising on grounds such as 'fairness' or 'good conscience', which are presented as even looser than unjust enrichment.

[32] *Baumgartner* v. *Baumgartner* (1987) 164 C.L.R. 137, 148 citing *Muschinski* v. *Dodds* (1986) 160 C.L.R. 583 at 620, per Deane, J. However, cf. at 154, where Toohey, J. equates this doctrine with unjust enrichment, which he appears to regard as a 'basis for decision'. This position is followed in *Marriage of Toohey* (1991) 14 Fam. L.R. 843, and by Kirby, P. (dissenting) in *Bryson* v. *Bryant* (1992) 29 N.S.W.L.R. 188 at 205–9.

[33] See, e.g. *Baumgartner* v. *Baumgartner* (1987) 164 C.L.R. 137 itself; *Hibberson* v. *George* (1989) 12 Fam. L.R. 725; *Lipman* v. *Lipman* (1989) 13 Fam. L.R. 1. For decisions which avoid this tendency, see e.g. *Arthur* v. *Public Trustee* (1988) 90 F.L.R. 203; *Public Trustee* v. *Kukula* (1990) 14 Fam. L.R. 97; *Woodward* v. *Johnson* (1991) 14 Fam. L.R. 828; *Miller* v. *Sutherland* (1991) D.F.C. 95–102; *Macchi* v. *Scott* (1991) D.F.C. 95–104. See further S. Gardner (1993), 109 L.Q.R. 263 at 276–8.

[34] See *Bryson* v. *Bryant* (1992) 29 N.S.W.L.R. 188 at 204–5, per Kirby, P. (dissenting).

[35] See D. W. M. Waters, Law of Trusts in Canada (2nd ed., 1984), 388; *Rawluk* v. *Rawluk* (1990) 65 D.L.R. (4th) 161 at 183–4, per McLachlin, J.; *Muschinski* v. *Dodds* (1986) 160 C.L.R. 583 at 614–15, per Deane, J.

defendant's subsequent bankruptcy, and/or being made traceable into the hands of subsequent alienees. On this view, the court order alone would have the proprietary effect. The plaintiff's claim to that order would have no such effect. So, for example, if the defendant became bankrupt before the action, the plaintiff's claim would be no more than an ordinary debt in the bankruptcy. This would entail a sharp difference between remedial constructive trusts and their institutional counterparts, which have proprietary effect from the date of the underlying facts, irrespective of whether a court finds itself enforcing them at any stage.

This position has not, however, been adopted by the Canadian judges.[36] The Canadian material regards the proprietary effect of remedial constructive trusts as attaching not merely to the court's order for disgorgement, but to the plaintiff's claim itself. The proprietary effect is thus held to arise at the date of the facts which will eventually move the court to make the disgorgement order.[37] A package of consequences follows.[38] The plaintiff's claim takes priority in the defendant's bankruptcy, even before the time of the action;[39] (presumably) the plaintiff is able to

trace the property in question into the hands of alienees, likewise; and the plaintiff can take advantage of the fact that the property in question has increased in value since the underlying facts occurred.[40,41]

If the remedial constructive trust's ultimate disgorgement order is preceded by this proprietary package arising from the underlying facts, though, remedial constructive trusts might be seen as by no means dissimilar from their institutional counterparts.[42] How, then, do they differ? The answer is apparently as follows. With an institutional constructive trust, the court's role is the merely mechanical one of recognising and if necessary vindicating the trust. With the remedial constructive trust, however, the court has a discretion. Assuming that the necessary underlying facts are present, the court is still faced with a decision whether to grant or withhold the proprietary remedy, as opposed to ordering personal restitution.[43]

That said, it is not clear how great the difference is. One view is apparently that, whilst the remedial constructive trust dates from the relevant facts if it arises at all, its existence depends upon whether a court, in its discretion, decides to give a proprietary

---

[36] It has been urged by some writers as the correct way to regard the English law of proprietary estoppel: see, e.g. D. J. Hayton [1990], Conv. 370 at 372, P. Ferguson (1993), 109 L.Q.R. 114 at 120–3; cf. D. J. Hayton (1993), 109 L.Q.R. 485. The authority to support this view (though neither cites it) is *Maharaj v. Chand* [1986] A.C. 898. Against it, however, seem to be *Dillwyn v. Llewelyn* (1862) 4 De G.F. & J. 517, *Inwards v. Baker* [1965] 2 Q.B. 29, *Jones v. Jones* [1977] 1 W.L.R. 438, *Griffiths v. Williams* (1977) 248 E.G. 947, *Re Basham* [1986] 1 W.L.R. 1498 (inchoate estoppel accepted as binding legatees and intestate successors); *Voyce v. Voyce* (1991) 62 P. & C.R. 290 (inchoate estoppel accepted as binding volunteer donee); *Hopgood v. Brown* [1955] 1 W.L.R. 213, *Ward v. Kirkland* [1967] Ch. 194, *E. R. Ives Investments Ltd. v. High* [1967] 2 Q.B. 379, *J. T. Developments Ltd. v. Quinn* [1991] 2 E.G.L.R. 257, *Ashburn Anstalt v. Arnold* [1989] Ch. 1 (inchoate estoppel accepted as binding purchaser for value); *Plimmer v. City of Wellington Corporation* (1884) 9 App. Cas. 699, *Pennine Raceway Ltd. v. Kirklees Metropolitan Council* [1983] Q.B. 382 (inchoate estoppel accepted as 'interest in land' requiring compensation under compulsory purchase or planning control legislation).

[37] See, e.g. *Rawluk v. Rawluk* (1990) 65 D.L.R. (4th) 161 at 176, per Cory, J., citing Canadian and U.S. academic authority.

[38] *L.A.C. Minerals Ltd. v. International Corona Resources Ltd.* (1989) 61 D.L.R. (4th) 14 at 51, per La Forest, J.

[39] See *Chase Manhattan Bank N.A. v. Israel–British Bank (London) Ltd.* [1981] Ch. 105.

[40] As in *Rawluk v. Rawluk* (1990) 65 D.L.R. (4th) 161.

[41] P. B. H. Birks, *An Introduction to the Law of Restitution* (revised ed., 1989), 375–7 questions the idea that these consequences should come as a package in this way. He labels the ability of a plaintiff to claim the present value of the property in question as the 'second measure' of restitutionary relief, in contrast to the 'first measure', which is the value of the enrichment as originally conferred. He points out that the choice of measure is in principle separate from the question whether the claim, whether to the first or the second measure, should be protected in bankruptcy and against alienees. The courts propounding remedial constructive trusts have paid little atten-

tion to this question, bundling the second measure with these proprietary effects without much thought. It could be said that in this they have allowed themselves to think in terms of the defendant, from the date of the underlying facts, holding particular property *on trust for* the plaintiff, rather than remaining true to the idea that remedial constructive trusts are purely remedies, albeit retrospectively proprietary if awarded. (This criticism is put, for other reasons, by McLachlin, J. in *Rawluk v. Rawluk* (1990) 65 D.L.R. (4th) 161 at 188.) However, there are now signs of fresh thought: see *Peter v. Beblow* (1993) 101 D.L.R. (4th) 621, where the minority seemed prepared to countenance what would in effect be a charge based on the first measure.

[42] See further see G. Elias, *Explaining Constructive Trusts* (1990), 155–68.

[43] The dissentients in *Rawluk v. Rawluk* (1990) 65 D.L.R. (4th) 161 would have withheld the proprietary remedy. McLachlin, J. at 188 criticises the majority for not recognising the element of discretion. An alternative view is that the majority recognised the discretion, but decided, in their discretion, that a proprietary response was appropriate (see per Cory, J. at 176–7).

[44] See G. G. Bogert and G. T. Bogert, *The Law of Trusts and Trustees* (rev. 2nd ed., 1978), para. 472; and *Rawluk v. Rawluk* (1990) 65 D.L.R. (4th) 161 at 185–6, per McLachlin, J. (who appears, however, to be unaware that she is saying anything controversial): 'When the court declares a constructive trust, at that point the beneficiary obtains an interest in the property subject to the trust ... [which] ... may be taken as extending back to the date when the trust was "earned" or perfected. ... The significance of the remedial nature of the constructive trust is not that it cannot confer a property interest, but that the conferring of such an interest is discretionary and dependent on the inadequacy of other remedies for the unjust enrichment in question. ... [E]ven where the tests for constructive trust are met [i.e. an unjust enrichment is found] the property interest does not automatically arise. Rather, the court must consider whether other remedies to remedy the injustice exist which make the declaration of a constructive trust unnecessary or inappropriate.' Note too A. W. Scott and W. F. Fratcher, *The*

remedy under it.[44] On this view, where a remedial constructive trust exists, it will give the same effects as an institutional constructive trust arising upon the same facts; but whereas the institutional constructive trust exists or not as a direct function of a legal rule, the existence or otherwise of the remedial constructive trust depends upon the discretion of a court, normally considering the matter retrospectively. The dominant view, however, is rather that given in the American Law Institute's *Restatement of the Law of Restitution*,[45] that even a remedial constructive trust arises from the operative facts themselves, as a matter of law, and the element of discretion is only as to the grant or refusal of an order for specific restitution in vindication of the trust. On this view, the remedial constructive trust, which is not a creature of discretion,[46] exists independently of the grant or refusal of the remedy, which is discretionary.[47] Remedial constructive trusts so envisaged are differentiated from their institutional counterparts on the following lines. Institutional constructive trusts entitle a beneficiary to curial vindication by proprietary remedy more or less as of right: they are like bankers' drafts, containing the promise of proprietary relief on demand. Remedial constructive trusts, on the other hand, entitle a beneficiary only to ask the court for such a remedy in its discretion: they are like raffle tickets, conferring a chance.[48]

So the discretion of a court over the grant of a remedy is viewed as essential to the idea of a remedial constructive trust. On the one view, this discretion controls the very existence of the trust (whether necessarily from the date of the underlying facts, or possibly from some other time, such as the date of the judgment); on the other view, the trust's existence is automatic but its vindication is discretionary. It is clear, too, that the discretion in question is a relatively wide one. To be sure, that is not obvious on a first reading of the materials. The customary treatment is to say that the characteristic order for proprietary restitution will not be made where an order for personal restitution would be 'adequate'. The *Restatement of Restitution*, indeed, makes it sound as though this means only that the personal order will be used if it makes no difference, but as soon as there is any advantage to the plaintiff in a proprietary order, a personal order will ipso facto not be adequate and she will have ('is entitled to') the proprietary order.[49] There is little, if any, discretion in that position. In fact, however, the idea of adequacy is taken more broadly than that. In its name, proprietary orders are granted or withheld by reference to the relative moral positions of the parties;[50] or by reference to external factors such as, in particular, the damaging effect of a proprietary order on the defendant's other creditors or on third parties with whom the defendant has dealt.[51] In reality, then, 'adequacy' is the deceptively bland name for a clearly normative exercise. In principle, of course, it would be possible to put the refusal of proprietary relief on these multifarious grounds into the form of a collection of rules; but in practice, it is apparent that it is regarded as left to the—it follows very wide—discretion of the court.[52]

Law of Trusts (4th ed., 1989), vol. V, para. 462: the defendant 'is not compelled to convey the property because he is a constructive trustee; it is because he can be compelled to convey it that he is a constructive trustee'; and A. W. Scott (1955), 71 L.Q.R. 39 at 41: 'a constructive trust, unlike an express trust, is a remedial and not a substantive institution. The court does not give relief because a constructive trust has been created; but the court gives relief because otherwise the defendant would be unjustly enriched; and because the court gives this relief it declares that the defendant is chargeable as a constructive trustee.' It is clear, however, that despite these remarks Professor Scott does not adhere to the view to which they point: see n. 45 below.

[45] (1937), pp. 664–5. See also A. W. Scott and W. F. Fratcher, *The Law of Trusts* (4th ed., 1989), vol. V, para. 462.4: this appears to be Professor Scott's considered view, despite the apparently contradictory remarks cited in n. 44 above.

[46] Though remember that it depends on a finding of unjust enrichment, which is discretionary.

[47] On the strength of this, Goulding, J. in *Chase Manhattan Bank N.A.* v. *Israel–British Bank (London) ltd.* [1981] Ch. 105 concludes that the existence of a remedial constructive trust under New York law is a matter of substantive, rather than procedural/remedial law. By way of illustration, in *Knight Newspapers* v. *Comr. of Internal Revenue* 143 F. 2d 1007 (1944) the trustee of a remedial constructive trust was held never to have been the beneficial owner of the property in question, and so not liable to tax upon it, in an action which was not for the property's recovery.

[48] The coherence of this analysis of remedial constructive trusts (though not its existence) is questioned by D. W. M. Waters, in *Equity and Contemporary Legal Developments* (ed. S. Goldstein, 1992), 482–7.

[49] American Law Institute, *Restatement of Restitution* (1937), 665. For an analysis on these lines, see *L.A.C. Minerals Ltd.* v. *International Corona Resources Ltd.* (1989) 61 D.L.R. 14 at 51–2, per La Forest, J.

[50] See *Rawluk* v. *Rawluk* (1990) 65 D.L.R. (4th) 161, where the majority thought the personal order was not adequate, and granted the trust remedy, because it respected her human rights better (per Cory, J., at 177). Note too *L.A.C. Minerals Ltd.* v. *International Corona Resources Ltd.* (1989) 61 D.L.R. (4th) 14 at 51–2, per La Forest, J., that 'the moral quality of the defendants' acts' is a factor in favour of proprietary relief.

[51] See *Rawluk* v. *Rawluk* (1990) 65 D.L.R. (4th) 161 at 187–8, per McLachlin, J., citing D. W. M. Waters, *Law of Trusts in Canada* (2nd ed., 1984), 391–3. See also *L.A.C. Minerals Ltd.* v. *International Corona Resources Ltd.* (1989) 61 D.L.R. 14 at 75–7, per Sopinka, J., and the discussion by D. W. M. Waters (1990), 69 Can. Bar. Rev. 455 at 461–6.

[52] See *Hunter Engineering Co. Inc.* v. *Syncrude Canada Ltd.* (1989) 57 D.L.R. (4th) 321 at 384, per Wilson, J.: the choice of remedy 'is a question to be decided on the facts of each case since the remedy of constructive trust is a discretionary one imposed as and when equity requires it.' See too *L.A.C. Minerals Ltd.* v. *International Corona Resources Ltd.* (1989) 61 D.L.R. 14 at 17, per Wilson, J.; and *Atlas Cabinets and Furniture Ltd.* v. *National Trust Co. Ltd.* (1990) 68 D.L.R. (4th) 161 at 174–5, per Lambert, J. La Forest, J. in *L.A.C. Minerals* at 51 insists that the discretion must be exercised in a structured way, but

There is a further view of remedial constructive trusts, though, which adds an extra element of discretion. It can be seen in the Australian decision, *Muschinski* v. *Dodds.*[53] There, the court was keen to protect third parties who had dealt with the property in question before the time of the judgment, and who would be injured if a constructive trust came into effect from the date of the underlying facts. The court ordered a remedial constructive trust, but explained that it should take effect only from the date of judgment.[54] It seems clear that this dating of the trust was not seen as fixed for all cases, but was selected as apt for this case, in an exercise of what was regarded as a discretion. This approach is favoured by Professor Waters as the way forward for remedial constructive trusts. He argues that a court should be able to deploy the proprietary remedy for unjust enrichment with total discretion as to such issues as from what date the proprietary consequences should flow, and against whom they should be effective, and whether they should include increase in value of the property in question.[55]

The centrality of discretion

We thus arrive at the position that the distinctiveness of remedial constructive trusts from their institutional counterparts is seen as lying in their dependence upon a court's discretion. This discretion is to be found in the initial decision whether to declare an unjust enrichment (or in Australia, though perhaps to a lesser extent, in the decision whether to find a contribution to a failed joint venture). It is also to be found in the consequent decision whether to order proprietary relief (and, at any rate in Australia and in the eyes of Professor Waters, in the details of what the effects of it should be).[56]

Formally, the two discretions lie in tandem.[57] In both practice and general discussion, however, they are often run together, so that the overall effect is of one large discretionary jurisdiction. This further emphasises the centrality of discretion to the way in which remedial constructive trusts are conceived. In *Pettkus* v. *Becker,*[58] for example, Dickson, J. remarks: 'The equitable principle on which the remedy of constructive trust rests is broad and general; its purpose is to prevent unjust enrichment in whatever circumstances it occurs.' And in *Rawluk* v. *Rawluk,*[59] Cory, J. speaks of the U.S. concept of the remedial

---

apparently has a very wide idea of the relevant considerations: at 47–8 he seems to suggest that the encouragement of commercial morality is one.

[53] (1986) 160 C.L.R. 583. There is little sign of this approach in the Canadian authority to date; though cf. *Atlas Cabinets and Furniture Ltd.* v. *National Trust Co. Ltd.* (1990) 68 D.L.R. (4th) 161 at 170, 173, per Lambert, J. A.

[54] See (1986) 160 C.L.R. 583 see at 615, 623, per Deane, J. However, Deane, J. also speaks in terms reminiscent of the Canadian approaches, or even of institutional constructive trusts: 'notwithstanding that the constructive trust is remedial in both origin and nature, there does not need to have been a curial declaration or order before equity will recognise the prior existence of a constructive trust' (at 614). This material seems to lead D. W. M. Waters, in *Equity and Contemporary Legal Developments* (ed. S. Goldstein, 1992) 456 to regard the Australian view of constructive trusts as not truly remedial at all, but that is surely to overlook the actual order in the case.

[55] D. W. M. Waters, in *Equity and Contemporary Legal Developments* (ed. S. Goldstein, 1992), especially 499–505.

[56] This discussion has taken no account of the suggestion by P. B. H. Birks, in *Equity and Contemporary Legal Developments* (ed. S. Goldstein, 1992), 335 et seq., that the proprietary remedy for subtractive restitution should be seen as the resulting, rather than constructive, trust. The focus of the present discussion is the discretionary treatment of (i) what constitutes unjust enrichment and (ii) when proprietary relief is warranted (and what precise form it should take). Birks' discussion deals explicitly with neither. He presumably assumes his own (non-discretionary) theory as regards unjust enrichment. As to proprietary response, he proposes that it should lie (i.e. a resulting trust should arise) upon the trigger of 'a situation in which the transfer was not intended to enure to the transferee's benefit'. Yet he senses that this is over-inclusive, as embracing ordinary breach of contract where there has been a prepayment: to give proprietary relief here would massively disrupt the accustomed handling of insolvency. He first seeks a more refined definition of the trigger, which would exclude the problem, but admits to finding this difficult (loc. cit. at 357–9). In the end, he proposes that the resulting trust should discontinue in the problem case, as a matter of policy (loc. cit. at 362). There is arguably a whiff of discretion about this presentation, but Birks would be equally entitled to say that his position could be readily cast into a firm rule.

[57] See *L.A.C. Minerals Ltd.* v. *International Corona Resources Ltd.* (1989) 61 D.L.R. (4th) 14 at 48, per La Forest, J.' *Atlas Cabinet and Furniture Ltd.* v. *National Trust Co. Ltd.* (1990) 68 D.L.R. (4th) 161 at 174, per Lambert, J. A. Canadian law recognises an intermediate step between them: that a proprietary order cannot be made unless the defendant presently holds property 'causally connected' with her enrichment by the plaintiff: see *Pettkus* v. *Becker* (1980) 117 D.L.R. (3d) 257 at 277; *Sorochan* v. *Sorochan* (1986) 29 D.L.R. (4th) 1 at 8 ff. In practice, however, the Canadian cases takes a discretionary approach to this as well. Dickson, C. J. in *Sorochan* v. *Sorochan* at 10 comments that the requirement of causal connection too is to be viewed with 'flexibility', so as 'to ensure equitable and fair relief in the myriad of familial circumstances and situations where unjust enrichment occurs.' In *Peter* v. *Beblow* (1993) 101 D.L.R. (4th) 621 McLachlin, J. is ostensibly exigent about the requirement (at [10–11]), but in fact takes an extremely cavalier approach to assessing it (at [15]); while Cory, J. argues that the required connection should be 'inferred' in family property cases (at [25–6, and 27]), and a constructive trust imposed so as to achieve 'equity and fairness' (at [28–9]). Cory, J. seems close to disputing the rightness of the requirement at all, as opposed to an approach of imposing a trust in favour of the plaintiff on any property of the defendant, in the way of a charge. This is not in fact unthinkable: see *Space Investments Ltd.* v. *Canadian Imperial Bank of Commerce Trust Co. (Bahamas) Ltd.* [1986] 3 All E.R. 75 at 77.

[58] (1980) 117 D.L.R. (3d) 257 at 276. Note also the way in which Dickson, J. in *Pettkus* v. *Becker* (1980) 117 D.L.R. (3d) 257 at 273 and McLachlin, J. in *Rawluk* v. *Rawluk* (1990) 65 D.L.R. (4th) 161 at 186 cite *Moses* v. *Macferlan* (1760) 2 Burr 1005 at 1012 as authority for the discretionary nature of remedial constructive trusts: when Lord Mansfield, C. J. was speaking only of the discretionary nature (as he apparently saw it) of the notion of unjust enrichment itself.

[59] (1990) 65 D.L.R. (4th) 161q at 169–70.

constructive trust as 'a broad restitutionary device that could be invoked in a wide variety of situations to compel the transfer of property to a claimant by the defendant in order to prevent the unjust enrichment of the title holder.' The same judge continues:[60] 'The review of the cases decided by this court from *Murdoch* v. *Murdoch*[61] to *Sorochan* v. *Sorochan*[62] demonstrates the importance that has been attached to the use of the remedy of constructive trust to achieve a division of property that is as just and equitable as possible.' And in *Hunter Engineering Co. Inc.* v. *Syncrude Canada Ltd.*,[63] Wilson, J., asserting that 'unjust enrichment giving rise to a constructive trust' is not confined to family cases, comments: 'Indeed, to do so would be to impede the growth and impair the flexibility crucial to the development of equitable principles.'[64]

II. Thinking About Discretion

The remedial constructive trust is thus essentially a jurisdiction to decide, as a matter of discretion, whether to identify a situation as warranting a disgorgement order with proprietary effect. In a moment we shall reflect upon the desirability of the law maintaining such a phenomenon. But to prepare ourselves, we must develop a proper understanding of what we mean by discretion, and by its conventional opposite, rules.

Rules and discretions: blurring the contrast

The discussion so far has assumed a sharp contract between rules and discretions. It is becoming orthodox to note, however, that such discussions are unreal. In reality, the distinction between rules and discretions is by no means an absolute one. It is rather a matter of degree: a matter of the adjudicative process being more or less constrained, but never totally constrained or unconstrained. And even when that truth is absorbed, it is important to realise that, to do its business, the law uses a mixture of relatively constrained and relatively unconstrained

devices.

Imagine, for example, an area of law which appears to consist purely of rules.[65] In reality, rules do not exist which dictate the legal response in every case. The first point here is a scepticism whether such rules could exist even in theory, given the necessary use of language to convey them. So it is standard to see legal rules as comprising a core of relatively settled significance, surrounded by a greater or smaller penumbra of more doubtful significance.[66] But there are other sources of indeterminacy besides this. For example, even the apparently routine application of settled rules depends on the finding of particular facts, and fact-finding will reflect the individual approach of the fact-finder,[67] and differences in the resources, attitudes, and activities of the parties. Whether or not those concerned are aware of the latitude inherent in what they are doing, the process involves discretions (not only of the judge) which condition the ultimate legal response.[68] Further, one can also reflect that the greater the complexity of the rule or set of rules involved, the wider the range of results which could plausibly be derived from them. Such a state of affairs once more leaves the judge to exercise choice, again with some influence from the inputs of the parties, as to the standard which will in fact decide the case. It would be wrong to exaggerate, of course. The upshot is not that judges are merely loose cannons. The image of core and penumbra can usefully be deployed regarding matters such as fact-finding and the handling of complex rules too, and the element of core must not be underestimated. But the point remains that *complete* fixity of standards is illusory. The reality is that legal response is not, and cannot be, generated in the manner contemplated by a pure model of rules, but involves a substantial element of discretion.

Coming at the matter from the other direction though, the modern orthodoxy is that even overt discretions do not generate complete fluidity of standards. The most radical statement to this effect is

---

[60] Ibid. at 180.

[61] (1973) 412 D.L.R. (3d) 367.

[62] (1986) 29 D.L.R. (4th) 1.

[63] (1989) 57 D.L.R. 321 at 383; approved in *L.A.C. Minerals Ltd.* v. *International Corona Resources Ltd.* (1989) 61 D.L.R. 14 at 49, per La Forest, J.

[64] The approach of general flexibility is noted, with disapproval, by McLachlin, J. in *Peter* v. *Beblow* . . . at [6].

[65] See K. O. Hawkins, in *The Uses of Discretion* (ed. K. O. Hawkins, 1992), 35–8.

[66] So, in the present discussion, it has been asserted that the concept of unjust enrichment as used in the Canadian cases represents a discretion. Yet to say 'where there is unjust enrichment, give restitution' sounds like a rule. The point is that, at any rate as those cases use it, the meaning of 'unjust enrichment' is substantially open.

[67] For a striking example in the material under discussion, see the division of the British Columbia Court of Appeal over the facts in *Atlas Cabinets and Furniture Ltd.* v. *National Trust Co. ltd.* (1990) 68 D.L.R. (4th) 161. See also S. Gardner (1993), 109 L.Q.R. 263, arguing that the impact of remedial constructive trusts in the family property sphere has been achieved only by fabricating the necessary facts. (Although remedial constructive trusts are avowedly discretionary, it has never, of course, been suggested that their invocation confers a special licence to invent facts.)

[68] For a discussion of fact-finding as discretion, see D. J. Galligan, *Discretionary Powers* (1986), 33–7.

[69] See particularly R. M. Dworkin, *Taking Rights Seriously* (1977), 31–9, 68–71. Dworkin has returned to the subject, without apparently a major change of position, in *Law's Empire* (1986), especially ch. 7.

that of Professor Dworkin.[69] He argues that judicial discretions, properly understood, never do more than require the judge to interpret a fixed standard in order to apply it. He contends that this process of interpretation and application is itself governed by fixed standards which are discernible in the surrounding law. It should therefore not entail any latitude as to the law's response, but on the contrary should lead merely to the enunciation of the single right answer. On this view, there seems in fact to be no substantive (as opposed to formal) space between rules and discretions, the latter being assimilated to the former. This account, however, may seem unsatisfying. It is far from clear that judicial discretions, whether statutory or common law, are seen by either legislatures or the judges themselves as never leaving the judges to settle their own standards. And more fundamentally, it seems implausible that there is a single right way of interpreting and applying open-textured standards, to be discovered in the values of the surrounding law: if anything, the extant law seems to reflect the tension between a plurality of competing values.[70]

However, a powerful body of sociological material has grown up over recent years which also concludes that discretions are in practice usually constrained.[71] The message of this material is less grandiose than Dworkin's, because it makes no claim as to what the constraining factors should be. The central idea is that when a person exercises discretion over some issue as a matter of routine, they will often tend to develop a set of standards by which the cases coming before them classify themselves as 'good' or 'bad', and the outcome follows accordingly. They will thus view themselves as having much less discretion than a reading of the enabling rule would lead one to suppose.[72] Various sources have been identified for this tendency. One group would include simple laziness; a desire for, or pressure to deliver, productivity; and a sense that like cases ought to be treated alike. Constraints of this kind would predicate the disposal of cases by more or less automatic reference to particular criteria, but would have little to say about what those criteria should be. Another group of influences would come at the matter from the other direction, emphasising the claim of particular matters to be the criteria which decide the outcomes of discretionary decisions. This group would include structural fac-

tors such as background culture, training, socialisation, and the occupation of a position within an organisation with certain traditional standards, whether the decision-maker or indeed the organisation was conscious of these or not.

This broad point, however, conceals a considerable range of truths. At one extreme, it may sometimes be possible to predict the actual pattern of outcomes by reference to such factors. For example, work shows that the various discretions of the criminal process—over arrest, prosecution, plea-bargaining, conviction, sentencing—are exercised in a highly regular manner, by reference to the proximity of the accused's relationship with the victim; the accused's respectability; and the accused's social status.[73] At the other extreme, structural conditioning may sometimes increase, rather than reduce, the extent of discretion. For example, immediately after the Judicature Act 1875 some English judges sought to maintain the individuality of equity after the fusion with the common law by emphasising the discretionary nature of equitable doctrines.[74] More generally, some judges appear to cultivate an image as free spirits, or innovators: perhaps because of their relationship with other members of the court, or with an eye to promotion, or to popular acclaim.

Maintaining critical distinction

So the operation of rules involves discretion, and the operation of discretion involves rules. It is important, however, not to allow this perception to lull us into thinking that there are therefore no further distinctions to be drawn, or choices to be made.

In the first place, the blurring of the contrast between rules and discretions does not mean that everything reduces to a single point midway between the two. It is clear that some areas of decision are more constrained than others:[75] that there remain separable ideas of 'rules' and 'discretion' as a matter of substance. The point is simply that the question whether a decision is governed by a rule or a discretion in this substantive sense (i.e. the question of the degree of constraint upon it) does not necessarily correlate with the presence of a rule or a discretion in the formal sense of those words, based on the appearance of the thing. (In what follows, we shall need to be careful to distinguish between the two sense. It is hoped that the context will make the mat-

[70] Cf. D. J. Galligan, *Discretionary Powers* (1986), 14–20. See too e.g. N. E. Simmonds and D. Howarth, in *Jurisprudence: Cambridge Essays* (ed. H. Gorss and R. Harrison, 1992).

[71] See generally K. O. Hawkins, in *The Uses of Discretion* (ed. K. O. Hawkins, 1992), 38–44; C. E. Schneider, ibid., 79–87; D. J. Galligan, *Discretionary Powers* (1986), 128–37.

[72] See R. Lempert, in *The Uses of Discretion* (ed. K. O. Hawkins, 1992), ch. 6; also D. J. Galligan, *Discretionary Powers*

(1986), 12–14.

[73] See M. P. Baumgartner, in *The Uses of Discretion* (ed. K. O. Hawkins, 1992), ch. 4.

[74] See S. Gardner (1987), 7 O.J.L.S. 60.

[75] D. J. Galligan, *Discretionary Powers* (1986), 11–14, argues plausibly that constraint is a matter of degree, rather than wholly present or absent; disagreeing with the view presented by R. M. Dworkin, *Taking Rights Seriously* (1977).

ter clear.) Moreover, it is certainly meaningful to discuss the question of how constrained or unconstrained we want legal determinations to be.

And we must also retain our sense of a second distinction. There are clearly differences in the derivation and content of the various constraints. The regularising factors which the sociologists have identified as constraining apparent discretions are not necessarily disclosed, may lack democratic derivation, and may be normatively improper. For example, there is evidence that the various determinations required by the criminal justice process are conditioned, sub silentio, by the face of the accused person.[76] Even if they constrain decisions in the same way, standards such as these are evidently to be differentiated from those established by public legislation.

The value of rules

Certain desiderata are promoted when the adjudication of some matter is relatively constrained—that is, when it is governed by a rule, in the substantive sense of the word. Many, though perhaps not all, of these desiderata are located under the idea of the Rule of Law.[77]

Constraining adjudication promotes judicial efficiency, and also consistency of decision-making, so that like cases are treated alike, and unlike cases differently. These are important benefits which can be claimed for all adjudication based on rules. There may be further benefits too, but these depend on the source and nature of the operative constraints. When the constraints are publicly known, they typically allow those affected by the branch of law in question to plan their activities with assurance so as to prevent disputes arising, and also so as to resolve them efficiently if they do arise. When the constraint lies in private regularising factors, however, this will not be the case. When the constraint has been developed by a respectable procedure, such as by legislation or judicial articulation, a high degree of rationality can also be claimed for the outcomes indicated, in that these outcomes have been determined on the basis of sustained thought and experience and collective wisdom. This will not necessarily be the case, however, where the constraint lies in private, even unconscious, regularising factors, for the rationality of these factors may itself be suspect.

The desiderata are thus delivered to some extent where adjudication is relatively constrained, though this delivery is not always perfect, and in particular may be compromised where the constraint does not lie in the lines of a publicly legislated prescription. On the other hand, the desiderata are certainly prejudiced, albeit perhaps to differing extents, when the adjudication is relatively unconstrained. Then, the judge is left to weigh matters on the day, which is less efficient. Like cases are less likely to be treated alike, and unlike cases differently. Those affected by the law in question are not helped to plan with assurance to prevent disputes arising, or to resolve them efficiently if they do arise. And only a lesser degree of rationality can be claimed for outcomes.

The value of discretion

It might be assumed from this that although governance by rules is not perfect, relatively unconstrained adjudication—that is, adjudication by discretion (in the substantive sense)—is certainly an embarrassment which, if ineradicable, should at least be kept to a minimum. That position is a tenable, and indeed a common, one, but it is not inevitable. It is founded on certain assumptions, which are the assumptions of liberal modernism. The contributions of the Marxists and the post-modernists teach us to query the inevitability of these assumptions as a matter of principle, and their cultural transience may be seen in other nations' operation of non-liberal political systems and in earlier Western legal systems' resort to mysticism. Even if one ranges less widely, however, and is content to maintain a liberal modernist rubric, the primacy of constrained adjudication is not inevitable. One might say that although the considerations favouring it are desirable, they may not be all-important: so that in principle they could be outweighed by countervailing advantages of discretion. What are these advantages?

The main argument for discretion takes as its basis the idea that the law, when it deals with a type of situation, aims to promote some purpose. For example, the rule that we must buy a television licence has the purpose of funding the B.B.C. The argument then proceeds with the notion that the law's purpose may sometimes be better promoted if it is not procrustenated into a rule but left as a discretion. That is, 'substantive rationality' is seen as more effective than 'formal rationality'.[78] This is classically seen as the case where the factors relevant to the achievement of the purpose are complicated, and trying to express the right path through them in the form of a rule would

---

[76] R. Hood, *Race and Sentencing* (1992).

[77] See e.g. D. J. Galligan, *Discretionary Powers* (1986), 61–4; C. E. Schneider, in *The Uses of Discretion* (ed. K. O. Hawkins, 1992), 68–79; cf. N. Lacey, ibid. 368–70.

[78] The terms come from M. Weber, *Economy and Society* (ed. G. Roth and C. Wittick, 1978). For a discussion, see D. J. Galligan, *Discretionary Powers* (1986), 64–72.

either be too difficult, or likely to lead to results significantly at variance with the underlying purpose.[79] There are shadings to this point. For example, the putative rule might be clearly inappropriate, leading to 'rule-compromise discretion'; or there might be a hope that such a rule might emerge, but a feeling that experience on the ground would help to clarify its shape, leading to 'rule-building discretion'.[80]

It has been observed that the need for this kind of discretionary response is more common in, and associated with the needs of, modern societies with an active State. Such societies generate a 'public law' culture, to which discretions are natural, in contrast to the 'private law' approach centred on rules.[81] They do so for a variety of reasons, including the point that the legislature is too busy to stop and formulate clear rules; the point that the politicians distrust the formal legal process as not necessarily sympathetic to their aims, and prefer to keep the implementation of their purpose in the more responsive hands of their own officials; and the point that today's societies are so complex, and the active State's goals so sophisticated, that implementing them often requires considerable fine-tuning on the ground.[82] At the same time, it has also been suggested that substantive rationality is generally more fashionable nowadays than it once was, a discretionary approach being favoured also in areas away from State activity—the domain of 'private law' treatment, whose natural currency is rules.[83] It may be debated whether this development is a product of the foregoing; it may at any rate perhaps be seen as reflecting a sense that even the traditionally 'private law' aspects of society demand a more complex appreciation and handling than they formerly received.

Finally, a distinct phenomenon is the use of discretions to promote some end other than furthering or settling the law's ostensible purpose. That is, the legislative purpose might be clear, and it might be admitted that the purpose could be promoted as well, if not better, by a rule than by a discretion; but a discretion is still preferred for some collateral reason. To prefer discretion for a collateral reason in this way is not necessarily discreditable: the collateral reason might well be as valid a desideratum as the purpose of the rule or discretion itself. Such a collateral reason might, for example, be a wish to see the parties themselves play a greater role in the resolution of legal questions affecting them. Investing the adjudicator with discretion would help foster a creative dialogue between the adjudicator and the parties, when a rule would keep everyone at arms' length.[84] Another collateral reason might be a wish to husband scarce appellate resources. Coupled with a régime whereby questions of law (rules) may be appealed whilst discretionary decisions may not,[85] the use of discretions rather than rules will result in more cases stopping at first instance level.[86] A third example might be a desire to keep the advisory and advocacy work associated with some legal question in the hands of a particular professional group. Where the question is governed by a discretion, practitioners who regularly operate in the area concerned are likely to be much more efficient and successful than outsiders at divining the likely outcome:[87] the advantage seems likely to be much smaller where the question is governed by a rule. Assuming (as seems plausible) that clients will perceive this point, governance by discretion rather than rule will have the effect of creating a de facto monopoly over the work

---

[79] See C. E. Schneider, in *The uses of Discretion* (ed. K. O. Hawkins, 1992), 62–6; D. J. Galligan, *Discretionary Powers* (1986), chs. 3 and 4.

[80] The terms come from C. E. Schneider, loc. cit. n. 79.

[81] The terms are those of D. J. Galligan, *Discretionary Powers* (1986), 86–8.

[82] See further D. J. Galligan, *Discretionary Powers* (1986), 72–80, 85–8.

[83] See e.g. R. M. Unger, *Law in Modern Society* (1976); P. S. Atiyah, *From Principles to Pragmatism: Changes in the Function of the Judicial Process and the Law* (1978); G. H. Treitel, *Doctrine and Discretion in the Law of Contract* (1981); F. Schauer (1987), 85 Michigan L.R. 847. For discussion, see D. J. Galligan, *Discretionary Powers* (1986), 80–1; C. E. Schneider, in *The Uses of Discretion* (ed. K. O. Hawkins, 1992), 58–60.

[84] See especially J. Handler, in *The Uses of Discretion* (ed. K. O. Hawkins, 1992), ch. 10. Similarly, note how recent decisions in criminal law have often left normative questions of criminal law to the jury (e.g. *R. v. Ghosh* [1982] Q.B. 1053, rendered still more important by *R. v. Gomez* [1992] 3 W.L.R. 1067): the jury being seen as representatives of the public, the public became participants in the criminal process.

[85] Which is intelligible, since (pace Dworkin) where discretion rather than a rule is involved there is no right to a single, 'correct' outcome.

[86] This point may be visible in e.g. *George Mitchell (Chesterhall) Ltd. v. Finney Lock Seeds Ltd.* [1983] 2 A.C. 803, on 'reasonableness' in the Unfair Contracts Terms Act 1977. It may also have affected the development in criminal law mentioned in n. 84: leaving matters in the discretion of the jury helps make convictions 'appeal-proof', as minimising the danger of misdirection.

[87] See M. Galanter (1974), 9 Law and Society Review 95.

[88] This may have been a factor in the flowering of discretion in late nineteenth century English equity, after the Judicature Acts had formally admitted common lawyers to this material: in practice, the emphasis upon discretion would have tended to confine the work to the Chancery specialists. See S. Gardner (1987), 7 O.J.L.S. 60. (It may be speculated whether a similar phenomenon has not been operating in the law of New South Wales since its amalgamation of courts of law and equity in 1972.) Is the same idea also to be seen in the very discretionary handling of judicial review in the modern law? Indeed, *O'Reilly v. Mackman* [1983] 2 A.C. 237 may be seen as confirming the effect; *Roy v. Kensington and Chelsea and Westminster Family Practitioner Committee* [1992] 2 W.L.R. 239 as some attempt by the excluded group to recapture some of the territory thus monopolised. More generally, discretion may set a premium on the work of the Bar, by reducing the law's accessibility to solicitors.

III. The Use of Discretion in Remedial Constructive Trusts

With these insights into the phenomena of rules and discretions, let us return now to assess the discretions which we saw earlier to be essential to remedial constructive trusts. We can straightaway be more precise about the nature of those discretions. The meaning of 'unjust enrichment', and also of its Australian counterpart, does not (quite) formally involve a discretion. That is, the law does not (quite) announce on its face that the matter rests with the judge in the individual case. By contrast, the question whether proprietary relief should issue (and, perhaps, what form it should take) is formally put into discretion: the leading authorities are quite explicit that this is so. But we can now understand that these formal presentations do not tell us one way or the other whether there is a substantive discretion, in either of the two facets of the matter. The formal presentation of unjust enrichment as bound by rules is not conclusive, because the rules might be so open-textured as in reality to confer a discretion. In fact, we saw earlier that this is indeed the case. Equally, both that discretion and the one which is formally announced regarding the issue of proprietary relief might in reality be constrained by factors which are not declared on the fact of the law. In that case, the law's handling of this area would, substantively speaking, be conducted by rules after all.

So far as that goes, it seems reasonably clear that the judges who have shaped this area do see it as relatively unconstrained: that is, as involving genuine substantive discretions. That does not, however, mean that in practice it necessarily is. There might be constraints which the judges do not readily acknowledge. In exercising the discretions, for example, the judges will almost inevitably be subject to constraints arising from factors such as their upbringing (do they tend to come from a particular section of society?), training (to what kinds of philosophies are they exposed?), and socialisation (is the Bench heavily influenced by the values of the Bar?). There is no doubt much to be said on this theme in every jurisdiction. The task is perhaps best left to those imbued in the affairs of the jurisdiction in question, and will not be taken further here. But if, after reflection on these lines, we do not like what we see, one response might be to recast the law into legislated rules, so that the constraints are settled overtly and democratically.

As a result of such background influences, it may be that there is very little substantive discretion left about this area of the law. But let us take it that that is not the case, and that we can still meaningfully detect discretion in the law regarding remedial constructive trusts. The task now is to decide whether the law is well advised to deploy discretion here, or whether it would do better to use rules (in the substantive sense) instead. As we have seen, the central point of using discretion rather than rules is that discretion offers a better means than a rule of promoting some purpose of the law: here, the proprietary remedying of unjust enrichment. At the same time, we should remember that there might be some collateral object as well as or instead of this purpose. There might, for example, be pressure on appellate resources, or monopolistic tendencies by the Bar or sections of the Bar, in a particular jurisdiction, and the use of discretion in remedial constructive trusts might be a response to that. If so, the validity of this object would need to be considered, as well as the question whether it is well served by remedial constructive trusts. But again, this work would be best undertaken by those familiar with the jurisdiction. We shall confine ourselves to assessing the central proposition, that the proprietary remedying of unjust enrichment is best served by the individualised treatment which discretion offers.

Before coming to that, though, we should briefly look sideways at institutional constructive trusts. By contrast with remedial constructive trusts, these are thought to be characterised by their use of rules rather than discretions. We can use our new understanding to assess this idea. It is reasonably clear that institutional constructive trusts are, at least for the most part, presented as governed by rules.[89] But that only tells us about the formal aspect of the matter. If the rules are open-textured, the law might substantively proceed by discretion (depending on the extent to which the discretion was constrained by unannounced factors). As might be expected, the relevant rules vary on this matter, but certainly, many of the most prominent ones contain major points of open texture. Consider, for example, the uncertainty as to the import of the doctrine 'equity will not permit a statute to be used as an instrument of fraud';[90] the invention of agreements regarding family property;[91] the variable import of the doctrine of notice,

---

[89] Thus in *Rawluk* v. *Rawluk* (1990) 65 D.L.R. (4th) 161 at 183–4, McLachlin, J. speaks of 'the traditional English view of the constructive trust as a limited doctrine applying in limited, clearly defined cases.'

[90] See especially D. R. Hodge [1980], Conv. 341 (the mean-

ing of 'fraud'); and J. D. Feltham [1987], Conv. 246, and T. G. Youdan [1988], Conv. 267 (the response once 'fraud' is discovered).

[91] As in *Grant* v. *Edwards* [1986] Ch. 638.

as used in tracing;[92] and the uncertain principles governing the choice between 'first in, first out' and pari passu reckoning as between the claims of innocent contributors to a mixture of trust funds.[93] Moreover, even when it is established that a person has rights under an institutional constructive trust, there must be a degree of discretion as to whether she be awarded an actual remedy in vindication of those rights.[94] At the end of the day, then, this alleged difference between remedial and institutional constructive trusts is at least somewhat ephemeral. But that need not detain us. It really does not matter whether so-called remedial constructive trusts are detectably different from their so-called institutional counterparts. What does matter is whether the law's use of remedial constructive trusts—that is, its approaching the proprietary response to unjust enrichment by discretion rather than rules—is commendable or not. It is to this question that we now come.

Should 'proprietary response to unjust enrichment' be a matter of discretion?

There is certainly nothing self-evident or inevitable about the use of discretion in this context. As we have seen, the authorities envisage two discretions in tandem: one over the finding of unjust enrichment, the other over the grant (and perhaps the fashioning) of proprietary relief. But a loose view of each of these matters is famously and vehemently opposed by Professor Birks.[95] Each could in principle be governed by rules, and Birks puts forward very detailed proposals as to what those rules should be. To some extent, the rules are already there, in the shape of concrete rationes decidendi of authoritative judicial decisions (or statutory provisions). However, there are also very large areas of the subject—especially the definition of unjust enrichment—regarding which matters are currently more fluid. This is certainly true in England, and seems so too in Australia and even common law Canada. But that does not mean that that is how matters will remain. The gaps could (and in Birks' view should) be filled by the development of such rules, rather than by continuing discretion.

That, for example, is how Lord Goff apparently saw the future in his two recent essays in the field.[96] But he also seemed to envisage that such rules will develop incrementally. As they do so, it would not be inaccurate to say that the judges will be exercising a discretion. But this discretion is of the rule-building variety. Rule-building discretion suffers from the same problems, considered above, as all other discretion. It differs, however, in that these problems are essentially transient: a temporary price which must be paid for the development of sound rules for the future.

One can find portraits of the Canadian material in terms of rule-building discretion. In particular, the rule-building rubric seems to be the thrust of Professor Waters' remark that the task of the courts in the area under discussion is 'to continue sharpening the edges of the criteria which must be satisfied before the claimant can obtain constructive trust relief'.[97] Apparently to similar effect, Professor Waters has also written that remedial constructive trusts, founded in unjust enrichment, are to be contrasted with Lord Denning's 'new model' constructive trust, founded on justice and conscience. ' "Justice and conscience" is a more uncertain perimeter to constructive trust intervention than is unjust enrichment. What the courts in Canada have now to do . . . is to determine what are unjust enrichment situations, as the courts determined duty of care situations after the formulation of the principle of negligence liability in Donoghue v. Stevenson[98] in

---

[92] Especially after *Polly Peck International Plc.* v. *Nadir* (*No. 2*) [1992] 4 All E.R. 769 at 781–2.

[93] See *Barlow Clowes International Ltd.* v. *Vaughan* [1992] 4 All E.R. 22.

[94] She would lose her remedy, for example, if she came to court with unclean hands. Cf. the old material discussed in *Tinsley* v. *Milligan* [1993] 3 All E.R. 65.

[95] P. B. H. Birks, *An Introduction to the Law of Restitution* (revised ed., 1989), especially 19 (unjust enrichment) and 378 (proprietary relief). See too R. Goff and G. Jones, *The Law of Restitution* (3rd Ed., 1986), 12–16.

[96] *Woolwich Building Society* v. *I.R.C.* (*No. 2*) [1992] 3 All E.R. 737 at 764; *Lipkin Gorman* v. *Karpnale Ltd.* [1922] 4 All E.R. 512 at 534.

[97] D. W. M. Waters, in *Where is Equity Going? Remedying Unconscionable Conduct* (1987); cited in *Baumgartner* v. *Baumgartner* (1987) 164 C.L.R. 137 at 153–4. Waters' view may have changed, however. In his more recent contribution, in *Equity and Contemporary Legal Developments* (ed. S. Goldstein, 1992), 457, he seems to envisage a jurisdiction involving more discretion (notably, over the date from which and the parties against whom, proprietary effect should operate); and

he seems to envisage that this discretion would be enduring rather than rule-building. However, he does not consider the matter explicitly; and it would certainly not be impossible for him to say that, although he is arguing for more variables in the incidence of remedial constructive trusts, he wants the choices over these variables to be eventually handled by rules.

[98] [1932] A.C. 562. The analogy with negligence is a favourite theme of commentators on remedial constructive trusts. Professor Waters' use of it here is slightly unusual. It is more commonly aimed at showing unjust enrichment as a generic, open-textured cause of action, rather than merely an umbrella term for a collection of separate rules: much as *Donoghue* v. *Stevenson*, *Dorset Yacht Co. Ltd.* v. *Home Office* [1970] A.C. 1004, and *Anns* v. *Merton L.B.C.* [1978] A.C. 728 depict negligence. For this approach, see P. D. Maddaugh and J. D. McCamus, *The Law of Restitution* (1990), 23–5, and G. B. Klippert, *Unjust Enrichment* (1983), ch. 2. But Waters' treatment of the open texture of unjust enrichment as a stage on the way to more a concrete formulation, was to receive its negligence echo in the way that those decisions have now been overtaken by *Murphy* v. *Brentwood D.C.* [1991] 1 A.C. 398.

1932. ... [Most] existing constructive trust situations can be reconciled with the principle of unjust enrichment prevention, as the *Restatement [of Restitution]* and the American literature show, and in charting the future Canadians have the advantage of fifty past years of American experience and precedent, whatever course we choose to pursue. Much charting has been done, and the shoals observed.'[99]

The judgments in the leading Canadian decisions themselves, however, do little to support this view that they are engaged in rule-building.[100] There is certainly little evidence that the judges concerned are looking forward to a time of sharper delineation. On the contrary, there is evidence that they regard the discretions involved in remedial constructive trusts to be wholesome for their own sake.[101] In particular, this position forms part of the ratio decidendi of *Rawluk* v. *Rawluk*.[102] The question there was whether the common law response of a remedial constructive trust based on unjust enrichment should continue to be deployed in family property cases, when a new legislative régime of community property had been introduced by the Ontario Family Law Act 1986. McLachlin, J., dissenting, argues that it should not. Her judgment contains forceful expressions of the discretionary quality of remedial constructive trusts, but she is clear that the discretions were aimed at rule-building, and she believes that with the advent of the 1986 Act the rules must now be considered built. Given this, in her view, the remedial constructive trust should bow out, its discretion being no longer appropriate.[103] But the majority decided otherwise. In their view, the common law should continue to be used, because, per Cory, J.: 'It enables the courts to bring that treasured and essential measure of individualized justice and fairness to the more generalized process of equalization provided by the Act.'[104] Employing this discretion, it was felt right to award a remedial constructive trust, giving the claimant more generous relief than the statutory régime would have done.

Cory, J. is clearly thinking not in terms of rule-building discretion. Instead, he is claiming that discretions are enduringly more apt than rules to

resolving the type of case in question. This is a more difficult position than that of McLachlin, J. Where discretion is employed to build rules, it may be conceded that it is not ideal, but its disadvantages may be put down as a temporary price worth paying. Where discretion is intended to be a permanent feature of the area of law in question, that is not possible. In this case, it must be shown that discretion is positively the better approach. Is that claim sustainable?

Family property cases

The answer may depend on the context in which the remedial constructive trust is to be deployed. The classic type of case to which these trusts have been applied—as in *Rawluk* v. *Rawluk*[105] itself—is of course the dispute over family property on the breakdown of the relationship. Discretionary resolution is par excellence the technique of family law, which characteristically presents complex, variable situations where the best way to achieve the legislative aim is arguably to juggle with the circumstances of the parties in close, individualised detail. That seems as true with property questions as with others. In particular, taking a discretionary approach to unjust enrichment in this context may be a way of dealing with what is otherwise a very difficult problem.[106] A standard libertarian analysis, which is enshrined in the authorities, tells us that there is either no enrichment to be discovered, or that it is not unjust for one to be retained, where the plaintiff does work for the defendant not intending to recoup for it, or where the defendant, accepting the work (reasonably), does not understand the plaintiff to expect recompense. We may well feel content with such thinking where the parties are in an arm's-length relationship, when they can be expected to look out for their own interests. In a family context, however, that is not the case. Where parties in such relationships do work for each other, but have no developed thoughts of its recompensability, we may feel that it is unsatisfactory to withhold relief. For such people cannot be expected to look out for themselves: on the contrary, they have committed

[99] D. W. M. Waters, *Law of Trusts in Canada* (2nd ed., 1984), 393.
[100] This is noted, relatively agnostically, in P. D. Maddaugh and J. D. McCamus, *The Law of Restitution* (1990), 21–7; and G. B. Klippert, *Unjust Enrichment* (1983), ch. 2.
[101] See e.g. *James More & Sons Ltd.* v. *University of Ottawa* (1974) 49 D.L.R. (3d) 666 at 676, per Morden, J.: 'Where a court, on proper grounds, holds that the doctrine of restitution is applicable, it is not necessary to fit the case into some exact category, apparently established by a previous decision, giving effect to the doctrine. Just as the categories of negligence are never closed, neither can those of restitution [*sic*]. The principles take precedence over the illustrations or examples of their application.'

[102] (1990) 65 D.L.R. (4th) 161.
[103] (1990) 65 D.L.R. (4th) 161 at 189–91: 'Both the statutory remedy and the remedy of constructive trust are on the facts of this case, directed to the same end. ... The scheme under the Act is relatively clear and simple. ... Grafting the remedy of constructive trust on to this scheme would add uncertainty and promote litigation. ... Note also McLachlin, J.'s concern at the discretionary employment of proprietary relief for unjust enrichment in *Peter* v. *Beblow* (1993) 101 D.L.R. (4th) 621, 643–4.'
[104] (190) 65 D.L.R. (4th) 161 at 181.
[105] (1990) 65 D.L.R. (4th) 161.
[106] What follows is developed at greater length in S. Gardner (1993), 109 L.Q.R. 263.

199

themselves to trust and collaborate with one another. This commitment may therefore be seen as taking the place of thoughts as to recompense in the establishment of an unjust enrichment. But (at any rate outside marriage) the identification of trust and collaboration in a relationship, and the attribution of a given item of work to these values, is not a clear-cut matter. The exercise may thus be best served by leaving the judge the discretion to take the measure of the situation in the round, with a view to seeing whether such a non-libertarian restitutionary response seems warranted. So although one might query the advisability of maintaining the common law régime as a rider upon a statutory one, as in *Rawluk* v. *Rawluk*,[107] in principle is it unsurprising that the law should approach family property disputes via a discretion.[108]

But such a discretionary approach is less apt where, broadly, it is important that people should know their legal position independently of proceedings in court. This is classically seen as exemplified by the case of the purchaser of (or grantee of some right in) the property in question. If the property is held to have been the subject of a constructive trust at the time of the sale, the transaction will be upset. If there is doubt as to the circumstances in which this will occur, it can be said that there is injustice to the individual purchaser who is thus caught unawares, and damage to the economy in that future potential purchasers of similarly-circumstanced property will fight shy, or will have to incur increased transaction costs in trying to evaluate the situation which confronts them. So the conclusion is that the law should avoid using discretions where commerce would be affected in this way, and instead use rules, so that those concerned know better where they stand the problems would be reduced.

Unfortunately, a case can both be a family property dispute, so demanding discretion, and involve questions of commerce, so calling for rules. For example, the property at the centre of a family dispute may

well have been mortgaged. The Canadian and Australian authorities reveal an awareness of this worry.[109] The standard response is an inclination to exercise the discretion *inter partes* in such a way as not to prejudice the third party.[110] Is this the best approach? It could be said to be the worst of both worlds. The remedy which is otherwise appropriate *inter partes* is cut back;[111] indeed, proprietary effect is denied just when it would be valuable. Yet the third party is still not told exactly where she stands, ahead of time, as she wants to be. The problem might be met equally well, if not better, by an approach which settles the allocation of property *inter partes* rather by rules fixing upon facts visible to third parties, and then allows the results, as being predictable, to affect third parties. This may be English law's approach. It is certainly protective of third parties,[112] but it will ultimately hold them bound by family property entitlements;[113] it may, therefore, be no accident that it also determines the incidence of family property entitlements largely by rules, especially the rule requiring 'direct financial contribution'.[114]

As a matter of policy *inter partes,* however, this particular rule is commonly felt to be unsatisfactory. Could the law retain the advantages of proceeding by rules but adopt rules of a more wholesome content? Would attention to a broader range of contributions require a discretionary approach? It may well be so, for the reason suggested earlier. Particularly where non-financial contributions are concerned, the whole matrix of the relationship and of the parties' activities will need to be examined in order to reach valid conclusions about the basis upon which the contributions were made and received. (Whereas money contributions pretty obviously warrant recognition.) The ability to react to such cases is thus lost if we insist on settling entitlements by rules, so as to make these entitlements visible to third parties. If we are to remain sympathetic to third parties, we thus appear to have the choice between ruling such cases out, as

---

[107] (1990) 65 D.L.R. (4th) 161.

[108] Cf. *Mallett* v. *Mallett* (1984) 156 C.L.R. 605, where the High Court of Australia affirmed that the jurisdiction to reallocate property upon dissolution of a marriage (Family Law Act 1975, s. 79) should be exercised by reference to the circumstances of the individual case and not constrained by even a presumption of equal shares.

[109] See e.g. D. W. M. Waters, *Law of Trusts in Canada* (2nd ed., 1984), 394–5, and in *Equity and Contemporary Legal Developments* (ed. S. Goldstein, 1992), 499–504; *Rawluk* v. *Rawluk* (1990) 65 D.L.R. (4th) 161 at 187–8, 191, per McLachlin, J.; *Muschinski* v. *Dodds* (1986) 160 C.L.R. 583 at 615, 623.

[110] Ibid. The inclination is either to deny proprietary relief altogether (see *Peter* v. *Beblow* (1993) 101 D.L.R. (4th) 621, 640, per Cory, J.); or, at any rate in Australia, to grant proprietary relief, but make the proprietary effect date only from the court order (see *Muschinski* v. *Dodds* (1986) 160 C.L.R. 583). Given the goal of protecting third parties, both treatments make the

same assumption about how it must be achieved: by stopping proprietary relief where a third party comes in. Neither explores whether proprietary relief might be capable of coexistence with the protection of third parties, as adumbrated in the text.

[111] When D. W. M. Waters, in *Equity and Contemporary Legal Developments* (ed. S. Goldstein, 1992), 457 argues against the view that proprietary effect is (necessarily, or even normally) retroactive, he may lose sight of this point. Proprietary effect from the date of the underlying facts is normally justified because that is the date when their respective obligations and rights become justified. From the parties' point of view, the date of the court order is essentially adventitious.

[112] See e.g. *Bristol & West Building Society* v. *Henning* [1985] 1 W.L.R. 778; *Abbey National Building Society* v. *Cann* [1991] 1 A.C. 56.

[113] *Williams & Glyn's Bank Ltd.* v. *Boland* [1981] A.C. 487.

[114] *Lloyds Bank Plc* . v. *Rosset* [1991] 1 A.C. 107; see S. Gardner (1991), 54 M.L.R. 126.

English law presently does, and responding to them by a discretion but placing heavy shackles on it to protect third parties, as the work on remedial constructive trusts suggests. Or is there some third possibility?[115]

Commercial contracts

Commercial contracts constitute another area in which it is commonly seen as right for the law to deal in terms of entitlements fixed independently of court proceedings, again so that those involved in trade—this time, the parties themselves, as well as third party creditors—should know where they stand. From this point of view, it would be inappropriate for the law to take a discretionary approach to proprietary relief for unjust enrichment in this area, except in a rule-building operation.

It is not clear how the Canadian decisions stand over this issue. Unpredictability in commerce is mentioned as a worry by Cory, J. in *Peter* v. *Beblow*.[116] But he seems to take it for granted that remedial constructive trusts must be enduringly discretionary, so that to restore predictability they should simply be eschewed (or at any rate 'limited') in this area. He does not appear to contemplate solving the problem instead by developing some rules about their incidence. The question came to the fore in *Hunter Engineering Co. Inc.* v. *Syncrude Canada Ltd.*,[117] but the discussion there is equivocal. The majority found for the defendant, holding that there was no unjust enrichment. The nub of the reasoning seems to be a perception that the doctrine of unjust enrichment must not be used to make for the parties a deal which they might have, but had not, made for themselves.[118] This position might be presented as a rule that the parties' own arrangements take primacy, so that there is no discretion to be exercised. Such a rule would allow parties and creditors to know where they stand. However, the majority judgment does not content itself with a crisp statement of that kind. Instead, it gives a protracted account of why there was no unjust enrichment on the facts. This makes it sound as though the court regarded itself as exercising the usual discretion about discovering unjust enrichment or not in the individual case, the primacy of the parties' own arrangements merely being a factor in that operation.[119]

If the point is indeed to give those involved confidence in their position, this approach seems a muddle. Acceptable levels of certainty could be restored, simultaneously with preserving the ability to give proprietary relief for unjust enrichment, by the development and articulation of rules. To a large extent the law would doubtless want to follow the parties' own arrangements. Sometimes, however, it would want to override them: the laws of contract and restitution contain many provisions of this kind. Either way, those involved will be enabled to know where they stand if the law operates by rules rather than by discretion. This thinking has obvious intuitive appeal, and enjoys a wide following, at any rate in England. On the other hand, that is not to say that it is beyond challenge or refinement.

Discretion as to purpose

So far we have been thinking about the discretions in remedial constructive trusts on the basis that the underlying purpose is clear (appropriate proprietary response to unjust enrichment), and the discretions are just the vehicle for implementing that purpose; we have been thinking about whether they are a more suitable vehicle than rules. Finally, however, we should notice that the material on remedial constructive trusts contains some suggestion that the discretions go deeper than this. It sometimes looks as though the discretion extends to the underlying purpose itself, so that remedial constructive trusts may be used to further legal projects which are settled only by the judge on the day.

There is some evidence that Canadian judges diverge over whether unjust enrichment is really what they are pursuing. We see this in particular in a passage in which Lambert, J. A. explains that an unjust enrichment analysis is applicable to both family and commercial contexts, but: 'In a domestic relationship, equality of the parties to the relationship should normally be the standard of fairness. But, in a business relationship, honest dealing not equal

---

[115] P. Ferguson (1993), 109 L.Q.R. 114, for example, suggests basing entitlements upon rules in the narrow band ('direct financial contribution') to which English law presently reacts, and allowing discretionary reaction to other cases *with prospective effect only.* D. J. Hayton [1990], Conv. 370 at 380–4 took a similar line. It seems, though, he now proposes that discretionary reaction should more readily affect third parties, apparently because he now devalues the policy of sympathy for them: (1993) 109 L.Q.R. 485 at 488–9.

[116] (1993) 101 D.L.R. (4th) 621, 639].

[117] (1989) 57 D.L.R. (4th) 321.

[118] See especially (1989) 57 D.L.R. (4th) 321 at 351, *per* Dickson, C. J.

[119] See also *LAC Minerals Ltd.* v. *International Corona Resources Ltd.* (1989) 61 D.L.R. (4th) 14, where the court awarded proprietary rather than personal restitution in a commercial unjust enrichment (breach of confidence) case, but Sopinka, J. (McIntyre, J. concurring) dissented, saying that the constructive trust would only exceptionally, if ever, lie for breach of confidence. Sopinka, J. offered no real reasoning for this assertion, and D. W. M. Waters (1990), 69 Can. Bar. Rev. 455 at 465–6, plausibly suggests that his point was in effect that proprietary intervention is unsuitable in commercial matters. If so, however, the fact that Sopinka, J. himself does not make the point so crisply leaves one with the sense that, even for him, everything lies in discretion.

dealing should set the standard of fairness.'[120] The reference to 'fairness' as the purpose of the unjust enrichment analysis threatens to betoken the lack of any predetermined reference point, and the threat is confirmed when we learn that, via 'fairness', the analysis has different purposes in family matters and in commerce. And the purpose which Lambert, J. A. mentions for the family context, equalisation of property, is certainly different from the purpose of unjust enrichment as it is normally understood, namely the return of the plaintiff's contribution. It must be said, however, that Lambert, J. A.'s approach is unusual among the leading Canadian decisions, which preponderantly base their response upon the quantum of the claimant's contribution, in a true unjust enrichment analysis.[121] It would be interesting, though, to know how matters are handled in the general run of first instance cases.

Signs of discretion as to purpose are also evident in the Australian material. Although Australian law's analysis is supposedly aimed at the retrieval of the plaintiff's input to a joint venture, as explained in *Muschinski* v. *Dodds*,[122] *Baumgartner* v. *Baumgartner*[123] contains the following passage: 'Equity favours equality and, in circumstances where the parties have lived together for years and have pooled their resources and their efforts to create a joint home, there is much to be said for the view that they should share the beneficial ownership equally as tenants in common, subject to adjustment to avoid any injustice which would result if account were not taken of the disparity between the worth of their individual contributions either financially or in kind.' The proviso at the end may bring matters back, but the overall sense

of this passage seems to be that the *Muschinski* v. *Dodds* analysis can, where appropriate, entail community property rather than restitution.

Maintaining discretion as to the law's purpose in this way is quite different from using discretion to implement a settled purpose, and it is probably fundamentally irreconcilable with the idea of the Rule of Law. Where the purpose is settled, it will be reconcilable with democracy; either the legislature settled the purpose itself, or the purpose was publicly known and the legislature could have changed it. That is not the case where the purpose is unknown until announced by the judge on the day. And where the purpose is settled, all cases will be exposed to essentially the same exercise. It is still a desideratum that like cases should be treated alike; it is known that they may not be, but this is understood as a criticism. This is not so, however, if the discretion extends to the purpose itself, for then, the judge is invited to decide for herself where the case should lead, and so it will be entirely natural for like cases to be treated differently.[124]

Discretion as to purpose is thus highly objectionable. The objections are less acute, however, when the discretion consists in the judges' deciding whether to change the law so as to reflect a different set of values from that reflected hitherto. In this exercise, they are using what may, to adapt the terminology used earlier, be called 'purpose-building' discretion.[125] An instance might be the debate, and change of direction, between *Williams & Glyn's Bank Ltd.* v. *Boland*.[126] on the one hand, and, on the other, the more recent decisions such as *Abbey National Building Society* v. *Cann*.[127] What we see here may

---

[120] *Atlas Cabinets and Furniture Ltd.* v. *National Trust Co. Ltd.* (1990) 68 D.L.R. (4th) 161 at 171

[121] Clearly to this effect are *Pettkus* v. *Becker* (1980) 117 D.L.R. (3d) 257; *Murray* v. *Roty* (1983) 147 D.L.R. (3d) 438; *Herman* v. *Smith* (1984) 42 R.F.L. (2d) 154; *Sorochan* v. *Sorochan* (1986) 29 D.L.R. (4th) 1; *Everson* v. *Rich* (1988) 53 D.L.R. (4th) 470. B. Hovius and T. G. Youdan, *The Law of Family Property* (1991), 136–41 take this to be the right approach. But cf. *Rawluk* v. *Rawluk* (1990) 65 D.L.R. (4th) 161 at 189, per McLachlin, J., that the Ontario Family Law Act 1986 is 'directed to the same end' as the common law of remedial constructive trusts, when the Act operates to equalise spouses' entitlements. (In *Peter* v. *Beblow* (1993) 101 D.L.R. (4th) 621, 652, McLachlin, J. talks of 'the expectations of most parties . . . to share in the wealth generated from their partnership' (similarly Cory, J. at 642), but in context it is clear that this does not necessarily mean that the shares should be equal: they are still supposed to reflect the values of the parties' respective contributions.)

[122] (1986) 160 C.L.R. 583.

[123] (1987) 164 C.L.R. 137 at 149–50.

[124] For some further, subtle, reflections, however, cf. D. J. Galligan, *Discretionary Powers* (1986), 78–80, 81–4.

[125] However, not all judges have eschewed even the less defensible forms of discretion as to purpose. The Australian case of *Mallett* v. *Mallett* (1984) 156 C.L.R. 605, discusses the jurisdiction to reallocate family property upon a divorce (Fam-

ily Law Act 1975, s. 79), and holds that it is discretionary. Gibbs, C. J. remarks (at 607–8) that the discretion extends to deciding the purpose of the jurisdiction: 'The Family Law Act was passed at a time when great changes had occurred, and were continuing to occur, in the attitudes of many members of society to marriage and divorce, but when it was (as it is now) difficult, if not impossible, to say that any one set of values or ideas is commonly accepted, or approved by a majority of the members of society. Conflicting opinions continue to be strongly held as to the nature of marriage, the economic consequences of divorce and the effect, if any, that should be given to the fault or misconduct of a party when a court is making the financial adjustments that divorce entails. It is not surprising that given this diversity of opinions Parliament did not require the power conferred by s. 79 to be exercised in accordance with fixed rules. On the contrary, it has conferred on the court a very wide discretion to make such order as it thinks fit . . .' Gibbs, C. J. may possibly have thought that the right approach would soon become clarified, so that the discretion would be of the merely 'purpose-building' kind discussed in the text. But there must be a strong suspicion that he envisaged rather an ongoing discretion as to purpose, the judges settling in individual actions what the Parliament could not settle in the legislation. To adapt the terminology used earlier, this would be a 'purpose-compromise' discretion.

[126] [1981] A.C. 487.

[127] [1991] 1 A.C. 56.

be justified as the irreducible minimum of discretion as to purpose which is required if the higher courts are from time to time to alter the direction of the law so as to reflect what they see as a change in prevailing social values. Once a new leading authority is decided, the course of the law would be expected to follow the newly settled purpose for some time.

This may be the way to regard the signs of discretion as to purpose in the Canadian and Australian cases on remedial constructive trusts.[128] In particular, the experimentation with equality of property may indicate that the courts are toying with the idea that an analysis aimed at reimbursing contributions does not meet the essential nature of the claim in some family cases. If so, they are arguably right. The essence of the claim may be rather that, by their rela-tionship, the parties have engaged to provide for each other's overall well-being in a way which transcends the keeping of separate accounts which is implicit in reimbursing contribution. It seems likely that some family relationships will be of this closer kind, and should command a response like equality of property; whilst others are of the looser kind to which a restitutionary approach is more appropriate.[129] Of course, once these two types of case, and the proper response to each, have been identified, there may still be room for discretion as to the identification of a given fact-situation as involving the one head or the other, and then as to the application of the appropriate response. But that is the more acceptable, conventional form of discretion.

---

[128] The Canadian material contains at least one passage explicitly taking this 'purpose-building' stance. In *Pettkus* v. *Becker* (1980) 117 D.L.R. (3d) 257 at 273, Dickson, J. remarks that unjust enrichment is a 'malleable principle' which can be 'shaped' 'so as to accommodate the changing needs and mores of society, in order to achieve justice.'

[129] For development of this suggestion, see S. Gardner (1993), 109 L.Q.R. 263 at 289–95.

15. Non-Marital Property

JOHN EEKELAAR

1. Introduction

A VAST literature has developed in the common law jurisdictions on the way their courts have responded to the resolution of disputes between unmarried former cohabitees over their property holdings. Some of the debate has drifted into doctrinal disputations about the nature of constructive or resulting trusts, and, in particular, whether there is or should be any distinction between constructive trusts and estoppels. I think this is unfortunate because in such debates it is easy to lose sight of the true nature of the problems which the litigants have brought to the courts for a solution.

These problems have not only confronted common law courts. In an article on cohabitation without marriage in Poland, Szlezak[1] cites a case where unmarried cohabitees jointly built a house on land belonging to the man. The woman contributed large sums of money. Her claim for recovery on the basis of unjust enrichment was rejected because the court decided that her contributions had been made on a sufficient legal basis (*viz.*, the intention to contribute to the well-being of the union), but the court went on to declare her joint owner of the house, even though strictly she could have been so constituted only by express conveyance by the man. Other doctrines have been used in civil law countries, such an unjust enrichment and implied partnership.[2] Sweden has passed legislation.[3] The point of making these references is that they show, what should be clear enough, that these are not problems *of* legal doctrine, but that there is a common set of issues which pose problems *for* legal doctrine. It is the task of legal doctrine to find solutions, not to bury itself within introspective analyses about itself.

An outstanding contribution towards such an attempt has been made by Simon Gardner in his article, 'Rethinking Family Property'.[4] Gardner provides a penetrating analysis of the social issues that are at stake and also of the legal doctrines that have been deployed to deal with them. My contribution, after his, must be modest. However, I would like to offer some reflections on the issues from a wider, family law, perspective.

2. Gardner's Thesis: Collaboration and Trust, Communality

Gardner's argument, crudely summarized, starts by pointing out that the common intention which in England is standardly proclaimed as the juristic basis for the 'constructive' trust (in Canada it would be called a 'resulting' trust), is often fictitious. I had made a similar point in an earlier article[5] when I argued that the cases showed that common intention was neither *necessary* nor *sufficient* to establish a constructive trust. Not necessary, because there were occasions where it was imputed where the facts showed clearly its absence,[6] and (I might have added) it would be inferred without more if there had been a direct financial contribution to the purchase. Not sufficient, because *as a matter of law* the courts barred 'ordinary domestic activities' from being used as evidence from which such intention might be inferred.[7] But, whereas I suggested that an alternative approach might be found in the more flexible doctrine of proprietary estoppel, which is grounded on the protection of a belief, reasonably held and acted upon by the non-owner that he or she either has or will acquire an interest in the other's property, Gardner rejects this. He points out that the idea that proprietary estoppel allows beliefs about the future whereas common intention does not, is not well-founded. More importantly, he argues that common intention is to be understood objectively, so that if an owner who secretly intends otherwise gives indications of readiness to share, this can allow a finding of common intention as well as a reasonable belief that such an intention existed. Furthermore, he argues that where the evidence shows that the owner communicated a negative attitude over property sharing, thus barring a finding of common intention, this should equally prevent a finding of 'reasonable belief'. He subjects the majority judgments in the Canadian decision of *Pettkus* v. *Becker*[8] to devastat-

---

[1] Andrzej Szlezak, 'Cohabitation without Marriage in Poland' (1991) 5 *International Journal of Law & the Family* 1 at 8–9.

[2] See Mary Ann Glendon, *The Transformation of Family Law* (Chicago, 1989), ch. 6 for an extended, comparative account.

[3] This is referred to below, at note 56.

[4] (1993) 109 *Law Quarterly Review* 263.

[5] John Eekelaar, 'A Woman's Place—A Conflict between Law and Social Values' [1987] *Conveyancer and Property Lawyer* 93.

[6] The cases, cited by both Gardner and myself, are *Eves* v. *Eves* [1975] 1 W.L.R. 1338 and *Grant* v. *Edwards* [1986] Ch. 638.

[7] See *Burns* v. *Burns* [1984] Ch. 317.

[8] (1980) 117 D.L.R. (3d) 257.

ing criticism for doing otherwise. Both doctrines, Gardner concludes, should be rejected as resting on fictions. He then proposes two alternative approaches, one drawn from unjust enrichment and grounded in the mutual collaboration and trust between the parties and the other drawn from fiduciary relationships and the law of trusts, based on the 'communality' inherent in the parties' relationship.

I am in complete agreement with Gardner that it is necessary to 'rethink' these issues. I will look more closely at his proposal at the end of this paper. But first I wish to re-examine the 'common intention' and 'reasonable expectation' positions for, in the absence of any fundamental change, we need to find the best solutions we can from existing doctrine.

3. Common Intention or Reasonable Expectation?

Gardner produces powerful arguments for suggesting that a claim based on 'reasonable beliefs' (whether classified under the rubric of proprietary estoppel or unjust enrichment[9]) is no more likely to succeed than a claim based on 'common intention'. Indeed, he suggests claimants may be worse off under a 'reasonable belief' doctrine because there is no 'tradition' of 'inventing' grounds for such belief, although he also remarks that if 'reasonable belief' was permitted to ground a claim where there had been no direct financial contribution (which is ruled out under the 'common intention' doctrine), 'invention' might actually increase.[10]

I am not completely persuaded by these arguments. The attraction of proprietary estoppel, at any rate over 'common intention', lies in its potential for development rather than its 'tradition'. I do not know whether Gardner wishes to draw a distinction between proprietary estoppel, based on 'reasonable belief', and a wider doctrine that has developed in New Zealand based on 'reasonable expectations'. He himself refers to the fact that, as applied in New Zealand, this doctrine poses the question: would a reasonable person in the claimant's position have expected an interest?[11] Were proprietary estoppel to be applied in this way in England, there is no basis for Gardner's fear that 'only women who actually raised the question of property ownership with their partner, and received a positive response, would continue to gain their interests'. This seems to assume that some express or implied representation

by the owner must be established and that the non-owner acted on this. Yet that which is reasonable to expect a person to do can be deduced not only from that person's behaviour, but also by reference to the community ethos of what would be 'the right thing to do'. If a woman gives up her employment, leaves her dwelling, moves into a man's house, bears his child and runs the house, it must be possible to infer *from those facts alone* that she had a reasonable expectation not to be turned out without any 'compensation'. One may reasonably expect another to act fairly, even honourably, without a preliminary discussion. One need not strain to imply some representation. It would not, I think, be 'invention' to hold that someone like Mrs. Burns[12] (as she called herself), who bore her partner two children, brought them up and looked after the home for nineteen years, had a 'reasonable expectation' of some share in the family's capital assets without having to produce evidence of express discussion of the question. Richardson, J. expressed this well in the leading New Zealand case, *Gillies* v. *Keogh*:[13]

'Whatever the position in other countries, it seems to me that social attitudes in New Zealand readily lead to expectations, by those with apparently stable, enduring de facto relationships, that family assets are ordinarily shared, not the exclusive property of, one or the other, unless it is agreed otherwise. . . .'

Even *Eves* v. *Eves*[14] and *Grant* v. *Edwards*[15] are sustainable on the basis of 'reasonable expectation'. In the former, the man told the plaintiff (who was pregnant by him) that he would have put the house in their joint names but did not because she was too young. In the latter case (in which the woman was also pregnant by the man with whom she moved in), the excuse was that if the conveyance had been in joint names, that would have prejudiced the woman in her divorce proceedings. These were excuses, and, as Gardner correctly points out, the fact that these *were* excuses indicates that the men never did *intend* to confer beneficial interests. The inference of a *common* intention was therefore improper, or at the very least, fictitious. But, by the same token, the fact that they were *excuses* for refraining from granting a share in the properties for prudential reasons of a temporary nature could give rise to a reasonable expectation and belief that the men did indeed intend to grant a share in the properties and would do so when the alleged temporary impediment was removed.

---

9 See *Gillies* v. *Keogh* [1989] 2 N.Z.L.R. 327 at 330–1.
10 See (1993) 109, *Law Quarterly Review* at 268–9.
11 See *Gillies* v. *Keogh* [1989] 2 N.Z.L.R. 327.
12 See *Burns* v. *Burns*, above, note 7.

13 [1989] 2 N.Z.L.R. 327 at 347.
14 [1975] 1 W.L.R. 1338.
15 [1986] Ch. 638.

I will return to the issue of 'reasonable expectation' later, as it embodies an ambiguity which should be resolved. But at this point I hope I have shown that the 'reasonable expectation' rationale may frequently apply, without 'invention', in circumstances where 'common intention' would fail without resort to invention. But the advantage of the former rationale is not simply one of intellectual comfort. There is a strong practical reason for preferring it. This was strikingly illustrated in *Hammond* v. *Mitchell*.[16] This cohabitation, which began with a chance encounter between a 40-year-old man, who was separated from his wife, and a 21-year-old woman in Epping Forest, lasted eleven years, produced two children and £450k assets. Waite, J. adopted the 'common intention' requirement. He observed that in cases like this, it was necessary to make orders for discovery early in the proceedings because

'the primary emphasis accorded by the law in cases of this kind to express discussions between the parties . . . means that the tenderest exchanges of a common law courtship may assume an unforeseen significance many years later when they are brought under equity's microscope and subjected to an analysis under which many thousands of pounds of value may be liable to turn'.

All this, he added, should be pleaded in the greatest detail. It is no surprise that the case involved a nineteen-day hearing and £125k costs, one party being on legal aid.

But if we abandon the need to pretend that we are giving effect to some kind of agreement, such absurdity is unnecessary. The plaintiff need produce evidence only of the 'social facts': the history of the relationship, her bearing of his children, patterns of employment, the way moneys were used, the acquisition and disposal of properties. These can, in themselves, show a pattern from which reasonable expectations may be inferred. The burden of proof then shifts to a defendant who wishes to contradict such expectations to produce evidence that, by reason of his words and conduct, such expectations could not have been reasonably held, as indeed the owner was able to do in *Gillies* v. *Keogh*.[17] If one adds to this the fact, already referred to, that 'domestic' behaviour may form part of such social facts (which it cannot in order to infer common intention), we can see that a considerable gap has opened up between this doctrine and that of common intention.

4. Constitutive Rights or a Remedial Claim? The Problem of Third Parties

If there is any merit in the argument above, *viz.*, that the doctrine of constructive trusts based on 'common intention' as propounded in *Gissing* v. *Gissing*[18] rests on a different basis from proprietary estoppel, especially as represented by a 'reasonable expectation' doctrine, it follows that the tendency to equate the two cannot be right. Yet the conflation has been made at the highest level. In *Lloyd's Bank* v. *Rosset*[19] Lord Bridge referred to the two interchangeably.

'The finding of an agreement or arrangement to share in this sense can only, I think, be based on evidence of express discussions between the partners, however imperfectly remembered and however imprecise their terms may have been. Once a finding to this effect is made it will only be necessary for the partner asserting the claim to a beneficial interest against the partner entitled to the legal estate to show that he or she has acted to his or her detriment or significantly altered his or her position in reliance on the agreement in order to give rise to a *constructive trust or proprietary estoppel.*'[20]

Patricia Ferguson has argued against the conflation of the two concepts in the pages of the *Law Quarterly Review*.[21] Her target is D. J. Hayton, who wishes to reduce the two doctrines to a common principle of unconscionability.[22] Ferguson suggests, first, that there may be a difference in the *onus of proof* between 'constructive trusts' and 'proprietary estoppel'. But she is referring to the 'onus of proof' in a particular context, *viz.* what must be proved by way of detrimental reliance. In her view, the authorities suggest that to constitute sufficient reliance in the former case, the plaintiff's conduct must be directly related to the agreement (at least, where express), in the sense that it would not have occurred 'but for' the agreement. The estoppel cases, she claims, apply a looser test, demanding no more than evidence of detrimental activity consequent to the representation relied on: the onus then shifts to the defendant to show there was no reliance.[23]

I do not wish to make anything of this point because Ferguson takes the 'estoppel' doctrine in its English 'undeveloped' form which requires evidence of some kind of representation by words or conduct by the defendant. If you do that, the onus of proof regarding reliance may indeed matter. But if you accept a more developed doctrine of 'reasonable expectation', as has occurred in New Zealand, the

---

[16] [1991] 1 W.L.R. 1127.
[17] Above, note 9.
[18] [1971] A.C. 886.
[19] [1991] 1 A.C. 107; see also *Austin* v. *Keele* (1987) 61 A.L.J.R. 605 at 609 (Privy Council).
[20] [1991] 1 A.C. 107 at 132, italics supplied.

[21] 'Constructive Trusts—A Note of Caution' (1993) 109 *Law Quarterly Review* 114.
[22] 'Equitable Rights between Cohabitees' [1990] *Conveyancer and Property Lawyer* 370.
[23] (1993) 109 *Law Quarterly Review* at 119; citing *Greasley* v. *Cooke* [1980] 1 W.L.R. 1306.

issue becomes different because the nature of the evidence necessary to establish a prima facie case changes. Now all the plaintiff needs to do is to lead evidence about the 'social facts', as described above. It is unnecessary to use these to establish representation by the defendant. The court determines whether this generates a reasonable expectation of a property share. If it does so, the defendant can escape only by proving that the plaintiff could not reasonably have held such an expectation.

Ferguson's second point is of more moment. She argues that, where a constructive trust is established, the beneficiary's interests vest at that time and may prevail against the after-acquired interests of a third party. So, in *Rosset* it was assumed that, had the non-owner's claim succeeded, her interests would have had priority over those of a subsequent mortgagee. But if the rights arising under estoppel do so only from the date of the court order, it would be unfortunate, she says, to follow Hayton and reduce both situations to a common one of 'unconscionability' because this would weaken a cohabitee's position against third parties, who could acquire the property free of the plaintiff's claim. Ferguson therefore presses for the 'constructive trust' solution, for this establishes beneficial interests in the plaintiff cohabitee earlier, usually when the property is acquired. Elsewhere in this volume, however, Gardner points out that the decisions indicate that the plaintiff's proprietary interest acquired under the estoppel doctrine can affect third parties from a date *prior* to the court order.[24]

These points reveal the latent conceptual traps laid by such doctrinal analyses. The sequence runs:

1. The remedy *inter partes* must be proprietal (constructive trusts, estoppel) because a personal remedy would improperly arrogate to the court a 'discretionary' power to re-distribute property similar to that possessed by courts exercising the divorce jurisdiction;[25]

2. *Unless* the plaintiff's interest is proprietal, the plaintiff's *security of occupation* will be not be protected against third parties;

3. *Because* the plaintiff's interest is a property interest, it puts the plaintiff in a privileged position

against third parties such as unsecured creditors and beneficiaries to his/her partner's estate.

Proposition (1) may be rejected; transfer of property from the defendant to the plaintiff cohabitee need not be grounded solely on a property claim, but can be supported by independent legal justification, and any policy qualms of trespassing into the territory of the divorce courts should have disappeared in the modern social climate. Nevertheless, it is the misfortune of its entanglement with constructive trusts and proprietary estoppel that even the members of the New Zealand Court of Appeal, in *Gillies* v. *Keogh*,[26] spoke of the 'reasonable expectations' claim an establishing a proprietary interest against the defendant, although Cooke P. was careful to point out that he was *not* considering the implications vis-a-vis third parties, other than to affirm that, of course, bona fide purchasers for value without notice would be unaffected.[27] It would be better to admit that the nature of the 'reasonable expectations' claim has moved so far from a claim that a proprietary interest was established *ab initio* that it should be seen in its true light as a *compensation* claim, operating against the defendant personally.

Since Proposition (2) may equally be rejected, it matters not that the plaintiff's claim is of a personal rather than proprietary nature. Hayton has suggested[28] that the occupation of a plaintiff who does not have a proprietary claim may be protected against a third party who 'deliberately or recklessly' fails to ask the occupying cohabitee whether he or she claims an interest in the home on the grounds that such a third party may be held to have acted unconscionably. This may be unduly complicated.[29] A simpler solution is to enact, as has been done in Sweden,[30] that, whatever the respective property interests of the cohabitees, the consent of each is required for dealings in the family home. But in England even this may not be necessary, as we shall see.

Proposition (3), if upheld, might be over-protective of cohabitees, putting them in a better position against the unsecured creditors of their insolvent partners than a spouse is vis-a-vis his or her insolvent partner's unsecured creditors (unless he or she had a similar proprietal interest) and it may be sig-

---

[24] Above, at 190, note 36.
[25] For the same reason the House of Lords rejected Denning, L. J.'s attempts to use section 17 of the Married Women's Property Act 1882 to re-distribute marital property between divorcing parties prior to the significant expansion of the statutory power of the court to make such redistribution in 1971: *Pettitt* v. *Pettitt* [1970] A.C. 770.
[26] Above, note 9.
[27] [1989] 2 N.Z.L.R. 327 at 331.
[28] David Hayton, 'Constructive Trusts of Homes—A Bold

Approach' (1993) 109 *Law Quarterly Review* 485.
[29] It is possible that Hayton's solution might work, but, as admirable as the intentions are, one cannot but think that they assume a world populated by lawyers. He writes about a cohabitee: 'If she makes no claim to an interest under a purchase money resulting trust but claims that she has the foundation for a proprietary estoppel remedy to be declared by the court, whether a co-ownership share or a life interest or an equitable charge for a sum of money . . .'. *Ibid.*, at 488–9.
[30] See below, note 56.

nificant that Cooke, P. reserved his position on the point.[31] Whether or not a cohabitee (or a spouse) should be so protected is, of course, an interesting policy question. But it is one that should be provided clearly and on its own merits, and need not be predetermined by the *a priori* categorization of the nature of the remedy *inter partes* or the grounds upon which that remedy is exercised.[32]

To argue that a proprietal claim is not a necessary prerequisite for the provision of adequate remedies for cohabitees, both *inter se*, and against third parties, is not of course to maintain that a cohabitee should in no circumstances be allowed a proprietary remedy against his or her partner. There can be no objection to a plaintiff attempting to prove (which may be difficult) that the owner holds the relevant property on trust on the basis of agreement, express or implied and, if successful, the appropriate consequences will follow. But such claims should be exceptional; they should not constitute the usual basis for resolving disputes relating to the property of former cohabitees.

5. 'Reasonable Expectations'

Assuming that an intention-based, proprietal, doctrine of constructive trusts can be separated from a wider, personal, 'reasonable expectations' doctrine, it is now necessary to examine the latter doctrine more closely.

I indicated earlier that the doctrine suffered from a troubling ambiguity. This can best be illustrated through an analogy. Suppose a post-doctoral student works under the direction of a distinguished science professor. The student's efforts produce significant results. The professor publishes these in a paper to which the student substantially contributed. It is clear, both from a consideration of institutional practice and broader considerations of fairness, that the student can reasonably believe (or expect) that the professor *should* acknowledge him in the publication. Whether he believes that the professor *would* do so may be more complex. Possibly the professor and student are on very goods terms; the professor is known as a woman of integrity who always looks to the needs of her students. In such a case, the student's expectation is not only that the professor should make the

acknowledgement, but that she would do so. But the professor may be (and be known to the student to be) a less reliable character: she is out primarily to promote her own career; she may have been less than generous in her treatment of previous students. Yet our student got on reasonably well with her, and in any case wanted to pursue the research for his own purposes. While the moral norm remains, the reasonableness of the expectation that the professor would abide by it may be harder to establish.

We may well see a parallel between these relationships and those between sexual partners. Here the reasonable expectation doctrine encounters difficulty. If its purpose is to determine, even on the basis of an 'objective' assessment of that other's conduct, whether the non-owner expected, on reasonable grounds, that the other *would* make provision, rather than whether he *should* make such provision, the adjudicative task is extraordinarily difficult (though not impossible). It is hard enough to know what the student expected of the second type of professor. How can we evaluate the nuances of the parties' sexual relationship? Certainly, if we need to make such a finding, claims are more likely to succeed against the generous and kind than against the unfeeling and selfish. But it is anyway difficult to resist a slippage between 'would' and 'should'. You tend to think most people will do what they 'should'.

Yet it has proved hard for courts to confront the question: how *should* the owner behave towards his or her former partner? (I call this 'the normative issue'). The language is usually couched in terms suggestive of prediction of what the other would ordinarily do.[33] The courts seem determined to elucidate what the partners themselves expected. This is understandable. I have argued elsewhere that the principles applied to court-ordered property and financial provision on divorce reflect underlying assumptions as to the normative structure of marriage.[34] Similarly, a view of what someone *should* do on termination of unmarried cohabitation assumes the existence of a normative model of non-marital cohabitation. Precisely to what is an unmarried partner, who enters a domestic relationship, committing himself or herself? Since our own society has not answered, or even posed, that question, it is not surprising that the courts have been unwilling to consider it.[35] I think it

---

[31] Above, note 27.
[32] Sir Peter Millett has written: 'The advantage which (a proprietary remedy) affords a plaintiff over the unsecured creditors of an insolvent defendant makes it imperative that the circumstances in which it will be granted should be known in advance': 'Bribes and Secret Commissions' (1993) 1 *Restitution Law Review* 7 at 9.
[33] See the quotation from Richardson, J. in *Gillies* v. *Keogh*, above at note 9. Cooke, P. referred to the 'reasonable expecta-

tions' of *both* parties.
[34] John Eekelaar, *Regulating Divorce* (O.U.P., 1991), ch. 4.
[35] It should be stated, however, that the approach taken by the Australian courts (see *Baumgartner* v. *Baumgartner* (1987) 164 C.L.R. 137), and advocated by Hayton (above, note 28), that a remedy should be given against a defendant who has acted 'unconscionably' poses more directly the question: what *should* the defendant have done? The answer is, however, left very open-ended.

is necessary to face that question more resolutely and that reasonable expectation should be judged on a normative, and not a predictive, basis.

Gardner faces the normative issue squarely. His contention is that the courts should look at the element of collaboration and trust in the relationship. It is this, rather than fictitious constructions of what the parties may or may not have thought, or believed, or expected, which grounds the claim. These elements can be used to 'modify' the traditional bases of unjust enrichment, overcoming, for example, the rule allowing the recipient of services to treat them as given free (unless it is clear, for example, that the services were requested or expected to be recompensed) or the difficulties of showing the enrichment was 'unjust'.[36] Alternatively, or in addition, the joint fiduciary relationship in which the partners may find themselves can impose on each an obligation on each to hold half the property for the benefit of the other: what Gardner calls 'communality'. He allows for opting out, but subject to principles of undue influence.

This analysis goes to the heart of the problem and I have much sympathy with it. But I am concerned that the *form* of the solution offered may create significant practical problems. It is indeed a strength of the approach that it allows for the variety of domestic arrangements. Some relationships may remain at the level of trust and collaboration; others may start and remain on a basis of communality. In yet others, 'modified' unjust enrichment may merge into 'communality'. The problem, however, with deploying two distinct juristic doctrines to respond to these different types of relationship is that the conceptualization, which will often be murky and contested, will dictate the consequences. For example, a party to a 'communal' relationship will have the proprietary remedies of trust law, whereas a party to a 'lesser' relationship will have the less clearly defined remedies of unjust enrichment law.[37]

This raises my most serious difficulty with the proposal. It would, at a stroke, introduce a matrimonial property régime into English law. 'As far as marriage is concerned', Gardner writes, 'communality seems incontestably the right approach'.[38] But can we con-

template such a step through manipulation of existing legal doctrine? How widely is the scope of property to be held on trust to be drawn? New Zealand[39] draws a distinction between separate and matrimonial property, and makes a further division within the latter between domestic and 'balance' property. The presumption of equal sharing applies differently between these subdivisions. There is a further modification for short marriages. It should also be noted that the Act does not create property rights during marriage; it only allocates the mode of sharing on divorce. In 1986 Ontario *moved from* a system of equal sharing of family assets (defined as property devoted to *joint use*) to a régime of 'equalization' of net assets.[40] The complexities of European systems are well known.[41]

I do not believe that these complex issues can safely be dealt with by anything less than statutory reform. But should we even consider such a reform? The New Zealand legislation has been criticized within New Zealand. 'In essence,' it has been said, 'the equal division of existing assets has not produced an equal financial result between husband and wife when the marriage has ended.' What is important, it is claimed, is not a retrospective exercise, but 'to provide the spouses with an equal chance in the future'.[42] The reasons are clear, and have been demonstrated time and again: where children have been born into a marriage, mothers are invariably in a worse position than fathers because their income and capital resources are less and they usually have more people in their household (i.e. the children).[43] In addition, as Maccoby and Mnookin have shown in the most recent study, while usually continuing to be the parent who provides the greater day-to-day care for the children, after separation from the father, the mother will usually become the major economic provider as well (though women's incomes remain steadily lower than those of men, and income transfers redress this only marginally).[44] Even the Scandinavian countries, which 'invented' the idea of the 'deferred community' in the 1920s, imposing equal division on divorce or separation, are retreating from that approach.[45]

In the case of married people, it might be retorted

[36] These problems for 'unjust enrichment' are discussed by Gardner at (1993) 109 *Law Quarterly Review* at 284–5.

[37] For the nature of remedies of unjust enrichment law, see A. Burrows, *The Law of Restitution* (Butterworths, 1992) at 28–9 and Peter Birks, *An Introduction to the Law of Restitution* (O.U.P., 1985), 77. See also the discussion in Birks at 377–8, of the position on insolvency.

[38] (1993) 109 *Law Quarterly Review* at 291.

[39] Matrimonial Property Act, 1976.

[40] Family Law Act, 1986.

[41] For a discussion, see Mary Ann Glendon, *The Transformation of Family Law* Chicago, (1989), 116 et seq.

[42] Caroline Bridge, 'Reallocation of Property after Marriage Breakdown' in M. Henaghan and B. Atkin (eds), *Family Law Policy in New Zealand* (O.U.P., 1992), at 247.

[43] See John Eekelaar, 'Equality and the Purpose of Maintenance' (1988) 15 *Journal of Law & Society* 188.

[44] E. Maccoby and R. Mnookin, *Dividing the Child* (Harvard U.P., 1992), especially ch. 10.

[45] See Ingrid Lund-Andersen, 'Towards an Individual Principle in Danish Law' (1990) 4, *International Journal of Law & the Family* 328. The matter is discussed further, in the light of the Scottish provisions, in John Eekelaar, *Regulating Divorce* (O.U.P., 1991) at 78.

that this does not matter because, in countries with jurisdiction to re-allocate property on divorce, like Australia and the United Kingdom, such re-allocation will be made in any event according to the principles considered appropriate. This is probably the main reason why proposals for various forms of community of property made by the Law Commission have gathered dust.[46] Indeed, the notion of dissolving a marriage as if it had been a business partnership, selling its assets and sharing them equally, is particularly inapt in most cases where children had been born into the union. Community of property may have more impact in the case of the insolvency or death of one of the spouses. But even in these situations, as has been said earlier, there are other ways of protecting the 'family' interests against creditors or other claimants to the estate than the retrospective implication of property interests.[47]

So it may be true that the impact of 'communality' between married people would not be great. In which case it may be asked—why embark on the exercise? But the lesson is a deeper one than that. If communality, involving retrospective construction of shared property interests, may not be the optimal solution for married people, why should it be right for the unmarried? We have not yet solved our problem: what is it reasonable to expect that an unmarried cohabitee *should* do when the cohabitation finishes?

5. A Pragmatic Approach

To attempt to answer this problem, we need to start, not with doctrine, but with an understanding of what problems faced by separated former cohabitees need resolution. We can learn from the research on divorce, which has shown that the problems of divorced couples who have jointly reared children are entirely different from those of childless divorcees. This has prompted calls for treating such divorces differently.[48] Reviewing western European laws, Mary Ann Glendon expresses it in these words:

Most divorces involve relatively young couples with minor children. Such couples typically have few assets other than the family dwelling, which may be leased, mortgaged, or owned. One way or another, courts everywhere, with more

or less aid from legislation, endeavor to preserve the marital home or its use for the needed period of time for the custodial spouse and children. Thus, in terms of the outcomes of a very large group of cases, one can say that a new marital property regime has emerged—one which applies in the majority of divorces—and that its basic features are similar everywhere. Only Sweden has cast it in statutory form: possession of the home and its contents are to be awarded to the spouse 'who needs it most'.[49]

If this is a universal response to the problems confronting young divorced people with children, why should it be different if the parties did not marry? That is why, when referring to various cases earlier in the paper, I stressed that the female cohabitees had borne their partners' children. These women will usually either be left to look after the children or, if the cohabitation ceases when the children have left home, suffer impaired earning power and gravely reduced prospects for old age as a result of having brought them up. The fundamental point is that it is *child-bearing* and not *marriage* which changes the lives of most women. We should therefore think of these disputes as typically being between *parents*, not *simply* between people who had merely 'lived together'.

So let us first look at the case of an unmarried mother left with the children. The 'maintenance' rights of these children against their father have been, since 1987, the same as for marital children.[50] As far as income provision is concerned, this has been substantially[51] replaced by the Child Support Act 1991, which makes no distinction between marital and non-marital children. Child support can, and in the case of payments under the 1991 Act, *does*, include payments for the children's carer. So a former cohabitee *should* make child support payments, whatever he may have said, represented or expected. But what of property? Section 12 of the Family Law Reform Act 1987 made the following significant insertion into the Guardianship of Minors Act 1971, now re-enacted in amended form in paragraph 1 of the First Schedule to the Children Act 1989:

1. (1) On an application made by either parent of a child, ... the court may— (a) in the case of an application to the High Court or a county court, make one or more of the orders mentioned in sub-paragraph (2); ...
(2) The orders referred to in sub-paragraph (1) are ... (e)

---

[46] See principally Law Commission, *Family Law: Third Report on Family Property. The Matrimonial Home (Co-Ownership and Occupation Rights) and Household Goods*, Law Com. No. 86 (H.M.S.O., 1978); Law Commission, *Family Law: Matrimonial Property*, Law Com. No. 175 (H.M.S.O., 1988).

[47] Although it must be admitted that the protection of family interests against creditors in England is not very satisfactory. See David Brown, 'Insolvency and the Matrimonial Home—the Sins of their Fathers' (1992) 55 *Modern Law Review* 284.

[48] John Eekelaar and Mavis Maclean, *Maintenance after*

Divorce (O.U.P., 1986); Mary Ann Glendon, *Abortion and Divorce in Western Law: American Failures and European Challenges* (Harvard U.P., 1987), 93; J. Thomas Oldham, 'Putting Asunder in the 1990s' (1992) 80 *California L.R.* 1091 at 1129.

[49] Mary Ann Glendon, *The Transformation of Family Law* (Chicago, 1989) at 234.

[50] Family Law Reform Act, 1987.

[51] But not completely: e.g. for payments of school fees, or where a child is disabled, or where the father is very wealthy.

an order requiring either or both parents of a child (i) to transfer to the applicant, for the benefit of the child, or (ii) to transfer to the child himself, such property to which the parent is, or the parents are, entitled (either in possession or reversion) as may be specified in the order.'

In *K.* v. *K* (*minors: property transfer*)[52] a judge ordered that the entire interest of an unmarried father in the joint tenancy of a council house be transferred to the mother 'for the benefit of the children'. So the house was now solely in the mother's name. The Court of Appeal rejected the father's argument that such an order could only be made if it conferred some financial or proprietary benefit on the children. 'Benefit' was to be interpreted widely. It is clear that maintaining a home for the children would be included. There therefore appears to be jurisdiction to settle the family home in cohabitation cases involving children in the same way as in divorce cases. A court may now hold that a father *should* transfer the home to the mother if the children need it.[53]

In practice, therefore, I believe English law already provides the mechanisms for solving the major problems likely to be faced by cohabitees, who are parents, and stipulates what ought to be done. But the solutions are not complete. Take the period *after* the last child has left home. The court might take the view that the father should recover the capital value of the house at that point. If so, it might require its sale.[54] But there is no power to order a division of the proceeds between unmarried parents. Or the cohabitation might terminate when the children have already left, as in *Burns* v. *Burns*.[55] A solution could be achieved through statutory extension of the existing provisions. One might envisage an insertion such as the following (in italics) in sub-sub-paragraph (e) to sub-paragraph (2) of Schedule 1 of the Children Act 1989:

(e) an order requiring either or both parents of a child (i) to transfer to the applicant, for the benefit of the child, or *for the benefit of a parent who has contributed substantially, whether by means of providing care or other resources, to the care of the child*, or (ii) to transfer to the child himself, such property to which the parent is, or the parents are, entitled (either in possession or reversion) as may be specified in the order.'

A similar insertion could be made into sub-paragraph (1) of paragraph (2), which allows the court to

make a periodical payments order 'to the applicant for the benefit of the child' or 'to the child himself'. It would make clear that courts could hold that a former cohabitee was potentially liable to make provision, by property transfer or otherwise, to the person who substantially cared for their child.

These would not be radical departures. They simply extend to the post-caregiving period provisions allowing support of the carer *during* the caregiving period. Their enactment would almost completely suffice to deal with the financial and property problems that arise between former cohabitees. By linking the jurisdiction to child-rearing issues, the 'open' normative issues in the 'reasonable expectations' doctrine become more focused. The decision-makers are directed to the norms and practices of analogous cases that are routinely dealt with in the divorce jurisdiction. But should we, nevertheless, go further?

There remain three possible areas of concern. One occurs during the period of the cohabitation. Should a non-owning cohabitee be required to obtain the consent of his or her partner dealings with the home and household goods? This protection has recently been provided in Sweden.[56] It must be repeated that, were it thought appropriate to provide such protection, it need not require creating a proprietary interest, for example, by retrospective constructive trust, in favour of the non-owner. Protection of *enjoyment* of property (through a consent requirement) is conceptually separate from the issue of ownership (which concerns entitlement to capital value). European countries make no linkage between the two. Nor should it be necessary to resort to uncertain extensions of the principle of unconscionability. A provision, such as the Swedish, could be enacted in England (at least where the cohabiting parents have children in the house) but it should be remembered that such protection is not given to married couples unless they register or enter a notice of caution under the Matrimonial Homes Act 1983. However, the *practical effect* of the House of Lords' decision in *William & Glyn's Bank* v. *Boland*[57] is such that third parties dealing with the owner of the *home* will standardly seek the consent of any other adult currently in occupation, irrespective of marital status. So it may not be necessary to do anything. If, through any misfortune, the *Boland* doctrine were to suffer judicial reversal, Parliament should either enact its effect

---

[52] [1992] 2 All E.R. 727.

[53] This solution is very similar to that adopted in Sweden under the Cohabitees (Joint Homes) Act 1987, which allows such transfers on the basis of needs. See below, note 56.

[54] This is achieved in divorce cases under so-called *Mesher* or *Martin* orders. These are explained in *Clutton* v. *Clutton* [1991] 1 All E.R. 340.

[55] Above, note 7.

[56] Cohabitees (Joint Homes) Act 1987. See David Bradley, 'The Development of a Legal Status for Unmarried Cohabitation in Sweden' (1989) 18 *Anglo–American Law Review* 322. In addition to imposing the consent requirement, the statute imposes a 'forced share' in a deceased's cohabitee's estate in favour of a former partner.

[57] [1981] 1 A.C. 487.

statutorily or impose a consent requirement for dealings in a family home.

The second area of concern is whether, even if the law were to be amended as has been suggested, there should *nevertheless* be some general principles upon which the property of non-married cohabitees should be allocated. The answer to this must clearly be 'yes'. There should be grounds for claiming a share in resources to which a partner has contributed, whether or not a child had been born into the union. But it will be apparent that I do not believe that a development in trusts law along the lines of the 'communality' envisaged by Gardner, attractive though it seems, is either necessary or even desirable. Would it be better, then, to enact a measure similar to the New South Wales De Facto Relationships Act 1984? This permits an application for a property adjustment order to be made by a party to a de facto relationship lasting more than two years (or into which a child is born) and the court may make such order 'as to it seems just and equitable' having regard to (a) financial and non-financial contributions made directly or indirectly to the acquisition, conservation or improvement of property or resources and (b) contributions, including those of a homemaker or parent, to the welfare of the other partner or a child. A proposal along similar lines has been made for Scotland.[58]

The significant difference between this provision and standard provisions on divorce is that it does not include a reference to the *future* needs of the partners, and it is criticized for this reason by Rebecca Bailey-Harris.[59] We have seen that English law to a large extent *already* allows financial and property orders to be made in favour of a former cohabitee on the basis of the future needs of a child, and, with small amendments, could be extended to take into account the future needs of a one-time caregiver. But as far as recognizing *past* contributions unconnected with child-rearing are concerned, some such provision has merit. Yet we may not need one. In 1987 the Alberta Law Reform Commission recommended against the adoption of such legislation in Alberta on the grounds that the remedies provided through the Canadian law of constructive trusts was sufficient, even if it did not recognize the contributions of a homemaker.[60] Perhaps we could say the same of English law, provided the statutory amendments concerning children and former caregivers suggested

above were enacted, and proprietary estoppel developed towards the New Zealand 'reasonable expectations' solution.[61]

Finally, attention would need to be paid to the position of a former cohabitee after the death of his or her partner. Although Sweden has made provision for a 'forced' share for the survivor, the Scottish Law Commission recommended against this, preferring a power to apply for a discretionary provision.[62]

6. Conclusion and Reflections

In conclusion, it is worth relating the position advocated above to some of the wider issues canvassed in this volume. First, the integrity of the distinction between proprietary and personal claims is maintained. I have argued that a cohabitee-plaintiff should be entitled to seek to prove that a beneficial interest is vested in him or her by producing evidence that this was expressly so declared or that such a common intention can be implied. The main benefit accruing from this will be that the capital value of this interest will be beyond the reach of third party claims against the plaintiff's partner (especially by unsecured creditors and beneficiaries to his/her estate). *Occupation* rights, it has been argued, are in *practice* secured against third parties by the operation of the *Boland* doctrine, whether or not the plaintiff has a beneficial interest; if this is thought to be inadequate, the solution (it has been suggested) is best found through a statutory consent requirement for dealings in a family home.

Because of the effect on third-parties, it is right that the establishment of such beneficial interests be strictly applied, although it is conceded that the proprietary estoppel cases create some doctrinal uncertainty here. Of course property concepts, like other legal concepts, serve social ends and *could* be imposed *ex post* (or their effect achieved by some other means) on the basis of a 'discretionary' appreciation of the context. But *general* legal concepts would collapse into incoherence without a framework which can sustain them. Hence the criticism of the potential wide and uncertain use of an apparently *proprietal* remedy within the context of 'reasonable expectations". A central purpose of this paper has been to demonstrate that the results which it is often sought to achieve through such remedies can normally be achieved in other ways which are

---

[58] Scottish Law Commission, *Report on Family Law*, Scot. Law Com. No. 135 (1992), para. 16.23.

[59] Rebecca Bailey-Harris, 'Property Division on Separation: will the Married and the Unmarried pass at the Crossroads?' (1985) 8 *U.N.S.W. Law Journal* 1.

[60] Alberta Institute of Law Research and Reform, *Towards*

Reform of the Law Relating to Cohabitation outside Marriage, 1987.

[61] It is notable that such principles have not been developed in Scots law: Scot. Law Com. No. 135 (above, note 58), para. 16.17.

[62] Scot. Law Com. No. 135, above note 58, para. 16.37.

clearer, cheaper and represent more considered policy choices. So legislation could ordain that a proportion of the value of an insolvent cohabitee's property be withheld from unsecured creditors in favour of the cohabitee's partner, as it might (but does not, in English law) do for an insolvent's spouse; or that a former cohabitee should have a prior call on a proportion of his or her deceased's partner's estate, as is indeed the case with respect to spouses.

But most disputes are confined to the (former) cohabitants themselves. Here it is argued that the 'reasonable expectations' doctrine provides the best *background principle* for determining these disputes, but that the very flexibility which makes it appropriate to operate *inter partes* disqualifies it, without more, from operating *erga omnes*. Furthermore, because the doctrine raises the difficult 'normative issue', it has been suggested that its application in the family context be mediated through statute in cases where the former cohabitees are parents of a common child or children. By linking the application of the principle closely to the jurisdiction which is exercised where similar issues arise between married parents, the courts will be provided with a 'map' to guide them in the application of the normative issue. This would in practice cover almost all the cases where substantial difficulty arises, leaving those falling outside this context to the background principle itself.

16. Proprietary Rights as Remedies

PETER BIRKS

LONG the leading scholar in the field, and the author of the leading treatise,[1] Professor Donovan Waters has exercised great and beneficial influence on the Canadian law of trusts. One pillar of his international reputation has been his advocacy over a period of some thirty years of the remedial as opposed to the substantive or institutional understanding of the constructive trust.[2] His participation in this seminar offers an opportunity which an agnostic in this matter cannot let pass. This paper therefore has modest analytical objectives. Its purpose is to identify the obstacles to reception of the remedial faith. It must be understood throughout as continually asking whether these difficulties are real or not.

1. The Meaning of 'Remedial'

Elias, in his study of constructive trusts, a difficult but profound work, comes to the conclusion that nobody has succeeded in formulating a rigorous interpretation of the word 'remedy' as used of the constructive trust.[3] An unstabilized concept is always dangerous, and the underlying difficulties crop up continually. Baffling sentences of this kind are almost inescapable: 'While it may indeed be accurate to state that English law does not regard the constructive trust as a remedy in the sense that it regards the injunction as a remedy, it can hardly be said that a litigant seeking the imposition of a constructive trust is not seeking a remedy.'[4]

There has to be some sorting out. We may safely concentrate on the proprietary implications and lay aside uses of the language of constructive trust which are directed, arguably superfluously, to bolstering a conclusion that a defendant is under an obligation to account, a form of words itself abused as often as not to mean only that he must pay. The mysteries of 'remedial' then reduce to an inquiry about all property rights. What, if any, meaning can be given to the notion of a remedial property right?

A first step is to say with more precision what we

intend, on the proprietary plane, when we affirm that one person holds an asset on a constructive trust for another. There are these separable points: (i) that other has a proprietary interest in the asset; (ii) that proprietary interest is equitable and not legal; (iii) that equitable proprietary interest, though possibly less than full ownership, is of a higher nature than a lien or a 'mere equity', since these lesser interests can subsist without there being any necessity to describe the parties as being in the relationship of trustee and cestui que trust; (iv) that proprietary interest does not originate directly from the intent of the parties, the word 'directly' here allowing for the possibility that their intent may not have been irrelevant. Of these the key points for most purposes are the proprietary right and its non-consensual origin. The question is whether such a right can be called a remedy.

A second preliminary step is to pause to consider the word or words with which 'remedy' is contrasted. Often in the law it is the contrast within an opposing pair of words that matters, as when common law is paired against equity, statute or civil law. In this paper the inquiry is conducted in terms of remedy and right. The question is whether the rights undoubtedly implied by a constructive trust differ from the generality of rights in some way which, without denying their quality as rights, can be satisfactorily identified by the adjective 'remedial'.

The elusive contrast between 'remedy' and something else is also often discussed as an opposition between 'remedy' and 'institution' or 'substantive institution'.[5] These pairings are more impenetrable. They are to be understood in this way: the only sense in which the property rights implied by a constructive trust can be contrasted with rights generally as being specially remedial entails denying their nature as inferences of substantive law from facts which happen in the world (substantive institutions) and insisting on their being, by contrast, merely the creatures of a later judicial discretion to redress the grievance which the facts threw up (remedies). This

[1] D. W. M. Waters, *The Law of Trusts in Canada*, 2nd edition (Toronto, 1984).

[2] The starting point was: D. W. M. Waters, *The Constructive Trust: The Case for a New Approach in English Law* (London, 1964), see esp. 7–26 and 73.

[3] G. Elias, *Explaining Constructive Trusts* (Oxford, 1990) 159, 163.

[4] A. J. Oakley, *Constructive Trusts*, 2nd edition (London, 1987) 11.

[5] *Rawluk v. Rawluk* (1990) 65 D.L.R. (4th) 161, 169 (Cory, J.),

183–9 (McLachlin, J.). Cf. J. L. Dewar, 'The Development of the Remedial Constructive Trust' (1982) 60 Can. B.R. 265; M. Cope, *Constructive Trusts* (Sydney, 1992) 12–15, 24–6, 48–9. This language appears to go back to a singularly opaque passage by Roscoe Pound: R. Pound, 'The Progress of the Law, 1918–1919', (1919) Harv. L.R. 420–3. It is to be noted that he thought the same about the equitable lien: 'A like remedial device, easily confounded with a substantive institution, is the imposition of an equitable lien' (423). On liens, see text from n. 8 below.

will seem very unclear, but it will become clearer below.[6]

1(1) Proprietary Rights Arising as Facts Happen

There are many examples of non-consensual proprietary rights which indisputably arise as facts happen in the world beyond the court. In order to minimize controversy, let us take three examples of such rights which do not imply a constructive trust: first, the undivided shares which arise at law when fluids mix; secondly, the equitable lien which arises when a person receives a payment which diminishes a loss already made good by his insurer; and, thirdly, the power to rescind and revest after misrepresentation.

When oil owned by one person is mixed with oil belonging to another, the immediate effect is co-ownership of the whole. That is, each contributor acquires an undivided share in the mass, measured by his contribution. If the ascertainment of the shares is evidentially impossible, then, if the evidential difficulty was created by the wrongful act of one party, that party will forfeit his interest to the other, who will thus become owner of the whole.[7] Can the undivided co-ownership of each contributor or, where the penal rule operates, the sole ownership of one contributor be called a remedy? The answer is yes. The facts create a problem and, in that one contributor will certainly be out of possession, potentially a substantial grievance. The proprietary interests which arise are the law's response to and thus constitute the cure or remedy for the difficulty. However, if those new proprietary rights are referred to as remedies, there is no contrast to be found in that usage between 'remedy' and 'right' or 'substance' or 'institution'.

Let us turn to the equitable lien. *Lord Napier and Ettrick* v. *Hunter*[8] involved Lloyds names who had incurred losses but had taken out stop-loss policies up to fixed maxima. The stop-loss insurers paid out, and the names subsequently recovered larger sums from those whose negligence had caused their losses. There was no doubt that the names who recovered damages diminishing the loss which had been paid were personally liable to repay the stop-loss insurers, but the question was whether the latter also had some species of proprietary right in the damages. If yes, they would have priority in a name's insolvency. The House of Lords held that the stop-loss insurers did have such a proprietary right, and that that right was by nature an equitable lien. The further question was left open whether that lien first

came into existence when the fund of damages was received by the names or, before that, had already attached to the claims against the tortfeasor. It was sufficient on the facts that the lien attached to the money received. What is absolutely clear is that in such a case the lien is engendered by the facts, not by the court.

Again this proprietary right can be called a remedy. The insurer has a grievance, which consists in the fact that his insured has been doubly indemnified at his expense. The law responds with a personal claim and, it now seems, with a lien on the receipts which have diminished the loss. Those rights, personal and proprietary, are the insurer's remedies. But again there is no contrast in that usage between 'remedy' and 'right' or between 'remedy' and any of the other words which are sometimes pressed into service to create an opposing pair ('institution' or 'substance').

Thirdly, the power to revest in oneself an asset the property in which has passed, voidably, to another. *Car and Universal Finance Co.* v. *Caldwell*[9] shows that the victim of misrepresentation loses title to his asset but acquires instead a power *in rem*, a power to alter the legal status of that asset and, in particular, to vest it in himself. The case also tells us that the exercise of the power does not require communication with the person in possession, so long only as reasonable steps are taken to make manifest the intention to exercise it. The power is itself a proprietary right, albeit a fragile one. And it is, equally, a remedy for a grievance of the victim. The power to revest is both right and remedy.

In *Chase Manhattan Bank* v. *British Israel Bank*[10] Goulding, J., had to ask himself, in order to deal with a conflicts question, 'whether the equitable right of a person who pays money by mistake to trace and claim such money under the law of New York is conferred by substantive law or is of a merely procedural character.'[11] He was driven to conclude that 'save in very special circumstances it is as idle to ask whether the court vindicates the suitor's substantive right or gives the suitor a procedural remedy, as to ask whether thought is a mental or cerebral process.' That is to say, in his opinion it was a matter of synonyms used to describe the same phenomenon from slightly different standpoints.

In our examples that is certainly true of 'right' and 'remedy'. The contributor to a fluid mixture, the insurer who pays up before the loss is diminished and the victim induced by misrepresentation to

---

[6] Part 1(2) below, text to n . 14.
[7] *Indian Oil Corporation Ltd.* v. *Greenstone Shipping S.A.* [1988] Q.B. 345.
[8] [1993] A.C. 713.

[9] [1965] 1 Q.B. 525.
[10] [1981] Ch. 105.
[11] At 124.

transfer his car all acquire what is analytically a proprietary right but functionally a remedy for the mischief arising on the facts. These rights imply no constructive trust. If and so far as those non-consensual proprietary rights which do subsist within a constructive trust are of the same kind in this one crucial respect, namely that they arise as the relevant facts happen, they must be similarly incapable of being 'remedies' in any sense opposed to 'right'. If that is correct, just as with the rights *in rem* themselves, so with the constructive trust within which they exist there cannot be distinct remedial conception of that trust.

At risk of labouring the point, the reason is that it is true of all rights which arise by operation of law when certain facts happen that, if they are referred to as remedies for the problem posed by those facts, their being so described does not change their nature as rights; it merely adds a functional comment: they are rights which, in contrast to those which are facilitative in the sense that they are recognized in order to give effect to what people want, are raised regardless of intent to help solve a problem or rectify a mischief.

An important recent case serves to conclude this part. In *A.-G. for Hong Kong* v. *Reid* ([1993] 3 W.L.R. 1143) the Privy Council, declining to follow *Lister* v. *Stubbs*,[12] held that the victim of bribery could assert a proprietary interest in assets in which the bribe had been traceably invested. To the extent that the tracing exercise was possible, the Attorney-General would thus be beneficially entitled under a constructive trust to the land in New Zealand bought by the corrupt prosecutor, Reid. The case presented to the Privy Council by counsel for the Attorney-General argued for what is expressly referred to as a 'remedial constructive trust'. It is evident from the advice written by Lord Templeman that the trust arose as the facts happened, since his Lordship's reasoning turns partly on the proposition that at the very moment that Reid received the bribe the doctrine in *Walsh* v. *Lonsdale*[13] bit on his obligation to surrender it to the Attorney-General: equity regarded that as done which ought to be done and therefore conceived the transferee as already the owner of the money. His Lordship did not himself use the term 'remedial constructive trust'.

If anyone were now to describe the *Reid* trust as remedial, that adjective could only be saying that the proprietary interest which arises on such facts is brought into existence to deal with a problem, namely the problem of corruption and the danger that a corrupt person might cling on to some of his ill-gotten gains. That functional or teleological comment could not create any contrast between the *Reid* trust and a trust in which the rights were 'substantive' or 'institutional'.

The lesson is that there is this weak sense of 'remedial' in which all non-consensual rights can be so described; it adds nothing interesting to 'right' and must never be allowed to create a distinct category. Much of what is found in books on remedies is only about remedies in this weak sense. For example, a close study of the measure of damages for torts or breach of contract is no more a study of the remedy for those occurrences than of the right born of them. Finally, it is worth rubbing in that this weak sense in which the constructive trust is indubitably and invariably a remedy not only does not set it apart but also obviously cannot suggest either that it can be understood other than in terms of the facts upon which it arises or that it should be immune to the law's ordinary concern for certainty. The weak sense of 'remedial' cannot make the constructive trust special in any way at all.

1(2) Judicial Remedies and Pre-Existing Rights

We have been looking at a usage of the word 'remedy' in which it is a synonym for 'substantive right', albeit one which takes its own functional perspective: the 'right' is a 'remedy' because it comes into existence to remedy a mischief. The word 'remedy' can be used in a narrower sense. The rights which a person has, even if they are not facilitative but remedial in the weak sense above, are not self-executing. That is, even if they arise to correct bad facts, they are in themselves corrective only in theory. In a narrower or stronger sense, therefore, a remedy is something practical which can be done towards realizing those theoretical rights. An extra-judicial or self-help remedy is something practical which you can do yourself to correct a grievance, and a judicial remedy is something which a court can do to help realize rights—a money judgment, for example, or an Anton Piller order or a Mareva injunction. We can leave the extra-judicial remedies aside.

It is important to notice that even now we have not created a clear opposition between 'remedy' and 'substantive right'. Within the category of remedies in the narrower sense (judicial remedies, things that a court can do to help realize rights), an important distinction has to be made between those which are discretionary and those which are not. The reason is that there is no real contrast between 'right' and 'non-discretionary remedy'. For example, the practical help given to a plaintiff by a money judgment at

---

[12] (1880) 45 Ch. D.1.

[13] (1882) 21 Ch. D.9.

common law is imperfectly distinguishable from his pre-existing right. That is because, from the moment the facts happened upon which the plaintiff's entitlement arose, one component of that entitlement was the right to that judgment. In other words, the plaintiff's pre-existing entitlement could be described as including the right to the judgment and the further rights which accrue to a plaintiff by virtue of the judgment.

It is different with remedies which are discretionary, which can be abruptly contrasted with rights. Such remedies may be available to deal with troublesome facts which disclose no perfect pre-existing rights, as for example judicial review of administrative action or Mareva injunctions. Or they may be available in support of pre-existing rights, as an order of specific performance is available in some cases in support of the right created by contract. Subject to a difficult point to be made below about discretions so well settled as to be merely technical, so long as a judicial remedy is described as discretionary, it cannot logically be said that the particular form of practical help which that remedy implies is part of the plaintiff's pre-existing entitlement. The entitlement of citizen who suffers a breach of natural justice can be described in terms of a right to turn to the courts but, beyond that important generality, cannot be said to include a right to judicial review in any of its forms; but the modern equivalents of certiorari, mandamus and prohibition are remedies, remedies which are not rights, in the courts' discretionary armoury for redressing administrative grievances.

The genuine opposition between 'right' and 'remedy' which is found here contradistinguishes entitlements inhering in individuals independently of judicial pronouncements ('rights') and, on the other hand, discretionary judicial pronouncements which, if they confer rights on an individual, do so by their own virtue and not merely by way of declaration or realization of a pre-existing entitlement ('remedies').

There is an acute difficulty at this point which must be noticed but which will not be pursued. Should a further distinction be made between remedies which are merely technically or marginally discretionary and remedies which are substantially discretionary? Probably the answer is yes. Specific performance is technically discretionary but the discretion has so settled down that it is perfectly possible to describe the facts upon which a party will have a right to that remedy. On the other hand in the Family Division residence and contact orders in respect of children and property adjustments upon divorce are substantially discretionary.[14] It is impossible ahead of the exercise of the discretion to describe a claimant's entitlements. Without formally making this distinction, which once made would acknowledge a pre-existing entitlement to a remedy which was only technically discretionary and would therefore in effect classify technically discretionary remedies with non-discretionary remedies, the model for what follows is the substantial discretion.

It is only here, in the category of discretionary things that a court may do, that one could hope to find a role for a remedial as opposed to substantive trust. Although the word 'substantive' will never be happy in the other corner,[15] the contrast would imply that trusts in general arose when facts happened in the world (substantive trusts or trusts connoting rights inferred by substantive law from facts), but that constructive trusts came into existence only when, in the exercise of a discretion, the court chose to create them. Strictly, the remedy should be called, not constructive trust, but declaration of constructive trust, the declaration being the practical step taken and the constructive trust being a bundle of new rights thus brought into existence.

If there were such a discretionary constructive trust in the court's armoury of remedies, its range would still need to be known. That is to say, the question would still remain to be answered whether the discretion to declare and thus create a constructive trust was general, in the sense that the court might create constructive trusts whenever that seemed a good response to a bad situation, or particular, in the sense that the court might have the discretion to create constructive trusts only to correct certain limited species of bad situations.

Wide ranging or not, the elaborate language ought never to conceal the fact that a remedial constructive trust of this kind necessarily implies, indeed is, a discretion to vary property rights. The premiss of the discretion is that on the facts which have happened the plaintiff has no pre-existing proprietary right in any relevant assets in the defendant's possession. If he did have such a right and that right were equitable, there would in these terms be a 'substantive' trust, a trust inferred by law from facts as and when they happened. Upon that premiss, that no entitlement *in rem* had arisen on the facts, the court would then have the discretion to raise as constructive trust or, in other words, to confer an equitable proprietary interest in those assets. It is notorious that when unmarried couples split up there is often a problem

---

[14] Children Act, 1989, ss. 8–12; Matrimonial Causes Act, 1973, ss. 24 and 24A.

[15] Cf. text to n. 5 above.

as to ownership of their former home. A jurisdiction which claims to be able to solve that kind of problem through remedial constructive trusts, and uses 'remedial' in the strong sense, must be claiming a non-statutory discretion to vary property rights.

1(3) A discretion to vary property rights?

If the remedial constructive trust entails the discretionary adjustment of property rights, these and only these are the terms in which debate should be conducted: Is it desirable for the courts, in relation to some or all kinds of grievance, to have a discretion to vary property rights? And should that right be claimed without a statute?

The tradition of the law has always been against powerful discretions to adjust property rights. In Lord Nottingham's words, the way would be 'opened to the Lord Chancellor to construe or presume any man in England out of his estate.'[16] In exceptional situations such a discretion has been conferred by statute. For example, under the Variation of Trusts Act 1958, the court is given a discretion to consent to arrangements on behalf of those who for one reason or another cannot consent for themselves and, although this was probably never intended, the order of the court does itself effect the variation.[17] Again it has been found necessary to give the court such a discretion when married couples divorce.[18] To notice a long-standing aversion to discretion interference with property rights is not, of course, to make the case against it, though it might be thought to shift the onus to the advocates of a judicial power of that kind.

It is true that proprietary consequences follow hard upon an unsatisfied judgment. But a special justification is needed to explain a departure from that order of events. A judgment for the surrender of items of property inflicts loss, as does a money judgment, but, unlike a money judgment, also entangles itself in the complexities both of unwanted consequences for third parties and of individual economic priorities. The latter point is important and often neglected. Taking money from people makes them worse off and narrows their options, taking specific things is a more erratic instrument of justice, because of their subjective value: the same 'adjustment' will cause vastly different degrees of pain, depending on the sentiments and tastes of the loser.

Do the courts in fact claim any such discretion or

do they regard the rights implied by a constructive trust as arising as inferences from the relevant facts as they happen? We have seen that in England the newest example, the proprietary rights in the assets in which a bribe is invested, indisputably arises as the facts happen.[19] The long story of the attempt to solve the problems of unmarried divorce might in substance be said by some to be tantamount to the assertion of a discretion but in form it has been exactly the opposite. The effort has all been directed to finding substantive doctrines to coax socially satisfactory consequences from the facts themselves. Common intention and proprietary estoppel are of that kind.

In the U.S.A. there has been a notorious disagreement as to whether a constructive trust is the creature of the relevant facts or of the court order. *Scott on Trusts* favours the former view: the constructive trust arises as the facts happen: 'It would seem that there is no foundation whatever for the notion that a constructive trust does not arise until it is decreed by a court.'[20] *Bogert on Trusts and Trustees* nevertheless takes the opposite line, conceding that the order of the court has retrospective effect to the time at which the fats happened.[21] Elias cites *U.S.* v. *Fontana*[22] as decisively, and explicitly, in favour of Scott's view.[23] Questions of priorities between a lien claimed by the U.S. Revenue and an interest under a constructive trust claimed by the employer of Fontana would have been resolved in favour of the Revenue if a constructive trust arose only with the order of the court. But the court held that it arose when the facts happened, so that the employer's interest took priority.

In Canada the Supreme Court was obliged to face up to the same question in *Rawluk* v. *Rawluk*.[24] The majority affirmed the position taken by *Scott on Trusts*. A married couple separated after twenty-nine years. Most of the assets were in the husband's name. The wife was entitled to a statutory equalization in money on the basis of a valuation made as on the day of their separation. However, because the value of the assets had risen after the valuation date, it had become very much in her interest to establish that she already had a large interest in them by that date. The larger her interest, the less would be caught by the now unfavourable equalization machinery.

The wife successfully established that she was and prior to the valuation date already had been entitled

---

[16] *Cook* v. *Fountain* (1676) 3 Swanston App. 585, 586.
[17] *Re Holt's Settlement* [1969] 1 Ch. 100.
[18] Matrimonial Causes Act, 1973, ss. 24 and 24A. The prevalence of informal 'marriage' is leading to the statutory extension of this discretion to the technically unmarried.
[19] *Attorney-General for Hong Kong* v. *Reid*, text before n. 12 above.

[20] A. Scott and W. Fratcher, *The Law of Trusts*, 4th ed., vol. 5 (Boston, 1989), #462.4, p. 323.
[21] G. G. Bogert and G. T. Bogert, *The Law of Trusts and Trustees*, revised 2nd edition (St. Paul, 1978), #472, from p. 30.
[22] 528 F. Supp. 137 (1981).
[23] Elias n. 3 above, 162.
[24] (1990) 65 D.L.R. (4th) 161.

to a half share under a constructive trust. Cory, J., with whom Dickson, C. J. C., Wilson and L'Heureux Dubé, JJ., agreed, continued to describe the trust as 'remedial' but expressly approved the statement from *Scott on Trusts* quoted above which flatly denies that a constructive trust arises other than when the relevant facts happen.[25] Having decided that the statutory machinery had not been intended to displace the operation of the constructive trust, Cory, J., had no difficulty in reaching a conclusion very favourable to the wife.

MacLachlin, J., with whom La Forest and Sopinka, JJ., agreed, dissented. She maintained that the statutory machinery had displaced the constructive trust as a means of reconciling the conflicting interests of the parties. In her view, moreover, the Canadian constructive trust was a discretionary remedy: 'The significance of the remedial nature of the constructive trust is not that it cannot confer a property interest but that the conferring of such an interest is discretionary and dependent on the inadequacy of other remedies for the unjust enrichment in question.'[26]

In the light of *Rawluk* it is not easy to know how to interpret the earlier decision in *Lac Minerals Ltd.* v. *International Corona Services Ltd.*[27] There Corona found a goldfield, largely on land which they did not own. Looking for a joint-venturer, they entered into conversations with Lac, which, when it had found out enough information, bought the necessary claims for itself. Lac having developed the goldfield, Corona successfully claimed to be entitled to it under a constructive trust, their interest being subject to a lien in Lac for the development input. In the Supreme Court of Canada both the majority, in favour of proprietary interest, and the minority, preferring to award compensatory damages clearly regarded themselves as having a choice: should they give a money judgment or vary the existing property rights? Moreover, they have been congratulated precisely for separating cause of action and remedy or, in other words, satisfying the requirements of certainty as to the ground of liability while insisting upon a discretion as to remedy.[28] That supposes a view of the constructive trust as something the courts may do if they see fit or, in short, a discretion to vary property rights.

Rawluk appears to require us to say that the *Lac* court was not contemplating a discretion exercisable from case to case but was rather weighing the policies which once and for all would determine whether misuse of confidential information does or does not give rise to proprietary consequences.

Under that interpretation, the question becomes whether, given that proprietary rights can arise when certain troublesome facts happen, acquisitive abuse of confidential information is or is not one such set of facts. And the Lac answer is yes. Hence the proprietary right which the victim acquires in the proceeds of an abuse of confidential information is, like the right in respect of a bribe which was recognized in *Reid*, a proprietary right engendered by the facts. It is not the creature of the court; it is not the consequence of a judicial discretion to vary property rights.

However, *Rawluk* or not *Rawluk*, the Supreme Court of Canada continues to treat the constructive trust as conferring on it a loosely constrained discretion to adjust property rights without statutory authority. In *Peter* v. *Beblow*[29] an unmarried couple had split up after twelve years. The question was whether the woman's long service in running and maintaining the home entitled her to an interest in the home or gave her only a personal claim for restitution of the money value of her work. She was held to be entitled under a constructive trust to the entire interest in the home. Cory, J., was now in favour of the maximum of discretionary flexibility. McLachlin, J., with whom Iacobucci, J., agreed, showed herself more inclined than Cory, J., to rein in the discretion. Nevertheless, she saw the issue as turning on three rather open-textured questions, whether a money judgment for reasonable remuneration would be adequate, whether there was a sufficient nexus between the wife's input and the asset in which a property interest was sought, and whether the interest in that asset could be matched to the value of her input. The loose grip of these questions was revealed in McLachlin, J.'s conclusion that the woman should have the entire interest in the house. She supported that conclusion by aggregating all the assets and reckoning the house as a fair reflection of her contribution to the joint-venture and her entitlement to one half of its aggregated surviving value.

McLachlin, J.'s views expressed in her dissent in *Rawluk* have clearly remained unchanged. The proprietary interest continues to be at the court's discretion, within guidelines very loosely set by the principle against unjust enrichment. In substance she has used *Peter* v. *Beblow* to extend to unmarried divorce the discretions statutorily available upon married divorce, a programme expressly indicated early in her judgment.[30] Oakley, who favours the view that there can be no constructive trust without

[25] At 176. Cf. Gardner above, n. 36 and text thereafter.
[26] At 185.
[27] (1989) 61 D.L.R. (4th) 14.
[28] J. D. Davies, 'Duties of Confidence and Loyalty', [1990]

L.M.C.L.Q. 4, answered by P. Birks, 'The Remedies for Abuse of Confidential Information' [1990], L.M.C.L.Q. 460.
[29] (1993) 101 D.L.R. (4th) 621.
[30] At p. 648.

a court order, has rightly pointed out that *Rawluk* has less weight in this matter than one easily supposes and that the majority could have reached their decision without adopting the Scott view of the manner and time in which a constructive trust comes into existence; the Bogert view would have sufficed.[31] McLachlin, J., is evidently of the same view.

With the possible exception of Canada, where the position now seems confused although *Rawluk* seems unlikely have much long-term effect, no jurisdiction appears to accept the remedial constructive trust in the only sense in which it can be usefully contrasted with other trusts. In that sense the remedial constructive trust is the creature of judicial discretion, and, as such, is a complex and, as some might say, deceptive assertion of a non-statutory discretion to vary property rights.

1(4) Two Special Cases

There are two figures which might be candidates to be considered remedial proprietary rights within the strong sense of that term which has just been considered. On closer inspection they are not. One may be described as the right arising where value can be traced through substitutions. The other is what Professor Goode has called a *ius ad rem*.

(i) *Tracing value through substitutions.* Suppose a simple series of substitutions in an uncontroversial context: a trustee takes money from the trust and puts it into an empty bank account and later withdraws it and buys a car. On these facts the process of tracing shows that the value taken from the trust in the form of money, exchanged for a claim against the bank and, reversing that exchange, withdrawn from the bank, is now invested in the car. Then comes a second and separate question: what right does the cestui que trust have in the car? On these facts that is not in doubt. He may assert that in equity the car is his. We need not for the moment decide whether the trust is constructive or resulting. In *El Ajou* v. *Dollar Land Holdings*[32] Millett, J., said that it was an old-fashioned institutional resulting trust, a classification with which it is very difficult to disagree.

A third question arises. At what moment in the story did the car become his? According to *Cave* v. *Cave*[33] it became his as soon as it was bought. The trust money was his, and in equity the claim against

the bank became his as soon as it was acquired, the money taken from the bank was his as soon as it was delivered to the trustee, and the car became his as soon as the legal property passed to the trustee. There are strong arguments in favour of a different analysis namely that the facts conferred on the cestui que trust a power to vest the substitutes in himself, a right analogous to that which arises in relation to the original asset under a voidable transaction. On this analysis he could have vested the earlier substitutes in himself but did not, and only by asserting his claim to the car did he vest it in himself.[34] The facts conferred a proprietary interest on him but that interest was initially only a power *in rem*, and only when the power was exercised did the interest crystallize as full equitable ownership.

It is not necessary to arbitrate between these two analyses. In this context, it is only relevant that neither produces a 'remedial property' in the strong sense. On the *Cave* analysis, the proprietary interest is raised immediately by the happening of the facts. In the power analysis the inchoate right, the power, is likewise born of the facts, and so also is the crystallized right. The crystallized right is born of the initial facts plus acts of the power-holder which suffice for the exercise of the power. Even here there is no discretionary intervention by the judges. Uncrystallized and crystallized, the plaintiff's right is not something which the courts may or may not concede. Hence, supposing it exists, the power to claim assets in which relevant value traceably survives is remedial only in the weak sense. The same is true of the right produced by the exercise of that power.

(ii) *Professor Goode's* ius ad rem. Professor Goode interprets the remedial constructive trust as implying a *ius ad rem*.[35] There are situations in which a person has a claim to have a particular asset conveyed to him, say an elephant. The general difficulty with such claims is that the limits on specific performance and specific delivery usually reduce them to money. And if the requirements for specific performance are satisfied the doctrine of *Walsh* v. *Lonsdale* confers an immediate equitable property on the person entitled. Nevertheless, there are some indications that it is possible for there to be a *tertium quid*: a claim that a thing be transferred to the claimant which the court will order to be transferred without triggering the

---

[31] A. J. Oakley, 'The Effect of the Imposition of a Constructive Trust' in S. Goldstein (ed.), *Equity and Contemporary Legal Developments* (Jerusalem, 1992) 427, 436–7. He also points to the evidence of *Muschinski* v. *Dodds* (1986) 160 C.L.R. 583 that, whichever rule is right, a court can depart from it. There the constructive trust was expressly given effect only from the publication of the judgments in order to ensure that its imposition did not imperil third parties.

[32] [1993] B.C.L.C. 735, 753.
[33] (1880) 15 Ch. D. 639.
[34] Further discussion: Birks, 'Mixing and Tracing, Property and Restitution' (1992) 45 (2) C.L.P. 69.
[35] R. Goode, 'Property and Unjust Enrichment', in A. S. Burrows, ed., *Essays on the Law of Restitution* (Oxford, 1991) 215, esp. 222, 237–44.

maxim that equity regards that as done which ought to be done or at least without triggering it until the order is actually made.[36]

It is slightly confusing to call such rights '*ad rem*', since analytically they are simply rights in personam which lay on the defendant the duty to convey a thing. Whatever the best name, we do not in this context need to determine whether the *tertium quid*, essentially a specifically performable obligation immune to *Walsh* v. *Lonsdale* until the court order, actually exists. Even if it does, it does not provide an example of a remedial property right in the strong sense. For the personal claim that the thing be transferred arises on the relevant facts and is not a property right at all; and, as for the order to transfer, those same facts which create the personal claim will either include or exclude the right to the order for specific delivery. In other words the property right born of the court order will either arise, contingently, as part of the package of entitlements created by the facts or it will not arise at all.

2. A Different Kind of Obstacle

We noticed above that if there were a non-statutory discretion to vary property interests there would still be a question as to its range, whether it was available to deal with all bad situations or only some. The assumption of those who have argued for the remedial constructive trust has been that its availability should be limited to situations in which the defendant has been unjustly enriched at the expense of the plaintiff. In short it would be a remedy only for unjust enrichment.

This could never work. There is no correlation between unjust enrichment and constructive trusts. That is, constructive trusts do not always respond to unjust enrichment and the trust response to unjust enrichment is not always a constructive trust. Each limb of that proposition calls for very extensive treatment, but both will have to be covered very briefly.

Professor Hayton says, very neatly, 'Constructive trusts can remedy other injustices besides unjust enrichment.'[37] and Elias's study shows that constructive trusts are founded on different rationalia. Some pursue the goal of what he calls 'perfection': they serve to perfect a commitment which the defendant

has made and which he should honour. Others pursue the goal of restitution for unjust enrichment. Others again have the aim of effecting reparation for loss.[38]

One might instance mutual wills and secret trusts as providing examples of constructive trusts which respond to other problems, but the point is sufficiently made for present purposes by the fact that there is no doubt that some constructive trusts serve to fulfil induced expectations. In *Pascoe* v. *Turner*[39] the plaintiff had made it very clear to the defendant that the house in which he had installed her was hers. She executed improvements in reliance on that belief. It might have been possible to conclude that he was thus enriched at her expense to the extent of about £200. But the decision was that he held the whole fee simple on trust for her. We need not dwell on the merits of that result. The only relevant point is that it could not conceivably be explained on the basis of unjust enrichment. Neither the legal fee simple nor its value had been received by the man at the woman's expense. The principle against unjust enrichment cannot explain relief which goes beyond restitution of enrichment which has been obtained at the plaintiff's expense. *Pascoe* was an expectation trust, not an unjust enrichment (or restitution) trust.

It cannot be sufficiently emphasized that a plaintiff who relies on unjust enrichment makes no case for any relief beyond restitution of the enrichment obtained at his expense. In *Gillies* v. *Keogh*[40] Sir Robin Cooke, P., aimed for a sensible rationalization of the rules which distribute the equitable interest in a home between unmarried partners who split up. He said that the key idea was that equity responded to the reasonable expectations of the parties. But he also seemed to suggest that this approach would produce results in line with those which had been produced elsewhere by looking for the partners' common intention or at the degree by which one of them would be unjustly enriched at the expense of the other. The same results were reached by different courts through different language: 'Normally it makes no practical difference in the result whether one talks of constructive trust, unjust enrichment, imputed common intention or estoppel.'[41] If that is true, it is only true because some courts have mistakenly abused of the very limited remedial potential of

---

[36] The possibility of such an animal has become less by reason of *Attorney-General for Hong Kong* v. *Reid* [1993] 3 W.L.R. 1143 and in particular because of Privy Council's treatment of *Metropolitan Bank* v. *Heiron* (1880) 5 Ex. D. 319 where both Brett, L. J., and Cotton, L. J., contemplated situations in which *Walsh* v. *Lonsdale* would not operate until the decree (but 'perilously close to the long vacation' [1993] 3 W.L.R. 1143, 1149 G).

[37] D. Hayton, 'Constructive Trusts: Is the Remedying of Unjust Enrichment a Satisfactory Approach?' in T. G. Youdan

(ed.), *Equity, Fiduciaries and Trusts* (Toronto, 1989) 205, 210.

[38] Elias n. 3 above, esp. 1–7, 48–85.

[39] [1979] 1 W.L.R. 431.

[40] [1989] 2 N.Z.L.R. 327.

[41] [1989] 2 N.Z.L.R. 327, 331. One flaw in this series is that whatever else it may be a constructive trust is a legal response to an event while the other three matters mentioned are events to which the law responds.

unjust enrichment. A trust which responds to induced expectations will differ not only in origin but also in quantum from one which arises from unjust enrichment.

There are two ways in which unjust enrichment can be illegitimately enlisted to the business of fulfilling expectations. One is overtly to break the logical link between unjust enrichment and restitution. A court which splits the ground of liability from the 'remedy', thus affirming that once an unjust enrichment has been established the possible responses are at large, will wrongly believe itself free to do things for which no case has been made. In *Sorochan* v. *Sorochan*[42] an unmarried couple had lived together for 42 years. The woman had done all the labour that farmer's wives could conceivably be expected to do. She successfully established a beneficial interest under a constructive trust in a severed one third of the farm and a personal entitlement to a substantial sum of money. Nobody would quarrel with the substance of that result. But it was reached on the basis of the man's unjust enrichment even though it is virtually impossible to explain as restitution strictly of his gain at her expense.

That the man did so gain is carefully established. But in the court's separated selection of the most appropriate response quite different ideas creep in, in particular: '[I]n assessing whether a constructive trust is appropriate, we must direct our minds to the specific question of whether the claimant reasonably expected to receive an actual interest in property and whether the respondent was or ought reasonably to have been cognizant of that expectation.'[43] This has nothing to do with unjust enrichment: a plaintiff who establishes that the defendant has been unjustly enriched at his expense simply makes no proposition which supports a right to have expectations fulfilled. It could be defended, if at all, only by a rigorous distinction, too delicate perhaps for forensic realities, between quantum of recovery (strictly no more than the gain at the plaintiff's expense) and the mode or manner of recovery (personal or proprietary).[44]

The second illegitimate extension of unjust enrichment into honouring expectations involves a switch from the plus-and-minus sense of 'at the expense of' to the 'by doing wrong to' sense. It is, as we have seen, evident that Pascoe was not enriched by his legal fee simple at Pearl Turner's expense in the subtractive plus-and-minus sense (it did not come from

her) and by the same token that attributing to her the full equitable interest did not reverse any such enrichment. But by changing the sense of 'at the expense of' we seem to be able to reach the contrary conclusion. In retaining the legal fee simple and endeavouring to evict her, he was enriching himself at her expense—that is, by committing a wrong to her, that wrong consisting in his resiling from the assurance which he had given her that the house was hers. There is an obvious *petitio principii*. The question was whether Pascoe must give up his house to Turner, but this 'wrong' analysis supposes as its starting point that he was bound to do so. Without that assumption there is no wrong on which the non-subtractive sense of 'at the expense of' can bite.

In *Baumgartner* v. *Baumgartner*,[45] where the High Court of Australia had to consider the rights to their home of partners who had split up, Toohey, J., appeared to think that, if it was unconscionable in the man to retain the land, it could equally be said that he was unjustly enriched by retaining it.[46] The truth is that both characterizations attach easily enough once one has decided the principal question: ought the entitled partner concede the interest in question? But neither can help till that question has been answered. A similar error has crept into attempts to use unjust enrichment to overcome the doctrine of privity.[47]

Because unjust enrichment is tied by its own logic to restitution of the enrichment to which the plaintiff points it cannot be used to fulfil expectations; no more can it be enlisted to solve the socio-economic problems created by new forms of marriage and complicated by an unstable housing market. When constructive trusts venture into these fields they venture beyond the law of unjust enrichment.

The other limb of the proposition that there is no correlation between unjust enrichment and constructive trusts is that other kinds of trust do respond to unjust enrichment. The resulting trust is centrally involved. A great deal of the law of restitution coheres around the elementary proposition 'I didn't really mean him to have it.' When a mistaken payment is recovered, it is because the payor 'didn't mean it' in the sense that his decision was impaired by the mistake. When a payment made for a consideration which fails is recovered, it is because the payor 'didn't mean it' in the sense that his decision was from the beginning conditional and in the events

---

[42] (1986) 29 D.L.R. (4th) 1.
[43] At p. 24.
[44] Lip service to something of this sort can be seen in the judgment of McLachlin, J., though definitely not in that of Cory, J., in *Peter* v. *Beblow* (1993), 101 D.L.R. (4th) 621, although what the court there actually does shows that even McLachlin, J., did not feel not firmly constrained by the logic

of restitution for unjust enrichment.
[45] (1987) 164 C.L.R. 37.
[46] At p. 154.
[47] *Trident-General Insurance Co. Ltd.* v. *McNiece Bros. Pty. Ltd.* (1988) 80 A.L.J.R. 574 (esp. Gaudron, J.): cf. K. B. Soh, 'Privity of Contract and Restitution' (1989), 105 L.Q.R. 4.

which have happened the condition was never purified. Resulting trusts are of this kind and these sub-kinds. An apparent gift is presumed not to have been meant unless either it was made in a gift-giving relationship (advancement) or it is proved to have been fully intended. A dedicated transfer which fails, either because it was a transfer on a trust which proves ineffective or because it was a transfer for a particular application which cannot be pursued, produces a resulting trust because from the beginning the transferor's intent was conditional and the condition has never been purified. Moreover a resulting trust carries back to the impoverished plaintiff exactly the enrichment which would otherwise be subtracted from him. In short the resulting trust effects restitution and, almost tautologously, responds to unjust enrichments within established and well-documented species of that disturbingly abstract genus.

It is difficult to know why the resulting trust has not been regarded as the law of trusts' principal contribution to the law of unjust enrichment. If it were true that resulting trusts rested ultimately on a genuine intention to create a trust or if it were true that they could be said to anticipate and prevent rather than reverse unjust enrichment, it would be right to have excluded them. But closer inspection falsifies both of these anti-restitutionary hypotheses.[48]

3. Conclusion

The agnosticism declared at the outset seems to boil down to these points. All rights which arise by operation of law are in a weak or inert sense remedial: they arise to deal with a problem. In the only strong or active sense that can be given to it, the remedial constructive trust is a judicial discretion to vary property rights and, as such, an object of suspicion. The fact that in one context, namely unmarried divorce, most legislatures are likely to agree on the need for such a discretion should not conceal the fact that, had the debate taken place in more accessible language, the project would have found few supporters. The sanctity of property and its immunity to discretionary 'adjustment' are deeply rooted in legal thought. This is dictated by respect for the individual and individual preferences and by the fear of prejudicing third parties.

So far as the project was linked to unjust enrichment it was flawed from the outset for want of any correlation between the constructive trust, remedial or not, and that particular cause of action. The forced correlation has had bad consequences. Unjust enrichment is a specific ground of liability with a restricted remedial potential. Those who favour the strong remedial notion of the constructive trust neglect that truth and compel unjust enrichment to do things beyond the power of its own logic to explain. The centrality in the law of restitution for unjust enrichment of the resulting trust has also been obscured. Nobody has suggested that the resulting trust is also remedial, not at least in the strong sense. It is to be hoped that nobody will. Property rights should not only be sacrosanct once in being but also stable in origin. That is, it should always be possible to know the facts upon which they arise. The notion of a remedial constructive trust ought therefore to be expelled from the law, partly because it is hopelessly incoherent and partly because, when compelled to be coherent, it reveals itself as noxious.

It often happens, however, that a scientific advance which will not quite work turns out none the less to have been a stage in the solution of a larger difficulty at first imperfectly perceived. In this case the more important and more difficult problem may turn out to have been a reclassification of trusts and trust obligations based on more accessible descriptions of the facts which bring them into being. Elias's work within constructive trusts should be enlarged. The aims which he found that constructive trusts pursued—perfection, restitution and reparation—can bear translation to, or at least relation to, more familiar language. Legal consequences generally can be said to be triggered by consent, wrongs, unjust enrichment and other events. The rights implied by trusts, and hence trusts themselves as the shell within which those rights subsist, will not turn out to be an exception. Indeed an exception is probably not a logical possibility, given the nature of the fourth term. The mysteries of implied, resulting and constructive sow early confusion. An intelligible classification would be a great advance.

---

[48] These paragraphs sum up an argument made at greater length in Birks, 'Restitution and Resulting Trusts' in S. Goldstein (ed.), *Equity and Contemporary Legal Developments* (Jerusalem, 1992) 335–74. More advanced research in a similar direction is being prosecuted by Robert Chambers (St. Peter's College, Oxford). One crucial question is the question whether evidence of affirmative evidence of a defective intent (a mis-

taken intent to give or an intent formed under undue influence or mental disability) suffices rebut a resulting trust. If it does, the notion that such a transferor has a 'mere equity' survives but the resulting trust itself has to absorb a contradiction, namely that which founds the trust when presumed, when affirmatively proved destroys it.

17. A State of Flux

J. D. DAVIES

THE series of seminars has had, for its subject, the Frontiers of Liability. Such a subject does not raise only the question of what the rules may be at the frontier. It also raises the question of the effect of the changing rules at the frontier on adjacent territories of law and on established divisions of the law (including, to Professor Birks' dismay, that between property and obligation). Our conception of the categories within which we usually envisage our rules of law as falling is affected. This is manifestly an issue that arises when we think about Constructive Trusts, but I will return to that later. For I want to start with Family Property Law, an area that is discussed in each paper, and in depth. I share the reservations expressed in one of those papers—and by many others in the course of the seminar—on whether it is a good way of approaching Constructive Trusts; but it serves to introduce the subject.

Each main Common Law jurisdiction recognized that there was a need for the judiciary to tackle the problems created by the changing fact situations within Family Property Law. The judiciary is to be commended for having done so, and for what has in consequence been achieved. But what has been achieved is not a complete solution, and the methods employed in doing so are easy to criticize.

The aim in each jurisdiction was to move to a solution through the existing resources of the law, by developing one or more of the various doctrines that might be available in order to provide a solution. In the United Kingdom there was development of the notion that where legal title is placed is not conclusive of where beneficial title should be. Development of the notion was based on common intentions, which may have been supportable in days of marriage vows and capital payments. But it was bound to run into trouble when the fact situations from which intentions were to be inferred became more complex. Findings of intentions to share in the beneficial ownership of property should not be founded on inadequate evidence; or on artificial interpretation of the facts. There is a role for common intentions, but it must not be strained into creating property rights which do not correspond with the reality. On that basis, however, the common intentions doctrine does not take us sufficiently far along the road of solving the Family Property problem.

Something more can be achieved by looking at representations given by one party to the other, in their own right. Representations do not fall to be considered only in the search for common intentions. Contract can only rarely assist in this area, but representations may lead to a remedy under the notion of Estoppel. After a late start, Australian law in particular might choose to use its present enthusiasm for Estoppel in this way. But this route is no more capable of providing a complete solution for the problems of Family Property law than a doctrine based on common intentions is. Representations need to be clear—straining towards an end has to be avoided here too—and they are not readily provable in this area. Moreover the remedy in Estoppel, as well as being discretionary, is also limited by reference to the detriment suffered.

A solution along the lines of a Constructive Trust can also be canvassed—which I believe to be a quite different solution to the 'common intentions' method. It is not dependent on intentions being common or on representations being clear, but relies to a greater extent on expectations that have in various ways been induced. Conduct is not excluded either, and the analysis tends to be retrospective as well as prospective. The solution is in fact remedial; and since it may lead to an award of a share in the beneficial ownership of property, can fairly be termed a Remedial Constructive Trust. It runs fewer risks of artificiality than other solutions for the simple reason that it has fewer components. But it is unstructured, objective, and must run the risk of being labelled discretionary. That label could certainly not be avoided if expectations were to be included, as Mr. Eekelaar would want them to be, whether or not they were induced expectations.

Canada has adopted a different solution, that of unjust enrichment. That is due, I think, not to a different social environment but to proximity to the United States. The papers reveal different views on its success as a solution to the problems of Family Property law. Mr. Gardner sees the artificiality in it; Professor Waters says it works. I cannot resolve their difference of opinion, but I am impressed with the method of assessing the success or otherwise of the solution which is adopted by Mr. Patrick Parkinson in his article in this year's *Toronto Law Journal*. Appellate cases provide less of a guide than those at first instance and, I would add, the views of those who advise on the settling of disputes out of court.

Mr. Gardner in his article in this year's *Law Quarterly Review* pursues a path of modified unjust enrichment and what he terms communality. He believes that 'trust and collaboration' can guide our footsteps in the exercise of the discretions that are involved. But I fear that what he has done is to replace artificiality with a desideratum. His attempt at a middle road also attracts Professor Birks' fire at anything that detracts from a rigorous link between an unjust enrichment and its restitution. So that unjust enrichment also fails to provide a ready alternative to the other solutions canvassed.

The judiciary was right to tackle the changing problems of Family Property Law. But it is wise to recognize that there are limitations to the doctrines that were developed in consequence. There is straining and artificiality in extending them to the extent that many think is needed in Family Property Law, and they should be reined in. A statutory base might be preferable for what the judiciary is doing; which might go some way to placate Professor Birks who fears for the sanctity of property—though to my mind Equity has been varying property rights from its earliest days. And such a base could be developed to take in the powers that Mr. Eekelaar advocates. But I doubt whether the statutory base could ever be formulated in more than rather general statements—compare the legislation regarding de facto couples that exists in some jurisdictions. Nor do I see it satisfying Mr. Gardner's wish to see discretions move towards rules; though he would not then be able to call the result undemocratic. If a choice has to be made between rules that could lead to artificiality and individualized treatment of cases, I would opt for the latter; not because I welcome uncertainty, but because I do not see the alternative—at least in the Family Property area.

Remedial Constructive Trusts are but a small part of the above discussion. They came within it since they are a device whereby, following the exercise of a discretion, a plaintiff achieves a proprietary remedy—which is how Remedial Constructive Trusts are regarded in each of the papers. It is to the genus that I now turn, and immediately there is a difficulty, for the papers have different focuses and objectives. Professor Birks focusses on rights themselves, and says firm things concerning the intrinsic logic of Restitution. Mr. Gardner focusses on discretions, using unjust enrichment more widely than Professor Birks would allow. Professor Waters considers Canadian law, where unjust enrichment is an established doctrine, and develops strongly a line between liability and remedy. I fear that no clear impression emerges of Remedial Constructive Trusts. But that may well be inevitable. For I doubt whether it is right to see them as a genus able to be provided with specific characteristics.

I am back with the subject of the series—Frontiers of Liability. At frontiers of liability we are also at a point where categories of liability become unsure of themselves. We must not make assumptions about the categories any more than about the rules; and asking the right questions becomes important. At one level, we can simply ask when, and why, the courts give a remedy with a proprietary consequence after the exercise of a discretion; an inquiry that would include Estoppel among other things. But I doubt whether by pursuing that inquiry we would learn much of value concerning a supposed genus of Remedial Constructive Trusts.

The questions I would ask relate to Trusts more generally. I believe that Trusts in an area that is losing what core it had, and is reverting to Equity. Expressly created trusts have been upheld in the courts that are very loose in character—they are draftsman not concept led. In some instances their origin is through contract, not settlement. Resulting trusts too are diffuse. And so for constructive trusts. They have all developed from the notion of the trust or in the alternative, as Mr. Gardner recognizes, the notion of trusteeship. But they can be very different in character from both their origin and from each other. They can be described as for instance Dr. Elias has described them, but I see relatively little gain in seeking to discern specific qualities in them. It is more a matter of how each of them can best be made to work. Thus each instance of a Constructive Trust that has been taken into the law needs to be examined in respect to the facts to which it relates in order to see how well it works in the context of those facts. Some are close to trusts and can legitimately be said to bring a 'Relationship' into being. Maybe they can be termed 'Institutional'; though I would not worry unduly about the definition of, or seek to expand, such a category; others are more like liabilities of a new sort; and I recall how Hoffman, L. J.'s paper of a year ago gave instances of what seem in effect to be liabilities created by Equity to reach circumstances, particularly circumstances concerning economic loss, that are beyond the range of the Common Law. There is no unity of concept in what has resulted from the developing of Constructive Trusts or Trusteeship. I agree with those who wish to jettison the phrase 'Constructive Trust' as lacking definition and usefulness. Even more so then, the phrase 'Remedial Constructive Trust'. It is not a case of the more adjectives, the better.

I doubt the value of seeking to develop the law at these frontiers through relying on the origin of the liabilities in older trust law. In some cases it will be apposite to draw on history, in others not. I found Professor Waters' line between liability and remedy more illuminating. I find it so for four main reasons. First, it seems right in principle to start with liability and proceed to remedy. We need to begin by knowing the ground of, and justification for, a liability. This can be clouded by approaching a matter of liability via a particular remedy. We have derived the law of Constructive Trusts from other varieties of trust with their attendant trust remedy, and have developed it sufficiently far from its origins for us to need to emerge from the cloud. A remedy *in personam* is the more appropriate, and should be seen as the primary, remedy for some of the liabilities that have developed within Constructive Trusteeship. Second, and following from that, we will be better placed to consider the appropriateness for particular instances of a personal or a proprietary remedy. Trust rationales and mechanisms should not force us to conclusions that we do not want. Thus I would take no objection if the recovery of illegitimate profits from a defendant who was the malefactor was treated on a different basis to recovery of those profits from third parties or in an insolvency. Third, and to be contrasted with expansion of 'Institutional Constructive Trusts', it enables us to appreciate the courts' role in determining what the incidences of a 'Constructive Trust' remedy are to be. I believe it to be an important role—and I would not stop short of enabling the courts to determine the date from which the remedy they are providing is to be effective. Fourth, the manner in which discretions are best exercised becomes clearer. Their exercise in relation to establishing a liability must be very different, and considerably more dangerous, than in relation to choosing a remedy. The distinction becomes vital if, as I believe to be the case, it will be difficult for rules to develop out of discretions in the way that Mr. Gardner would wish.

Whether all this can assist in diminishing the hostility with which many commercial lawyers regard developments that involve Constructive Trusts, I do not know. But if it is accepted—and no voice at the seminar was raised in protest—that Family Property Law is a unique area, so that provision of a remedy in that context does not imply recognition of an 'Institution' or concept that must apply elsewhere, maybe something will have been achieved.

It may also help in diminishing hostility if it is further accepted that the title of the seminar—'Remedial Constructive Trusts'—is not really helpful. Again I heard no voice in protest when that question arose during the seminar. The phrase may be more a reaction against 'Institutional' than a definitive step forward. It may be wiser to accept that Equity is expanding in scope, while the Trust as understood by earlier generations of Equity lawyers is contracting. It may be a matter of new wine and old bottles; and that the word that can confuse most of all is 'trust'. Such a conclusion does not in itself take us further forward, but it may serve to demystify. I hope that those in practice, especially in the commercial sphere, may derive comfort from it.